DELISTING OF STOCK CORPORATIONS IN EUROPE AND BEYOND

This book examines delisting – and the difficult questions it raises around investor protection – from the perspectives of the company, shareholders, trading venues and supervisory authorities.

Delisting is analysed with a view to finding common ground in the EU, and exploring whether delisting should be part of the EU project of a Capital Markets Union. In order to answer the question of harmonisation at the European level, the book also considers approaches in jurisdictions outside Europe. In particular, the book looks at the legal situation in Australia, Hong Kong, India, South America and the USA.

Offering a comprehensive and authoritative discussion of the major questions for listed companies who want to go private, the book will be of great interest to academics, lawmakers, supervisors, lawyers and judges.

The book's companion website (bloomsbury.pub/delisting-stock-corporations) provides access to reports and questionnaires on specific EU member states.

Online resources to accompany this book are available at bloomsburyonlineresources.com/delisting-of-stock-corporations-in-europe-and-beyond-rationales-forms-and-perspectives. If you experience any problems, please contact Bloomsbury at: onlineresources@bloomsbury.com

Delisting of Stock Corporations in Europe and Beyond

Rationales, Forms, and Perspectives

Edited by
Vassilios Tountopoulos
and
Rüdiger Veil

•HART•
OXFORD • LONDON • NEW YORK • NEW DELHI • SYDNEY

HART PUBLISHING
Bloomsbury Publishing Plc
Kemp House, Chawley Park, Cumnor Hill, Oxford, OX2 9PH, UK
1385 Broadway, New York, NY 10018, USA
Bloomsbury Publishing Ireland Limited, 29 Earlsfort Terrace, Dublin 2, D02 AY28, Ireland

HART PUBLISHING, the Hart/Stag logo, BLOOMSBURY and the Diana logo are trademarks of Bloomsbury Publishing Plc

First published in Great Britain 2025

A catalogue record for this book is available from the British Library.

A catalogue record for this book is available from the Library of Congress.

Library of Congress Control Number: 2025945746

ISBN: HB: 978-1-50997-478-8
ePDF: 978-1-50997-480-1
ePub: 978-1-50997-479-5

Typeset by Compuscript Ltd, Shannon

PREFACE

This book explores the complex issue of delisting – and the challenging questions delisting raises regarding investor protection – from the perspectives of companies, shareholders, trading venues, banks, and supervisory authorities. It examines delisting in the context of the European Union, aiming to identify common ground across Member States and to assess whether delisting should form part of the EU's broader Capital Markets Union initiative. To address the question of harmonisation at the European level, the book also considers legal approaches beyond Europe. In particular, it analyses the regulatory frameworks in Australia, Hong Kong, India, South America, and the United States. A companion website (bloomsbury.pub/delisting-stock-corporations) offers access to detailed reports and questionnaires covering selected EU Member States.

We are grateful to the authors for their excellent contributions to this book. They presented drafts of their chapters at a conference held on Chios Island on 9 and 10 June 2023, under the auspices of the University of the Aegean, Ludwig-Maximilians-Universität München, and the Union of Greek Listed Companies.

The idea for this conference had taken shape a year earlier during a joint vacation on the Peloponnese. It emerged quickly after we had exchanged views on the challenges issuers face in accessing capital markets. The basic concept of the project was already outlined that same evening. Our subsequent research revealed a striking lack of comparative legal scholarship on delisting which only increased our enthusiasm. However, without the expertise of our colleagues, it would not have been possible to approach the topic of delisting from such a wide range of perspectives. The conference fostered an invaluable exchange of ideas among the authors and helped to conceptualise and structure this book.

This book represents the provisional final part of the work carried out within the research project the *Codification of European Capital Markets Law.* We are deeply grateful to the German Research Foundation (Deutsche Forschungsgemeinschaft) for supporting the project and thereby making it possible to explore the harmonisation of delisting.

Eva Litina and Koray Çavuşoğlu provided outstanding support in organising the conference, for which we are deeply grateful. Anna-Lena Vogt and Felix Müller took on the demanding task of editing the manuscripts. They handled this responsibility with impressive dedication and contributed significantly to the creation of a coherent and seamless volume. We extend our sincere thanks to them.

Vassilios Tountopoulos and Rüdiger Veil
Chios and Munich, April 2025

CONTENTS

CONTRIBUTORS

Mikel Ataun is a Lawyer at Pérez-Llorca Abogados, SLP.

Gaia Balp is Associate Professor of Business Law at Bocconi University, Milan, Italy.

Jens-Hinrich Binder is Professor of Law, Chair for Private Law, Corporate Law, Banking and Capital Markets Law at Eberhard-Karls University of Tübingen, Germany, visiting Professor of Financial Law at Università Cattolica del Sacro Cuore, Milan, Italy, and Judge (part-time) at the Stuttgart Court of Appeals, Germany.

Jonathan Chan is Assistant Professor at Faculty of Law, McGill University, Canada.

Katrin Deckert is Associate Professor at Association nationale des Sociétés par Actions (ANSA), France.

Martin Gelter is Professor of Law at Fordham University School of Law, USA.

Carsten Gerner-Beuerle is Professor of Commercial Law, Faculty of Laws, University College London. UK, and Global Distinguished Professor of Law, Notre Dame Law School, USA.

Paolo Giudici is Professor of Business Law at the Free University of Bozen-Bolzano, Italy.

Juan Pablo González is Professor of Securities Law at Pontificia Universidad Javeriana, Colombia and Partner at Esguerra JHR.

Pamela Hanrahan is Emerita Professor at University of New South Wales Business School, Senior Fellow Melbourne Law School, and Consultant Johnson Winter Slattery, Sydney, Australia.

Elif Härkönen is Senior Associate Professor at Linköping University, Sweden.

Harpreet Kaur is Vice-Chancellor at the National Law University, Jodhpur, India. She was Professor of Law at National Law University Delhi and is on deputation. She has been a Fulbright Nehru Scholar and a Fulbright Scholar in Residence.

Chee Keong (CK) Low retired in July 2022 after some three decades as an Associate Professor in Corporate Law at CUHK Business School, Hong Kong.

Athanasios Kouloridas is Assistant Professor of Corporate and Capital Markets Law at Athens University of Economics and Business, Chairman of the Greek Union of Listed Companies, and Managing Partner at ABLAW, Greece.

Ioannis Ktistakis is a Judge at the European Court of Human Rights and Associate Professor at the Democritus University of Thrace, Greece.

Ioannis Linaritis is Assistant Professor of Commercial Law at the Democritus University of Thrace, Faculty of Law, Greece. He is a Member of the Associated Researchers Group of the European Banking Institute e.V., Attorney-at-law member of the Athens Bar Association, MBA (International Banking & Finance).

Tak Yip (TY) Low is Judicial Assistant at the Hong Kong Court of Final Appeal.

Heikki Marjosola is Associate Professor of Financial Law at the University of Helsinki, Finland.

Jessica Östberg is Associate Professor at Linköping University, Sweden.

Andrés Recalde is Professor of Business and Corporate Law at Universidad Autónoma of Madrid, Spain. He is a member of the European Company Law Expert Group (ECLE).

Steve Thel is Wormser Professor of Law at Fordham University School of Law, USA.

Ulrich Torggler is Professor at the Department of Commercial and Business Law at the University of Vienna, Austria.

Vassilios Tountopoulos is Professor of Commercial Law at the University of the Aegean, Greece.

Christoph Van der Elst is Professor of Business Law and Economics at Tilburg University, The Netherlands and Ghent University, Belgium.

Rüdiger Veil is Professor for Corporate Law and Capital Markets Law at Ludwig Maximilian University Munich, Germany.

Anna-Lena Vogt is a Research Fellow and Doctoral Candidate at the Chair of Civil and Corporate Law at Ludwig Maximilian University Munich, Germany.

Daniel Mert Yilmaz is a Research Assistant and Doctoral Candidate at the University of Vienna, Austria.

PART I

Fundamentals of Delisting

1

Delisting in EU Capital Markets Law: Forms, Goals and Rationales

VASSILIOS D TOUNTOPOULOS*

I. Introduction: Delisting Terminology

Every effort to approach delisting from a comparative law perspective begins with one basic question. What exactly is delisting? The answer to this question is not as simple as it might appear. Globally, there is no unanimous definition of delisting.[1] Even the term 'delisting' itself is not used in all legal orders. Instead, terms such as discontinuance,[2] deletion, withdrawal and removal[3] are often used. In the literature we can also find terms such as 'going private'[4] and 'going dark'.[5] The differences are not only at the level

* Professor of Commercial Law at the University of the Aegean, Greece.

[1] A legal definition of delisting does not exist in many legal orders. See eg, for German law W Groß, '§ 39 BörsG' in *Kapitalmarktrecht, Kommentar zum Börsengesetz, zur Börsenzulassungs-Verordnung, zum Wertpapierprospektgesetz und zur Prospektverordnung*, 8th edn (Munich, Verlag CH Beck, 2022) para 11; N Ilyevich, *Delisting – Parallele zum Übernahmerecht, Probleme und Lösungsmöglichkeiten* (Baden-Baden, Nomos Verlag, 2019) 26.

[2] See Directive 2001/34/EC on the admission of securities to official stock exchange listing and on information to be published on those securities [2001] OJ L184/1 Art 18, para 2: 'The competent authorities may decide that the listing of the security be discontinued where they are satisfied that, owing to special circumstances, normal regular dealings in a security are no longer possible.'

[3] See Directive 2014/65/EU on markets in financial instruments and amending Directive 2002/92/EC and Directive 2011/61/EU (recast) [2014] OJ L173/349 Arts 52, para 1 and 69, para 2.

[4] K Lehn and A Poulsen, 'Free Cash Flow and Stockholder Gains in Going Private Transactions' (1989) 44 *Journal of Finance* 771, 774, define a going private transaction 'as one that converted a free standing, publicly traded corporation into a privately held corporation'. According to the European Private Equity and Venture Capital Association, as cited by A Astashov in 'Three Essays on Private Equity/Trois essais sur le capital-investissement' (Doctoral thesis, Université Lumière Lyon 2 2017) 3, a PTP (Public To Private) transaction is defined as 'a transaction involving an offer for the entire share capital of a listed target company by a new company Newco – and the subsequent re-registration of that listed target company as a private company. The shareholders of Newco usually comprise members of the target company's management and private equity providers. Additional financing for the offer is normally provided by other debt providers'. See also DA Zetzsche, 'Going Dark under German Law' (2014). Available at: www.ssrn.com/abstract=2387712: 'Going-private transactions include all transactions which result in the withdrawal of a class of securities listed on a regulated stock exchange from listing on the regulated market.'

[5] CCH Sanders, *Anlegerschutz bei Delisting zwischen Kapitalmarkt- und Gesellschaftsrecht, Eine Untersuchung zum deutschen Recht unter Berücksichtigung des britischen und US-amerikanischen Rechts* (Berlin, Duncker & Humblot, 2017) 29: 'Ein vollständiger Börsenrückzug wird auch als "Going Private" oder

of terminology. In the US, the terms 'going private' and 'going dark' are not synonyms. When a firm goes private, it becomes fully private, whereas stocks of a firm going dark can still be traded on pink sheets over-the-counter. Moreover, in many legal orders a distinction is drawn between termination of listing on a specific exchange and termination of admission to a market,[6] where admission to a market is considered as a prerequisite for listing on a stock exchange.[7] In other legal orders, delisting is distinguished from deregistration.[8] Nonetheless, delisting is usually linked to deregistration of a company as a public company.[9]

In this chapter we take a broad and functional approach to delisting. From this perspective, the legal nature of delisting (as an administrative act[10] or as an act of private law) is irrelevant. It is also irrelevant whether the delisting is the primary objective of a transaction and/or its sole effect. Delisting is simply considered as the *actus contrarius* of listing. While rules on listing regulate the entry mechanism to the market, delisting rules establish the procedures for exiting the market. Accordingly, we define delisting as *the permanent (non-temporary) removal of a financial instrument from a regulated market/stock exchange.*[11]

Of course, the removal of a financial instrument from a Multilateral Trading Facility (MTF) is also considered as 'delisting' *lato sensu*. In fact, 'delisting' from an alternative market has become a quite common phenomenon in recent years. Nonetheless, according to EU capital markets law, a company qualifies as listed only if its securities are admitted to trading on a regulated market.[12] Accordingly, delisting refers to companies admitted to trading (listed) on regulated markets. It is therefore a paradox, at least from a European law perspective, to speak about 'delisting' from an MTF. Moreover, the requirements for a security to be admitted to trading on an MTF are substantially different from those for regulated markets, while delisting from an alternative market in some Member States is not governed by statutory provisions.[13] The general market rules apply. Therefore, when reference is made to delisting, a distinction has to be drawn between delisting from a regulated market and removal from an MTF.

"Going Dark" bezeichnet.' ['A complete withdrawal from the stock exchange is also referred to as "Going Private" or "Going dark".'].

[6] For German Law, see K Krug, *Der Rückzug von der Börse, Widerstreitende Interessen von Groß- und Minderheitsaktionären beim Delisting* (Baden-Baden, Nomos Verlag, 2019) 32; Sanders ibid 25 f.

[7] ibid 32 f.

[8] In the US, the term deregistration refers to the removal of all the company's securities from the exchange/regulated market, thus absolving the company from any financial reporting obligations with regard to the authority regulating the abovementioned exchange/regulated market. The term delisting refers to the removal of a certain class of securities issued by a company from the trading on an exchange/regulated market.

[9] In US Law, see the differentiation between delisting and deregistration.

[10] On delisting as an administrative act, see Sanders (n 5) 28.

[11] See D Magni et al, 'Defining the Relationship Between Firm's Performance and Delisting: Empirical Evidence of Going Private in Europe' (2022) 13 *Journal of the Knowledge Economy* 2584, 2585: 'Delisting is that process happening when a firm chooses to remove its stock from list of a regulated market …'. See also Sanders (n 5) 26: 'beschreibt ein Delisting den Rückzug einer Aktiengesellschaft von der Börse durch Beendigung der Zulassung der Wertpapiere zum Börsenhandel' ['delisting describes the withdrawal of a stock corporation from the stock exchange by cancellation of the admission of the securities to stock exchange trading'].

[12] N de Luca, *European Company Law*, 2nd edn (Cambridge, Cambridge University Press, 2021) 422, 423: '… a company qualifies as listed or publicly traded only provided that its securities are admitted to trading on a regulated market …'.

[13] For German Law, see Krug (n 6) 38.

Moreover, although delisting refers to all types of financial instrument (bonds, options, etc), the most important form of delisting refers to shares. Accordingly, this chapter will focus on the delisting of shares. As a consequence of share delisting, the shares are no longer traded on the regulated market/stock exchange and public reporting requirements are eliminated. Moreover, due to its permanent character, delisting is differentiated from suspension[14] and trading halts which are temporary in character. Furthermore, delisting should be distinguished from freeze-outs, where the controlling shareholder exercises a legal right to buy out the shares of the minority. A freeze-out is usually, but not necessarily, followed by delisting.

II. Data on Delisting

A market is an organised platform linking fund providers to fund seekers. Fund providers usually prefer to allocate funds to companies with positive results and growth expectations, while fund seekers aim to secure financing on the best possible terms. Therefore, it is self-evident that fund providers are not willing to invest in distressed companies without growth expectations and listed companies have no incentive to remain listed on a stock exchange when the listing costs exceed the benefits. From this point of view, listing on a stock exchange is not a one-way street. The smooth functioning of the market presupposes the existence of a mechanism to allow companies that do not wish to remain on the market and do not meet the conditions for listing to exit the market either voluntarily or compulsorily.

Delisting has more than just a theoretical importance in global capital markets. As mentioned in the OECD Corporate Governance Factbook, although overall global market capitalisation increased from USD 84 trillion in 2017 to USD 105 trillion by the end of 2020, 'the net number of listed companies continued to decline from approximately 41,000 in 2017 to slightly over 40,000 in 2020'.[15] More specifically, since 2005, 'almost 30,000 companies have delisted from the stock markets globally'.[16] More specifically, between 2005 and 2019, there were nearly 8,000 delistings of European companies, over 5,000 delistings of US companies and approximately 1,300 delistings of Japanese companies.[17] Moreover, it is reported that from 1995 to 2005 more than 25 per cent of European listed firms went private.[18] According to another report, the number of listed companies in OECD economies declined from 30,000 in 2000 to about 22,000 in 2020.[19]

[14] See Directive 2001/34/EC on the admission of securities to official stock exchange listing and on information to be published on those securities [2001] OJ L184/1 Art 18 para 1: 'The competent authorities may decide to suspend the listing of a security where the smooth operation of the market is, or may be, temporarily jeopardised or where protection of investors so requires.'

[15] OECD, *OECD Corporate Governance Factbook 2021* (Paris, OECD Publishing, 2021) 18.

[16] ibid, 12.

[17] ibid, 21.

[18] C Djama, I Martinez and S Serve, 'What Do We Know About Delistings? A Survey of the Literature' (2014). Available at: www.hal.science/hal-00937899/document 2.

[19] OECD, *Understanding Delistings from the Portuguese Stock Market* (2020). Available at: www.lexpoint.pt/Fileget.aspx?FileId=36194 17.

By comparing the number of total listed companies and the number of delisted companies it becomes clear that delisted companies have not been replaced by new listed companies and that there has been a decline in the number of listed companies. In other words, after 2000, the number of delisted companies has often outnumbered new listings both in the US and Europe,[20] where there has been a decrease in the number of listed companies in each year from 2008 to 2019.[21] Starting from the year 2000, there has been a decreasing trend in the number of listed companies in almost all European markets. The largest decline has been in the Netherlands (75 per cent), France (61 per cent) and Portugal (61 per cent).[22] Against this trend, the number of listed companies in Europe grew marginally in 2021.[23] In contrast, markets in China and Japan have witnessed an increase in the number of listed companies during the same timeframe (2000–2021).[24] More specifically, in the last two decades, the number of listed companies in China has tripled.[25]

Considering the practical significance of delisting, it is essential to examine the factors contributing to the overall reduction in the number of listed companies within the OECD region. Nevertheless, any attempt to do this in a systematic manner is not easy due to the heterogeneity of the forms of delisting.

III. Forms of Delisting

As already indicated, delisting is a multifaceted phenomenon. It appears in many different forms. The main differentiation is between voluntary and mandatory (compulsory) delisting. Voluntary delisting is based on a decision of the listed company. That means that the listed company decides of its own accord to delist and the delisting occurs 'at the request of the company'. This form of delisting seems to be the prevailing one[26] and is certainly the most debated form of delisting in many European legal orders. Contrary to voluntary delisting, mandatory delisting is imposed by the authorities and/or the exchange. Mandatory delisting mainly occurs when a listed company fails to meet the listing requirements.

In between the voluntary and mandatory form of delisting lie some hybrid forms where delisting is pursued by the company and/or its shareholders; nonetheless it is imposed by the relevant authorities without a decision/request of the company or automatically comes into effect, especially in cases of cold delisting.[27] This is described as the transformation of a listed company resulting in its delisting, especially the merger by

[20] B Fidanza, O Morresi and A Pezzi, *The Decision to Delist from the Stock Market, Theory and Empirical Evidence of Going Private* (Cham, Palgrave Macmillan, 2018) 1 ff.

[21] OECD (n 15) 21.

[22] OECD (n 19) 17.

[23] D Pintacasi and A Thomadakis, '2022 ECMI Statistical Package: key findings, ECMI Research Report No19/January 2023'. Available at: www.ecmi.eu/sites/default/files/ecmi_stat_pack_2022_-_key_findings.pdf 3.

[24] OECD (n 19) 17.

[25] ibid 18.

[26] Magni et al, 'Defining the Relationship Between Firm's Performance and Delisting' (n 11) 2586: 'Voluntary delisting is the predominant reason for delisting in the stock markets in continental Europe.'

[27] On cold delisting see Härkönen and Östberg, Chapter 13 in this volume.

absorption of a listed company by an unlisted company. In order to avoid circumvention of the relevant provisions, such forms of delisting are usually considered as voluntary delisting resulting in the application of all relevant provisions in favour of minority shareholders.

Other forms of delisting are downlisting[28] and cross-border delisting.[29] In downlisting, a company delists its shares from a regulated market to list them on an MTF with lower costs and fewer obligations.[30] Although the terms are sometimes used interchangeably,[31] downlisting is not the same as downgrading. Downgrading refers to a situation where the shares are traded in another category of the same market.[32] In cross-border delisting, a company delists its shares to list them on another regulated market abroad.

Another form of delisting is partial delisting. Partial delisting refers to a company which is listed on several markets but chooses to delist from one or more of them yet remains listed on another one. We can further distinguish partial delisting based on the following criterion: whether a company is listed on several markets in the same legal order or in different legal orders. In the former case, the partially delisted company remains listed in the same legal order. In the latter case, the partially delisted company remains listed abroad.

Despite the differences in the above-mentioned forms of delisting, all have some common characteristics. It goes without saying that all forms of delisting affect the rights of (minority) shareholders. Before addressing this issue, we have first to analyse the rationales behind delisting.

IV. Delisting Rationales

The rationales for delisting have been subject to a considerable number of studies, especially in the US. Nonetheless, the studies differ in terms of (a) the factors and reasons explored, (b) the methodologies employed, (c) the time periods covered, and (d) the geographical locations examined. Additionally, some studies focus primarily on firm-level factors, while others incorporate macroeconomic variables. Notwithstanding the above, it is generally accepted that delisting is the result of a complex equation with multiple variables and different weighting factors. Accordingly, the rationales for delisting vary significantly. Moreover, given the complexity and heterogeneity of the forms of delisting, it is accepted that when analysing delisting rationales we have to distinguish between mandatory and voluntary delisting.

[28] On downlisting see Balp, Chapter 11 in this volume.

[29] On cross-border delisting, see Gerner-Beuerle and Chan, Chapter 12 in this volume.

[30] BGH, Beschl. v. 8.10.2013 – II ZB 26/12 ('Frosta'), NJW 2014, 146, 149 para 15.

[31] See BVerfGE 132, 99 using the term downgrading as a synonym of downlisting. See also N Ilyevich, *Delisting – Parallele zum Übernahmerecht* (2019) 27: 'Der Wechsel aus dem regulierten Markt in den Freiverkehr … wird inzwischen von der ganz herrschenden Meinung als Downlisting bezeichnet. Teilweise findet immer noch der Terminus Downgrading Anwendung' ['The switch from the regulated market to the unregulated market … is now referred to by the prevailing opinion as downlisting. In some cases, the term downgrading is still used'].

[32] See on downlisting Balp (n 28).

A. Voluntary Delisting

As mentioned above, in voluntary delisting the Company decides to delist. Accordingly, voluntary delisting is linked to the decision of the competent organ and/or the controlling shareholders of the listed company to delist. The rationales for voluntary delisting have been described in the financial literature since the mid-1980s.[33] Analysis of delisting is traditionally linked to and examined together with the question why companies decide to go public. As mentioned above, the rationale behind this is that delisting is considered as an *actus contrarius* to listing. Therefore, delisting rationales are examined in parallel with listing rationales. Hence, if a listing motive ceases to exist, a delisting reason may be established. Nonetheless, it has to be pointed out that although listing and delisting reasons are often inversely correlated, listing and delisting reasons are not always symmetrically opposed. The fact that listing costs increase does not automatically lead to a delisting decision.

Usually, a delisting decision is based on a cost-benefit analysis, a trade-off between the costs and benefits of listing and delisting.[34] More specifically, there is an expectation that being listed is associated with multiple benefits. These benefits are not only financial in nature. They are interpreted broadly and include, among others, enhanced visibility,[35] credibility, better access to multiple sources of financing and ready access to equity through secondary offerings. These benefits are compared with the costs associated with being listed, such as listing fees and compliance costs. When the costs outweigh the benefits, the listed company can decide to voluntarily delist.[36] In other words, the delisting decision is made when the costs of listing exceed the benefits of going public or the benefits of going public are less than the costs of listing.[37]

This analysis depends heavily on the market situation and the special characteristics of the company in question. Therefore, a cost–benefit analysis does not produce – always and for all companies – the same outcome. The weighting factor for each specific characteristic/criterion may vary substantially based on the particularities and needs of each company. Hence, a well-financed company does not have the same needs as a company with limited financial flows and extensive funding needs. Accordingly, a listed company may consider compliance costs to be a decisive criterion, whereas another company may consider the unexploited value potential to be a decisive criterion. Be that as it may, such motives will not usually lead to a delisting decision on their

[33] Djama, Martinez and Serve, 'What Do We Know About Delistings?' (n 18) 3. See especially H DeAngelo, L DeAngelo and EM Rice, 'Going Private: Minority Freezeouts and Stockholder Wealth' (1984) 27 *The Journal of Law & Economics* 367.

[34] See ST Bharath and AK Dittmar, 'Why Do Firms Use Private Equity to Opt Out of Public Markets? (2010) 23 *The Review of Financial Studies* 1771, 1772: 'We argue that since the nature of the theories of going public are trade-off type theories, the reverse is also true. When the costs of having lesser control exceed the benefits of liquidity, firms will reverse their decision, that is, firms will exit the public markets and go private.' See also CCH Sanders (n 5) 43.

[35] See H Mehran and S Peristiani, 'Financial Visibility and the Decision to Go Private' (2010) 23 *The Review of Financial Studies* 519.

[36] OECD (n 19) 16.

[37] I Martinez and S Serve, 'Reasons for Delisting and Consequences: A Literature Review and Research Agenda' (2017) 31 *Journal of Economic Surveys* 733, 740 with further references.

own, but only when several motives are at play. Again, the delisting decision is not a binary question; instead it is a very complex decision.

In terms of theory, there have been several attempts to systematise delisting incentives. In the financial literature, a distinction is usually drawn between traditional motivations, motivations derived from agency theory and motivations related to financial structure.[38] According to another view, incentives for delisting can generally be divided into the following groups: (a) operational disadvantages due to the stock exchange listing, (b) a non-functional stock exchange listing, as well as (c) unexploited value potentials.[39] In this analysis we will follow the latter categorisation. Again, this distinction is only for systematic reasons.

i. Non-Functional Listing/Financing Alternatives

As already indicated above, a company decides to go public to achieve benefits, such as financing, credibility, better access to multiple sources of financing and ready access to equity through secondary offerings, better visibility, etc. If the market does not offer or no longer offers these benefits, the expectations of the listed company are not fulfilled and, consequently, the listed company does not have any reason to remain listed, especially if liquidity deteriorates.[40] In an illiquid market the price formation mechanism is not reliable and small volume transactions can affect share prices. Moreover, illiquid shares are not covered by analysts. Accordingly, there is no market visibility for the shares or the listed company. Another important delisting driver is the emergence of private equity funds offering better financing alternatives. If a company has access to better financing alternatives, the listed company no longer has any reason to remain listed.

ii. Operational Disadvantages Due to Listing/Listing Costs

Listing a company increases costs dramatically. The costs incurred by a listed company can be both direct and indirect. Direct costs contain ongoing costs following an IPO, including, among others, listing fees imposed by exchanges and regulatory bodies, trading fees, clearing and depository fees, etc. The most important direct listing costs are listing fees, which are usually calculated at a flat rate fee determined by market capitalisation. Usually, a minimum and maximum cap fee applies. Listing fees are a basic source of income for exchanges. Nonetheless, exchange fees differ widely across exchanges.[41]

[38] Djama, Martinez and Serve (n 18) 3.

[39] M Pfüller and D Anders, 'Delisting-Motive vor dem Hintergrund neuerer Rechtsentwicklungen' (2003) 6 *Neue Zeitschrift für Gesellschaftsrecht* 459, 460. See also, in the same direction, C Riedel, *Freiwilliges und zwangsweises Delisting im deutschen und südkoreanischen Recht, Eine rechtsvergleichende Untersuchung* (Berlin, Peter Lang, 2017) 45 f.

[40] See Bharath and Dittmar, 'Why Do Firms Use Private Equity' (n 34) 1771. See generally on the relationship between liquidity and delisting AWA Boot, R Gopalan and AV Thakor, 'Market Liquidity, Investor Participation, and Managerial Autonomy: Why Do Firms Go Private?' (2008) 63 *The Journal of Finance* 2013.

[41] J Macey and M O'Hara, 'The Economics of Stock Exchange Listing Fees and Listing Requirements' (2002) 11 *Journal of Financial Intermediation* 297.

Indirect costs include costs incurred to comply with regulatory provisions. Indirect costs include the cost of a mandatory market sponsor and/or market maker, the drafting of financial statements according to special provisions, the (re)organisation costs of the company according to regulatory requirements such as MAR and corporate governance codes (providing for board diversity and various committees), the convening of shareholder meetings according to the relevant provisions, the disclosure of inside information, etc. Indirect listing costs are also considered to include the increase of legal and compliance risk for the listed company taking into consideration the high monetary sanctions imposed on listed companies for violation of capital markets rules as well as investor actions against issuers based on a violation of capital markets rules.

Given the ever-mounting listing costs, delisting is considered as a way to reduce the economic and managerial burden of continued increased costs and regulatory compliance, especially with regard to the reporting and disclosure requirements of the Capital Markets regulation. Accordingly, 'delisting' is no longer accompanied by negative connotations. Rather, it can be a prudent business decision aimed at improving a company's efficiency to the benefit of shareholders, particularly where a company is not otherwise enjoying the advantages of being a public company.

From this point of view, the Sarbanes Oxley Act (SOA) was one of the main drivers of, if not the catalyst for, delisting in the US.[42] More specifically, 77 per cent of foreign companies which delisted from the US markets allegedly did so due to the high cost of compliance with stock exchange rules.[43] A major segment of these companies made specific reference to the SOA. Moreover, other studies have found a positive correlation between the IFRS and the propensity to delist.[44] According to another study, regulatory requirements and corporate governance standards, by increasing the information burden, may induce companies to leave the public equity market. However, when overall governance improves, fewer going private transactions happen.[45]

[42] P Hostak et al, 'An Examination of the Impact of the Sarbanes–Oxley Act on the Attractiveness of U.S. Capital Markets for Foreign Firms' (2013) 18 *Review of Accounting Studies* 522, 555: 'These results suggest that SOX played a distinct role in driving our sample firms away from the U.S. markets'; S Chaplinsky and L Ramchand, 'What Drives Delistings of Foreign Firms from U.S. Exchanges?' (2012) 22 *Journal of International Financial Markets, Institutions and Money* 1126, 1147: 'we conclude that SOX appears to be a significant enough force to prompt reassessment of firms' listing decisions, leading those with strong governance at home and low net benefits from a U.S. listing to delist'; A Marosi and N Massoud, 'Why Do Firms Go Dark?' (2007) 42 *The Journal of Financial and Quantitative Analysis* 421, 441: 'Consistent with anecdotal evidence, we find that the compliance cost – as measured by audit fees – and the passage of the Sarbanes-Oxley Act are among the major driving forces behind a firm's decision to go dark. Firms with fewer growth opportunities, greater insider ownership, lower institutional ownership, lower market momentum, and higher leverage are also more likely to go dark'; C Leuz, A Triantis and TY Wang, 'Why Do Firms Go Dark? Causes and Economic Consequences of Voluntary SEC Deregistrations' (2008) 45 *Journal of Accounting and Economics* 181, 182: 'The Sarbanes–Oxley Act of 2002 (SOX), and in particular its internal control requirements in Section 404, are frequently cited as catalysts in this recent movement to "go dark"'; E Engel, RM Hayes and X Wang, 'The Sarbanes–Oxley Act and Firms' Going-Private Decisions' (2007) 44 *Journal of Accounting and Economics* 116.

[43] Hostak et al, ibid 524.

[44] EF Gutierrez, M Vulcheva and M Rykaczewski, 'The Cost-Benefit Tradeoff of Securities Market Regulation: European Firms' Delisting Around Major Regulatory Shocks' (2022). Available at: www.ssrn.com/abstract=2903679.

[45] S Thomsen and F Vinten, 'Delistings and the Costs of Governance: A Study of European Stock Exchanges 1996–2004' (2014) 18 *Journal of Management & Governance* 793: '… the tendency to go private is found to be lower, when the quality of overall governance is high'.

Moreover, it must also be pointed out that listing costs are not equally important for all firms. Delisting is especially connected with certain characteristics of firms that influence their ability to afford listing costs.[46] More specifically, larger firms are better placed to amortise fixed costs, while small firms are more likely to go private. The rationale behind this is that for smaller companies, public company compliance costs have increased significantly as a percentage of revenues. Moreover, low-performing firms seem to be more motivated to go private compared to other listed firms.[47]

iii. Unexploited Value Potentials, Undervalue Elimination and Capital Structure

The financial literature adequately describes how going private transactions could create significant wealth gains for target stockholders. Four suggested sources of stockholder gains in these transactions include: (1) tax savings; (2) redistribution from bondholders; (3) mitigation of agency problems; and (4) asymmetric information.[48]

More specifically, if a stock market undervalues the company, the persons controlling the company may opt for delisting to benefit from the difference between the stock market valuation and the real valuation. In the same vein, controlling shareholders can use private information to take their companies private before performance improvements, when the market prices of minority shares does not incorporate this future improvement.[49]

The capital structure can also be a good reason for a company to voluntarily delist its shares. This is the case if the company has no need to raise funds to finance growth opportunities. Moreover, delisting may be linked to low growth opportunities/prospects[50] and large free cash flow.[51] At the same time, going private allows the firm and its shareholders to have the actual availability of the cash flows produced, thereby

[46] Engel, Hayes and Wang 'The Sarbanes–Oxley Act and Firms' Going-Private Decisions' (n 42) 116, 143: 'the abnormal returns associated with the passage of SOX are positively related to firm size and share turnover; (3) smaller firms with high inside ownership experience higher going-private announcement returns in the post-SOX period compared to the pre-SOX period'; Leuz, Triantis and Wang, 'Why Do Firms Go Dark?' (n 42) 181, 192: '... going-dark firms are significantly smaller than firms that choose to continue reporting despite the fact that both satisfy the threshold rule for deregistration'; Thomsen and Vinten, 'Delistings and the costs of governance' (n 45) 821: 'Presumably, the benefits of being listed are larger for large firms while fixed administration costs are easier to carry for large firms'; C Weir, M Wright and L Scholes, 'Public-to-Private Buy-Outs, Distress Costs and Private Equity' (2008) 18 *Applied Financial Economics* 801: 'we also find that UK PTPs are more likely to be younger ... and be smaller than firms remaining public'.

[47] See generally Djama, Martinez and Serve (n 18) 6: '... a performance problem associated with high costs from financial distress is another possible incentive for a firm to go private'; Thomsen and Vinten (n 45) 811; Weir, Wright and Scholes, 'Public-to-private buy-outs', ibid 803.

[48] Lehn and Poulsen, 'Free Cash Flow and Stockholder Gains' (n 4) 772, 773.

[49] LA Bebchuk and M Kahan, 'Adverse Selection and Gains to Controllers in Corporate Freezeouts' in RK Morck (ed), *Concentrated Corporate Ownership* (Chicago, University of Chicago Press, 2000) 247, 249.

[50] C Weir and M Wright, 'Governance and Takeovers: Are Public-To-Private Transactions Different from Traditional Acquisitions of Listed Corporations?' (2006) 36 *Accounting and Business Research* 289; C Weir, D Laing and M Wright, 'Incentive Effects, Monitoring Mechanisms and the Market for Corporate Control: An Analysis of the Factors Affecting Public to Private Transactions in the UK' (2005) 32 *Journal of Business Finance & Accounting* 909: '... there is some evidence of lower growth opportunities'.

[51] Lehn and Poulsen (n 4) 771; Magni et al (n 11) 2584: 'We find that a high level of stock market performance, associated with high level of free cash flows, promotes going private as a means of anticipating and preventing future value decreases.'

avoiding them being employed in projects with negative net present value. Moreover, it is argued that if a firm no longer needs access to the equity market and is not financially constrained, the decision to go private may reveal its preference for alternative sources of financing, such as debt.[52] Furthermore, it is argued that a listed company with a low level of debt may have a greater probability of delisting.[53]

iv. Ownership Concentration/Control Change

Delisting is very often the consequence of the change of control. Shareholders who acquired control of the company often want to exit the market, usually for reasons already mentioned above under (i) to (iii). Indeed, as a matter of principle, controlling shareholders want to expropriate wealth and maximise their benefits to the detriment of minority shareholders. Freezing out minority shareholders and delisting is an efficient means to achieve this goal as well as to reduce the responsibility placed upon and monitoring of executives by market and regulatory authorities. Moreover, controlling shareholders will choose to exit the market when faced with threats to their control.[54] The difficulties of share transferability due to delisting creates a safety net for controlling shareholders. Accordingly, the protection of control and information asymmetry can justify a positive link between ownership and delisting.[55]

Be that as it may, delisting is very often linked to ownership concentration. A high concentration rate is usually positively correlated to delisting. It is observed that the higher the proportion of shares in the hands of small investors (with a stake under 5 per cent), the more difficult the approval process at the general meeting will be. Thus, it is observed that companies with a low free float are more prone to delisting,[56] since there is a decrease in the costs involved in the acquisition of shares circulating on the market that enable delisting.

Moreover, there is evidence that concentration of votes is a crucial condition for conducting PTP transactions.[57] This aspect is well-founded because: (1) higher concentration reduces the cost of coordinating the delisting process; and (2) the higher the concentration of control, the easier the process of having delisting approved by the competent company organ.[58] In a relevant study in Germany covering an investigation period from 8 October 2013 to 30 June 2015, the free float of the delisting candidates was only 8.86 per cent (median 7.81 per cent), while that of the control group was 45.56 per cent (median 44.42 per cent).[59]

[52] Martinez and Serve, 'Reasons for Delisting and Consequences' (n 37) 742.

[53] Fidanza, Morresi and Pezzi, *The Decision to Delist from the Stock Market* (n 20) 136.

[54] Weir and Wright, 'Governance and takeovers' (n 50) 289.

[55] Fidanza, Morresi and Pezzi (n 20) 142.

[56] M Michelsen and C Klein, '"Privacy Please!" The Public to Private Decision in Germany' (2011) 5 *Review of Managerial Science* 49, 53.

[57] ibid 49.

[58] ibid.

[59] B Karami and R Schuster, *Eine empirische Analyse des Kurs- und Liquiditätseffekts auf die Ankündigung eines Börsenrückzugs am deutschen Kapitalmarkt im Lichte der "FRoSTA"-Entscheidung des BGH, 2015, 33* (2015). Available at: www.bewertung-im-recht.de/downloads/delisting-studie.php.

B. Mandatory/Compulsory Delisting

As mentioned above, in mandatory/compulsory delisting the financial instruments of a company are removed from the exchange by the competent authorities, ie capital market authorities and/or stock exchanges, without a prior decision from the listed company. The mandatory removal usually occurs due to a substantial failure of the company and/or a breach of the listing conditions. Substantial failure can include bankruptcy, liquidation and discontinuation of business.[60] The listing conditions and the reasons resulting in mandatory delisting are not the same in all legal orders. The financial literature mainly focuses on the following three questions:[61]

(1) *Whether certain characteristics of firms (also regarding newly listed companies) influence the probability of mandatory delisting.* To address this question, some studies focus on performance,[62] stock returns[63] and (ineffective) governance[64] and examine whether there is a positive correlation between delisting and these characteristics.

(2) *How strictly market authorities and stock exchanges enforce the mandatory delisting rules on minimum listing requirements.* Macey et al highlight the flexibility of the control enforced by US market regulators, noting that some firms continue to trade for months after a rule violation.[65] This flexibility could be explained by the delisting dilemma.[66] Stock exchanges are profit-seeking entities and delisting of companies makes their profits sink and increases legal risks. Moreover, the cost of the investigation that the market regulator will incur to detect a violation should also not be excluded from the equation. However, not to delist a failed company could harm investors and cause reputational damage to the exchange. Finding the equilibrium point is particularly difficult, resulting in the delisting dilemma. Some exchanges resolve the issue by strictly applying the listing rules, while other exchanges adopt a more lenient approach. This question is also linked to the question of how the competent supervisory authority uses its powers to delist a company.

(3) *What are the firm's strategies with regard to the risk of mandatory delisting?* This question is linked to the fundamental question of whether the company wishes to remain listed. If this is the case, the listed company will take measures to address the reasons for the delisting. If not, the listed company will accept the delisting decision and eventually accelerate the delisting process. Besides, as mentioned above, involuntary delisting could be the end result of a series of voluntary actions by listed companies.

[60] See Binder, Chapter 9 in this volume.

[61] Martinez and Serve (n 37) 750.

[62] See eg S Peristiani and G Hong, 'Pre-IPO Financial Performance and Aftermarket Survival' (2004) 10 *Current Issues in Economics and Finance* 1 focusing on pre-issue profitability.

[63] GP Baker and RE Kennedy, 'Survivorship and the Economic Grim Reaper' (2002) 18 *Journal of Law, Economics & Organization* 324.

[64] A Charitou, C Louca and N Vafeas, 'Boards, Ownership Structure, and Involuntary Delisting from the New York Stock Exchange' (2007) 26 *Journal of Accounting and Public Policy* 249.

[65] J Macey, M O'Hara and D Pompilio, 'Down and out in the Stock Market: The Law and Economics of the Delisting Process' (2008) 51 *The Journal of Law & Economics* 683, 711.

[66] ibid 709. See also S Kastl, *Der Rückzug kapitalmarktfähiger Unternehmen von der Börse* (Baden-Baden, Nomos Verlag, 2016) 88: 'Für die Börse bzw. ihre Börsenträger ist das Delisting ein zweischneidiges Schwert' [translated 'Delisting is a double-edged sword for the stock exchange and its exchange operators.'].

Moreover, mandatory delisting rules also have to be examined from a geopolitical point of view.[67] Indeed, capital market rules have recently been used to achieve specific political goals. ESG rules are the most prominent example from an EU law perspective.[68] In the same vein, mandatory delisting rules have also been instrumentalised to achieve political goals. We refer to the issue of delisting of Chinese companies from US markets, which is linked to heavy political tensions and controversies between the US and China.[69] The problem began with the SOA and the creation of the Public Company Accounting Oversight Board (PCAOB). The latter has raised concerns for years about China-based companies failing to comply with audit requests.[70]

As a result, in 2020 the Holding Foreign Companies Accountable Act (HFCAA) was enacted.[71] The latter provides that publicly traded firms in the US must have their auditors scrutinised by American regulators. The legislation bans securities trading by public companies who fail to meet auditing requirements for two consecutive years. The collapse of Luckin Coffee, a Chinese beverage-delivery group listed on Nasdaq which was caught manipulating its sales figures in 2021, has increased pressure on Chinese companies.[72]

Although checking financial statements is a very important issue, it is well argued that the US rules on delisting are also aimed at reducing Chinese companies' access to American investors' money. The fact that even before the HFCAA was passed, the US had already expelled a number of big Chinese firms like China Telecom, China Mobile and China Unicom,[73] confirms this view. It is not by chance that the US administration in parallel moved to punish Chinese companies involved in supporting China's military and security services. Many companies – from aerospace to telecommunications – were placed on the Commerce Department's 'entities list' which bars US businesses from conducting commerce with those companies, including investments.

In December 2022 the Public Company Accounting Oversight Board (PCAOB) said that it had gained full access to inspect and investigate Chinese companies.[74] Nonetheless, amid the escalating trade and tariff war between the US and China, the

[67] See generally CJ Milhaupt, 'The (Geo)Politics of Controlling Shareholders, Law Working Paper No 696/2023' (2023). Available at: https://papers.ssrn.com/sol3/papers.cfm?abstract_id=4406516.

[68] See eg EU High-Level Expert Group on Sustainable Finance, *Financing a Sustainable European Economy, Final Report 2018* (2018). Available at: www.finance.ec.europa.eu/system/files/2018-01/180131-sustainable-finance-final-report_en.pdf (hereafter Expert Group on Sustainable Finance, Final Report 2018).

[69] See generally TKP Leung and LHW Lei, 'The Economy of the Sino–US Conflict: Its Impact on Chinese Firms Listed in the US and Hong Kong as a Financial Hub' (2022) 28 *Asia Pacific Business Review* 680.

[70] See generally T Gu, Y Jiang, and D Simunic, 'The Value of the PCAOB's International Audit Oversight on U.S. Listed Foreign Companies: Evidence from an Initial Enforcement Breakdown' (2023) 19 *Journal of Contemporary Accounting & Economics* 1.

[71] See generally Q Bu, 'The Anatomy of Holding Foreign Companies Accountable Act (HFCAA): A Panacea or a Double-Edged Sword?' (2021) 16 *Capital Markets Law Journal* 503.

[72] See on this case PC Lee, 'Fraud at Luckin Coffee: The Rapid Rise and Downfall of China's Starbucks' (2021) 25 *Asian Case Research Journal* 409.

[73] See the NYSE news release from 31 December 2020 'NYSE to Commence Delisting Proceedings in Securities of Three Issuers to Comply with Executive Order 13959'. Available at: https://s2.q4cdn.com/154085107/files/doc_news/NYSE-to-Commence-Delisting-Proceedings-in-Securities-of-Three-Issuers-to-Comply-with-Executive-Order-13959-2020.pdf.

[74] See C Prentice, X Yu and S Heavey, 'Chinese firms avert delisting as U.S. audit watchdog gets full inspection access' (2022). Available at: www.reuters.com/business/us-pcaob-says-is-able-inspect-firms-china-first-time-2022-12-15/.

US' Secretary to the Treasury recently said that 'everything's on the table when it comes to removing Chinese companies from American stock exchanges'.[75] This fact confirms our analysis that mandatory delisting rules can be used to achieve geopolitical goals. It highlights the trend of the world dividing into two economic and financial spheres, each governed by increasingly different rules and principles.

V. Contrasting Interests in (Voluntary) Delisting

Delisting either in the form of mandatory or of voluntary delisting affects the interests of many parties, ie issuers, shareholders, directors, market operators, potential investors etc. At a macro level, delisting also affects the attractiveness of the financial market and the interests of the national economy.

From a financial point of view, the importance of delisting is also reflected in share prices after the announcement of a delisting. More specifically, studies looking at the German capital market show that without share price stabilising mechanisms (e.g. appraisal rights), a delisting announcement has a negative impact on the share price.[76] If, on the other hand, stabilising mechanisms intervene, no price losses are observed. In the US, the local findings show that the market reaction to the going dark decision is on average negative,[77] while the market's reaction to firms going private (via an LBO or a freeze-out) is significantly positive.[78] By contrast, as a matter of principle, it appears that downlisting does not result in statistically significant share price losses.[79]

Hence, it is clear that the conflict of interest between the parties involved does not arise with the same intensity in all cases.

In the case of mandatory delisting, the issue is quite simple. Delisting is the result of the failure of the listed company and/or the violation of the listings provisions. Allowing eg a company involved in serious fraud to continue trading harms both investors and market reputation.[80] This fact leaves no option other than to delist. As a consequence, prospective investors are protected from fraud and assured of firm quality, while the reputation of the market is also protected. The question is the extent and nature of the violation leading to a mandatory delisting as well as the competent organ that has to decide on it.

[75] See The Economic Times Online, 'Delist Chinese stocks from US indices? Trump administration says 'everything's on the table''. Available at: https://economictimes.indiatimes.com/news/international/global-trends/delist-chinese-stocks-from-us-indices-trump-administration-says-everythings-on-the-table/articleshow/120128240.cms.

[76] Sanders (n 5) 45; M Jonas et al, *Abschlussbericht im Auftrag der Bundesrepublik Deutschland, vertreten durch das Bundesministerium für Finanzen, zur Frage: "Bietet die regelmäßige Anknüpfung von Delisting-Angeboten an den 6-Monats-Durchschnittskurs einen angemessenen Schutz für Anleger?"* (2022). Available at: www.grantthornton.de/globalassets/1.-member-firms/de-germany/pdf-download/bericht_bmf_delisting_final.pdf; Karami and Schuster, *Empirische Analyse des Kurs- und Liquiditätseffekts auf die Ankündigung eines Börsenrückzugs* (n 59). See also K Çavuşoğlu, Questionnaire Germany Q 35.

[77] Leuz, Triantis and Wang (n 42) 198, 204.

[78] See also Fidanza, Morresi and Pezzi (n 20) 149: 'To summarize, involuntary delisting typically produces negative effects on value whereas voluntary delisting produces positive effects that, in any case, depend on the geographical location. Governance characteristics and the tax profile of an LBO can also justify these results'.

[79] See Balp (n 28).

[80] Macey, O'Hara and Pompilio, 'Down and out in the Stock Market' (n 65) 710.

In contrast to mandatory delisting, voluntary delisting is a more complex matter. A listed company which decides to delist is not, by definition, a failed company. Very often quite the opposite is true. Hence, delisting is usually not a one-way street for the issuer; rather it is one of several options from which the issuer can choose. The choice to delist or to remain listed obviously affects the interests of the parties involved, especially when the management is both the purchaser of the public shares and the agent for the sellers.[81]

Moreover, as mentioned above, there are a variety of forms of delisting based on different conditions and resulting in different consequences.[82] While downlisting and partial delisting do not significantly affect the interests of the parties, due to the fact that the company remains listed on a (regulated) market, full delisting is associated with many legal and financial consequences for both issuers and shareholders. Therefore, it is very difficult to describe the affected interests abstractly and uniformly. Nonetheless, as a general rule, we could argue that the interests primarily affected in voluntary delisting are, on the one hand, the fundamental rights of companies and, on the other hand, the rights of (minority) shareholders.

A. Issuers

As mentioned above, in specific cases, voluntary delisting may be the appropriate decision for a listed company. If the costs of listing obviously exceed the listing benefits, the listed company does not have any option other than to exit the market. In such cases, the interest of the company can fully justify the delisting. What is more, delisting can be a means to achieve a corporate goal. From this point of view, delisting is associated with fundamental rights of the listed company such as financial freedom, corporate mobility and freedom of establishment.[83] Accordingly, restrictions on delisting are considered as restrictions on fundamental freedoms of the listed company. These restrictions have to pursue a legitimate goal and be in accordance with the principle of proportionality.

B. Shareholders

A delisting decision as such does not directly affect the shares of the shareholders nor their legal status. Shareholders still own the shares after the delisting of the company and their rights as shareholders are recognised. Nonetheless, delisting could negatively affect the shareholders from a financial point of view. In order to examine how delisting affects shareholders, we have to take into consideration that shareholders are

[81] DeAngelo, DeAngelo and Rice, 'Going Private: Minority Freezeouts and Stockholder Wealth' (n 33) 400: 'Because management is both purchaser of the public shares and agent for the sellers, going private frequently evokes charges of unfair treatment of minority stockholders. Indeed, some members of the legal community have called for a per se prohibition of these transactions based on the assertion that any productive gain from going private is small while the potential for exploitation of minority stockholders is large.'

[82] See III above.

[83] See Gerner-Beuerle and Chan (n 29).

not all in the same position, nor do they pursue the same goals. Therefore, we have to distinguish between the different categories of shareholders, ie minority and majority shareholders.

i. Minority Shareholders

More specifically, for minority shareholders, the shareholding in a listed company is mainly used for capital investment purposes.[84] Disposal of shares through an efficient market is therefore an important criterion for their investment.[85] As a general rule, an efficient market is a guarantee that: (a) the shares can be disposed of without high transactions costs and (b) at a fair price according to the price formation mechanism. Instead, delisting affects the liquidity of the shares and consequently the possibility of the shareholders selling their shares and disinvesting. Moreover, delisting leads to a limitation of information flows from the company to shareholders. In the same vein, obligations aiming at the protection of shareholders (such as insider-dealing prohibitions, director-dealings announcements and transparency of shareholdings), do not apply after the delisting of the company, while supervision of the company by the competent authorities also ceases. Therefore, the interests of minority shareholders usually do not align with a delisting decision.[86] Of course, this is not the case or not to the same extent, when (a) the market is inefficient, ie illiquid and the shareholders could not – even before the delisting decision – dispose of their shares at a fair price and (b) a company decides to partially delist and/or downlist.

ii. Controlling Shareholders

Controlling shareholders of a listed company are usually concerned with achieving entrepreneurial goals. Unlike minority shareholders, controlling shareholders do not primarily intend to dispose of their shares through the market. They rather intend to secure and safeguard their control. In case of disposal of their shares, controlling shareholders will usually suffer a discount on their shares or have to share the control premium with other shareholders. At the same time, as indicated above, in the case of

[84] BVerfGE 100, 289, 303.

[85] ibid: 'Shareholdings in listed stock companies allow the shareholder, at least in times of a functioning capital market, practically at any time … to invest or disinvest his capital as he sees fit. The share is so attractive from the point of view of the small shareholder precisely because he does not tie up his capital for a long period of time but can sell them again almost all the time.'

[86] See in this direction AA Sommer Jr, '"Going Private": A Lesson in Corporate Responsibility' (1974) *Law Advisory Council Lecture, Notre Dame Law School*. Available at: www.sec.gov/news/speech/1974/111474sommer.pdf: 'I speak today of a newer and currently, at least, more disquieting fad. That is the fad of "going private". Daily we read of companies which are offering to buyout all, or substantially all, of their shareholders, thus enhancing the control of the controlling shareholders and freeing the corporation of the "burdens" of being publicly held. In other instances, clever and indeed most imaginative devices are used to afford the small shareholders little, if any, choice in the matter. What is happening is, in my estimation, serious, unfair, and sometimes disgraceful, a perversion of the whole process of public financing, and a course that inevitably is going to make the individual shareholder even more hostile to American corporate mores and the securities markets than he already is.'

delisting, controlling shareholders usually intend to expropriate wealth and maximise their benefits to the detriment of minority shareholders.

C. Directors

Directors of a listed company are exposed to the pressure from market participants. The new legal framework provides for draconian sanctions against directors for violations of capital markets rules. In some provisions, culpability is not required. At the same time, extensive disclosure obligations can give rise to actions against directors. Accordingly, legal risks and market pressure speak in favour of delisting since it reduces oversight and control by the authorities. On the other side, it is argued that as soon as the firm is delisted, managers lose prestige and visibility.[87] Be that as it may, it is generally accepted that voluntary delisting reduces and minimises the agency costs between managers and shareholders.

VI. Basic Questions Regarding Voluntary Delisting

In section V above, we analysed in broad terms the contrasting interests of the issuer, the shareholders and the directors in voluntary delisting. From this analysis it is clear that the issue of voluntary delisting should not be fully left up to the parties themselves. Due to the allocation of powers and the possibility of expropriation by controlling shareholders, a regulatory intervention is necessary. As indicated above, the extent and the nature of the regulatory intervention is linked to the form of delisting. It is self-evident that a decision on partial delisting does not affect the interest of the parties the same way as full delisting does. The same applies mutatis mutandis to downlisting. Therefore, in this analysis we will focus on full delisting. As mentioned above, the latter is the most debated form of delisting.

The basic questions regarding regulation of voluntary full delisting, also discussed in the legal literature, address the following issues: (a) the competent organ to take the delisting decision and the conditions for the decision being taken,[88] (b) the protection of minority shareholders and (c) the role of the competent authorities. These issues are not separate but highly interrelated.

A. Decision on Voluntary Delisting

The first question refers to the organ competent to take the delisting decision and the conditions for the decision being taken. This question is linked to the internal distribution and allocation of powers in a public company. This issue is globally much debated. As a general remark, the competence of the board of directors ensures flexibility in decision-making, while the competence of the general meeting gives a voice

[87] Fidanza, Morresi and Pezzi (n 20) 167.
[88] See Van der Elst, Chapter 3 in this volume.

to shareholders and guarantees the legalisation of the relevant decision. Further issues to be regulated are the quorum and majority requirements with regard to the delisting decision. A high quorum and majority requirement makes the delisting decision more difficult, nonetheless minority shareholders are better protected.

B. Protection of Minority Shareholders

As indicated above, the competence of the general meeting to decide on delisting offers some protection to the minority shareholders.[89] Again, the protection offered is linked to the quorum and majority requirements. A delisting decision that can be adopted with simple quorum and majority requirements does not usually hinder the majority shareholder from implementing its delisting plan to the detriment of minority shareholders. Nonetheless, this is not the case if the decision has to be taken with high quorum and supermajority requirements.

The protection of minority shareholders can also be achieved through the recognition of statutory veto rights. Nonetheless, the recognition of such rights would make the delisting decision very difficult.

A very well-recognised method to protect minority shareholders from delisting is also the recognition of exit/appraisal rights. Granting an exit/appraisal right means that in the event of a delisting, the shareholder has the right to receive the full price of its shares. The question in such a case is how to calculate/determine the fair price. In the same vein, a mandatory offer at a fair price would fully protect the minority shareholders in case of delisting.[90]

All these are forms of procedural ex ante protection of minority shareholders. Nonetheless, protection for shareholders could also be provided ex post.[91] Examples of ex post protection include the possibility of dissenting shareholders to challenge the relevant delisting decision as well as in case of an appraisal right to challenge the price determination.[92]

C. Role of Competent Authorities and Stock Exchanges in the Delisting Procedure

The final question refers to the role of the competent authorities and stock exchanges in the delisting procedure. The main questions here are whether the competent authorities and stock exchanges should have the right to monitor the delisting procedure, to check that the legal requirements are met and eventually to impose additional conditions in favour of minority shareholders in order to allow the delisting.

[89] See generally on this issue de lege ferenda CS von Berg, *Der Marktrückzug des Emittenten, Dynamische Marktstrukturregulierung im Schnittfeld von Kapitalmarkt- und Gesellschaftsrecht* (Tübingen, Mohr Siebeck, 2018) 452 f.

[90] See Recalde and Ataun, Chapter 4 in this volume.

[91] See Giudici, Chapter 5 in this volume.

[92] ibid.

VII. European Law

Despite the great importance of this matter, European law does not regulate delisting as an integrated phenomenon. Reference to (mandatory) delisting is made in Article 18 of the Listing Directive[93] as well as in MiFID II.[94] According to Article 18 of the Listing Directive, the competent authorities may (a) decide to suspend the listing of a security where the smooth operation of the market is, or may be, temporarily jeopardised or where protection of investors so requires and/or (b) discontinue the listing of the security where they are satisfied that, owing to special circumstances, normal regular dealings in a security are no longer possible. A similar provision is also included in MiFID II. According to its Article 69(2), the competent authorities are given the power to require the removal of a financial instrument from trading, whether on a regulated market or under other trading arrangements.[95] Moreover, MIFID II contains provisions regarding the powers of market operators to remove financial instruments from trading on a regulated market,[96] multilateral trading facility (MTF) or organised trading facility (OTF),[97] which no longer comply with the rules of the regulated market, MTF or OTF, unless such suspension or removal would be likely to cause significant damage to the investors' interests or the orderly functioning of the market.

Nonetheless, the above provisions only regulate the powers of competent authorities and markets operators in the context of mandatory delisting. No reference is made to voluntary delisting. Voluntary delisting remains subject to regulation at Member State level. Hence, national provisions have to determine the competent organ of the company to decide on the delisting, the quorum and the majority requirement for the decision of the competent organ, the minority rights and the protection of dissenting shareholders, the delisting procedure, etc.

National provisions on delisting vary widely between Member States. Even the legal nature of such provisions (company law rules or capital markets rules[98]) is not clear cut in all Member States. Hence, we are far from a harmonised legal environment on delisting. Another factor that makes harmonisation on delisting more difficult are the different listing rules within European markets. As mentioned above, though market operators are given the power to remove financial instruments from trading if they do not comply with the listing rules, this power is not used the same way by all. Besides, due to the competitive relationship between exchanges, an exchange-driven harmonisation at European level is very unlikely.

Moreover, the different domestic rules on civil procedure regarding actions for compensation add a further degree of difficulty, thus resulting in legal uncertainty and cost increases at European level.

[93] Directive 2001/34/EC on the admission of securities to official stock exchange listing and on information to be published on those securities [2001] OJ L184/1.

[94] Directive 2014/65/EU on markets in financial instruments and amending Directive 2002/92/EC and Directive 2011/61/EU (recast) (MiFID II) [2014] OJ L173/349.

[95] MiFID II [2014] OJ L173/349 Art 69, para 2.

[96] ibid, Art 52.

[97] ibid, Art 32.

[98] See generally von Berg, *Der Marktrückzug des Emittenten* (n 89) 446 f.

VIII. The EU Listing Initiatives and Delisting

At the EU summit held on 9 February 2023, EU leaders stressed that the capital markets union is crucial for Europe to remain a continent of production and innovation. On 8 October 2024, the European Council adopted the Listing Act, a package of measures (i) reviewing the Prospectus Regulation, the Market Abuse Regulation, MiFIR and MiFID,[99] (ii) repealing the Listing Directive[100] and (iii) introducing a new directive regulating multiple vote share structures.[101] The Listing Act aims to simplify listing requirements, including post-listing, in order to make public capital markets more attractive for EU companies and facilitate access to capital for SMEs.

Nonetheless, listing is not an end in itself. It is an effective means of funding if specific conditions are met. It makes no sense to regulate listing while leaving delisting unregulated. Delisting rules are always a criterion for a company to go public, especially if a listed company has access to better financing alternatives. Moreover, there is no point in facilitating the listing of a company on a market if that company is subsequently delisted. Accordingly, it seems that support for listing is not possible without studying and regulating delisting.[102] From this point of view, the lack of European provisions regarding delisting as an integrated phenomenon remains a paradox and is in contrast with the goal of incentivising listing at European level.

The aim of this book is precisely to examine legal aspects of delisting in EU capital markets law, its forms, goals and rationales.

[99] See Regulation 2024/2809 amending Regulations (EU) 2017/1129, (EU) No 596/2014 and (EU) No 600/2014 to make public capital markets in the Union more attractive for companies and to facilitate access to capital for small and medium-sized enterprises [2024] OJ L2024/2809.

[100] See Directive 2024/2811 amending Directive 2014/65/EU to make public capital markets in the Union more attractive for companies and to facilitate access to capital for small and medium-sized enterprises and repealing Directive 2001/34/EC [2024] OJ L2024/2811.

[101] See Directive 2024/2810 on multiple-vote share structures in companies that seek administration to trading of their shares on a multilateral trading facility [2024] OJ L2024/2810.

[102] See, from this point of view, COM(2022) 761 final 6: '… The proposal focuses on alleviating the regulatory requirements that can deter a company from deciding to list or to remain listed'. See also COM(2022) 761 final 2:' … the features of the ecosystem that determine the cost of listing services, geopolitical instability, Brexit, COVID-19, central bank policy and inflation – have all had (and will continue to have) an impact on whether to list, when and where to list, and whether to remain listed in the EU. Regulatory requirements and the associated costs and burden, however, are also important factors in a company's decision to list and remain listed.'

2

Delisting in the Light of the ECHR

IOANNIS KTISTAKIS*

I. Introduction

When a stock is removed from the exchange listings, it is considered delisted. This can be a voluntary action initiated by the company or a compulsory action initiated by the exchange if the stock no longer meets listing requirements (B and C).[1] Each has its own characteristics in the light of the European Convention on Human Rights (ECHR). However, the main (procedural) issue before the European Court of Human Rights (ECtHR) remains the question of the victim status of the applicant (A).

II. Can the Shareholders Claim Victim Status before the ECtHR?

According to Article 34 of the ECHR, the ECtHR can examine applications from 'any person, non-governmental organisation or group of individuals'. The case law of the ECtHR has shown that the 'non-governmental organisation' category includes companies, which may therefore claim the status of victims.

Article 1 of Protocol No 1 expressly stipulates that legal persons are entitled to the peaceful enjoyment of their possessions, but other provisions, which use terms such as 'everyone' or 'no one', have also been interpreted as protecting both natural and legal persons, including companies. For example, companies have long been recognised as

* Judge at the European Court of Human Rights and Associate Professor at the Democritus University of Thrace, Greece.

[1] Article 18 of Directive 2001/34/EC on the admission of securities to official stock exchange listing and on information to be published on those securities [2001] OJ L184/1 (Listing Directive) provides the following: '(1) The competent authorities may decide to suspend the listing of a security where the smooth operation of the market is, or may be, temporarily jeopardised or where protection of investors so requires. (2) The competent authorities may decide that the listing of the security be discontinued where they are satisfied that, owing to special circumstances, normal regular dealings in a security are no longer possible.'

having the right to free expression under Article 10 of the ECHR.[2] Companies also have the right to respect for their home under Article 8 of the ECHR.[3]

A share in a company with an economic value, together with various rights attached to it which enable the shareholder to exercise influence over the company, may be considered a 'possession'.[4] This includes an indirect claim on the company's assets, including the right to share in those assets in the event of liquidation, but also other corresponding rights, in particular voting rights and the right to influence the conduct and policies of the company.[5] In *Lekić v Slovenia*, the Grand Chamber of the ECtHR accepted that the mere possession of a share created interests of a proprietary nature and that the lack of, inter alia, assets did not take the applicant's share out of the ambit of Article 1 of Protocol No 1.[6]

Then, as a matter of general principle, established in the case *Agrotexim v Greece*,[7] shareholders cannot be seen as victims of acts and measures affecting their companies. While reiterating this general principle, in *Albert and Others v Hungary*,[8] the Grand Chamber of the ECtHR clarified two situations which constitute an exception to the above principle.

The first exception, to the general principle excluding the victim status of shareholders in respect of measures affecting their companies, is the situation 'where the company and its shareholders are so closely identified with each other that it is artificial to distinguish between the two'.[9] Although companies with a separate legal personality are not normally to be identified with their shareholders, the ECtHR has accepted that there are situations where it would 'serve no purpose to distinguish between the two'[10] and has allowed the shareholders to proceed with their complaints about the proceedings or events affecting their companies.[11] The ECtHR points out that the reason for accepting victim status in such cases is that there is 'no risk of differences of opinion among shareholders or between shareholders and a board of directors as to the reality of infringements of the rights protected under the Convention and its Protocols or

[2] *Sunday Times v UK (No 1) Series A no 30* (1979) 2 EHRR 245.

[3] *Société Colas Est and Others v France ECHR 2002–III 131* (2002).

[4] *Sovtransavto Holding v Ukraine* (2002) ECHR 2002–VII 133 para 91; *Shesti Mai Engineering OOD and others v Bulgaria* App no 17854/04 (ECtHR, 20 September 2011) para 77; and *Sebeleva and others v Russia* App no 42416/18 (ECtHR, 1 March 2022) para 39.

[5] *Company S and T v Sweden* App no 11189/84 (ECtHR, 11 December 1986) 50 DR 121; *Reisner v Turkey* (ECtHR, 1 December 2016) para 45; and *Marini v Albania* App no 3738/02 (ECtHR, 18 December 2007) para 165.

[6] *Lekić v Slovenia* [GC] App no 36480/07 (ECtHR, 11 December 2018) para 71.

[7] *Agrotexim and Others v Greece* Series A no 30 (1996) 21 EHRR 250 paras 65 f; *Olczak v Poland* App no 30417/96 (ECtHR, 7 November 2002) para 57; *Lekić v Slovenia* [GC] (n 6) para 111; *Albert and Others v Hungary* [GC] App no 5294/14 (ECtHR, 7 July 2020) para 122; and *Papachela and AMAZON SA v Greece* (ECtHR, 3 December 2020) para 37.

[8] *Albert and Others* (n 7) para 124.

[9] ibid para 135.

[10] *Nassau Verzekering Maatschappij NV v the Netherlands* App no 57602/09 (ECtHR, 4 October 2011) para 21.

[11] For instance, in *Pine Valley Developments Ltd and Others v Ireland* Series A no 222 (1991) 14 EHRR 319, where the third applicant (Mr Healy) was the sole shareholder of the second applicant (Healy Holdings) which wholly owned the first applicant (Pine Valley), the Court noted that 'Pine Valley and Healy Holdings were no more than vehicles through which Mr Healy proposed to implement the development' (para 42).

concerning the most appropriate way of reacting to such infringements'.[12] This group has included cases brought by shareholders of small or family-owned or family-run companies or cooperatives, notably where a sole owner of a company has complained about the measures taken in respect of his or her company[13] or where all shareholders of a small cooperative applied to the ECtHR as applicants.[14] It has also included cases where one shareholder in a family-owned firm had lodged an application under the ECHR, while the remaining shareholders at least did not object to this.[15]

The second type of situation in which the ECtHR may disregard the company's distinct legal personality and allow its shareholders to bring complaints about the company's rights, concerns the existence of 'exceptional circumstances, in particular where it is clearly established that it is impossible' for the affected company to bring the case to the ECtHR in its own name.[16] In cases falling within this category, the mere existence of measures of outside supervision or control, which had been imposed on the company in issue due to its financial or other difficulties, was generally viewed as an important factor, but not the only one.[17] The ECtHR pointed out that the burden had been on the shareholders to demonstrate (i) either that an official who had been tasked with looking after the company's interests had been unable or unwilling to raise the grievances in issue either at the domestic or Strasbourg level,[18] (ii) or that the ECHR complaint had concerned a matter, such as the removal of a regular manager and the appointment of a trustee, in respect of which there had been a difference of opinion between the trustee and the shareholders,[19] (iii) or concerned various actions of the trustee affecting the interests of the shareholders. In each case, the matter had been such that its potential impact could have had a serious effect on the shareholders' situation, directly[20] or indirectly.[21] The shareholders must put forward weighty and convincing reasons to show that it is practically or substantially impossible for the company to have

[12] *Ankarcrona v Sweden* ECHR 2000-VI 573.

[13] For instance, as early examples, *Yarrow and Others v the United Kingdom* App no 9266/81 (ECtHR, 28 January 1983) 30 DR 155; and *Dyrwold v Sweden* App no 12259/86 (ECtHR, 7 September 1990); and, as recent examples, *SC Fiercolect Impex SRL v Romania* App no 26429/07 (ECtHR, 13 December 2016) paras 38–41; *Vujović and Lipa DOO v Montenegro* App no 18912/15 (ECtHR, 20 February 2018) paras 29 f; and *Vladimirova v Russia* App no 21863/05 (ECtHR, 10 April 2018) paras 40 f.

[14] *Jafarli and Others v Azerbaijan* App no 36079/06 (ECtHR, 29 July 2010) paras 38–42.

[15] *Khamidov v Russia* App no 72118/01 (ECtHR, 15 November 2007) paras 123–26; *Kin-Stib and Majkić v Serbia* App no 12312/05 (ECtHR, 20 April 2010) para 74; *Rysovskyy v Ukraine* App no 29979/04 (ECtHR, 20 October 2011) paras 46–49; and *KIPS DOO and Drekalović v Montenegro* App no 28766/06 (ECtHR, 22 October 2019) paras 86 f.

[16] *Agrotexim and Others* (n 7) para 66; *Lekić* (n 6) para 111; *CDI Holding Aktiengesellschaft and Others v Slovakia* App no 37398/97 (ECtHR, 18 October 2001) para 4; *Meltex Ltd and Movsesyan v Armenia* App no 45199/09 (ECtHR, 17 June 2008) para 66; *Veselá and Loyka v Slovakia* App no 54811/00 (ECtHR, 13 December 2005); *GJ v Luxembourg* App no 21156/93 (ECtHR, 26 October 2000) para 24; *Feldman and Slovyanskyy Bank v Ukraine* App no 42758/05 (ECtHR, 21 December 2017) paras 28 f; and *Vladimirova v Russia* App no 21863/05 (ECtHR, 10 April 2018) paras 40 f.

[17] *Albert and Others v Hungary* [GC] (n 7) paras 124, 138 f and 143.

[18] *Agrotexim and Others* (n 7) para 70; *Albert and Others* (n 7) para 144.

[19] *Credit and Industrial Bank v Czech Republic* App no 29010/95 (ECtHR, 21 October 2003) para 51; *Camberrow MM5 AD v Bulgaria* App no 50357/99 (ECtHR, 1 April 2004); *Capital Bank AD v Bulgaria* ECHR 2005-XII 37; *International Bank for Commerce and Development AD and others v Bulgaria* App no 7031/05 (ECtHR, 2 June 2016) paras 90–92; and *GJ v Luxembourg* (n 16) paras 23 f.

[20] *Sprl ANCA and Others v Belgium* App no 10259/83 (ECtHR, 10 December 1984) 40 DR 175.

[21] *GJ v Luxembourg* (n 16) para 24.

recourse to the ECHR bodies through the organs established by its statutes and that they should therefore be allowed to bring the application on behalf of the company.[22]

III. Voluntary Delisting

In considering the issue of voluntary delisting, it becomes evident that the primary victims of the decision taken by the company's competent bodies are the minority shareholders, who may not approve the delisting initiative. There is no relevant case law of the ECtHR on the issue of the loss of property rights of minority shareholders. Nevertheless, the ECtHR has generally held that in horizontal relations there may be public interest considerations which may impose some positive obligations on Contracting States. Thus, even in cases involving disputes between individuals or companies, certain measures necessary to protect property rights may be required.

For instance, in *Zolotas v Greece (No 2)*[23] the applicant was unable to claim the funds in his bank account due to a lack of transactions on it for over twenty years. The ECtHR held that the Greek state had a positive obligation to protect citizens and, in view of the potentially adverse consequences of limitation periods, to require banks to inform the holders of dormant accounts when the limitation period was about to expire, thus giving them the opportunity to stop the limitation period from running. The failure to require the provision of such information would be liable to upset the fair balance that must be struck between the requirements of the general interest of the community and the requirements of the protection of the fundamental rights of individuals. However, in the context of ordinary economic relations between private parties, such positive obligations are much more limited. Consequently, the ECtHR has repeatedly emphasised that Article 1 of Protocol No 1 cannot be interpreted as imposing a general obligation on Contracting States to cover the debts of private entities.

Finally, it is important to note that the issue of voluntary delisting may give rise to questions concerning the right of access to the national court. In several cases brought against the Czech Republic,[24] the ECtHR was asked to examine a systematic problem: the restriction of the applicants' access to a national court to assess the validity of general meetings of shareholders and the decisions taken at those meetings with a view to excluding minority shareholders from various companies. In all these cases, the minority shareholders' right of access to the courts was found to have been violated. In 2011, the relevant Czech legislation was amended, and minority shareholders now have access to the national courts to challenge the decision of the general meeting that deprived them of their shares. Although they cannot obtain the annulment of the resolution, the substance of their claims, whether the resolution was adopted in violation of

[22] *Albert and Others* (n 7) paras 144 f.

[23] *Zolotas v Greece (No 2)* ECHR 2013-I 359.

[24] *Kohlhofer and Minarik v the Czech Republic* App nos 32921/03, 28464/04 and 5344/05 (ECtHR, 15 October 2009); *Pekárny a cukrárny Klatovy, a.s. v the Czech Republic* App nos 12266/07, 40059/07, 36038/09 and 47155/09 (ECtHR, 12 January 2012); *Chadzitaskos and Franta v the Czech Republic* App nos 7398/07, 31244/07, 11993/08 and 3957/09 (ECtHR, 27 September 2012); and *Minarik v the Czech Republic* App no 58874/11 (ECtHR, 22 November 2012).

the law or the company's internal statutes, will be heard, and finally decided in a dispute before the Czech court.[25]

IV. Compulsory Delisting

The issue of compulsory delisting is more complex than might be initially apparent. The compulsory nature of delisting is related to the intervention of public authorities in the stock market, which consequently affects the right to property under Article 1 of Protocol No 1.

A share in a company is considered a 'possession', under the ECHR case law. It represents a form of ownership in the company, and this ownership carries with it certain economic rights. This encompasses an indirect claim to the assets of the company, including the right to a share in those assets in the event of liquidation, but also other corresponding rights, in particular voting rights and the right to influence the conduct and policy of the company. It is notable that in *Pintar and Others v Slovenia*,[26] the ECtHR held that Article 1 of Protocol No 1 applied to the cancellation of the applicants' shares, even if the government's objection concerning their questionable economic value were to be upheld.

With regard to the nature of the interference with the company's shares, it appears that the compulsory delisting does not affect the shares in terms of their existence, but rather changes the manner in which they are now traded outside the capital market. In this instance, compulsory delisting cannot be regarded as a deprivation of property; rather, it can be considered a control of use.

In the event that the control of the use of the company's shares is affected, the relevant requirements of the ECtHR's case law must be considered. These include the tests of legality, legitimate interest, and fair balance.

No relevant case law of the ECtHR exists on delisting cases per se. Therefore, analogies can be drawn with relevant issues.

A. Requirement of Legality

The mere existence of a legal basis in domestic law does not, in itself, satisfy the principle of legality. In addition, the legal basis must possess a certain quality, namely that it must be compatible with the rule of law and provide freedom from, or guarantees against, arbitrariness. Furthermore, the principle of legality requires that the applicable provisions of domestic law are sufficiently accessible, precise and foreseeable in their application.

The necessity of foreseeability is frequently intertwined with the requirements of non-arbitrariness and procedural safeguards. Consequently, a legal rule is deemed

[25] *Fischer v the Czech Republic* App no 24314/13 (ECtHR, 22 February 2022) para 31.
[26] *Pintar and Others v Slovenia* App nos 49969/14 et al (ECtHR, 14 September 2021) para 91.

'foreseeable' if it offers a degree of protection against arbitrary interference by public authorities. In this context, the case of *Korporativna Targovska Banka AD v Bulgaria* is of interest.[27] The applicant bank's grievance was that the withdrawal of its licence, which was followed almost automatically by the Sofia City Court's decision to declare the applicant bank insolvent and order its liquidation, constituted an interference with its property. The ECtHR unanimously held that the interference was unlawful, citing the applicant bank's lack of opportunity to challenge the reasons for the Central Bulgarian Bank's decision to withdraw its licence. It had already been established that the Central Bank was unable to obtain judicial review of the applicant bank's decision through proper representation. Moreover, the Central Bank's decision lacked any accompanying procedural safeguards. The applicant bank was not informed that the Central Bank would adopt the decision in question, nor was it given the opportunity to object to it, either before or after the decision was taken. These procedural safeguards were expressly excluded by domestic law. Additionally, there was no avenue for challenging the Central Bank's decision before a non-judicial authority.

In ascertaining whether the condition of judicial review has been satisfied, the ECtHR must take a comprehensive view of the applicable procedures. Furthermore, even in situations where no individual procedural deficiencies in themselves affect decisively the proportionality of a forfeiture measure, the ECtHR must consider their cumulative effect.[28] In cases where the applicants did not have the possibility of effectively challenging the measure, the ECtHR has found that an excessive burden had been borne by them.[29] The ECtHR checks whether the procedure applied provided the applicant a fair possibility of defending his or her interests.[30]

B. Legitimate Interest

Any interference by a public authority with the peaceful enjoyment of property can only be justified if it serves a legitimate public interest.

It can be reasonably assumed that the 'smooth operation of the market' and the 'protection of investors' could be cited as a legitimate interest directly provided by EU law.[31]

It is pertinent to note that in the case of *Minarik v the Czech Republic*,[32] the question of whether the applicant had effective access to the courts in relation to his action

[27] *Korporativna Targovska Banka AD v Bulgaria* App no 46564/15 and 68140/16 (ECtHR, 30 August 2022).

[28] *AGOSI v the United Kingdom* Series A no 108 (1986) para 55; *Bowler International Unit v France* App no 1946/06 (ECtHR, 23 July 2009) paras 44 f; *Jokela v Finland* ECHR 2002-IV 1 para 45; *Denisova and Moiseyeva v Russia* App no 16903/03 (ECtHR, 1 April 2010) para 59; and *Microintelect OOD v Bulgaria* App no 34129 (ECtHR, 4 March 2014) para 44.

[29] *Hentrich v France Series A no 296* (1994) para 49; *Könyv-Tár Kft and Others v Hungary* App no 21623/13 (ECtHR, 16 October 2018) para 59; and *Uzan and Others v Turkey* App No 19620/05, 41487/05, 17613/08 and 19316/08 (ECtHR, 5 March 2019) para 215.

[30] *Bäck v Finland* ECHR 2004-VIII 249 para 63; *Družstevni Záložna Pria and Others v the Czech Republic* App no 72034/01 (ECtHR, 31 July 2008) paras 94 f.

[31] See Listing Directive (n 1).

[32] *Minarik* (n 24) paras 32 and 37.

against the decision of the company's general meeting to dissolve the company and divide its assets between two new companies was addressed. The ECtHR upheld defender's argument that a different understanding of the national legislation, which would give minority shareholders an unlimited right to challenge the decision of the majority shareholder in court, could lead to a practical impossibility of transforming companies and to a destabilisation of commercial relations, with serious consequences for the economy of the Czech Republic.

C. Fair Balance Test in the Context of Article 1 of Protocol No 1

The first of the important factors in the fair balance test is whether there were other less intrusive measures which the authorities could reasonably have resorted to in pursuit of the public interest. However, their possible existence does not in itself render the contested legislation unjustified. Provided that the legislature remains within its margin of discretion, it is not for the ECtHR to say whether the legislation was the best solution to the problem or whether the legislature's discretion should have been exercised in a different way.[33]

The second important factor for the balancing test under Article 1 of Protocol No 1 is whether the applicant attempted to take advantage of a weakness or a loophole in the system.[34] Similarly, in *G.I.E.M. S.R.L. and Others v Italy*,[35] the ECtHR held that the degree of fault or negligence on the part of the applicants, or at least the relationship between their conduct and the offence in question, may be considered in assessing the proportionality of confiscation. A person's qualification as an accountant was one of the decisive reasons for deciding that reimbursing excess contributions without interest was proportionate.[36]

Finally, relevant factor to be taken into consideration is the investment risk. In the important decision *Mamatas and Others v Greece*[37] concerning the haircut of Greek state bonds during the Greek economic crisis, the ECtHR stated the following:

> In addition, the Court considers that an investment in bonds cannot be risk-free. Between the issue of such a security and its maturity, there is normally a fairly long period during which unforeseeable events may occur which could have the effect of considerably reducing the solvency of the issuer, even if that issuer is a State, and therefore lead to a subsequent loss of assets for the creditor.

[33] *James and Others v United Kingdom* Series A no 98 (1976) *8 EHRR 123* para 51; *Koufaki and Adedy v Greece* App nos 57665/13 and 57657/13 (ECtHR, 7 May 2013) para 48.

[34] *National & Provincial Building Society, Leeds Permanent Building Society and Yorkshire Building Society v the United Kingdom* Series A no 7 (1997) para 109; *OGIS-Institut Stanislas, OGEC Saint-Pie X and Blanche de Castille and Others v France* App nos 42219/98, 54563/00 (ECtHR, 27 May 2004) paras 69 and 71.

[35] *G.I.E.M. S.R.L. and Others v Italy* (merits) [GC] App nos 1828/06 et al (ECtHR, 28 June 2018) para 301.

[36] *Taşkaya v Turkey* App no 14004/06 (ECtHR, 13 February 2018) paras 49 ff.

[37] *Mamatas and Others v Greece* App nos 63066/14, 64297/14 and 66106/14 (ECtHR, 21 July 2016) para 117.

V. Conclusions

The ECHR does not recognise the freedom to conduct a business, as is the case with the much more recent provision of Article 16 of the Charter of Fundamental Rights.[38] Instead, the ECHR recognises a right to property which, under certain conditions (defined by Strasbourg's case law), protects the right of majority or minority shareholders to peacefully enjoy their shares in the event of compulsory delisting. Finally, in both types of delisting, both companies and shareholders have the right to effectively challenge before a national court the relevant internal or state decisions on the matter, in accordance with the provision of Article 6 paragraph 1 of the ECHR (right to fair trial).

[38] Charter of Fundamental Rights of the European Union [2016] OJ C202/389.

PART II

Voluntary Delisting in EU Member States

3

Voluntary Delisting and Shareholder Protection from a Corporate Law Perspective

CHRISTOPH VAN DER ELST*

I. Introduction

Companies often use the stock market to finance their activities, reduce their debt, transform their growth trajectory, offer exit opportunities for founders or other incumbent shareholders, thrust the company into the public spotlight and increase the credibility due to the pre-IPO screening.

However, not all initial public offerings end up being successful. Furthermore, the regulatory requirements of a stock exchange listing are burdensome and costly, and the market pressure for short-term results can be difficult to align with the company's strategy. In addition, the liquidity of the trading in the shares may be low, reducing the interest of market participants and putting the company in a negative light. In short, the interest in the securities of the stock exchange listed company can make it necessary to consider delisting. While the rules and procedures for listing are abundant, those for delisting are often not so clear, if they exist at all.

While a delisting of its securities can be in the interest of the company, it is not necessarily in the interest of all corporate incumbents. Especially for small and minority shareholders the decision to leave the stock exchange can be detrimental and mean 'the final nail in the coffin for a stock'.[1] For example, in an older study by Sanger and Peterson the stock price drop on the day of the delisting announcement is approximately

* Professor of Business Law and Economics at Tilburg University, The Netherlands and Ghent University, Belgium.

[1] J Khort, 'Protection of Investors in Voluntary Delisting on the U.S. Stock Market' (2014) *Uppsala Faculty of Law Working Paper 4/2014* 4. Note that although this chapter focuses on the US, it provides a detailed overview of a number of specific delisting issues in 25 jurisdictions, including many jurisdictions covered in this chapter, including Australia, France, Germany, Hong Kong, India, Italy, the Netherlands, Spain, Sweden, the UK and the US.

8.5 per cent.[2] After the going private transaction, the shareholders are tied to the company and only have few options to transfer their shares. Shareholders are deprived of an easy exit mechanism at a market price and have to search for a purchaser that values the shares appropriately, which can be quite cumbersome, if possible at all.

Regulators all over the world have different levels of interest in the specific problems that delisting gives rise to, resulting in procedures for delisting transactions that are laid down in different regulatory frameworks in different jurisdictions. Those regulations are confronted with many different questions. First, while there is minor discussion whether a delisting should be facilitated, it is more debated which conditions should be complied with before a delisting can become effective and which corporate parties should be involved in the delisting process, especially for the protection of the (small) shareholders. The company is being run by a corporate body, commonly a board of directors, while the persons affected by the delisting are primarily the holders of the securities, although many others, like bondholders or employees can be influenced, too. Second, in addition to these corporate incumbents, there is also the market operator that monitors the market for securities trading, which is often a listed company itself, setting specific standards for its listed customers as well as a market supervisory agency. Do these parties have to be involved and, if so, which interests do they have to consider?

In this chapter I focus on the position of minority shareholders in a voluntary delisting transaction of a company listed on a main or regulated market in a number of European Member States. 'Voluntary' indicates that the company takes the decision or agrees with the initiative to delist its securities with voting rights from the trading activities of the stock exchange, considering that some corporate incumbents do not necessarily support this delisting. I emphasise the delisting procedure largely from a company law perspective as other chapters address it from other legal angles. However, the structure of the acts on company law differs substantially between jurisdictions, obliging us to take into account other laws and rules for functional approach reasons. For example, the UK Companies Act does not address delisting of the securities of the company, but the rules can be found in the FCA Listing Rules, requiring a shareholders' special resolution, whereas the Companies Act does focus on the squeeze-out mechanism which follows a takeover bid and which is generally considered part of securities law. Moreover, the Euronext Amsterdam Announcement 2004–41 refers to an exit and delisting arrangement, which is further developed in Book 2:92a of the Dutch Civil Code. Also, the Columbian law for the financial sector and the securities market explicitly empowers the general meeting of the company to take the delisting decision.

The chapter is (largely) based on a questionnaire that legal scholars of different European jurisdictions answered in 2023,[3] and supplemented with an overview of

[2] GC Sanger and JD Peterson, 'An Empirical Analysis of Common Stock Delistings' (1990) 25 *The Journal of Financial and Quantitative Analysis* 261. Note that this study is about involuntary delistings. Economic literature points at significant shareholder gains for voluntary delistings, but these studies envisage the delisting that takes place after another transaction like a buy-out or freeze-out. For an overview see I Martinez and S Serve, 'Reasons for Delisting and Consequences: A Literature Review and Research Agenda' (2017) 31 *Journal of Economic Surveys* 740.

[3] Questionnaires.

the delisting processes in five other non-European jurisdictions. The jurisdictions are: Australia, Austria, Colombia, Cyprus, Finland, France, Germany, Greece, Hong Kong, India, Italy, Spain, Sweden, the UK and the US. For the references to the different legislative and regulatory frameworks I refer to the answers to the questions on voluntary delisting.

In the next section I briefly sketch the different scenarios within which a voluntary delisting takes place. I focus on a company that only has one class of securities, shares with voting rights, listed on the regulated or main market of the stock exchange and on the procedural elements including the valuation of the shares in a functional approach. The delisting can be the consequence of a transaction, trigger a transaction or stand alone. In the second section I illuminate which of the scenarios the different jurisdictions provide for. Section three examines the different corporate bodies that are engaged in the voluntary delisting as well as third parties that can be involved and how this involvement protects the (minority) shareholders. Depending on the jurisdiction, the board of directors, the general meeting of shareholders, a supermajority shareholder, promotor or acquiror and a market operator or supervisor are involved in the delisting process. The (in)voluntary exit of the minority shareholders and the consideration of the compensation for the transfer of the shares is discussed in section four. Section five questions the efficiency of some of the choices in the procedures of voluntary delistings and concludes.

II. Voluntary Delisting Decision in a Transactional Perspective

A decision to voluntarily delist rarely stands alone, although now and then the voluntary delisting is indeed not preceded, accompanied, or followed by any other transaction or decision. Figure 3.1 presents the common scene in which a voluntary delisting decision takes place. In a large number of jurisdictions, a transaction like a successful takeover or some types of mergers result in the concentration of all (or as good as all) securities in the hands of one party, making the listing of those securities superfluous. In some of these processes, the ensuing delisting of the securities are referred to as a 'cold delisting'. These M&A and takeover transactions are heavily regulated in most jurisdictions, depending on the nature of the transactions, in company or securities laws. The regulatory frameworks within which these transactions take place, offers (more or less) instruments for (minority) shareholders to protect their interests. The delisting of the securities follows the transaction and accompanying protective mechanisms will not be addressed in this chapter.

In a number of jurisdictions, the voluntary delisting of its securities can be taken, independently from any preceding transaction, by the company's board of directors, the general meeting of shareholders or the (supermajority) shareholder(s acting in concert). In some jurisdictions the shareholders (and eventually other parties like the bondholders or creditors) are not offered any specific right when the company takes the decision to delist. It can be considered a stand-alone decision like many others that the company takes. When this decision is taken in compliance with the regulations – there are often specific conditions in the listing rules of the market operator envisaging the interest of the market participants, in particular the investors – there is limited room for the shareholders who disagree with the delisting decision to challenge it, but to exit the company and sell their shares before the delisting becomes effective.

Figure 3.1 Voluntary Delisting in Perspective

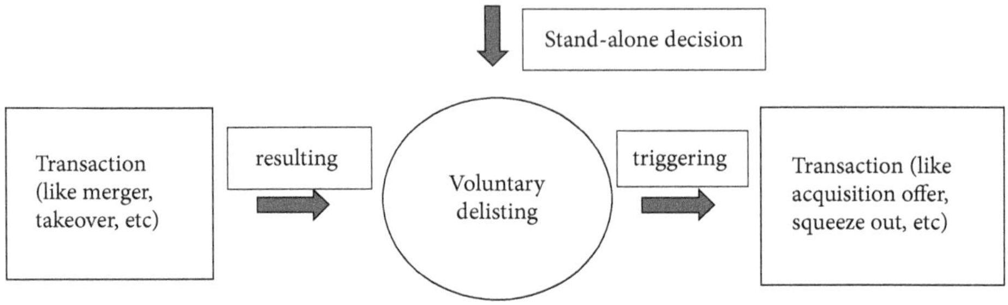

In a number of other jurisdictions, the regulators of the securities markets, company and/or securities laws provide additional mechanisms to protect shareholders' interests. In those jurisdictions, the decision to delist triggers specific mechanisms like an acquisition offer to all or only the opposing shareholders, or squeeze out transactions resulting in the concentration of all securities 'in one place'. The next sections address the different ways in which the jurisdictions with developed stock exchanges offer protection to the shareholders of companies who take the decision to voluntarily delist, other than through a 'cold delisting' or a market migration.

III. The Voluntary Delisting Landscape

While most jurisdictions provide in their current approach for eternal life for companies,[4] eternity is not expected as all jurisdictions provide for procedures for the (voluntary) liquidation of companies. Commonly, jurisdictions empower the general meeting of shareholders as the competent body to take a decision to dissolve the company. It can be argued that if a company can decide to end its corporate existence as a separate legal entity, it must also be possible to take the less far-reaching decision to delist its securities from a stock exchange. However, whereas becoming a stock exchange listed company is decided at the company level, being exposed to the public is seen in all jurisdictions as a matter that transcends corporate law. Therefore, securities (exchange) law in most jurisdictions addresses issues related to stock exchange listing and also stock exchange delisting. It has a major effect on the procedural issues of a delisting. Contrary to a voluntary liquidation, a delisting is in many and even most jurisdictions not only an exclusive matter of the company itself but made dependent

[4] Some jurisdictions provide for a fixed term. The French legislator determines in Art L. 210-2 of the French Commercial Code that the term of a company cannot exceed 99 years.

on another corporate action. It offers (minority) shareholders protection that goes beyond the corporate law shareholder protection mechanisms.

In Greece and Sweden, securities market law explicitly refers to a voluntary delisting of the securities. The Swedish Securities Market Act states in chapter 15, section 11 that 'Delisting of a financial instrument that has been admitted to trading must also take place at the request of the person at whose request the instrument has been admitted to trading',[5] but Nasdaq as the market operator can postpone the delisting if it is considered appropriate from the public point of view. The same goes for Greece, but the Hellenic Capital Market Commission, not the market operator, can set conditions for the delisting of securities.

Most jurisdictions are less explicit in their national securities law but refer for the delisting to the regulatory agency or the stock exchange listing rules. All facilitate delisting, but upon conditions the company (or other parties like a large shareholder or acquiror) must comply. *Cyprus* sets out the conditions for a delisting in a regulatory decision of the Council of the Cyprus Stock Exchange, which was authorised by the securities and Cypriot stock exchange laws. Similarly, the *Finnish* Act on Trading in Financial Instruments empowers the trading venue to set the rules for delisting, hence the Nasdaq providing the conditions in its Main Market Rulebook. This approach is found in non-European jurisdictions as well. The US Securities and Exchange Act empowers the Securities and Exchange Commission which, next to setting general standards of compliance with national rules, further refers to the Stock Market Rules. Similarly, although somewhat more complex, the Australian Corporations Act provides the stock exchange operator ASX Limited and the supervisory authorities with the powers to regulate delisting (which is especially to be found in chapter 17 of the ASX Listing Rules). In the UK, the Financial Services and Markets Act 2000 allows voluntary delisting in accordance with the Financial Conduct Authority Handbook. The company must apply to the Financial Conduct Authority for a delisting.

Other jurisdictions explicitly exclude the right of the company to a purely voluntary delisting that is unilaterally decided by the company's competent body. Austria and Germany combine a company's delisting request with a (preceding mandatory) takeover or a market migration. The Austrian securities law (s 38) further requires certain terms of listing ranging from one to three years depending on the type of preceding action (market migration or takeover). Both jurisdictions explicitly add to these limited options of delisting that a delisting must not contradict with the protection of the investors, signalling that the interests of the shareholders must be considered. In practice, the majority shareholder will take over the company, although it does not exclude other avenues such as a hostile takeover bid. The Spanish approach is similar but reverses the steps. If the company's general meeting takes the decision to delist the shares from the market, Article 65 of the Spanish Securities Act obliges the company to seek a public acquisition offer. The Columbian Financial Law (Decreto unico 2555) provides in Article 5.2.6.1.3 that a company intending to cancel the registration of its shares in the National Registry of Securities and Issuers and trading on the stock

[5] The original version of the provision reads: 'Avnotering av ett finansiellt instrument som har tagits upp till handel ska även ske på begäran av den efter vars begäran instrumentet har tagits upp till handel.'

exchange must inform its intention in a notice in two newspapers when and where the general meeting of shareholders will decide on the delisting. The general meeting's decision triggers an acquisition offer.

A similar approach is to be found in India. The company cannot voluntarily delist but the Delisting Regulations of the Securities and Exchange Board of India (SEBI) foresee that the acquiror or the promotor of the company can file a delisting procedure.

In two jurisdictions, France and the Netherlands, the Euronext stock exchange provides for a voluntary delisting procedure. In both countries Euronext Rule Book I gives the authority to the Relevant (local) Euronext Market Undertaking to delist *at the request of the relevant issuer*. In France, the Monetary and Financial Code refers to the removal from trading of a financial instrument in Article L. 420-10, but only by the market operator or by the chairman of the French securities and exchange commission (AMF, *Autorité des marchés financiers*), a voluntary delisting at the request of the issuer is not being provided for. However, the highest court, the Cour de Cassation, rejected the proposition that a delisting on the initiative of the issuer is not possible. The delisting must be decided upon by the market operator, but this does not prevent a company from initiating this process by requesting such a decision to delist. Article L. 433-4 of the same Code empowers the French AMF to determine the procedure for a buy-out offer by a supermajority shareholder, leading to the delisting of the shares. The procedure is to be found in Article 236-1 to 236-7 of the AMF General Regulation. The 2019 Loi PACTE modified Article L. 433-4 of the Monetary and Financial Code substantially. Furthermore, chapter four of Euronext Rule Book II: Specific rules applicable to the French regulated markets, provides in its latest 2019 edition in the delisting procedure that Euronext Paris is the market authority that decides the delisting of the securities of an issuer that requested its delisting. In the Netherlands, the local Euronext Market Undertaking issued next to the general Euronext Rule Book I, already in 2004, Announcement 2004–41 that contains the delisting process, referring to the supermajority shareholder taking the initiative for the delisting, not the company. Case law is very scarce, but the validity of this Euronext Amsterdam Announcement was never contested.

Italy is familiar with the absence of a legislative framework for voluntary delisting. The securities law provides in a procedure for market migration and the Civil Code refers to an exit right for certain shareholders upon delisting. There is no explicit provision for a voluntary delisting of the company's securities, which creates legal uncertainty. The delisting based on an issuer's request can be disputed, notwithstanding Euronext Rule Book I. Therefore, in Italy, alternative schemes are being used which end the conditions for being stock exchange listed.

This overview shows that there is a wide variety of regulations for securities delisting but also that an issuer can seldom take a delisting decision unilaterally. In the few European jurisdictions where an issuer is empowered to do so, this commonly triggers a sell-out mechanism for the opposing shareholders. Almost all jurisdictions add requirements to a 'voluntary' delisting of the securities. The requirements may be that delisting is only possible in very specific circumstances, often involving (some kind of) takeover or migration to another market, or depends on the discretion of the market operator or sometimes the supervisory agency. As the market operator is often itself a private entity, this kind of private ordering is common practice. The discretion of the operator or agency can be flexible, like in Sweden or strict, like in Austria, resulting in a very limited number of acceptable delisting reasons. It could also be that it is not the issuer who decides to delist but an acquiror or promotor, as is the case in India. Not many jurisdictions disclose the reasons for these limitations to voluntary delisting, but both Germany and Austria point at the interests of the investors (the delisting should not even be allowed when their interests would be violated in the latter countries). In short, when the securities market is involved, companies can seldom act completely autonomously, different from a voluntary liquidation decision.

IV. The Actors in a Voluntary Delisting Procedure

When a voluntary delisting is not forbidden, which is seldom the case, the delisting transaction raises the questions as to which corporate body or bodies can initiate and decide on this transaction and which instruments the shareholders are offered or can use to protect their interests.

The previous section showed that the voluntary delisting of the securities of a company is approached differently in the various jurisdictions. The (process of) delisting is either triggered by another event (predominantly a takeover or a related transaction like a merger) or is (sometimes) triggering another event, such as a takeover or exit rights for shareholders. A stand-alone delisting process is rarely found in legislative or regulatory frameworks. The event and process resulting in delisting, taking place either before or after the delisting, affect the protection of (minority) shareholders.

In the majority of cases, a corporate body is involved in the decision to have the company's securities voluntarily delisted from the listing tables. In some jurisdictions it is a shareholder – in the position of an acquiror, promotor, or large shareholder – that is in charge of the delisting (whereby it is questionable whether this can be called a 'voluntary' delisting).

A large number of jurisdictions leave this voluntary delisting decision to the board of directors. This is the case in the US, but also in Australia, Austria, France, Germany, India, Finland, the Netherlands and Sweden. In the latter three countries, the allocation of the right to decide on a delisting to the board of directors flows from the general company law rule that it is the board of directors that is in charge of the management of the company. There is some uncertainty due to the absence of a specific legal rule or case law of the jurisdictions' supreme courts. In Colombia, Cyprus, Greece, Hong Kong, Italy, Spain and the UK, the (extraordinary) general meeting is in charge of the delisting decision. Like for some countries where there is some uncertainty as to the power of the board of directors for taking this decision to delist, in Italy it is unclear if the (extraordinary) general meeting of shareholders must vote on the delisting.

The dichotomy between the powers of the board of directors and the right of the general meeting of shareholders should not be overemphasised, as a more balanced approach is de facto applied in many jurisdictions.

First, if the board of directors is responsible for the delisting decision, other corporate bodies, especially the general meeting of shareholders, can also be involved.

This is the case in Austria. Section 95(5)(no 15) and section 148(2a) of the Austrian *Aktiengesetz* explicitly engages both the supervisory board and the general meeting of shareholders in the delisting process. The board of directors can only decide a delisting with the approval of the supervisory board and support by a decision of the general meeting of shareholders taken with a 75 per cent majority of the votes. Similarly, in India the shareholders' approval, voting for this special resolution, must be obtained within 45 days after the board's approval according to section 11(1) of the SEBI Delisting Regulation 2021. Note that the board of directors must also appoint a peer review company secretary who must prepare a special due diligence report. The board of directors of Australian companies must make a request to the ASX Limited stock exchange operator to remove the securities from the stock exchange list. In the case of voluntary delisting, which is not preceded by a successful control transaction, ASX Limited supports the practice that the company obtains the shareholders' approval through a special resolution according to its Guidance Note 33 (section 2.7) whereby the stock exchange can exclude certain shareholders from voting when the delisting is considered to confer benefits to the latter at the expense of the other shareholders including situations whereby some shareholders have an informational advantage over other shareholders after the delisting.

Second, some jurisdictions in which the board of directors must take the decision of the delisting, the board must comply with other requirements. For example, in India, the board must certify its compliance with all securities law provisions, that the delisting is in the interest of the shareholders of the company,[6] and that the acquiror is in compliance with the provisions of the securities laws.

Third, when the board of directors is in charge of the delisting process, it can voluntarily address and engage the shareholders in the general meeting. This was, for example, the case for Geojunxion. This Dutch company was established in the 1980s and originally developed navigation maps and later apps for signalling alerts (eco-alerts, health alerts and the like). The company had one major customer and three large shareholders holding 31 per cent, 11 per cent and 7 per cent of the shares, the other shareholders owning each less than 3 per cent of the shares. The company had been listed on the Amsterdam Euronext stock exchange for more than 20 years and before the financial crisis of 2008 its shares were trading at more than €16 but plummeted thereafter. Since early 2022, its stock price further dropped from €2 to less than €1. Similar to other small companies listed on Euronext Amsterdam, the company did not appoint an external auditor. At its 2022 general meeting, it sought authorization for the board to select an external auditor and outlined potential alternatives if no auditor could be found, including the possibility of delisting the company.[7] The company contacted all six Dutch firms that were licensed to perform an external audit, but none of them accepted the invitation. There is a mandatory external audit for listed companies to which the Euronext Rulebook explicitly refers. The Euronext market operator

[6] Note that the SEBI rules mention the requirement of an alignment with the interests of the shareholders explicitly.

[7] GeoJunxion NV, *Presentation to the shareholders at the general meeting* (15 November 2022). Available at: www.geojunxion.com/wp-content/uploads/GeoJunxion_AGMS-Presention_15Nov_2022_FINAL.pdf (on file with the author) 32.

is authorised to delist the shares if the company does not have an external auditor which was, for several years, the case for Geojunxion. Euronext provided a timeframe for resolving the absence of an external auditor. In May 2023, Euronext informed Geojunxion that the delisting would become effective if no auditor was elected as of 6 November 2023. The absence of an external auditor was also a breach of a bank covenant in a convertible loan agreement. During the annual meeting in 2023, the board of directors informed the shareholders (again) of the different options and the board's preference for a delisting of the shares, which would mean that all assets would be sold to a third party, and the company would then be liquidated. The shareholders were also provided with a fairness opinion. At an extraordinary meeting attended by 65 per cent of the shareholders,[8] this plan was approved with an overwhelming majority of more than 99 per cent for each of the agenda items related to this transaction: the sales transaction, the dissolution and the appointment of the liquidator. The approval rates of the disinterested shareholders, which the company voluntarily presented, were between 98 per cent and 99 per cent. According to Euronext's website, the company has not been active (listed) since January 2024. Note that, Geojunxion preferred voluntary delisting over the involuntary delisting initiated by the market operator. For companies listed on the different Euronext markets (including Amsterdam, Brussels, Dublin, Lisbon, Milan, Paris and Oslo) a voluntary delisting, combined with a transaction that results in a type of exit (liquidation in Geojunxion's case) is not suffering from the 'pure' involuntary delisting by Euronext in accordance with rules 6905/1 and 6905/2 of Rulebook I. Although understandable, this does not provide any kind of exit route for the shareholders before or after the removal of the securities.

Finally, the governance structure of listed companies in a number of jurisdictions is such that the (executive) board of directors is monitored by a supervisory board. This is common in the Netherlands, Germany and Austria where, in the latter country, the law explicitly involves the supervisory board.

Conversely, in all jurisdictions where the general meeting oversees the delisting decision, the board of directors is responsible for the organisation (and the agenda) of the general meeting of shareholders; only if this responsibility is not taken in compliance with the companies acts, will jurisdictions offer alternatives for organising the meeting.[9]

The different organs that oversee the delisting decision affect the protection of the shareholders. When the board of directors triggers the delisting, it must consider the directors' duty to act in the best interests of the company. In many jurisdictions this is embedded in their fiduciary duties and includes the interests of all the shareholders. However, the interests of the company can and will overrule the interests of the minority shareholders if the listing does not offer the appropriate visibility and recognisability, amongst other advantages. An unlisted company (generally) offers minority shareholders less investor protection. Disclosure and liquidity levels depend on the jurisdiction.

[8] Given the ownership structure of the company, several small shareholders attended the meeting. If all shareholders had attended, this could have determined the outcome of the vote at the general meeting.

[9] Such as a shareholder's right to convene a meeting or to apply to a court to have a meeting convened.

In most jurisdictions, shareholders can vote on the delisting resolution based on their own interests. However, minority shareholders do not always receive better protection when the general meeting of shareholders has the authority to decide about the delisting.

Some countries apply minimum quorum rights for validly holding a general meeting of shareholders. This is the case in Italy (20 per cent of the share capital with voting rights but the articles of association can opt for another (more stringent) threshold), Spain (25 per cent of the share capital, first call) and Cyprus (three members in person), all offering no real protection for minority shareholders who oppose a delisting, as in all the cases known to us, the company counts shareholders who own and control large voting blocks. This is different in Hong Kong where, when a delisting is structured in a scheme of arrangement, 75 per cent of the voting shareholders must be present. In Greece, where no quorum exists, a supermajority approval right serves as an important indirect quorum requirement.

Minority shareholders can be better protected when the resolution to delist the (shares of the) company is set very high, which is the case in a number of jurisdictions including Hong Kong, Cyprus and Greece. In Greece, according to Article 17 of Law 3371/2005, more than 95 per cent of the total voting share capital is required for the delisting decision. In the former two countries 90 per cent of the voting securities must approve the scheme (Hong Kong) or resolution (Cyprus). In some other countries, large minority shareholder(s) (possibly acting in concert) can vote down the resolution. This is the case in India,[10] Austria and the UK where shareholders with 75 per cent of the attending shares with voting rights in the latter two countries and two-thirds of the votes in the former country must approve the delisting resolution. The UK FCA Listing rules offer minority shareholders further protection if the company has a controlling shareholder. In the latter case, the cancellation of listing must be approved not only by 75 per cent of the attending shareholders with voting rights but also with a majority of the votes attached to the shares of the independent shareholders. A controlling shareholder is one who controls more than 30 per cent of the votes to be cast at the general meeting. The UK is the only country that provides this specific kind of veto right for minority shareholders in a voluntary delisting process.[11]

Like for the quorum requirements, in countries such as Columbia, minority shareholders are not offered any specific protection, as the decision to delist is taken using a regular majority of the votes.[12]

It is relevant to note that, in some jurisdictions, the decision on voluntary delisting is directly or indirectly taken outside the company. The Netherlands serves as an example. It follows from the Euronext Amsterdam Announcement 2004–41 that a shareholder(s) who hold(s) 95 per cent of (a certain type of) shares or depository receipts can request the delisting of this class of securities if the issuer agrees. The general Euronext Rulebook does not provide for a request of the supermajority shareholder(s),

[10] As well as in Italy, but see supra regarding the uncertainties of the delisting procedure.

[11] See also the Geojunxion case (n 7), where the general meeting minutes disclose the voting results of the disinterested shareholders.

[12] Note that Columbian law offers opposing minority shareholders an exit mechanism.

only of the issuer (or competent authority or Euronext). The Announcement 2004–41 explicitly provides for the issuer's consent,[13] but the initiative for delisting is taken by the supermajority shareholder. The consent of the issuer refers to the involvement of the board of directors of the company. In practice, and although this old Announcement 2004–41 does only provide for a delisting started by the issuer in case the company's shares or receipts are listed on another exchange, it is usual that the delisting is the result of an acquisition or takeover resulting in a squeeze-out process and the termination of both the listing and the listing agreement, which is approved by Euronext Amsterdam. Hence, the company publicly announces that it addresses the stock exchange to end the listing of its financial instruments, rather than the shareholder who holds more than 95 per cent of those financial instruments. In other European Member States, it is common for an acquiror or current shareholder to launch a takeover bid. If successful, this is followed by a squeeze-out procedure, leading to the delisting of shares. This process results in the acquiror legally owning all the shares, thus ending their market trading. Similarly, in India the SEBI Delisting Regulation explicitly refers to the acquiror initiating the delisting: Regulation 8(1) starts with 'On the date when the acquirer(s) decides to voluntarily delist the equity shares of the company, it shall make an initial public announcement to all the stock exchanges'.[14] The delisting rules related to the takeover are discussed in Chapter 4 of this volume.

When the shareholders are empowered to take part in the voluntary delisting process of the company, the resolution can differ in different jurisdictions. Spain provides a good example. According to Ley 6/2003, Article 65 grants the general meeting of shareholders the approval right for the delisting. Further, the law requires that a takeover offer must be launched – an exit right – and that the meeting must approve the price of the shares. Therefore, the shareholders must be provided with a detailed report that justifies this price. Also, in India where a delisting is initiated by the acquiror, shareholders are explicitly involved in determining the price of the shares: 'Public shareholders holding the equity shares of the company, which are sought to be delisted, shall be entitled to participate in the reverse book building process.'[15] In Colombia, a vote for delisting triggers another right or duty. Article 5.2.6.1.3 of the Decreto Unico 2555 of 2010 states that the shareholders that do not take part in the general meeting or vote against the delisting obtain an exit right; the shareholders who vote for the delisting must make the public acquisition offer.

Note that, in some jurisdictions, the companies' securities must remain listed for a minimum term after the initial public offering. The Austrian *Börsengesetz* makes mandatory term of at least three years in case the delisting is initiated with a takeover bid and one year in case the shares are traded or will be traded on another regulated market (or an equivalent outside the European Union).[16]

[13] With the exception of the delisting request when the shares or depository instruments are also listed on another regulated and liquid market.

[14] Securities and Exchange Board of India (Delisting of Equity Shares) Regulations, reg 8, para 1.

[15] ibid reg 19.

[16] Austrian *Börsengesetz*, section 38, §6.

V. Delisting and the Financial Position of the (Minority) Shareholders

In several countries an exit right of the shareholders resulting from or related to the delisting decision and the consideration of the compensation for the securities flow from another transaction. In Austria, the delisting is the result of an offer aimed at the acquisition of all shares admitted to trading; the price must be at least the average stock market price of the securities weighted according to the respective trading volumes of at least five trading days before the intended day of stopping trading was announced. When this price is obviously below its actual value, the price must be set appropriately by using other means, such as the discounted cash flow method. Shareholders can challenge this offer price unless they hold more than 50 per cent of the securities that are subject to the offer they have already accepted. Also, the Takeover Commission can apply for a review of the offer price. Similarly, the German delisting follows the request of the management after a takeover to acquire all the securities for which the delisting is requested, has been made. According to Section 39(3) of the German *Börsengesetz*, the consideration shall at least be the weighted average domestic stock exchange price during the six months before the announcement of the takeover. There are three exceptions: in case of illiquidity, a violation of the requirement to publish insider information or a violation of the market manipulation rule during the aforementioned six-month period. Contrary to Austria, Germany does not provide for any other exception, resulting in the debate whether this list is exhaustive. In India, the acquiror will provide an indicative price which must be higher than the floor price for which a reference is being made to the SEBI takeover regulations of the Securities and Exchange Board of India. In that regulation the acquiror must determine this floor price depending on the regime that is applicable. For example it will be the volume weighted average market price of such shares for a period of 60 trading days immediately preceding the date of the public announcement of the acquisition or the volume weighted average price paid or payable for acquisitions, whether by the acquiror or by any person acting in concert with him during the 52 weeks immediately preceding the date of the public announcement.[17]

Voluntary delistings that are not the consequence of a control transaction (frequently a takeover) but are independent decisions taken by a company organ or a third party (like a supermajority shareholder) question whether and, if so under which conditions, the shareholder can exit the company. This could be the case if the decision was taken by the general meeting and the shareholder opposes the delisting which was approved by the appropriate majorities, the shareholder suffers from the reduced liquidity of the trading in the shares of the unlisted company.[18] As discussed, a number of jurisdictions offer additional protection rights to the shareholders, like an appraisal or exit right.

[17] See Regulation 8 of SEBI's Substantial acquisition of Shares and Takeovers Regulation 2011.

[18] This is similar in jurisdictions where the decision to delist rests with the board of directors. However, in these cases, a shareholder is aware of this risk when entering the company.

In Spain, voluntary delisting is accompanied by an offer of the company to all the holders of shares (as well as subscription right owners and convertible bondholders), except those shareholders that approved the delisting resolution (and immobilised the securities according to Article 10(2) of Real Decreto 1066/2007).[19] The offer price must be approved by the general meeting. This price must be based on different methods: the theoretical accounting value based on the latest financial statements, the net asset value of the company, the weighted average price of the securities during the six months period preceding the announcement of the exclusion proposal, the value of the consideration in a public acquisition offer that has been made in the year preceding the date of the exclusion request, other valuation methods that are commonly accepted in the international financial community (like discounted cash flow or a multiple). The accompanying valuation report must justify the relevance of the different methods.

The Columbian delisting process starts with calling a general meeting of shareholders with the resolution to delist the company. When the majority of the attending shareholders approve the delisting, the supporting shareholders must start the acquisition offer within three months after the general meeting, pro rata of their participation. An independent expert acknowledged by the Columbian SFC (Superintendencia Financiera de Colombia) determines the offer price. The company must pay the expert's appraisal costs.

In the Netherlands a voluntary delisting that is not the result of a preceding takeover bid in combination with a squeeze-out procedure in accordance with book 2:359c of the Dutch Civil Code, will either start with a request for delisting as part of a squeeze-out procedure under Article 2:92a of the Civil Code, or as a delisting request in compliance with Euronext Amsterdam Announcement 2004–41. Both mechanisms start with the request of a supermajority shareholder (or shareholders) holding (in concert) more than 95 per cent of the share capital. Under Article 2:92a of the Civil Code, the shareholder addresses the Enterprise Court of Amsterdam requesting the other shareholders to transfer their shares to the plaintiff. The Court will appoint one of three experts to prepare a report of the value of the shares on a specific date, set by the Court. The experts are entitled to inspect all books, records and other data of the company. The Court will (based on the reports) determine the consideration for the compensation. The plaintiff will publish the day, place of payment and price in a national daily newspaper and inform in writing the shareholders of whom he knows the address. If the delisting follows the procedure of Euronext Amsterdam Announcement 2004–41, the supermajority shareholder must offer an exit arrangement to the remaining shareholders. The request for delisting will provide the terms and conditions of the offer. The Announcement identifies four different admissible exit arrangements of which an offer of the issuer to buy the remaining shares in the market is the most likely.[20] In that case it is the company's board of directors

[19] There are a number of exceptions to this rule, such as when the shareholders decide unanimously for the delisting (see Art 1(b) of the Real Decreto 1066/2007).

[20] The other three refer to a public offer for listed shares which will take place in the regime of takeovers and squeeze-outs (see Book 2:259c) or the buyout arrangement of Book 2:92a of the Civil Code, or an arrangement that meets the requirements of Euronext Amsterdam Authority which will result in a public offer

(and supervisory board) which determines the consideration of the compensation. Euronext Amsterdam monitors the exit arrangement in its approval of the request for delisting. In recent history there has been only one example of this type of delisting. The shareholders were offered a share price 6.5 per cent higher than the price at which the supermajority shareholders acquired the shares that passed the threshold of 95 per cent of the shares, a premium of 4.4 per cent compared to the weighted average market price of these shares in the preceding period of three months, as well as a premium of 4.8 per cent compared to the weighted average market price of these shares in the preceding six months.

France also provides for a squeeze-out procedure as an exit route for delisting the shares, which was not preceded by a (recent) takeover offer.[21] Article 236-3 of the AMF General Regulation offers the majority shareholder(s) holding at least 90 per cent of the shares or voting rights in a French listed company admitted to trading on a regulated market the right to file a buyout offer for the remaining equity securities as well as securities giving access to the capital or voting rights. The price at which the offer is made must be higher than the price determined by calculating the average stock market prices, weighted by trading volume for 60 trading days prior to the publication of the notice of the offer to the AMF who informs the market. Note that France also offers a sell-out route for the minority shareholders under Article 236-1 of the AMF General Regulation. Thereafter the company can apply for a delisting of its securities with Euronext Paris in accordance with Article P.1.4.2 of Euronext Rulebook II with the specific rules applicable to the French regulated markets.

When the delisting decision has been taken by the general meeting of shareholders, the delisting of a Cypriot company can take place 15 days thereafter. As the decision requires the approval of more than 90 per cent of the represented securities, the Cypriot regime does not offer an automatic exit right, but the minority shareholders can file a case. If the decision is to be considered an oppression of the minority shareholders, the court can, under Article 202 of the Cypriot Companies Act, order the company to acquire the shares of these shareholders. An expert or auditor will determine the consideration of the compensation.

Shareholders of Italian companies that delist – taking into account these legal uncertainties – have a specified exit right. According to Article 2437 *quinquies* of the Civil Code, a shareholder who did not participate in the resolution resulting in the delisting has a withdrawal right. Shareholders who did not participate include those who opposed the resolution or abstained from voting. The shareholder must inform the company of its intention to exit the company by offering its shares. The shareholder opposing the resolution will know the consideration when exiting the company – the arithmetic average of the closing process in the six months preceding the publication of the notice convening the meeting. The articles of association can provide for different criteria but cannot result in a consideration that is lower than this. Article 2437*ter* of the

(TM Stevens, 'Listing and Delisting' in MCA van den Nieuwenhuijzen (ed), *Financial Law in the Netherlands* (Alphen aan den Rijn, Kluwer Law International, 2010) 171, 193 f.

[21] Here, the situation of a French company listed on Euronext Paris is addressed. The Euronext Rule Book II also provides for a specific delisting procedure in case of a foreign company listed on Euronext Paris.

Civil Code continues to state that this value needs to be available at least 15 days before the date of the general meeting.

In light of the uncertain status of delisting there is also ambiguity. The shareholder must inform the company within 15 days after the resolution that leads to delisting. According to the Euronext market rules, the Milan Euronext Market Undertaking will set a date when the delisting becomes effective. This will be more than 15 days after the company's decision to delist. Should the shareholder exiting the company assess which consideration offers the best return, taking into account that the request to exit the company blocks the shares, which must be deposited at the registered office?

Some jurisdictions do not offer shareholders any exit right. This is the case in the UK. The shareholders receive a circular with extensive information related to the proposal for delisting and vote on the special resolution for delisting taking into account the dual majority if there is a controlling shareholder: 75 per cent of the shareholder must support the resolution and 50 per cent of the attending independent shareholders (votes) must approve the delisting. When the resolution is approved, the company will be delisted not less than 20 business days following the passing of the resolution, so shareholders have enough time to exit the company via selling the shares on the stock exchange. As there can be a greater number of shares from exiting shareholders compared to the demand for shares from interested investors, the stock price can fall significantly. Only when the company also passed a resolution to reregister as a private company, can minority shareholders address the court to cancel the resolution in accordance with section 98 of the Companies Act 2006; the court can take any order including the purchase of the shares of its members. However, this action is not available in case of a 'pure' voluntary delisting. Delistings in other common law countries like Australia and the US seem to proceed in the same way. Neither the US nor Australian delistings offer minority shareholders exit rights. Minority shareholders that want to exit the company before the delisting must do so between the announcement of the delisting and the day of delisting. In Australia, minority shareholders will have at least one month; in the US it can be less. When the company decides to delist its securities, it has four business days to file a Form 8-K. Next, the company must submit a written notice to the stock exchange and inform the public and must file an SEC Form 25 to delist. The former notice to the exchange must be sent at least ten days before Form 25 is filed. The delisting becomes effective 10 days after Form 25 is filed. It must be seen separately from the requirement of registration with the SEC, for which other rules apply. Therefore, companies that have delisted their securities, but are still registered with the SEC, must still comply with a list of disclosure requirements. Delisting from the Swedish, Finnish or Greek stock exchange does not offer the shareholders another exit right than the option during the time between the announcement of the delisting and the last trading day, to sell their shares.

Note that other jurisdictions also offer a minimum period of time after the announcement of the delisting and the date when the delisting becomes effective. Euronext Amsterdam offers 'in principle 20 trading days after publication of the decision', similar to the UK date of delisting of securities 'which must be not less than 20 *business days* following the passing of the resolution', although the latter results de facto in four weeks.

VI. Assessment and Conclusion

Voluntary delistings of securities are not harmonised and many different systems co-exist. In some countries – predominantly common law countries – it is a strategic decision of the board of directors; in others, the general meeting must approve the delisting. The former group of countries let the interests of the companies prevail, hence they leave it to the board, while the latter jurisdictions, among which are many civil law countries, endorse the shareholder interests more openly. It seems at odds with the law and finance theory. Note that in some countries where the board of directors takes the delisting decision, the market operator or supervisor has some discretionary power to guide the decision, sets conditions and takes into account the interests of the (minority) shareholders.

In countries where the general meeting of shareholders votes on the delisting, there are some peculiarities that are harder to explain from a legal or law and economics perspective. First, some jurisdictions set a minimum term during which the securities of the company must remain listed. Those jurisdictions set requirements for liquidation and dissolution that are less stringent, which does not seem very logical. Second, some jurisdictions combine the right of delisting with a mandatory bid or squeeze out. The offer can be in the common interest of the minority shareholders, the majority shareholder (who in some countries is required to offer this exit route to the shareholders) and the company, if sufficient resources are available for this buy-out and the squeezed-out shareholders receive an appropriate compensation. There are large differences in the way this is done: in some jurisdictions, the price is set by an independent expert, while in others, the courts determine the price or take the weighted average stock price over a certain period before the delisting or use a combination of different valuation techniques. This shows that there is no optimal mechanism to protect the interests of the minority shareholders in this process. Third, in some jurisdictions the subsequent offer only addresses the shareholders that voted against the delisting (or abstained from voting). If not all information is in the market at the time of the meeting,[22] the shareholders who voted for it are locked in. This problem can be aggravated in Columbia where the shareholders that vote for the delisting must participate in the takeover bid, potentially creating numerous collaboration and financial issues and problems.[23]

How to conclude? In short, this assessment shows that balancing the interests of all parties involved in a voluntary delisting decision cannot be achieved by one harmonised approach.

[22] Consider, for example, a pandemic.
[23] Some of these issues are addressed in Columbian law (see Art 5.2.6.1.4 of the Decreto Unico 2555/2010).

4

Voluntary Delisting: Procedures and Shareholder Protection under Takeover Law

ANDRÉS RECALDE AND MIKEL ATAUN*

I. The Rationale for Delisting

A. Origins and Grounds for Going Private

Over the last 20 years a massive outflow from capital markets has led to a significant decline in the number of listed companies. The phenomenon is well illustrated by the fact that many companies have directly opted to leave European and American regulated capital markets by way of a voluntary request to delist,[1] as well as a decrease in IPOs.[2]

* Andrés Recalde, Professor at Universidad Autónoma of Madrid Professor of Business and Corporate Law at Universidad Autónoma of Madrid, Spain, and Mikel Ataun, Lawyer at Pérez-Llorca Abogados, SLP.

[1] OECD, *OECD Corporate Governance Factbook 2021* (Paris, OECD Publishing, 2021) 18: Almost 30,000 companies of the OECD area delisted from the stock markets since 2005. Even if this is a global case, in Europe it is particularly relevant. Over the period 2005–19 almost 8,000 delisting of European companies occurred (ibid 21). Figures have not changed significantly later; since 2017 the number of listed companies increased, but the increase was mainly driven by emerging economies. The Stock Exchange of Hong Kong reflects the trend in the opposite direction, where the number of listed companies has grown significantly (see Low and Low, Chapter 16). On the contrary, advanced economies have maintain the decrease in the number of listed companies (OECD, *OECD Corporate Governance Factbook 2023* 13). In the EU, data show a significant number of annual delisting not only affecting regulated markets: 523 in 2018 (227 of regulated markets, 75 on SME Growth Markets, and 221 on other MTF), 497 in 2019 (195, 74 and 156 for each market), 477 in 2021 (181, 102 and 194) (see European Commission, 'Commission Staff Working Document, Impact Assessment Report, SWD(2022) 762 final' on the Proposal of the Listing Act available at eur-lex.europa.eu/legal-content/EN/TXT/?uri=CELEX:52022SC0762#footnote22.The phenomenon goes back to some years before; in the USA, between 1995 and 2004 more than 9,000 firms delisted from US stock exchanges and markets (J Macey, M O'Hara and D Pompilio, 'Down and Out in the Stock Market: The Law and Economics of the Delisting Process' (2008) 51 *The Journal of Law & Economics* 683). Alternative market segments, however, have been established across jurisdictions and are becoming an increasingly common listing alternative, as Multilateral Trading Facilities (MTFs) in Europe and growth segments in other regions generally impose simplified requirements for listing, supporting market dynamism and capital markets growth (see data in OECD, *Corporate Factbook 2023* (above) 14).

[2] In the 1990s, European non-financial companies – mainly from the UK, Germany, France and Italy – played a leading role in the global scene in terms of initial public offerings (IPOs), accounting for 41% of all

In fact, markets are not seen to be flexible enough to accommodate companies' financing needs – particularly SMEs, who do not consider listing as an easy and affordable means of financing. At the same time, market capitalisation has also clearly declined.[3]

There are various reasons why a company may decide to delist. These are mainly related to the procedures and costs that listed companies have to bear to maintain their listing on a stock exchange.[4] Companies are often not interested in complying with these complex corporate and market requirements, or the disclosure duties that may also harm business efficiency, reducing the company's confidentiality.

However, leaving the stock markets may be driven by other factors, such as overall strategies that serves the interests of the company, the directors, the controlling shareholder(s) and the minority shareholders. Companies often proceed to delisting after a change of control. The goal of delisting is to increase the value of the company, which ultimately will also benefit shareholders. If delisting eliminates significant compliance costs, shareholders will benefit in the long run. Another common factor that may explain the delisting decision is that the majority shareholders want to retain control. The management body may also try to avoid shareholder pressure (either through short-termism or long-termism), which limits their power to manage the company. Finally, the new controlling shareholder usually intends to squeeze out the remaining minority, when squeeze-out legal procedures do not apply.[5]

A valuation of the company or its shares below the expectations of shareholders or management can also be a factor which may induce companies to leave a regulated market.[6]

B. The Need to Protect Minority Shareholders in a Voluntary Delisting

Even if delisting does not mean a fundamental legal change for the shareholders, it also significantly affects them. Delisting impacts the liquidity of the shares, since they will no longer be transferable in a market that facilitates the encounter of buyers and sellers. In fact, the automatic and direct consequence of delisting is that shareholders will be deprived of the ability to monetise their investment in a regulated market. In fact, the company's decision to delist modifies the legal and financial condition that determined

capital raised, with over 3,500 listings during that period. Since then, IPOs have declined both in absolute and relative terms. European non-financial companies raised only 24% of the total equity capital raised via IPOs during the 2001–11 period, dropping to 19% between 2012 and 2022 (OECD, *Factbook 2023* (n 1) 15, as opposed to the relevant increase of the significance of IPOs in China in terms of global markets).

[3] These data are crucial for the Listing Act and the initiative of the Parliament (2020) that lead to the report calling for a 'further development of the Capital Markets Union (CMU): improving access to capital market finance, in particular by SMEs, and further enabling retail investor participation'.

[4] DA Zetzsche, 'Going Dark Under German Law – Towards an Efficient Regime for Regular Delisting' (2013) 4 *Revue trimestrielle de droit financier* 1, 2 f; N Ilyevich, *Delisting – Parallele zum Übernahmerecht, Probleme und Lösungsmöglichkeiten* (Baden-Baden, Nomos Verlag, 2019) 19 f; P Girgado, 'La OPA de exclusión' in J Juste and A Recalde (eds), *Derecho de OPAs* (València, Tirant Lo Blanch, 2010) 215 f.

[5] PL Davies, S Worthington and C Hare, *Gower: Principles of Modern Company Law*, 10th edn (London, Sweet & Maxwell, 2016) 863.

[6] Zetsche, 'Going Dark' (n 4) 4 f.

the issuing and tradability of the shares in a regulated market. This makes life easier for directors as they will be free from reporting and organisational duties. However, if the company and directors are exempt from these duties, shareholders conversely might be harmed by the non-application of regulatory provisions and supervision, primarily established to protect them.

The loss of tradability of shares as a result of an amendment to the articles of association restricting the free transfer of shares is typically dealt with by company law. The regulation varies from country to country. However, it is usually provided that the decision shall be taken either by an enhanced majority at the shareholders' meeting or may even require the unanimous consent of all shareholders. In addition, to compensate for the reduced liquidity of shares resulting from restricted transferability, some jurisdictions provide dissenting shareholders with an exit right.[7]

Obviously, delisting is not an amendment of the articles of association that regulates the negotiability of the shares.[8] Hence, the above-mentioned company law provision would not be applicable to delisting. However, delisting has a similar impact on the attractiveness of the shares as it amends their characterisation as negotiable instruments. The risk of losing liquidity is particularly serious for those who do not have a real possibility to liquidate their investments.[9] In the same way that company law considers the restriction of the transferability of shares in the articles of association of a public limited company, the reduction in their tradability in the stock market as a result of delisting is also subject to legal provisions.

The loss in the share's liquidity may also knock down the value of the company and its shares.[10] The value of financial instruments is strongly associated with the possibility to sell them in the market. Logically, if investors find it more difficult to sell their shares outside a regulated market, the price will fall as a result of delisting.[11] Furthermore, the mere risk of a loss of liquidity may induce shareholders to sell their shares as soon as possible ('rat race') which will result in a drop in the share price.

On the other hand, delisting means a material change in the legal status of shareholders once the shares are no longer admitted to trading on a regulated market.

[7] In many legal systems, company law protects shareholders when the transferability of shares is restricted by an amendment of the articles of association: in Germany s 180(2) AktG requires the consent of all the affected shareholders; in Italy shareholders who have not approved the resolution introducing restrictions to the transferability have a withdrawal right towards the company (Art 2437(g) Codice civile); in Spain a much weaker provision is provided, since Art 123(1) LSC only provides that the shares will not be submitted to the introduced restrictions of the transferability during a *vacation period* of three months.

[8] We will not deal with this issue, which is analysed in Chapter 3 of this book.

[9] P Maume, 'The Parting of the Ways: Delisting Under German and UK Law' (2015) 16 *European Business Organization Law Review* 255, 259; A Heidelbach, 'BörsG § 39' in E Schwark and D Zimmer (eds), *Kapitalmarktrechtskommentar*, 5th edn (Munich, C.H.Beck, 2020) marginal no 13; M López Martínez, M, 'Artículo 10. Oferta por exclusión' in J García de Enterría and J Zurita (eds), *La regulación de las OPAs, comentarios sistemático del RD 1066/2007, de 27 de julio* (Civitas Ediciones, Madrid, 2009) 255, 258 f; M Gimeno Ribes, 'La Exclusión Voluntaria de la Cotización Bursátil' (2017) 36 *Revista de Derecho Bancario y Bursátil* 91 IV.2.

[10] An empirical confirmation of the drop of the share prices is not easy to reach, since data over the prices cannot be found after leaving the market. Despite this, a study on 63 firms delisted on the New York Stock Exchange (NYSE) in 2002, 58 of which were later traded on an organised over-the-counter (OTC) market, established that the shares experienced an average drop of 50% (Macey, O'Hara and Pompilio, 'Down and Out in the Stock Market' (n 1) 691–98).

[11] Maume, 'The Parting of the Ways' (n 9) 259.

Capital market law is governed by the principle of investor protection.[12] Efficient markets depend on investor confidence in the regulation of issuers and transactions and in the oversight provided by the supervisory authority. Market flight would mean that issuers and their trading would no longer be subject to these investor protection rules.

To sum up: The decision to delist comes at a 'price', namely a reduction in effective shareholder protection. Various legal tools provide a functional approach to balancing this risk. They are designed to compensate for the adverse effects on shareholders resulting from the reduced tradability of the shares and from the fact that they are not listed on a regulated market.

II. A Comparative Summary of the Tools Provided to Protect Shareholders

A. The Terms of the Debate

Even if shareholders cannot reasonably expect eternal continuity of listing and the company's freedom to delist should be preserved, this decision should also be subject to conditions. The need to protect investors is not in dispute, but the real issue is how to strike the right trade-off between protecting the shareholder and flexibility in the management of the company. Overly strict regulations that could block or prevent the company from making a legitimate and free decision to leave the market should be excluded. Additionally, the mechanism must be proportional to the loss suffered by shareholders.

As it has been described, shareholders may be harmed by the mere decrease in shares' liquidity. Going private also excludes the application of capital markets rules provided to protect investors. The main issues arise when the real impact that investors suffer from exiting the regulated markets cannot be quantified, or if the level of negative impact on shareholders is slight. This could be the case when delisting is accompanied by a request to relist in a regulated market of another country (cross-border delisting), or into a less-regulated market (downlisting). In these cases, liquidity will not fully disappear, even though it might decrease. Special protection measures would not be required at the same level if orderly trading of the security is guaranteed after the decision to go private; eg if, after delisting has been carried out, listing is requested in another market with similar expectations of liquidity and similar regulation and supervision standards.[13]

However, there is an obvious link between the need for protection after delisting and the ownership structure of the company. In companies with a high degree of equity concentration, the decision to delist may be made by the controlling shareholder on its own without the need to obtain the consent of other shareholders or the controlling

[12] R Veil (ed), *European Capital Market Law*, 3rd edn (Oxford, Hart Publishing, 2022) 29 f, 269.

[13] K Hopt, 'Das Dritte Finanzmarktförderungsgesetz – Börsen- und kapitalmarktrechtliche Überlegungen' in J Basedow, K Hopt and H Kötz (eds), *Festschrift für Ulrich Drobnig zum siebzigsten Geburtstag* (Tübingen, Mohr Siebeck, 1998) 525 f, 534.

shareholder shall often be able to veto the decision. Hence, the aim of protecting shareholders who suffer the loss of marketability is only significant for minority shareholders, not for the controlling shareholders, who promoted the measure.

Shareholder protection can be based on capital market regulation or on company law. However, the two models should not be seen as watertight compartments, but as a whole. It is better to understand the content, rather than the systematic location, of the legal mechanisms that protect shareholders. What matters is whether the power to decide on delisting is vested in the shareholders (possibly with a qualified majority, which would strengthen the protection of minorities), and whether shareholders have the right to leave the company with fair financial compensation.

B. The Reduction of Regulatory Requirements

Many jurisdictions have opted to reduce the regulatory framework for delisting, extending companies' free discretion to make such decision. In the USA, the SEC regulation for delisting[14] opts for a self-regulatory model,[15] thus giving the power to establish the conditions of delisting to the Stock Exchange. Rule 500 at the NYSE demonstrates the evolution towards lesser regulatory requirements and a more flexible policy. Originally the rule[16] prescribed that a company could not apply for delisting unless at least two-thirds of the shares were cast in favour of delisting; in addition, no more than 10 per cent of the shares could be cast in opposition to the move. These requirements were heavily criticised. In 1999, the rule was amended and the shareholders' majority requirements were abolished.[17] In the case of American issuers, a company's decision would only be conditioned to (1) the approval of the audit committee and (2) a majority of the company's full board of directors. However, delisting would only take place after a grace period of a maximum of 60 days and the duty to notify the 35 largest shareholders.[18]

C. Provisions Relating Only to the Power of Decision

Similarly, the United Kingdom has also excluded any strong legal requirements imposed for delisting, as a compelling minority protection might increase the willingness of

[14] Rule 12d2-2(d) Securities Exchange Act provides that this application should be submitted to the rules of the stock exchange operator.

[15] This also the case for Australia, where the market operator has a strong discretion to approve or reject the request for delisting (see Hanrahan, Chapter 15 in this volume). Scandinavian countries also opted for a flexible model that limits shareholder protection. In Sweden and Finland no offer for sale of the shares of the company is needed to call for delisting. Generally, the decision on requesting for delisting can be taken by the board of directors (this happens in Finland and according to an extended opinion of the academia in Sweden), without the need for a resolution from a shareholders' meeting (J Östberg, Questionnaire Sweden Q 2 and H Marjosola, Questionnaire Finland Q 2).

[16] Rule 500 was a Great Depression measure introduced in the 1930s (Maume (n 9) 263).

[17] On 17 November 1997, the NYSE filed with the Securities and Exchange Commission a proposal for reforms along these lines, which the SEC accepted. See www.sec.gov/files/rules/sro/9731not.htm.

[18] In 2003, Listing Rule 500 was completely discarded, despite criticism from the US Securities and Exchange 37 Commission (SEC) (Maume (n 9) 264).

investors to acquire a minority stake controlled by a single shareholder.[19] The Financial Conduct Authority (FCA) is competent for most aspects of admission (via the UK Listing Authority), market supervision and enforcement. In May 2014 – also in July 2024 – the FCA amended Listing Rule 'Cancelling Listing').[20] The regulator tried to ensure that minority shareholders have a proper say in the delisting decision. A company with a controlling shareholder, which intends to delist from a premium listing segment, requires the approval of a 75 per cent overall majority, as well as a (regular) majority of the votes attached to the shares of the independent shareholders voting on the resolution.[21] If the issuing company has a controlling shareholder, a majority in value of the certificates representing shares in issue at the time of the meeting that are: (i) held by holders of certificates other than the controlling shareholder; and (ii) that are voted on the resolution are required.

D. The Assignment to Shareholders of an Exit Right as a Condition for Delisting

In contrast to the previous models, based on flexible capital markets requirements, or requirements referring to the company's body competent to request delisting, other countries combine both types. On the one hand, they are based on corporate law provisions associated with majorities needed to adopt the decision, since the request of delisting must be approved by a resolution of the shareholders' meeting. On the other hand, they give shareholders an exit right with a fair compensation or at a regulated price, allowing them to sell the shares to the company or to another shareholder.

In some jurisdictions this exit right has been designed as a withdrawal right that can be enforced against the company. In Italy, since 2004,[22] shareholders who did not participate in the decision to request delisting and who do not want to remain shareholders of the company are paid by the company according to the withdrawal right provisions.[23]

[19] Davies, Worthington and Hare, *Gower* (n 5) 863.

[20] An issuer must satisfy the requirements applicable to it in Listing Rules 5.2.5 R to Listing Rules 5.2.11CR and Listing Rules 5.3 before the FCA will cancel the listing of its securities at its request.

[21] A listed company that intends to exit the market must essentially meet two requirements: on the one hand, it must obtain the agreement of at least 75% of the shareholders at the shareholders' meeting (Listing Rules 5.2.5 [2] FSA); on the other hand, it must communicate the exact date of exit from the market, which must be set at least twenty days in advance of the approval of the resolution at the meeting (Listing Rules 5.2.5 [1] FSA) (see J Chan and C Gerner-Beuerle, Questionnaire UK Qs 3 and 4).

[22] '*Se le azioni sono quotate sui mercati regolamentati hanno diritto di recedere i soci che non hanno concorso alla deliberazione che comporta l'esclusione dalla quotazione*' (Art 133 TUF; the general regulation of the withdrawal right is in Art 2437*quinques* of the codice civile, the Italian civil code).

[23] Art 2437*quinquies* codice civile. Previously, a withdrawal right was only recognised in the case of structural modifications (merger, division), and according to securities regulation (Art 131 TUF) (M Notari, 'Il recesso per esclusione dalla quotazione nel nuovo art. 2437-quinquies c.c.' (2004) 4-6 *Rivista del Diritto Commerciale e del Diritto Generale delle Obbligazioni* 529; A Daccò, 'Art. 2437-quinquies' in P Abbadessa and GB Portale (eds), *Le società per azioini, Tomo II* (Milan, Giuffrè Editore, 2016) 2552; A Pacciello, 'Articolo 2347-quinquies' in G Niccolini and A Stagno d'Alcontres (eds), *Società di capital, Commentario, Vol. 2* (Naples, Jovene, 2004) 1140 ff).

Other European countries have opted to condition the delisting to a previous takeover bid over the shares; this must be addressed to all shareholders and must comply with the takeover regulations. This is a common provision in several European countries.[24]

This combination of company law and securities market regulation was established in Germany, although here the regulation has experienced an interesting evolution. Originally, just as the admission to listing, which requires a resolution of the shareholder's meeting, the act of delisting also demands a similar resolution adopted by the majority that is required to amend the articles of association.[25] The German Supreme Court (BGH) ruled in the *Macrotron* case (2004) that only the shareholders' meeting had the power to decide on delisting.[26] However, reputable scholars argued that requiring a resolution by the shareholders' meeting with a qualified majority would be an excessive burden, and would not contribute to effective protection. In the usual case of a controlling shareholder interested in promoting delisting, their decisive influence on the approval of the resolution would render the meeting futile from the point of view of minority shareholder protection.[27] Hence the power of the shareholders' meeting was restricted by the German Constitutional Court (BVerfG),[28] which questioned whether the holding of shares was part of the content of the constitutional right to property.[29] Subsequently, the BGH ruled in the *Frosta* case (2013) that delisting is a management decision for which the directors are competent, rejecting the need for a resolution of the shareholders' meeting. As a consequence, minority shareholder protection was left to the listing authorities and to securities law. A general rule provides that delisting should not harm investors (section 39(2) sentence 2 BörsG) and, consequently, if delisting is made at the request of the issuer or a controlling shareholder, it is conditional on a public tender offer to purchase all shares, submitting the bid to the general takeover regulation (section 39(2) sentence 3 number 1 BörsG).[30]

[24] See Q 9 of the European Questionnaires. For Germany, see s 39(2) sentence 3 no 1 BörsG in conjunction with § 31 of the Securities Acquisition and Takeover Act (*Wertpapiererwerbs- und Übernahmegesetz*; hereafter: WpÜG); for Spain, see Art 65.1 LMVSI and Art 10 of the Royal Decree 1066/2007 on Takeover Bids and for Austria s 27.1.a *Übernahmegesetz* and s 38.6 *Börsengesetz*. France and Greece also provide a similar protection based on the shareholders' power to sell their shares after a takeover has been launched (see K Deckert, Questionnaire France Q 9 and A Kouloridas, Questionnaire Greece Q 9).

[25] M Lutter, 'Gesellschaftsrecht und Kapitalmarkt' in M Lieb, U Noack and HP Westermann (eds), *Festschrift für Wolfgang Zöllner, Zum 70. Geburtstag, Band I* (Cologne, Carl Heymanns Verlag, 1999) 363, 380 f.

[26] This is linked to court resolutions that increased the shareholders' powers, giving implicit competences to the general meeting when shareholders could be affected. Seminal in this regard, see the *Holzmüller* case of the BGH from 1982 (BGHZ 83, 122): 'there are decisions covered by the formal exclusive attribution of management's power to manage and represent the company, as well as by the wording of the articles of association, which nevertheless so profoundly affect the rights deriving from the status of shareholder and the interests inherent in the shareholders' ownership of the company's assets that the management cannot reasonably assume that it can take them on its sole responsibility without involving the general meeting'.

[27] Hopt, 'Das Dritte Finanzmarktförderungsgesetz' (n 13) 536 f; Maume (n 9) 263. However, the resolution may be challenged by the minority shareholders.

[28] BVerfG, Judgment of 11 July 2012–1 BvR 3142/07, 1 BvR 1569/08 (2012) 66 *Zeitschrift für Wirtschafts- und Bankrecht* 1378.

[29] Zetsche (n 4) 11.

[30] A similar regulation is provided, see U Torggler, Questionnaire Austria Q 9.

However, the mandatory offer as a condition for delisting has been criticised on similar grounds to those used to reject the need for a shareholder resolution. In particular, it was cautioned that the risk of a possible mandatory takeover bid in the future could increase the cost of delisting and discourage companies from going public. It was also warned about the uncertainty of these decisions and the incentives they might create for litigation over the bid price.[31] That is why listed companies look for alternatives to an ordinary delisting decision to avoid the mandatory offer. 'Cold delisting' is the most frequently used. This occurs when a listed company undergoes a merger or other corporate restructuring (spin-off, conversion) and the acquiring or receiving company is not listed. This results in the former listed company being delisted.[32]

E. Preliminary Conclusion

The legal culture of some European countries is deeply imbued with the idea that the transfer of shareholdings cannot be left to the discretionary will of the directors or the majority of shareholders. Shareholders must be afforded adequate protection since the delisting decision impacts them deeply. However, the trade-off between a company's freedom to delisting and investor protection mechanisms varies. Flexibility is consubstantial to efficient business management and benefits shareholders at the end. Legal measures cannot make delisting too difficult or expensive. Excessive protection and overregulation reduce management's ability to run the company and might ultimately harm shareholders. A regime that is rigidly focused on protecting dissenting shareholders will distort the balance and allow the minority to impose its will on the majority. And at the end of the day, strong layers of protection discourage companies from listing on regulated markets and make going public less attractive.[33]

Some systems do not interfere at all with the decision-making capacity of the management (USA, UK, Sweden, Finland, Australia); investor protection hence only relies on free market development. In other countries, there is a general mandatory rule that delisting should not be detrimental to investors, that is accompanied with some technical provisions, giving strong leeway to the supervisor (Germany).[34]

In the majority of jurisdictions company law requires a resolution of the shareholders' meeting (UK, Spain, Greece, Italy). Protection is intensified when supermajorities are required for this resolution. This implicitly gives a veto right to shareholders overcoming the threshold necessary for the supermajority. In other jurisdictions,

[31] This is not, however, unanimously accepted. As it has been pointed out, listing in a stock market cannot always be seen as equivalent to liquidity. A non-regulated market may have a similar degree of liquidity and protection as a regulated market. A mandatory compensation disregards this crucial aspect (Zetsche (n 4) 14, 16). Some stock exchanges could and would set listing requirements with adequate investor protection, and shareholders would press issuers to list at this stock exchange even if there was only a small chance of ensuring higher stock prices.

[32] Some jurisdictions do not allow cold delisting. In such cases, listed companies looked for alternatives to avoid launching a mandatory bid for such a cross-border merger when the remaining company is listed in another regulated market.

[33] Maume (n 9) 261.

[34] In Germany s 39(2) sentence 2 BörsG.

however, the decision to delist is regarded as a purely managerial act, and the power to take it is therefore vested in the directors (eg Germany, USA, Sweden, Finland, the Netherlands).

Many European systems protect minority shareholders by allowing them to exit the company. This is either in the form of a withdrawal right (eg in Italy) or by granting them the ability to sell their shares in a mandatory delisting takeover bid (eg Germany, Austria, Greece, Spain, Cyprus).

None of these alternative solutions conclusively offer the strongest protection to minority shareholders. Indeed, there is no natural way to regulate delisting, nor is there a definitive line of reasoning to determine the appropriate shape or level of protection that should be afforded to shareholders. It not only depends on the details of the regulation, and on the costs involved, but also on the structure of equity ownership and on the depth and the liquidity of the market.[35]

III. The Delisting Takeover

The main objective of delisting regulation is to strike a balance between the need for flexibility to decide whether the company remains on the market, and protecting minority shareholders against the detrimental effects of such a decision. In the following, we will focus on the protection provided to minority shareholders through the granting of an exit right shaped as a mandatory takeover bid. First, the key differences between a delisting takeover and an ordinary takeover must be identified (see A below). It must be determined what person or entity is standing to launch the offer and who, where applicable, would be obliged to launch it if a request for delisting is going to be made (see B below). A takeover has often been considered an obstacle that hinders delisting; however, if the costs of the offer were not material, it should not be deter companies from taking this decision. These costs usually will not matter if the bid is targeted at a small number of people or if a significant proportion would not be in a position to accept it. (see C below).

On the other hand, the possibility of exceptions must be considered in the context of the definition of the scope of the delisting takeover. The main issues arise if an exit from the stock market is the result of other corporate transactions, when the flight from the market was not the direct intention of the company (below D.i). The potential disadvantages for shareholders should be taken into account if the delisting is accompanied by the company's request to be listed on another market with less stringent regulation (below D.ii) or on another market in another country but subject to similar regulation (below D.iii). Similarly, the mandatory bid should be considered if alternative legal instruments would provide sufficient protection for the interests of minority shareholders (below D.iv). Finally, the acquisition of control as a result of a refinancing or restructuring operation aimed at rescuing the company is usually considered as an exception to the corresponding mandatory bid; the question is whether this should also apply from the point of view of the delisting bid (below D.v).

[35] Maume (n 9) 259.

The other factor to be taken into consideration is the price of the tender offer, which is less dependent on the quantity, rather on how the price is to be fixed (below F). Finally, some remarks shall be made on the execution procedure applicable to delisting (below G).

A. General Takeover Provisions or Special Takeover Regime for Delisting

Countries that make delisting conditional on the prior launch of a takeover bid often subject the latter to the general regime governing takeovers.[36] In particular, disclosure as well as the procedure regulation on takeovers, including the duration of the offer period, also govern the delisting takeover. There is no reason why the application of these provisions should be limited to offers which follow or are aimed at the acquisition of control and they should not be extended to offers that do not involve a shift of control.[37]

The disclosure regulation of takeover bids is intended to provide the addressees of the bid with adequate and timely information about its characteristics to enable them to make an informed decision. In some jurisdictions the board of directors will issue a report giving the reasons and motivations for delisting and the price offered. This report must be made available to shareholders.[38] The information that is required to make an informed decision is the same if the takeover has been launched to acquire control of a listed company, when an already controlling shareholder makes an offer to increase their shareholding in the target company, or when the aim of the offer is to give shareholders the right to exit the company before delisting takes place.

However, the application of the entire takeover bid regime is not straightforward. In fact, the Takeover Directive 2004/25/CE[39] only regulates bids that have been launched in the context of a change of control; it does not deal with the delisting offer. In fact, the aim of shifting the control underlying an ordinary takeover bid is completely different from the objectives of the delisting. The delisting offer is imposed by law to guarantee that minority shareholders do not have to remain in a company, whose shares would no longer be tradable on a stock market. This exit from the company must be made for a fair consideration, which compensates the shareholders for the material, legal and financial changes to their shares due to the risk associated with the lack of liquidity, which is detrimental to the investment.

The hostility to a mandatory delisting bid is coherent with the opposition that an extended scholar doctrine adopts against the mandatory bid rule, provided in the directive after a change of control (Article 5).[40] The mandatory delisting takeover has

[36] In Germany, see s 39(3) sentence 2 BörsG; in Spain, see Art 65.2 LMVSI and Art 10.5 Royal Decree 1066/2007 on Takeover Bids.

[37] A Recalde and M Winner, 'Public Takeovers' in R Veil (ed), *Regulating EU Capital Markets Union, Volume I: Fundamentals of a European Code* (Oxford, Oxford University Press, 2024) 444, 461.

[38] FCA Handbook, ch 5 LR 5.2.5. In Spain, see Art 65.3(2) LMVSI and Art 10.5 RD 1066/2007.

[39] Directive 2004/25/EC on takeover bids [2004] OJ L142/12.

[40] JL Hansen, 'The Mandatory Bid Rule: Unnecessary, Unjustifiable and Inefficient, Nordic & European Company Law Working Paper No. 18-01' (2018). Available at: www.papers.ssrn.com/sol3/papers.cfm?

often been controversial. It has been described as an inefficient formula that incurs significant time and documentation costs[41] and hinders the flexible functioning and adaptability of listed companies. In fact, a mandatory delisting takeover bid is said to make a company's decision not to remain on the stock exchange more expensive.

However, the rationale of the mandatory bid is partially different in ordinary takeover cases than in those of delisting. In an ordinary takeover, the mandatory bid is a consequence of the change of control in the company and aims either to guarantee an equal distribution of the control prime among the shareholders or to allow minority shareholders to leave the company after its acquisition of control from a third party. The reasoning behind this is that shareholders should not have to bear the consequences of the new controlling shareholder making the company's most important decisions.

In the case of delisting, the mandatory delisting takeover is intended to allow shareholders to leave the company before they suffer any damage that may result from delisting, due to the loss of liquidity, derogation of a special protecting regulation and lack of supervision. In this case, the special purpose explains why some general provisions of takeover regulation should be excluded. For example, there is no justification for applying the neutrality rule that prevents directors from taking a decision to oppose the offer, when the delisting request comes from the issuing company as a self-bid.

B. Who is Legitimate and/or Obliged to Launch a Delisting Tender Offer?

In a delisting tender offer, there are two potential scenarios depending on who is entitled or obliged to launch the delisting takeover bid: (i) the bid may be launched by the company that issued the listed shares; or (ii) the bidder may be a shareholder, in particular a majority shareholder, or a third party aiming to take full control of the company and prevent it from remaining listed on a regulated market.[42] In practice, the two alternatives are common.[43] Even if the takeover is launched by a third party, the application

abstract_id=3112100; M Habersack, 'Non-Frustration Rule and Mandatory Bid Rule – Cornerstones of European Takeover Law' (2018) 15 *European Company and Financial Law Review* 1, 28 f; J García de Enterría, *La OPA obligatoria* (Madrid, Civitas Ediciones, 1996) 135 f. For the pros and cons of the mandatory bid rule and the relationship between the general rule and the exceptions see R Skog and E Sjöman, 'No Rule, Just Exemptions? Mandatory Bids in Sweden and in the EU' (2014) 11 *European Company and Financial Law Review* 393; M Winner, 'Does the European Union Have a Mandatory Bid Rule?' in RJ Gilson et al (eds), *Festskrift till Rolf Skog* (Stockholm, Norstedts Juridik, 2021) 1179 ff.

[41] J Winter et al, 'Report of the High Level Group of Company Law Experts on Issues Related to Take-over Bids in the European Union' in G Ferrarini et al (eds), *Reforming Company and Takeover Law in Europe* (Oxford, Oxford University Press, 2004) 65; the Winter report considered that the introduction of a divestiture obligation was a more efficient means of achieving the same end.

[42] This is a common situation. As the Questionnaires show, it is the rule in Germany (s 39 BörsG) and Spain (Arts 65.1 and 65.2 LMVSI: the bid could also be launched by another person or entity but delisting must be approved by the shareholders meeting, Art 10.4.2 RD 1066/2007), see K Çavuşoğlu, Questionnaire Germany Q 12 and A Recalde and M Ataun, Questionnaire Spain Q 12.

[43] LM Guntermann, 'Self-Tender Offer und Delisting' (2021) 24 *Neue Zeitschrift für Gesellschaftsrecht* 1621. In Spain, statistics show that among the 21 cases of delisting takeovers, in nine cases the bid was made by the issuing company, and in 12 cases it was the major shareholder.

for delisting must be made by the shareholders' meeting and executed by the board of directors. A bidder trying to acquire control of a listed company is not competent to request delisting; no person or entity other than the issuing company can request to delist to the regulated market.[44]

There are differences between the two possibilities, but they are not material. They could have consequences for the offer price. Indeed, in a share buyback by the issuing company, the majority shareholder will be interested in a higher price; meanwhile, if the delisting bid is made by the majority shareholder, it will be interested in offering the lowest price.[45]

If the bidder is the largest shareholder, it will usually also have access to non-public/insider information. Insider dealing would occur if the bidder used this information to buy shares before the delisting bid was made. In Germany, the bidder in a takeover bid is usually a majority shareholder who offers the other shareholders to buy their shares before applying for delisting. However, in the frequently quoted case of 'Rocket Internet Co.' in 2020, the listing takeover came from the issuing company itself.[46] A case of self-insider trading was highlighted due to the asymmetric information in the hands of the bidder (the issuing company) and the shareholders. The assumption that the risk of abuse is greater if the issuer launches the bid to acquire its own shares than in cases of a shareholder or a third party being the bidder, though, is not self-evident.

A self-insider dealing was identified in a takeover for delisting in the Italian Supreme Court resolution in the *Cremonini* case, when the bidder was the major shareholder.[47] However, the risk of breaching the prohibition of insider dealing is no different from ordinary takeovers and should not necessarily be applicable according to the MAR provisions on information created by one person.[48]

The main differences between a takeover bid launched by the company or by a shareholder concern company law. The bid shall be subject to the regulation on the acquisition of own shares by the company, including the maximum threshold of the share capital that may be acquired. However, this threshold can usually be exceeded if the acquisition of the own shares is carried out by the company in a public bid aimed to redeem the shares.[49]

[44] Girgado, 'La OPA de exclusión' (n 4) 221.

[45] On the price to be paid in the delisting takeover bid see E below.

[46] Among the offer documents published on BaFin's website only in one other case the issuer – and not a majority shareholder – had submitted the delisting takeover offer (Guntermann, 'Self-Tender Offer und Delisting' (n 43) 1622).

[47] Cassazione civile, 12 May 2020. Mr Cremonini, major shareholder and president of the board of a group of companies active in the food industry, decided at the beginning of 2008 to delist a listed company (Cremonini spa). Before announcing the takeover for delisting, Mr Cremonini started, through a newly created company, to buy shares of Cremonini spa at a price lower than the one decided for the delisting. Consob sanctioned him for insider dealing (S Lombardo, 'Some Reflections on the Self-Insider and the Market Abuse Regulation – The Self-Insider as a Monopoly-Square Insider' (2021) 18 *European Company and Financial Law Review* 2, 9 f.

[48] Lombardo, 'Some Reflections on the Self-Insider' (n 47) 30 f, defends that in a pre-bid acquisition of shares by the major shareholder (see n 66) the exemption of Art 9.6 MAR should prevail over the rule of Art 9.5 MAR authorising the use of information created by the offeror.

[49] There is no particularity here with respect to the ordinary takeover regime. The case is expressly provided in Spain (Art 12 Royal Decree 1066/2007 on Takeover Bids), subject to the general takeover bid regulation (M López Martínez, 'Artículo 12. Oferta pública de adquisición por reducción de capital mediante adquisición

On the other hand, if the delisting request and the launch of the takeover bid are made by the company, they require a resolution of the shareholders' meeting; this could be subject to judicial challenge, allowing review even for substantial grounds or unfairness.[50] A successful challenge would justify the reversal of the delisting request by the management of the stock exchange. Thus, it might be justified to exclude the need for a resolution of the shareholders' meeting, to avoid such judicial control over the delisting.[51]

Delisting may be promoted by a third party; the delisting takeover bid shall usually be launched by the major shareholder. Although launching a delisting tender offer does not necessarily depend on a prior process of acquisition of control, both procedures may go hand in hand. The bidder launching a voluntary takeover bid with the purpose of acquiring control of a company, may be also interested in delisting the company. The bidder seeks to delist, to manage and, if necessary, restructure the company without the restrictions and constraints inherent on listed companies. The simplest and most expeditious way of achieving delisting is to exercise the squeeze-out right; however, this is conditional on having acquired the percentage of the necessary share capital necessary.[52]

The prospectus of the takeover bid should also state that a delisting request is intended. In this case, as will be explained (below D.iv), a new delisting bid would not be necessary if the original bid met the requirements of a delisting bid.

C. The Addressees or Beneficiaries of the Bid

Delisting impacts on the liquidity of all the securities issued by the company. The tender offer must thus be addressed not only to the holders of ordinary shares, but also to holders of non-voting shares, convertibles and exchangeable debentures, as well as warrants or other securities and financial instruments giving an option to acquire or subscribe shares. They all would suffer in the same way from the loss of tradability and the exit from the regulation and supervision of the stock exchange.

However, the mandatory tender offer will only apply to financial instruments giving an option to acquire or subscribe shares or other securities issued by the company itself. If the options or the subscription right had a contractual nature and were given by a shareholder vis-à-vis another shareholder no takeover bid is imposed for these instruments. In fact, it would be unreasonable to require an offer directed at warrants issued

de acciones propias' in J García de Enterría and J Zurita (eds), *La regulación de las OPAs, comentarios sistemático del RD 1066/2007, de 27 de julio* (Civitas Ediciones, Madrid, 2009) 312).

[50] For Germany, see T Eckhold, '§ 61 Delisting' in R Marsch-Barner and FA Schäfer (eds), *Handbuch börsenno-tierte AG, Aktien- und Kapitalmarktrecht*, 4th edn (Cologne, Otto Schmidt, 2018) 2085 marginal no 73.

[51] For Germany see s 246a AktG. Guntermann (n 43) 1625: neither the risk of a challenge, nor the mere challenge claim already brought, implies that the resolution is without effect; a challenge to the resolution of the shareholders' meeting resolution has no suspensive effect. See also, in Spanish law, Art 207.II LSC.

[52] In Spain, the percentage to execute a squeeze out is at least 90% of the voting rights (see Art 116.1 LMVSI and Art 47.1 of the Royal Decree 1066/2007 on Takeover Bids). If this percentage is not reached, the bidder could also promote the company's exit from the stock market by means of an ordinary delisting takeover bid Art 82.2 LMV and Art 10 Royal Decree 1066/2007 on Takeover Bids).

by financial intermediaries, if the company is not committed to issue or deliver shares in exchange.

Usually, the right to sell is given to shareholders regardless of whether they were in favour of delisting, they dissented or abstained, or did not even attend the shareholder's meeting when the company approved the resolution. However, in some jurisdictions, the offer may not be extended to shareholders who voted in favour of the delisting resolution in the shareholders' meeting.[53] This solution is coherent with the shaping of an exit right in the form of a withdrawal right. This would only be applicable to dissenting shareholders, who voted against the resolution for delisting or the corporate transaction (eg a merger or a split-off) causing delisting.[54]

However, excluding those shareholders who voted in favour of the delisting could eventually lead to strategic voting at the shareholders' meeting with the sole purpose of retaining the right to exit. This could jeopardise the transaction.

D. The Scope of the Mandatory Takeover Bid

Delisting shall often be made with the sole and direct objective of going private. However, a so-called 'cold delisting' may also result from other company transactions, eg a resolution to convert a listed public company into a limited liability company, a merger if the acquiring company is not a listed company, or a complete division of a listed public limited company into several unlisted companies. However, delisting from a regulated stock exchange may be part of an application process to be listed on another regulated market of another country (cross-border delisting). It could also be aimed to be listed on a less regulated market, such as a multilateral trading facility (downlisting).

We will focus on the effect of these operations from the point of view of the duty to undertake a takeover. As mentioned above (II.A), the legal perspective should always consider the real prejudice that would be caused to shareholders by each one of these transactions.

i. Cold Delisting

A cold delisting occurs when a company undertakes a merger or any other kind of corporate restructuring operation (merger, division, conversion), which leads to a situation where the previous listed company will no longer be traded on the stock exchange. In Germany this was the usual path followed by companies for delisting, particularly when the strong conditions imposed by *Macrotron* jurisprudence were ruling.[55]

[53] See for Spain Recalde and Ataun, Questionnaire Spain (n 42) Q 13: The takeover bid does not have to be launched to those shareholders who approved the delisting resolution at the shareholders' meeting if they freeze out their shares until the end of the takeover bid procedure (Art 10.2 b RD 1066/2007).

[54] See for Italy Art 2437-quinquies Civil code and G Balp, Questionnaire Italy Q 13.

[55] As it was highlighted between 2003–10, cold delisting was the main delisting strategy, with 66.89% (196 of 293) of transactions; in 23.55% (69 of 293) of the cases, the delisting was the side effect of an issuer's insolvency or dissolution; only 9.56% (28 of 293) transactions were regular delisting (Zetsche (n 4) 5; see also M Habersack, '§ 40 Delisting' in M Habersack, PO Mülbert and M Schlitt (eds), *Unternehmensfinanzierung am Kapitalmarkt*, 4th edn (Cologne, Otto Schmidt, 2019) 1335, 1351).

In these cases, delisting would also be the consequence of a voluntary decision of the company, even if these decisions were not directly oriented to the exit of the regulated market but the result of the merger or division. Cold delisting may also be the forced consequence of the corporate restructuring operation eliminating the legal or structural requirements for the shares to continue to be admitted to the regulated market. Removing these requirements would lead to their listing either expiring or simply being revoked. The merger of the company could also have been driven by the direct intention of the company to go private as it would be the only instrument to achieve the delisting of the company. In both cases, delisting will be forced by a decision of the stock exchange management or the market supervisor.

There are no material differences in the potential damages for shareholders in an ordinary delisting and in a cold delisting. In both cases, they will become shareholders of an unlisted company, hence they will suffer from the loss of marketability of their shares and from the reduction of protection that was conferred by market regulation and supervision. Therefore, the protection given to shareholders in an ordinary delisting should apply in the same way in cold delisting.

Similarly, if through a merger or division, the shareholders of a listed company subject to a regulated market become shareholders of a listed company on another market with a similar level of regulatory and supervisory protection, they will not suffer any detriment. Hence, no takeover bid should be imposed.[56] Company law provisions ensuring the appropriate exchange ratio in a merger should be sufficient to protect shareholders.

From the point of view of the competence to carry out the operation, no issue arises, as a resolution of the shareholders' meeting is always required to approve corporate transactions that result in a cold delisting.

If an exit right is required to compensate shareholders for the loss of tradability of their shares, this is not usually covered by company law. A takeover bid should therefore be available in the case of cold delisting, as well as in the case of an ordinary delisting. This is sometimes expressly recognised,[57] as the same result could be promoted by the authors' interpretation.[58]

The takeover by the company should be launched as a condition for the merger to proceed and ultimately lead to the delisting of the acquired company.[59] The imposition

[56] For Spain, see Recalde and Ataun, Questionnaire Spain (n 42) and Art 11c RD 1066/2007.

[57] See Q 18 of the Questionnaires. In Austria s 27e(1) Übernahmegesetz and s 38(6)–(8) BörsG; in Spain Art 65.1(2) LMVSI provides that corporate transactions whereby the shareholders of the listed company may become, in whole or in part, shareholders of another unlisted entity shall be assimilated to delisting; if the outcome company does not obtain admission to trading of its shares within three months of registration of the corporate transaction in the Companies Register, the case shall be treated as a case of delisting (Art 10.1 sentence 2 of RD 1066/2007). Even if a shift of control is the result of a merger that is carried out for industrial reasons, is usually provided as an exception to the duty to launch a takeover bid, the duty to launch the bid would not be avoided when the transaction leads to delisting.

[58] In Germany, even if s 39 BörsG does not provide structural measures as a case of delisting (see Çavuşoğlu, Questionnaire Germany (n 42) Q 18), this could be achieved under company law and such measures may have consequences under stock exchange law. However, authors have said that this cannot consist on the application of s 39(2) sentence 3 and (3) BörsG by analogy (Habersack, '§ 40 Delisting' (n 55) 1351; Eckhold '§ 61 Delisting' (n 50) marginal no 82 f).

[59] Even in Italy the withdrawal right in the case of a structural modification shall be activated and the shareholder can request the reimbursement of the shares' value, from the moment the general meeting

of the takeover obligation is a way to avoid the risk that the merger and delisting would become effective without giving shareholders a right to exit, which would be justified in the same way as in an ordinary delisting.

ii. Downlisting

The company's decision to request listing in another market may lead to delisting from the regulated market where the shares were previously listed. A case of downlisting occurs when the shares no longer are traded on a regulated market (as defined by European law), but an application has been made to be traded on a Multilateral Trading Facility (MTF). MTFs might be more or less efficient from a marketability point of view. However, they will never be subject to the same regulatory provisions and supervisory regime established for regulated markets. Therefore, MTFs do not meet the regulatory requirements, nor do they afford investors with a similar level of protection.

As a logical consequence, the request for listing in a less regulated and supervised market that follows the exit from listing in the regulated market, should be assimilated to requirements and shareholder protection imposed in an ordinary delisting. In fact, legal systems that impose the duty to launch a takeover bid before delisting do not provide for an exception for the case of downlisting, which is treated like regular delisting.[60]

iii. Market Migration

When a company migrates from one regulated market to another one subject to the equivalent regulation and supervision, there would not be any need to afford shareholders with the exit right embodied in the delisting mandatory takeover. In Europe the equal level playing field reflects a regulation affording a similar level of shareholders' protection. The migration would not effectively affect the investors' ability to trade with the shares to a lower extent, neither would it have an impact on the protection arising from the regulation or the supervision of the market. If a company applies for delisting of shares admitted to a European regulated market, and at the same time applies to be admitted to trading in another stock exchange, or in the market of another EU Member State, no tender offer should be launched.

However, this exemption does not apply automatically; it will require an express waiver from the supervisory authority.[61]

A similar conclusion should be reached in the case of delisting from one or more regulated stock exchanges in one European Member State, but trading continues on

approves the resolution, and the shareholder communicates her/his will to exercise the right, and not after the transaction is executed (Pacciello, 'Articolo 2347-quinquies' (n 23) 1142).

[60] See Q 14 of the Questionnaires. See also G Balp, Chapter 11 in this volume.

[61] The Spanish LMVSI approved in 2023 expressly provides it (Art 65.4 *in fine*). However, even before, in 2019 the Spanish National Securities Market Commission approved alternative procedures to delist in cases such as the delisting from the Spanish stock market of Bayer Aktiengesellschaft ('Bayer'). Such alternative procedures guaranteed a similar protection to shareholders than a mandatory takeover bid.

at least one stock exchange in the same country. This is a so-called partial delisting, in which there is obviously no concern about investors protection or a less regulatory protection.[62]

iv. Exceptions to the Mandatory Takeover Bid in Soft Delisting and Squeeze Out

Legal systems that require a mandatory takeover bid prior to delisting sometimes provide for the possibility of waiving this requirement if alternative procedures are available that offer similar protection to shareholders. The takeover bid will usually be exempt if a previous takeover voluntary bid was launched, and this bid met the requirements of an ordinary delisting, particularly in terms of the consideration offered or addressees of the bid. This exception avoids the cumbersome and unnecessary process of double takeover bids.

In Spain, an 'intermediate' or 'soft delisting' procedure may exclude a subsequent mandatory bid if the offeror stated in the prospectus of a previous takeover bid his intention to delist, and maintains a purchase order of sale for the entire capital at the same price as that of the previous bid, for at least one month in the six-month period following the end of the previous bid of the offeree company and the price, as provided for ordinary delisting was justified by a valuation report. The sale should be facilitated by a purchase order for those securities, at the same price as that of the previous bid, for a reasonable time following the end of the previous bid,[63] particularly when a bid was previously made for all the securities at a price equal to or higher than that required in delisting takeover.[64]

The duty to launch an offer should also be excluded when company law allows squeeze-out or sell-out rights, whose special regulation covers all the need of shareholders' protection. This, in short, refers to a typical case of an exception to the delisting takeover bid. In fact, the right of a majority shareholder to force minority shareholders to sell their shares is subject to strict conditions. These sometimes include the prior launch of a public offer for the entire capital. This is also considered an exception to the obligation to launch a takeover bid.[65] Shareholders entitled to sell their shares cannot demand, in addition, that a takeover bid will be submitted to them. The shareholders' right to have an offer made as a condition on delisting is only granted when they reach a certain level of dispersion.[66]

[62] For Germany W Groß, *Kapitalmarktrecht*, 8th edn (Munich, C.H.Beck, 2022) § 39 BörsG marginal no17.
[63] For Spain, see Recalde and Ataun, Questionnaire Spain (n 42) Q 11 and Art 11.d) of the RD 1066/2007 on Takeover Bids.
[64] However, according to Spanish law, the previous offer would not suffice. The exception would only apply if, as a result of the bid, the bidder had attained at least 75% of the target company's voting capital rights and the sale of all the securities was facilitated by a purchase order at the same price as that of the previous bid, for at least one month during the six-month period following the end of the previous bid (Art 65.2 LMVSI and Art 11d) RD 1066/2007).
[65] As to Spanish law, see Arts 47 and 48 RD 1066/2007.
[66] Habersack (n 55) 1351.

v. Exemptions to the Mandatory Delisting Bid after an Acquisition of Control in the Framework of an Insolvency or Restructuring Procedure

Some national laws provide for an exemption from the obligation to launch a takeover bid in the case of an acquisition of control resulting from a refinancing operation aimed at restoring the financial viability of a company.[67] There are good reasons to argue that the same exemption should apply to delisting takeover bids.[68] In any case, the same rationale would justify a similar exception when the acquisition of control is adopted in accordance with Directive (EU) 2019/1023.[69] This exemption has not been provided even if the restructuring plan and the legal procedure can be used as a tool for covert takeovers. After the transposition of the Directive into national law, in several cases restructuring plans have been used to take control of companies without the shareholders' consent.[70] This is made possible by loopholes in the Directive and the lack of substantive controls in national legislation against the fraudulent or dishonest use of plans.[71]

In the context of a restructuring procedure aimed at saving a listed company in an insolvency risk, mandating the takeover bid as a condition of acquiring the control or delisting can be an obstacle that hampers the rescue operation and makes it costlier. Companies in financial distress often need flexibility to explore a range of options to stabilise their operations and improve their financial health. The need for a delisting takeover bid would require significant capital resources to purchase outstanding shares, potentially diverting them away from addressing the company's operational and financial issues. By allowing for voluntary delisting without the need for a takeover bid, companies can streamline their restructuring efforts, focusing on financial recovery and operational improvements without the added complexity and expense of a formal takeover process.

Furthermore, the delisting mandatory bid would impose unnecessary constraints on a company's ability to manage its refinancing strategy. This flexibility can be crucial in enabling a company to navigate financial challenges efficiently, ensuring that the focus remains on long-term viability and sustainability rather than on procedural requirements that may not add value to the refinancing process.

[67] In Spain, Art 8 d) Royal Decree 1066/2007 on Takeover Bids. In Germany, the supervisory authority may, on application, exempt the offeror from the obligation to launch a bid if, inter alia, this appears justified in view of the objective pursued by the acquisition of control. This has been used to waive the obligation in the case of a takeover to rescue a company in financial difficulties.

[68] S Korch, 'Delisting und Insolvenz' (2020) 20 *Zeitschrift für Bank- und Kapitalmarktrecht* 285 f.

[69] Directive (EU) 2019/1023 on preventive restructuring frameworks, on discharge of debt and disqualifications, and on measures to increase the efficiency of procedures concerning restructuring, insolvency and discharge of debt, and amending Directive (EU) 2017/1132 (Directive on restructuring and insolvency) [2019] OJ L172/18.

[70] In Germany see S Mock, '(Einseitige) Bezugsrechtsgewährung in Restrukturierungsplänen, Restrukturierungsübernahmerecht Ante Portas?' (2024) 27 *Neue Zeitschrift für Gesellschaftsrecht* 769, 772.

[71] Critical of these implications resulting from the implementation of the restructuring Directive in Spanish law without providing a material control see FJ León and N Latorre, 'La Buena Fe en las Reestructuraciones Empresariales y la Necesidad de Evitar el Fraude (Planteamiento General y Derecho Comparado)' (2025) *Diario La Ley* no 10648.

Finally, and more seriously, the mandatory bid would provide shareholders with an option to exit at the market price prior to restructuring, the cost of which would be borne by the creditors who are being asked to contribute to the financial rescue of the company.

An exception for the mandatory bid in these cases would recognise the financial and operational challenges faced by companies in distress and allow them to focus on restructuring their debt and stabilising their operations without the additional burden of a mandatory takeover bid.

In practice, a way to skip the obligation to launch a delisting takeover bid to delist a company could be through a typical corporate transaction used by companies facing economic difficulties to restructure their capital and improve their financial situation. This would be made by way of a capital reduction to zero or to a very low amount, which eliminates accumulated losses and cleans up the balance sheet, and a subsequent capital increase carried out immediately, injecting new funds into the company.[72] This capital increase can be subscribed either by existing shareholders or by creditors (debt-to-equity swap). In the latter case, those who subscribe the new shares take control of the company and dilute the old owners, at least if, as is the case under Spanish law, the former shareholders are not given a pre-emption right on the new shares.

In such an operation, the listed shares would have been redeemed and the old shareholders would no longer remain. However, the new shares would no longer be listed which would have avoided a delisting takeover bid. In such a natural delisting, the minority shareholders would not be harmed in any way by the absence of a delisting takeover bid, as the share capital would be reduced to zero.

E. Consideration of the Takeover Bid

As was mentioned above, in most countries that give an exit right to shareholders as a condition for delisting, this takes the form of a right to accept a takeover that must be offered for the shares. The launch of such a takeover bid is mandatory as is the main aspect of the price, which is laid down by the regulation. The main objection that scholars raise to a mandatory takeover bid as a condition for delisting is that such a takeover makes delisting more expensive and may be a deterrent to legitimate corporate decisions.

In a delisting framework, the costs associated with the takeover bid have been identified as the main obstacle to this decision. The offer to minority shareholders of a right to sell the shares and exit from the company is a reasonable protection tool. However, if the mechanism to fix the delisting takeover bid price is not efficient, the delisting takeover could become too costly.[73] In such cases, the duty to launch an offer might be considered a 'loss of liquidity premium' similar to the 'control premium' that is often paid in an ordinary takeover.

[72] This mechanism is well known as a means of refinancing and is regulated in the event that the reduction in capital falls below the minimum capital requirement, eg in Germany s 222 AktG, in Austria s 181 AktG, in France Art L224-2 Code de commerce; in Spain Art 363 LSC, where this is named an 'accordion' operation.

[73] Maume (n 9) 262; López Martínez, 'Artículo 10' (n 9) 260.

However, such a 'loss of liquidity premium' may not be justifiable, when the majority shareholder has already paid a 'control premium' to acquire a percentage of the share capital that allows it to make the main corporate decisions, eg a capital increase, the distribution of dividends, structural modifications or the dissolution of the company. The delisting decision is not more detrimental to minority shareholders than these corporate decisions, therefore, the extra price to be paid for having the possibility to delist the company should be paid when acquiring control of the company, not when executing the delisting decision, just like the other corporate decisions listed above.

The actual extent to which a takeover bid increases the costs of delisting will depend on the price at which the takeover bid should be offered and the manner in which that price must be set and paid.[74] A price that is too high may deter the company from proceeding with a delisting taken on a rational commercial basis.

i. Nature of the Consideration

In order to offer a liquid alternative to shareholders who wish to sell their shares in view of the loss of marketability resulting from delisting, it is usually provided that the price should be paid in cash (monetary consideration).[75] In fact, only a cash offer fully guarantees that shareholders will not suffer a loss of liquidity as a result of the delisting.

It could be considered whether offering other shares admitted to trading in a European regulated market as consideration would be enough to compensate for the loss of tradability. The liquid shares could be sold easily in their corresponding stock exchange and this option would prevent potential bidders having to find external financing. However, the legislators' option requiring a consideration in cash is easy to understand in a delisting promoted by the company, since the company would only be able to offer shares of other companies which may significantly change the shareholders' investment decision.

A more flexible solution could be allowed in the case of an acquisition by a shareholder or a third party. However, allowing shares to be offered as consideration in a delisting offer, while not drastically reducing liquidity, may involve additional costs for the shareholder, such as having to appoint custodians or being subject to new stock exchange rules different from those applicable to their original shares. The ability to sell shares admitted to trading may not provide adequate compensation for these additional costs.

ii. Price-setting Mechanisms

The mechanisms for setting the consideration of the offer vary among the different countries that establish a mandatory delisting takeover. The bidder sometimes lacks

[74] In Spain in 2023, the Spanish supervisory authority did not allow the majority shareholder of the hotel owner company 'NH' to launch a delisting offer because the proposed price was considered too low. Finally delisting failed, which shows how forcing a high bid price may discourage delisting.

[75] In Germany, s 39(2) BörsG; in Spain, according to Art 10.3 RD 1066/2007 the delisting offer may only be made in the form of a purchase and sale, and the entire price must be paid in cash.

the information necessary for the accurate determination of the intrinsic value of the company. In German law it is only required that the consideration of the delisting offer shall be equal or higher than the weighted average domestic stock exchange price of the securities during the six months prior to the publication of the delisting offer.[76] This valuation mechanism based on the stock exchange price is an easy mechanism to determine. If the bidder is, at the same time, the issuer, it has all the information to assess whether the stock market price reflects the true value of the company. If the issuing company launches the delisting offer after the share price has collapsed, this could be a breach of the duty of loyalty that company law imposes on directors to defend the interests of shareholders.

However, the regular stock market price of the shares has risks if the delisting takeover is tendered at a time when the market price is favourable to the bidder. In general, this should not be considered unlawful. It is simply a market risk that an investor must bear. If the offer is made with non-public inside information or on the basis of inaccurate information that has already been published, the case may be relevant from the point of view of market abuse regulation (insider trading or manipulation). This is not a specialty of delisting, but the consequence of its submission to the general regime.

Another risk may arise if the issuer does not immediately publish inside information that directly affects the price or publishes incorrect inside information that directly concerns the issuer (that would entail a breach of Article 17 MAR,[77] market manipulation when the bidder profits of the low prices of the shares in the late months).[78] The lower value may be due to unlawful misconduct, resulting from a breach of the duty of transparency, when the issuer does not immediately publish inside information that directly affects the price or publishes inside information which is incorrect. This would be the case if the major shareholder bought shares at a lower price knowing that he or the issuing company was going to make a delisting bid. This could constitute a breach of the prohibition on market manipulation or insider dealing. The acquisition of shares by the major shareholder is likely to be considered insider dealing,[79] as held by the Italian Supreme Court in the *Cremonini* case,[80] for the acquisition of shares by the major shareholder prior to a delisting bid.

When the securities of the issuer to which the delisting offer is addressed have been quoted on less than one-third of the trading days during the six months preceding to the publication of the offer and, if several successively quoted prices differ from each other by more than 5 per cent (section 39(3) sentence 4 BörsG), the stock market price mechanism to set the price should be complemented. The consideration to be paid

[76] See Q 9 in the Questionnaires.

[77] Regulation (EU) No 596/2014 on market abuse (market abuse regulation) repealing Directive 2003/6/EC of the European Parliament and of the Council and Commission Directives 2003/124/EC, 2003/125/EC and 2004/72/EC [2014] OJ L173/1.

[78] In Germany (see Çavuşoğlu, Questionnaire Germany (n 42) Q 9) the issuer is obliged to pay the difference between the consideration stated in the offer and the consideration corresponding to the value of the company determined on the basis of a valuation report (H Krause, 'Fragen zur angemessenen Gegenleistung bei Übernahme-, Pflicht- und Delisting-Angeboten' in S Grundmann, H Merkt and PO Mülbert (eds), *Festschrift für Klaus J. Hopt zum 80. Geburtstag* (Berlin, De Gruyter, 2020) 599 ff).

[79] Lombardo (n 47) 9 f.

[80] ibid.

should correspond to the intrinsic value of the company based on a valuation of the issuing company determined by external auditors.

Apart from those cases, it has been controversial whether a price calculation mechanism only based on regular stock exchanges prices is effective if the bidder chooses to launch the delisting offer when the stock market price of the shares had collapsed due to exogenous reasons (eg, the pandemic caused by Covid-19).[81] The stock exchange price mechanism might not be effective when the stock market price has changed abruptly due to exogenous reasons, as it would not reflect the true value of the share. Alternatives to stock exchange price mechanisms should be considered, to set the bid price based on non-market criteria. A possible solution for the inefficiency of the stock exchange price mechanism could be that the offer would have to include a valuation report prepared by an independent expert using other valuation methods.[82] This procedure might diminish the risks of manipulation and avoid, in principle, the risk that the bidder may launch the delisting offer at a time when the share price does not represent the intrinsic value of the company due to exogenous reasons.

However, the circumstances determine when a valuation report providing a different form of setting the consideration of the offer should be carefully considered. To require that the consideration of the delisting offer should be settled within a mandatory independent valuation report, may have undesirable consequences. In particular, if the setting of the bid price is based on non-market criteria, it can lead to considerable increases in the costs associated with delisting and become time-consuming.[83] In practice, the consideration proposed in the valuation report in the delisting offers according to non-market criteria shall usually be significantly higher, therefore, it will increase the price in the delisting takeover and may deter companies from delisting.

In practice, it can mean a case of overregulation, that may cause strategical behaviours and even lead issuers to seek other alternatives to achieve the objective of

[81] In Germany, the delisting request of 'Rocket Internet' made by its major shareholder at the time where the stock prices were low because of Covid-19, triggered a public debate on the appropriateness of valuing the delisting offer at market prices. However, the German legislator does not seem to consider a change in current legislation.

[82] Such is the case in Spanish law (see Recalde and Ataun, Questionnaire Spain (n 42) Q 9). An evaluation report fixing the price of the offer must be carried out by the delisting request. The valuation report contains a detailed rationale for the proposal and the price offered based on the results obtained by using the following methods. The price cannot be lower than the higher of (i) the *equitable price* according to general takeover legislation (highest price that the bidder – or persons in concert with the bidder – have paid or agreed upon in respect of the same securities over the 12 months prior to the announcement of the delisting offeror) and (ii) the price resulting from taking into account, jointly and with justification of their respective relevance, different criteria such as the book value of the company and, if applicable, of the consolidated group; break-up value of the company and, if applicable, of the consolidated group; average weighted price of the securities over the six-month period immediately prior to the announcement of the delisting proposal by means of the publication of a significant event, regardless of the number of sessions at which they have been traded; value of the consideration previously offered, in the event that a takeover bid has been made over a period of one year prior to the date of the resolution on the request for delisting; other valuation methods applicable to the specific case and generally accepted by the international financial community, such as discounted cash flows, company multiples and comparable transactions or others. The report also contains the rationale for the relevance of each of the methods employed in the valuation.

[83] The above mentioned 'NH Case' in Spain (n 73) illustrates how some jurisdictions imposing a higher offer price than market price deny the self-regulating ability of the market to determine the price of the shares. It also shows that a more rigorous regulation to fix the price may be deterrent from delisting.

delisting. The risk of a sharp fall in the value of the shares impacting on the bid price, is a market risk that a shareholder must always count with. There is no reason why this risk should not be considered in the context of delisting.

F. Enforcement

To ensure compliance with the obligation to launch the takeover bid, the supervisor can make use of the most common enforcement mechanisms, such as administrative fines. However, the need for effective instruments is likely to require provisions that link the requirements imposed by two bodies (market operator and public officer of the commercial register) or, as the case may be, the establishment of private enforcement mechanisms, such as civil liability, in the case of the breach of the duties.[84]

The most effective measure is undoubtedly to make delisting conditional on the launch of the takeover bid. In the case of cold delisting, if the corporate transaction has been, the supervisor could also deprive majority shareholders of their voting rights by preventing them from benefiting from the transaction.

G. Execution of Delisting

Even if the delisting application comes from the company or a shareholder, the delisting execution requires authorisation from the management of the stock exchange where the securities are listed, and/or from the public supervisor. Nonetheless, a previous authorisation will usually be required from the public supervisory body, which must verify compliance with the takeover bid requirement. It must also be verified that the obligations referring to disclosure and to the content of the bid document have been complied with.[85]

According to the ordinary takeover regime, delisting shall only take place after the offer has been settled through the central securities depository and the result of the bid has been published. This will determine the end of the takeover procedure according to general takeover legislation. Once it has been established that all the conditions for delisting have been met, the stock exchange operator shall immediately take the necessary steps to exclude the company from the list, without any further requirements.

Some jurisdictions provide for a grace period from the moment of the delisting request to its execution (eg three months for the Frankfurt Stock Exchange, NYSE, etc). This grace period may be a sensible addition to shareholder protection. However, this tool is not very effective. If shareholders are to suffer the loss of tradability of their shares,

[84] Recently, private enforcement tools have become more and more widespread. This has happened mostly in Italy, even if France and Germany have been more reluctant (P Agstner and D Marchesini Mascheroni, 'Breach of the Mandatory Bid Rule: Minority Shareholders' Protection in the Public vs. Private Enforcement Debate' (2020) 17 *European Company and Financial Law Review* 726).

[85] For Germany see Guntermann (n 43) 1625; for Spain see Arts 10.7 and 21 of the Royal Decree 1066/2007 on takeover bids.

this will not be avoided by their being able to sell the shares during an extended period after the request for delisting. Grace periods can even become particularly cumbersome for the company if the prescribed time frame is too long, delaying the delisting process. Small investors might face problems because they are usually detached from company management and will not be able to ascertain, prior to the delisting announcement, whether other investors are interested in buying or selling shares.

IV. The Protection of Shareholders in Mandatory Delisting

In the above cases, delisting is always the result of a voluntary decision by the company. However, delisting is sometimes imposed by the regulated market operator or the public supervisor, although, in the latter case, the market operator is ultimately responsible for implementing the delisting.

Mandatory delisting happens if the company does not comply with the legal burdens and conditions for remaining listed, specifically in the case of companies with little liquidity. The market operator or the public supervisor may revoke the listing authorisation following not only an issuer's application to withdraw shareholders from listing, but also when the requirements that should be fulfilled to remain listed no longer apply. When the requirements to remain listed are lost, the question of whether the decision of supervisory authorities or market operators is a regulated one, or discretionary will depend on the way in which the law describes the situations that should lead to withdrawal from the market.

In such cases of loss of liquidity, problems of legal strategy arise, which explains the authorities' reluctance to impose delisting. The suspicion of buy-back programmes by the company of its own shares, which can become a tool to reduce liquidity and thus put pressure on the supervisor to decide to delist the shares, must be understood. There is a risk that loss of liquidity may be stimulated by the company to facilitate the circumvention of the shareholder protection regime provided for by an opt-out evasion of the law. Indeed, the decision of the public authority or market operators may not be an easy one to take. A mandatory delisting ordered by the market operator's supervisory authority may ultimately end up penalising shareholders twice over.[86]

In any case, the practice of market operators or public authority who do not rigorously enforce compliance with the criteria for continued listing is understandable. Their reluctance to force delisting is also explained by the conflict of interest in which they find themselves, as delisting impacts on trading venues by depriving them of revenues from fees and commissions linked to the listing of securities.

Thus, the decision of supervisors and market operators not to react immediately in case a company does not meet the legal conditions to remain on the market can be easy to understand, as forced delisting may further harm shareholders (and the market). In effect, the delisting decision would force shareholders to remain in a company with even

[86] In Spain, Baron de Ley, S.A, executed various buyback programmes before launching the delisting offer. In the end the target of the takeover was 7.49% of the capital.

less liquidity and which would no longer be subject to market regulation and supervision. In this sense, cases of forced delisting should be conditional on not conflicting with investor protection.

It is not possible to go into the numerous issues raised by this case in depth. But probably the appropriate composition of the interests of the market and potential investors on the one hand, and of the shareholders of the company affected by the loss of the conditions for continued admission to trading on the other hand, would justify to oblige the company to launch a takeover bid, prior to the mandatory delisting of the company.

V. Conclusion

A voluntary delisting is a situation that may be grounded on different legitimate rationales. However, delisting also means a loss of liquidity of the shares and the regulation and supervision to which listed companies are subject and which is governed by investor protection no longer applies.

In this chapter it has been argued that the takeover bid conditioned to a voluntary delisting is an effective mechanism to protect minority investors. It assigns shareholders with the right to exit the company. The same effect could also be reached by other means, such as a withdrawal right, traditionally contemplated in company law to protect shareholders from a loss of transferability.

However, this exit right may sometimes not be an efficient instrument for the intended purpose. The need to file a delisting tender offer implies significant time and documentation costs that require the use of internal resources and highly qualified external consultants at a high financial cost. The costs associated with the mandatory offer have been considered the main obstacle to the company's freedom to agree to the delisting.

What makes the exclusion of contribution more expensive is the price to be paid. This depends on the number of potential recipients of the bid and the price they must be offered. There are two ways to fix the price of the bid. On the one hand, in some countries, the price must be fixed according to the average market price; on the other hand, other countries require a more rigorous regulation, requiring an independent expert valuation report as price setting mechanism for the delisting takeover consideration that may be based in non-market criteria. This could lead to establish a consideration significantly higher than the market price and may hinder potential delisting decisions unjustifiably.

The intersection of mandatory and voluntary delisting rules also raises difficulties from the perspective of shareholder protection. The automatic delisting of the company by the market operator when the company does not meet the liquidity requirements may result in a double detriment. The supervisor should be particularly wary of strategic attitudes. A reasonable solution could be to impose a takeover bid on the company prior to delisting.

5

Mechanisms of Ex Post Shareholder Protection

PAOLO GIUDICI*

I. Introduction

A delisting can be a decision of the company, taken by the company's board, with or without a shareholder's resolution. A delisting can also be the consequence of a takeover bid, where the bidder declares that it wants to buy all the shares in order to delist the company and go private. However, delisting can also be the consequence of a decision by the regulator or the market operator (the stock exchange). The position of minority shareholders and their right to challenge the decision that leads to the delisting of the company's shares depends on the given scenario. A separate analysis is therefore necessary.

II. Voluntary Delisting

A. When the Company can Delist at Will

The first scenario is the one where the decision to delist and go private is taken by the company. In this scenario it is important to understand whether the national law allows the issuer to delist at any moment, independently from the concentration of the shares in the hands of a controlling shareholder or a controlling coalition of shareholders, or whether the decision to delist can be taken exclusively when the free float is reduced below a certain minimum level. A typical threshold for requesting to be delisted is the reduction of the free float below 5 per cent, which is generally the result of a takeover bid aimed at delisting the company. Another issue is whether the delisting decision needs to be approved by the shareholders.

Of course, the most interesting and extreme case is the one where the issuer is entitled to delist at will and the decision can be taken by the board of directors. Minority

* Professor of Business Law at the Free University of Bozen-Bolzano, Italy.

shareholders might be damaged by the company's decision to delist, even if there is a long span of time running from the decision to delist to the actual delisting of the shares. In this span of time the price of the shares can start to collapse, since buyers might disappear from the market. Minority shareholders who are not able or do not want to sell their shares at a falling price will become shareholders of a private company. Indeed, the decision to delist might be also part of an attempt by the controlling shareholder to force minority shareholders to sell their shares at a very low price, thereby squeezing them out. Accordingly, minority shareholders might suffer serious damage from the company's decision to delist at will.

In the US, a company can delist after the board approves the action. Therefore, at least theoretically, minority shareholders are exposed to opportunistic behaviour. However, delisting is usually part of a going private transaction (such as a freezeout merger), which is an instrument that eliminates minority shareholders from the corporation and is governed in large parts by state corporate law and fiduciary duties. Thus, the US is less of an outlier than it appears. Minority shareholders are protected by the principles of fair dealing and fair price. Under certain conditions, they also enjoy an appraisal right.[1] It is well known that dissenting shareholders' appraisal litigation is common in the US, and that minority shareholders are ready to enforce their right to surrender the shares in exchange for a fair value in court.

In Sweden, a company can delist at will. Sweden might seem an outlier as well. However, the board must act in the interests of the company and of all of the shareholders (not just the majority) and, if the admission requirements are still met, the reasons for the delisting application must be of sufficient strength to justify the exposition of shareholders to the disadvantages of delisting. Minority shareholders are protected by general company law rules against conflicted decisions of the shareholder meeting that give an undue advantage to a shareholder or a third party to the detriment of the company or a shareholder. When the decision is taken by the board, shareholders could bring an action against the directors if their decision gave an undue advantage to a shareholder or a third party to the detriment of the company or a shareholder. Accordingly, shareholders – particularly minority shareholders – are protected by general company law rules.

Other jurisdictions try to prevent minority shareholders from being exposed to the risk of opportunistic behaviour from the company or its controlling shareholder ex ante. They can adopt many different strategies.

B. Jurisdictions where the Company can Delist Only when the Free Float has become Very Small

The first legal strategy is to allow the company to delist exclusively when a certain concentration level of the shares in the hands of a controlling shareholder or a controlling

[1] See M Gelter and S Thel, Chapter 15 in this volume; for a comparison between the US and Europe *see* M Ventoruzzo, 'Freeze-Outs: Transcontinental Analysis and Reform Proposals' (2010) 50 *Virginia Journal of International Law* 841.

coalition has been reached. This concentration should not necessarily depend on a previous takeover bid.

I understand from the Dutch chapter that, as mentioned, this is the rule in the Netherlands, where the board can start the delisting process if 95 per cent of the shares are in the hands of a shareholder or a coalition of shareholders. This is also the rule in Greece, where 95 per cent of the total voting rights are required to approve the delisting. This is, at least implicitly, also the rule in France, where the board can decide to delist but, according to Euronext rules, it is up to the market operator to approve the delisting, provided that the financial instrument no longer meets the admission conditions and the delisting is not likely to significantly harm the interests of investors or to compromise the orderly functioning of the trading platform.

However, this strategy is less common than one might expect, probably for good reason. When there is a concentration of the ownership of the shares and therefore a reduction in the free float, somebody is buying shares on the market and there is at least some buyer pressure on prices. Moreover, almost all jurisdictions, including Europe, have rules on block-holder disclosure, ie rules concerning transparency of major holding and voting rights. Accordingly, minority shareholders know who is buying and can understand whether the buyer is accumulating a position from which to launch a takeover bid aimed at delisting the company or is accumulating share ownership to reach the threshold that lets the company board apply for a voluntary delisting. In this situation, minority shareholders can protect their position by selling the shares on the market and leaving the company or by buying shares on the market to prevent the threshold from being exceeded and negotiating with the controlling shareholder.

Furthermore, there are cases where the company has very good reasons to delist but cannot do so if 5.001 per cent of the minority shareholders oppose the delisting. This can create a situation where the minority shareholders can seek to extract wealth from the other shareholders by forcing them to buy the shares at an excessive price. Accordingly, many jurisdictions seek to find a different balance between the protection of minority shareholders and the interest of the company to be delisted.

C. Jurisdictions where the Company can Delist at Will after a Resolution of the Shareholder Meeting

The second legal strategy is therefore to allow the company to request a delisting after a resolution of the shareholder meeting that approves the action. Needless to say, the resolution is meaningless if there is a controlling shareholder who has already decided to delist the company. Accordingly, the law may require that requests for the cancellation of the listing are to be approved by a supermajority (e.g. 75 per cent) at a meeting of the shareholders, or by a majority of minority resolutions. These rules apply in Australia and in the UK, where the board of directors can take the decision to delist and then 75 per cent of shareholders voting on the resolution must approve the delisting at the general meeting. In the UK, moreover, if the issuer has a controlling shareholder, defined as a shareholder who controls more than 30 per cent of the votes to be casted at the general meeting, then a majority of independent shareholders voting on the resolution must also approve the delisting at the general meeting.[2] In Sweden there are circumstances where the decision to delist must be taken by the general meeting.[3]

Then there are two different sub-sets of policy strategies. The first is not to protect the minority shareholder any further, unless that shareholder brings an action claiming that it suffered unfair prejudice or was oppressed. The second is to protect dissenting minority shareholders by giving them the right to exit the company at a fair price (appraisal right).

(i) No Further Protection (No Exit Right)

The first strategy is the one followed, with some differences, by the UK, Sweden and Australia. In the UK, shareholders are protected according to general principles such as unfair prejudice or the duty of shareholders to act bona fide for the benefit of the company, but the national report underlines that those remedies have a limited scope of application, and it is rare that minority shareholders succeed on these claims. Accordingly, civil actions might be very difficult for minority shareholders. Australia protects minority investors through the oppression remedy. It gives a shareholder standing to make an application to a court for relief if the delisting is contrary to the interests of the company's shareholders as a whole, or is oppressive to, unfairly discriminatory against, or unfairly prejudicial to a security holder or security holders. There is also an 'unacceptable circumstances' remedy that can be obtained through the Takeovers Panel. My understanding is that Australia protects minority shareholders more than the UK.

(ii) Some Form of Exit Right is Given to Dissenting Shareholders

The second strategy for the national law is to add another layer of protection, offering to minority shareholders who disagree with the decision to delist the right to exit the company at a fair price. Accordingly, private enforcement in this scenario depends on general company law rules concerning shareholder resolution and exit rights, and on company or capital markets law concerning the assessment of fair price.

In Spain, generally speaking, the delisting decision must be taken by the general meeting; the company should launch a tender offer to provide dissenting shareholders with the right to sell their shares and leave the company. This is a form of exit right. The dissenting shareholder has the right to receive a fair price; the law states the criteria to be followed to assess this.[4] I do not know what type of discretion exists on which method to follow in the assessment and therefore whether the Spanish model can give occasion for price disputes equivalent to appraisal litigation.

The Italian model is slightly different. First it must be noted that in Italy, even though the delisting resolution is explicitly considered by a specific provision of the Civil Code, it is debated whether this provision actually means that the company

[2] See J Chan and C Gerner-Beuerle, Questionnaire UK.
[3] See J Östberg, Questionnaire Sweden.
[4] See A recalled and M Ataun, Questionnaire Spain.

can delist at will with a straightforward and simple delisting resolution of the shareholders' meeting.[5] I think that the company can do it. In any event, listed companies can also be delisted through a 'cold delisting', through the merger by incorporation into a non-listed company, which requires a shareholder resolution. In both cases the resolution is subject to a supermajority voting requirement (66,66 per cent) and shareholders who have not cast their vote in favour of the delisting are granted an appraisal right. The dissenting shareholder should be paid a value equal to the average market price of the shares in the last six months before the publication of the notice convening the shareholders' meeting. Since the price is assessed through a mathematical calculation that uses market data, litigation is very limited, differently from the US, where appraisal proceedings require the judge to determine the 'fair value' of the corporation's shares. It remains to be seen what happens in cases where the reference to stock exchange prices is not significant because of market abuse or illiquidity of the market.

I understand that in Finland the common way for a company to delist is through the merger by incorporation into a non-listed company. We have a scenario which is similar to the Italian one, where dissenting shareholders have an exit right.[6]

D. Allowing the Company to Delist Following a Board Decision and Giving Shareholders the Right to Exit

Another strategy is to allow the company to delist and to give the power to take the delisting decision to the board, but to grant exit rights to the shareholders. In Germany shareholders have no veto rights. The delisting decision should be taken, at least in principle, by the executive board. However, minority shareholders have the right to receive an offer by the issuer, with the requirements for the price of the offer subject to a detailed regulation, similar to the Italian one but more detailed since it also makes reference to cases where the calculation based on stock exchange prices should not be followed because there were market abuses that influenced the price of the shares or the market was not sufficiently liquid. From this perspective, the German rules appear to be more advanced than the Italian ones.[7]

E. Assessment

The private law protection of minority shareholders depends on the framework adopted by each jurisdiction. In the US dissenting shareholders' appraisal litigation is widespread. In Italy, appraisal right litigation is almost absent because the valuation of the company's shares is not left to the assessment of a court and appears very rigid. In Spain it looks like there is room for some litigation on the fair price of the tender offer that

[5] See G Balp, Questionnaire Italy.
[6] See H Marjosola, Questionnaire Finland.
[7] See K Çavuşoğlu, Questionnaire Germany.

the company must launch in order to be delisted, and the same is true for Germany, where minority shareholders can invoke the presence of market abuses or an illiquid market to challenge the exit price determined by reference to stock exchange prices. In jurisdictions like Sweden, the UK, Australia, minority shareholders are protected by general company law rules and there are no specific rules aimed at regulating a delisting scenario. In particular, dissenting shareholders have no specific appraisal/exit rights. Finally, I assume that when the delisting decision is subject to the approval of the market operator or the securities watchdog, minority shareholders can challenge that approval in court.

III. Takeover Bid

In Europe, delisting is usually triggered by a takeover bid. We have mentioned the fact that Spain requires a tender offer by the issuer equivalent to a takeover bid when the company wishes to be delisted.

For all EU member states the Takeover Directive[8] applies, including the right of squeeze-out (Article 15) and the right of sell-out (Article 16). Therefore, the main issue is whether minority shareholders can challenge in court the price of the offer that brought the offeror to reduce the free float to a level where the company can apply for a delisting request or can challenge the price of the squeeze-out or sell-out.

For instance, imagine a situation where a minority shareholder alleges that the price of the takeover bid that preceded the squeeze-out/sell-out phase was unfair because of market manipulation or any of the other circumstances that made the offer appear more appealing than it really was, and that as a consequence the bidder reached the 90–95 per cent threshold and was able to delist the company. Alternatively, imagine a situation where the same shareholder alleges that the offer document was misleading and therefore the offeror succeeded in reaching the squeeze-out/sell-out threshold because the offer price appeared more convenient than it really was. In such situations, the question arises as to whether dissenting shareholders are allowed to stop the delisting process or whether they can only assert claims for damages. In both cases, it should be understood what instruments dissenting shareholders possess to get information from the market operator or the securities authority concerning trades, prices, and potential market abuses affecting the price of the shares, or to access information concerning the relationship between the offeror and the board of directors of the target and any other information that can reveal the existence of a misrepresentation aimed at favouring the success of the takeover bid and the ensuing delisting of the company. Accordingly, private enforcement depends, as usual, on the mechanisms that are available to the dissenting shareholder to gather information against the defendant (discovery) or against the market operator or the securities authority. This is an area of capital markets law that is not duly investigated in the literature. In many jurisdictions, minority shareholders have no access to information gathered by the market operator or the securities

[8] Directive 2004/25/EC on takeover bids [2004] OJ L142/12.

authority, and therefore it is extremely difficult for them to provide evidence of market abuse. Italy is a case in point, since information gathered by the securities authority is subject to secrecy and cannot be disclosed to third parties.

Private enforcement also depends on the possibility of pooling claims together through class actions or other mechanisms of claim aggregation. Of course, the position of dissenting shareholders should be very easy to aggregate, since they are all in the same position.[9] However, not every country makes this aggregation of identical claims easy.[10]

Another issue concerns litigation costs, ie whether the English rule or the American one is applicable, or any alternative and intermediate form of cost shifting rules.[11] With regards to costs, a further issue is whether third-party litigation funding is available and admitted.[12] Another matter that can facilitate private enforcement is the participation of the securities authority in the litigation as amicus curiae or something similar. Imagine this situation. It is discovered that there was massive market manipulation affecting the share price that went undisclosed at the time of the takeover bid. The securities authority fined the bidder but of course could not do more, because the bid was successful and the company went private. Minority shareholders sue the bidder who contests the existence of any market manipulation before the civil court. Here one issue is whether the assessment of the securities authority that led to the fine obliges the court to hold that there was market abuse, ie whether the existence of market abuse can be disputed or not by the bidder. If it can be disputed, the subsequent question is whether the authority can be called into the litigation to support the minority shareholders' assertion that there was market abuse, or whether it can voluntarily join the litigation as amicus curiae or something similar.

IV. Delisting Imposed by the Regulator or the Market Operator

This case is interesting because it would be potentially possible for a group of shareholders to increase their shares in the company to the point where the free float becomes almost inexistent in order to 'force' the regulator or the market operator to delist the company's shares. In this case the controlling shareholders or the issuer would not pay an exit price to dissenting shareholders. Minority shareholders would therefore have

[9] RA Epstein, 'Class Actions. Aggregation, Amplification and Distortion' (2003) *The University of Chicago Legal Forum* 475.

[10] BT Fitzpatrick and RS Thomas (eds), *The Cambridge Handbook of Class Actions, An International Survey* (Cambridge, Cambridge University Press, 2021); A Uzelac and S Voet (eds), *Class Actions in Europe, Holy Grail or Wrong Trail?* (Cham, Springer, 2021).

[11] S Antill and SR Grenadier, 'Financing the Litigation Arms Race' (2023) 149 *Journal of Financial Economics* 218; G Dari-Mattiacci and M Saraceno, 'Fee Shifting and Accuracy in Adjudication' (2020) 63 *International Review of Law and Economics* 1.

[12] S Peyer, 'Competition Litigation Funding' in B Rodger, M Ferro and F Marcos (eds), *Research Handbook on Private Enforcement of Competition Law in the EU* (Cheltenham, Edward Elgar Publishing, 2023); C Veljanovski, 'Third Party Litigation Funding in Europe' (2012) 8 *Journal of Law, Economics and Policy* 405.

only one way to protect their interest, starting legal action against the regulator or the stock exchange. If I am not wrong, however, no chapter in this book refers to a similar case that actually took place in Europe at least.

V. Conclusion

The previous analysis has shown that the mechanisms of ex post shareholder protection are very different. The law generally does not leave minority shareholders at the mercy of the board of directors or the controlling shareholders. The mechanisms adopted depend on the way in which the delisting of the company is pursued. The most interesting case is the one where it is the issuer that decides that it is time to be delisted, whether through its board of directors or through a resolution of its shareholders, and whether through a straightforward withdrawal from the listing (when this is allowed) or alternative procedures such as the merger through incorporation into a non-listed company. In this case there is no common instrument to protect minority shareholders, but jurisdictions can use, singularly or cumulatively, different instruments: strict enforcement of the board's fiduciary duties, supermajorities, majority of minority resolutions, anti-oppressive or anti-abusive instruments, exit rights in the form of appraisal rights or rights to receive a cash offer.

The delisting of the company through a takeover bid and the following use of squeeze-out and sell-out rights is the most common way of delisting companies in Europe. In this case minority shareholders can accept the offer to leave the company before it goes private and the problem is the pressure to tender in a scenario where market prices might be manipulated or the information provided for by the bidder misrepresents the real situation, pushing shareholders to sell at prices that do not reflect the real value of the deal.

The delisting of the company can also be decided by the regulator or the stock exchange. In this situation minority shareholders might be forced to challenge the delisting decision of the regulator or the stock exchange and this is of course outside the boundaries of corporate law. This scenario is potentially very interesting, even though no similar case has been reported by the national chapters.

PART III

Perspectives of Delisting in EU Member States

6

Delisting from the Company's Perspective – Corporate Governance

ATHANASIOS KOULORIDAS*

I. Introduction

In recent years delisting has grown to be a significant phenomenon for public markets, since, in absolute figures, there have been financial periods in which instances of delisting outnumbered new listings in most major exchanges.[1] The phenomenon has received considerable attention in the relevant literature. Studies test various hypotheses on the reasons for delisting and the economic impact of delisting in shareholders' value. However, attention has been given primarily to the impact of delisting and going-private transactions on shareholders' protection and the orderly operation of public markets. While this is obvious, since in the case of delisting, shareholders are, in principle, deprived of the liquidity offered by the market and the investor protection associated with rules applicable to listed companies, little or no attention has been given to delisting as a corporate decision taken in the light of the best interest of the issuer.

Although the notion of the company's interest may vary among jurisdictions, nowadays there is an overall consensus, at least in Europe, that the company's interest does not necessarily equal the financial interests of the shareholders. It has grown to cover both the separate best interests of the company as a legal person and owner of its own assets[2] as well as the interests of various stakeholders such as voluntary and involuntary partners of the company like employees, creditors, customers, society

* Asst Professor of Corporate and Capital Markets Law, Athens University of Economics and Business, Chairman of the Greek Union of Listed Companies, Managing Partner ABLAW.

[1] See, among others, Tountopoulos, Chapter 1 in this volume and further bibliography therein; I Martinez and S Serve, 'Reasons for Delisting and Consequences: A Literature Review and Research Agenda' (2017) *31 Journal of Economic Surveys* 733.

[2] For example, the German Corporate Governance Code states in principle 1: 'The Management Board is responsible for managing the enterprise *in its own best interests*,' Whereas in the foreword, it is stated that in so doing it needs to take into account 'the interests of the shareholders, the enterprise's workforce and the other groups related to the enterprise (stakeholders) to ensure the continued existence of the enterprise and its sustainable value creation (the enterprise's best interests)'. For an analysis of the German approach see H Fleischer, 'A Guide to German Company Law for International Lawyers: Distinctive Features, Particularities,

and, more recently, the environment ('enlightened shareholder value theory').[3] In this context, despite the negative effect that a going private decision may have on the marketability of the shares issued by the listed company and owned by its shareholders, delisting may be in the 'best interest' of the company and its business. How is this conflict between the legitimate interests of the shareholders, whose property's marketability and legal rights associated with it are diminished by delisting, on the one hand, and the company's interest in securing and promoting its business by going private, on the other, to be resolved?

This chapter seeks to shed light on the delisting phenomenon from the company's perspective. After all, the decision to delist is bestowed upon the organs of the company and primarily relates to the company as the issuer of the listed securities. The analysis is structured in three parts. Its first part is an attempt to analyse the overwhelming literature on the reasons for delisting decisions and the impact of delisting on shareholder value. Based on the classification of the various findings, its second part seeks to identify the various interests and the conflicts that arise. Conflicts are identified at three levels: (a) the market level, eg between the private interests of the issuer and its shareholders and the public interest of the market or between market operators; (b) the company level, between the interest of the issuer and the interest of the holders of listed securities; and (c) the principal level, between the interest of major shareholders or managers and the interest of minority shareholders. The third part examines the mechanisms of company law or capital markets law used in different jurisdictions. The analysis is based on questionnaires which were answered by legal scholars from different European jurisdictions in 2023. It also attempts to assess the effectiveness and efficiency of various mechanisms and whether EU-wide convergence and further harmonisation is required.

II. Empirical Studies

A. Delisting Methods

In various market reports, delisting is usually classified by the method it is effectuated. So, delisting may take place due to a merger, in which case a listed or even an unlisted company absorbs the delisted entity, or leverage buyout transactions, or takeover offers and squeeze outs of minority shareholders, or company failures such as insolvency. The method may vary between markets. For example, in the UK and the US, the initiators are mainly other listed entities or private equity funds whereas

Idiosyncrasies' in H Fleischer, JL Hansen and WG Ringe (eds), *German and Nordic Perspectives on Company Law and Capital Markets Law* (Tübingen, Mohr Siebeck, 2015).

[3] For example, the Companies Act 1980, s 172 incorporates into UK company law the principle of enlightened shareholder value by appending to the directors' duty to 'promote the success of the company for the benefit of its members as a whole' a list of matters to which directors are required to 'have regard' in discharging the duty. With respect to value creation and the interests of stakeholders see among others MC Jensen, 'Value Maximization, Stakeholder Theory and the Corporate Objective Function' (2001) 14 *Journal of Applied Corporate Finance* 8, 16.

in Europe the dominant form of delisting, most likely due to the concentrated shareholder ownership of most listed firms, is a going private transaction after a takeover offer or a merger with minority squeeze out.[4] From that perspective, delisting may be regarded as a 'natural' phase in the firm's life cycle[5] and is characterised by strong heterogeneity.[6] Delisting may also take place involuntarily because a listed entity fails to meet numerical or qualitative criteria set by the market operator. However, underneath these instances there are more intrinsic reasons for delisting.

B. Reasons for Delisting

Most empirical studies identify regulatory costs as a crucial driver of delisting. As Martinez and Serve (2017) rightfully observe in their analysis of the existing delisting literature, 'the cost saving rationale is omnipresent in analysis of the phenomenon'.[7] Studies report a decrease in IPOs due to increases in regulatory requirements.[8] Conversely, reducing compliance costs seems to have a positive correlation with listings and new IPOs[9] or an increase in investments in innovation following IPOs.[10] Other studies investigate the introduction of strict regulation and its effect on the number of delistings.[11] For example, despite a steady increase in the total number of US firms, the number of firms listed on US stock exchanges declined by about 50 per cent from its peak of 8,090 firms in 1996 to 4,266 firms in 2019.[12] This trend, established as an abnormal US phenomenon called the 'US Listing Gap',[13] has recently

[4] I Martinez and S Serve, 'The Delisting Decision: The Case of Buyout Offer with Squeeze-Out (BOSO)' (2011) 31 *International Review of Law and Economics* 228; M Ventoruzzo, 'Freeze-Outs: Transcontinental Analysis and Reform Proposals' (2010) 50 *Virginia Journal of International Law* 842.

[5] T Shumway, 'The Delisting Bias in CRSP Data' (1997) 52 *The Journal of Finance* 327; C Weir and M Wright, 'Governance and Takeovers: Are Public-To-Private Transactions Different from Traditional Acquisitions of Listed Corporations?' (2006) *Accounting and Business Research* 289.

[6] Martinez and Serve, 'Reasons for Delisting and Consequences' (n 1).

[7] ibid.

[8] PJ Engelen et al, 'The Effects of Stricter Regulation on the Going Public Decision of Small and Knowledge-Intensive Firms' (2020) 47 *Journal of Business Finance & Accounting* 188.

[9] M Dambra, LC Field and MT Gustafson, 'The JOBS Act and IPO Volume: Evidence That Disclosure Costs Affect the IPO Decision' (2015) 116 *Journal of Financial Economics* 121; CM Lewis and JT White, 'Deregulating Innovation Capital: The Effects of the JOBS Act on Biotech Startups' (2023) 12 *The Review of Corporate Finance Studies* 240.

[10] M Dambra and MT Gustafson, 'Do the Burdens to Being Public Affect the Investment and Innovation of Newly Public Firms?' (2021) 67 *Management Science* 594.

[11] C Leuz and PD Wysocki, 'The Economics of Disclosure and Financial Reporting Regulation: Evidence and Suggestions for Future Research' (2016) 54 *Journal of Accounting Research* 525.

[12] G Lattanzio, WL Megginson, and A Sanati, 'Dissecting the Listing Gap: Mergers, Private Equity, or Regulation?' (2023) 65 *Journal of Financial Markets* 100836. However, see BE Eckbo and M Lithell, 'Merger-Driven Listing Dynamics' (2023) *Journal of Financial and Quantitative Analysis*, 11 December. Available at: www.cambridge.org/core/services/aop-cambridge-core/content/view/2FE20241AD8A16DFAB4790658BE28561, who show that the dramatic post-1996 US listing decline by approximately 50% – often attributed to declining listing benefits – has been reversed as the 'missing' firms de facto continue to exist inside their public acquirers.

[13] C Doidge, GA Karolyi and RM Stulz, 'The US Listing Gap' (2017) 123 *Journal of Financial Economics* 464. According to their data analysis, the US listing gap is consistent with a decrease in the net benefit of a listing for US firms. Since the listing peak in 1996, the propensity to be listed is lower for all firm size categories and industries, the new list rate is low, and the delist rate is high. The high delist rate accounts for 46% of the listing gap and the low new list rate for 54%.

been reported to have increased significantly due to US stock market regulation.[14] Similar delisting gaps after listing picks are found in other jurisdictions.[15] In line this with trend, many studies document that the introduction of the Sarbanes–Oxley Act in the US in 2002 and other US reforms, such as amendments to codes of best practice of the major US exchanges and the associated compliance costs, significantly increased the probability of firms delisting.[16] Other studies find similar results for EU corporate governance codes[17] and the introduction of IFRS for listed companies.[18] Evidence also shows that a major incentive in going private through leverage-buyout transactions is cost cutting.[19]

Since listing and regulatory costs apply to all listed companies it is reasonable to expect that companies of a smaller size are more likely to be affected. So, delisting is closely related to the ability of the company to afford listing costs. Empirical evidence supports this size effect across various markets.[20] According to such empirical evidence, smaller firms are less efficient in absorbing increases in listing costs, hence smaller firms are more motivated to go private when compliance costs increase. The findings are consistent with other empirical studies' findings that the insolvency rate of listed firms is higher for companies with lower market capitalisation.[21]

[14] Lattanzio, Megginson and Sanati, 'Dissecting the Listing Gap' (n 12).

[15] Eckbo and Lithell, 'Merger-Driven Listing Dynamics' (n 12) who, by investigating other jurisdictions, find that four-fifths of countries experience listing peaks followed by a 'U.S.-style' decline, but with their peaks distributed widely over the period from 1980 to 2020, they find that in non-US. economies, post-peak listing declines tend to reflect outflows of firms from public markets rather than retentions within public acquirers.

[16] SB Block, 'The Latest Movement to Going Private: An Empirical Study' (2004) 14 *Journal of Applied Finance* 36; E Engel, RM Hayes and X Wang, 'The Sarbanes–Oxley Act and Firms' Going-Private Decisions' (2007) 44 *Journal of Accounting and Economics* 116; E Kamar, P Karaca-Mandic and EL Talley, 'Going-Private Decisions and the Sarbanes-Oxley Act of 2002: A Cross-Country Analysis' (2008) 25 *The Journal of Law, Economics & Organization* 107; C Leuz, A Triantis and TY Wang, 'Why Do Firms Go Dark? Causes and Economic Consequences of Voluntary SEC Deregistrations' (2008) 45 *Journal of Accounting and Economics* 181; A Marosi and N Massoud, 'Why Do Firms Go Dark?' (2007) 42 *The Journal of Financial and Quantitative Analysis* 421.

[17] M Berninger, M Klug and D Schiereck, 'Börsenrückzüge infolge steigender Corporate-Governance-Anforderungen – Empirische Evidenz von 13 europäischen Kapitalmärkten' (2018) 70 *Schmalenbachs Zeitschrift für betriebswirtschaftliche Forschung* 351; S Thomsen and F Vinten, 'Delistings and the Costs of Governance: A Study of European Stock Exchanges 1996–2004' (2014) 18 *Journal of Management & Governance* 793.

[18] G Pownall and M Wieczynska, 'Deviations from the Mandatory Adoption of IFRS in the European Union: Implementation, Enforcement, Incentives, and Compliance' (2018) 35 *Contemporary Accounting Research* 1029 and MI Vulcheva, 'International Accounting Standardization across Countries with Unequal Enforcement – Questionable Benefits at a High Price?' (PhD dissertation, Emory University 2011).

[19] K Lehn and A Poulsen, 'Free Cash Flow and Stockholder Gains in Going Private Transactions' (1989) 44 *The Journal of Finance* 771.

[20] US: ST Bharath and AK Dittmar, 'Why Do Firms Use Private Equity to Opt Out of Public Markets? (2010) 23 *The Review of Financial Studies* 1771; Engel, Hayes and Wang, 'The Sarbanes–Oxley Act and Firms' Going-Private Decisions' (n 16); RL Kieschnick, 'Free Cash Flow and Stockholder Gains in Going Private Transactions Revisited' (1998) 25 *Journal of Business Finance & Accounting* 187; Leuz, Triantis and Wang, 'Why Do Firms Go Dark?' (n 16); H Mehran and S Peristiani, 'Financial Visibility and the Decision to Go Private' (2010) 23 *The Review of Financial Studies* 519; UK: H Aslan and P Kumar, 'Lemons or Cherries? Growth Opportunities and Market Temptations in Going Public and Private' (2011) 46 *The Journal of Financial and Quantitative Analysis* 489; E Kashefi Pour and M Lasfer, 'Why Do Companies Delist Voluntarily from the Stock Market?' (2013) 37 *Journal of Banking and Finance* 4850; EU: Thomsen and Vinten, 'Delistings and the Costs of Governance' (n 17).

[21] PJ Seguin and MM Smoller, 'Share Price and Mortality: An Empirical Evaluation of Newly Listed Nasdaq Stocks' (1997) 45 *Journal of Financial Economics* 333.

Similarly, a number of studies document a positive relationship between relatively poor performance and the decision to delist. For example, studies in the US identify a negative correlation between sales and assets growth and delisting in the US market.[22] Similar findings are reported for the UK and the EU, also indicating that firms that delist are relatively worse performing in terms of operating results such as sales, return on assets profit margins or stock performance,[23] or that they have fewer growth opportunities.[24] Also, companies with a lack of growth opportunities, no need for public equity or an inability to attract investor interest and institutional investors have a higher probability of going private.[25] Finally, lower financial visibility is found to be a pivotal factor in a company's decision to go private.[26] Financial visibility is the ability of a company to attract an adequate level of investor interest and recognition and is measured by analyst coverage.

Illiquidity is also an important factor in delistings. Many studies show the influence of low transaction volumes in a listed security on the delisting decision,[27] meaning that the more liquid a firm is, the less likely it is to go private[28] and vice versa. In addition, many studies systematically confirm that delisted companies are undervalued, which leads to the outcome that undervaluation is a predominant going private factor.[29]

Ownership structure also seems to be a relevant factor. In companies with concentrated ownership, larger investors may have the incentive to use control to extract private benefits from going private, such as limiting agency, monitoring costs or distributing

[22] Lehn and Poulsen, 'Free Cash Flow and Stockholder Gains' (n 19). See also Doidge, Karolyi and Stulz, 'The US Listing Gap' (n 13); WS Kim and EO Lyn, 'Going Private: Corporate Restructuring under Information Asymmetry and Agency Problems' (1991) 18 *Journal of Business Finance & Accounting* 637.

[23] Kashefi Pour and Lasfer, 'Why Do Companies Delist Voluntarily?' (n 20); Martinez and Serve, 'The Delisting Decision' (n 4); Thomsen and Vinten (n 17); M Wright et al, 'Leverage Buyouts in the UK and Continental Europe: Retrospect and Prospect' (2006) 18 *Journal of Applied Corporate Finance* 38.

[24] Weir and Wright, 'Governance and Takeovers' (n 5); C Weir, D Laing and M Wright, 'Incentive Effects, Monitoring Mechanisms and the Market for Corporate Control: An Analysis of the Factors Affecting Public to Private Transactions in the UK' (2005) 32 *Journal of Business Finance & Accounting* 909; C Weir, D Laing and M Wright, 'Undervaluation, Private Information, Agency Costs and the Decision to Go Private' (2005) 15 *Applied Financial Economics* 947.

[25] W Bessler et al, 'Why do Firms Down-List or Exit from Securities Markets? Evidence from the German Stock Exchange' (2023) 17 *Review of Managerial Science* 1175 and relevant literature therein; Bharath and Dittmar, 'Why Do Firms Use Private Equity to Opt Out of Public Markets?' (n 20); Martinez and Serve (n 4); Mehran and Peristiani, 'Financial Visibility' (n 20).

[26] P Halpern, R Kieschnick and W Rotenberg, 'On the Heterogeneity of Leveraged Going Private Transactions' (1999) 12 *The Review of Financial Studies* 281; Martinez and Serve (n 1); Mehran and Peristiani (n 20).

[27] See, among others, AK Achleitner et al, 'Private Equity Acquisitions of Continental European Firms: the Impact of Ownership and Control on the Likelihood of Being Taken Private' (2013) 19 *European Financial Management* 72; Bharat and Dittmar (n 20); Kashefi Pour and Lasfer (n 20); Mehran and Peristiani (n 20); Martinez and Serve (n 4).

[28] Bharath and Dittmar (n 20); Martinez and Serve (n 4); Mehran and Peristiani (n 20).

[29] E Croci and A Del Giudice, 'Delistings, Controlling Shareholders and Firm Performance in Europe' (2014) 20 *European Financial Management* 374; Halpern, Kieschnick and Rotenberg, 'Heterogeneity of Leveraged Going Private Transactions' (n 26); RJ Maupin, CM Bidwell and AK Ortegren, 'An Empirical Investigation of the Characteristics of Publicly-Quoted Corporations Which Change to Closely-Held Ownership Through Management Buyouts' (1984) 11 *Journal of Business Finance & Accounting* 435; Weir and Wright (n 5); Weir, Laing and Wright, 'Incentive Effects, Monitoring Mechanisms and the Market for Corporate Control' (n 24); Weir, Laing and Wright, 'The decision to go private' (n 24).

free cash flows.[30] Hence there is empirical evidence that concentrated ownership is positively correlated with the likelihood of going-private transactions.[31] The same applies for companies with high managerial ownership.[32] Managers may wish to protect themselves from hostile takeovers[33] or to extract private benefits for the firm, especially for firms with higher and steady cash flows[34] and lower institutional ownership.[35] Conversely, companies with strong corporate governance structures are less susceptible to delisting.[36]

On the other hand, delisting decisions are not necessarily driven by private interests of the managers or the controlling shareholders. Empirical studies support the argument that the delisting process may be undertaken to enhance the sustainability of the company[37] or to maintain a high level of the company's performance and social responsibility.[38] Also, other studies categorise as potential reasons for managers' or major shareholders' decisions to go private more interest aligning perceptions such as the reduction of agency costs.[39] Restrictions through listing rules or the market on managerial incentive plans may be overcome by going private. Consequently, more risky and complex transactions may successfully take place if the management team has better incentives achieved with a management buyout or through a private company.[40] Finally, alternative sources of financing such as debt[41] or tax benefits – savings

[30] D Magni et al, 'Defining the Relationship Between Firm's Performance and Delisting: Empirical Evidence of Going Private in Europe' (2022) 13 *Journal of the Knowledge Economy* 2584.

[31] Achleitner et al, 'Private Equity Acquisitions of Continental European Firms' (n 27); D Cumming et al, 'Pre-Going Private Ownership Around the World' (2019) 30 *British Journal of Management* 692.

[32] L Fauver and A Naranjo, 'Derivative Usage and Firm Value: The Influence of Agency Costs and Monitoring Problems' (2010) 16 *Journal of Corporate Finance* 719; M Pagano and A Röell, 'The Choice of Stock Ownership Structure: Agency Costs, Monitoring and the Decision to Go Public' (1998) 113 *The Quarterly Journal of Economics* 187.

[33] Weir and Wright (n 5).

[34] Maupin, Bidwell and Ortegren, 'An Empirical Investigation' (n 29); T Opler and S Titman, 'The Determinants of Leveraged Buyout Activity: Free Cashflow vs. Financial Distress Costs' (1993) 48 *The Journal of Finance* 1985.

[35] Marosi and Massoud, 'Why Do Firms Go Dark?' (n 16).

[36] N Chancharat, C Krishnamurti and G Tian, 'Board Structure and Survival of New Economy IPO Firms' (2012) 20 *Corporate Governance: An International Review* 144; A Charitou, C Louca and N Vafeas, 'Boards, Ownership Structure and Involuntary Delisting from the New York Stock Exchange' (2007) 26 *Journal of Accounting and Public Policy* 249; Leuz, Triantis and Wang (n 16).

[37] M Del Giudice et al, 'The Micro Level Actions Undertaken by Owner-Managers in Improving the Sustainability Practices of Cultural and Creative Small and Medium Enterprises: A United Kingdom–Italy Comparison' (2017) 38 *Journal of Organizational Behavior* 1396; IN Dubina, EG Carayannis and DFJ Campbell, 'Creativity Economy and a Crisis of the Economy? Coevolution of Knowledge, Innovation, and Creativity, and of the Knowledge Economy and Knowledge Society' (2012) 3 *Journal of the Knowledge Economy* 1.

[38] RVD Jordão and VR de Almeida, 'Performance Measurement, Intellectual Capital and Financial Sustainability' (2017) 18 *Journal of Intellectual Capital* 643.

[39] L He, 'Do Founders Matter? A Study of Executive Compensation, Governance Structure and Firm Performance' (2008) 23 *Journal of Business Venturing* 257; L Renneboog, T Simons and M Wright, 'Why do Public Firms Go Private in the UK? The Impact of Private Equity Investors, Incentive Realignment and Undervaluation' (2007) 13 *Journal of Corporate Finance* 591.

[40] H DeAngelo, L DeAngelo and EM Rice, 'Going Private: Minority Freezeouts and Stockholder Wealth' (1984) 27 *The Journal of Law & Economics* 367. In their sample, they found that going-private transactions did not result in a systematic exploitation of minority shareholders.

[41] Bharath and Dittmar (n 20); Martinez and Serve (n 4).

associated with debt financing[42] – impact a company's decision to exit the market, especially when financial visibility is low and equity financing scarce.[43]

C. Down-Listing

Empirical evidence also suggests that a viable alternative to delisting for some companies is the so-called down-listing, meaning an issuer voluntarily transferring to a lower market segment with fewer regulatory requirements, either in the form of a regulated market or, more commonly, in the form of a growth market – a multilateral trading facility.[44] Such empirical studies provide evidence consistent with a cost–benefit analysis.[45] The same reasons identified above as leading to a decision to delist are identified as reasons for down-listing, such as inferior growth opportunities, no need for further financing, low stock liquidity, smaller firm size, poor operating performance, stricter disclosure requirements and higher regulatory costs.[46] It is also anticipated that this trend is likely to increase with the introduction of a more ambitious ESG regime, in particular with the entry into force of the implementing measures for the CSRD in the EU Member States, since this regime will apply to listed SMEs but not to unlisted SMEs or those admitted to trading in an MTF. Also, the reporting standards that non-listed SMEs may voluntarily follow will be different and less cumbersome than reporting standards that listed SMEs will need to adhere to.

D. Impact on Value

Empirical findings on the financial impact of delisting on shareholders and the company's value are consistent with the heterogeneity of the reasons for going private. Announcements of mandatory delistings are found to be closely associated with value decreases, in the form of reduced trade volumes, share price dilution and increases in effective spreads and volatility.[47] This is reasonable since a mandatory delisting is

[42] Halpern, Kieschnick and Rotenberg (n 26); S Kaplan, 'Management Buyouts: Evidence on Taxes as a Source of Value' (1989) 44 *The Journal of Finance* 611; Kieschnick, 'Free Cash Flow and Stockholder Gains' (n 20); However see Weir, Laing and Wright, 'Incentive Effects, Monitoring Mechanisms and the Market for Corporate Control' (n 24) and Weir, Laing and Wright, 'The Decision to Go Private' (n 24) where, as far as the UK is concerned, tax benefit hypothesis is not validated.

[43] Bharat and Dittmar (n 20); Kashefi Pour and Lasfer (n 20); Martinez and Serve (n 4).

[44] Berninger, Klug and Schiereck, 'Börsenrückzüge' (n 17). For further analysis on down-listing see G Balp, Chapter 11 in this volume.

[45] See eg, Bessler et al, 'Why do Firms Down-list or Exit from Securities Markets?' (n 25). The paper identifies 518 firms that listed on the Prime Standard at least once during the sample period of which 243 firms left this market segment. Of these firms, 107 downlisted and transferred to lower market segments and 136 firms exited the public equity market for the following reasons: 61 firms merged, 53 were insolvent, and 22 firms went private.

[46] Bessler et al (n 25).

[47] GP Baker and RE Kennedy, 'Survivorship and the Economic Grim Reaper' (2002) 18 *The Journal of Law, Economics, and Organization* 324; V Panchapagesan and I Werner, 'From Pink Slips to Pink Sheets: Market Quality Around Delisting From NASDAQ' (2004) *Working Paper Ohio State University* Charles A Dice Center for Research in Financial Economics. Available at: https://ssrn.com/abstract=565325; GC Sanger

bad news for the shareholders and is mainly due to failure of the company to meet the market requirements and hence is perceived as a form of sanction or a result of poor performance.[48]

Whereas empirical evidence on mandatory delisting shows consistent value depreciation for shareholders, empirical findings on delisting show the exact opposite. Voluntary delisting does not generate wealth losses. As one should expect, if delisting is done for cost-cutting reasons or more flexibility in business decisions and restructuring or for the distribution of free cash flows, delisted firms should generate greater returns for shareholders. Moreover, if such delistings are accompanied by buyout transactions, such wealth gains should manifest themselves as a premium that the acquirer is willing to pay to take the company off the market. Consistent with the above assumptions, the majority of studies quantifying cumulative abnormal returns (CARs) on the announcement of delisting find positive CARs which vary among the US, the UK and the EU, being higher in the US and lower in the EU.[49] Also, a sizeable number of studies find considerable tax benefits.[50]

Findings, however, are less conclusive when it comes to ownership structure and corporate governance. One should expect that, due to conflict of interests, transactions that involve major shareholders or high managerial ownership would be less profitable for minority public shareholders, and this should not have been the case in companies with strong corporate governance or in countries with increased shareholder protection. However, the majority of empirical evidence does not support the above hypotheses and is inconclusive at best. For example, whereas one study finds that the increase in shareholder value is greater in companies with strong corporate governance such as the existence of independent directors,[51] another finds that weak corporate governance and poor investor protection generate higher CARs.[52] Similarly, on the one hand, empirical evidence suggests that deals involving family owners[53] or concentrated ownership with increased control rights[54] generate higher returns, while, on the other hand, other studies find no correlation between family ownership and higher CARs[55] or link low managerial ownership with higher returns.[56] Also, whereas one would expect that undervalued or smaller firms when going private will generate less CARs, studies

and JD Peterson, 'An Empirical Analysis of Common Stock Delistings' (1990) 25 *Journal of Financial and Quantitative Analysis* 261.

[48] Martinez and Serve (n 1).

[49] For a very useful and detailed account of the relevant studies and their findings see Martinez and Serve (n 1) and further references therein.

[50] For the US see Kieschnick (n 20); Halpern, Kieschnick and Rotenberg (n 26); Kaplan, 'Management Buyouts' (n 42). For the EU see Achleitner et al (n 27).

[51] Lee, CI et al, 'Board Composition and Shareholder Wealth: The Case of Management Buy-outs' (1992) 21 Financial Management 58.

[52] Weir, Laing and Wright, 'Incentive Effects, Monitoring Mechanisms and the Market for Corporate Control' (n 24); Weir, Laing and Wright, 'The decision to go private' (n 24).

[53] M Geranio and G Zanotti, 'Equity Markets Do Not Fit All: An Analysis of Public-to-Private Deals in Continental Europe' (2012) 18 *European Financial Management* 867.

[54] S Boubaker, A Cellier and W Rouatbi, 'The Sources of Shareholder Wealth Gains from Going Private Transactions: The Role of Controlling Shareholders' (2014) 43 *Journal of Banking & Finance* 226.

[55] Croci and Del Giudice, 'Delistings, Controlling Shareholders and Firm Performance' (n 29).

[56] Renneboog, Simons and Wright, 'Why Do Public Firms Go Private in the UK?' (n 39). However, DeAngelo, DeAngelo and Rice, 'Going Private' (n 40), find the opposite.

suggest the opposite, validating the hypothesis that voluntary delisting for such reasons creates value.[57]

E. Interim Summary

The analysis of the rich empirical literature generates very interesting results. Delisting is characterised by strong heterogeneity. However, overall, most studies provide evidence consistent with a cost–benefit analysis. Listed entities decide to go private if the listing costs outperform the expected benefits from retaining the listing status. Consistent with the above findings, most voluntary delistings, as opposed to mandatory ones, are reported to generate positive returns, even in cases of undervalued or smaller companies. Even in cases with increased probability of conflicts of interests, returns seem to remain positive. If this is the case, why is delisting that targeted? Could it be a regulatory fallacy?

III. Conflicts of Interest

The agency theory traditionally identifies the company as a structure of conflicting interests at various levels. The analysis of the empirical studies on delisting also identified conflicts of interest as a plausible explanation of various going-private transactions. Moreover, the identification of the various levels of conflicts involved in a delisting decision could be an important determinant for any regulatory intervention. It could also provide an explanation of the need to regulate such conflicts over and above the mechanisms used under the normal operation of company law for the regulation of other conflicts of interest. In addition, delisting may also occur because of a decision of the regulatory authority or the market operator, as in the case of mandatory delisting. In that respect, in the case of delisting, conflicts may arise at three levels:[58]

(i) between the private interests of the issuer and its shareholders and the public interest of the market;
(ii) the interest of the issuer and the interest of the holders of listed securities; and
(iii) the interest of major shareholders or managers and the interest of minority shareholders.

A. Conflicts at Market Level (the Public Interest)

Mandatory delisting may occur when a listed company fails to meet listing requirements or continuing obligations as set by the market operator or the applicable law. Interestingly enough, this area of the delisting phenomenon is the only part for which there is some harmonisation effort at EU level. More precisely, Article 52 of

[57] Geranio and Zanotti, 'Equity Markets Do Not Fit All' (n 53); A Sannajust, 'Motivations and Performance of Public to Private Operations: An International Study' (2010) 6 *Journal of Modern Accounting and Auditing* 1.
[58] See also Tountopoulos (n 1) with a slightly different classification.

MiFID II[59] provides that 'a market operator may suspend or remove from trading a financial instrument which no longer complies with the rules of the regulated market unless such suspension or removal would be likely to cause significant damage to the investors' interests or the orderly functioning of the market'. Furthermore, Article 69 of MiFID II grants to the supervisory authority the same power, without the qualifications provided for in Article 52.[60]

The exercise of or the failure to exercise the aforementioned powers may conflict with the best interests of the issuer or the shareholders. For example, a market operator delists an issuer due to low liquidity or low free float. Exchanges make money from trade volume. While low liquidity or low free float could constitute a failure to comply with listing requirements, it may have detrimental effects for the issuer and especially the shareholders, who are deprived of the protection afforded to shareholders in listed companies.

Similarly, market operators, being for-profit organisations, may not exercise their power to remove a financial instrument even if the issuer fails to comply with listing rules. As a matter of fact, empirical evidence seems to suggest that this is the norm.[61] Martinez and Serve (2017) note a 'gap between the strictly defined listing criteria and the flexible enforcement of delisting'. Similarly, Macey and O'Hara identify inherent conflict of interest problems as 'the delisting dilemma' the solution of which cannot be left to markets.[62] Such failure or delay may have detrimental effects on any recovery or restructuring plan of the issuer or on existing and, more importantly, new shareholders who enter the company in the interim. This issue imposes another problem: a thinning of the market due to competition among market operators. If it is the issuer that initiates the delisting procedure, it may select an exchange where the market operator demonstrates greater leniency towards listing requirements, eg liquidity or free float thresholds. This could lead to a race to the bottom among market operators. However, there is no empirical evidence on this subject matter. Also, market migration and its efficiency pose an EU harmonisation issue. Greater mobility on this subject matter could further enhance market integration, whereas barriers imposed in the ability of an issuer to migrate from a market of one Member State to a market of another Member State are to be scrutinised under EU freedoms, such as the free movement of capital, the freedom of establishment and the freedom to provide services.

Finally, conflicts may also arise when market operators act de jure or de facto as national competent authorities.[63] As for-profit organisations, the dual status of such entities reasonably causes concerns as to the independence of their judgement and discretion on the exercise of public authority and power.[64]

[59] Directive 2014/65/EU on markets in financial instruments and amending Directive 2002/92/EC and Directive 2011/61/EU (recast) (MiFID II) [2014] OJ L173/349.

[60] For further analysis on mandatory delisting see H Marjosola, Chapter 8 in this volume.

[61] ibid, and further analysis therein.

[62] JR Macey, M O'Hara and D Pompilio, 'Down and Out in the Stock Market: The Law and Economics of the Delisting Process' (2008) 51 *The Journal of Law & Economics* 683.

[63] For example, see Questionnaires on France, Germany and Netherlands and further analysis in Marjosola (n 60).

[64] On the role of public authorities and market operators see Marjosola (n 60).

While one could argue that the above issues relate to mandatory delistings only, it should not be ignored that mandatory delisting may also be seen as a manifestation of an unsuccessful listing or as an indirect form of late voluntary delisting, where the company is either obliged to delist due to infringements of market rules or deliberately and knowingly fails to comply to initiate its delisting. Similar conflicts may also arise in the context of a voluntary delisting, such as when national competent authorities need to approve a request for a voluntary delisting and, in doing so, they have the discretion to approve or to impose further conditions or requirements.[65] Authorities may fear reputational risks and impose additional expensive conditions for the delisting entity such as the requirement to provide an exit right to minority shareholders.[66]

Conflicts may also arise when an issuer decides to delist with the purpose of migrating to another exchange. A market operator or a national authority may have the incentive to delay or frustrate such transfer, whereas on the other hand it may be for the benefit of the migrating company on multiple levels. A market migration may mean for the issuer more liquidity, additional investors, foreign investors, greater visibility or access to more equity funds. This is the case when an issuer transfers its listing from a peripheral smaller exchange to a bigger market. Apart from the profit or visibility impact that the transfer of a big firm has on the small national exchange, more national stock exchanges have a symbiotic relationship with national economies. Such market migration may be an issue of national importance, especially when such market migration is accompanied by a seat transfer to the host state.

B. Conflicts at Company Level (the Best Interest of the Issuer)

One notable characteristic of a listing status is the following: whereas the decision for the listing is normally taken by the company organs, such a decision creates positive externalities to the issuer's shares which are owned by its shareholders. It is not only that the value of the shares issued by the company and held by the shareholders mirrors the value of the company and follows its upwards and downwards movements, as if in any other business decision, but also, following a listing, the shares owned by the shareholders, as their property, obtain special rights and characteristics with the most notable one that of marketability. Once the issuer decides to delist, such a decision affects the properties of the shareholders' shares. Delisting the issuer means delisting the shares owned by the shareholders. Such shares will no longer be marketed, so the shareholders are deprived of an important quality of their property, which could also be the legal foundation for their subscribing for or acquiring the said shares.

In addition, once a company goes private, shareholders are deprived of the protection afforded to them under legislation applicable only to listed companies. Corporate

[65] For example, in the UK or Greece.

[66] For example, although not required directly by law, and irrespective of the fact that the delisting decision is taken with a supermajority of 9% of the total share capital of the issuer, the Hellenic Capital Market Commission requires that a takeover offer is made as part of the delisting process unless a mandatory takeover bid has preceded the delisting request.

governance requirements, disclosure and transparency requirements, market abuse and takeover law provisions apply only in the case of listed companies. Problems also arise for foreign investors who end up holding unlisted shares in another jurisdiction with considerable barriers in exercising their rights.

Consequently, and irrespective of whether delisting has a negative financial impact on the owners of the listed shares,[67] it has two inherent negative consequences for shareholders who in principle are deprived of (a) the liquidity offered by the market and (b) the investor protection associated with rules applicable to listed companies.[68]

On the other hand, the decision to delist may be based on solid and reasonable grounds for the issuer. The majority of empirical studies explored in Part I.A provide strong evidence that such decisions are based on a cost–benefit analysis. If the issuer's benefits from listing do not justify listing costs, its board has a duty to act in the best interest of the company. After all, as indicated already in the introduction of this chapter, the company's interest does not necessarily coincide with the financial interests of its shareholders but in most jurisdictions, it has outgrown them. For example, an innovation company may face issues with market disclosure requirements which signal important information to competitors. A company based on its financial performance and its size struggles with listing and compliance costs. An old established company operating in a saturated market has considerable free cash flows and is not in need of additional equity financing. Another company, due to its size and low free float, has lower liquidity and market visibility and is constantly undervalued. After all, the decision to make a capital increase or for a major shareholder to offer shares in the market to increase free float lies with the shareholders. Another company may need restructuring, and such restructuring will be more flexible and less painful for the company and its shareholders if it is done behind the market curtains.

Also, in many cases, when shareholders entered the company, some of these characteristics may have already existed. Why should an investor be afforded protection from delisting if entering a company with extremely low free float and/or with low or no liquidity at all, and subsequently the company is delisted because of that? In addition, things may have substantially changed for issuers after initial listings. Regulation may have increased, and new requirements may have been imposed. Empirical findings suggest that the introduction of new regulation such as Sarbanes–Oxley Act in the US or corporate governance codes in the EU resulted in a wave of delistings.[69]

C. Conflicts at Principal Level (the Agency Problem)

The motives of the issuer for delisting may not always be based on a cost–benefit rationale and may be more self-serving in nature. After all, decisions at company level are made by humans who may advocate their own personal interests. The analysis of the empirical studies in Part I.A revealed that personal interests may be a crucial factor

[67] See IID. above.
[68] For further analysis on the shareholders' perspective see C Van der Elst, Chapter 3 in this volume.
[69] See IIB above.

for delisting decisions.[70] In companies with concentrated ownership, larger investors may have the incentive to use control to extract private benefits from going private, such as limiting agency or monitoring costs or by distributing free cash flows. Hence there is empirical evidence that concentrated ownership is positively correlated with the likelihood of going-private transactions. The same applies for companies with high managerial ownership. Managers may wish to extract private benefits for the firm, especially for firms with higher and steady cash flows and lower institutional ownership, or to protect themselves from hostile takeovers. Conversely, companies with strong corporate governance structures are less susceptible to delisting. Even if other empirical findings suggest that such going private transactions are not value-decreasing for the shareholders,[71] and especially for minority investors, an issue of the distribution of wealth gains and fair treatment arises.[72]

D. Interim Summary

From an issuer's perspective, in any given delisting decision conflicts may arise at three levels. At a market level, conflicts may arise primarily in cases of market migration or where the market operator or the national competent authority has a discretion in effectuating a mandatory bid or in approving a voluntary bid. Second, at a company level, while a delisting decision may be in the best interest of the issuer it has two inherent negative consequences for shareholders since they are, in principle, deprived of (a) the liquidity offered by the market and (b) the investor protection associated with rules applicable to listed companies. So, a weighing of the relative importance of the company's interest versus the protection of shareholders' interests is inevitable. Third, at principal level, a delisting decision may be a manifestation of normal agency problems especially in companies with concentrated ownership or strong managerial control. The questions that follow are how such conflicts are addressed by the various jurisdictions under question, whether special rules exist, or if such treatment lies with the normal operation of company or capital markets law and whether the current status is efficient in addressing such risks or creates unwanted costs for the issuer.

IV. Legal and Regulatory Mechanisms

The heterogeneity that is present in the empirical findings on the delisting phenomenon, repeats itself when it comes to the analysis of the various mechanisms used by various jurisdictions to regulate delisting. The analysis that follows is based on a questionnaire that legal scholars of different European jurisdictions answered in 2023.[73] Any additional source or reference is identified in the relevant footnote.

[70] ibid and relevant footnotes.
[71] See IID. above.
[72] With respect to shareholders' protection see Part II for further analysis.
[73] Questionnaires.

A. Addressing Issuer's Concerns in Market Level Conflicts

As identified above, at a market level, conflicts may arise primarily in cases of market migration or where the market operator or the national competent authority has a discretion in effectuating a mandatory bid or in approving a voluntary bid.

Not all jurisdictions have special rules on market migration. In certain jurisdictions, the retention or parallel seeking of a listing in an EEA-regulated market waives the obligation to otherwise make a mandatory offer or to offer an exit opportunity to minority or dissenting shareholders. This is the case, for example, in Austria and Germany with the additional requirement that the said regulated market has equivalent prerequisites for a delisting.[74] Similarly, in France, the Euronext rules allow for an exemption from a requirement to make a squeeze-out offer for minority holdings in the case of market migration provided that a sales facility is provided by the issuer, providing priority to existing shareholders to sell their securities on the most liquid market at no expense.[75] Conversely, in the Netherlands, the issuer needs to provide for an exit mechanism even in cases of market migration.

In other Member States the regulation of market migration is only circumstantial. For example, in Greece, no approval by the Hellenic Market Commission is required for the delisting in case of a merger where the shareholders of a listed company receive shares listed in another regulated market in Greece.[76] This is not the case, however, with straightforward voluntary delistings. Equally, in certain jurisdictions rules exist at rule book level of certain exchanges.[77] For example in the UK, the London Stock Exchange, which operates and regulates AIM, may waive the shareholder vote requirement for AIM delistings[78] if the issuer's securities 'are already or will be admitted to trading on an EU or UK regulated market or an AIM Designated Market to enable shareholders to trade their AIM securities in the future'.[79] In Spain, while there are no specific rules on market migration, the Comisión Nacional del Mercado de Valores (CNMV) can authorise delisting without having to launch a takeover bid when another procedure with equivalent shareholders' protection has been implemented.[80] On the extreme side, in Italy, market migration is the only reason for which delisting is allowed.[81] Overall, most jurisdictions address market migration in a more flexible way and establish directly or implicitly exemptions from normal procedures and primarily the requirement to provide an exit for minority shareholders. This is

[74] Section 38 para 8 no 2 of the Börsegesetz 2018 (BörseG) for Austria and s 39 para 2 sentence 3 no 2 of the Börsengesetz (BörsG) for Germany.

[75] Euronext Rule Book II, Art P 1.4.4. Euronext Paris can waive this obligation if the issuer remains listed on a regulated market operated by another Euronext market operator, with the same settlement system.

[76] See art 17, para 5 of law 3371/2005. However, only one regulated market operates in Greece.

[77] Such as in the UK, Sweden and Spain.

[78] Normally 75% of the shareholders present at the general meeting must approve the delisting. See J Chang and C Gerner-Beuerle, Questionnaire UK.

[79] London Stock Exchange, *AIM Rules for Companies* (1 January 2021). Available at: www.docs.londonstockexchange.com/sites/default/files/documents/AIM%20Rules%20for%20Companies%20%2801012021%29_1.pdf, Guidance Notes to Rule 41.

[80] Art 65 para 4 of Ley 6/2023 of 17 March 2023 (LMVSI) and art 11(e) of Royal Decree 1066/2007 of 27 July 2007.

[81] Art 133 of Legislative Decree No 58 of 24 February 1998 (TUF).

an obvious policy choice since minority shareholders, albeit needing probably to deal with lack of proximity with the new market, still have a market exit and are still afforded similar investor protection. The latter is in most cases an explicit or implicit prerequisite in most jurisdictions. However, certain jurisdictions[82] seem to have a different approach and require an exit mechanism, even if the company is still listed elsewhere.

Things are even more heterogeneous when it comes to the other potential subject of conflict: Market's discretion on mandatory and voluntary delisting. Even in mandatory delisting, where there seems to be a basis for harmonisation as the basic powers of the market operators and the designated national competent authorities are provided in Articles 52 and 69 of MiFID II, the current situation looks far from harmonised in terms of processes. First, in certain jurisdictions it is the market operator who also acts as the competent authority,[83] whereas in others there is a separation.[84] In some, the competent authority has no say on delistings,[85] in others, even the delisting conditions are not set out in law but only in the rulebook. Also, the discretion level differs. In some jurisdictions the operator or the authority have full discretion[86] either explicitly or through the ambiguity of the wording on delisting reasons,[87] providing, for example, additional grace periods,[88] in others limited discretion. Nonetheless, a norm that applies in all jurisdictions is that mandatory delisting seems to work more as a sanction on issuer's actions or failures to comply with listing rules or capital markets regulations. Also, in almost all jurisdictions the issuer is provided with a response time and has a right to appeal against the delisting decision, however the extent of such right and the competent courts (civil or administrative) differ.[89]

Discretion also differs in cases of voluntary delisting. In some jurisdictions, authorities have no power to approve the delisting which lies with market operators,[90] while in others, authorities or market operators, acting as authorities, have limited power to review the legality of the process, and the fulfillment of the conditions and prerequisites imposed by the law and the market rules,[91] in other cases they have greater discretion,[92] and even the right to introduce additional requirements or measures mainly for the protection of the minority investors.[93]

Also, great ambiguity exists as to the interpretation in practice of the overriding principle that exists in almost all jurisdictions, under which a market operator or the competent authority, as the case may be, may not delist a security 'if such a

[82] France and the Netherlands.
[83] Austria, Germany, Cyprus and Sweden.
[84] Italy and Greece.
[85] Austria, the Netherlands (however AMF can dictate Euronext), Germany and Sweden.
[86] Greece and the Netherlands.
[87] Germany and Italy.
[88] See eg France, Greece and Sweden.
[89] For further analysis see Marjosola (n 60).
[90] See eg Spain, where the Spanish Securities Market Commission (Comisión Nacional del Mercado de Valores, the 'CNMV') approves the takeover process which is a prerequisite for the delisting (art 21 RD 1066/2007).
[91] Austria, Italy (to the extent that voluntary delisting is permitted), UK and Sweden.
[92] The Netherlands.
[93] Greece.

measure could significantly harm the interests of investors or the orderly functioning of the market'.[94] It should be noted that, under EU law, the meaning of circumstances constituting significant damage to investors' interests and the orderly functioning of the market is quite restrictive. According to Article 80 of Regulation (EU) 2017/565[95] such circumstances occur at least:

> (a) where it would create a systemic risk undermining financial stability, such as where the need exists to unwind a dominant market position, or where settlement obligations would not be met in a significant volume; (b) where the continuation of trading on the market is necessary to perform critical post-trade risk management functions when there is a need for the liquidation of financial instruments due to the default of a clearing member under the default procedures of a CCP and a CCP would be exposed to unacceptable risks as a result of an inability to calculate margin requirements; (c) where the financial viability of the issuer would be threatened, such as where it is involved in a corporate transaction or capital raising.

As the wording of the provision reveals this is not a maximum harmonisation rule and Member States may include other circumstances as well.[96]

Based on the above analysis, and even though the powers of market operators and regulatory authorities is an area of delisting regulation that should be more harmonised due to the intervention attempted through MiFID II, the general regulatory picture across the EU remains quite fragmented. The fragmentation is further augmented due to different processes and regulatory structural idiosyncrasies of each Member State. However, fragmentation is translated to cost for the issuer and the efficient operation of the markets. The most notable example is market migration. Fragmentation is bad for liquidity. Mobility of capital is crucial for a single market where that better serves the interest of the issuer in seeking additional equity capital and more liquidity. In addition, an issuer seeking dual listing may refrain from doing so if this increases its liability. For example, if delisting from one market required the issuer to make a mandatory bid with respect to that market, even if retaining a listing in another, more liquid market, this could work as a disincentive for further expansion into additional markets. Also, a lack of transparency on the discretion and the exercise of powers of authorities and market operators can have the same effect. Needless to say, the flexibility on the enforcement of delisting that certain market operators may demonstrate could lead to reverse competition among exchanges and a race to the bottom and thinning of markets, especially when competition among exchanges increases and technical and national barriers decrease.

Since fostering competition among market participants with a goal of a single capital markets union is the predominant policy choice, the issues of market migration and the harmonisation of the discretion in delisting should be addressed. This requires an EU-wide initiative. The first step has been done using the abovementioned provisions of MiFID II which, a few years after their transposition, need to be further

[94] See Marjosola (n 60).

[95] Commission Delegated Regulation 2017/565/EU supplementing Directive 2014/65/EU as regards organisational requirements and operating conditions for investment firms and defined terms for the purposes of that Directive [2017] OJ L87/1.

[96] See also ibid, Art 80 para 3.

enforced and improved. Harmonising the rules on market migration and the market operators' powers and supervision would facilitate a level playing field and provide companies with the ability to move more easily to new markets, where they can access more liquidity or meet their financing needs. For example, it seems like there is no sense in requiring an exit mechanism when a company delists from an EEA stock exchange and has or requests a listing on another EEA exchange. Shareholders can equally be protected by exchanging their old listed shares for new listed shares. Any cash-out requirement operates as a clear barrier to exit and causes market fragmentation. Such approaches need to be reviewed under the main freedoms of the EU Treaties and also from a competition law perspective, maybe as an abuse of dominant position if the market which introduces such rules has a dominant position at national or EU level.

Furthermore, clear rules and their acceptance by the relevant market operators and central securities depositories to minimise barriers to entry for companies are of paramount importance. While harmonising delisting requirements in general may not be necessary, the need for harmonisation is more important when it comes to facilitating cross-border listing. Also, there seems to be an inherent fallacy in the argument that there is a necessity to harmonise listing requirements but not those for delisting.

B. Addressing Issuer's Concerns in Company and Principal Level Conflicts

When it comes to private interests that emerge at the level of the company or the shareholders, most jurisdictions address potential conflicts with two main mechanisms that are also evident in other instances of the agency problem: (a) regulating the decision-making for the delisting, and (b) providing for an exit mechanism for shareholders. Of course, the implementation of the said mechanisms and the actual mix of rules differ from country to country.

As far as the decision-making process is concerned, there are jurisdictions that assign the competence of making the delisting decision to the board of directors,[97] whereas others require a general meeting decision. In some jurisdictions, while the board is primarily responsible, there may be instances when it shares competence with the general meeting. For example, in Sweden, a practice note issued by the Swedish Securities Council ('SSC'), a self-regulatory body seems to ascribe the competence between the board of directors and the general meeting. If admission requirements are still met and there are no good reasons for delisting, a general meeting resolution taken with a 90 per cent supermajority is the best practice. Moreover, in France, there are no special rules on the competence of the delisting decision, so the decision lies with the board of directors. Surprisingly enough, market rules require an ordinary resolution by the general meeting for down-listing, while the decision on a pure delisting lies with the board. In Austria, the approval of the supervisory board is required and, if the company

[97] Sweden, Germany, France and the Netherlands.

is listed there, an extraordinary resolution of the general meeting with a three-quarters majority is required.

Furthermore, the quorum and the majority rules differ greatly among jurisdictions, with some leaving the matter to the normal operation of company law and others introducing special rules. In general, where the matter is bestowed to the board, regular company law rules apply.[98] Conversely, where a general meeting resolution is required, majority and quorum rules differ considerably, but, in general, a simple majority requirement is the exception. In Greece, a majority of 95 per cent of the total share capital is required, whereas in Cyprus and Hong Kong 90 per cent of the capital represented in the meeting is required with minimal quorum rules. Italy requires an extraordinary resolution in accordance with company law rules. The UK's approach is very interesting, requiring a 75 per cent majority and, if a major shareholder holds more than 30 per cent, a simple majority of independent shareholders present in the meeting. On the other hand, a simple majority suffices in Spain.

When it comes to ex ante investor protection through the provision of an exit mechanism, it seems that most continental European jurisdictions have some form of protection in one way or another, unlike common law jurisdictions where no such a requirement is imposed by law. This does not mean, however, that the delisting mechanisms used do not include public offers or cash out mergers for shareholders. In the UK,[99] Sweden and Cyprus no exit mechanism exists. Similarly, neither US nor Australian delistings offer the minority shareholders exit rights. In the US, depending on the form of delisting, shareholders are afforded an appraisal right.[100] In the US and Australia minority shareholders who want to exit the company before the delisting must do so in the time between the delisting announcement and the day of delisting.[101]

In continental Europe, a mandatory bid requirement is omnipresent in most jurisdictions, whether explicitly or implicitly. In Greece for example, although there is no explicit requirement, in order to approve a delisting Hellenic Capital Market Commission requires that a mandatory offer is made for the remainder of the shareholders, unless the initiating the delisting shareholder has reached the 90 per cent threshold immediately before through a mandatory takeover bid. This is required regardless of the fact that the decision was taken with a special majority of 95 per cent of the total share capital. In Austria and Germany, a takeover bid is required as a prerequisite for the market operator to approve the delisting. In France, a requirement for a public offer (delisting offer) is required in cases of illiquidity, meaning that the major shareholder holds shares representing at least 90 per cent of the total share capital of the issuer. In Italy, dissenting shareholders are afforded a withdrawal right in cases of cold delisting or pure delisting, where permitted. In the Netherlands, a requirement to make a public offer is imposed by the market rules.

Furthermore, notice should be given as to the EU interpretation of the interest of investors in cases of delisting under Articles 52 and 69 of MiFID II. In almost all

[98] For example, in the Netherlands it is a simple majority while in Germany it must be unanimous.

[99] However, a withdrawal right exists in case a company changes its status from public to private. However, this is not necessary and after a delisting the company can continue to trade as a plc.

[100] See M Gelter and S Thel, Chapter 14 in this volume.

[101] See Van der Elst (n 68).

continental European jurisdictions, law and regulation seems to suggest that in assessing the interests of the issuer versus the interests of shareholders in the context of a delisting, the ability of the investors to cash out their investments and hence to protect the economic value of their investment by requiring a mandatory offer or a similar exit opportunity is crucial. However, this is not the stance taken in Article 80 of Regulation (EU) 2017/565.[102] Under Article 80, circumstances constituting significant damage to the investors' interests and the orderly functioning of the market relate more with systemic risk, post trade risk management and the financial stability of the issuer. Also, even where the Member State identifies additional circumstances other than those provided in the EU regulation, according to paragraph 3 of the said regulation the following factors should be taken into account:

> (a) the relevance of the market in terms of liquidity where the consequences of the actions are likely to be more significant where those markets are more relevant in terms of liquidity than in other markets; (b) the nature of the envisaged action where actions with a sustained or lasting impact on the ability of investors to trade a financial instrument on trading venues, such as removals, are likely to have a greater impact on investors than other actions; (c) the knock-on effects of a suspension or removal of sufficiently related derivatives, indices or benchmarks for which the removed or suspended instrument serves as an underlying or constituent; (d) the effects of a suspension on the interests of market end users who are not financial counterparties, such as entities trading in financial instruments to hedge commercial risks.[103]

If the ability of the shareholders to recoup or exit their investment and be compensated for the delisting by the issuer, or third parties acting on its behalf, is such a crucial part of the investors' interests for most jurisdictions, why is it totally absent from the only EU provision about delisting which specifically defines the terms 'investors' interests' and 'orderly functioning of the market'? Even the wording of letter b of paragraph 2

> the nature of the envisaged action where actions with a sustained or lasting impact on the ability of investors to trade a financial instrument on trading venues, such as removals, are likely to have a greater impact on investors than other actions

has more the notion of a subsidiarity test rather than a specific requirement to assess the impact of the delisting decision on the value and the marketability of the investor's shares. It seems that EU law defers the issue of shareholder protection in cases of delisting to national company law and takeover regulation, as it remains entirely silent in the provision where a reference to delisting would be most appropriate.[104]

Could it be that Member States have gone too far with the imposition of capital markets rules that require the 'compensation' of minority shareholders in the context of delisting? It seems that there is a divergence between EU policy in this aspect and

[102] See above.

[103] Art 80 para 2 of Regulation 2017/565 (n 95).

[104] Art 52 para 3 of MiFID II (n 59) states that the 'Commission shall be empowered to adopt delegated acts in accordance with Article 89 to list situations constituting significant damage to the investors' interests and the orderly functioning of the market referred to in paragraphs 1 and 2 …' (emphasis added).

national choices. How is damage to the investors' interests different when one assesses why a delisting should not take place compared to when it takes place?

The above regulatory 'overemphasis' on the protection of financial interests of minority shareholders in a delisting is also exposed by the relevant empirical findings. First, as identified above,[105] voluntary delisting is usually associated with higher returns and not with value destruction. Conversely, mandatory delisting results in value decreases and losses for shareholders. So, if the rule seeks to protect the economic interest of investors, why is it not applicable where it is needed the most? Why should there be a difference in the first place? Why, if a company does not meet the liquidity or free float requirements of a market, can it be delisted without an exit being offered to investors, while if the company decision comes from the company investor is protected? In addition, if providing an exit market for shareholders is to protect their financial interests in the context of a voluntary delisting, why are CARs greater in the US and the UK where there is no such requirement, compared to continental European markets,[106] where such investors' protection is the cornerstone of delisting laws and regulations?

The debate on shareholders' protection in the context of delisting is not new. As early as the 1970s, it was widely believed in the United States that managerial interests in going-private transactions often led to the unfair treatment of public shareholders. This concern gave rise to extreme proposals at both the academic and policy levels regarding the regulation of such transactions, including suggestions for their outright prohibition[107] or considerable restrictions such as a ban on managers voting their shares when seeking approval from the general meeting.[108] Among the proposals examined was that the firm paid a fair price to minority shareholders. However, the policy developed eventually by the SEC in 1979 required extensive disclosure of the fairness of going-private transactions.[109]

This leads to the question: is there a less-expensive alternative to balancing the interests of the issuer and that of the minority shareholders? One idea would be to limit any exit right offered to dissenting shareholders only. However, such an approach would create incentives for minority shareholders to stand against any delisting proposal just to have access to such protection. Another alternative would be for opposing shareholders to seek judicial protection either with the purpose of cancelling the transaction on the grounds of unfair treatment or by being granted access to some form of an appraisal remedy. Again, such a proposal would put into jeopardy the finality of the transaction, which is of paramount importance for public markets.

[105] See II D above.

[106] ibid. For a very useful and detailed account of the relevant studies and their findings see Martinez and Serve (n 1) and further references therein.

[107] V Brudney and MA Chirelstein, 'A Restatement of Corporate Freezeouts' (1978) 87 *The Yale Law Journal* 1354.

[108] For a more detailed account see DeAngelo, DeAngelo and Rice (n 40) who report that, according to the *Wall Street Journal*, the SEC froze approximately 20 going-private transactions between 1974 and 1975 while exploring alternative policy choices.

[109] Securities Act Release No 33-6100 of 1979, SEC Rule 1.

The least-expensive solution is provided by corporate law and corporate governance: the decision for delisting will be approved by the general meeting of shareholders based on full disclosure made by the board of the reasons behind the decision, all potential conflicts and alternative solutions examined. Traditionally, decisions affecting the characteristics of the shares issued require the approval of shareholders in a general meeting. This is the case in most jurisdictions with mergers, issuance of shares of a different class or type, any alterations in the rights attached to any given class of shares etc.

However, such an approach is not a panacea. Depriving managers of the appropriate decision may provide a solution against managerial self-dealing, but it does not offer any protection from major shareholder self-dealing. One way would be to require an increased quorum and majority for a delisting decision. However, even supermajority requirements may not be enough in companies with concentrated ownership, while putting extreme quorum or majority rules such as 90 per cent does not offer any solution because either such quorum or majority rules are unattainable for many listed companies with dispersed ownership or require a mandatory offer as a prerequisite in order to be achieved.

Hence, the most efficient approach is that of the UK. The general meeting by virtue of an extraordinary resolution has the competence to decide on the board's proposal for delisting, which must be accompanied by a full disclosure of reasons, conflicts and other related party interests in the form of a circular to the general meeting. If there is a major shareholder who, directly or indirectly, alone or with other related parties, holds over 30 per cent of the shares of the company then the delisting needs to be approved by the majority of the remaining (independent) shareholders. International Financial Reporting Standards could be a basis for defining related parties.

The aforementioned solution does not preclude the acquisition of minority interests as a protection afforded to minority shareholders. If the proposed transaction is motivated by self-dealing, independent shareholders will not vote in favour, hence the initiating major shareholder or management will need to make a mandatory bid. However, this would allow for a financially justified delisting that has the approval of the shareholders to proceed without additional costs.

An alternative approach would be that a relaxation from any requirement to provide an exit with minority shareholders would be granted in case of downlisting, since shareholders still have access to a market, have a greater level of protection compared to private companies stemming from the applicable market rules and the market abuse directive and, in certain Member States, takeover law.

V. Conclusion

The phenomenon of delisting has become increasingly significant in recent years, often outnumbering new listings in major exchanges. While much of the literature has focused on the impact of delisting on shareholders and market operations, this chapter has explored delisting from the company's perspective, emphasising the potential benefits for the issuer despite the negative consequences for shareholders.

Delisting decisions are driven by various factors, including regulatory costs, poor performance, low liquidity, and concentrated ownership. Empirical studies suggest that voluntary delistings often result in positive returns for shareholders, whereas mandatory delistings typically lead to value decreases. This highlights the importance of understanding the motivations behind delisting and the conflicts of interest that may arise.

Conflicts can occur on three levels: market, company and principal. At the market level, issues such as market migration and the discretion of market operators and regulatory authorities play a crucial role. At the company level, delisting decisions can deprive shareholders of liquidity and investor protection. At the principal level, personal interests of managers and major shareholders can influence delisting decisions, potentially leading to self-serving actions.

To address these conflicts, various jurisdictions employ mechanisms such as regulating the decision-making process and providing exit mechanisms for shareholders. However, the regulatory landscape remains fragmented, with significant differences in processes and rules across jurisdictions. Harmonisation at the EU level, particularly regarding market migration and the discretion of market operators, could enhance market efficiency and liquidity.

Ultimately, balancing the interests of the issuer and minority shareholders is crucial. While providing an exit mechanism for shareholders can protect their financial interests, it is essential to ensure that delisting decisions are made transparently and fairly, with appropriate shareholder approval. The UK approach, which requires a majority vote from independent shareholders in cases of concentrated ownership, offers a promising solution to mitigate conflicts and ensure fair treatment.

In conclusion, delisting is a complex decision that involves weighing the benefits for the issuer against the potential negative impact on shareholders. A harmonised regulatory framework and transparent decision-making processes can help address conflicts and promote the best interests of both the company and its shareholders.

7

Delisting – The Perspective of the Trading Venue – Market Rules

KATRIN DECKERT AND ANNA-LENA VOGT*

This chapter examines the role of market operators managing trading venues, notably regulated markets, in the context of a company's delisting.

The delisting decision, in the strict sense of the term, is generally taken, *in fine*, by the market operator. Delisting can also be initiated by other players (company; market authority) as it can be voluntary or involuntary. Voluntary delisting means that the company chooses to do so on its own, i.e. at its own request. On the other hand, involuntary (also mandatory or compulsory) delisting initiated by market operators generally occurs as a sanction when the company does not meet the requirements set by the exchange on which it is listed or listing requirements by national laws. Another main cause is bankruptcy or liquidation of the listed company. As a result, involuntary delisting is often a sign of poor financial health or poor corporate governance, and more generally aberrant behaviour. On the contrary, voluntary delisting can often be motivated by economic reasons in accordance with the company's interest and strategy.[1]

During the period 2005–2019, there were almost 8,000 delistings of European companies, over 5,000 delistings of US companies and around 1,300 delistings of Japanese companies.[2] Delisting is relatively frequent in the European Union, especially in recent years, and particularly on the regulated markets operated by Euronext.[3] More precisely, 133 companies were delisted from Euronext in 2023, 58 in 2022, 100

* Dr Katrin Deckert, Associate Professor and Consultant at Association nationale des Sociétés par Actions (ANSA), and Anna-Lena Vogt, Research fellow and doctoral candidate at the Chair of Civil Law and Corporate Law of Prof. Rüdiger Veil at Ludwig-Maximilian-University Munich.

[1] E Kashefi-Pour and M Lasfer 'Why Do Companies Delist Voluntarily from the Stock Market?' (2013) 37 *Journal of Banking & Finance* 4850–60; I Martinez and S Serve, 'Reasons for Delisting and Consequences: A Literature Review and Research Agenda' (2017) 31 *Journal of Economic Surveys* 733, 739; D Magni et al, 'Defining the Relationship Between Firm's Performance and Delisting: Empirical Evidence of Going Private in Europe' (2022) 13 *Journal of Knowledge Economy* 2584, 2586; see also A Recalde and M Ataun, Chapter 4 in this volume.

[2] OECD, *Corporate Governance Factbook 2021* (1 September 2021) 21. Available at: www.oecd.org/en/publications/oecd-corporate-governance-factbook-2021_783b87df-en.html.

[3] For a general and updated overview of different stock exchanges including Euronext, see Baker McKenzie, *Cross-Border Listings Guide*, 10th edition (2024). **Available at:** https://resourcehub.bakermckenzie.com/en/resources/cross-border-listings-guide.

in 2021 and 80 in 2020.[4] As to cases of involuntary delisting, empirical data available mostly concentrates on delisting in the US.[5] Europe, on the other hand, is generally lacking specific data on involuntary delisting, as statistics provided list general reasons for delisting decisions, but do not reveal further information on criteria underlying the decision or who initiated it (market operator/supervisory authority).[6] However, it can be observed that delistings are largely voluntary.[7] The data clearly shows that (involuntarily) delisting is more reactive, occurring generally after the revelation of the firms' difficulties – exchanges eventually delist companies after malfeasance or insolvency has been made public – rather than proactive – exchanges discover and remove dishonest companies.[8] Indeed, one hypothesis is that exchanges as profit-seeking entities delist out of economic considerations when it appears that firms are unable to pay their current listing fees.[9] Nevertheless, we can observe a certain reluctance on the part of the market operator to issue delisting.[10]

Thus, the question arrives as to the extent to which market operators are willing or not to delist companies, and consequently to facilitate delisting or not. Are they even faced with a 'delisting dilemma'?[11]

The first question to be asked concerns the interests of market operators, and the existence, at least potential, of conflicts of interest with which they have to deal facing delisting decisions (I). A second question relates to the legislative, regulatory and/or judicial supervision of market operators, which could eventually prevent or resolve such conflicts (II).

I. Existence of Conflicts of Interests

Are market operators faced with conflicts of interests?[12] Today, market operators are for-profit companies that are often themselves listed on the stock exchange. When deciding whether or not to delist a company, do they take into consideration economic

[4] Euronext, *Fact Book 2023* (22 March 2024). Available at: https://live.euronext.com/en/resources/statistics/factbook.

[5] I Martinez and S Serve, 'Reasons for Delisting and Consequences: A Literature Review and Research Agenda' (n 1); see also A Charitou, C Louca and N Vafeas, 'Boards, Ownership Structure, and Involuntary Delisting from the New York Stock Exchange' (2007) 26 *Journal of Accounting and Public Policy* 249.

[6] For example, Euronext, *Factbook 2023* (n 4) 17 companies have been removed due to 'bankruptcy' or 'compulsory liquidation', other reasons are 'Squeeze out', 'Merger' and 'Non-compliant issuer'; Oxera, *Primary and secondary equity markets in the EU, Final report* (2020). Available at: www.oxera.com/insights/reports/primary-and-secondary-equity-markets-in-the-eu/: 64 out of 320 delisted companies between 2017–2019 from Borsa Italiana, Euronext, London Stock Exchange and Nasdaq Stockholm were forced to delist or financially distressed.

[7] ibid.

[8] J Macey, M O'Hara and D Pompilio, 'Down and Out in the Stock Market: The Law and Economics of the Delisting Process' (2005) *SSRN* 30. Available at: https://papers.ssrn.com/sol3/papers.cfm?abstract_id=58340; G Min and KY Jin, 'Relational Enforcement of Stock Exchange Rules' (2021) 47 *Brigham Young University Law Review* 149, 153 ff.

[9] Macey, O'Hara and Pompilio, 'Down and Out in the Stock Market' (n 8) 30; Martinez and Serve (n 1).

[10] See, for example, evidence from the US, showing that market operators continue trading for months after the issuer violated delisting rules: J Macey, M O'Hara and D Pompilio, 'Down and Out in the Stock Market: The Law and Economics of the Delisting Process' (2008) 51 *Journal of Law and Economics* 683, 711.

[11] Macey, O'Hara and Pompilio (n 8) 28.

[12] For a more in-depth analysis, see in particular P Barban, *Les entreprises de marché* (Fondation Varenne, 2015) 611.

factors and/or related political and social factors? Is investor protection also a rationale for delisting?

To address those questions, it is first necessary to determine whether market operators benefit or not from delisting (A), and then whether delisting is needed to protect investors (B).

A. Benefits and Costs of Delisting

Today's market operators are for-profit companies and often publicly traded, which need to make a profit to remain at least economically viable. Their own market capitalisation (or share price) depends, among other things, on the number of companies listed on the exchanges they operate. A decrease in listings generally correlates with a negative impact on their own profits. Are they therefore in a position to make an appropriate, conflict-free decision on whether or not to delist a company? Are they always able to correctly assess the costs and benefits of delisting? To answer this question, the following point has first to be assessed: Do market operators benefit from delisting or not?

There is no doubt that delisting is beneficial for sparsely traded securities. Indeed, it is too costly – not only for listed companies but also – for market operators to list firms whose trading is only sporadic or whose free float is very small, i.e. the market for their securities shows a worrying lack of liquidity.[13] The relationship between the market operator and the listed company must remain profitable, and market rules are designed to guarantee that.

Alternatively, it can be argued that market operators, as profit-seeking companies, earn their living from the fees associated with trading.[14] More generally, it is economically important for the trading platform not to result in losses. The more companies listed, the higher the returns for the trading venue. The richness of the exchange's catalogue of listed companies is one of the main criteria for valuation of the market operator. As a result, exchanges have little or no incentive to delist companies since their revenue streams depend on listing fees, resulting in relaxation of enforcing stock exchange rules by the operator itself.[15]

However, and this is where the relationship between listing and delisting comes into play, market operators, who in the past actively sought new listings by lowering listing standards in order to generate more revenue,[16] may today be tempted to delist such lower quality companies. In effect, this is a way for market operators to eliminate these listing 'mistakes' without having to bear the costs of their initial poor listing decision.[17] This furthermore benefits market operators, as it maintains the signaling value attached to listing. Indeed, exchanges traditionally provide not only a range of services

[13] Macey, O'Hara and Pompilio (n 10) 686.

[14] For a more general analysis, see also J Macey and M O'Hara, 'The Economics of Stock Exchange Listing Fees and Listing Requirements' (2002) 11 *Journal of Financial Intermediation* 297.

[15] Min and Jin, 'Rational Enforcement of Stock Exchange Rules' (n 8) 153 ff.

[16] M Kahan, 'Some Problems with Stock Exchange-Based Securities Regulation' (1997) 83 *Virginia Law Review* 1509, 1518; see also IOSCO, *Final Report: Evolution in the Operation, Governance and Business Models of Exchanges: Regulatory Implications and Good Practice* (2006). Available at: www.iosco.org/library/pubdocs/pdf/IOSCOPD779.pdf.

[17] Macey, O'Hara and Pompilio (n 10) 711.

to investors and issuers (standardised rules, transactions monitoring, etc.), but also a signaling function. The value of the 'signal' associated with listing on a specific trading venue may be preserved through delistings, notably by expelling errant companies.[18] In addition, the market operator itself is subject to supervision by the respective national supervisory authorities. This indirectly obligates him to comply with and enforce their rules in order to avoid sanctions or investigations from a reputational point of view.[19]

In line with the previous idea, protecting the reputation of the trading venue and of the listed companies is becoming increasingly important today. It permits an increase in the trading venue's own value, particularly in the context of intense competition between exchanges for listings.[20]

Although this increased competition may also be, at least partly, responsible for the reticence to delist companies. Indeed, competition among trading venues has grown considerably in recent years, and exchanges in the EU, and even worldwide, are faced today with a new competitive reality.[21] Whereas they were once sheltered quasi-monopolies, exchanges now have to contend with a multitude of competitors operating regulated or non-regulated markets. This is necessarily leading to changes in their business models and governance.

While some exchanges have begun to compete intensively on listing fees, and sometimes even on listing conditions, to attract new companies, delisting is not, for the moment at least, a priority. This is probably also because delisting often concerns companies with low market capitalisation. Trading venue operators thus allow companies to remain listed, with delisting only occurring after months of violating stock exchange rules and practices, in particular listing requirements.[22]

Finally, it is also worth mentioning that a too high level of difficulty for delisting, especially for voluntary delisting, could discourage companies from listing. As exchanges evolve to meet these new economic realities, a kind of competition could emerge in this field too.

B. Protection of Investors Through Delisting

Is investor protection, *one of the most important objectives of the securities regulation* across countries,[23] also a rationale for delisting which is taken into consideration by

[18] ibid 686 f.

[19] Min and Jin (n 8) 167.

[20] For a detailed study of the competition among exchanges issue, see PC Hautcoeur, A Rezaee and A Riva, 'Competition among Securities Markets: Stock Exchange Industry Regulation in the Paris Financial Center at the Turn of the Twentieth Century' (2018) *INCAS Discussion Paper Series* 2018 #08. Available at: https://halshs.archives-ouvertes.fr/halshs-01863942; E Cantillon and PL Yin, 'Competition Between Exchanges: A Research Agenda' (2011) 29 *International Journal of Industrial Organization* 329–36; SB Ramos, 'Why Do Stock Exchanges Demutualize and Go Public?' (2006) *Swiss Finance Institute Research Paper* No. 06–10. Available at: https://ssrn.com/abstract=890268.

[21] Cantillon and Yin, 'Competition Between Exchanges' (n 20); J Macey and M O'Hara, 'From Markets to Venues: Securities Regulation in an Evolving World' (2005) 58 *Stanford Law Review* 563.

[22] See, for example, analysis by Min and Jin (n 8).

[23] See, in particular, International Organization of Securities Commissions (IOSCO), 'Objectives and Principles of Securities Regulation' (May 2003). Available at: www.iosco.org/library/pubdocs/pdf/ioscopd154.pdf. This document sets out 30 principles of securities regulation, which are based upon three objectives of

market operators when taking a decision to delist or not? In other words, is delisting necessary to protect (potential) investors?

That argument relies on the idea that investors draw inferences and make trading decisions based on the fact that a company is listed on a given exchange (signalling function). Market operators must therefore ensure that only companies who meet the standards of the exchange, particularly their market rules, are traded on them, otherwise investors would be misled. However, while this is conceivable in specific situations (delisting in the event of company fraud for example), at least two problems may arise here. Firstly, it is difficult to know how important the trading venue really is for individual (retail) investors: would there be more investors in each company if it were listed on a specific exchange rather than another? And do investors rely on the integrity of listed companies, because simply being listed would mean that they have complied with the underlying standards and rules? Secondly, if investor protection is really the rationale for delisting, why do market operators allow companies that do not comply with the listing requirements to remain traded without being delisted?

The various arguments developed here would support the thesis that market operators do not always adequately and objectively weigh up the costs and benefits of delisting taking into account the protection of investors,[24] at least not beyond considering their own reputation protection and the signaling certain listings have. They are intrinsically interested parties when it comes to delisting, at least in decisions that leave discretionary power to the market operator.[25] In particular, the profit-seeking incentives of exchanges may not always be compatible with the general interests of capital markets and investor protection, in the short and long term.

II. Resolution of Conflicts of Interest

How can these conflicts of interest be resolved? By legal, regulatory and/or judicial supervision of trading venue operators (A)? And how much leeway do market operators really have regarding the delisting (or not) of companies (B)?

A. Articulation of Rules on Delisting

In many countries worldwide, delisting is subject to different levels of control. It is generally carried out in compliance with the procedures laid down by law and/or market rules. In addition, financial market authorities in many States have also been invested with regulatory powers in this field. Finally, the courts are involved in delisting decisions, sometimes only indirectly.

securities regulation: protection of investors; ensuring that markets are fair, efficient and transparent; and the reduction of systemic risk.

[24] Subjectivity with which the NYSE applies its own listing standards: Macey, O'Hara and Pompilio (n 10) 687.

[25] Excluding, naturally, cases of automatic delisting, when the company ceases to exist.

(i) Legal Framework: Grounds for Delisting

In the EU, the rights and obligations of market operators, but also listed companies and financial market authorities regarding delisting, are generally set by regulatory requirements on national level. Those rules are not widely harmonised at the European level, at least as far as details are concerned. More precisely, Articles 32 and 52 of MiFID II[26] only establish few general obligations for national competent authorities and trading venues relating to the (suspension and) removal of certain financial instruments from trading on a regulated market, multilateral trading facility (MTF) or organised trading facility.[27] Article 52(1) of MiFID II states that '[w]ithout prejudice to the right of the competent authority under Article 69(2) to demand suspension or removal of a financial instrument from trading, a market operator may suspend or remove from trading a financial instrument which no longer complies with the *rules of the regulated market* unless such suspension or removal would be likely to cause significant damage to the *investor's interests* or the *orderly functioning of the market*'.

While some national legal frameworks provide grounds or criteria for delisting initiated by market operators,[28] others solely refer to market rules as grounds for delisting.

Table 7.1 Delisting initiated by market operators in national legal frameworks

Country	Legal Framework	Grounds for Delisting by Market Operator
Germany	§ 39(1) BörsG	Orderly exchange trading is no longer guaranteed in the long term after discontinued listing (§ 25(1) BörsG). Issuer fails to fulfil obligations arising from admission (e.g. disclosure duties). Admission requirements are no longer fulfilled.
Finland	Chapter 3, Section 11 ATFI (1070/2017)	Failure to fulfil requirements of stock exchange's rules. Removal is necessary due to fair practice or rules on stock exchange. Considering investor protection and a functional market.
Sweden	Chapter 15, Section 11 SMA	Failure to fulfil admission requirements of stock exchange. The issue seriously breached obligations under SMA or other statutory Act. Delisting does not significantly damage investor or functioning of the market.

(continued)

[26] Directive 2014/65/EU on markets in financial instruments and amending Directive 2002/92/EC and Directive 2011/61/EU [2014] OJ L173/349.

[27] Where a regulated market, MTF or OTF removes a financial instrument or a related derivative from trading, *as a consequence of its rules*, the respective venue must make this decision public and notify its National Competent Authorities (NCAs). Depending on the reasons for the removal, the NCA must make this decision public, and if so, remove that instrument, or related derivatives, from trading not only on other regulated markets, MTFs, and OTFs, but also systematic internalisers under its jurisdiction. It also must communicate this to ESMA and other NCAs. Notified NCAs then also have the obligation to remove from trading the instrument or derivative on regulated markets, MTFs, OTFs, and SIs under their respective jurisdictions. However, the relevant NCAs have the discretion not to apply the removal where this could cause significant damage to investors' interests or the orderly functioning of the market.

[28] For example, in India, where grounds on mandatory delistings are statutorily provided: H Kaur, Chapter 17 in this volume.

Table 7.1 ***(Continued)***

Country	Legal Framework	Grounds for Delisting by Market Operator
Austria	§§ 17(1), 38(4) BörseG	Issuer no longer meets prerequisites for listing (change of corporate form, free-float-requirement). Issuer obtained listing under false pretenses/wilfully providing false information. Repeated breaches of obligations e.g. disclosure duties. Requirements of the regulated market (market operator's terms and conditions, major incidents with influence on stock price). Not against investor interests and a functional market.
Greece	Article 52, Law 4514/2018	Non-compliance with market rules. Not in case of significant damage to investor interest and orderly functioning of the market.
Cyprus	Article 53, Law 87(I)/2017	Non-compliance with market rules. Not in case of significant damage to investor interest and orderly functioning of the market.
Netherlands	Article 5:32g, Law of Financial Supervision	Substantial breaches of market rules. Failure to fulfil listing requirements. Not in case of significant damage to investor interest and orderly functioning of the market.
France	Article L. 420-10 I Monetary and Financial Code	Instruments or conditions of its trading no longer obey platform rules. Not against investor interests and orderly platform functioning.
Spain	Article 20, RD 21/2017	Non-compliance with market rules. Not in case of significant damage to investor interest and orderly functioning of the market.
Italy	Article 66-ter, CLF	Non-compliance with market rules. Not in case of significant damage to investor interest and orderly functioning of the market.
US	Section 12(d), SecuritiesExchange Act	Rules of the Exchange (with regard to investor protection).
India	Securities Contract (Regulation) Rules [1957], Rule 21(d)	Delisting on statutory provided grounds: Losses during the three consecutive years and negative net worth, trading suspension for more than six months, infrequently trading of securities for the past three years, company/promoters/directors have been penalised for regulatory/statutory/contractual infraction with certain fine, minimum public shareholding below specified threshold, addresses of company/promoters/directors is not known.

Only a few legal frameworks provide statutorily defined grounds for delisting issued by the market operator. India, however, provides a list of reasons in which cases a trading venue can make a delisting decision and does not recourse on market rules. The German Börsegesetz on the other hand only states that a market operator *may* justify compulsory delisting on the ground that an orderly exchange trading is no longer guaranteed in the long term and the management of the market operator has discontinued the listing (§ 25(1) sentence 1 no 2 BörsG), or because the issuer fails to fulfil obligations following the delisting.[29] Pursuant to § 39(8) BörseG Austria, a withdrawal of the admission is possible in the case that the issuer does not meet the general conditions for an admission anymore.[30] Similarly, the Swedish provision refers to the delisting (market operator *shall* delist) if the issuer does not fulfil the admissions requirements which apply for admission to trading, or where the issuer has seriously breached its obligations under the Swedish Companies Act.[31] However, it can be detected that the regulation of special cases as grounds for delisting (eg insolvency) differ in the national frameworks.[32] Most jurisdictions do not specify grounds for delisting, as they leave specification to the market operator's rules or the 'fair practice' of the market, giving market operators regulatory authority.

(ii) Market Rules

As seen, there are generally only a few legal or governmental/administrative requirements in the context of delisting initiated by market operators (except notably for public buy-out and squeeze outs, that often precede a delisting). Market rules play a particularly important role not only in most EU Member States, but in almost all jurisdictions. Trading venues operators thus use their market rules to implement, to varying degrees of scope and complexity, delisting requirements and criteria.[33]

Euronext, operating several regulated markets in the European Union,[34] provides a good illustration here. The integration of Euronext's regulated markets has indeed been accompanied by the harmonisation of its market rules. As a result, a single Euronext Rule Book governs today trading on all Euronext securities and derivatives markets; it contains both harmonised[35] and non-harmonised[36] (local) rules,[37] in particular with

[29] § 39(1) BörsG; see K Çavuşoğlu, Questionnaire Germany Q24.

[30] See U Torggler, Questionnaire Austria Q22.

[31] Chapter 15 Section 11 SMA (Swedish Companies Act); see J Östberg, Questionnaire Sweden Q24.

[32] See for insolvency as grounds for issuer's delisting in national regulations JH Binder, Chapter 9 in this volume.

[33] PG Mahoney, 'The Exchange as Regulator' (1997) 83 *Virginia Law Review* 1453; analysing differences in exchanges' listing rules Oxera, *Primary and Secondary Equity Markets in the EU* (n 6) 39 f.

[34] Securities Markets i.e. in Amsterdam, Brussels, Dublin, Lisbon, Milan, Oslo and Paris; and Derivatives Markets i.e. in Amsterdam, Brussels, Lisbon, Milan, Oslo and Paris.

[35] Euronext, Rule Book I contains the Harmonised Rules, including rules of conduct and of enforcement, designed to protect the markets, as well as rules on listing, trading and membership.

[36] Rule Book II and Notices applicable to Euronext Amsterdam, the regulated market operated by Euronext Amsterdam NV; Rule Book II and Notices applicable to Euronext Brussels, the regulated market operated by Euronext Brussels SA/NV.; Rule Book II and Notices applicable to Euronext Dublin, the regulated market operated by Euronext Dublin (The Irish Stock Exchange plc); Rule Book II and Notices applicable to Euronext Lisbon the regulated market operated by Euronext Lisbon – Sociedade Gestora de Mercados Regulamentados, S.AI; Borsa Italiana Rules and accompanying Instructions (Rule Book II) and Guide to the Parameters applicable to regulated markets operated by Borsa Italiana S.p.A.; Rule Book II and Notices applicable to Euronext Paris the regulated market operated by Euronext Paris S.A.; Rules applicable to the regulated markets operated by Oslo Børs ASA.

[37] Available at: www.euronext.com/en/regulation/euronext-regulated-markets.

regard to delisting. Article 6905/1 Euronext Rulebook I enumerates, *without limitation*, reasons for removal of securities by the market operator: failure to comply with rules pursuant the application, issuer as legal entity ceases to exist, bankruptcy, ongoing delisting would conflict with the maintenance of an orderly and efficient market and developments in connection with an issuer, also in the context of the EU Sanction List, have occurred that could harm the reputation of Euronext as a whole.

Similarly, the Nasdaq Nordic Member Rules contain conditions for delisting.[38] Besides general rules for all exchanges, Nasdaq Nordic lays down specific rules consistent with the respective national legal framework. For Nasdaq Stockholm, shares may be removed in the event of an application for bankruptcy and a significant failure to fulfil admission requirements or the failure to pay fees, which could not be restored in a period of time set by the market operator and there are no other means to remedy.[39] Nasdaq Helsinki on the other hand allows termination of trading if the requirements of the Rulebook are no longer fulfilled or it is otherwise necessary based on the listed companies' actions, which are in contradiction to the legislation, regulations of the operation of the exchange or good market practice.[40] The specific Nasdaq Helsinki Main Market Rule Book specifies that in the case of substantial changes in the issuer which imply that the issuer could be regarded as being an entirely new company, a delisting is possible.[41]

In Italy, market rules allow Borsa Italiana to revoke the listing in the case of a prolonged lack of trading or in circumstances that interfere with the maintaining of a normal and regular market.[42] Deciding on the revocation, the market operator shall consider special circumstances: average daily turnover and number/frequency of securities traded, the distribution of the instruments in public, the involvement in insolvency proceedings, a liquidation of the issuer, an adverse opinion by the statutory auditor and a prior suspension of the instruments.[43] Where delisting ensues the exercise of squeeze-out and sell-out rights, the securities *shall* be delisted and withdrawn.[44]

Market rules, specifying delisting by the market operator himself, also play a crucial role outside the EU. Within the US, for example, the NYSE Rules state that securities will be suspended or struck if they fall below certain qualitative or quantitative criteria (number of total stockholders, trading volume, public float, market capitalization, stock price),[45] securing a minimum standard as a guarantee of quality. In case of

[38] Nasdaq Nordic, including Copenhagen, Helsinki, Iceland and Stockholm. The Nasdaq Nordic Member Rules contain a general part with overall rules, as well as specific rules in Supplement A-D. Available at: www.nasdaq.com/docs/2025/01/02/Nasdaq_Nordic_Main_Market_Rulebook_1_Jan_2025.pdf.

[39] ibid Supplement D Nasdaq Stockholm, Part G, Section 29 and J Östberg, Questionnaire Sweden (n 31) Q 22.

[40] Nasdaq Nordic (n 38) Supplement B Nasdaq Helsinki, Part G, Section 25 and H Marjosola, Questionnaire Finland Q24.

[41] Section 2.16 Nasdaq Helsinki Regulated Market Rule Book. Available at: www.nasdaq.com/docs/2024/12/20/NASDAQ-HELSINKI-RULEBOOK-FOR-ISSUERS-OF-EXHCHANGE-TRADED-NOTES-Dec-18-2024.pdf.

[42] Art 66-ter CLF (Consolidated law on financial intermediation Italy) and Rules of the Markets Organised and Managed by Borsa Italiana, Art 2.5.1(1)(b). Available at: www.borsaitaliana.it/borsaitaliana/regolamenti/regolamenti/marketrules27012025.en_pdf.htm; see also G Balp, Questionnaire Italy Q24.

[43] Borsa Italiana Rule Book, Art 2.5.1(5) (n 42).

[44] ibid Art 2.5.1(6).

[45] Securities Exchange Act, Section 12(d); NYSE Rule 801.00; see also M Gelter and S Thel, Chapter 14 in this volume.

possible liquidation, bankruptcy, violation of securities law and the listing agreement, the exchange may evaluate the issuer's continued listing.[46]

Overall, delisting initiated by market operators refers to issuers misconduct, especially regarding obligations following listings on the market, their (long-term) financial performance, events with (major) influence on the stock price, compliance with market rules, contributing to the orderly functioning of the market, and substantial changes in the issuer itself that could justify the decision for removal of the financial instruments.[47] Even though grounds for delisting are specified, in most jurisdictions, by market rules, specific criteria the market operator has to take into consideration are lacking in most frameworks, with the exception of India, Borsa Italiana, Euronext and NYSE. However, most frameworks are non-exhaustive when it comes to criteria and circumstances the market operator has to consider. Both the legal frameworks following Article 52 of MiFID II and the recourse on market rules to define grounds for delisting leave discretionary power to the market operators over the delisting decision and their underlying criteria, as the failure to fulfil obligations leave room for interpretation, allowing a possible subjectivity in applying delisting standards.[48]

(iii) Pros and Cons of Self-regulation and Statutory Law

Market rules are drafted and enforced by the market operators. Generally, market rules and their amendments must be submitted to the competent national regulator; in most cases a governmental (financial markets) authority or agency and approved beforehand.[49] The latter is therefore often authorised to monitor the rules of a trading venue to ensure they comply with the legal framework. To take the example of Euronext again, the regulators in Belgium, France, Ireland, Italy, the Netherlands, Norway and Portugal approve the relevant market rules, either collectively (Book I) or in respect to their own jurisdictions (Book II).

This – often controlled – self-regulation by market operators is a typical method of regulating financial markets. The benefits of and limits to self-regulation in this field have attracted a great deal of attention over the past years.[50] The main inconvenience of self-regulation is that its basis is merely contractual, consequently it does not

[46] NYSE, Rule 802.01.

[47] See also with an overview on reasons for mandatory delisting U Torggler and D Yilmaz, Chapter 19 in this volume, VII. A.

[48] Naturally not in cases of automatic delisting, for example, if the issuer as the legal entity ceases to exist or in cases of liquidation.

[49] Also, for example, in the US, Section 19(b) Securities Exchange Act authorising the SEC to approve or disapprove exchange rules, and Section 19(c) to add new rules.

[50] For example, CFA Institute Centre for Financial Market Integrity, *Self-Regulation in the Securities Markets: Transitions and New Possibilities (2013).* Available at: www.cfainstitute.org/sites/default/files/-/media/documents/article/position-paper/self-regulation-in-securities-markets-transitions-new-possibilities.pdf; ICSA International Council of Securities Associations, *Self-Regulation in Financial Markets: An Exploratory Survey* (2006). Available at: https://icsa.global/sites/default/files/Self-RegulationFinancialMarkets.pdf. See also ST Omarova, 'Wall Street as Community of Fate: Toward Financial Industry Self-Regulation' (2011) 159 *U Pa Rev* 411. For a more general analysis, see P Rawlings, A Georgosouli and C Russo, 'Regulation of Financial Services: Aims and Methods' (2014) Queen Mary University of London, Centre for Commercial Law Studies. Available at: www.qmul.ac.uk/ccls/media/ccls/docs/research/020-Report.pdf; V Winship, 'Enforcement Networks' (2020) 37 *Yale Journal on Regulation* 274, 278; NS Ellis, LM Fairchild and HD Fletcher, 'The NYSE

have the impact of a statutory law applied and enforced by a public authority.[51] But self-regulation is flexible, close to market practices and fits in with the ever-evolving complexities of the securities markets.

Anyway, the debate between statutory and 'light' non-statutory rules, and how best to implement them, needs to be considered in the context of delisting. Firstly, increasing competition between trading venues has created – or could create – new incentives for all players to be more competitive and provide exchange rules likely to attract new companies.

Secondly, delisting may not be as important as admission to trading, but it is nevertheless an important part of the listing requirements puzzle. And delisting is an issue which can greatly benefit from the advantages of self-regulation without suffering its drawbacks.

Thirdly, statutory law should set general rules or standards for delisting (qualitative/quantitative criteria, grounds for delisting), excluding, for example, automatic delisting, whereas the rules of market operators specify the terms and conditions of those rules, for example due to a delegation of power.[52] Moreover, market rules often stipulate that the delisting request submitted at the issuer's initiative must comply with national laws and regulations,[53] suggesting that there are 'higher-level' rules for setting delisting conditions. Market rules may therefore provide for arrangements of a contractual nature, but they remain infra-legislative rules nonetheless.[54]

Consequently, market rules – and therefore the market operator's final decision – on delisting must never harm the interests of investors and compromise the orderly functioning of the trading platform or financial markets in general. These are indeed the main objectives of financial markets regulation, in all jurisdictions, which must always be taken into account by the market operator.

In this sense conflicts of interest may not be completely avoided or resolved, but they can at least be limited. In addition, purely discretionary use on the part of the market operator is also excluded.

B. Market Operator's Discretionary Power

The various requirements covering delisting are often complex. Added to this complexity of delisting rules is the not insignificant discretion that market operators have in applying them: 'a market operator *may* suspend or remove from trading a financial

Response to Specialist Misconduct: An Example of the Failure of Self-Regulation' (2010) 7 *Berkeley Business Law Journal* 102, 128.

[51] This ambivalence is at the origin of the difficulties in qualifying market rules: are they contractual rules, and therefore private, or regulatory, and therefore public in nature? The market company is in fact a commercial company, and the relations between the market company and the members of the market are contractual; at the same time, these rules are generally issued under a legislative authorisation and approved by a state authority.

[52] R Vabres, 'Entreprise de marché – Radiation demandée par un émetteur et protection des investisseurs' (2017) *Droit des sociétés no 3* comm 48.

[53] For example, Euronext, Rule Book I (Harmonised Rules) Rules 6905/1 ff.

[54] ibid.

instrument'.[55] But does that discretion really give market operators considerable latitude in determining when and how to apply their delisting rules, supporting the thesis that market operators do not always adequately and objectively weigh up the costs and benefits of delisting taking into account the protection of investors?

(i) Actual Discretionary Power?

Pursuant to most national legal frameworks and market rules, the market operator *may* decide to delist a financial instrument, giving them discretionary power to delist or not to delist. Out of the countries under survey, only Sweden and Austria statutorily limited discretionary powers of the market operator in certain cases. In Austria, the financial instrument *has to* be suspended from trading if it does not meet the requirements of the regulated market.[56] Similarly, the Swedish Securities and Exchange Act states that securities *shall* be suspended (under certain conditions).[57]

Even if the delisting decision is left to the discretion of the market operator, in reality however, they have little real room for discretion when it comes to delisting of companies, since their decision is generally based on – more or less – objective criteria,[58] creating the possibility of reviewing the delisting decision. In addition, public policy considerations (notably investor and financial markets protection) must be taken into account by the market operator, as the decision to delist a financial instrument should not cause 'significant damage to the investors' interests or the orderly functioning of the market' (MiFID II, Article 52(1)). Therefore, discretionary powers are at least limited, statutorily or by general capital markets principles, or could in some cases even be reduced to zero if there are important reasons in favour of investor protection or the orderly functioning of the market that do not justify any other decision.[59]

(ii) Supervision and Review of Delisting Decisions

As a consequence of linking delisting decisions by the market operator to the fundamental principles of capital markets law, the considerations before removing a financial instrument may be reviewed by the regulator and/or the judges.[60] This follows the idea that powerful public authorities ensure effective use of the market

[55] MiFID II, Art 52(1).

[56] § 17(1) BörseG (Austria), requirements meaning prerequisites for listing, obtaining the listing under false pretenses through willingly providing false information, repeatedly breaching obligations.

[57] Chapter 15, Section 11 SMA, circumstances including non-fulfilment of admission requirements, seriously breach of obligations under SMA or another statutory act.

[58] See for national legal framework and market rules criteria above II.A.i.; see, for example, especially NYSE and Borsa Italiana, laying down (quantitative/qualitative) criteria for a delisting decision, and Euronext Rulebook, providing grounds for delisting.

[59] For Germany, for example, A Heidelbach, '§ 39 BörsG' in E Schwark and D Zimmer (eds), *Kapitalmarktrechts-Kommentar*, 5th edn (München, CH Beck, 2020) no 8: narrow interpretation of § 39 BörsG.

[60] The possibility for (administrative/general) courts to review IV the delisting decision differ within the jurisdictions. Generally, the Questionnaires show no specific data on actual cases.

operator's self-regulatory powers.[61] In the MiFID II regime, the power of market operators to remove financial instrument is 'without prejudice to the right of the competent authority under Article 69(2)',[62] creating a parallel system for delisting decisions, limiting the above described conflict of interests market operators are facing. Furthermore, supervision is often guaranteed by intervention powers of national supervisory authorities, which could contain the right to approve a delisting decision, or to require or initiate it.[63] A system of 'enforced self-regulation' is provided, which allows flexibility in market rules on the one hand, but on the other hand ensures enforcement of such rules.

III. Conclusion

What is the right way to handle delisting, and more specifically who should make the delisting decision? While delisting has traditionally been the responsibility of the market operator, it seems that this issue is being reconsidered today, especially following MiFID II and the system of 'enforced self-regulation'. The fact that stock exchange companies are also for-profit companies suggests that market rules are not always being enforced consistently and strictly, with exchanges making use of their discretionary powers in favour of their own financial interests. As seen, these discretionary powers can be limited by strict qualitative/quantitative criteria and statutorily provided grounds for delisting. Although most Member States recourse to market rules, the main principles of capital market law (investor protection and functioning of the market), pursuant to Article 52 of MiFID II, limit the discretionary powers to the extent that the decision is possibly subject to supervision by judges and supervisory authorities. The procedure leading to delisting and the reviewable (qualitative/quantitative) criteria that have to be considered are not always sufficiently developed in depth either by the legislator and/or financial markets authority or by the market operator, which is also regrettable. Indeed, market operators must give reasons for their decision to delist or not to delist. This requirement is an expression of overall principles in the case of a decision whose consequences have an impact on the legal position of a listed company. Nevertheless, it would be desirable that market operators always specify and clarify in a transparent manner the criteria they use in the context of delisting, as silence leads to uncertainty.

In any case, there is no single approach that policymakers and regulators can adopt to (re)design the framework for delisting.

[61] A Héritier and S Eckert, 'New Modes of Governance in the Shadow of Hierarchy: Self-regulation by Industry in Europe' (2008) 28 *Journal of Public Policy* 113.

[62] MiFID II, Art 52(1).

[63] For an overview on the Role of Public Authorities and differences in national jurisdictions, see H Marjosola, Chapter 8 in this volume.

8

Mandatory Delisting of Stock Corporations in the Shadow of Hierarchy: The Role of Public Authorities

HEIKKI MARJOSOLA*

I. Introduction

This chapter examines the role of public authorities in Europe in imposing mandatory delisting of shares in publicly listed companies and in overseeing and reviewing mandatory delisting decisions taken by operators of trading venues. Mandatory delisting is a matter of quality assurance, ie ensuring that listed firms fulfil certain minimum requirements for listings and adhere to the binding rules of the marketplace. Accordingly, a mandatory delisting generally occurs due to a breach of specified listing criteria or as an end result of financial difficulties, restructuring, or liquidation.[1]

The purpose of the chapter is twofold: first, it will present the current structure of regulatory powers in EU Member States, which is primarily based on the Markets in Financial Instruments Directive (2014/65/EU, MiFID II).[2] MiFID II ensures that the use of regulatory powers by the operators of marketplaces, such as in the case of involuntary delisting decisions, is subject to adequate public oversight. To that end, MiFID II requires that National Competent Authorities (NCAs), which should be public authorities, are given powers to impose delisting on delinquent companies that are both parallel and superior to those of trading venue operators. This structure of powers, which was already adopted in MiFID II's precursor Directive 2004/39/EC (MiFID I),[3] is in line with the prevailing view according to which for-profit marketplaces

* Associate Professor of Financial Law at the University of Helsinki, Finland.

[1] The empirical evidence on mandatory delisting is predominantly from the United States and the UK. See I Martinez and S Serve, 'Reasons for Delisting and Consequences: A Literature Review and Research Agenda' (2017) 31 *Journal of Economic Surveys* 733, 754 f, 764.

[2] Directive 2014/65/EU on markets in financial instruments and amending Directive 2002/92/EC and Directive 2011/61/EU (recast) (MiFID II) [2014] OJ L173/349.

[3] Directive 2004/39/EC on markets in financial instruments amending Council Directives 85/611/EEC and 93/6/EEC and Directive 2000/12/EC of the European Parliament and of the Council and repealing Council Directive 93/22/EEC [2004] OJ L145/1.

operating in a competitive environment face conflicts of interests that prevent them from ensuring the protection of investors and orderly functioning of markets. The idea is that the 'shadow of hierarchy' of powerful public authorities ensures that operators of trading venues, mindful of the intervention powers of NCAs, perform their regulatory role more effectively.[4]

Reviewing the submitted Member State questionnaires, this chapter shows that the implementation of the MiFID II-based structure of powers has resulted in national approaches of surprising diversity. In some Member States, market operators can still act as NCAs, while public authorities in most Member States perform only a formal oversight function. Moreover, even where public authorities are given intervention powers that match the letter of MiFID II, there is scant evidence of these powers being put to practice. In other words, despite 'the MiFID revolution' securities exchanges continue to exercise significant regulatory functions largely unchecked by public authorities. This finding challenges the view according to which self-regulation plays only a minor role in post-MiFID European securities markets.[5]

The chapter also finds fundamental divergences in Member States' legal systems with regard to remedies given to companies and/or their shareholders against delisting decisions. Two types of models are distinguished. In what is termed the 'private law model', followed in Sweden and the Netherlands, disputes over delisting decisions are adjudicated as if they were contractual in nature. Accordingly, the affected shareholders and/or the companies must challenge delisting decisions in general courts. In the 'public law model', which is the model followed in most of the reviewed Member State jurisdictions as well as the United Kingdom, the delisting decisions are challenged before supervisory authorities or administrative courts even where the challenged decision is adopted by an operator of a trading venue. In contrast to the contractual private law model, the public law model views operators of trading venues as regulatory entities performing a public function.

In addition to such a positive analysis of EU and Member State laws, this chapter also revisits the traditional debate about the role of self-regulation in securities markets, particularly with respect to delisting of stock corporations. Sections II and III will accordingly describe the historical market conditions and shifts in policies which since the 1990s led to the gradual decline of stock exchanges as autonomous self-regulatory organisations (SROs). Against this background, section IV turns to EU law, particularly the structure of regulatory powers as imposed by the MiFID-regime. The analysis of EU Member State jurisdictions, along with the United Kingdom, will be the topic of section V, which will also assess the case for more public oversight of delisting in the EU. Section VI concludes.

[4] The term 'shadow of hierarchy' is adopted from political science literature, where it has been used, inter alia, to characterise the need for public intervention powers as a precondition for the development of effective self-regulation. See eg A Héritier and S Eckert, 'New Modes of Governance in the Shadow of Hierarchy: Self-Regulation by Industry in Europe' (2008) 28 *Journal of Public Policy* 113.

[5] See eg IOSCO, *Regulatory Issues Arising from Exchange Evolution, Final Report* (2006). Available at: www.iosco.org/library/pubdocs/pdf/IOSCOPD225.pdf; J Carson, 'Self-Regulation in Securities Markets, World Bank Policy Research Working Paper 5542' (2011) 11 f, 25–28. Available at: www.documents1.worldbank.org/curated/en/337711468340157842/pdf/WPS5542.pdf.

II. The Decline of Self-Regulation in Securities Markets

Securities exchanges have provided classic examples of self-regulatory organisations (SROs), given their historical role as private institutions that establish, monitor compliance with, and enforce rules of conduct applicable to securities markets.[6] Extensive self-regulation by marketplaces was generally supported by superior information and experience as well as better incentives of marketplaces compared to governmental regulators.[7]

The general trend since the 1990s has nevertheless been towards a diminished role of exchange SROs and a corresponding increase in the regulatory role of public authorities.[8] This gradual shift from private to public has been due to two intertwined market transformations: the first is increased competition and market fragmentation. Technological advances and attendant shifts in transaction costs caused the interests of certain exchange members to deviate from the interests of the exchanges – often organised as non-profit cooperatives – as a collective. The exchanges' broker-dealer members, in particular, which were now able to set up their own trading venues, became direct competitors of exchanges for listings and trading volume.[9] In Europe, regulation played a critical role in the transformation. The adoption of MiFID I, implemented in 2007, accelerated competition among exchanges and alternative trading venues. Most importantly, MiFID I abolished national rules concentrating trading in listed national companies on national exchanges. As a result, incumbent marketplaces gradually lost market share to Multilateral Trading Facilities (MTFs) and other new platforms.[10]

The increased competition gradually gave rise to the second transformation, the restructuring of exchanges as for-profit corporations. Starting in the late 1990s, most major stock exchanges adapted to the competitive environment by demutualising and publicly listing their shares.[11] European exchanges were among the earliest adopters of the for-profit corporate model.[12]

The combination of self-regulation with profit-seeking in a competitive environment was considered problematic. Macey and O'Hara argued that many regulatory functions performed by exchanges were 'diametrically at odds with their corporate

[6] Carson, 'Self-Regulation in Securities Markets' (n 5) 5–8, noting that 'the most common form of formal SRO in the securities markets arena still is a securities exchange'.

[7] PG Mahoney, 'The Exchange as Regulator' (1997) 83 *Virginia Law Review* 1453, 1455.

[8] See eg IOSCO, *Regulatory Issues* (n 5).

[9] JR Macey and M O'Hara, 'From Markets to Venues: Securities Regulation in an Evolving World' (2005) 58 *Stanford Law Review* 563, 571; RS Karmel, 'Turning Seats into Shares: Causes and Implications of Demutualization of Stock and Futures Exchanges' (2002) 53 *Hastings Law Journal* 367, 400–02; IOSCO, *Issues Paper on Exchange Demutualization, Report of the Technical Committee of the International Organization of Securities Commissions* (2001). Available at: www.iosco.org/library/pubdocs/pdf/IOSCOPD119.pdf.

[10] G Ferrarini and P Saguato, 'Regulating Financial Market Infrastructures' in in N Moloney, E Ferran and J Payne (eds), *The Oxford Handbook on Financial Regulation* (Oxford, Oxford University Press, 2015) 577 f.

[11] IOSCO, *Issues Paper on Exchange Demutualization* (2001) 3. Available at: www.iosco.org/library/pubdocs/pdf/IOSCOPD119.pdf (reporting that 'the trend towards stock exchange demutualization is being driven largely by heightened competition and changes in technology').

[12] Carson (n 5) 25.

mandates to maximise profits'.[13] IOSCO also reported that new business models and the competitive environment raised inevitable questions 'as to whether the role that exchanges play as setters and enforcers of rules may need to be modified'.[14] The theory was that the pursuit of profits in a competitive market for listings and trading volume lowered the trading venues' enforcement incentives as well as their regulatory standards, particularly with respect to listing and delisting.[15]

The transformations accelerated changes in policies and regulations, resulting in a clear shift towards intensified public oversight of exchanges. However, the regulatory responses to the market evolution varied considerably, and exchanges and self-regulatory organisations retained an important regulatory role in several jurisdictions.[16] In Europe, the transfer of regulatory functions to public authorities was considered to be most visible. The adoption of the Market Abuse Directive (2003/6/EC), the Prospectus Directive (2003/71/EC), and MiFID I collectively meant that most self-regulatory responsibilities of exchanges were transferred to government regulators.[17]

III. The Case for Public Oversight of the Delisting Process

The exchanges' incentives surrounding their decision as to whether and when to delist a company – ie to remove or deregister a listed company from trading on a stock exchange – became particularly complex due to the competitive, for-profit environment. The case for more public oversight of the delisting process was strongest in mandatory delisting decisions. Literature shows that for-profit stock exchanges operating in a competitive environment will not necessarily base the delisting decision solely on the defined delisting criteria but consider other factors as well.[18] Evidence from the United States in particular showed that firms often continued to trade for months after violating listing rules.[19] The explanation was that for-profit exchanges, which make money from trading volume, do not have the necessary incentives to delist firms, especially when firms are large and the stock liquid.[20] This forbearance was to a degree limited by reputational

[13] Macey and O'Hara, 'From Markets to Venues' (n 9) 566.

[14] IOSCO (n 5) 6 f.

[15] ibid 10; M Kahan, 'Some Problems with Stock Exchange-Based Securities Regulation' (1997) 83 *Virginia Law Review* 1509, 1518; Macey and O'Hara (n 9); for a more critical view on increasing public oversight, see AC Pritchard, 'Self-Regulation and Securities Markets' (2003) 26 *Regulation* 32.

[16] For an overview of regulatory responses, see IOSCO (n 5) 11–22.

[17] Carson (n 5) 25–28; see also Ferrarini and Saguato, 'Regulating Financial Market Infrastructures' (n 10) 577 (noting that 'the role of exchanges in the regulation and supervision of listed issuers has been reduced and replaced by public regulation and supervision, which has correspondingly widened its scope of application').

[18] For a review of empirical literature, see Martinez and Serve, 'Reasons for Delisting and Consequences' (n 1) 754 f.

[19] JR Macey, M O'Hara and D Pompilio, 'Down and Out in the Stock Market: The Law and Economics of the Delisting Process' (2008) 51 *The Journal of Law & Economics* 683, 711; Martinez and Serve (n 1) 754 (noting a 'gap between the strictly defined listing criteria and the flexible enforcement of delisting').

[20] Macey, O'Hara and Pompilio ibid, 710f (noting the failure to delist the notorious corporate miscreants such as Enron and WorldComm before their problems became public).

effects attached to trading errant companies.[21] Small and infrequently traded issuers, which are more expensive to trade, faced a higher risk of mandatory delisting.[22] But even for such issuers the delisting regime may not work optimally. Insofar as such firms entered the market due to lower listing standards and relaxed quality control, the investors end up bearing the costs of eventual delisting.[23]

Rule enforcement of stock exchanges is therefore subject to complex 'push and pull factors'.[24] It has even been suggested that balancing the (social) costs and benefits of delisting would require no less than 'an omniscient social planner'.[25] Because of such inherent conflict of interest problems, Macey, O'Hara and Pompilio argued that solving 'the delisting dilemma' cannot be left to markets.[26] An optimal delisting policy, providing protection for both current and future investors, therefore requires public oversight.[27]

The need for public oversight in the case of voluntary delisting has received much less attention in literature. In many cases, delisting can be in the interests of the company following a cost–benefit analysis. Studies have found that firms generally choose to delist only if the net expected benefits of listing are negative. Common reasons for exiting the markets have included, eg, insufficient growth opportunities, lower profitability or liquidity, poor operating performance, or high regulatory costs.[28] Going private can benefit the company by realigning the incentives of managers and shareholders, thus improving the firm's governance structure.[29] However, manager-shareholders may seek to delist to protect their control rents, thus externalising further costs to non-controlling shareholders.[30] In Europe, voluntary delisting is particularly circumspect because of a stronger concentration of ownership. While the presence of large shareholders implies fewer conflicts of interest between shareholders and managers, it increases agency costs between large and minority shareholders. Large shareholders may seek delisting, just as controlling managers, to extract private benefits of control.[31] Studies on European

[21] ibid 710.

[22] ibid.

[23] ibid 711.

[24] G Min and K-Y Jin, 'Relational Enforcement of Stock Exchange Rules' (2021) 47 *Brigham Young University Law Review* 149, 153.

[25] Macey, O'Hara and Pompilio (n 19) 710.

[26] ibid.

[27] ibid 712.

[28] For evidence from the German market, see W Bessler et al, 'Why Do Firms Down-List or Exit from Securities Markets? Evidence from the German Stock Exchange' (2023) 17 *Review of Managerial Science* 1175; see also Martinez and Serve (n 1) 740–43 (also citing empirical literature) and Oxera Consulting LLP, *Primary and secondary equity markets in the EU, Final report* (2020). Available at: www.oxera.com/wp-content/uploads/2020/11/Oxera-study-Primary-and-Secondary-Markets-in-the-EU-Final-Report-EN-1.pdf, 77f.

[29] The seminar paper presenting this argument is MC Jensen, 'Agency Costs of Free Cash Flow, Corporate Finance, and Takeovers' (1986) 76 *The American Economic Review* 323; for a review of empirical literature testing this hypothesis, see Martinez and Serve (n 1) 745–49; see also S Kaplan, 'The Effects of Management Buyouts on Operating Performance and Value' (1989) 24 *Journal of Financial Economics* 217.

[30] Martinez and Serve (n 1) 749.

[31] ibid 750; see E Croci and A Del Giudice, 'Delistings, Controlling Shareholders and Firm Performance in Europe' (2014) 20 *European Financial Management* 374 (finding no such evidence).

markets have shown that high pre-listing ownership concentration increases the probability of going-private transactions.[32]

It is therefore evident that more than self-regulation is required to ensure the protection of minority shareholders also in voluntary delisting scenarios. Even those who generally view exchange self-regulation favourably note that exchanges should not be relied on in matters such as the enforcement of fiduciary duties.[33]

The focus of this chapter will be on mandatory delisting, particularly due to breach of listing standards or statutory rules.[34] As mentioned above, European jurisdictions have led the transition internationally towards consolidation of regulatory and supervision functions in government authorities.[35] The following section takes a closer look at the structure of powers imposed by the current MiFID regime.

IV. The Structure of Regulatory Powers in the EU

MiFID II harmonises the structure of powers with regard to delisting financial instruments from trading. First, the directive seeks to ensure that all trading venue operators have the power to suspend or remove from trading an instrument which no longer complies with the market rules unless the suspension or removal would likely cause significant damage to the investors' interests or the orderly functioning of the market. The rule is identical for operators of regulated markets[36] and for market operators and investment firms operating multilateral trading facilities (MTF) and organised trading facilities (OTF).[37] Where necessary, to support the objectives of the delisting, all operators of trading venues[38] are obliged to delist certain derivatives[39] that relate or are referenced to the delisted financial instrument.

The role of public authorities under MiFID II is twofold. First, where a market operator or investment firm uses its power to delist a financial instrument, the competent authority, in whose jurisdiction the delisting occurred, must require that the instrument and derivatives (where relevant) are also delisted from other regulated markets and trading venues which fall under its jurisdiction. This obligation exists only where the instrument is delisted due to suspected market abuse, a takeover bid or non-disclosure of inside information under MAR and where the delisting would not cause significant damage to the investors' interests or the orderly functioning of the market.[40]

[32] AK Achleitner et al, 'Private Equity Acquisitions of Continental European Firms: the Impact of Ownership and Control on the Likelihood of Being Taken Private' (2013) 19 *European Financial Management* 72.

[33] Pritchard, 'Self-Regulation' (n 15) 34.

[34] See Part II of this book on governance of the voluntary delisting process.

[35] Ferrarini and Saguato (n 10) 577.

[36] MiFID II, Art 52(1).

[37] ibid Art 32.

[38] In this chapter, the term 'operator of trading venues' is used in accordance with Art 2 of the Commission Implementing Regulation to include both (a) a market operator operating a regulated market, an MTF or an OTF and (b) an investment firm operating an MTF or an OTF. See Commission Implementing Regulation (EU) 2017/1005 laying down implementing technical standards with regard to the format and timing of the communications and the publication of the suspension and removal of financial instruments pursuant to Directive 2014/65/EU of the European Parliament and of the Council on markets in financial instruments [2017] OJ L153/1.

[39] As referred to in MiFID II, Annex I, s C, paras (4)–(10).

[40] MiFID II, Art 52(2) sub-para 2 and Art 32(2) sub-para 2.

A similar obligation applies to competent authorities with regard to cross-listed financial instruments or derivatives.[41] Articles 32 and 52 of MiFID II, as well as Commission Implementing Regulation 2017/1005, ensure that all delisting decisions, whether by operators of trading venues or by NCAs, are published and communicated in a timely and efficient manner.

Second, MiFID II vests NCAs with powers that are both parallel and superior to operators of trading venues. The powers of market operators are without prejudice to the right of the competent authority to demand delisting. Accordingly, the supervisory powers of competent authorities must include *at least* the power to require the removal of a financial instrument from trading, whether on a regulated market or under other trading arrangements.[42] The competent authorities designated by the Member States must be public authorities.[43]

The MiFID regime therefore shifts regulatory responsibilities regarding delisting only partially from trading venues to public authorities. Operators of trading venues continue to perform an important regulatory role as first-line monitors of their NCA-authorised rulebooks. MiFID II therefore ensures regulatory effectiveness primarily by requiring that operators of trading venues establish and maintain effective arrangements and procedures for the regular compliance monitoring.[44] Their decisions, just as the decisions of NCAs, must also be subject to the right of appeal before a tribunal.[45] The role of NCAs is primarily to stay informed[46] and to make use of their intervention powers when needed.

Against this structure and division of powers, the view that self-regulation plays only a minor role in post-MiFID European securities markets appears exaggerated.[47] The approach is better described as 'enforced self-regulation', a regulatory model in which firms within an industry are charged with developing and implementing regulatory standards (as approved by authorities) while the government retains oversight and powers to enforce compliance.[48] In fact, the regulatory system is broadly similar to the one operating in the United States, where the Securities Exchange Commission (SEC) monitors and regulates stock exchanges which, in turn, regulate their members and listed companies.[49] However, the above-described provisions of MiFID II, which establish the regulatory structure in broad and flexible terms, tell little about how the powers have been implemented, organised and used in Member States. This will be the topic of the following section.

[41] ibid Art 52(2) sub-para 5 and Art 32(2) sub-para 4.

[42] ibid Art 69(2) sub-s n.

[43] ibid, Art 67(1). Delegation of powers to private entities is prohibited. The only exception is provided by Art 29(4), which concerns registering and monitoring of so-called tied agents of investment firms.

[44] ibid, Art 31(1) (MTFs and OTFs) and Art 54(1) (regulated markets).

[45] ibid, Art 74.

[46] MiFID II also mandates that the operators of trading venues inform relevant NCAs immediately of significant infringements of their rules or of any disorderly conduct that may indicate that the provision of MAR have been breached. See MiFID II, Art 31(2) (MTFs and OTFs) and Art 54(2) (regulated markets).

[47] Carson (n 5) 25–28.

[48] I Ayres and J Braithwaite, *Responsive Regulation: Transcending the Deregulation Debate* (Oxford, Oxford University Press, 1992).

[49] For a brief overview of SEC powers, see Min and Jin, 'Relational Enforcement' (n 24) 161–63; the SEC also has a last resort power under the US Securities Exchange Act of 1933, s 15 USC 78l 12(j), to revoke the registration of a security.

V. Governing the Delisting Procedure in EU Member States and the UK

A. NCAs and their Powers

The above-described regulatory structure of MiFID II accommodates a variety of Member State systems that are surprisingly diverse, particularly with respect to the role of public authorities. The majority of jurisdictions have opted for the MiFID-prescribed model of 'enforced self-regulation' where public agencies oversee and/or may initiate compulsory delisting of financial instruments. This is the case for Austria, Cyprus, Finland, France, Greece, Italy, Spain and Sweden in all of which a designated public authority enjoys some form of intervention powers parallel and superior to those of operators of trading venues. Even within this family, however, the chosen approaches differ significantly. In countries such as Cyprus and Greece, the designated competent authorities act as effective gatekeepers, not just overseeing but approving delisting decisions by market operators.[50] In Finland, Italy, Spain and Sweden such an approval procedure does not exist, but public authorities have, at least in formal terms, powers to require delisting of a financial instrument. In France, in contrast, the market operator (Euronext) itself acts as the NCA with wide autonomy to decide on delisting, but delisting can also be imposed by a decision of the Chair of the Autorité des marchés financiers (AMF). In Austria, the Finanzmarktaufsicht (FMA) is designated as the NCA with the power to require the market operator to remove financial instruments from trading. However, the FMA has no competence to challenge the delisting decision by the market operator, which acts as a 'public entity' under the supervision of the FMA.

Germany and the Netherlands are both closer to a pure self-regulation mode with a more limited oversight role by public agencies. In Germany, the market operator (Börse) acts as the NCA subject to general oversight by the competent supreme state authority (oberste Landesbehörde), which is also known as the exchange supervisory authority (Börsenaufsichtsbehörde). The powers of the latter authorities do not, however, include any powers to demand delisting of financial instruments. In the Netherlands, the Dutch Authority for the Financial Markets (AFM) acts as the NCA but it does not have independent powers to order delisting; where there exists a suspicion of market abuse or a take-over bid or if the AFM considers that delisting would be in the interest of investors, the AFM must *request* the Court of Rotterdam to exclude a security from trading.[51]

In the UK, delisting a financial instrument is not generally possible without consent of the Financial Conduct Authority (FCA). In the case of voluntary delisting, for instance, the issuer technically requests the delisting, and the competent authority subsequently cancels the listing.[52]

[50] In Cyprus, the Cyprus Stock Exchange is a non-profit public sector entity.

[51] Law of Financial Supervision (*Wet op het financieel toezicht*), Art 5:77e.

[52] This is not, however, the case for the Alternative Investment Market, where the London Stock Exchange plc approves the delisting.

The NCAs and their powers are summarised in Table 8.1.

Table 8.1 The powers of NCAs regarding delisting

Country	National Competent Authorities (NCA)	NCA powers in delisting
Austria	The *Finanzmarktaufsicht* (FMA) acts as the designated NCA but the market operator (*Wiener Börse AG*) acts as 'a public entity' under the supervision of the FMA.	The NCA has the power to require the market operator to remove financial instruments from trading eg if the market operator fails to act on its own. The FMA has no competence to challenge the delisting decision by the market operator in the case of voluntary delisting.
Cyprus	The Cyprus Securities and Exchange Commission The Central Bank of Cyprus	Delisting decision is taken ex officio by the Stock Exchange Council or upon the issuer's application but it is subject to approval by the Cyprus Securities and Exchange Commission. Both NCAs have the power to require removal of financial instruments from trading.
Finland	The Finnish Financial Supervisory Authority (FIN-FSA)	The decision on delisting of shares is made by the Nasdaq Helsinki Listing Committee. The NCA may order a stock exchange to remove a financial instrument from trading. The NCA must, prior to making the decision, hear the stock exchange unless the urgency of the matter or another special reason otherwise requires. In voluntary delisting, the NCA does not review or approve the market operator's decision. The market operator may nevertheless request the NCA to verify the operator's decision to delist / not to delist.
France	The Market operator (Euronext) acts as the NCA.	The market operator as the NCA may remove a financial instrument from trading. Delisting can also be required by the Chair of the *Autorité des marchés financiers* (AMF).
Germany	The market operator (Börse) acts as the NCA.	Mandatory delisting can be imposed only by the Börse. The market operator is supervised by the competent supreme state authority (*oberste Landesbehörde*), also known as the exchange supervisory authority (*Börsenaufsichtsbehörde*), but the authority does not have powers regarding delisting.

(continued)

Table 8.1 ***(Continued)***

Country	National Competent Authorities (NCA)	NCA powers in delisting
Greece	The Hellenic Capital Market Commission (HCMC)	The NCA may decide to delist a security at the request of the exchange or on its own initiative. The competent authority must approve delisting decisions by market operators.
Italy	The *Commissione Nazionale per le Società e la Borsa* (CONSOB)	Mandatory delisting may be imposed by either *Borsa Italiana* (the market operator) or by Consob. Consob may also prohibit the enforcement of a delisting decision by the market operator within five open market days from receipt of the communication from the market operator if it considers the decision contrary to the purpose of ensuring transparency, orderly trading and investor protection.
The Netherlands	The Dutch Authority for the Financial Markets (AFM)	Mandatory delisting decisions are the responsibility of the market operators. The AFM can nevertheless request the Court of Rotterdam to exclude a security from being traded after the AFM has signalled Euronext Amsterdam of a suspicion of market abuse or a take-over bid or if it is generally in the interest of investors.
Spain	The Spanish Securities Market Commission (*Comisión Nacional del Mercado de Valores,* CNMV)	The operator of a regulated market may decide to delist a financial instrument independently of the NCA. The CNMV may impose mandatory delisting. The CNMV also has wide powers to establish whether the conditions or requirements for delisting are met, and this includes the possibility to require additional terms in voluntary delisting.
Sweden	The Swedish Financial Supervisory Authority The market operator (Nasdaq Stockholm)	Mandatory delisting is primarily the responsibility of a market operator who also acts as the NCA. In addition, the Swedish Financial Supervisory Authority can order the exchange to delist an instrument.
The UK	Financial Conduct Authority (FCA)	The FCA has wide discretion to cancel listings. The London Stock Exchange may also remove a financial instrument from trading, but delisting is not generally possible without consent of the FCA. In the case of the AIM, the London Stock Exchange plc approves voluntary delisting decisions.

It is surprising that several Member States appear to have designated market operators – private for-profit corporations – as NCAs. This contradicts Article 67(1) of MiFID II, which requires that NCAs are public authorities and bans the delegation of discretionary powers to private entities. A likely reason for this is the Listing Directive 2001/34/EC,[53] which concerns admission to and suspension and discontinuance of 'official listing' by NCAs. Unlike in MiFID II, the Listing Directive does not require that NCAs are public authorities. Its functions can therefore be carried out by trading venues themselves.[54] The concept of 'official listing', which is not defined in the Listing Directive, is ambiguous, and the Act has in general become outdated.[55] Noting that only a few Member States continue to apply the directive, the 2022 EU listing act package proposed to repeal the Listing Directive.[56]

B. Grounds for Mandatory Delisting

MiFID II requires that both market operators and NCAs supervising them may remove from trading an instrument which no longer complies with the rules of the market, provided that this would not cause significant damage to the investors' interests or the orderly functioning of the market.[57] Although Articles 32(1) and 52(1) only refer to the suspension or removal of a financial instrument as a result of breaches of market rules, it is evident that the operators should have similar powers in situations of suspected market abuse, a takeover bid or non-disclosure of inside information under MAR.[58] This minimum requirement has been implemented in Member States in various ways, both in statutory rules and in applicable market rules. The most significant difference concerns the level of discretion granted to NCAs and market operators.

At one end of the spectrum are Member States implementing MiFID II in faithful adherence to its wording ('may remove'), thus giving market operators and NCAs discretion to determine the existence of conditions justifying delisting. In Finland, for instance, the Nasdaq Helsinki Main Market Rulebook, which essentially replicates statutory requirements implementing MiFID II, provides that the Nasdaq Helsinki Listing committee *may decide* that trading in a share is terminated

[53] Directive 2001/34/EC on the admission of securities to official stock exchange listing and on information to be published on those securities [2001] OJ L184/1.

[54] See N Moloney, *EU Securities and Financial Markets Regulation*, 4th edn (Oxford, Oxford University Press, 2023) 197.

[55] ibid 196f.

[56] European Commission, 'Proposal for a Directive of the European Parliament and of the Council amending Directive 2014/65/EU to make public capital markets in the Union more attractive for companies and to facilitate access to capital for small and medium-sized enterprises and repealing Directive 2001/34/EC' COM(2022) 760 final. For an impact assessment see European Commission, 'Commission Staff Working Document, Impact Assessment Report' SWD(2022) 762 final.

[57] See Section IV above.

[58] See eg MiFID II, Art 32(2), subpara 2, which states that the NCAs must require the market operators to suspend or remove financial instruments related or referenced to the suspended or removed financial instrument where the decision was 'due to suspected market abuse, a take-over bid or the non-disclosure of inside information about the issuer or financial instrument infringing Articles 7 and 17 of Regulation (EU) No 596/2014 …'.

when (a) the share or the issuer no longer fulfils the requirements of the Rulebook; or (b) delisting is otherwise necessary based on the issuer's actions being in contradiction with the legislation or regulations on the operation of the exchange, the Nasdaq Rulebook, or with the good practice in securities markets. The only explicit requirement limiting the discretion is, in line with MiFID II's requirements, that delisting may not result in significant harm to investors or risk proper functioning of the financial markets.[59] The powers of the Finnish Financial Supervisory Authority (the FIN-FSA) are similar but more circumscribed: the FIN-FSA may order a delisting in the event of a *material breach* of certain statutory rules such as the Finnish Securities Markets Act or MAR or the rules of the stock exchange. However, the FIN-FSA may also order a stock exchange to remove a financial instrument from trading if there is 'another compelling reason' for doing so. Again, such an order cannot be issued if the order would significantly harm investors or impair the orderly functioning of the market.

The regulatory systems in Cyprus, Greece, Italy and Spain are broadly comparable to the Finnish system although the specific grounds for mandatory delisting vary.[60] In Greece, as mentioned above, the discretionary powers of market operators are structurally limited by oversight of the NCA, which makes the ultimate decision on delisting. In the Netherlands, market operators also have a wide discretion to impose mandatory delisting due to substantial breaches of market rules or failure to fulfil listing requirements.[61] However, the powers of the NCAs are more limited than in the first group. As noted in Section IV, the AFM can only request the Court of Rotterdam to exclude a security from being traded after having notified Euronext Amsterdam of its suspicion of market abuse, a takeover bid, or where it considers that delisting would generally be in the interest of investors.[62]

Germany stands out as the Member State with the least discretion given to public authorities or market operators to impose involuntary delisting. Public authorities have no powers to impose delisting themselves or review decisions by market operators.[63] The powers of Deutsche Börse as the market operator (and NCA) are also more limited under the applicable law (*Börsengesetz)*.[64] The management board of the Börse may revoke the admission of securities to trading on the regulated market only if (a) orderly exchange trading is no longer guaranteed *in the long term* and the management of the market operator has already discontinued the listing or (b) the issuer fails to fulfil admission obligations even after it has been given a reasonable period of time to comply. According to the literature, this provision must be interpreted narrowly due to the substantial impact of delisting on the issuer. For instance, whereas insolvency of an issuer would constitute a conceivable case for justifying delisting (ie trading would no longer be guaranteed in the long term), illiquidity or a minority squeeze-out would not per se constitute such cases.

[59] See s 25 (Supplement B) of the Nasdaq Helsinki Main Market Rulebook.

[60] For a comparison of differences in listing rules and ongoing obligations in European exchanges, as of 2019, see Oxera Consulting LLP, *Primary and secondary equity markets in the EU* (n 28) 39–42.

[61] Art 5:32g of the Law of Financial Supervision. The relevant Euronext Rulebook also provides an open-ended list of appropriate grounds that may trigger delisting. See Art 6905/1 of the Euronext Rule Book I.

[62] See Table 8.1 and n 51.

[63] See Table 8.1.

[64] ibid and BörsG, s 39(1).

In the final group of Member States are Austria and Sweden, which also limit the use of discretion by market operators. Unlike in Germany, where the limitations primarily serve the interests of issuers, the applicable Swedish and Austrian laws stipulate certain conditions under which the market operators (both of which also act as NCAs) *must* delist a financial instrument. In Austria, the *Börsengesetz* provides that the market operator (Wiener Börse AG) must delist an issuer that (a) does not meet certain prerequisites for a listing anymore (eg change of corporate form or free-float-requirement); or (b) has obtained the listing under false pretences or through wilfully providing false information; or (c) has repeatedly breached its obligations such as disclosure duties.[65] In addition, the market operator has discretion to delist a financial instrument when the issuer fails to meet the general conditions for an admission, eg the fair, proper, efficient and free trading of the financial instrument. In Sweden the regulatory structure is similar, although the grounds for involuntary delisting differ in detail.[66] In Sweden, just as in Austria, such a delisting decision pursuant to the express statutory requirement may be postponed if it is in the public interest.

In the UK, the FCA has wide discretion to cancel listings 'if it is satisfied that there are special circumstances that preclude normal regular dealings in them'.[67] The London Stock Exchange may also, at its own initiative, suspend or remove from trading a security 'which no longer complies with the rules unless such a step would be likely to cause significant damage to the interests of investors or the orderly functioning of the financial markets'.[68] In general, however, delisting is not possible without consent of the FCA.

C. Remedies – Public and Private Law Approaches

A review of the questionnaires shows divergences also in legal systems with regard to the range and type of remedies available for companies and/or their shareholders against involuntary delisting decisions. Most Member States, as well as the UK, follow a 'public law model' in which delisting decisions can be challenged before supervisory

[65] BörseG, S 38, para 4. However, if the protection of investors is not at risk, the market operator may grant a grace period for an amendment of the situation in cases of categories (a) and (c) (S 38(4) sentence 2 BörseG).

[66] Under the Swedish Securities Markets Act a securities exchange must decide that a financial instrument shall be delisted, where the instrument does not fulfil the admission requirements which apply for admission to trading or where the issuer has seriously breached its obligations under SMA or other statutory act or at the request of the Swedish National Debt Office pursuant to c 14, s 3, para 1, sub-s 1 of the Resolution Act (2015:1016) or at the request of a foreign resolution authority pursuant to the national legislation implementing Art 64(1)(c) of the Bank Recovery and Resolution Directive 2014/59/EU. A securities exchange may in addition to the above delist a financial instrument where it is not likely that the delisting would cause significant damage to the investors or the functioning of the market.

[67] Under Listing Rules 5.6.23–29 such circumstances may include, but are not limited to, situations where: '1) the securities are no longer admitted to trading as required by these rules; or 2) the issuer no longer satisfies its continuing obligations for listing, for example if the percentage of shares in public hands falls below 10% (the FCA may however allow a reasonable time to restore the percentage, unless this is precluded by the need to maintain the smooth operation of the market or to protect investors); or 3) the securities' listing has been suspended for more than six months; or 4) the securities are equity shares with a standard listing issued by a closed-ended investment fund where the closed-ended investment fund no longer has a premium listing of equity shares.' For more details, see J Chan and C Gerner-Beuerle, Questionnaire UK.

[68] Rules of the London Stock Exchange, LSE Rule Book (1 July 2019) G 1510.

authorities and/or administrative courts. This is the case regardless of whether the challenged decision was adopted by an operator of a trading venue or an NCA (where they are not the same entity). There is some divergence within this family, however, especially regarding standing. In Finland, for instance, the delisting decision can be challenged before administrative courts both by the issuer and each of its shareholders independently. When compulsory delisting is imposed by the market operator, the FIN-FSA as the NCA acts as the first instance. In Germany, the issuer may take legal action against the delisting decision of the market operator (which acts as the NCA), which is considered an administrative act. But shareholders have no standing, although the law in this regard is subject to debate.[69] The regime is similar in Cyprus, where the issuer (but not shareholders) can challenge, under administrative law, the delisting decision of the market operator or the NCAs. The same model is followed in Austria where the issuer (but not shareholders) can appeal to the Federal Administrative Court (*Bundesverwaltungsgericht)* and from thereon to the Austrian Supreme Administrative Court (*Verwaltungsgerichtshof*).

The systems also differ with respect to the standard and scope of review: whereas in Finland and in Germany the administrative courts may also review the merits of delisting decisions,[70] this is not the case eg in Cyprus or Greece.

The public law model therefore views operators of trading venues as regulatory entities performing a public function. This is not the case in jurisdictions following a 'private law model', ie France, the Netherlands and Sweden, where disputes over delisting decisions are adjudicated as if they were contractual in nature. This means that a decision imposing involuntary delisting must be challenged before general courts which can also review the merits of the challenged decision. In France, for instance, an issuer may challenge the delisting decision of the Relevant Euronext Market Undertaking before the Paris Commercial Court.[71] In the Netherlands, the relevant court is the Court of Amsterdam. The situation is different, however, where the challenged delisting decision is imposed by the NCA resorting to its MiFID II-based powers. In Sweden, the relevant court in such a case would be an administrative court. In the Netherlands, the relevant tribunal would likely be the Court of Rotterdam, which reviews possible orders by the AFM to seek delisting of financial instruments. In France, where the Chair of the AMF enjoys a rare personal prerogative to impose delisting, the competent court reviewing the challenged decision would presumably be the Administrative Court of Paris, although this appears to be uncertain.[72]

D. Law in Action?

The above-described divergences across Member States are arguably significant and question the level of harmonisation achieved by the current MiFID II regime. However,

[69] See K Çavuşoğlu, Questionnaire Germany.

[70] In Germany, however, the relevant courts have the power to examine the reasons for delisting only in cases of obligatory delisting.

[71] See K Deckert, Questionnaire France.

[72] ibid.

turning from the 'law in books' to 'law in action', the differences diminish in importance. Although granular data on mandatory delistings in Europe is generally lacking,[73] it is evident that mandatory delistings are rare compared to other reasons for exits from public markets, such as buyouts, squeeze-outs or mergers and acquisitions.[74] The questionnaires confirm that companies are forced to delist relatively rarely. Most importantly, supervisory authorities appear to play no visible role. In Member States such as Finland, France, the Netherlands, Italy and Spain, the questionnaires do not report a single case where public authorities would have resorted to their authority to bypass the market operator by ordering delisting.[75] A notable exception is Greece where there have been 76 cases of mandatory delisting since 2012, out of which six have been imposed by a decision of the NCA (HCMC). Sweden, with a much larger market, has since 2007 seen only 13 cases of mandatory delisting from regulated markets and 36 from the MTF (First North). The majority of these has been due to bankruptcy or non-fulfilment of the listing requirements; only a few are due to breaches of applicable rules. Nasdaq Stockholm, as the market operator, and NCA has taken all the decisions. Again, no cases have been reported in which the Swedish Financial Supervisory Authority would have used its last resort powers to order delisting.[76]

This appears problematic given the market transformations discussed above.[77] If the increased competition among for-profit marketplaces indeed leads to lower standards and lax enforcement, as the theory predicts, one would expect public authorities to play a more significant role. The continued shrinking of European public equity markets, both in terms of the number of listed companies,[78] and the total number of shares traded,[79] will not increase the incentives of for-profit marketplaces to impose mandatory delisting. In other words, more marketplaces are competing for less liquidity and a smaller number of firms. This exacerbates 'the delisting dilemma' which, as argued by Macey, O'Hara and Pompilio, cannot be solved by markets themselves.[80]

Does this indicate a regulatory and enforcement failure in EU capital markets? Of course, the near absence of mandatory delistings imposed by public authorities is not necessarily because of low standards and lax enforcement. Regardless of salient corporate fraud scandals such as Wirecard,[81] there is no empirical research suggesting

[73] For instance, the data on mandatory delistings, where available, does not differentiate between reasons for exits but groups delistings due to financial difficulties or breach of listing requirements into one category. The data does not reveal whether delistings were initiated by the trading venues or supervisory authorities. See Oxera Consulting LLP (n 28) 73–78 and the European Equity Market Reports by the Federation of European Exchanges. Available at: www.fese.eu/statistics/european-equity-market-report/.

[74] See Oxera Consulting LLP (n 28) 73–78.

[75] Not all the questionnaires have been able to ascertain this, but it is evident that any examples would be rare.

[76] However, the Swedish authority has decided to suspend the trading in shares of several companies.

[77] See Section III.

[78] See Oxera Consulting LLP (n 28) 25–30. The data also shows that most delistings in large markets such as France, Germany and the UK are either voluntary going-private transactions or due to mergers or acquisitions.

[79] ibid 34 f.

[80] Macey, O'Hara and Pompilio (n 19).

[81] The Wirecard case is widely treated as an accounting and audit failure. See B García Osma, A Gisbert and B Navallas, *What are the wider supervisory implications of the Wirecard case? Public Oversight Systems for Statutory Auditors in the EU* (2020). Available at: www.europarl.europa.eu/RegData/etudes/STUD/2020/651383/IPOL_STU(2020)651383_EN.pdf.

widespread non-compliance by listed companies with financial reporting regulations or stock market rules in European markets. There could also be more than meets the eye. Instead of resorting to the big stick of delisting, which is often the only formal enforcement action available for operators of trading venues, the trading venues may seek to remedy non-compliance via informal negotiations and conversations.[82] The development of such informal systems of sanctioning is supported by the fact that regulations often allow or even require the operators of trading venues to apply grace or cure periods during which the delinquent firms can regain compliance.[83] Such cooperative compliance might – depending on the jurisdiction and allocation of powers – also include public authorities. The relationship between operators of trading venues and the public authorities regulating and supervising them could also be characterised as a relational contract, which induces cooperative compliance without heavy sanctions and visible interventions. In short, the number of mandatory delistings provides a poor metric for measuring the degree of compliance. Further empirical research in this area would be needed.

The negative association between listing/delisting standards and market competition is not straightforward in Europe either. Measured in terms of ease of entry and the number of market players, European markets appear highly competitive: 37 different exchange groups (out of which 26 groups were domiciled in the EEA) operated within the EEA area in 2021 and 2022.[84] Moreover, in terms of different trading infrastructures (regulated markets, MTFs, systematic internalisers), share trading in Europe takes place in a highly fragmented landscape.[85] At the same time, however, competition for listings between operators of regulated markets remains low. The number of cross-border listings in the EU is still modest and home-market bias is prevalent.[86] As noted by one study, 'more than 95% of European IPOs are on domestic exchanges which enjoy a virtual monopoly in their domestic markets'.[87]

Competition for primary market listings is unlikely to have an effect on the exchanges' listing standards. Listing fees, on average, generate a relatively small proportion of European exchanges' revenue compared to fees from trading cash and derivatives products. In 2022, listing fees generated on average 6 per cent of the European exchanges' total revenue.[88] The revenue breakdown was not significantly different in 2021, which saw members of the Federation of European Exchanges (FESE) register a record total of 534 IPOs.[89]

[82] From the perspective of the United States, see Min and Jin (n 24) 215 f.

[83] ibid.

[84] ESMA, *Evolution of EEA Share Market Structure Since MiFID II, ESMA TRV Risk Analysis* (2023) 6. Available at: www.esma.europa.eu/sites/default/files/2023-10/ESMA50-524821-2954_TRV_Article_EEA_share_market_structure_publication.pdf.

[85] ibid.

[86] Oxera Consulting LLP (n 28) 96–99. Cross-border listings also often take place within an exchange group such as Euronext. See ibid, 97.

[87] W Wright and EF Hamre, 'The Problem with European Stock Markets' (2021), New Financial. Available at: www.newfinancial.org/wp-content/uploads/2021/03/2021.03-The-problem-with-European-stock-markets-New-Financial.pdf.

[88] FESE, *Equity Market Report*. Available at: www.fese.eu/statistics/.

[89] FESE, *Exchanges in 2021: The Year in Statistics. A Summary of FESE Members' Trading Figures* (2022). Available at: www.fese.eu/app/uploads/2022/01/Exchanges-in-2021-report-summary-of-FESE-members-

However, if competition for equity listings is not high, competition for trading and liquidity has gradually intensified. Since the UK's withdrawal from the EU, shares traded on MTFs (especially on dark pools) have been highly concentrated; in 2022, 95 per cent of MTF trading took place in the Netherlands (57 per cent), France (29 per cent) and Germany (9 per cent). The same countries dominate intra-EEA cross-border share trading, which has diminished after Brexit. In 2021, 61 per cent of share trading volume was domestic, ie traded in the same country as the issuer of the shares (as opposed to only 41 per cent before Brexit).[90] Due to ongoing exchange consolidation driven by Euronext and Nasdaq, the competition is likely to become more intense.

This could have an adverse effect on listing standards. As Macey and O'Hara note, the exchanges' incentives to list more firms than would be optimal become stronger when the listed stocks end up being traded elsewhere.[91] Such gatekeeper failures predictably increase firm mortality and delistings following financial difficulties.[92] In such a scenario, the costs of failing firms would be borne by investors while the entire market would be affected by decreased investor confidence.

To conclude, restricting access to securities markets and denying the privilege of public trading is a public good that is crucial for enhancing market quality.[93] In Europe, modest competition for primary market listings combined with fierce competition for trading volume gives rise to complex externalities, which the markets will struggle to solve effectively. These developments and the slow but ongoing consolidation of market infrastructures[94] will ensure that the discussion on centralising a listing authority within Europe continues in the future.[95]

VI. Concluding Remarks

The established view is that Europe has been a global leader in consolidating regulation and supervision of securities markets in government authorities. In the United Kingdom, for instance, the regulatory body responsible for the *listing* of shares (Listing Authority) was transferred in 2001 from the London Stock Exchange to the (then) Financial Services Authority (FSA). In the EU, the transfer of regulatory functions was brought by several transformative directives such as the Market Abuse Directive, the Prospectus Directive and MiFID I.[96] As a result, it has been considered that self-regulation plays a

trading-figures.pdf; FESE, *European Exchange Report 2021*. Available at: www.fese.eu/app/uploads/2024/08/european-exchange-report-2021.pdf.

[90] ESMA, *Evolution of EEA Share Market Structure* (n 84) 9 f.

[91] Macey and O'Hara (n 9) 584.

[92] EF Fama and KR French, 'New Lists: Fundamentals and Survival Rates' (2004) 73 *Journal of Financial Economics* 229.

[93] Macey and O'Hara (n 9) 584.

[94] Wright and Hamre, 'The Problem with European Stock Markets' (n 87) 8.

[95] See E Avgouleas and G Ferrarini, 'A Single Listing Authority and Securities Regulator for the CMU and the Future of ESMA: Costs, Benefits, and Legal Impediments' in D Busch, E Avgouleas and G Ferrarini (eds), *Capital Markets Union in Europe* (Oxford, Oxford University Press, 2018).

[96] See n 17 and accompanying text.

minor role in European securities markets where it 'was never extensive because of its civil law system'.[97]

This view appears exaggerated, at least in the context of delisting of stock corporations. The implementation of the MiFID-based structure of powers has resulted in a wide variety of national approaches. MiFID II requires that public bodies designated as competent authorities must have the power to require delisting of financial instruments from trading.[98] As this chapter shows, there are still Member States where public authorities do not have such powers (Germany) or where such powers have been heavily circumscribed (the Netherlands). Even when public authorities have formal powers to delist or require the delisting of financial instruments, which is the case in most Member States, there is little evidence of these powers being put to practice.

However, neither the Member State questionnaires nor existing empirical literature suggest that European trading venues are under-enforcing their rulebooks or that NCAs are under-using their MiFID-based intervention powers. Trading venues could perform their regulatory roles effectively without strong enforcement. Cooperative compliance, both by operators of trading venues and listed companies, could be supported by informal negotiations overshadowed by the hierarchically superior powers of NCAs. We do not know, however, to what extent such relational dynamics are at play in Europe.[99]

The status of competition on European equity markets nevertheless suggests that there is cause for concern. The equity market infrastructure remains complex and heterogenous, and consolidation slow. National exchanges still enjoy a near-monopoly on primary market equity listings. But the competition for trading volume is getting fiercer, with increasing volume of transactions being directed to pan-European exchanges such as Aquis, Equiduct and Turquoise as well as to MTF dark pools. This means that listing and delisting decisions will have complex externalities, both positive and negative, which the exchanges will not fully internalise.[100] The declining trading fees – a more important source of revenue for regulated markets compared to listing fees – probably affects how the market operators perform their regulatory roles, both in terms of listing as well as delisting of stock corporations. Public authorities might need to step up to ensure the protection of investors, both current and prospective.

[97] Carson (n 5) 25.
[98] MiFID II, Arts 67(1) and 69(2) sub-s n.
[99] For the United States, see Min and Jin (n 24).
[100] Macey and O'Hara (n 9).

9

Delisting in the Issuer's Insolvency

JENS-HINRICH BINDER*

I. Introduction

Among the many aspects of regulatory frameworks for the delisting of securities, delisting in the issuer's insolvency prima facie presents the most straightforward case: If the company is forced to exit from trading on account of its financial difficulties and if, as a consequence, equity is written down in its entirety, there is a strong case for mandatory termination of the listing of the shares in the interest of prospective investors, and neither the issuer nor existing shareholders can claim a legitimate interest in the preservation of the status quo ante. On further inspection, however, the problem is considerably more complex than this simple consideration would suggest. To be sure, the fundamental reasoning, as such, remains true. In fact, it can also be extended to debt instruments. If the issuer is liquidated in formal insolvency proceedings, the case for the preservation of the listing of exchange-traded bonds is, at best, limited, and concerns about the protection of prospective investors appear to militate in support of the termination of trading also in this scenario.

At the same time, it has to be borne in mind that modern insolvency laws tend to be geared not exclusively towards liquidation, but alternatively also towards the restructuring as a going concern if and 'where creditors would not involuntarily receive less than in liquidation and the value of the debtor to society and to creditors may be maximized by allowing it to continue'.[1] These objectives may either be pursued in a single,

* Professor of Law, Chair for Private Law, Corporate Law, Banking and Capital Markets Law at Eberhard-Karls University of Tübingen, Germany, visiting Professor of Financial Law at Università Cattolica del Sacro Cuore, Milan, Italy, and Judge (part-time) at the Stuttgart Court of Appeals, Germany.
I would like to thank Vasilis Tountopoulos, Paolo Giudici, Athanassios Kouloridas, Rüdiger Veil and other participants in the Delisting Workshop at the University of the Aegean at Chios on 8 and 9 June 2023 and the international Working Group on Delisting for numerous insightful comments. Participants' responses to the questionnaire developed for the working group provided an indispensable source of information for the survey in Section III below. I am also indebted to Andrea Cardani for extremely helpful input on the legal and regulatory situation in Italy, as well as to Lina Nädele and Marianne Wesle for useful research assistance on other jurisdictions and relevant academic literature. The usual disclaimer applies.

[1] In the words of UNCITRAL's Insolvency Law Working Group, see United Nations Commission on International Trade Law (UNCITRAL), *Legislative Guide on Insolvency Law – Parts 1 and 2* (2005) 11 para 6.

unitary procedure or through alternative procedures with stronger or weaker functional links with one another.[2] Moreover, a wide range of jurisdictions have introduced procedural frameworks for the restructuring of corporate debt *outside* established insolvency proceedings, but in formal procedures that can be initiated prior to the relevant company fulfilling the established triggers of balance-sheet insolvency or illiquidity. Examples include so-called Schemes of Arrangement under Part 26 of the UK Companies Act 2006 and, more recently, arrangements established by the 2019 EU Directive on preventive restructuring frameworks.[3] If and when, as a result of either insolvency or pre-insolvency procedures, an issuer of securities survives as a going concern, the case for mandatory termination of the listing is evidently less compelling than in the case of traditional liquidation procedures – all the more so if the position of the relevant investors (shareholders or investors in debt instrument) is not written down in full. In such scenarios, the relevant securities are not (necessarily) cancelled, and to the extent they are not, remain a tradeable asset with a commercial value, so that the interest in the preservation of access to exchange-based trading does not necessarily fade away. In fact, preserving the listing, in such scenarios, may contribute to the restructuring efforts in that it facilitates the ongoing trading process, which may be attractive both for existing and incoming investors.

Moreover, and irrespective of the foregoing, the simple equation between insolvency and (mandatory) termination of the listing of securities ignores the fact that insolvency procedures – however structured and with whatever objective – generally are divided between the commencement stage and later stages. During the former, a decision is made, upon the application by the insolvent company or a debtor and on the basis of a (preliminary) assessment of the company's financial position, whether the conditions for commencement are met.[4] This is usually complemented with the imposition of safeguards, frequently including a stay of proceedings and executions, a freeze of payments, and the appointment of an interim administrator, in order to protect the debtor's estate against an outflow of value to the benefit of individual creditors (or other parties) and to the detriment of the creditors as a whole.[5] The actual liquidation or reorganisation procedure usually starts only upon the formal completion of the commencement stage. It is, again, evident that the ultimate decision to terminate, or indeed to uphold, the delisting must take these aspects into account and should be structured accordingly.

Finally, all differentiations sketched out above may require an intricate balance to be struck between the interests of the issuer and present investors on the one hand and prospective investors on the other hand with regard to the delisting decision. However, that balance may have to be calibrated differently depending on where exactly the relevant securities are listed. As has been noted already, some time ago,

Available at: www.uncitral.un.org/sites/uncitral.un.org/files/media-documents/uncitral/en/05-80722_ebook.pdf.

[2] ibid 17–19 paras 21–25 and 26–31 and paras 19–36; see, for an up-to-date assessment, N Tollenaar, *Pre-Insolvency Proceedings. A Normative Foundation and Framework* (Oxford, OUP, 2019) paras 1.15–1.33.

[3] Directive (EU) 2019/1023 on preventive restructuring frameworks, on discharge of debt and disqualifications, and on measures to increase the efficiency of procedures concerning restructuring, insolvency and discharge of debt (…) [2019] OJ L172/18; see also UNIDROIT (n 1) 21–26, paras 1–18.

[4] See, for further discussion, eg UNIDROIT (n 1) 56–57, paras 55–58.

[5] See, eg, ibid 83–94, paras 26–57.

delisting regimes may reflect the respective trading venue's interest in preserving their reputational capital, and signaling effects as to the value associated with the listing on that trading venue.[6] Markets or market segments with restrictive listing requirements, such as 'regulated markets' governed by harmonised European securities law,[7] will therefore be less tolerant of trading in securities issued by companies in financial distress, resulting in an early termination of the listing in insolvency, while markets or market segments with lower requirements may be kept open for a longer period.

It may be understandable in view of residual differences between national insolvency regimes that European securities regulation, from the first, rudimentary harmonisation of listing requirements with Council Directive 79/279/EEC[8] through MiFID II[9] up to the modifications introduced by the newly adopted 'Listing Act',[10] has so far refrained from harmonising conditions for the suspension or mandatory termination of a listing in the issuer's insolvency. Given the potential differences in the treatment of insolvent issuers and investors under national regimes, the absence of harmonisation in this regard is nonetheless conspicuous. The practical relevance is certainly high, judging from a significant percentage of insolvent issuers in mandatory delistings in major jurisdictions.[11] In this light, the present chapter undertakes to examine the case for harmonised rules on the delisting of securities in the issuer's insolvency. In order to prepare the ground, Section II below explores the economic position of issuers, investors and markets in relevant scenarios. Section III then turns to a comparative analysis of approaches currently in place in a variety of jurisdictions. Against this backdrop, Section IV discusses potential lessons to be learnt. Section V concludes.

In the interest of consistency, the term 'insolvency' will be used throughout this chapter in a broad, non-technical sense, covering formal liquidation or restructuring proceedings triggered by the issuer's financial problems and/or its inability to meet its obligations vis-à-vis its creditors. Specifically, this definition is meant to include also restructuring proceedings that can be initiated, on the application of the issuer or its creditors, prior to the issuer's balance-sheet insolvency or actual illiquidity.

[6] J Macey, M O'Hara and D Pompilio, 'Down and Out in the Stock Market: The Law and Economics of the Delisting Process' (2008) 66 *The Journal of Law and Economics* 683, 686.

[7] See, generally, eg, N Moloney, *EU Securities and Financial Markets Regulation*, 4th edn (Oxford, OUP, 2023) 104–05.

[8] See Directive 79/279/EEC coordinating the conditions for the admission of securities to official stock exchange listing [1979] OJ L66/21, Art 4 in conjunction with Schedules A–D; consolidated into Directive 2001/34/EC on the admission of securities to official stock exchange listing and on information to be published on those securities [2001] OJ L184/1 ch 2.

[9] Directive 2014/65/EU on markets in financial instruments (…) [2014] OJ L173/349, Arts 51 and 52.

[10] See Directive (EU) amending Directive 2014/65/EU to make public capital markets in the Union more attractive for companies and to facilitate access to capital for small and medium-sized enterprises (…) [2024] OJ L14/1.

[11] See eg, Italy (37 out of 457 delistings from Borsa Italiana between 1995 and 2021, see Borsa Italiana, *Companies Delisted from January 1995 to 30 December 2021* [2022]. Available at: www.borsaitaliana.it/borsaitaliana/statistiche/mediaitaliano/statistiche/mercatoprimario/2021/revoche.en.pdf; The Netherlands (two out of 76 delistings from Euronext Amsterdam between 2013 and 2023, see questionnaire on The Netherlands); USA (86 out of 320 delistings from NYSE and 229 out of 1,607 delistings from NASDAQ between 1999 and 2004, see Macey, O'Hara and Pompilio, 'Down and Out in the Stock Market' (n 6) 683).

II. Delisting and the Economics (and Law) of Corporate Insolvency

A. What Changes in Insolvency?

If and when a company approaches the vicinity of (balance-sheet and/or illiquidity) insolvency, the allocation of risk and opportunities between shareholders and creditors changes. With substantial losses, the net value of equity capital – the investment of shareholders as the residual owners of the company – is reduced accordingly. This is recognised also in the standard arrangements for the distribution of losses in insolvency, whereby share capital is written down first (and prior to any creditor's claims), and creditors' claims are written down pro rata to the extent that the debtor's assets prove insufficient for meeting all creditors' claims in full. Prior to completion of the liquidation process, however, as long as equity has not been written down in full, investors in equity capital remain entitled, on a pro-rata basis, to any profits the company may generate in present and future circumstances. If and as long as the company is allowed to continue trading despite a deteriorating capital base, this creates incentives for excessive risk-taking: With the original investment all but lost, shareholders have every reason to gamble, or support gambling by the company's directors. Even though the shares thus turn into a high-risk asset, however, further losses, as a result of new risks taken, will eventually materialise on the part of the company's creditors (who do not receive a risk premium of outstanding debt but stand to receive even less than they would receive if the company was liquidated right away), not by existing shareholders. Taken together, these considerations – and, indeed, the incentives of debtors and creditors in the face of a dwindling common pool of assets available to meet obligations in the vicinity of insolvency – have long become accepted as the fundamental rationale explaining the very existence of insolvency procedures, as well as core features such as a mandatory stay of proceedings upon their initiation and control by insolvency officials on behalf of the creditors as a whole.[12] As far as pre-insolvency restructuring procedures are concerned, they fit into this broader picture inasmuch as they are designed to facilitate a coordinated restructuring of companies that ultimately provides higher returns for the benefit of the creditors than would be achievable through conventional insolvency liquidation or reorganisation procedures.[13]

[12] Seminal works include T Jackson, *The Logic and Limits of Bankruptcy Law* (Washington DC, Beards, 1986); T Jackson, 'Bankruptcy, Non-Bankruptcy Entitlements, and the Creditors 'Bargain' (1982) 133 *The Yale Law Journal* 857; D Beard and T Jackson, 'Corporate Reorganizations and the Treatment of Diverse Ownership Interests: A Comment on Adequate Protection of Secured Creditors in Bankruptcy' (1984) 91 *The University of Chicago Law Review* 51; for a good recent review of the available literature and its critique, see, eg, Tollenaar, *Pre-Insolvency Proceedings* (n 2) paras 2.03–2.104.

[13] See, eg, Tollenaar (n 2) paras 3.06–3.08.

B. And What Follows?

While it is neither possible nor necessary to explore the fundamental considerations developed above in more detail for present purposes,[14] they are nonetheless crucial also for the understanding of the interests of issuers of, and investors in, listed securities in (the vicinity of) the issuer's insolvency, as well as of the interests of the trading venues in such circumstances. They should therefore inform relevant policy decisions on the design of regulatory approaches in this regard. Three implications in particular are worth noting:

First, with respect to equity and debt investors alike, the financial crisis of a company, from the occurrence of substantial losses to the moment where it meets balance-sheet or liquidity-based tests for the commencement of insolvency proceedings (and indeed beyond that point), is a continuum characterised by a shift in risks and incentives. Trivial though it may appear, this finding is nonetheless important in that it militates against black-and-white solutions regarding the listing of relevant securities. To the extent that the economic value of listed securities has not yet fallen to zero, both the issuer and indeed the existing investors may have an ongoing interest in the preservation of the listing as such. From the issuer's perspective, this interest may be motivated either by reputational aspects (an obligatory delisting might contribute to the bad perception of a failing firm, and might thus impact even on the availability of non-market based funding sources). Alternatively, it may be motivated by the costs that would have to be incurred in connection with a re-entry into the market in the course of a restructuring (eg, through a capital increase or the issuance of new bonds), or indeed by both factors at the same time.[15] From the existing investors' perspective, the preservation of the issuer's listing may be attractive as it facilitates flexible reactions, specifically: a hold-out combined with last-minute sales, to the incentives mentioned above. At the same time, depending on the circumstances, speculative investors hitherto unconnected with the issuer could use the opportunity to acquire a stake at low cost, particularly where they feel that there are prospects of recovery or they are interested in specific assets of the firm. For both types of actors, early termination (or even the suspension) of the listing of securities issued by failing companies will be outright harmful.[16]

Second, the shift in the risk profile of both equity and debt instruments will inevitably affect the risk assessment by investors and thus influence market prices, turning the relevant instruments into a highly speculative investment in all cases. These effects are particularly dramatic in the case of instruments listed in highly regulated markets with restrictive entry standards aiming at a high level of investor protection, as the relevant securities will no longer be suitable for (retail) investors interested in investments with moderate risk levels. In comparison with the first observation above, this consideration highlights problematic implications of continued trading for prospective (retail)

[14] ibid paras 2.03–2.104.
[15] See Macey, O'Hara and Pompilio (n 6) 710.
[16] ibid.

investors who are unfamiliar with the issuer's financial problems and who rely on the trading venue's enforcement of listing standards as a protection.

Third, it should be noted that the interest of market operators in the preservation of the listing (and the trading fees) may, in the circumstances, outweigh investor concerns that might require the suspension, or even termination of a failing issuer's listing. As has been discussed in the academic literature before, this may provide incentives to delay the suspension or termination of listings even in cases of serious breaches of listing requirements, including in the issuer's insolvency.[17]

All three observations taken together clearly reinforce the thesis that the problems associated with the delisting of securities issued by a failing company are way more complex than would appear at first sight.[18] The decision of whether to delist in relevant circumstances will meet a complex interest structure, and must thus strike a careful balance between the conflicting positions of current and prospective investors. While it may be simple to define an optimal obligatory delisting policy that balances the interest of issuers, current and prospective investors also in the case of failing issuers at an abstract level,[19] the operationalisation can be expected to be fraught with difficult policy choices – again, particularly in markets or market segments with high levels of investor protection.

C. Fundamental Questions

The above analysis can also be translated into a taxonomy of questions designed to inform the comparative survey of different jurisdictions below. At a very fundamental level, of course, it can be asked whether, in view of the conflicting interests discussed above, delisting in the issuer's insolvency should receive special treatment in laws or regulations at all. In this regard, much will depend on the characteristics of the respective delisting regime more generally. For instance, it is perfectly conceivable that the issuer's insolvency can, and will, be addressed under more general provisions governing the delisting of securities in cases of qualified breaches of listing requirements which, if applied adequately in the circumstances, might provide levels of protection equal or similar to more specific provisions. Moreover, the decision whether to delist or preserve an existing listing in response to the issuer's financial difficulties should also be reconciled with the applicable disclosure regime. Specifically, it may be conceivable – particularly in the case of markets or market segments with less restrictive entry criteria – that concerns about the protection of prospective investors may be addressed through disclosure rather than the suspension or outright termination of the listing.

[17] ibid 686 and 711 (citing evidence from US trading venues).

[18] See above, Section I.

[19] See Macey, O'Hara and Pompilio (n 6) 710 (arguing that '[a]n optimal delisting policy […] should provide optimal liquidity for a stock consistent with the exchange's interest of making, or at least not losing, money while protecting both current and future investors in the company').

If delisting in the issuer's insolvency is regulated, the question then becomes *who* should regulate – and in which ways (mandatory suspension and/or termination? on which conditions?). Several policy options appear to exist in this regard. While it is conceivable that relevant decisions can be made at the legislative level, it is also possible to allocate them to the discretion of the market operators or, indeed, to regulatory agencies, leaving them with some discretion to react depending on the circumstances of each particular case. If formal insolvency or pre-insolvency restructuring proceedings have been opened in relation to the issuer, it is also questionable whether insolvency courts and/or insolvency practitioners (liquidators, administrators) ought to play a role in the process.

III. Delisting in Insolvency: An Empirical Survey

A. Overview

As indicated above, it is by no means self-evident that the insolvency of the issuer (however defined) should be treated as a scenario that merits special regulation at all. Particularly in highly regulated markets with restrictive listing requirements, for instance, it is perfectly conceivable to treat the issuer's financial distress simply as a breach of general listing conditions, or to resort to more generally defined market distortions as grounds for the suspension or termination of a listing. The following survey of established approaches in selected jurisdictions explores whether insolvency scenarios have been addressed by specific legal and/or regulatory arrangements at all (below B), if so, which actor has adopted the relevant provisions (below C), and if relevant provisions on the termination and the suspension provide discretion (below D). As far as European jurisdictions are concerned, the focus – in line with the overall concept of the Delisting project whose results are published in the present volume – is mainly on arrangements for 'regulated markets' (and, thus, a market segment with restrictive entry criteria and ongoing disclosure requirements) for a small selection of EU jurisdictions. Other trading venues are not covered in detail. Moreover, the survey is restricted to legal and/or regulatory arrangements as such (as evidenced by the country questionnaires submitted within the context of the project) and does not extend to their practical operationalisation. The following subsection should not, therefore, be interpreted as a comprehensive comparative assessment of the EU as a whole, and its informative value is inevitably limited (but, arguably, not negligible).

B. Delisting in the Issuer's Insolvency: Is it Regulated at All?

European securities law does not provide for specific approaches for any market segment in this respect. For 'regulated markets' within the meaning of Article 4(1)(21) of

MiFID II,[20] ie, trading venues with restrictive listing and ongoing disclosure requirements,[21] it generally falls to (the operators of) regulated markets themselves to have in place 'clear and transparent rules regarding the admission of financial instruments to trading'.[22] As far as listing requirements are concerned, the relevant provisions originally were laid down in Article 6(1) in conjunction with Articles 42–51 (for shares) and Articles 52–63 (for debt securities) of Directive 2003/41.[23] For trading venues other than 'regulated markets',[24] no similar requirement exists. Competent authorities, within the current framework, have to be provided with general powers to 'require the suspension of trading in a financial instrument'[25] and to 'require the removal of a financial instrument from trading, whether on a regulated market or under other trading arrangements',[26] but neither is linked to specific scenarios. Market operators of 'regulated markets', by contrast, 'may suspend or remove from trading a financial instrument which no longer complies with the rules of the regulated market unless such suspension or removal would be likely to cause significant damage to the investors' interests or the orderly functioning of the market'.[27] While relevant listing requirements have been specified further in a Delegated Regulation,[28] neither instrument lists conditions for the suspension or termination of the listing in the issuer's insolvency. While the 2024 'Listing Act' has incorporated (in an amended form) the earlier provisions on listing requirements for shares (in Article 51a of MiFID II), EU securities regulation still refrains from harmonising corresponding *de*listing frameworks, leaving full discretion to Member States in this respect.

Against this backdrop, it is probably not surprising that EU Member States[29] have adopted different approaches with regard to the treatment of relevant scenarios in this respect. For example, delisting in the issuer's insolvency is regulated as a special case in Austria, France, Italy, The Netherlands and the Nordic Member States (Denmark, Finland, Sweden). A number of other EU jurisdictions (eg, Cyprus, Germany, Greece, Spain) and market operators in those jurisdictions, by contrast, have chosen *not* to address insolvency scenarios specifically, so that delisting decisions in relevant cases

[20] Defined as 'a multilateral system operated and/or managed by a market operator, which brings together or facilitates the bringing together of multiple third-party buying and selling interests in financial instruments – in the system and in accordance with its non-discretionary rules – in a way that results in a contract, in respect of the financial instruments admitted to trading under its rules and/or systems, and which is authorised and functions regularly and in accordance with Title III of this Directive'.

[21] See Moloney, *EU Securities and Financial Markets Regulation* (n 7) 193.

[22] Art 51 MiFID II.

[23] Directive 2001/34/EC on the admission of securities to official stock exchange listing and on information to be published on those securities [2001] OJ L184/1; under the 2024 'Listing Act', the relevant conditions will now be consolidated into MiFID II.

[24] That is multilateral trading facilities (MTFs) as defined by MiFID II, Art 4(22) or organised trading facilities (OTFs) as defined by MiFID II, Art 4(23); see generally Moloney (n 7) 104–05 and 470–74.

[25] MiFID II, Art 69(2)(m).

[26] ibid Art 69(2)(n).

[27] ibid Art 52(1).

[28] Commission Delegated Regulation (EU) 2017/568 supplementing Directive 2014/65/EU of the European Parliament and of the Council with regard to regulatory technical standards for the admission of financial instruments to trading on regulated markets [2017] OJ L87/117.

[29] For details, including on relevant provisions in national laws or regulations or exchange rulebooks, readers are referred to the country reports submitted for the purposes of this project. For specific approaches, see also below Section C.-E.

will be based on the general framework for obligatory delisting reflecting Articles 69(2) and 52(1) of MiFID II.

Non-EU jurisdictions are characterised by similarly diverse approaches. Specific regulations addressing delisting in the issuer's insolvency can be found, for example, in US securities regulation and in Switzerland, while Australia, Chile, and India all apply more general provisions allowing for delisting for reasons of investor and market protection. A special case is the United Kingdom, where the issuer's insolvency is not just regulated within the context of obligatory delisting,[30] but also provides for certain derogations from general provisions in the context of voluntary delistings.[31]

C. Who Regulates?

To the extent that delisting in the issuer's insolvency is regulated at all, the question then becomes who (i.e., the legislator, the securities regulator or, indeed, the trading venues) has issued the relevant regulators. This should not be mistaken as a merely formal matter. Given the incentive structure analysed before,[32] it is at least conceivable that delisting policies defined by market operators will be shaped by different considerations than those defined by the legislator or regulatory bodies, which may be concerned more about investor protection and less about the monetary interests of the trading venue.

Against this backdrop, it is particularly noteworthy that many EU[33] jurisdictions without specific regulations addressing delisting in insolvency scenarios tend to define relevant conditions in either primary legislation[34] or in regulations issued by regulatory agencies,[35] whereas in all EU jurisdictions[36] where relevant scenarios have been addressed in bespoke regulation at all the relevant provisions have been adopted by the trading venues themselves.[37] In other words, relevant provisions have been adopted on

[30] See Financial Conduct Authority (FCA), Listing Rule 5.2.12: 'Cancellation as a result of schemes of arrangement etc.'

[31] ibid Listing Rule 5.2.7: shareholder involvement and 75% approval for voluntary delisting not required if 'there is no reasonable prospect that the *issuer* will avoid going into formal insolvency proceedings'.

[32] See above at II. A.

[33] Due to the different regulatory framework, the picture is less coherent outside the EU, where relevant listing rules are frequently promulgated by the trading venues themselves (eg in Australia or the US).

[34] See, eg, Cyprus, Germany, Greece, Spain, The Netherlands (with additional powers in Euronext Listing Rules, see C Van der Elst, Questionnaire Netherlands Q 22 and 23).

[35] See, eg, the UK.

[36] An example for statutory regulation in this regard outside the EU is Chile, where relevant scenarios have been addressed in Art 5.2.6.2.1 of Decree 2555 of 2010; see JP Gonzáles, Questionnaire Chile Q 26; other jurisdictions have adopted relevant provisions in the respective listing rules: In the US, relevant provisions can be found, eg, in Sec 127 NYSE Company Guide. Available at: www.nyseamericanguide.srorules.com/company-guide/09013e2c853aa8db; in Switzerland, in Art 58(1)(2) of SIX's Listing Rules. Available at: www.ser-ag.com/dam/downloads/regulation/listing/listing-rules/sdx-lr-en.pdf.

[37] See, for Austria: Wiener Börse [Vienna Exchange], *Rules prime market* (20 February 2019) 16. Available at: www.wienerborse.at/uploads/u/cms/files/issuers/shares/rules-prime-market.pdf; for France: Art 6905/1(b) and (c) and Art P.1.4.6 of the Euronext Rulebook. Available at: www.euronext.com/en/regulation/euronext-regulated-markets; for Italy: Art 2.5.1(1)(b) in conjunction with Art 2.5.1(5)(b) of Borsa Italiana's Market Rules. Available at: www.borsaitaliana.it/borsaitaliana/regolamenti/regolamenti/marketrules-25032024.en_pdf.htm; for The Netherlands: Art 6905/1(b) of the Euronext Rulebook; for Sweden: Sec 29 of NASDAQ Stockholm Listing Rules. Available at: www.nasdaq.com/docs/2024/01/02/Nasdaq_Nordic_Main_Market%20_-_Shares_-_Rulebook_%28SWE%29_1_Jan_2024.pdf.

top of, and complementary to, the general statutory and/or regulatory regime transposing the requirements under Articles 52(1) and 69(2) of MiFID II in the relevant jurisdictions. This is surely attributable to the fact that, as mentioned before, EU law itself does not itself prescribe specific approaches in this respect, although Member States would have been free to legislate for specific decisions, tied to specific financial and/or procedural criteria, in legislation transposing the harmonised listing requirements.

D. Mandatory vs Discretionary Termination of Listing and Suspension of Trading

Significantly, all of the Listing Rules arrangements examined before provide for discretionary rather than mandatory delisting of securities in the issuer's insolvency. With the exception of Italy, where the Listing Rules include special provisions for both the suspension and the termination of the listing in relevant scenarios,[38] the focus is always on the ultimate revocation of the listing, not on suspension as an interim measure (which can always be imposed on the basis of more general powers, however). Neither of the examined jurisdictions thus provide for a multi-tiered system of graduated responses to financial irregularities, where specific measures (first a suspension of trading, followed by the revocation of listing) are triggered by specific circumstances (eg, the filing of an application for the commencement of insolvency proceedings, the adoption of safeguards in the commencement stage, the formal opening of such proceedings by the court, the appointment of a liquidator or administrator, etc).

IV. Context is Everything: The Case for Special Regulation

A. General Observations

Delisting in the issuer's insolvency – is there a case for special regulation? On the basis of both the economic perspective and the empirical survey, the answer cannot be formulated in the abstract, but will depend entirely on the broader regulatory context.

On the basis of the empirical survey of selected jurisdictions above, it may be tempting to identify two possible strategies: First, securities law or regulation could follow the lead of the applicable insolvency framework, and accept securities for trading unless and until they are cancelled in the insolvency procedure. Under this approach, the listing of securities would remain unaffected both by the application for and the formal initiation of insolvency proceedings (including, again, pre-insolvency reorganisation proceedings). Concerns about investor protection in view of the speculative nature of

[38] See Art 2.5.1 of Borsa Italiana's listing rules (n 37).

trading in distressed assets could be mitigated through enhanced disclosure requirements. Second and alternatively, the regulatory treatment with regard to the listing decision could follow considerations separate from the legal treatment of the relevant securities under the applicable insolvency law and induce suspension and/or termination irrespective of whether the relevant securities continue to exist.

On closer inspection, however, this categorisation turns out to be misleading. In fact, the choice is not between the termination or preservation of the listing as such, but rather one of the right timing. Even trading venues with less restrictive listing requirements will not uphold a listing indefinitely, but terminate it once trading in the relevant securities has ended.[39] In traditional insolvency procedures, this will occur, at the latest, when shares issued by an insolvent entity have been cancelled in the liquidation process. Whether suspension and/or termination of trading should occur at an earlier stage (eg, upon the filing of an insolvency petition or on the issuer's initiative to enter into formal restructuring procedures) or at a later stage (eg, upon the formal commencement of insolvency procedures) remains a matter of regulatory policy in all circumstances. The real choice in this respect is not between what could be characterised as "autonomous" concepts based exclusively on policy objectives set in securities regulation, where the fate of the listing is decided independently from the applicable insolvency treatment of the relevant securities (with concerns about market liquidity and investor protection as key determinants), on the one hand and 'heteronomous' concepts, where the delisting decision is fully contingent on insolvency law (and securities are traded until they are cancelled). Rather, it is always between different equally legitimate approaches to balance different regulatory objectives, namely (a) the preservation of market liquidity and (b) the protection of (retail) investors. As noted previously, what could be described as a 'hold-out' policy, i.e., the preservation of the listing until the ultimate legal fate of the relevant securities is settled by cancellation, may be perfectly consistent with the general policy framework established in some trading venues, particularly if coupled with enhanced disclosure obligations to protect current and prospective investors. Yet it may be inconsistent with regulatory frameworks seeking to restrict market access to a selected group of solid issuers subject to high entry and ongoing regulatory requirements.

B. Implications for EU Securities Regulation

Against the backdrop sketched out above, the broader regulatory context evidently matters also with regard to the implications of the foregoing in the context of EU securities regulation. Specifically, the distinctive segregation of market segments established by MiFID II is of fundamental relevance also in this respect. Given the strategy to establish 'regulated markets' as highly regulated market segments with high levels of investor protection,[40] it is rather obvious that a permissive stance with regard to the preservation of the listing of securities of issuers in financial problems

[39] See also Macey, O'Hara and Pompilio (n 6) 686 (suggesting that trading venues would usually terminate listing if they do no longer make profits in view of fading trading frequency).

[40] See n 21 and accompanying text.

would not be acceptable in this environment. Put simply, the very concept of 'regulated markets' would be inconsistent with the trading of distressed equity or distressed debt, or else the relevant trading venues would lose their appeal as highly regulated and, therefore, comparatively safe trading platforms designed to appeal to, and attract, professional and retail investors alike. For other, less restrictively regulated trading venues (ie, MTFs or OTFs),[41] by contrast, the case for restrictive, harmonised delisting regimes requiring the mandatory revocation of listings in insolvency scenarios simply does not exist.

These considerations are fully consistent with the current state of EU regulation as far as MTFs and OTFs are concerned, for which EU law does not prescribe either listing requirements or, indeed, specific delisting measures, and where trading venues are free to set and implement the relevant policies. Relevant scenarios, ranging from extraordinary financial losses through the filing of an insolvency application and the commencement of formal insolvency proceedings, arguably would all be subject to the ad hoc disclosure obligation under Article 17 of the 2014 Market Abuse Regulation,[42] so that investors can be said to be adequately protected through disclosure.

As noted before, however, the absence of a harmonised framework for the suspension and/or termination of the listing of securities in the issuer's insolvency seems more difficult to explain for 'regulated markets'. If ongoing trading of distressed equity or debt instruments is inconsistent with the very concept, there is a strong case both for a suspension of trading as an interim measure and for the revocation of the listing at least upon the commencement of formal insolvency proceedings. To be sure, the absence of bespoke regulation does not imply that relevant scenarios cannot be adequately addressed under the powers for competent authorities and market operators in Articles 69(2) and 52(1) of MiFID II. Indeed, as mentioned before, in jurisdictions without bespoke powers for either supervisory authorities or market operators, it is perfectly conceivable that suspensions or terminations may be based on more general powers facilitating such measures to protect investors and/or the orderly functioning of the market.[43] While authorities and/or market operators may have sufficient powers to respond adequately and effectively within the general frameworks transposing Articles 69(2) and 52(1) of MiFID II; however, it is worth recalling that the specific circumstances that might trigger such measures are not harmonised at all and that, moreover, both competent authorities and market operators retain a margin of discretion that is hardly limited in this respect. Given the incentive structure of market operators diagnosed above,[44] it seems at least possible that similar scenarios – again: the filing of an application, the adoption of safeguards in the commencement stage, the formal opening of insolvency proceedings, the appointment of a liquidator or administrator, etc. – might be treated rather differently across Member States, which would conflict with the overall objective to ensure a 'level playing field' through equal

[41] See above n 24 and accompanying text.
[42] Regulation (EU) No 596/2014 on market abuse (…) [2014] OJ L173/1.
[43] See, eg, K Çavuşoğlu, Questionnaire Germany Q 24; A Kouloridas, Questionnaire Greece Q 32; A Recalde and M Ataun, Questionnaire Spain Q 32.
[44] See II.A. above.

treatment of investors across all 'regulated markets' within the EU. To be sure, there is some empirical evidence as to the number of mandatory delistings based on the issuer's insolvency in some jurisdictions.[45] Yet both the legal (statutory and/or regulatory) basis and, indeed, the policy approaches taken by authorities and market operators arguably are far too opaque as to provide legal certainty and predictability of economic outcomes in this regard. If that assumption holds true and if similar cases were indeed treated differently across Member States, the case for harmonising EU legislation would be considerable. Such regulation could (and perhaps should) then define specific criteria triggering the suspension and, ultimately, the termination of listings in 'regulated markets' that are tied to specific steps of financial difficulties and procedural stages of formal insolvency procedures.

That said, the technical design of harmonising rules certainly would require a far more detailed assessment of established policies and practices in all relevant markets than could be carried out within the limits of the present chapter. In this context, residual differences between individual insolvency proceedings are likely to require a substantial degree of flexibility as far as the definition of the triggers for suspension and termination are concerned. Moreover, the delisting process would have to be reconciled with existing insolvency procedures as far as the role of courts and insolvency officials are concerned. Both aspects are likely to require a functional approach to the definition of triggers that fully reflects, and is consistent with, the normative frameworks established in Member States.

V. Conclusion

The key findings developed above can be summarised as follows. The intuitive notion that the commencement of insolvency or formal restructuring proceedings in relation to an issuer of listed (equity or debt) instruments should always trigger an automatic delisting may appear persuasive, but is overly simplistic – particularly with regard to restructuring proceedings. Instead, the delisting decision should reflect, and address, a complex set of (conflicting) interests, namely (a) the financial interests of the trading venue, (b) concerns about the preservation of market liquidity, and (c) the interest of current and prospective investors in view of the risks associated with the ongoing trading in distressed assets. Significantly, both within and outside the EU, there is currently no established standard of bespoke, insolvency-related regulations addressing delisting of, or suspension of trading in, securities following the insolvency of the issuer. While this can be perfectly acceptable for trading venues with less restrictive listing requirements, inaction in the event of an issuer's insolvency is inconsistent with restrictive markets with high standards of investor protection, such as 'regulated markets' as defined by EU securities regulation. While the absence of harmonisation can be explained on the grounds that obligatory delisting can usually be accomplished on the grounds of

[45] See n 11 above and accompanying text.

general listing requirements for regulated markets, the incentive structure of market operators and the wide margin of discretion granted to trading venues and competent authorities may well trigger substantial differences in the economic outcomes of similar scenarios across 'regulated markets' within the Member States. Subject to further comparative research into established policies and practices, this could well justify harmonising regulation to facilitate a 'level playing field' in this regard.

10

Perspectives of the Banks: Delisting Financing and Servicing

IOANNIS E LINARITIS*

I. Introduction: Banks v Capital Markets Financing

Financing through the equity and debt capital markets has been traditionally considered as the opposite of and alternative to conventional bank financing.[1] As firms are actively seeking to implement an optimal capital structure and most efficient liability management, they are often looking at the potential significant benefits which the listing of their equity or debt securities in regulated markets could generate for them and their stakeholders.[2] In Europe as well, progressively, successful companies substituted part of their bank-borrowed funds, with new financing obtained through the issuance of common or preferred shares, or corporate bonds, purported to be listed on the stock exchanges. This led not only to a restructuring of their balance sheet but, effectively, to a decrease in the significance of the banking sector, as a whole, in the modern financial world. Capital markets, including less-regulated trading venues, along with 'shadow banking' actors, claimed an important stake in corporate funding.[3]

* Assistant Professor, Democritus University of Thrace, Faculty of Law. Member of the Associated Researchers Group, European Banking Institute eV, Attorney-at-law, MBA (International Banking & Finance). For valuable comments and constructive discussion on the subject matter, the author would like to thank Mrs. Maria-Eleftheria Tiliakou, Attorney-at-law, MSc in Law and Finance (Oxon).

[1] F Allen, 'Stock Markets and Resource Allocation' in C Mayer and X Vives (eds), *Capital Markets and Financial Intermediation* (Cambridge, Cambridge University Press, 1993) 81; H Leland and D Pyle, 'Informational Asymmetries, Financial Structure, and Financial Intermediation' (1977) 32 *Journal of Finance* 371; S Myers and N Majluf, 'Corporate Financing and Investment Decisions When Firms Have Information That Investors Do Not Have' (1984) 13 *Journal of Financial Economics* 187; R Levine, 'Bank-based or Market-based Financial Systems: Which is Better?' (2002) 11 *Journal of Financial Intermediation* 398; J Bats and A Houben, 'Bank-based Versus Market-based Financing: Implications for Systemic Risk' (2020) 114 *Journal of Banking & Finance* 105776.

[2] R Brealey, S Myers and F Allen, *Corporate Finance*, 8th edn (Boston, McGraw Hill/Irwin, 2006); P Bolton and X Freixas, 'Equity, Bonds, and Bank Debt: Capital Structure and Financial Market Equilibrium under Asymmetric Information' (2000) 108 *Journal of Political Economy* 324.

[3] On the risks of excessive growth of banking in Europe as well as of substitute shadow banking, see M Pagano, S Langfield, V Acharya, A Boot, M Brunnermeier, C Buch, M Hellwig, A Sapir and I van den Burg, 'Is Europe Overbanked?' (2014) *ESRB: Advisory Scientific Committee Reports 2014/4*. Available at: www.ssrn.

Nevertheless, in the last two decades the widespread phenomenon of European firms delisting their securities has signalled a critical reversal of the aforementioned past trend.[4] Bank financing has regained pace, and this is neither an incidental, nor an unexpected development. In this chapter, we argue that banks play, indeed, a key role in stimulating and enhancing this reversal. The banking sector's 'come-back' is propelled by virtue of its multi-faceted influence, relationships and various complementary financial services offered to the listed entities, their major shareholders and management. This intriguing hypothesis is elaborated in the following sections. Section II portrays the major business activities and ancillary functions of credit institutions, which incentivise, support and facilitate voluntary delisting. Section III focuses on the legal features of bank credit facilities, as well as other financial services agreements. Section IV discusses key legal challenges and risks, originating from the aggressive involvement of banks into corporates' delisting operations. Conflicts of interests due to overlapping mandates and wide diversity of activities, along with concerns about potential risk of market abuse, necessitate the implementation of effective operational and governance safeguards, to ensure compliance with banks' contractual obligations and securities market regulation. Section V concludes by summarising the key contributions of the discussion and offering insights into potential future developments in the subject matter of this chapter.

II. Banks Business Activities and Statutory Functions in the Realm of Voluntary Delisting

Credit institutions form the most integral part of the international financial system and are subject to an extensive regulation and sophisticated licensing and supervisory regime. According to the applicable EU legislation, banks are authorised not only to accept deposits and grant all types of credits and loans to their corporate, SME, retail and individual market segments, but also to provide investment services, payment services and a complete spectrum of ancillary facilities to their diverse clientele.[5] Provision of relevant services typically takes place in the context of long-established bank-customer

com/abstract=3723325, T Adrian and An Ashcraft, 'Shadow Banking: A Review of the Literature' (2012) *FRB of New York Staff Report No 580*. Available at: www.ssrn.com/abstract=2175144, respectively.

[4] On the earliest evidenced waves of leveraged public to private transactions in the US and the UK, highlighting the comparative differences in the nature and extent of their debt financing, see indicatively M Jensen, 'The Eclipse of the Public Corporation' (1989) *Harvard Business Review*. Available at: https://hbr.org/1989/09/eclipse-of-the-public-corporation; considering going-private transactions along with takeovers, corporate breakups, divisional spin-offs and leveraged buyouts, as the most visible manifestations of a massive organisational change in the economy, M Wright, T Simons and L Renneboog, 'Why Do Public Firms Go Private in the UK?' (2007) 13 *Journal of Corporate Finance* 591.

[5] See Regulation (EU) 575/2013 on prudential requirements for credit institutions [2013] OJ L176/1; Directive 2013/36/EU on access to the activity of credit institutions and the prudential supervision of credit institutions [2013] OJ L176/338; and, indicatively, C Gortsos, *European Central Banking Law, The Role of the European Central Bank and National Central Banks under European Law*, Palgrave Macmillan Studies in Banking and Financial Institution Series (Cham, Palgrave Macmillan, 2020) 185, 194, 249; M Haentjens and P de Gioia Carabellese, *European Banking and Financial Law*, 2nd edn (Abingdon/New York, Routledge, 2020).

relationships, characterised by increased trust, access to valuable customer information and confidentiality.[6] Given their cornerstone role to the economy and applicable regulatory requirements, banks are recognised as highly trusted organisations, in the course of international public policy making. In that context, they are often assigned, by virtue of law, additional functions in the implementation of significant capital market transactions.[7]

Banks prove valuable also in the realm of voluntary delisting, ie, the form of delisting which is based on a decision of the listed company (as opposed to involuntary delisting, which is typically due to the failure on the part of a company to meet listing requirements). Most often, due to the legal requirements outlined in earlier chapters of this book, the feasibility of voluntary delisting is closely associated with the acquisition of shares of the minority, institutional or retail investors, either by the listed company itself, or by majority shareholder(s). Notably, according to the empirical evidence and the insights of bank industry professionals, such acquisition is rarely attempted through the use solely of equity capital. Instead, a close evaluation of specific instances of voluntary delistings reveal that the set-up of the process bears similarities with corporate takeovers and leveraged buy-out transactions, targeting a listed company.[8] Typically, such transactions are carried out by the dominant controlling shareholder(s) or a third-party acquiror, who rely heavily or exclusively on bank financing, rather than their own funds.[9] Indeed, banks' involvement in acquisition funding is often perceived by the markets as a positive signal regarding the entire project's profitability; this is related to the banks being widely regarded as financial intermediaries with superior information and evaluation capabilities, allowing them to identify bad

[6] See, indicatively, K Hopt, *Der Kapitalanlegerschutz im Recht der Banken* (München, CH Beck, 1975) 465; J Zerey, *Rechtliche Probleme der Finanzierung von Leveraged Buy-Outs und Tender Offers durch Banken in den USA und in der Bundesrepublik Deutschland* (Frankfurt am Main, Peter Lang 1994) 212. On the established common law jurisprudence that banks have a fiduciary duty not to divulge information which their clients have entrusted under an even implied condition that the information remain confidential, see J Clemente, 'Corporations: Conflicting Bank Duties in Tender Offer Financing' (1980) 10 *Seton Hall Law Review* 794, 797.

[7] See III.B.i. below.

[8] See A Cahn and D Donald, *Comparative Company Law*, 2nd edn (Cambridge, Cambridge University Press, 2018) 980; Zerey, *Rechtliche Probleme der Finanzierung* (n 6); A Kouloridas, *The Law and Economics of Takeovers: An Acquirer's Perspective* (Portland, Hart Publishing, 2008) 18; S Betton, BE Eckbo, K Thorburn, 'Corporate Takeovers' in BE Eckbo (ed), *Handbook of Empirical Corporate Finance, Volume 2* (Amsterdam, Elsevier/North-Holland, 2008) 297.

[9] See C Weir and M Wright, 'Governance and Takeovers: Are Public-to-private Transactions Different from Traditional Acquisitions of Listed Corporations?' (2006) 36 *Accounting and Business Research* 289; Y Amihud, B Lev and N Travlos, 'Corporate Control and the Choice of Investment Financing: The Case of Corporate Acquisitions' (1990) 45 *Journal of Finance* 603; M Goergen, J Frechnall-Hughes, 'Mix and Match Facilities and Loan Notes in Acquisitions' in G Gregoriou and L Renneboog (eds), *International Mergers and Acquisitions Activity since 1990: Recent Research and Quantitative Analysis* (Amsterdam, Elsevier, 2007) 135; M Faccio and R Masulis, 'The Choice of Payment Method in European Mergers and Acquisitions' (2005) 60 *Journal of Finance* 1345. According to V Vladimirov ('Financing Bidders in Takeover Contests' (2015) 117 *Journal of Financial Economics* 534) acquirers tend to finance their cash bids with equity only if they lack access to competitive bank financing (yet this leads to underbidding and lower takeover premiums), while acquirers with access to competitive bank financing use debt and overbid. On the positive relationship between investments in intangible assets and firms' decision to delist, which is accentuated by the availability of alternative sources of financing, see H Agyei-Boapeah, Y Wang, A Tunyi, M Machokoto, F Zhang, 'Intangible Investments and Voluntary Delisting: Mass Exodus of Chinese Firms from US Stock Exchanges' (2019) 27 *International Journal of Accounting & Information Management* 224.

acquisitions and fund only deals with a positive net present value.[10] Nevertheless, relevant credit support is granted in consideration of the respective interest payment costs, obligations, and securities provided. It is also envisaged to be secured ultimately by means of the listed (target') company's assets, rights and cash flows, after the delisting is completed.

In other words, banks get involved in voluntary delistings as principal financiers, serving the fundamental need to fund externally, in whole or in part, the takeover, buy-out, or buy-back bids addressed to the minority shareholders of the listed company.[11] Similarly, additional financing may be needed for the implementation of freeze-outs, cash-mergers or other corporate transformations resulting in the extinction of the listed shares of the minority,[12] as well as following the exercise of potential exit, or 'sell out' or appraisal rights of the latter. As elaborated in earlier chapters and the following section, those rights may be established by virtue of applicable company or capital markets law rules, in favour of the minority shareholders of the listed company which seeks voluntary delisting.[13]

During the previous years of historically low interest rates (2009–2022), banks marketed aggressively their credit products and services to their corporate clientele. As expected, they targeted the sub-group of listed companies and equity securities, characterised by limited free-float, market illiquidity, low analyst coverage, free cash flows and restricted growth opportunities,[14] along with dominant (controlling)

[10] In essence, the market may interpret the news about bank debt financing as a certification that a takeover will be profitable. See M Martynova and L Renneboog, 'What Determines the Financing Decision in Corporate Takeovers: Cost of Capital, Agency Problems, or the Means of Payment?' (2009) 15 *Journal of Corporate Finance* 290, 301; Leland and Pyle, 'Informational Asymmetries' (n 1); D Diamond, 'Financial Intermediation and Delegated Monitoring' (1984) 51 *Review of Economic Studies* 393; A Bharadwaj and A Shivdasani, 'Valuation Effects of Bank Financing in Acquisitions' (2003) 67 *Journal of Financial Economics* 113; S Lummer and J McConnell, 'Further Evidence on the Bank Lending Process and the Capital-Market Response to Bank Loan Agreements' (1989) 25 *Journal of Financial Economics* 99.

[11] See Zerey, *Rechtliche Probleme der Finanzierung* (n 6); T Papadopoulos, *EU Law and the Harmonization of Takeovers in the Internal Market* (Alphen aan den Rijn, Kluwer Law International, 2010); A Viandier, *OPA – OPE et autres offres publiques*, 4th edn (Paris, Lefebvre Dalloz, 2010). On the bank debt being utilised most for the majority (81%) of leveraged buyouts' non-equity financing, see U Axelson, T Jenkinson, M Weisbach and P Stromberg, 'Leverage and Pricing in Buyouts: An Empirical Analysis' (2007) *Swedish Institute for Financial Research Conference on The Economics of the Private Equity Market*. Available at: dx.doi.org/10.2139/ssrn.1027127. In the rarer case of corporate bonds buy-back and their subsequent delisting, banks are also usually employed to finance the respective issuer's bid addressed to its bondholders.

[12] See E Bajo, M Barbi, M Bigelli and D Hillier, 'The Role of Institutional Investors in Public-to-Private Transactions' (2013) *ECGI – Finance Working Paper No 350*. Available at: www.ssrn.com/abstract=2221420 ('in continental Europe, a tender offer accompanied by a freeze-out of minority shareholders is the modus operandi of bidders who wish to take a firm private'); L Bebchuk and M Kahan, 'Adverse Selection and Gains to Controllers in Corporate Freezeouts' in R Morck (ed), *Concentrated Corporate Ownership* (Chicago, University of Chicago Press, 2000) 247; H DeAngelo, L DeAngelo, and EM Rice, 'Going Private: Minority Freezeouts and Stockholder Wealth' (1984) 27 *Journal of Law and Economics* 367.

[13] Including those who had not accepted an earlier takeover bid, or expressly dissented, or been absent, during the relevant shareholders' general meeting resolving upon the delisting. On the different available routes to delisting and the established rights of the minority shareholders, see, analytically, III.A.ii. below.

[14] On the main financial drivers and reasons for voluntary delisting see, indicatively, K Lehn and A Poulsen, 'Free Cash Flow and Stockholder Gains in Going Private Transactions' (1989) 44 *The Journal of Finance* 771; D Magni, O Morresi, A Pezzi and D Graziano, 'Defining the Relationship Between Firm's Performance and Delisting: Empirical Evidence of Going Private in Europe' (2022) 13 *Journal of the Knowledge Economy* 2584; H Aslan and P Kumar, 'Lemons or Cherries? Growth Opportunities and Market Temptations in Going Public and Private' (2011) 46 *Journal of Financial and Quantitative Analysis* 489; I Martinez, S Serve and C Djama,

shareholders of such companies,[15] or other prospective owners, including private equity investors. Banks' argumentation has emphasized the high direct and indirect costs associated with the listing of securities listing, include ongoing financial obligations to the Exchanges, compliance with burdensome market regulations, extensive disclosure requirements and corporate governance rules. These downsides were accentuated by the fact that, due to the prevailing market conditions at that time, the anticipated benefits of listing seemingly remained unfulfilled.[16] In effect, banks first acted in the background as unofficial advisors, compiling strong cases for the listed companies to leave their particular regulated market. At the same time, they proactively presented the opportunity of their credit facilities' offering, aimed at financing the significant upfront cost of the delisting process. Whether such banking activities may be judged as complementary, cross-selling services, or an unethical conspiracy against the institutionalised capital markets, their expected outcome has been the increased demand for bank delisting financing.

In parallel, banks have engaged in auxiliary roles to further facilitate delistings. Their corporate finance services include guidance on the incorporation and capitalization of new entities (SPVs, 'shell corporations') which are set up to act as prospective acquirors in the context of tender offers (submitted by one or more financed parties, acting in concert).[17] Particularly in the context of takeover bids, according to the applicable capital market rules, credit institutions and authorised investment firms are appointed to assist as consultants or advisors, in the compilation of the analytical offer document, or prospectus, and relevant documentation and materials addressed to the investors of the target company;[18] in some cases, the financial capacity, meaning the

'Reasons for Delisting and Consequences: A Literature Review and Research Agenda' (2015). Available at: dx.doi.org/10.2139/ssrn.2591449; E Kashefi Pour and M Lasfer, 'Why Do Companies Delist Voluntarily from the Stock Market?' (2013) 37 *Journal of Banking & Finance* 4850.

[15] See L Enriques, 'European Takeover Law: Designing a Neutral Approach' in S Grundmann, B Haar, H Merkt, P Mülbert, M Wellenhofer, H Baum, J von Hein, T von Hippel, K Pistor, M Roth and H Schweitzer (eds), *Festschrift für Klaus J. Hopt zum 70. Geburtstag am 24. August 2010* (Berlin/New York, De Gruyter, 2010) 1789, observing that 'tender offers launched by the shareholders already controlling the company are normally with a view to delisting it', and characterizing them as 'functionally equivalent to self-dealing transactions. On the particular fact that controlling shareholders possess private information on a listed company's future profitability, which gives them advantage with respect to other investors, that can be used to take the company private at the most favorable time (before good performance, when the market price of minority shares does not incorporate this future improvement), along with an empirical challenge of the relevant hypothesis, see E Croci and A Del Giudice, 'Delistings, Controlling Shareholders, and Firm Performance in Europe' (2014) 20 *European Financial Management* 374; Bebchuk and Kahan, 'Adverse Selection' (n 12).

[16] See also Pour and Lasfer, 'Why Do Companies Delist?' (n 14); S Thomsen and F Vinten, 'Delistings in Europe and the Costs of Governance' (2007) *Department of Economics. Copenhagen Business School. Working paper 12-06.* Available at: www.ssrn.com/abstract=986603.

[17] See H-D Assmann, '§ 2 WpHG' in H-D Assmann, U Schneider, P Mülbert (eds), *Wertpapierhandelsrecht*, 8th edn (Köln, Otto Schmidt, 2023) no 190; G Lekkas, 'L'harmonisation du droit des offres publiques et la protection de l' investisseur – Etude comparée des règles en vigueur en France, au Royaume Uni et aux Etats Unis d' Amerique' (2002) 54 *Revue Internationale de Droit Comparé* 885; W Hitschler, 'Leveraged (Management) Buy-Outs, Bestimmungsfaktoren, Finanzierung und rechtliche Gestaltungsmöglichkeiten in der Bundesrepublik Deutschland' (1881) 45 *Betriebs Berater*; V Tountopoulos, 'Anlegerschutz bei unterlassenem Pflichtangebot nach europäischem Kapitalmarktrecht' (2014) 68 *Wertpapiermitteilungen* 337; G Psaroudakis, 'Acting In Concert' in *börsennotierten Gesellschaften: Eine rechtsvergleichende Untersuchung im europäischen und US-amerikanischen Kapitalmarktrecht einschließlich rechtsökonomischer, kartell- und beweisrechtlicher Aspekte* (Köln, Carl Heymanns Verlag, 2009).

[18] See III.B.i. below.

availability and adequacy of the bidder's funds, must be verified and certified by an authorised bank, as a mandatory step in the relevant takeover bid documentation.[19] Eventually, financing banks may participate in the delisting project management and closely follow the process and related corporate transformations.

III. Credit and Financial Services Agreements

A. Credit Agreements

Delisting financing is typically implemented through structured credit legal agreements. These are designed to address all uncertainties and potential contingencies of the envisaged process, while governing the contractual relationship of the credit institution with the borrower. The latter may be the listed company itself, but most often it is its major shareholder(s) and/or any special purpose vehicle (SPV) company established for the purpose of acquisition of listed securities. The relevant documentation typically includes additional contractual arrangements, to effectively secure the credit receivables and rights of the financing bank(s) until repayment.

(i) Purpose of the Credit

Credit institutions' credit committees and officers primarily consider that the purpose (objective) of the delisting financing falls outside typical managerial acts in a listed company. In contrast, credit is to be used to fund the acquisition of company securities, either by the listed company itself, or, most often, by its largest shareholder(s), or a different entity.[20] In that sense, the completion of the delisting will largely depend on the company stakeholders' evolving arrangements, and on the ultimate outcome of the potential tender offer to be addressed to the regulated market's investors, minority shareholders (or bondholders) of the listed entity.

In detail, the credit made available to the company will serve to settle the payment of purchase price to shareholders (or bondholders) who will tender their securities, or be squeezed out by the offeror, or may exercise their 'sell-out right', after the conclusion of the tender offer.[21] Notably, bidders are, in principle, not permitted to make tender or takeover offers conditional upon financing becoming available.[22] As a general observation, delisting finance differs materially from the conventional company financing, used to fund a company's working capital or investment expenditure. It instead presents

[19] See III.B.i. below and in 68.

[20] On the distinction between strategic bidders (usually companies active in a related type of business, such as competitors, suppliers, or customers) and financial bidders (typically private equity firms, looking for undervalued targets with a potential to generate high cash flow, often after a reorganisation, and subsequent sale once exit opportunities become sufficiently appealing), and discussion of empirical evidence regarding contrasting bid valuations, see A Gorbenko and A Malenko, 'Strategic and Financial Bidders in Takeover Auctions' (2014) 69 *Journal of Finance* 2513.

[21] On each relevant corporate act and related EU law provisions, see more analytically III.A.ii. below.

[22] See Kouloridas, *The Law and Economics of Takeovers* (n 8) 251.

notable similarities with other structured finance deals, such as project finance. From the bankers' perspective, what makes these credit deals attractive is that the underlying project, which in our case is the target (listed) corporate entity's business, most often presents sound financial capacity, liquidity and credible prospects for profitability. In view of the above, it is observed that the credit risk of the financing bank may be mitigated significantly, but only insofar as it manages to obtain security over or effective ultimate recourse to the assets of the target company.

(ii) Corporate Actions and Financing Scenarios

Nevertheless, contrary to project finance, the evolution of most voluntary delisting projects remains inherently uncertain, contingent upon the market developments and investors' ultimate decisions. As a result, the relevant credit assessment and legal agreements are necessarily more complex, as they are structured based on, and provide for, several possible scenarios, alternative borrowing terms and security packages.

(a) Financing Terms and Conditions in the Case of Successful Delisting

In the first (base') scenario, the bank-funded acquisition offer would be eventually accepted by the targeted shareholders of the listed company or at least by an adequate number of them, enabling the bidding entity to successfully acquire the desired predetermined shareholding. The probability of such a successful bid may be increased where the bidder has already secured binding commitments from significant minority shareholders.[23] Successful acquisition would allow the bidding entity to initiate and complete soon after, directly or indirectly, the desired delisting.

Alternative Corporate Actions Towards Delisting

The first method of delisting involves the acquisition of an increased shareholding which may suffice, in the first place, to allow the company and its shareholders to directly procure and adopt a valid shareholders' general meeting (and/or board of directors') resolution for delisting its securities. According to the second method, the acquired shareholding may allow for the dominant shareholder, first, to effect a squeeze-out of all remaining minority shareholdings, and subsequently, as the sole shareholder of the listed company, swiftly resolve to delist its securities.[24] As a third indirect option, if the acquired shareholding meets the required quorum and voting majority, the major

[23] See B Bachofer, *'Irrevocable Undertakings' – unwiderrufliche Andienungsverpflichtungen im Rahmen öffentlicher Übernahmen* (Berlin, Duncker & Humblot, 2016); M Wright, C Weir and A Burrows, 'Irrevocable Commitments, Going Private and Private Equity' (2007) 13 *European Financial Management* 757; Bajo, Barbi, Bigelli and Hillier, 'The Role of Institutional Investors' (n 12) 18; Kouloridas (n 8) 195.

[24] On the empirical evidence that the majority of voluntary delisting transactions, initiated by the historical controlling shareholders in continental Europe, are implemented following a buyout offer with squeeze-out (BOSO) operation, see also S Serve and I Martinez, 'The Delisting Decision: The Case of Buyout Offers with Squeeze-Out (BOSO)' (2011) 31 *International Review of Law and Economics* 228, concluding also that family controlling shareholders may prefer to take on debt, rather than increase capital to avoid reducing their controlling stake in the firm. On the evident similarities and the interchangeable use of 'squeeze-out' with 'freeze-out' terms, in Europe and the US, comparatively, see M Ventoruzzo, 'Freeze-outs: Transcontinental Analysis and Reform Proposals' (2010) 50 *Virginia Journal of International Law* 842.

shareholder(s) may adopt a valid resolution for a reverse merger of the listed company by means of acquisition (absorption) by the former (major shareholder), assumed to be a non-listed legal entity. That corporate transformation would result in the listed company ceasing to exist, thus practically to its delisting ('cold delisting').[25]

Remarkably, national laws on voluntary delisting vary considerably among different jurisdictions concerning the competent corporate body; where a general shareholders' meeting is the competent body, the quorum and voting majority is required to enact a resolution on delisting; in some cases, national laws require a substantially high voting majority for this purpose.[26] However, EU capital market law provides harmonised rules for the Member States regarding (a) the squeeze-out right, which is granted in favour of the dominant shareholder of a listed company, following a tender offer, and (b) the sell-out right, which is granted in favour of the remaining minority shareholders of a listed company, following a tender offer. More specifically, according to Article 15(2) of Directive 2004/25/EC,[27] Member States must ensure that an offeror is able to require all the holders of the remaining securities to sell him/her those securities at a fair price, either where the offeror holds securities representing not less than 90 per cent of the share capital carrying voting rights (and 90 per cent of the voting rights) in the offeree company,[28] or where, following acceptance of the bid, the offeror has acquired, or has firmly contracted to acquire, securities representing not less than 90 per cent of the offeree company's share capital carrying voting rights (and 90 per cent of the voting rights).[29] Conversely, according to Article 16(1)–(2) of Directive 2004/25/EC, Member

[25] See Tountopoulos, Chapter 1 in this volume; D Zetzsche, 'Going Dark Under German Law – Towards an Efficient Regime for Regular Delisting' (2013) *IFS – Propter Homines Chair Working Paper 3/2013*. Available at: www.ssrn.com/abstract=2387712, referring to the fact that, in the years 2003–2010, cold delisting was the main voluntary delisting strategy used in German capital markets, applied in 196 of 293 transactions; (in Greek) E Perakis, 'The "cold delisting" and its requirements' (2008) 14 *Dikaio Epixeiriseon kai Etairiwn* 487. On the comparable result of corporate freeze-outs, when they are structured as cash merger transactions, where the minority investors are forced to receive cash in exchange for their shares in the listed company being merged with a corporation wholly owned by the controlling shareholder, see Bebchuk and Kahan (n 12) 1 and Art 116 of Directive (EU) 2017/1132, which introduces common rules also for the case that a merger operation is permitted by the laws of a Member State to provide for a cash payment exceeding 10%.

[26] See analytically the complied Questionnaires on Delisting Q4; P Maume, 'The Parting of the Ways – Delisting under German and UK Law' (2015) 16 *European Business Organization Law Review* 255; Kouloridas (n 8) 239. On the substantial adverse costs of delisting to the detriment of the minority investors, see also J Macey, M O'Hara and D Pompilio, 'Down and Out in the Stock Market: The Law and Finance of the Delisting Process' (2005). Available at: www.ssrn.com/abstract=583401; Zetzsche, 'Going Dark Under German Law' (n 23) 5, 14, proposing that regular delisting should require a special minority shareholder resolution, along with an equal treatment obligation for controlling shareholders as an anti-corruption rule, and favouring a relevant self-ordering capacity of stock exchanges (in the examples of Toronto, Hong Kong, Singapore, Johannesburg Stock Exchanges).

[27] Directive 2004/25/EC on takeover bids [2004] OJ L142/12. See S Grundmann, *European Company Law: Organization, Finance and Capital Markets*, Ius communitatis series 1, 2nd edn (Cambridge, Intersentia, 2012) 751; Enriques, 'European Takeover Law '(n 15) 10, 12, 21; P Pohlmann, 'Rechtsschutz der Aktionäre der Zielgesellschaft im Wertpapiererwerbs und Übernahmeverfahren' (2007) 36 *Zeitschrift für Unternehmens und Gesellschaftsrecht* 1.

[28] Member States may set a higher threshold that may not, however, be higher than 95% of the capital carrying voting rights and 95% of the voting rights.

[29] See Papadopoulos, *EU Law and the Harmonization of Takeovers in the Internal Market* (n 11) 114; M Burkart and F Panunzi, 'Mandatory Bids, Squeeze-out, Sell-out and the Dynamics of the Tender Offer Process' in G Ferrarini, K Hopt, J Winter and E Wymmersch (eds), *Reforming Company and Takeover Law in Europe* (Oxford, Oxford University Press, 2004) 753; Serve and Martinez, 'The Delisting Decision' (n 21); J Grant, 'Takeover Regulation and the Balancing of Interests' in J Grant (ed), *European Takeovers:*

States must ensure that, following a bid made to all the holders of the offeree company's securities for all of their securities, the holders of remaining securities can require that the offeror buys their securities from them at a fair price, under the same circumstances as provided for in Article 15(2).[30]

With regard to cold delisting, it is observed first that EU company law provides for harmonised rules of the Member States regarding the implementation of mergers or divisions (demergers). In essence, according to Articles 93(1) and 139(1) of Directive (EU) 2017/1132,[31] Member States are required to adopt legislation ensuring that a merger or a division shall require at least the approval of the general meeting of each of the companies involved in the merger or division, and such approval decision shall require a majority of not less than two-thirds of the votes.[32] The aforementioned Directive has been amended, recently, to further regulate the cross-border corporate transformations within the EU, including cross-border mergers and, for the first time, cross-border divisions of limited liability companies. According to Articles 126 and 160h of Directive (EU) 2017/1132, as amended following the adoption of Directive (EU) 2019/2121,[33] the general meeting of each of the merging companies and/or the company being divided shall decide, by means of a resolution, whether to approve the common draft terms of the cross-border merger or cross-border division, respectively.[34] However, all these EU company law provisions do not regulate further

The Art of Acquisition, 1st edn (London, Euromoney Books, 2005) 48; P Rühland, 'Das übernahmerechtliche Squeeze-out im Regierungsentwurf des Übernahmerichtlinie – Umsetzungsgesetzes' (2006) 9 *Neue Zeitschrift für Gesellschaftsrecht* 401; C Sellmann, 'Ausgleichs- und Verfahrensregelungen des Squeeze-out auf dem Prüfstand des Verfassungsrechts' (2003) 57 *Wertpapiermitteilungen* 1545; C van der Elst and L van den Steen, 'Squeezing and Selling Out: A Patchwork of Rules in Five European Member States' (2007) 4 *European Company Law* 19.

[30] See Papadopoulos (n 11) 115–18; L Enriques, 'The Mandatory Bid Rule and the Sell-out Right in the Takeover Directive: Harmonisation for its Own Sake?' in J Grant (ed), *European Takeovers: The Art of Acquisition*, 1st edn (London, Euromoney Books, 2005) 123; Burkart and Panunzi, 'Mandatory Bids '(n 26); K Hasselbach, 'Das Andienungsrecht von Minderheitsaktionären nach der EU-Übernahmerichtlinie' (2005) 34 *Zeitschrift für Unternehmens- und Gesellschaftsrecht* 387.

[31] Directive (EU) 2017/1132 relating to certain aspects of company law (codification) [2017] OJ L169/46.

[32] See Grundmann, *European Company Law* (n 24) 684, as well as the subsequent provisions of Arts 93 and 139 of the Directive, exemplifying further the majority and quorum requirements and the additional shareholders vote procedures, in cases where there exists more than one class of shares affected by the merger transaction. Limited appraisal rights may be established by Member States for minority shareholders, in case of mergers carried out by a company holding 90% or more of the company being acquired. See, comparatively, A Seretakis, 'Appraisal Rights in the US and the EU' in T Papadopoulos (ed), *Cross-border Mergers: EU Perspectives and National Experiences* (Cham, Springer, 2019) 65; Ventoruzzo, 'Freeze-outs' (n 21); Serve and Martinez (n 21).

[33] Directive (EU) 2019/2121 amending Directive (EU) 2017/1132 as regards cross-border conversions, mergers and divisions [2019] OJ L321/1.

[34] On the cross-border mergers' regime review and discussion of protective measures for the minority shareholders, see T Papadopoulos, 'Reviewing the Implementation of the Cross-border Mergers Directive' in T Papadopoulos (ed), *Cross-border Mergers: EU Perspectives and National Experiences* (Cham, Springer, 2019) 3, 15. According to Arts 126a and 160i of the amended Directive, Member States shall ensure that at least the members of those companies who voted against the approval of the common draft-terms of the cross-border merger or cross-border division, have the right to dispose of their shares for adequate cash compensation, under specific conditions and requirements, provided that as a result of the cross-border merger or division they would acquire shares in the company resulting from the merger or division, which would be governed by the law of a Member State other than that of their company being merged or being divided, respectively. Member States may also provide for other members of the company being involved in cross-border mergers or divisions to have the aforementioned right.

the distinct cases where the company being acquired (absorbed) or divided, in the course of national or cross-border mergers or divisions, had listed its shares in a regulated market (or other trading venue). Thus, national laws and jurisprudence continue to diverge significantly, in respect of the applicable legal requirements of shareholders' quorum and voting majority, and of minority shareholders' rights, to implement relevant corporate transformations resulting in listed companies exiting, indirectly, the regulated capital markets.[35]

Bank Debt 'Push-Down'

From the perspective of the financing bank(s), a critical element of the successful acquisition of the listed company's shares is to render at least one of the three alternative corporate actions legally feasible to implement. In this context, credit legal agreements normally include special terms and conditions to ensure not only that delisting occurs (in one or several stages), but also that (if not from the beginning) then concurrently, or soon after the delisting, the bank receivables are effectively secured by means of recourse to company's own cash flows and encumbrances on its valuable real assets. In practice, where the borrower entity is different from the company, the delisting financing credit agreement includes important positive legal covenants (undertakings) of the borrower. The latter, apart from utilising the credit for the specific purpose of acquisition of the listed company's shares, promises to procure, as soon as possible, detailed resolutions of the competent corporate bodies and legal agreements, both of itself and of the target company, which will achieve the cornerstone bank objective.

Full assumption of relevant bank debt by the target company might take place contractually, by means of a respective legal agreement, between the borrower (bidding entity), the target company and the credit institution.[36] The same outcome can also be achieved through the company law mechanism of merger of the borrower (bidding entity) with the target company, which will result (*uno actu*) to the amalgamation of the total assets and liabilities of the merged entities and cancellation of the shares of the acquired (absorbed) entity.[37] As a result of the implementation of either of such contractual or company arrangements, the financing bank's credit exposure will be effectively 'pushed-down', i.e. directed against a solvent operating company, equipped with significant assets and adequate cash flows to support the repayment of the bank debt. In that sense, ultimately, the respective credit risk of such, typically long-term delisting financing, would justifiably be weighted lower than initially, thus

[35] While in some jurisdictions, the capital market law provisions on voluntary delisting, which are established in favour of minority shareholders (such as required increased quorum or vote, or a compulsory cash offer) apply expressly also in the case of cold delisting (or other hybrid forms of delisting), to avoid those rules' circumvention, this is not always the case. See Tountopoulos (n 25); M Habersack, '"Macrotron" – was bleibt?' (2012) 176 *Zeitschrift für das gesamte Handelsrecht und Wirtschaftsrecht* 463; Zetzsche (n 23) 9, and the analytically complied Questionnaires on Delisting (n 23) Q18.

[36] See M Lutter and HW Wahlers, 'Der Buy-Out: Amerikanische Fälle und die Regeln des deutschen Rechts' (1989) 34 *Die Aktiengesellschaft* 3. Yet, on the demanding EU company and capital markets law legal requirements of any such a related party agreement, at least for the burdened target company, see analytically III.A.b.below.

[37] See Art 89 Directive (EU) 2017/1132.

presenting the involved credit institution with the benefit of improved risk-adjusted profitability.[38]

(b) Financing Terms and Conditions in the Case of Unsuccessful Delisting

In the adverse scenario, the acceptance rate of the bank-funded tender offer would prove inadequate for the exercise of any of the three alternative corporate actions described above, so that the legal requirements for delisting would not be met. Given that risk, it is observed that the delisting financing terms should be carefully formulated, to safeguard the bank's interests in the event of such an adverse outcome.

Borrowing Entity Credit Risk

It is obvious that, if the target company is the borrower, the incremental credit risk for the bank appears less significant, because the credit assessment and credit security is made and obtained, in the first place, against an operating company. Yet, even in such a lower-risk scenario, the use of external finance by the borrower to acquire their own shares would have immediate company law implications and activate special regulatory requirements for the target company. As the validity of the relevant bilateral or open-market transactions entered into by the listed entity and their adherence to the mandatory EU capital maintenance rules relies on compliance with such requirements,[39] verifying that those are met is critical to ensure the legality of the related bank funding.

From the creditors' perspective, in the most common case where the borrower is not the target company, the circumstances are materially different and present more difficulties. Here, the financing bank would, of course, request to obtain real security (pledge) over all the borrower's shares in the target company. Ideally, the bank would be interested in making the target company guarantee the debt, or in rendering it, in a different way, jointly liable with the borrowing entity. At the very least, the credit risk related to the delisting financing would be substantially mitigated if the bank obtained adequate encumbrances over the target company's assets, as third-party security for the debt of the bidding entity. Those encumbrances could take the form of collateral, security over real estate assets, or pledges over commercial receivables, bank deposits, investment securities, or any other available target company rights.

Legal Restrictions for the Provision of Target Company's Guarantee and Encumbrances

Nevertheless, EU company law establishes broad preventive rules with regard to listed (and non-listed) companies' financial assistance for the acquisition of their own shares by third parties. According to Article 64 of Directive (EU) 2017/1132, Member States

[38] On the capital requirements of bank credit exposures following their risk-weighting, and their implications, see Art 111 f of Regulation (EU) 575/2013; C Gortsos, *The Single Supervisory Mechanism (SSM) – Legal aspects of the First Pillar of the European Banking Union* (Athens, Nomiki Vivliothiki, 2015) 145; B Sutorova and P Teplý, 'EU Banks' Profitability and Risk Adjustment Decisions under Basel III' (2014) 62 *Ekonomický časopis* 667.

[39] See Directive (EU) 2017/1132, Arts 61–63; Grundmann (n 24) 231.

may permit companies (falling within the scope of the Directive) to, directly or indirectly, advance funds, make loans or provide security, with a view to the acquisition of their shares by a third party; yet such transactions are subject to special conditions and requirements stipulated in the Directive.[40] Clearly, any undertaking or pledge over the target company assets in favour of the financing bank, aiming to secure the obligations of the borrower entity bidding for the company's remaining shares, falls under the ambit of the aforementioned provisions. In essence, the relevant transactions should take place under the responsibility of the administrative or management body of the target company, at fair market conditions. This is particularly important with regard to the interest or guarantee fee payable to the target (listed) company and the security provided to it for any such loans, advances and guarantees. The credit risk standing of the prospective acquiror must have been duly investigated. Notably, the potential acceptance of the company's own shares (whether already owned, or to be acquired by the prospective acquiror) as collateral is not expected to qualify as appropriate (fair) security; it will be treated, both legally and accounting-wise, as an acquisition of the company's own shares.[41]

Furthermore, any such financial assistance transactions must be submitted by the administrative or management body to the shareholders' general meeting of the target company for prior approval. In principle, such approval is to be granted at least by a majority of not less than two-thirds of the votes attaching to the securities or the subscribed capital represented.[42] The administrative or management body must present a written report to the general meeting, indicating: (a) the reasons for the transaction; (b) the interest of the company in entering into such a transaction; (c) the conditions on which the transaction is entered into; (d) the risks involved in the transaction for the liquidity and solvency of the company; and (e) the price at which the third party is to acquire the shares. This report shall be submitted to the companies' register for publication. The aggregate financial assistance granted to third parties shall at no time result in the reduction of the company net assets below the amount specified in Article 56 of Directive (EU) 2017/1132.[43] Additional requirements and formalities are applicable in the examined case, where the financial assistance is

[40] ibid Art 64(2)–(5); E Wymeersch, 'Reforming the Second Company Law Directive' (2006) *Financial Law Institute Working Paper No WP2006-15* 22. Available at: ssrn.com/abstract=957981; N Vervesos, 'Legal Capital in European and Greek Company Law: Its Importance and the Mechanisms for its Protection Embodied in the Principles of Raising and Maintenance of Legal Capital. More Specifically, the Prohibition of Financial Assistance for the Acquisition of Own Shares' in A Antapasis et al (eds), *Honorary Volume for Professor N Rokas* (Athens, Nomiki Vivliothiki, 2012) 132; G Sotiropoulos, *Kredite und Kreditsicherheiten der GmbH zugunsten ihrer Gesellschafter und nahestehender Dritter: eine Studie zu §§ 30, 43a GmbHG* (*Heidelberg v Decker*, 1996); Enriques (n 15) 13, concluding that EU Directive provisions are curbing leveraged buy-out activity, however little; Cahn and Donald, *Comparative Company Law* (n 8) 985, also contrasting with the ex-post remedial model adopted by US federal and state corporate law, which leaves companies free to engage in the forms of leveraged acquisition financing they find most beneficial, while eliminating any resulting damaging by challenging them judicially as breach of directors' fiduciary duties.

[41] ibid Arts 65, 60, 61, 63, 64.

[42] ibid Art 83. Yet, the laws of the Member States may lay down that a simple majority of the votes specified in the first paragraph is sufficient, when at least half the subscribed capital is represented.

[43] ibid Art 60. In the context of relevant calculation, any reduction of the net assets that may have occurred through the acquisition, by the company or on behalf of the company, of its own shares, is also taken into account. Furthermore, the company shall include, among the liabilities in the balance sheet, a reserve, unavailable for distribution, of the amount of the aggregate financial assistance.

extended to the parent company (or to individual members of the administrative or management body of the company).[44] In the context of such 'related-party transactions', Member States must ensure through adequate safeguards that the relevant transaction does not conflict with the target company's best interests.[45] Additional transparency requirements are established by virtue of the amended Article 9c of the Directive 2007/36/EC, on the exercise of certain rights of shareholders in listed companies.[46] In this context, Member States may provide that relevant disclosure is accompanied by a report assessing whether the transaction is fair and reasonable from the perspective of the company and of the shareholders who are not a related party, including minority shareholders.

Substitute Commitments and Covenants of the Borrower to Facilitate Repayment

The above mandatory rules, which impose complex and onerous obligations on the target listed company, make it difficult and unlikely in practice for the company to provide its financial assistance to the bidding company, in the form of guarantee or encumbrances. Under such circumstances, the financing bank is incentivised to analyse closely the financial standing of the target company, along with the prospective borrower, as well as to evaluate the existing and anticipated (in the adverse scenario) future influence of the latter in the former. Depending on the outcome of the above analysis, the financing bank may request and obtain additional effective commitments from the borrower, which are capable, even in the absence of target-company guarantees or encumbrances, to mitigate the credit risk to a tolerable level. Typically, the financing bank will seek assurances that, even if the credit-facilitated delisting exercise fails, the borrower would still be in position to legitimately extract adequate cash proceeds from the target company, within a predetermined period, to repay the delisting credit facility. Such verification is related first to the reasonably expected current and medium-term available liquidity of the target company, in conjunction with the implementation of specific corporate actions of the latter, i.e. mainly augmented profits distributions and extensive reduction of capital of the target company.

In effect, following careful financial and legal due diligence, the financing bank is expected to impose meaningful positive covenants on the borrower, as regards the future exercise of its shareholder voting rights in the target company. Given that delisting financing will result to the increase of borrower (bidding company) proportionate

[44] On the concept and diverse cases of 'parent undertaking', see in detail Directive 2013/34/EU, Art 22 on the annual financial statements, consolidated financial statements and related reports of certain types of undertakings [2013] OJ L182/19.

[45] See Directive (EU) 2017/1132, Art 65. On the significant risks embedded in related party transactions, see from the EU law literature, indicatively, L Enriques, G Hertig, H Kanda, and M Pargendler, 'Related Party Transactions' in R Kraakman, J Armour, P Davies, L Enriques, H Hansmann, G Hertig, K Hopt, H Kanda, M Pargendler, W-G Ringe and E Rock (eds), *The Anatomy of Corporate Law, A Comparative and Functional Approach*, 2nd edn (Oxford, Oxford University Press, 2009) 153; T Katsas, 'Disclosure as a Legal Instrument against Potential Abusive Behaviour in the Case of Related Party Transactions' in V Tountopoulos and R Veil (eds), *Transparency of Stock Corporations in Europe: Rationales, Limitations and Perspectives* (London, Bloomsbury Publishing, 2019) 71.

[46] As amended by Directive (EU) 2017/828 amending Directive 2007/36/EC as regards the encouragement of long-term shareholder engagement [2017] OJ L132/1. On the inherent nature of delisting (it being understood as a majority v minority conflict) as related party transaction, see Zetzsche (n 23) 5.

influence in the target company, the former will commit to ensure that the latter will hold and preserve specific pre-agreed level of cash and cash-equivalent financial instruments (typically sight or short-term bank deposits, money market funds), free of any charge or lien, until the delisting funding facility is repaid. Verification of the relevant liquidity will usually be agreed by appointing company auditors or external auditors to carry out checks on extracts from the target company accounts. Concurrently, the borrower (bidding company) will also undertake to propose to the target company's competent corporate bodies (board of directors, shareholders' general meeting) that they vote in favour of the maximum distributions of profits and capital return from the target company to its shareholders, to facilitate and accelerate the repayment of the delisting financing.

In essence, a parallel due diligence of the target company by the financing bank[47] would be critical to reasonably determine these substitute terms and provisions of the delisting financing, which should apply in the adverse scenario of an unsuccessful delisting process. Those may involve (apart from requirements regarding the target company's financials and borrower's conduct) the prolonged duration of the credit facility, or even step-up credit interest rate.[48] The protracted transfer of liquidity from the target company to the borrower company should take place in conformity with the mandatory provisions of EU company and capital markets law, with regard to legal capital maintenance and listed companies corporate governance. In particular, Article 56 of Directive (EU) 2017/1132 stipulates detailed requirements and thresholds, as regards allowed distributions of company profits to its shareholders.[49] The Directive also establishes thresholds, additional prerequisites and formalities that apply to lawfully enact a reduction of legal capital. More specifically, Article 75 of the Directive (EU) 2017/1132 provides for specific procedures and safeguards to protect the interests of the creditors of the target company, before the released amount of capital is returned proportionally to its shareholders[50] (including the borrower, who aims to use it for the repayment of the bank's credit facility). The reduction of capital requires express shareholder approval, granted at the company's general meeting by a majority of at least two-thirds of the votes attaching to the securities or the subscribed capital represented.[51]

[47] On the challenges and limits of such parallel due diligence exercise, from the market integrity and equal treatment of shareholders' points of view, see IV.B. below.

[48] See below.

[49] It is provided that, except for cases of reductions of subscribed capital, no distribution to shareholders (including, in particular, the payment of dividends and of interest relating to shares) may be made when on the closing date of the last financial year the net assets as set out in the company's annual accounts are or, following such a distribution, would become, lower than the amount of the subscribed capital plus those reserves which may not be distributed under the law or the statutes of the company. Anyway, the amount of a distribution to shareholders may not exceed the amount of the profits at the end of the last financial year plus any profits brought forward and sums drawn from reserves available for this purpose, less any losses brought forward, and sums placed to reserve in accordance with the law or the statutes.

[50] See Grundmann (n 24) 685.

[51] See Arts 73 and 83 Directive (EU) 2017/1132. Yet, the laws of the Member States may lay down that a simple majority of the votes specified in the first paragraph is sufficient, when at least half the subscribed capital is represented.

(iii) Other Terms and Conditions

(a) Interest Rate and Duration

From a legal structuring and contracting perspective, the delisting financing agreements typically take the form of a fixed maturity loan, rather than a revolving credit facility. Applicable credit interest rate may be set as either fixed or floating. Financial literature observes that leveraged buyouts sponsored by private equity firms receive favourable loan terms, both in loan interest rates and covenant structure. This finding underscores the importance of bank relationships, which are strengthened through repeated interactions with professional investors, as their loan transactions are more frequent and larger in scale compared to those of traditional borrowers.[52] These relationships can indeed mitigate inefficiencies from information asymmetry; in practice, the involved banks may progressively gain confidence in these borrowers' due diligence processes and understand more aptly the risk characteristics of the target company.

As mentioned, the duration of the loan is strongly associated with the prospects for its repayment in the adverse scenario where delisting will not ultimately occur and the relevant credit obligation will neither be assumed nor guaranteed by the target company. To accommodate such a possibility, the bank debt may be also divided into several tranches, some of which may be contingently available. Depending on the commercial circumstances, the financing bank may decide to grant an interim, short-term credit facility (commonly called 'bridge finance'),[53] to accelerate the approval and execution of funding of a prospective delisting opportunity. In such a case, the credit documentation will typically include the most important positive and negative covenants of the borrower, adequate interim security arrangements and provisions for the structure of the subsequent, main long-term credit agreement. While some of these conventional credit facilities may be amortising, the majority tend to be structured as interest only, with a final 'bullet' repayment of the principal ('balloon payment').[54]

Depending on the desired amount of delisting financing, its investment appeal and the banking relationships of the bidding and the target companies, it may take the form of a syndicated loan or corporate bond loan.[55] In the latter case, the respective loan

[52] See V Ivashina and A Kovner, 'The Private Equity Advantage: Leveraged Buyout Firms and Relationship Banking' (2011) 24 *Review of Financial Studies* 2462, also referring to the favourable pricing of those loans by banks, to cross-sell other fee business.

[53] On the historical position of commercial banks as dominant providers of bridge or transaction financing for large, cash acquisitions in the US, see Betton, Molson, Eckbo and Thorburn, 'Corporate Takeovers' (n 8) 43.

[54] See Axelson, Jenkinson, Weisbach and Stromberg, 'Leverage and Pricing in Buyouts' (n 11). Such repayment terms normally address the interests of most borrower entities, for deferring the payment of all or significant part of bank debt, until final maturity date, while also providing for optional early-prepayment grounds.

[55] On the leveraged acquisition financing banks usually motivated to structure and price their loans, so that they can be syndicated in the aftermarket, see Ivashina and Kovner, 'The Private Equity Advantage' (n 52) 2474.

receivables and rights of the originating creditor bank(s) are effectively securitised, into corporate bond securities, initially held by the originating bank(s). Securitisation allows for increased transferability of the delisting financing, within the local and international banking community, presenting the opportunity for partial deleveraging of the originating credit institution and, correspondingly, lower capital requirements, throughout the term of the relevant credit facility.[56]

(b) Covenants

Delisting financing agreements typically include additional positive and negative covenants for the borrower entity, which pertains both to its own corporate affairs and those of the target company. More specifically, the borrower is usually asked to rigorously exercise all its available legal rights, including control, monitoring, information and audit, either directly, as a major shareholder, or indirectly, through the appointed members of the board of the target company, to ensure the persistent, sound management of the latter. The credit agreement may also provide for extraordinary circumstances, which are considered material for the increase in the embedded credit risk of the borrower's entity. Depending on the medium-term evolution of significant financial characteristics of the target company (eg, its solvency or leverage ratio, liquidity or debt/cashflow level[57]), the agreement might include ancillary economic terms and rights for the bank creditor(s). These terms could range from a quasi-automatic step-up (increase) in the loan interest rate to the early unilateral termination of the credit facility.

Financing bank(s) may also request to obtain, contractually, early notification, or even approval rights, as regards specific significant commercial transactions or corporate activities of the target company. Notably, relevant bank rights could be served even more effectively if the corresponding financial security agreements provided for a simultaneous pledge of the voting rights of the borrower's shares (in the target company) in favour of the bank. However, such aggressive contractual measures would come with undesirable consequences, especially as regards potential immediate assumption of control of the target company by the financing bank itself, in accordance with the applicable accounting rules. In essence, the assumption of majority voting rights in listed entity would trigger manifold onerous company law, competition law, as well as capital market law obligations and formalities, to be imposed onto the credit institution(s).[58] For this reason, financing bank(s) normally prefer to contractually associate their right to exercise the voting rights of the pledged shares in the target

[56] Bond loan structures also offer complementary advantages and cost efficiencies, in that case of ultimate miscellaneous creditors, since their respective legal rights and interests are to be established, monitored and pursued duly, by the nominated bond loan representative (typically either the originating bank, or the bank with largest credit exposure), acting on behalf of all bondholders (creditors) with a duty of care owed to them.

[57] On the identification of 'maximum debt to EBITDA' as the most significant financial covenant in relevant financing transactions, according to industry participants and evidence, see Ivashina and Kovner (n 52) 2474.

[58] Including, indicatively, potential merger control notification, disclosure of major (indirect) shareholding, mandatory cash tender offer to minority, inclusion of borrower entity accounts in the bank's consolidated financial statements etc.

company, only with the hypothetical future case of unilateral termination of the credit facility, especially in case of borrower's default.

Conversely, the borrower entity is expected to contractually undertake to refrain from the granting of any lien, encumbrance, pledge, financial security, or burden on any of its assets (especially, on its pledged shares in the target company), in favour of any third party other than the financing bank(s), as well as avoiding any additional credit from third parties. In a similar respect, the borrower promises to refrain from amending its corporate objective, from any corporate transformation (other than the potential envisaged merger with the target company), as well as other (prohibited') actions, without the express prior consent of the financing bank(s).

(c) Default and Disclosure

To safeguard the rights of the delisting financiers, credit documentation would provide for several events of default. These typically include default on any repayment obligations of the borrower, as well as material breach of terms and conditions of the credit facility (especially of the covenants exemplified above). Widely identified events of default, such as initiation of insolvency or administration or liquidation proceedings against the borrower, 'cross-default' of the latter in respect of other financial obligations, the material deterioration of the financial condition or business or commercial prospects of the borrower and material litigation against the latter and invalidity or imperfection of any security agreement, are also applicable in the context of the delisting financing agreements. What is more important here is that the financing bank may negotiate and insist that similar circumstances be formulated as events of default, additionally regarding the target company. The rationale behind such a view is that any material deterioration of the latter's financial condition would be expected to result in a radical decrease in the value of the corresponding shareholding of the borrower (being its main asset and fundamental collateral of the credit facility). This would have a severe negative impact on the repayment prospects of the credit facility.

Having explored the contractual framework of the delisting credit facilities, it should be observed that their terms and conditions are confidential in principle. However, in the frequent case that any such facility is utilised to fund a related tender offer, according to Article 6(3)(l) of the Directive 2004/25/EC, the offer document[59] must include information concerning the bid financing, including its sources. It has been suggested, indeed, that details should be provided to the public investors regarding the debt facilities (or other instruments entered into) used to finance that offer (and even, to refinance the existing debt or working capital facilities of the offeree company).[60]

[59] On the bank financial services and involvement in the preparation of that offer document, or prospectus, and their submission to the competent capital market authority, see III.B. below.

[60] See the extensive provision of UK Takeover Code, Art 24.3, referring expressly to information regarding the amount of each facility or instrument, repayment terms, interest rates, including any 'step up' or other variation provided for, any security provided, a summary of the key covenants, names of the principal financing banks, time by which the offeror will be required to refinance the acquisition facilities and of the consequences of its not doing so by that time etc.

B. Financial Services Agreements

Financial services related to a potential delisting opportunity, or an actual delisting operation, often involving a tender offer (takeover bid), subsequent squeeze-out and/or merger, are provided to the interested parties under services agreements.

(i) Identification of Services

The relevant financial agreements outline the services performed by the contracting credit institution, investment firm or other involved financial institutions, which may be engaged separately or jointly. Contractual provisions may refer to a variety of investment banking and consultancy services, such as (a) assistance to the interested entities in considering alternative options available to formulate and structure their bids and acquire minority shareholdings in the target company, (b) examination of potential strategic and financial buyers of the listed entity, (c) structuring a tender offer, especially with regard to target company valuation and pricing of the offer, taking into account the prevailing market conditions, (d) cooperation in the formation of the 'delisting story', to increase the appeal of the offer and address the potential concerns of creditors, or any authority supervising the target company, associated with the prospective delisting and corporate transformation, (e) assistance in the drafting of the investor presentations and offer document (or prospectus) to be submitted to the competent capital markets authority, (f) cooperation in the preparation of the relevant agreements' documentation, and (g) contacts and meetings with institutional investors[61] and other significant minority shareholders' (before and during the execution of a relevant tender offer). It is noted that the tender offer and takeover offer documents fall within the definition of financial promotions; thus, they typically need to be issued or approved by an authorised person, usually the offeror's investment bank or financial adviser (investment firm).[62]

Interestingly, most agreements would expressly exclude the provision of services which could be considered as 'investment advice', as defined in Article 4(1) of the Markets in Financial Instruments Directive (EU) 2014/65 (MiFID II).[63] In essence, a professional investment advice service has been regulated in most jurisdictions, by means of imposing significant tasks and rules of conduct to the authorised financial advice provider and its personnel (investment advisors), while the investment advice should in principle be tailored to the characteristics, risk appetite and needs of its recipient, after their comprehensive assessment.[64] On those grounds, the involved credit

[61] On the significant and active role of institutional investors (having superior financial training, adequate time and bearing fiduciary duties towards own clients) in minority shareholders receiving a higher takeover premium in the context of delisting operations, see Bajo, Barbi, Bigelli and Hillier (n 12).

[62] See Kouloridas (n 8) 74.

[63] Directive 2014/65/EU on markets in financial instruments and amending Directive 2002/92/EC and Directive 2011/61/EU ('MiFID II Directive') [2014] OJ L173/349. 'Investment advice' means the provision of personal recommendations to a client, either upon its request or at the initiative of the investment firm, in respect of one or more transactions relating to financial instruments.

[64] See in particular MiFID II Directive, Arts 24 p 4(a) and 7, 25 regarding the required analytical precontractual information and categorisation of clients, the assessment of suitability and appropriateness and

institutions normally verify and make explicit reference to the professional client status, sophistication and securities markets' experience of their counterparty. In that context, they denote that any advice, if ever provided in the course of the agreed services, is furnished by way of information only, not by way of a recommendation to the bidding entity, the target entity or to any of their shareholders.

Financial services may also be requested, particularly regarding the issuance of a 'fairness opinion', regarding a prospective or pending tender offer to minority shareholders, or a proposed merger or division involving the listed entity, which has the potential to eventually result in the delisting. The engaged bank (or investment firm or auditor) undertakes to perform an objective professional assessment of the value of both the listed target company and the minority shareholdings, and to opine on the fairness of the tender offer price addressed to the latter.[65] The fairness opinion may be requested by the bidding entity, or by the management of the target company, in the context of its statutory and/or fiduciary duties.[66] The relevant valuation is calculated typically with the weighted use of the generally accepted corporate finance valuation methods. These include (mainly) the methods of discounted future cash flows, accounting book value (net assets), comparable transactions, capital market multipliers (P/E, P/BV, EV/EBITDA), and the (pre-offer) stock market price and fluctuation.[67] The inferences of the above methods are to be deduced, by utilising the appointed institution's proficient resources, specialist information, ample financial data, and expertise. The deliverable normally takes the form of a dual report, where its full comprehensive version (addressed solely to the client) includes the economic assumptions applied by the issuer of the report, valuation calculations and results, justification of the weights

reporting to them, R Veil, 'Investment Advisory Services' in R Veil (ed), *European Capital Markets Law*, 3rd edn (Oxford/Portland, Hart Publishing, 2022) 613.

[65] On the valuation exercise fundamentals, see J Coates, '"Fair Value" as a Default Rule of Corporate Law: Minority Discounts in Conflict Transactions' (1999) 147 *University of Pennsylvania Law Review* 1251, focusing on minority discounts and control premiums, in a discussion of Delaware courts' jurisprudence, Bebchuk and Kahan (n 12). According to Directive (EU) 2017/1132 amended provisions, regarding the independent expert report to be furnished to the shareholders during proposed national and cross-border mergers and divisions (Arts 96, 125, 142, 160 f), that report must include the expert's opinion as to whether the cash compensation and the share exchange ratio are adequate. On the apparently limited impact of a fairness opinion on the success of a launched tender offer and possible explanation, see Bajo, Barbi, Bigelli and Hillier (n 12) 18.

[66] On the relevant requirement imposed by the regulated markets, see indicatively Arts 261 ff of the Règlement général de l' Autorité des Marchés Financiers. On the assignment of an independent fairness opinion, as means to fulfil the duty of neutrality and draw up the objective opinion document of the management body of the offeree company facing a takeover bid, as established by virtue of Directive 2004/25/EC, Art 9(2)–(5) see Papadopoulos (n 11) 119; (in Greek) G Papachristou, 'Fairness Opinion – Duty of Faith and Rule of Business Judgment in the Field of Acquisitions and Mergers' (2008) 14 *Dikaio Epixeiriseon kai Etairiwn* 834. On the foundation of US law respective fiduciary duties, see F Easterbrook and D Fischel, 'Proper Role of a Target's Management in Responding to a Tender Offer' (1981) 94 *Harvard Law Review* 1161.

[67] See Brealey, Myers and Allen, *Corporate Finance* (n 2) ch 6. As per the aforementioned provisions of Directive (EU) 2017/1132, related to the report and opinion of the appointed independent expert, when the latter assesses the cash compensation, he shall consider any market price of the shares in the merging companies prior to the announcement of the merger proposal or the value of the companies excluding the effect of the proposed merger, 'as determined *in accordance with generally accepted valuation methods*'. See also Art 9c of amended Directive 2007/36/EC stipulating that the report assessing whether the transaction is fair and reasonable from the perspective of the company and of the shareholders who are not a related party, should '*explain the assumptions it is based upon together with the methods used*'; (in Greek) I Linaritis, 'The Experts' Opinion in Company Mergers and Divisions' (2022) 28 *Episkopisi Emporikou Dikaiou* 1.

attributed to the different valuation methods, minority discount applied, consequential value range for each minority share, as well as the related opinion on the fairness of the proposed acquisition price per share. A shorter summary is also prepared, for public use and reference of all market participants, which may include only the economic assumptions applied, the resulted value range for each minority share, as well as the related opinion of the engaged bank (or other professional entity) on the fairness of the proposed acquisition price.

Moreover, in case the bidding entity is legally required, or commercially incentivised, to submit a financial capacity certification, along with its tender offer for the minority shareholdings, a bank may be required or called upon to provide such a distinct financial service.[68] Under the relevant agreement, the credit institution will undertake to issue the requested document addressed to the competent capital markets authority and/or be relied upon by the market investors. The issuance of such a certificate is made contractually conditional upon the bidder providing evidence of his readily available funds, or irrevocable unconditional equity commitments,[69] otherwise approved debt financing (from the same or different banking institution(s)), for the full amount required to buy out all remaining minority shares of the listed target company. In particular, the equity commitments will be audited by the bank's legal advisors to verify their due authorisation, binding effect, unconditionality, enforceability and effectiveness to establish a direct civil claim of the bidding entity against each of the committing entities (being typically limited partners or shareholders of the bidding entity), regarding their committed funding.

(ii) Remuneration

As remuneration for the bank's range of offered financial services, other than the provision of credit, the engaging entity undertakes to pay commission fees.[70] Such remuneration may be negotiated and structured to include a fixed part (base fee') and/or a variable part. The latter may become payable only upon the closing of the tender offer transaction and be calculated based on the total purchase amount of the shares tendered by the minority and acquired by the bidding entity. Alternatively, the parties may enter into a success fee arrangement. In this context, the bidding entity agrees to

[68] See Art 327b(3) AktG '… the dominant *shareholder must submit to the Managing Board a declaration from an authorised credit institution, through which the latter guarantees the fulfillment of the obligation of the main shareholder to immediately provide the minority shareholders with the specified cash consideration amount for their shares.*'; Art 24.8 of the UK Takeover Code 'When the offer is for cash or includes an element of cash, the offer document must include confirmation by an appropriate third party (eg the offeror's bank or financial adviser) that resources are available to the offeror sufficient to satisfy full acceptance of the offer'; Art 9§4 Greek Law 3461/2006; Zetzsche (n 23) 6; Kouloridas (n 8) 120. On the role of banks as designated depositary of tender offers, see A Fleischer and R Mundheim, 'Corporate Acquisition by Tender Offer' (1967) 115 *University of Pennsylvania Law Review* 317, 337.

[69] On the private equity funds institutional setup, capital calls and use of limited partners commitments as collateral, see E Gourier, L Phalippou and M Westerfield, 'Capital Commitment' (2022) *Netspar Discussion Paper No 06/2014-035*. Available at: ssrn.com/abstract=2490430; Ivashina and Kovner (n 52) 2472.

[70] On the considerable legal and investment banker fees involved with the preparation of necessary takeover documents, identification of target company ('finder's fee'), arrangement fees, underwriting fees and fees to valuation experts, see Kouloridas (n 8) 120.

pay the retained credit institution an incentive fee,[71] either fixed or proportional to the total purchase price amount, in case that a predetermined target acquisition shareholding is accomplished, so that the desired delisting of the target company can proceed successfully. Typically, all expenditures necessary for, or related to, the bank's financial services provision, such as lawyers, accountants, due diligence-related fees, are borne by the engaging entity.

(iii) Liability and Other Additional Terms

Considering the sophistication of the contracting parties, the potential civil liability for acts or omissions by the retained banks during the provision of their financial services is narrowly defined. The engaging entity is responsible for providing the appointed bank with all updated information and material developments relating to itself and the target entity, which are relevant for the performance of the assigned services.[72] Bidder entity (or target entity) assumes responsibility for coordinating and implementing any due diligence investigations, which may prove necessary, so the appointed bank can proceed to the specific professional valuation, fairness opinion or capacity certification services. Banks normally avoid any obligation to advise or opine on any solvency or liquidity issues of the target company.

Similarly, unless expressly stated in the financial services agreement, even if the bank undertakes to assist it will not be obligated to complete the approval process by the competent authority of the potential offer document or prospectus that may need to be prepared in connection with the particular offer and delisting operation. In the same respect, the appointed bank would normally not accept responsibility for the accuracy and completeness of the statements and information included in any such offer document or prospectus; the preparation of the latter is normally assumed by the bidding entity, in cooperation with its legal advisors. The bidder and target entities normally undertake the responsibility for assessing the commercial benefits and implications of their engaged banks' financial services, reports and proposals. This assessment includes an evaluation of the services provided and deliverables also from the perspective of the best interests of their shareholders.

Reports, informative advice or proposals of the involved bank in connection with its engagement are procured confidentially, for the information of the appointing entity, its competent decision-making bodies, senior management and any other involved professional advisors, to help in their consideration of the particular tender offer and delisting transactions. Thus, they are normally not to be disclosed to any third party, or referred to publicly, in the context of the engaging entities' announcements or other communications, unless such disclosure is provided for in the relevant scope of services undertaken, or in the applicable law rules (as is the case for the financial capacity certificate or summary fairness opinion).

[71] See D Barron, 'The Incentive Problem and the Design of Investment Banking Contracts' (1979) 3 *Journal of Banking & Finance* 157.

[72] In essence, the appointed bank will assume the accuracy and completeness of any furnished financial, accounting and other information provided, without necessarily carrying out an independent verification.

The engaging entity would be liable to compensate the appointed bank, in case the former's representations about its legal and financial capacity to proceed to the relevant acquisition or tender offer transaction, prove materially inaccurate or misleading and result in the bank's pecuniary or reputational harm. Correspondingly, the appointed bank is expected to exhibit professional conduct and diligence in the course of its financial services. It should act in good faith with respect to its assignment, in particular any professional assessment and independent opinion to be furnished in the context of a tender offer.[73] In that respect, the appointed bank should, in principle, disclose timely any circumstances or events, which might influence its standpoint, or perception, or its specific services' outcome or content, avoiding any conflict of interests; such highly controversial issue and appropriate internal mechanisms are elaborated in the subsequent Section (IV.A). Obviously, the bank must comply, in performing its tasks, with the provisions of all applicable laws and regulations of any relevant jurisdiction.

Finally, taking into consideration the numerous participants in the financial markets, who may be adversely affected by the desired delisting, the engaging entity is usually asked to indemnify the appointed bank against any losses, claims, damages or liabilities to any third person arising out of, or in connection with, its financial services engagement. Nevertheless, any such contractual indemnification arrangements are to govern the relationship between the parties. Thus, they are not relevant, when examining the potential establishment of a damaged third party's civil claim addressed against the bank directly, based on a particular statutory provision of national securities markets law, or general tortious liability.[74] In the special case of the financial capacity certification service, if the bank, in giving the relevant capacity confirmation, acted responsibly and took all reasonable steps to assure itself that sufficient financial resources were readily available to the offeror (to satisfy an acceptance in whole of their tender offer to the minority of the listed target entity), then it will not be expected to produce the purchase price itself, nor compensate the minority investors, if the offeror eventually fails to fulfil his obligations.[75]

IV. Challenges and Legal Risks

The multifaceted business activities and services provided by the banks, described in the previous sections, which are offered to the bank's international clientele, do raise particular legal challenges and risks. At first sight, the inherent credit risk is notable in the context of any preparatory tender offer or leveraged acquisition finance transaction.

[73] On the relevant liability issues see C Hermann, *Fairness Opinion und Haftung* (Baden-Baden, Nomos Verlag, 2015); T Möllers, 'Verfahren, Pflichten und Haftung, insbesondere der Banken, bei Übernahmeangeboten' (2002) 31 *Zeitschrift für Unternehmens- und Gesellschaftsrecht* 664.

[74] On the liability of banks for negligent misstatements and the potential concurrent liability of banks in tort and contract, even in common law jurisdictions, see C Vaupel, 'Die Haftung der Banken für die Richtigkeit der Angebotsunterlage bei Umtauschangeboten nach dem WpÜG' (2002) 56 *Wertpapiermitteilungen* 1170; J Wadsley and G Penn, *The Law Relating to Domestic Banking*, 2nd edn (London, Sweet and Maxwell, 2000) 135, 176.

[75] See expressly Art 24.8 of UK Takeover Code.

This risk is typically addressed by the involved bank, by means of effective legal documentation and acceptable security, as discussed above, along with efficient processes for the approval, diversification and management (including partial hedging[76]) of relevant credit exposures. In addition, material operational risks arise for the credit institutions, which are set to actively support the various delisting opportunities and operations. This section focuses on the circumstances creating the potential for increased bank organisations and officials' conflicting interests (corporate and personal). These may not only result in substandard bank services but also, possibly, in economic losses for the parties involved in a particular delisting process. Even more importantly, the same grounds may well jeopardise both the integrity and efficiency of financial markets as well as the protection of investors, ie, the twin cornerstone objectives of capital markets legislation.[77]

A. Diverging Roles and Conflicts of Interests

(i) Circumstances of Concern

The root of the question lies in the modern international paradigm of banks as full-service financial institutions. In essence, credit institutions engage simultaneously in lending and financing, advisory, underwriting, principal investing, sales and trading, research and investment management activities, with a variety of clients and counterparties, corporate, retail, governmental, institutional and individual. When a bank is appointed to grant credit or provide financial services to enable a particular delisting opportunity, it is expected to utilise its extensive industry knowledge, transactional expertise and capital markets insights for the benefit of its client. However, the same credit institution may usually be providing concurrently, or seek to provide, similar or other kind of financial services to the appointing client's competitors or investors, who normally have different, and sometimes opposing, investment strategies, interests and objectives.

In more detail, the appointed credit institution may engage in market making, trade execution, clearing, custody, margin lending and other financing activities, by acting either as an agent for buyers and sellers by executing their orders in the market, or as a principal supplying liquidity directly to market participants. During this principal investing activity, the appointed bank may trade and have positions (in its own accounts, or as a custodian for its clients) in the equity, debt, derivatives and/or other financial instruments of the targeted company, or of its appointing client or borrower (if the latter is a listed entity as well). The bank may also engage in brokerage, investment advisory services, personal trust services, wealth advisory services and private banking services, which normally allow for discretion over client assets with respect to

[76] On the use of market- and over the counter- derivatives, including Interest rate swaps, foreign exchange swaps, credit default swaps and synthetic securitisations, as techniques to manage and reduce bank inherent risks, see indicatively Brealey, Myers and Allen (n 2) chs 20, 26.

[77] See indicatively R Veil, 'Concepts and Aims of Capital Markets Regulation' in R Veil (ed), *European Capital Markets Law*, 3rd edn (Oxford/Portland, Hart Publishing, 2022) 24.

the purchase or sale of any financial instrument. For such services, the bank receives brokerage commissions, advisory fees, fiduciary trust fees, lending fees and interest from its clients. From the target company perspective as well, the appointed bank may possess or have the right to exercise (eg, as security for loans granted) voting and other rights associated with the targeted minority shareholdings, on behalf of its clients, or as a principal.

The appointed credit institution may also perform investment research and analysis services addressed to the community of institutional investors. On the public side, the same bank may manage mutual funds, hedge funds, private equity funds, funds of funds and similar accounts, and provide other asset management services and investment advice. Those funds and investment accounts, irrespective of whether they are managed actively or passively, may own the listed target company securities. Investment funds, managed or advised by the bank, may also be a potential seller, or buyer for the target entity minority shareholdings, which are meaningful in the context of a voluntary delisting transaction. Under these roles of manager or advisor, the bank is expected to earn management, advisory and performance-based fees from the investment funds and accounts. Additionally, the bank officials and employees (including, without limitation, the investment banking team appointed to support the delisting financing and/or delisting operation) may have invested in these funds or have agreed to receive earn-out fees, depending on their performance.

Finally, the general credit activity of the banks may result in any of the corporate or individual clients to whom the bank provides loans, acting as potential competitive buyers for the acquisition of the target company-hunted shareholdings. In that sense, the proceeds of some credit facilities, which have been granted to other clients may be used, ultimately, against the successful implementation of the envisaged (either directly financed, or indirectly supported by means of other financial services) delisting.

(ii) Measures

Clearly, each credit or financial services agreement that the involved bank enters into, establishes and imposes distinct commercial and legal obligations, duties and responsibilities on it, owed directly to its counterparty.[78] For instance, in the course of investment portfolio management, where the bank frequently has discretion over client assets, it is required by law and the relevant contract to fulfil a fiduciary responsibility to its clients (professional or individual investors, investment funds etc., as detailed above) in making decisions to purchase, sell, hold or vote, or take any other action with respect to, any financial instrument. Such duties and responsibilities obviously cover the relevant portfolio management actions with respect to the listed securities of the target company as well.

[78] On the duties to bank customers, including depositors, borrowers, trust beneficiaries and other stakeholders, beyond the purely contractual debtor-creditor relationship, in common law jurisdictions see indicatively Clemente, 'Corporations' (n 6) 797, 799; R Patterson, 'The Responsibilities of Banks in Financing Tender Offer Takeovers of Customers' (1981) 48 *The University of Chicago Law Review* 439.

In the past, it was held that a bank is not precluded, by a per se rule, from financing the takeover of a customer, merely because it held confidential information about them. But the more controversial question is whether the bank is allowed to use such internal non-public information of the target entity, to evaluate whether to finance a prospective bidder (or service a relevant delisting project).[79] Nevertheless, in our opinion, the involved bank needs to cautiously address these circumstances and potentially concurring roles, mandates and responsibilities, to be able to respond also to the demands of its engagement in each prospective delisting project. Before it undertakes contractual obligations related to acquisition finance, or to provisionally fund, support, or deliver any sophisticated financial services aimed at the successful accomplishment and execution of any delisting opportunity, the bank should assess whether such a mandate is compatible with the assignments, onto which it has already embarked in relation to the same target company. That important operational risk assessment obviously entails a detailed conflict-of-interest check within the bank, which will seek to reveal any potential contradictory professional tasks. As an example, if the bank had already been appointed by a strategic minority shareholder of the same listed target entity to provide investment advice to contest or avoid an existing or future tender offer, that appointment would be considered incompatible with the financing or supporting a delisting project for the same entity. In the event of such incompatibility, it seems prudent that the bank refrains from the later engagement, to avoid breaching its legal and contractual duties of care and loyalty towards both clients.

To avoid similar undesirable situations, resulting in missed business opportunities and increasing the bank's legal and regulatory risk, the banks may consider applying additional precautionary operational strategies, policies and reorganisation measures. Many have adopted or progressively transformed themselves into a more complex bank group structure, where their investment banking, securities proprietary trading, or private equity funds and other financial markets operations are segregated and/or divided into several different regulated legal entities, outside its core banking business legal entity, normally oriented to offering credit and deposit products and services.[80] Even when such segregation or division is not implemented, the banks may establish and maintain effective information barriers between their investment banking business unit, on the one hand, and their sales and trading and other asset and wealth management business units, on the other. Similar practices ('chinese walls') are often applied even within certain of those business units.

[79] See *American Medicorp, Inc v Continental Ill. Nat'l Bank* [1977] 475 F Supp. 5; *Washington Steel Corp. v TW Corp* [1979] 602 F.2d 594. According to the latter judgment, the bank is allowed to use any information in its files, on the rationale that, otherwise, banks might be forced to go blindly into loan transactions, arguably violating duties to their own depositors, while their discouragement from dealing with companies interested in acquiring interests in another bank customer would impede the free flow of a vitally important money supply.

[80] On the initiatives around relevant structural reform of banking systems, see M Lehmann, 'Volcker Rule, Ring-Fencing or Separation of Bank Activities: Comparison of Structural Reform Acts Around the World' (2014) *LSE Law, Society and Economy Working Papers 25/2014* 3. Available at: eprints.lse.ac.uk/60570/1/WPS2014-25_Lehmann.pdf.

More challenging situations may arise where the investment banking arm of the credit institution needs to obtain special market expertise from colleagues working in another arm, such as opinions or assessments relating to financing, hedging or market reaction to a particular delisting transaction. In that case, colleagues working for the other arm may need to be wall-crossed and monitored by the bank's compliance team, subject to specific procedures and restrictions. More generally, all these barriers should be subject to surveillance by the bank's internal control and compliance departments and form an integral part of their governance and regulatory risk management policies.[81] They will be scrutinised anyway by the financial institutions' supervisory authorities, during their ordinary evaluation processes and extraordinary assessments and audits.[82] In any event, the engaged bank is prohibited, in the context of the provision of its discussed services, from making use of, or exploiting any secret, confidential or proprietary information stemming from the bank-customer relationships with other clients.[83]

In all cases, given that these structural remedial efforts may not prove fully effective to avoid allegations regarding potentially conflicting roles, the banks may attempt to mitigate further their relevant inherent operational and reputation risk though the extensive use of general disclaimer disclosures. These are addressed to any prospective customer of the bank (including the prospective bidder, the target entity itself, its dominant individual or institutional shareholder(s), private equity funds), who are willing to obtain credit or employ the bank's financial services with regard to a particular delisting opportunity. In essence, the credit documentation or financial services agreements may specifically state that the contractual relationship of the bank with the appointing customer, and the particular financial services assigned, will not give rise to any fiduciary, equitable or contractual duties,[84] that would prevent or hinder the bank from providing similar services to other clients, or otherwise acting on behalf of them, or on its own account. In a similar context, the bank involved may expressly inform its customers that the former will not be required to account to the latter for any payment, remuneration, profit or benefit that it may obtain as a result of acting in such ways. More generally, banks are advised to emphasise that they will not bear any obligation to disclose to the assigning entity (nor will they use for the benefit of the latter), any non-public information relevant to the matters contemplated by their engagement, which (information) they may have acquired in the course of their other activities and relationships, or be subject to an obligation of confidence to another person.

[81] On 'compliance as a defense measure', elements of a compliance organisation and informational barriers, see particularly R Veil, 'Insider Dealing' in R Veil (ed), *European Capital Markets Law*, 3rd edn (Oxford/Portland, Hart Publishing, 2022) 212 and M Wuntenberg, 'Compliance Requirements' in R Veil (ed), *European Capital Markets Law*, 3rd edn (Oxford/Portland, Hart Publishing, 2022) 629, 661.

[82] On the supervisory powers of EU and national capital markets and banking authorities, see Gortsos, *The Single Supervisory Mechanism* (n 38) 145, 174, 207, Veil, 'Insider Dealing' (n 81) 216.

[83] See in particular Clemente (n 6); Hopt, *Der Kapitalanlegerschutz im Recht der Banken* (n 6) 465.

[84] On the legal effectiveness of such disclaimers of fiduciary duties, between advised, commercial parties of relatively equal bargaining strength, see *JP Morgan Chase Bank v Springwell Navigation Corporation* [2008] EWHC 1186 (Comm) [470], largely confirmed on appeal [2010] EWCA Civ 1221.

B. Market Abuse

(i) Standalone Inside Information and Related Dealings

The circumstances surrounding banks involved in the delisting operations present additional risks from perspective of financial market abuse. In essence, a delisting financing or servicing opportunity is likely to qualify as inside information.[85] This empirical assessment is based on the fact that the success of the delisting endeavour normally presupposes the acquisition of a substantial part of free-float securities of the target entity from its minority shareholders. Such an acquisition not only requires adequate funding and financial services provided to the bidding entity, but also it is crucially associated with the offering of an increased purchase price (premium), in comparison to the existing ('pre-announcement') market price of target shares.[86] Following the public launch of any relevant tender offer, it is expected that the stock price of the target entity will rise, at least during the period of the offer, to the level of such a bid. This is also expected in the case of a substantial minority shareholding acquisition over the counter, or a corporate transformation, which are deemed able to bring about a successful delisting. Practically, the market will anticipate a subsequent (voluntary or mandatory) tender offer or squeeze-out transaction, or sell-out rights to be established (as detailed in Section III), which would have to be priced, according to law, at the increased price of that last acquisition.

As a result, credit institutions, along with other professional entities and market participants, will have to abide by strict EU rules stipulated in the Market Abuse Regulation (EU) 596/2014 ('MAR') and relevant secondary acts. Based on factual evidence, the intended delisting may well be recognised as a 'protracted process', envisaged in Article 7(2)–(3) of the MAR, as currently in force.[87] It is noted that even an intermediate step in a protracted process shall be deemed to be inside information if,

[85] See on the relevant legal requirements, indicatively, H Krause, 'Begriff der Insiderinformation' in A Meyer, R Veil and T Rönnau (eds), *Handbuch zum Marktmissbrauchsrecht*, 2nd edn (München, CH Beck, 2023) § 6 no 21; M Ventoruzzo and S Mock, *Market Abuse Regulation, Commentary and Annotated Guide*, 2nd edn (Oxford, Oxford University Press, 2022) Art 7, B.7.3.

[86] On the observed substantial premiums of leveraged public to private transactions and the significant average positive market reaction to their announcement (30–40%), see Wright, Simons and Renneboog, 'Why Do Public Firms Go Private in the UK?' (n 4) 3; H-D Assmann, 'Übernahmeangebote im Gefüge des Kapitalmarktrechts, insbesondere im Lichte des Insiderrechts, der Ad hoc-Publizität und des Manipulationsverbots' (2002) 31 *Zeitschrift für Unternehmens- und Gesellschaftsrecht* 697; S Boubaker, A Cellier and W Rouatbi, 'The Sources of Shareholder Wealth Gains from Going Private Transactions: The Role of Controlling Shareholders' (2014) 43 *Journal of Banking and Finance* 226, commenting that empirical findings support the view that delisting transactions are expected to mitigate the inefficiencies induced by pre-transaction agency problems between controlling and minority shareholders, and concluding that relevant shareholder wealth gains reflect the potential additional value that will be created under private ownership, Zetzsche (n 23) 5.

[87] According to the applicable legal provisions, in the case of a protracted process, which is intended to bring about, or results in, particular circumstances or a particular event, those future circumstances or that future event, and also the intermediate steps of that process, which are connected with bringing about or resulting in those future circumstances or that future event, may be deemed to be precise information. See analytically C Di Noia and M Gargantini, 'Issuers at Midstream: Disclosure of Multistage Events in the Current and in the Proposed EU Market Abuse Regime' (2012) 9 *European Company and Financial Law Review* 484; Krause, 'Begriff der Insiderinformation' (n 85) § 6 no 129; ECJ, *Markus Geltl v Daimler AG* [2012] ECLI:EU:C:2012:397.

by itself, it satisfies the criteria of inside information as referred to in Article 7 of MAR. On such legal grounds, each and any of the different possible constituent steps of the whole delisting project, such as the financing of the prospective bidder, the fully documented tender offer, the exercise of squeeze-out right, the initiation and completion of a facilitating corporate transformation, and the delisting itself, can be regarded separately as 'inside information'. With regard to delisting financing, this qualification will be held valid, as long as, if the approval or disbursement, of the financing were to be made public, they would have a significant effect on the price of financial instruments (shares) of the target entity, as information which reasonable investors would be likely to use as part of the basis of their investment decisions.

Consequently, banks and bank officials in possession of such inside information must refrain from using it by means of acquiring on their own account or on behalf of any third party, directly or indirectly, financial instruments to which that information relates, particularly shares of the target entity (or bidding entity, if the latter is also listed entity).[88] With regard to their remaining business activities, and to be able to invoke the 'legitimate behaviour' safe harbour provisions of Article 9 of the MAR, banks should have established and maintained adequate and effective internal arrangements, procedures and measures, as noted in IV.A.2, which effectively ensure that the delisting financing or servicing inside information is not communicated in any way (including by recommendation, inducement or otherwise) to any of their employees or agents or clients who may eventually have implemented trades in the securities of the target entity,[89] without any knowledge of the inside information, but only in order to discharge their coexisting, non-conflicting professional duties.[90]

(ii) Disclosure Obligations and Constraints

Until recently, our conclusion that a delisting financing agreement may qualify as inside information would mean that, in the case of a prospective bidder, having its securities listed on a trading venue, Article 17 of the MAR would probably trigger his own obligation to disclose such a credit arrangement.[91] Nevertheless, imminent disclosure could be legitimately delayed, on the basis of Article 17(4) of the MAR, as this is indeed

[88] Art 8 MAR; (in Greek) G Sotiropoulos, 'Legal Issues of Bank Financing of Business Acquisitions' (2001) 6 *Dikaio Epixeiriseon kai Etairiwn* 256.

[89] See analytically MAR, Art 9(1).

[90] A further exemption is available, under additional legal requirements, for the banks and bank-affiliate investment firms which are authorised to execute orders on behalf of third parties, to the extent the orders for acquisition or disposal of financial instruments of the target entity were carried out legitimately in the normal course of the exercise of their employment and duties. See analytically MAR, Art 9(2); R Veil, 'Handelsverbot' in A Meyer, R Veil and T Rönnau (eds), *Handbuch zum Marktmissbrauchsrecht*, 2nd edn (München, CH Beck, 2023) § 7 no 59.

[91] On the triggers of the disclosure obligation, see indicatively L Klöhn, *Marktmissbrauchsverordnung: Verordnung (EU) Nr. 596/2014 über Marktmissbrauch* (München, CH Beck, 2018); Ventoruzzo and Mock, *Market Abuse Regulation, Commentary and Annotated Guide* (n 85) Art 17 B.17.28; J Payne, 'Disclosure of Inside Information' in V Tountopoulos and R Veil (eds), *Transparency of Stock Corporations in Europe: Rationales, Limitations and Perspectives* (Oxford, Hart Publishing, 2019) 103. On the significant stock exchange returns of bidding firms, at the announcement of takeover bids, also depending on the method of payment, see N Travlos, 'Corporate Takeover Bids, Methods of Payment, and Bidding Firms' Stock Returns' (1987) 42 *The Journal of Finance* 943.

likely to prejudice the legitimate interests of the bidder;[92] provided, additionally, that the delay of disclosure is not likely to mislead the public and the bidder is able to ensure the confidentiality of that information. Following the recent amendment of Article 17 of the MAR, by virtue of Article 2 of Regulation (EU) 2024/2809 ('EU Listing Act'), the disclosure requirement shall not apply to inside information related to intermediate steps in a protracted process as referred to in Article 7(2) and (3) of the MAR, where those steps are connected with bringing about or resulting in particular circumstances or a particular event. In effect, in the context of a protracted process, as defined above, only the final circumstances or final event shall be required to be disclosed, as soon as possible after they have occurred. However, issuers must ensure the confidentiality of the information which meets the criteria of inside information, until such time as that information is disclosed.[93] Therefore, strict confidentiality clauses of the credit or financial services agreement with the involved bank, as well as internal procedures of the latter, aiming at avoiding any communication of relevant information outside the engaged bank unit, are necessary and should be considered effective to meet these statutory requirements.

Market abuse rules impose additional constraints on the banks involved in a delisting endeavour. In essence, financing banks may not be able to perform thorough legal, financial, accounting and tax due diligence on the target listed entity.[94] In subsection III.A.ii, we concluded that assessing the credit risk profile of the target entity is meaningful, as it is intended to assume later (in a successful tender offer and subsequent corporate transformation) either part or allof the bank debt granted initially to the borrower (bidding entity). Nevertheless, even where the major shareholder is already controlling the target entity, the latter is not part of the credit agreement. More importantly, it remains bound by the company law principle (and exemplifying rules) of equal objective treatment of all its shareholders (investors) and the MAR disclosure regime. Thus, any selective flow of material financial information from the target firm (including, indicatively, unpublished financial results, business plan, assets), through its dominant shareholder or its appointed board members, ultimately towards the engaged credit institution, so that the latter adjusts its offered financing terms more aptly, should

[92] For example, due to increase of the price of shares of target entity, before the implementation of tender offer, thereby making the prospective acquisition more costly. On the exemplification on relevant exemption ground, see ESMA, *MAR Guidelines – Delay in the Disclosure of Inside Information* [2016] ESMA/2016/1478; R Veil, A Brüggemeier and M Göttler, 'Veröffentlichung von Insiderinformationen' in A Meyer, R Veil and T Rönnau (eds), *Handbuch zum Marktmissbrauchsrecht*, 2nd edn (München, CH Beck, 2023) § 10 no 106; L Klöhn and K U Schmolke, 'Der Aufschub der Ad-hoc-Publizität nach Art. 17 Abs. 4 MAR zum Schutz der Unternehmensreputation' (2016) 45 *Zeitschrift für Unternehmens- und Gesellschaftsrecht* 866.

[93] See in detail Art 2(6) Regulation (EU) 2024/2809 of the European Parliament and of the Council of 23 October 2024 amending Regulations (EU) 2017/1129, (EU) No 596/2014 and (EU) No 600/2014 to make public capital markets in the Union more attractive for companies and to facilitate access to capital for small and medium-sized enterprises, OJ L, 2024/2809, 14.11.2024. On the exclusion of intermediate steps disclosure in the recent reform of MAR, see R Veil, M Wiesner and M Reichert, 'Ad Hoc Disclosure under the EU Listing Act' (2023) 68 *Die Aktiengesellschaft* 57.

[94] On the particulars of due diligence exercise in the context of takeover bids, including the relevant obligations of the management of the target firm, in accordance with the MAR, Art 9(4) exemption rule, see also M Schiessl, 'Pflicht zur Gleichbehandlung konkurrierender Übernahmeinteressenten bei der Due Diligence?' in S Grundmann (ed), *Festschrift für Klaus J. Hopt zum 70. Geburtstag am 24. August 2010* (Berlin, De Gruyter, 2010) 2455; P Aubel, 'Due Diligence' in M Habersack, PO Mülbert and M Schlitt (eds), *Unternehmensfinanzierung am Kapitalmarkt*, 5th edn (Köln, Verlag Dr. Otto Schmidt, 2024) 1082.

be considered very hesitantly. In essence, such a flow may result in the bank itself being actively involved in the asymmetric transmission of corporate secret information of the regulated listed entity. This normally amounts to breaching the statutory company law and capital markets law duties of the latter, damaging minority shareholders, violating trading venue rules protecting public investors, thus causing harmful economic and reputational repercussions for the involved bank.

(iii) Shadowed Manipulation

Finally, banks should carefully monitor the use of debt funds advanced to prospective bidders and the evolution of the serviced delisting project. It has been mentioned that voluntary delisting opportunities arise especially in the case of listed entities' under-priced shares.[95] In such an environment, before submitting their tender offer, prospective bidders might be tempted to take part in unlawful schemes aimed at artificially driving down the market price of target securities. Such manipulative actions, which may be shadowed along with other financial market participants, with or without the cooperation of target entity management, would effectively frustrate minority shareholders and increase the probability of them opting to divest, by means of accepting a future tender offer by the majority shareholder or a takeover bid. As a result, market investors could be exploited, while the total cost of both the prospective acquisition of their minority shareholdings and the related delisting project would decrease considerably and benefit the bidder (borrower).

Clearly, any such conduct, especially the participation in market transactions or placement of orders, which would give, or be likely to give, false or misleading signals as to the supply of, demand for, or price of the target listed financial instruments, would qualify as market manipulation, according to Article 12 of MAR.[96] Notably, the prohibitive EU rules and sanctions are also directed against persons who collaborate or in any way facilitate market abuse.[97] From the banks' perspective, then, taking into consideration all their potential concurring roles, activities and services in the financial markets, it is vital to be able to demonstrate that they did not devise, finance, support, advise, recommend, accept, or even become ever aware of, any potential structural element of the relevant delisting project (including trading strategies or corporate transformation), which would be designed, purported, or even considered likely to result in market abuse, or even in any simpler form of loss, or even confusion, of the unsophisticated market investors.

[95] See Magni, Morresi, Pezzi and Graziano, 'Defining the Relationship Between Firm's Performance and Delisting' (n 14) 2584; Wright, Simons and Renneboog (n 4); Martinez, Serve and Djama, 'Reasons for Delisting and Consequences' (n 14); Pour and Lasfer (n 14).

[96] On further exemplification of manipulative acts, attention is drawn to the non-exhaustive indicators mentioned in Annex I of the Regulation, and Annex II of Commission Delegated Regulation (EU) 2016/522, see in detail L Teigelack, 'Grundlagen' in A Meyer, R Veil and T Rönnau (eds), *Handbuch zum Marktmissbrauchsrecht*, 2nd edn (München, CH Beck, 2023) § 12.

[97] See MAR, Preamble no 39; Teigelack, 'Grundlagen' (n 96) § 12 no 22.

V. Concluding Remarks

The preceding discussion has drawn attention to the commercial and legal aspects of the position of credit institutions in contemporary voluntary delistings. Banks usually act as prime sponsors of protracted projects resulting, ultimately, in publicly listed companies resolving to go private. Banks get involved early in the identification and promotion of relevant opportunities, while providing economic support for their implementation, in particular by offering attractive acquisition finance solutions. These are tailored according to the ambitious objectives and needs of the interested stakeholders, and the applicable EU and national legal frameworks regulating tender offers, squeeze-out, sell-out and 'cold delisting' operations. Borrowers, being typically the dominant shareholder(s), or a takeover bidder (including private equity investors), or – less frequently – the target company itself, enter into structured credit agreements. These include provisions for differentiated scenarios, depending on the successful or unsuccessful accomplishment of the project. Contractual terms and conditions, including adjustable interest rates, loan duration, covenants and security, are formulated after due diligence, to mitigate the inherent credit risk, by imposing significant obligations on the borrower, particularly the implementation of mergers, or other corporate transformations or acts affecting the target entity and (adversely) its listing status. Such terms are aimed at accelerating, to the extent legally feasible (particularly given the restrictions of EU company law), the assumption of bank debt by the target company, in effect securing bank recourse to the valuable assets and cashflows of the latter; or, in the adverse scenario, by compelling the borrower to extract, expeditiously yet lawfully, the necessary cash to repay the debt facility in a timely manner.

Complex delisting projects are further enabled and facilitated by the banking sector, through the provision of supplementary financial services. In the context of the latter, credit institutions offer indispensable intermediation to the assigning clients (including the listed company itself), with the minority (including the dissenting) shareholders, the capital markets' supervisory authorities, other market professionals and participants, including the institutional and retail investor community, in exchange for rewarding fees. Nevertheless, the concurring wide-ranging roles, mandates and responsibilities which modern banks are looking for and promise to their clientele, oblige them to adopt considerable operational measures, compliance procedures and safeguards. These are deemed necessary for the banks to identify early on, avoid and address efficiently all related regulatory, litigation and reputational risk, any conflicts of interest, unintended breaches of contractual and statutory duties, sub-standard performance or market abuse.

Undoubtedly, such close involvement in delisting projects signalled a major retaliation of the banking sector against capital markets' financing, which has unfolded with its own multiple gains, opportunities and challenges. Notably, the latter are far more widespread and controversial than the credit institutions' gains; by means of orchestrating, repetitively, the selective pulling of more public companies under the 'radar screen' of disclosure obligations and other safeguards covering them as long as listed, the banks' actions are prone to reinforce risks for the economy and investors, otherwise covered by the regulatory umbrella.[98] Nevertheless, these risks should not be overestimated. The incentives and risk appetite of dominant shareholders and private equity funds to engage with enthusiastic banks in frequent leveraged acquisition finance and subsequent delisting operations, increased along with the availability of inexpensive credit. Given the recent increase in interest rates (implying that such envisaged investments returns may no longer exceed the cost of borrowing), we may soon witness the pendulum's reversal: early repayments of delisting credit facilities and banks, reluctantly servicing more and more future public offerings.

[98] Cahn and Donald (n 8) 983. On the long-standing debate about the real economic merits of market-based versus bank-based financial structure, and the recent literature suggestions that financial crises prove economically more severe in bank-based than in market-based financial structures, see Bats and Houben, 'Bank-based Versus Market-based Financing' (n 1) 3.

PART IV

Delisting and Corporate Mobility in EU Member States

11

Downlisting

GAIA BALP*

I. Introduction

The decline of public equity markets in the Union has prompted the European Commission to take action to make listing more attractive.[1]

As reported in a study prepared for the Commission, 'the number of listings in the EU-28 declined by 12%, from 7,392 in 2010 to 6,538 in 2018', and an estimated '8,000–17,000 large companies in 14 EU Member States are eligible to list but not seeking to do so'.[2] Significantly, EU primary markets 'have failed to keep pace with a steady flow of delistings', with new listings net of delistings showing an overall negative balance over the period 2010–2018, despite variations across Member States.[3]

Reluctance to go public and delistings are not only a European phenomenon, but also affect other markets, including the United States, where the rise of a 'listing gap' has been reported as the product of low rates of new listings and high rates of delistings on the three major US stock exchanges, mostly motivated by merger activity among public companies.[4] In fact, there has been a global trend of declining IPO markets, in terms of the number of transactions, the amounts raised or market capitalisation, for as long as 20 years.[5]

* Associate Professor of Business Law, Bocconi University, Milan.

[1] Oxera Consulting Group, *Primary and Secondary Equity Markets in the EU. Final Report* (September 2020). Available at: www.data.europa.eu/doi/10.2874/496492, 12.

[2] ibid. Sweden and Italy are an exception to the EU-wide deteriorating trend, primarily due to successful growth markets: ibid 27.

[3] ibid 29 f, Figure 2.9. See also PF Russo, F Parlapiano, D Pianeselli and I Supino, *Firms' Listings: What is New? Italy versus the Main European Exchanges* (April 2020). Available at: www.bancaditalia.it/pubblicazioni/qef/2020-0555/index.html?com.dotmarketing.htmlpage.language=1.

[4] C Doidge, GA Karolyi and RM Stulz, 'The U.S. Listing Gap' (2018) 123 *Journal of Financial Economics* 464, 464 (reporting that the number of US firms listed on a US stock exchange fell from 8,025 in 1996 to 4,102 in 2012, a gap that exceeds 5,000). See also I Martinez and S Serve, 'Reasons for Delisting and Consequences: A Literature Review and Research Agenda' (2017) 31 *Journal of Economic Surveys* 733. See also RM Stulz, 'Public versus Private Equity' (2019) *Fisher College of Business Working Paper* No 2019-03-027. Available at: www.ssrn.com/abstract=3486578.

[5] European IPO Task Force, *European IPO Report 2020* (2020). Available at: www.fese.eu/app/uploads/2020/03/European-IPO-Report-2020.pdf, 10. For evidence on exits from the London Stock Exchange see BR Cheffins and BV Reddy, 'Will Listing Rule Reform Deliver Strong Public Markets for the UK?' (2023)

However, the gap between EU and US equity primary issuance is large and 'has widened significantly over the last five years. From 2018 to 2022, equity issuance in the EU represented 27 per cent, or less than one-third of that in the US'.[6] More importantly, and unlike in other economies, the decline in the absolute number of listings in the United States does not appear to be accompanied by a decline in the real competitiveness of US public markets. If the nominal number of companies listed on US exchanges is adjusted to include only transactions that actually remove corporate assets from the stock market (rather than also including transactions, such as public-to-public mergers and spinoffs, that do result in delisting yet merely shift corporate assets between public companies), the US listing gap tends to disappear. Therefore, the trend observed in US markets largely 'reflects movement of real assets between public firms', irrespective of the rise of private equity.[7] On the contrary, declining patterns recorded in other advanced and developing or emerging economies around the world have been found to 'tunnel assets out of the public markets', pointing to a real US listing advantage in terms of the merger-driven ability of major US stock exchanges 'to retain corporate assets under public management, which by extension preserves real investment opportunities for investors'.[8]

Weakening EU primary markets also account for shrinking secondary market liquidity, as the reduced number of companies present in the market has a negative impact on investor interest and trading. The Union's market capitalisation at the end of 2022 is 'less than one-third of US market capitalisation' and the 'turnover of EU shares (a measure of liquidity) remained completely flat from 2016 to 2022, while this measure increased by 40 per cent in the United States over the same period'.[9] Further still, 'more than half of the global equity trading volume takes place on US exchanges'.[10]

Ultimately, such developments contribute to making EU public equity markets less competitive than their much larger US (and Asian[11]) counterparts and less attractive to foreign investors. Not surprisingly, delistings from European exchanges to move trading to US exchanges are on the rise, as are dual listings in Europe and the United

86 *The Modern Law Review* 176–213, 178–81 (highlighting that 'unlike in the United States, the size of the companies traded on the LSE has not increased substantially enough to forestall a decline of the stock market, measured by aggregate market capitalisation, relative to the size of the UK economy, over the past 20 years').

[6] April Day, 'Equity-Market Liquidity Is Leaving Europe' (22 June 2023). Available at: www.afme.eu/news/views-from-afme/details/equity-market-liquidity-is-leaving-europe.

[7] BE Eckbo and M Lithell, 'Follow the Assets: Is the US Listing Gap 'Real'?' (2020). Available at: www.nhh.no/contentassets/3cd4b433648f4d4b903f0ed1e1daae56/ssrn-id3547581.pdf, 1–3 (for a more recent version of the paper see BE Eckbo and M Lithell, 'Merger-Driven Listing Dynamics' (2023) *European Corporate Governance Institute – Finance Working Paper* No 752/2021. Available at: www.ssrn.com/abstract=3547581).

[8] Eckbo and Lithell, ibid 4.

[9] Day, 'Equity-Market Liquidity Is Leaving Europe' (n 6).

[10] Markets4Europe, *Transforming Europe's Capital Markets. A Roadmap to a Capital Markets Union for Companies and Savers* (27 September 2019). Available at: www.markets4europe.eu/wp-content/uploads/2019/11/Markets4Europe-Roadmap.pdf, 11.

[11] Oxera (n 1) 26 and figure 2.6 (reporting that, despite the EU and US trends, the largest Asian stock exchanges 'have seen a significant increase in the number of listed firms' since 1990). See also Markets4Europe, *Transforming Europe's Capital Markets* (n 10) 11 f; Technical Expert Stakeholder Group (TESG) on SMEs, *Empowering EU Capital Markets for SMEs. Making Listing Cool Again. Final Report* (2021). Available at: www.finance.ec.europa.eu/document/download/ebb1a257-9ef2-4416-87b5-a1235157c351_en?filename=210525-report-tesg-cmu-smes_en.pdf, 21 f.

Sates, and new listings by European companies, including UK companies, directly on US exchanges[12] – particularly, but not exclusively, by companies owned by US-based venture and private equity funds. Efficiency in capital allocation, growth and innovation across the EU are thus potentially impaired.

As noted above, delistings play an important role in explaining such a downward trend in Europe. Data collected from Borsa Italiana and Euronext, London Stock Exchange and Nasdaq Stockholm main markets for the period 2017–2019 show that, net of involuntary and technical delistings, which account for around 24 per cent of all 320 recorded going-private transactions, *voluntary* delistings account for the bulk of all such transactions.[13] In particular, issuer requests for delisting account for 36.5 per cent, and M&A activity accounts for 29.4 per cent of the total number of delistings from the main markets.[14]

Interestingly, a further 6.8 per cent of voluntary delistings (or 22 transactions) in the same sample are motivated by the *downlisting* of securities to trading on multilateral trading facilities (AIM UK, AIM Italia, Euronext Growth Paris). Such transactions cannot be classified as public-to-private transactions, as removal from the regulated markets is functional to migration to trading on exchange-regulated markets, which, based on a cost-benefit assessment, prove to be more suitable to meet the financing needs of the issuer concerned:[15] an opportunity opened up by the rise of multilateral trading facilities competing with regulated markets following MiFiD I and the abolishment of the 'concentration rule' (a rule of order centralisation on regulated markets).

Downlisting is the process by which a listed firm withdraws completely from the regulated market, but resumes listing in at least one segment of an exchange-regulated market (or continues trading in such segment after departing from the regulated market), which is subject to less stringent regulatory requirements and offers issuers greater flexibility in terms of corporate governance and disclosure obligations while providing the same organised trading functionality as regulated markets, making these venues subject to common pre- and post-trade transparency rules for equity.[16] In essence, downlisted securities (and the underlying corporate assets) do not go dark

[12] Oxera (n 1) 90, 105 ff. See also, regarding Italy, Assonime, 'Corporate Governance in Italy: The Implementation of the Italian Corporate Governance Code 2021' (2022). Available at: www.assonime.it/attivita-editoriale/studi/Pagine/Report-on-Corporate-Governance-in-Italy-the-implementation-of-the-Italian-Corporate-Governance-Code_2021.aspx, iii (highlighting that 'investors are … negatively affected, in terms of missing opportunity, by the so-called "listing shopping," with a growing number of Italian companies accessing capital markets by listing on main international financial venues (eg New York), which offer a more competitive market and regulatory eco-system, in particular for medium-large and/or fast-growing companies'); A Noto, 'The New Competition For Listings' (2023) *Global Finance*. Available at: www.gfmag.com/capital-raising-corporate-finance/stock-exchanges-ipos-global-competition/, 14 (noting that 'cross-border IPOs on US exchanges, as a percentage of total US IPOs, have climbed steadily from 26% in 2021 to 39% in 2022. Today, the percentage of total US IPOs hailing from Europe, China or elsewhere comes to more than half: 52%').

[13] Oxera (n 1) 74. See also Federation of European Securities Exchanges (FESE), *Listed Instruments Survey 2022* (2022). Available at: www.fese.eu/statistics/#cmf, 8.

[14] Oxera (n 1) 74.

[15] ibid.

[16] See recital 7 to MiFIR (Regulation (EU) No 600/2014 on markets in financial instruments and amending Regulation (EU) No 648/2012 [2014] OJ L173/84). See generally D Busch and H Gulyas, 'Regulated Markets, Alternative Trading Venues & Systematic Internalisers in Europe' (2020) 75 *European Banking Institute Working Paper Series*. Available at: www.ssrn.com/abstract=3723660.

but move to another market, though second-tier and self-regulated, and continue to trade under a less prescriptive regime.

Given that high costs and burdensome compliance with stricter regulatory requirements imposed on firms listed on regulated markets are among the strongest determinants of delisting,[17] in a number of circumstances downward market mobility should arguably be expected to be attractive to issuers willing to reduce such costs. Downward mobility should also be expected to be preferable to delisting for both the issuer and its investors. In principle, a move to a junior market should allow the company to continue to take advantage of still better financing and visibility opportunities, while offering existing investors higher standards and better exit and trading opportunities than those typically available in private markets. However, based on the figures above, downlisting appears to be uncommon in the European Union.

This chapter examines whether, and if so under which conditions, downlisting to MTFs, which are characterised by simplified requirements but are nevertheless intended to ensure an adequate level of investment protection,[18] can be (part of) an answer to the cost–benefit problem associated with remaining listed on regulated markets and is preferable to a voluntary delisting from regulated markets altogether. After reviewing the regulatory status quo regarding downlisting in a number of EU jurisdictions and considering whether there is ground for giving companies more flexibility in deciding whether and how to leave regulated markets, this chapter assesses the arguments for and against harmonising the regulatory framework for downlisting.

II. The Regulatory Background Relevant to Downlisting in the EU

The regulatory environment for downlisting is very uneven and patchy across the EU. Such a diverse and uncertain landscape can arguably have a negative impact on European public equity markets, as it may further discourage going public.

A. EU-Level Regulation

At present, there is no EU-level regulation on downlisting, or even on transferring the category of listing within different segments of the regulated markets (downgrading). The lack of any EU-level regulation on downlisting depends on the fact that delisting at the issuer's request ('pure', or 'regular', voluntary delisting) – the major transaction, of which downlisting may be considered a subcategory – is not addressed either. In turn, the circumstance that delisting 'fits squarely into the nexus between company law and

[17] Oxera (n 1) 52, 78. See also Fit for Future Platform, *Facilitating small and medium sized enterprises' access to capital, Opinion 2022/SBGR2/04* (2022). Available at: www.commission.europa.eu/document/download/e2a20718-fb02-4a28-aaf7-be5d4f159ef5_en?filename=Final%20opinion%202022_SBGR2_04%20SMEs%20access%20to%20capital_fup.pdf, 8.

[18] See recital 133 to MiFID I, according to which the SME growth markets regulation included in the directive targets 'the correct balance between maintaining a high level of investor protection and reducing unnecessary administrative burdens for issuers.'

securities law' and that company law is mostly the product of non-harmonised Member State law, makes it indeed less easy to be captured by EU law.[19]

Current EU regulation only deals with upward market mobility and the process of transferring securities from trading on MTFs to trading on regulated markets (uplisting). Trading on MTFs, particularly SME growth markets as a more flexible sub-category of MTFs for small and medium-sized issuers as defined by Article 33 of Directive 2014/65/EU (MiFID II),[20] is not seen as 'a final step in the scaling up of issuers', but 'should enable successful companies to grow and move one day to regulated markets, in order to benefit from greater liquidity and a larger investors' pool'.[21] To facilitate the transition from an SME growth market to a regulated market, Article 14 of the Prospectus Regulation was amended in 2019 to allow issuers listed on an SME growth market to prepare a simplified prospectus (the one formerly available for secondary offerings only) for admission to trading on a regulated market of securities fungible with those previously issued, provided they have been continuously listed on the junior market for at least 18 months.[22]

Regulatory interventions, such as those just mentioned, implemented in the wake of the European Commission's 2015 CMU Action plan, proved to be insufficient to promote market-based financing.[23] In 2022, building on the measures previously adopted, the Commission launched the EU Listing Act package as part of its 2020 CMU Action Plan.[24] The Listing Act, which was formally adopted by the Council on 8 October 2024, comprises a regulation and two directives aimed at further improving access to public markets.[25] The package includes measures functional to facilitate listing by reducing the costs and burdens imposed on companies, particularly SMEs, and giving controlling shareholders greater flexibility in deciding how to distribute voting rights after admission to trading.

[19] P Maume, 'The Parting of the Ways: Delisting Under German and UK Law' (2015) 16 *European Business Organization Law Review* 255, 256 (explaining that while 'the decision to delist is a matter of internal corporate governance, the delisting process and its requirements are regulated under securities law').

[20] Directive 2014/65/EU on markets in financial instruments and amending Directive 2002/92/EC and Directive 2011/61/EU (MiFID II) [2014] OJ L173/349.

[21] See recital 15 to Regulation (EU) 2019/2115 amending Directive 2014/65/EU and Regulations (EU) No 596/2014 and (EU) 2017/1129 as regards the promotion of the use of SME growth markets (SME Listing Act) [2019] OJ L320/1.

[22] See Art 14(1)(d) of Regulation (EU) 2017/1129 on the prospectus to be published when securities are offered to the public or admitted to trading on a regulated market, and repealing Directive 2003/71/EC (Prospectus Regulation) [2017] OJ L168/12.

[23] See Technical Expert Stakeholder Group on SMEs, *Empowering EU Capital Markets for SMEs* (n 11).

[24] Communication from the Commission to the European Parliament, the Council, the European Economic and Social Committee and the Committee of the Regions, *A Capital Markets Union for people and businesses-new action plan, COM/2020/590 final* (2020). Available at: www.eur-lex.europa.eu/legal-content/EN/TXT/?uri=COM:2020:590:FIN (CMU Action Plan 2020).

[25] The Listing Act, published in the Official Journal of the European Union on 14 November 2024, includes: Regulation (EU) 2024/2809 amending Regulations (EU) 2017/1129, (EU) No 596/2014, and (EU) No 600/2014 to make the public capital markets in the Union more attractive for companies and to facilitate access to capital for small and medium-sized enterprise [2024] OJ L2024/2809; Directive (EU) 2024/2811 amending Directive 2014/65/EU to make public capital markets in the Union more attractive for companies and to facilitate access to capital for small and medium-sized enterprises and repealing Directive 2001/34/EC [2024] OJ L2024/2811; and Directive (EU) 2024/2810 on multiple-vote share structures in companies that seek admission to trading of their shares on a multilateral trading facility [2024] OJ L2024/2810. The Listing Act will be implemented gradually, with delays of 15, 18, and 24 months following its entry into force.

Despite being designed to respond to the decline of public equity markets in the EU, the Listing Act fails to address downlisting, or even regular delisting: in terms of market mobility, the Commission was satisfied with further improving the incentives for SMEs listed on MTFs to migrate to regulated markets.

Along these lines, the package includes amendments to the Prospectus Regulation to reduce the regulatory burden at the IPO and post-IPO stages. In particular, the amendments to Article 1(4) and 1(5) of the Prospectus Regulation introduce a new exemption from the prospectus requirement, under which firms issuing securities fungible with those already admitted to trading on (a regulated market or) an SME growth market, *including companies transferring from an SME growth market to a regulated market*, are not required to draw up and publish a prospectus. Instead, these firms are required to publish and file with the national competent authority a short summary document (the so-called Follow-on prospectus, as termed in the new Annexes IV and V to the Prospectus Regulation) containing a statement of compliance with ongoing and periodic reporting and transparency obligations and details of the use of proceeds and any other relevant information not already publicly disclosed.[26] By making the preparation of the transaction more efficient and less onerous, the EU Follow-on prospectus should 'facilitate an upgrade to a regulated market' of issuers whose securities have already been admitted to trading on an SME growth market continuously for at least the preceding 18 months, and 'enable issuers to benefit from an exposure to a broader base of investors'.[27]

The willingness to promote upward market mobility underpins further measures included in Directive (EU) 2024/2811, amending MiFiD II, in particular those aimed at facilitating the development and provision of investment research on listed SMEs and increasing their visibility, both by removing the market capitalisation threshold below which trading execution fees and research fees can be rebundled and by providing a framework for the development of a specific type of issuer-sponsored research (Recitals 4 and 5 to Directive (EU) 2024/2811, and Article 24 of MiFiD II, as amended).

B. Member State Regulation

The lack of an EU-level regulatory framework for downlisting is mostly not compensated for by Member State law. In fact, with very few exceptions, the rules for downlisting (if they exist at all) are not laid down in national statutory legislation. Secondary, non-legislative sources of regulation, such as those provided by national supervisory authorities and/or operators of regulated markets, do not make any provision for

[26] See European Commission, Explanatory Memorandum to the Proposal for a regulation of the European Parliament and of the Council amending Reg (EU) 2017/1129, (EU) No 596/2014 and (EU) No 600/2014 to make public capital markets in the Union more attractive for companies and to facilitate access to capital for small and medium-sized enterprises [2022] COM(2022) 762 final 19.

[27] Recital 35 to Regulation (EU) 2024/2809 and Art 14a(1)(b) and (c) of the Prospectus regulation, as amended. See also recital 39 of the same regulation.

downlisting either. For example, Euronext Rulebook I, which sets out harmonised rules for Euronext regulated markets, does not deal with downlisting at all.

Instead, rules relevant to downlisting are mostly set by market operators in their market-specific rulebooks (such as the Euronext Rulebooks II, applying to the individual Euronext market) or are derived from case law. Unsurprisingly, these rules diverge across jurisdictions, also depending on the broader, country-specific company law framework. Further still, in certain jurisdictions, downlisting is disregarded entirely at all levels of regulation and is treated identically to delisting.

As a result, and, unlike delisting,[28] the current regulatory landscape for downlisting is largely uneven and fragmented across EU jurisdictions. Without attempting to provide a more comprehensive analysis, some references to the regulatory framework relevant to downlisting in a number of illustrative jurisdictions may suffice to account for such diverse landscape in some more detail.

The most comprehensive framework for downlisting is provided in France. As an exception to other European jurisdictions, French law explicitly allows for downlisting, conditional on certain requirements. For securities traded on a regulated market to be downlisted to trading on an MTF, Article L421-14 V of the Monetary and Financial Code (*Code monétaire et financier* – CMF) stipulates that the issuer's market capitalisation must be less than €1 billion and that the target MTF must have rules on public offerings in place that are equivalent to those applicable in the regulated market of origin.[29] Additionally, the issuer's application for admission to trading on the relevant MTF must be approved by the shareholders' meeting at least two months prior to the intended date of admission to trading on the relevant MTF; the public must be notified at least two months before this date. Corresponding provisions are included in Article 223–36(1) of the General Regulation of the French supervisory authority (AMF GR), according to which the notice to the public must specify the reasons for migration and its consequences for the shareholders and the public, and include the provisional timetable for the move. Further still, under Article P 1.4.5 of Euronext Paris Rulebook II, the downlisting decision by the shareholders' meeting is to be made based on appropriate shareholder information about how the transfer would affect the issuer's periodic and ongoing disclosure regime. Finally, Article 223–36(2) AMF GR requires a second notice to the public to be disseminated by the board of directors immediately upon the making of the decision to implement the move, specifying the reasons for the transfer, the consequences for the public and the shareholders, the procedures and timetable for the transfer.[30]

[28] See, for a general overview of delisting regulation in the EU member states, M Zmysłowska, 'Protection of Interests of Minority Shareholders in the Case of the Delisting of a Company in the Light of Regulations Binding in Europe' (2023) 18 *Capital Markets Law Journal* 391–401.

[29] Under Art L433-3, II CMF (referred to in Art L421-14 V (I) CMF), a public offer is to be launched 'when any individual or legal entity acting alone or in concert … comes to hold, directly or indirectly, more than five-tenths of the capital or voting rights of a company whose registered office is located in France and whose shares are admitted to trading on a financial instruments market that does not constitute a regulated market in a Member State of the European Union or another State party to the Agreement on the European Economic Area, when the person managing this market submits a request to the Autorité des marchés financiers'.

[30] See also AMF, *Position/recommandation AMF no 2010-03 Questions – Réponses de l'AMF sur le transfert vers Euronext Growth d'une société cotée sur Euronext* (2010). Available at: www.amf-france.org/sites/institutionnel/files/private/2021-04/2010-03.pdf.

From a technical standpoint, given that downlisting entails a delisting from the regulated market and, simultaneously, a direct admission to trading on the MTF, a corresponding application is to be submitted by the issuer to the relevant market operator (Article P 1.4.1 of the Euronext Paris Rulebook II; Article 3.1.1 and Appendix 3 of the Euronext Growth Markets Rulebook I). The decision concerning admission to trading on the MTF is due within one month (Article 3.7.1 Euronext Growth Markets Rulebook I). Admission to trading on the MTF requires that a presentation document be filed with the relevant market operator and made public by the issuer, containing 'a detailed description of [the issuer's] shareholder base (in particular to prove that the Securities have already been placed in public hand) and a certificate from its Listing Sponsor that it has satisfied and continues to satisfy the reporting and disclosure requirements of the market on which it is already admitted to trading', alongside the latest annual financial statements, a cash position statement, data referred to share price performance and a statement of market disclosures made during the year preceding, as well as a presentation note summarising the essential characteristics of, and risks associated with, the issuer, its operation and securities (Euronext Growth Markets Rulebook I, Article 3.2.1(iii) and Appendix III).

Germany and Italy are on the opposite side; they are jurisdictions where the same rules apply to downlisting as to delisting.

In Germany, delisting and downlisting have undergone a fluctuating evolution strongly driven by case law. Following a 2012 ruling of the Constitutional Court that held that neither a shareholders' meeting nor a compensatory offer is required to protect shareholders' proprietary rights in the event of a delisting or downlisting,[31] in its '*Frosta*' ruling of 2013,[32] the Federal Supreme Court made (delisting and) downlisting much easier, compared to its previous 2002 ruling in the '*Macrotron*' case.[33] In *Frosta*, the Court established that (delisting and) downlisting no longer requires approval from the shareholders' meeting and a compensatory offer to minority shareholders. The Court reasoned that while the law protects shareholders' corporate and financial participation and organisational rights, it does not guarantee the tradability of securities, or the market liquidity associated with listing in general or listing in a specific market or market segment.

In 2015, following *Frosta* and the criticism associated with its ruling, the rules set out in section 39(2)–(3) of the Stock Exchange Act (*Börsengesetz – BörsG*) for delisting at the issuer's request were amended to provide a framework for investor protection. In spite of the fact that section 39(2)–(3) only explicitly regulates voluntary delisting, the

[31] BVerfG [2012] 1 BvR 3142/07, 1 BvR 1569/08 (arguing that delisting and downlisting do not, in principle, encroach on the scope of protection of share ownership since Art 14(1) of the German Constitution only protects the legal (right to sell a share at any time) and not the actual marketability (tradability) of the share).

[32] BGH, *Frosta* [2013] II ZB 26/12.

[33] BGH, *Macrotron* [2002] II ZR 133/01 (according to which delisting required a corresponding resolution by the shareholders' meeting and was associated with the obligation for the issuer to submit a compensation offer to the shareholders, whereby the offer could be reviewed in subsequent appraisal proceedings at the request of the shareholders; the same applied to a switch from the regulated market to the unofficial market (*einfacher Freiverkehr*), but not to the *qualifizierter Freiverkehr*: interestingly, downlisting to the qualified unregulated market – an exchange-organised unofficial market with simpler admission requirements and no follow-up obligations, such as the Open Market at the Frankfurt Stock Exchange – was held not to impair the shares' marketability and therefore did not require a mandatory offer).

same regime also applies to downlisting.[34] Specifically, section 39(2)–(3) BörsG requires an unconditional cash offer to be launched by the issuer, or its majority shareholders, to purchase all equity securities that are the subject of the delisting (or downlisting) at a price not lower than the volume-weighted average trading price during the six months prior to the publication of the offer. The decision to delist or downlist lies not with the shareholders but with the board of directors, in accordance with the *Frosta* ruling. Moreover, unlike under the *Macrotron* ruling, shareholders are granted no right to initiate an appraisal proceeding in court by which to challenge the price of the offer.

Italy entirely lacks any normative or private-ordering reference framework for downlisting. At the forefront, such state of affairs derives from the fact that – unlike in Germany – neither pure delisting is regulated, and that, therefore, the very legitimacy of a delisting at the issuers' request is still not undisputed, in spite of the permissive stance currently prevailing in doctrine. In fact, the only provision explicitly allowing securities to be removed from trading upon the issuer's request is enshrined in Article 133 of the Consolidated Act on Finance (CLF) which, however, refers to migration within regulated markets only. Covering the transfer to another (Italian or European) regulated market (provided that the target venue offers equivalent investor protection), Article 133 of the CLF and the corresponding rules set by Consob, the national supervisory authority (Article 144(2) of its Issuer Regulation), do not apply to downlisting. No provision concerning downlisting is included in the market rules set by Borsa Italiana, the Italian stock exchange, either.

As a consequence, downlisting requires a cumbersome two-step unbundled process to be put in place, by which to first effect the delisting from the regulated market and hence apply for a first admission to trading on the relevant MTF. Importantly, delisting from the regulated market triggers the application of Article 2437-*quinquies* of the Civil Code, under which shareholders (holding listed equities) who 'did not contribute to the resolution that determined delisting' – be it the resolution to merge into a non-listed entity or, where deemed possible, the pure delisting resolution – are granted the right to withdraw from the company. Upon withdrawal, the shareholder is to be paid by the issuer a value equal to the average market price of the shares in the last six months before publication of the notice of call of the shareholders meeting, unless the remaining shareholders buy the shares from the withdrawn shareholder at the same price (Article 2437-*ter*(3) Civil Code). As plainly derives from Article 133 CLF on market migration, pure delisting – even if actually aimed at downlisting – requires approval by the shareholders' extraordinary meeting and, as no dedicated track is provided upon delisting for admission to trading on an MTF, the ordinary listing regime fully applies.

No specific provision on downlisting is set out in the UK either. Therefore, downlistings require the company to submit both a motivated request to the FCA for cancellation of its equities' listing from the main market (see LR 5.3.1) and an application to the market operator for admission to trading on the AIM. Under the Listing

[34] N Ilyevich, *Delisting. Parallele zum Übernahmerecht. Probleme und Lösungsmöglichkeiten* (Baden-Baden, Nomos, 2015) 50 f.

Rules, unless a takeover offer is launched or other special circumstances apply, cancellation of listing of securities with a premium listing (but not with a standard listing) requires the company to obtain, at a general meeting, the prior approval of a resolution for the cancellation from a majority of not less than 75 per cent of the votes attaching to the shares voted on the resolution *and*, where an issuer has a controlling shareholder, a majority of the votes attaching to the shares of independent shareholders voted on the resolution (LR 5.2.5(2)).[35] An FCA-approved circular is to be sent to the holders of the relevant securities, and an announcement is to be made public, providing, amongst further things, a clear and adequate explanation of the subject matter giving due prominence to its essential characteristics, benefits and risks, and including the anticipated date of cancellation, which must be not less than 20 business days following the passing of the resolution for cancellation (LR 5.2.5(1)). The passing of the cancellation resolution by the shareholders' meeting is to be made public as well, in accordance with LR 5.2.5(4). If the FCA agrees to cancel the listing, it will notify the issuer to provide the date on which the cancellation will take effect and give details of the cancellation (LR 5.3.8).

Notwithstanding the applicability to downlisting of the aforementioned rules on delisting, the London Stock Exchange yet facilitates the transfer from the regulated market to the MTF in that it allows for a faster and more streamlined AIM admission process. The LSE's 'AIM Designated Market Route', introduced in May 2003, provides for a fast-track admission to AIM for 'eligible applicants': a category which includes not only the UKLA Official List (the Official List maintained by the FCA, acting in its capacity as the UK Listing Authority, in accordance with section 74(1) of the Financial Services and Markets Act), but also, amongst others, 'any UK or EEA Regulated Market or SME Growth Market and registered in accordance with the relevant laws'.[36] Under the AIM Designated Market Route, no admission document is required for the AIM listing if the eligible applicant has had its securities traded on an AIM Designated Market for at least 18 months prior to the date of admission to AIM. Instead of an AIM admission document, applicants are required to make a more detailed pre-admission announcement (as compared to the one normally required according to rule 3 of the AIM Rules for Companies)[37] that must include specified pieces of information. In addition, applicants admitted to a UK or EEA regulated market or SME growth market only must have a market capitalisation of at least £20,000,000 upon admission to the AIM and have their admission documentation on their home market and all disclosure required under the UK or EEA Market Abuse Regulation (as applicable) published in English.

[35] Interestingly, the same regime applies to downgrading from premium to standard listing: under LR 5.4A.4, a transfer of the listing of equity shares with a premium listing out of the category of premium listing requires not only that the shareholders and the public be notified about the background and reasons for, and the anticipated timing and the effects of, the proposed transfer, but also that the shareholders' meeting approves of the transfer with a majority of not less than 75% of the votes attaching to the shares voted on the resolution, and, where an issuer has a controlling shareholder, a majority of the votes attaching to the shares of independent shareholders voted on the resolution.

[36] London Stock Exchange, *The AIM Designated Market Route* (2020). Available at: www.docs.londonstockexchange.com/sites/default/files/documents/ADM%20template%20%2801012021%29.pdf.

[37] London Stock Exchange, *AIM Rules for Companies* (2021). Available at: www.docs.londonstockexchange.com/sites/default/files/documents/AIM%20Rules%20for%20Companies%20%2801012021%29_1.pdf.

III. How the Regulatory Environment Affects Downlisting

As the preceding analysis shows, downlisting requires a varied combination of different regulatory tools to be applied depending on the jurisdiction. The transfer of trading on MTFs is usually subject to disclosure obligations in the form of public announcements that set out the reasons and rationale of the transfer, and waiting periods may be imposed between the announcement and the day the downlisting comes into effect.

A resolution by the shareholders' meeting is a common requirement as well. However, the majority requirements may differ. For instance, under French law, downlisting is decided by a simple majority, while in Italy, it requires an extraordinary shareholders' meeting due to the lack of an ad-hoc regulation.[38] In the UK, a 75 per cent majority at the general meeting and a majority-of-the-minority requirement apply for premium-listing securities' delisting. On reverse, shareholder approval is not necessary under German law. Additionally, in some cases, the target MTF must have rules on public offerings in place that are equivalent to those applicable on the regulated market of origin (France, Italy).

Still in other cases, such as the UK, a fast-track admission to trading on the MTF is provided for issuers listed on the regulated market to facilitate the transfer.

But above all, where downlisting is not regulated separately from delisting, the shift can come with costly consequences that can disincentivise the move altogether. This is the case with Italy and Germany, where dissenting shareholders are granted an exit opportunity. On the contrary, remedies functionally similar to those triggered by downlisting under German and Italian law will usually apply under French law only upon voluntary delisting from the regulated market, in the form of a buyout or a voluntary offer to minority shareholders followed by a squeeze-out.[39]

Such different downlisting regimes, which can be either enabling or quite exacting – and deterring, through vagueness and uncertainty, or rigor and even over-protection of investors – can have practical consequences.

In effect, downlisting is quite frequent in jurisdictions where specific rules are set that provide issuers and investors with an adequate level of assurance as to the applicable rules, and where the transfer is not made prohibitively costly; it is not where no difference is made between downlisting and delisting.

In France, where market mobility is favoured in both directions and downlisting is subject to an ad-hoc regulation, 35 downlistings from Euronext Paris to Euronext Growth Paris took place between 2018 and 2021.[40] In 2023, there were eight shifts from Euronext

[38] A simple-majority requirement for the shareholders' resolution concerning downlisting also applies under NYSE Euronext Amsterdam, *Notice 2012-001 on Transfer from NYSE Euronext Amsterdam to NYSE Alternext* (2012). Available at: www.euronext.com/en/regulation/euronext-regulated-markets (also requiring a press release from the issuer announcing the transfer and containing details on its rationale, timetable and other relevant circumstances, and imposing a 30-days waiting period between the date of issuance of the press release announcing the transfer and the date of first admission to trading on the relevant Alternext Market(s)).

[39] See K Deckert, Questionnaire France Q 9, Q 11, Q 13.

[40] Data referred to France are drawn from F Annunziata and A Lambiase, *Euronext Growth Milan (ex AIM Italia) ed Euronext Growth Paris. Mercati di crescita per le PMI a confronto* (Milan, Egea, 2022) 29–31.

Paris to Euronext Growth Paris, and six in 2022.[41] Interestingly, downward mobility in France affects not only small-cap issuers, but also issuers with significant levels of capitalisation. On the contrary, upward mobility seems very limited; the fact that liquidity of French growth MTFs is not substantively dissimilar to that of the regulated markets is, arguably, among the factors that make upward mobility less attractive and, at the same time, downward mobility attractive.[42]

In the UK, the flow of market switches undertaken was mostly directed at the AIM, via the AIM designated market route. From the inception of AIM in 1995 to the end of 2006, 218 companies downlisted, while 56 companies switched from AIM to the main markets.[43]

In Italy, the regulatory vacuum and uncertainty surrounding delisting itself have certainly contributed to hindering any form of downward market mobility. As a matter of fact, no shift from the regulated market managed by Borsa Italiana to Euronext Growth Milan (formerly, AIM Italia) seemingly occurred between 2018 and 2023, while 63 voluntary delistings from the main market (net of migrations to other regulated markets) took place in the same period of time, mostly effected by means of mergers or takeovers. On the contrary, 25 MTF-listed issuers moved upwards to Euronext Milan in the same period of time.[44]

The most illustrative case is that of Germany, where the trend in downlistings shows a clear correlation with the regulatory evolution that has taken place. Many downlistings took place between 2013 and 2015: after the *Frosta* ruling, that greatly facilitated the transfer by removing both requirements of the approval from the shareholders' meeting and the cash offer to minority shareholders, and until the amendments to section 39(2)–(3) BörsG came into force, which reintroduced the cash offer requirement. After that, the number of downlistings dropped significantly.[45]

As the cases of Germany and Italy quite visibly show, regulation can indeed act as a roadblock to downward market mobility. The exit remedy dissenting shareholders are granted upon downlisting in either the form of withdrawal rights or the mandatory cash offer, and the corresponding costs imposed on issuers or the controlling shareholders, prevent mobility from the regulated markets to alternative venues otherwise potentially attractive for reducing the costs and compliance burdens associated with listing on the main markets.

[41] Euronext, *Fact Book 2023* (2023), *Fact Book 2022* (2022). Available at: www.live.euronext.com/en/resources/statistics/factbook.

[42] Annunziata and Lambiase, *Euronext Growth Milan* (n 40) 31.

[43] T Jenkinson and T Ramadorai, 'Does One Size Fit All? The Consequences of Switching Markets with Different Regulatory Standards' (2013) 19 *European Financial Management* 837–1050, 854.

[44] All data referred to Italy are retrieved from Borsa Italiana's 'Historical Statistics'. Available at: www.borsaitaliana.it/borsaitaliana/statistiche/statistiche-storiche/revoche-202311.en_pdf.htm; see the tables included in G Balp, Questionnaire Italy for more details.

[45] See J-M Hitz, S Koch and F Moritz, 'Downlistings in European Exchange-Regulated Markets: The Role of Enforcement' (2020) 39 *Journal of Accounting and Public Policy*, Article 106735. Available at: www.doi.org/10.1016/j.jaccpubpol.2020.106735, 4, 6, table 1. See also M Berninger, D Schiereck and D van de Vathorst, 'Der Abfindungsanspruch beim Rückzug aus dem regulierten Markt – eine empirische Evaluation der gesetzlichen Neuregelung' (2019) 31 *Journal of Banking Law and Banking* 329–49, 331 (finding that the delisting rate (the proportion of delistings in the period under review in relation to listed companies in the previous year) was 8.45% for the *Frosta* period, whereas since the new regulation came into force it has been just 2.52%).

IV. The Regulatory Environment for Downlisting: A Policy Perspective

Correlation between regulation and the actual practice of downlisting within the European Union requires consideration from a public policy perspective.

It is reasonable to assume that, when deciding to apply for admission to trading of securities on regulated markets, issuers also take into account the availability of workable exit opportunities, such as pure voluntary delisting or downlisting.[46] Inhibiting downward market mobility at the national level through regulation, or the absence of it, can therefore have weighty consequences.

First of all, divergent regulatory regimes for downlisting in EU jurisdictions can enhance competition between European trading venues by directing or redirecting listings towards the exchanges where the regulatory conditions for downlisting are clearer and less restrictive. Ultimately, this can contribute to enhancing a listing shopping phenomenon within the EU that is not, however, motivated by genuine competition between trading venues (in terms of the costs of trading, trading and post-trading fees, or the services offered by different facilities). Regardless of whether regulatory arbitrage can be beneficial for firms, investors and the economy, competition between stock exchanges induced by national regulation sharply contrasts with the 2020 CMU Action Plan objective of 'integrating national capital markets into a genuine single market' that protects and facilitates investments.[47]

In the Action Plan, the European Commission acknowledged that 'European capital markets remain fragmented along national lines' and announced its willingness to 'address barriers related to legal frameworks or barriers driven by long-established national practices' that hinder market integration.[48] Among the measures identified to counter market fragmentation, those referred to company law are, however, limited to further facilitating shareholder engagement by making voting easier for investors, and do not cover either delisting or downlisting.[49] Delisting and downlisting are not addressed by any action falling under the umbrella of EU securities law.

Second, if home bias is also accounted for – which is known to act as a determinant for companies often choosing to list on domestic exchanges[50] – hindered downward

[46] Precisely that reasoning underpinned the decision by the German legislator, back in 1997, to first introduce an ad hoc regulatory framework for delisting in the *Börsengesetz* and put an end to the then highly controversial issue of the admissibility of, and the conditions for, an issuer's voluntary withdrawal from the stock exchange: see Deutscher Bundestag, *Gesetzentwurf der Bundesregierung – Entwurf eines Gesetzes zur weiteren Fortentwicklung des Finanzplatzes Deutschland (Drittes Finanzmarktförderungsgesetz) BT-Drs. 13/8933* (1997). Available at: www.dserver.bundestag.de/btd/13/089/1308933.pdf, 57 (according to which such regulation would provide planning security for firms considering a listing on a domestic stock exchange, reduce reservations about such a step, and thus contribute to the fostering of equity capital funding).

[47] CMU Action Plan 2020 (n 24) 12.

[48] ibid.

[49] See Action 12 of the 2020 CMU Action Plan (n 24) 13, and related Annex.

[50] Data from the WFE, which classify listed companies as domestic and foreign, depending on their country of incorporation in relation to the stock exchange on which they are listed, show that domestic companies account for 92%, while foreign ones for the rest 8% of all listed companies. See World Federation of Exchanges (WFE), *Number of Listed Companies* (2022). Available at: www.focus.world-exchanges.org/articles/number-listed-companies, fig 5. See also ESMA TRV Risk Analysis, *Evolution of EEA Share Market Structure since*

market mobility can discourage listing altogether on venues subject to Member State regulation that fails to adequately address downlisting. Failing to ensure a level playing field among companies across the EU is contrary to the very goals outlined in the Listing Act package as part of the 2020 CMU Action Plan. Incentivising companies to list or remain listed on regulated markets as well as SME growth markets is an objective that could better be pursued if *all* deterrents were considered, including restrictions to the freedom to exit the market. Yet constraints to listing identified at the EU level are essentially limited to compliance costs, especially for SMEs.[51]

Finally, and strictly related, if the costs of trading on the regulated market outweigh the benefits, exchange-listed firms may decide to resort to delisting *tout-court* for lack of downward market mobility opportunities. It is, in fact, inherent in regulatory regimes within the EU that lack a regulation on the transfer of trading to an MTF, or that make it overly costly, that exchange-listed firms are fundamentally denied an alternative exit route that in many cases would be preferable to delisting. This, too, betrays the spirit of the Listing Act aimed at delivering on Action 2 of the 2020 CMU Action plan, to support companies' access to public markets.[52]

Against this backdrop, choosing to focus the regulatory efforts on listing and upward market mobility, whilst disregarding the flipside of departure from the market, is questionable from a public policy perspective. In 2017, the European Commission did actually publicly consult, amongst others, on the issue of (delisting and) downlisting. On that occasion, the Commission reasoned that

> [s]mall caps listed on regulated markets can find it increasingly difficult to comply with some regulatory requirements (such as the Transparency Directive, the Shareholders Rights Directive). Furthermore, many midcaps on regulated markets can feel that their market capitalisation makes them candidates for SME Growth Markets. In such a case, quoted SMEs may consider a voluntary transfer of their shares from a regulated market to a market with a lighter regulatory burden (ie the future SME Growth Markets).[53]

The Commission also considered that 'such transfers may imply some investor protection issues and can be difficult to organise for SMEs. In addition, the legal framework of such transfers can vary from one Member State to another'.[54] The Commission solicited feedback on whether there may be 'merits in introducing harmonised rules at EU level on voluntary transfer of listing from a regulated market to an SME Growth Market'.[55] Respondents were found to be 'equally split between those supporting and those opposing the harmonisation of the transfer, while a small group of them remained neutral';[56] apparently this led the Commission not to pursue the issue further.

MiFID II, ESMA50-524821-2954 (2023). Available at: www.esma.europa.eu/sites/default/files/2023-10/ESMA50-524821-2954_TRV_Article_EEA_share_market_structure_publication.pdf, 12.

[51] CMU Action Plan 2020 (n 24) 7.

[52] ibid 8.

[53] European Commission, *Consultation Document: Building a Proportionate Regulatory Environment to Support SME Listing* (2017). Available at: www.web.archive.org/web/20220215171650/https://ec.europa.eu/info/sites/default/files/2017-barriers-listing-smes-consultation-document_en.pdf, 12.

[54] ibid.

[55] ibid.

[56] European Commission, *Feedback Statement of the Public Consultation on Building a Proportionate Regulatory Environment to Support SME Listing* (2018). Available at: www.web.archive.org/web/20211123040216/https://ec.europa.eu/info/sites/default/files/2017-barriers-listing-smes-feedback-statement_en.pdf, 8.

For all that, it seems quite clear that if, on EU-average, delistings outpace new listings, policymaking aimed at revitalising European public equity markets should but most carefully consider exits alongside new listings. The regulatory approach eventually adopted in the EU fails instead to recognise that limits placed by national legislation on migration to non-regulated markets negatively affect the attractiveness of going public. It also fails to recognise that enabling downward market mobility might facilitate the return, one day, to trading on the exchanges, given that – differently from delisting – downlisting does not lead to the complete disapplication of capital market rules. More generally, the policy choices made at the EU level fail to account for the fact that different levels of investor protection in different Member States as a by-product of diverse national law can affect investors' confidence in public equity markets. The need for valorisation of listing transfer requirements in the European context is even more accentuated by virtue of the freedom of capital movements that characterises the single market. Restrictions to this freedom must be considered admissible if they are justified by the need to protect the investment and if they are proportionate to the aims pursued.

V. Interests Surrounding Downlisting: The Position of the Issuer and its Minorities

From an issuer perspective, downlisting could respond to a number of issues that may affect trading on the exchange and lead it to consider stepping down from the public market without however necessarily exiting trading definitively. Issues potentially conducive to such move include, most notably, slight growth opportunities, low capitalisation, low stock liquidity, low trading volume, low free float, small firm size, poor operating performance, stock undervaluation, and high costs of remaining listed, as the case may be.[57]

In such circumstances, downlisting should be preferable to delisting from the standpoint of investors too. After all, trading and price formation on MTFs are the same as on regulated markets, and prices on MTFs are still market prices. Unlike delisting, downlisting does not lead to an increase in information asymmetry between majority and minority shareholders, since significant disclosure obligations will continue to apply after the switch. Specifically, the same MAR-dictated transparency and disclosure requirements apply to firms whose stocks are traded on regulated markets and on MTFs. MTF-issuers are subject to the same regime as RM-issuers concerning ad hoc disclosures, the obligation to maintain insider lists and the rules on directors' dealings.

It would thus seem reasonable to assume that, differently from delisting, downlisting should not impact shareholders' wealth in terms of adverse price reactions upon announcement of the move that might force shareholders to sell stocks below their

[57] See generally W Bessler, J Beyenbach, MS Rapp and M Vendrasco, 'Why Do Firms Down-list or Exit from Securities Markets? Evidence from the German Stock Exchange' (2023) 17 *Review of Managerial Science* 1175–1211.

actual value due to supply pressure countered by low demand on the market. In principle, the transfer should not affect too deeply investors' ability to trade stocks after the switch, since growth markets are designed to ensure a certain level of stock liquidity on the secondary market. At least, the impact of downlisting should not be the same as with delisting, which causes stocks to be conclusively removed from trading.[58] If these assumptions were to hold, the very rationale of a cash consideration requirement as a tool by which to protect minority shareholders upon downlisting would be undermined.

Underpinning exacting regulatory regimes for downlisting and, specifically, those that require some form of cash consideration for the shareholders, is, nevertheless, precisely the concept that

> the tradability of shares which move from the regulated market to an exchange-regulated market is severely restricted. Affected shareholders may therefore not be able to realise the asset value bound up in the share or only do so with sometimes significant limitations. In particular, they can face share price losses because other investors will only invest in securities with uncertain opportunities to dispose of them at a discount.[59]

The cash offer mandated under German law was thus conceived as a means of striking a balance between majority and minority shareholders. For the same reason, Italian law grants dissenting shareholders the right to exit the company and be liquidated in cash at a price unaffected by the market's reaction to the switch.

However, empirical research seems to suggest that downlisting does not seem to affect shareholders' financial interests or their ability to trade, at least not as much as is assumed under German and Italian law.

A. Price Reaction Upon the Downlisting Announcement

Germany's oscillating evolutionary pattern of downlisting regulation made it an ideal setting for testing such assumptions through event studies that measure abnormal price reactions to the downlisting announcement and analyse bid-ask spreads over a period before and after the actual shift of trading to the MTF. The cash offer requirement did not apply during the 2013–15 period (it did apply before 2013 and has applied since 2015), making it possible to assess the actual need for the cash offer requirement as a compensatory measure. Further analyses referred to other markets are yet to be accounted for.

While evidence confirms that, in the absence of a mandatory compensatory offer, pure voluntary delisting from the regulated market reduces shareholders' wealth

[58] See Maume, 'The Parting of the Ways: Delisting Under German and UK Law' (n 19) 259 f.

[59] O Klepsch, 'Delisting: Stock Exchange Act – Requirement to Make Compensation Offer to Shareholders' (2016) *Bundesanstalt für Finanzdienstleistungsaufsicht – BaFin*. Available at: www.bafin.de/SharedDocs/Veroeffentlichungen/EN/Fachartikel/2016/fa_bj_1601_delisting_en.html, 2.

(irrespective of the reasons underlying the decision to delist[60]), no such conclusion can apparently be drawn in regard to downlisting.[61]

According to a recent report referred to the German market, commissioned by the Federal Ministry of Finance, *delisting* announcements before the amendment of section 39 BörsG led to statistically significant negative abnormal returns (ie to a loss of shareholder wealth). After the amendment of section 39 BörsG, the abnormal returns are smaller and sometimes even positive and it cannot be proven statistically that they are different from zero. A wealth loss of the shareholders, as it was observed before the amendment of section 39 BörsG, can therefore no longer be empirically proven. In this respect, the amendment of section 39 BörsG has improved the protection for investors.[62]

The evidence from the German market appears to be consistent with that from studies in the wider EU context, including the UK, which assume that an offer at a premium to the market price is made by the controlling shareholders to buy the minorities out and take the company private. Market reaction upon the delisting announcement is found to be *positive*, rather indicating shareholder wealth creation.[63] Moreover, the fact that the transaction is carried out by the controlling shareholder seems not to affect

[60] See Maume (n 19) 259 (noting that 'even if the purpose of delisting is to increase the company value in the long run, this has no immediate effect on share price … As market prices are based upon investor confidence, the mere danger of a loss of investment could make shareholders sell their shares as soon as possible ("rat race"), resulting in a decline in share price development').

[61] See generally Berninger, Schiereck and van de Vathorst, 'Der Abfindungsanspruch beim Rückzug aus dem regulierten Markt' (n 45) 338.

[62] See M Jonas, A Budzinski, C Deyerler and O Mehring, *Non-technical Summary of the Expert Report on Behalf of the Federal Republic of Germany, "Does the fact that delisting-offers are linked to the 6-month average share price provide adequate protection for investors?"* (2022) Research project fe 6/21. Available at: www.grant-thornton.de/globalassets/1.-member-firms/de-germany/presse/nt_summary_bmf_delisting_final.pdf. The full report is available in German only: M Jonas, A Budzinski, C Deyerler and O Mehring, *Abschlussbericht im Auftrag der Bundesrepublik Deutschland, vertreten durch das Bundesministerium für Finanzen, zur Frage: "Bietet die regelmäßige Anknüpfung von Delisting-Angeboten an den 6-Monats-Durchschnittskurs einen angemessenen Schutz für Anleger?"* (2022) Forschungsvorhaben fe 6/21. Available at: www.grantthornton.de/globalassets/1.-member-firms/de-germany/pdf-download/bericht_bmf_delisting_final.pdf. See also Berninger, Schiereck and van de Vathorst (n 45) 342; C Aders, D Muxfeld and F Lill, 'Die Delisting-Neuregelung und die Frage nach dem Wert der Börsennotierung' (2015) 11 *Corporate Finance* 389–99 (finding an average price reaction of -13.0% and an abnormal price reaction of -9.4% over a period of 20 days from the announcement of the delisting); M Doumet, P Limbach and E Theissen, 'Ich bin dann mal weg: Werteffekte von Delistings deutscher Aktiengesellschaften nach dem Frosta-Urteil' (2016) 68 *Schmalenbachs Zeitschrift für betriebswirtschaftliche Forschung* 253–77; B Karami and R Schuster, *Eine empirische Analyse des Kurs- und Liquiditätseffekts auf die Ankündigung eines Börsenrückzugs am deutschen Kapitalmarkt im Lichte der FRoSTA Entscheidung des BGH* (2015) Bewertung im Recht 35 available at www.hbfm.link/300; L Pilsl and L Knoll, 'Delisting und Börsenkurs' (2016) 69 *Der Betrieb* 181; C Thomale and A Walter, 'Delisting als Regulierungsaufgabe' (2016) 45 *Zeitschrift für Unternehmens- und Gesellschaftsrecht* 679–728, 712.

[63] See E Croci and A Del Giudice, 'Delistings, Controlling Shareholders and Firm Performance in Europe' (2014) 20 *European Financial Management* 374–405, 384. But see A Dasilas, C Grose and T Spyridis, 'Wealth Effects of Delistings Announcements in Europe' (2017) 14 *Investment Management and Financial Innovations* 67–79, 77 f (finding, for wide samples of delistings in the EU, negative wealth effects in the period preceding the delisting announcement, explained by information leakages and insider trading that affect stock prices even before the actual announcement; these effects are however less pronounced in voluntary delistings than in involuntary delistings).

returns for minority shareholders, since controllers 'do not appear to pay lower premiums to exploit minority shareholders'.[64]

On the contrary, in the case of a *downlisting*, the findings referred to the German context are that announcements 'do not lead to statistically significant negative abnormal returns, regardless of the regulatory environment in which the downlisting takes place'.[65] The conclusion drawn is that 'a wealth loss of the shareholders following the announcement of a downlisting cannot be empirically proven'.[66] More so, according to one further study referred to the current German setting, under which the switch requires a cash offer to be launched, a statistically significant *positive* price reaction was observed not only on the day of the announcement and the following day, but also for longer event windows, indicating that the shareholders are overcompensated by the cash offer.[67] Downlisting, combined with a mandatory compensation offer for investors, would thus seem to overcompensate the shareholders.

These findings are essentially consistent with those of previous research equally referred to the German context under the *Frosta* setting. Even if not all studies available show statistically significant price reactions to the downlisting announcement,[68] the effects are, at any rate, less negative than with pure voluntary delisting.[69]

Results are also in line with those referred to the UK market, based on which firms whose equities were downlisted from the LSE to the AIM did experience average negative announcement effects of around 5 per cent, which were not, however, found to be statistically significant.[70] Strikingly, if longer-term share price performance after the switch is considered too, a 'strong positive drift for the down-switchers in the year following the switch' was observed, with risk-adjusted cumulative returns averaging around 25 per cent over the first year after switching.[71] Such post-switch upward drift was

[64] Croci and Del Giudice ibid 387 (further finding no evidence that firms' operating performance increases after delisting: which suggests that 'controlling shareholders do not take their companies private to avoid sharing the operating performance improvement with minority shareholders').

[65] Jonas, Budzinski, Deyerler and Mehring, *Non-technical Summary of the Expert Report on behalf of the Federal Republic of Germany* (n 62).

[66] ibid.

[67] Berninger, Schiereck and van de Vathorst (n 45) 343.

[68] See Doumet, Limbach and Theissen, 'Ich bin dann mal weg' (n 62) 253–77 (finding cumulative average abnormal price reactions of 1.53% in the interval +/- 1 since downlisting announcement, and of 0.81% from announcement to following day, which are however not statistically significant. Upon delisting announcement, results are instead unambiguously negative and significant, recording a cumulative average abnormal price change of -11.73% in the interval +/- 1 since announcement of the delisting, and of -11.71% from announcement to the following day); Karami and Schuster, *Eine empirische Analyse des Kurs- und Liquiditätseffekts auf die Ankündigung eines Börsenrückzugs am deutschen Kapitalmarkt im Lichte der FRoSTA Entscheidung des BGH* (n 62) 38; Pilsl and Knoll, 'Delisting und Börsenkurs' (n 62) 185 (finding no statistically significant negative price reaction on the day of the announcement or in [-3;+3]); Thomale and Walter, 'Delisting als Regulierungsaufgabe' (n 62) 710, 717.

[69] Berninger, Schiereck and van de Vathorst (n 45) 338 f (providing a detailed overview of the results of previous empirical research). See also L Pasch, A-K Schmeling and D Starke, 'Determinants and Consequences of Downlistings: An Analysis in the Light of Conflicting Interests of Management, Controlling and Non-Controlling Shareholders' (2017). Available at: www.ssrn.com/abstract=3052274, 39 (finding the average cumulative negative price reaction upon the delisting announcement to be relatively low and further observing a positive price reaction in around 40% of cases).

[70] Jenkinson and Ramadorai, 'Does One Size Fit All? The Consequences of Switching Markets with Different Regulatory Standards' (n 43) 871.

[71] ibid 873.

found to be associated with significant improvements in firm operating performance.[72] Ultimately, this finding suggests that 'the switch to a less regulated environment can be beneficial to some companies'.[73] It should follow that in the case of downlistings the cash offer requirement is redundant, if not even over-protective of investors' financial interests.

Interestingly, in the German setting, price effects are again negative upon announcement of voluntary *delistings from MTFs* – a hypothesis that falls outside the scope of application of section 39 BörsG and hence does not trigger the cash offer obligation. Under the *Frosta* setting, statistically significant negative price effects were unambiguously observed for delisting from the *Freiverkehr* on the event day and in the interval [-1; 1] in all studies.[74] Price drops were also found to be higher in the case of delisting from an MTF than with delisting from the regulated market.[75] Such negative market reaction is further confirmed under the current legal setting.[76]

B. Impact of the Transfer of Trading on Stock Liquidity

The other issue raised by downlisting is the liquidity of downlisted securities. Whilst it is reasonable to assume that the tradability of stocks moving from the regulated market to an MTF may be restricted once the transfer has taken place, the extent and significance of any such restriction needs to be assessed.

As a measure of liquidity, most of the studies available analyse the bid-ask spread after the changeover: if transactions are infrequent, the bid-ask spread is high, indicating illiquidity and hence high transaction costs and low significance of stock prices. Once again, research based on the German environment seems to prevail in the European context. Its overall findings show that, contrary to current belief, there are no significant changes in the relative bid-ask spread. Therefore, the liquidity of stocks moving from the regulated market to an MTF does not necessarily decrease.[77]

It should be noted that previous studies (also in the German context) come to ambiguous conclusions, finding either a decline in share liquidity of around 3 per cent after the switch,[78] or an increase of around 1.90 per cent.[79] However, as these studies themselves acknowledge, liquidity was already low well in advance of the downlisting announcement.[80]

Because of the explanatory function they can serve, findings related to the bid-ask spread *before the announcement* of the downlisting cannot be overlooked when assessing

[72] ibid 879 f.
[73] ibid 884.
[74] ibid. See also Pilsl and Knoll (n 62) 185.
[75] ibid.
[76] Berninger, Schiereck and van de Vathorst (n 45) 343.
[77] ibid 346 (finding, for the sample of downlisted firms analysed, that liquidity decreases slightly after the switch takes effect, and subsequently increases); Pasch, Schmeling and Starke, 'Determinants and Consequences of Downlistings (n 69) 42.
[78] Doumet, Limbach and Theissen (n 62) 23.
[79] Karami and Schuster (n 62) 54.
[80] Doumet, Limbach and Theissen (n 62) 17; Karami and Schuster (n 62) 33, 60.

stock liquidity following the actual shift. According to a study, the liquidity of both delisted and downlisted securities is lower than that of comparable CDAX companies in the 220 days prior to the announcement.[81] The spread tends, however, to be lower for downlistings than for delistings, regardless of whether the cash offer requirement applies.[82] The fact that the shares in the downlistings cluster tend to have the lowest spreads, therefore the highest liquidity, is very much in line with the assumption that 'shares in the OTC market are generally considered to be less liquid'.[83] For delistings alone, another German study considering a period of +/-125 trading days around the delisting announcement finds a median bid-ask spread of 3 to 5 per cent, above the median of both the DAX (0.3 per cent) and the CDAX (1.25 per cent), confirming that delisted stocks were already illiquid before the announcement.[84] More generally, these results confirm that delistings and downlistings mostly concern essentially illiquid shares.

It would therefore seem that low liquidity is not necessarily causally associated with downlisting. The relative bid-ask spread is not significantly reduced following the actual downlisting and the tradability of the shares is not meaningfully impaired. Overall, these findings would seem to suggest that it is not the listing on the regulated market per se that determines liquidity, but rather further factors such as the issuer's size, free float and course of business, affiliation to a certain industry, the number of trading days and the number of securities traded, as well as price volatility.[85] These very factors, particularly low stock liquidity and the lack of perception by the market, indicate an issuer's limited benefits associated with listing and act as strong drivers for the decision to downlist.[86]

VI. Is there (Still) a Case for Harmonising Downlisting?

The empirical evidence summarised in the preceding paragraphs would appear to support the need to differentiate the rules applicable to downlisting from those applicable to delisting. On the one hand, there seems not to be a sound empirical basis for requiring that shareholders be mandatorily offered compensation upon downlisting. On the other hand, a cash offer or functionally similar mechanisms appear instead to be needed to protect the shareholders from a fall in stock prices in the event of a voluntary delisting from the regulated markets.

[81] Jonas, Budzinski, Deyerler and Mehring (n 62) 55 f.
[82] ibid.
[83] ibid, Non-technical Summary.
[84] Aders, Muxfeld and Lill, 'Die Delisting-Neuregelung und die Frage nach dem Wert der Börsennotierung' (n 62) 397–398; B Karami and R Schuster, 'Anlegerschutz beim Börsenrückzug im Spannungsfeld zwischen Rechtsdogmatik, Jurisprudenz und Rechtstatsachenforschung – Problemskizze und Würdigung aus ökonomischer Sicht' (2016) *Corporate Finance* 106, 119.
[85] Ilyevich, *Delisting. Parallele zum Übernahmerecht. Probleme und Lösungsmöglichkeiten* (n 34) 111.
[86] Pasch, Schmeling and Starke (n 69) 45.

Due to these findings, the inconsistency of the rules applicable to downlisting across Member States raises the question of whether, despite the missed opportunity of the Listing Act, downlisting should still be harmonised, at least to some extent.

Given that exchange-led convergence of self-regulatory measures for downlisting is unlikely to be achieved (due to the profit-seeking nature of market operators and competition between venues to attract issuers), harmonisation would appear to be an appropriate response to the issues arising from fragmentation of the relevant regulatory frameworks, which inherently contradict the spirit of any EU intervention aimed at countering the decline of European public equity markets (see IV).

The challenges of harmonisation are, however, considerable.

To begin with, the results of the empirical research carried out thus far should be interpreted with caution. The studies available are limited in number, the findings are not unambiguous, and the size of the samples analysed is often relatively small. Especially with regard to share tradability after downlisting to an MTF, a general conclusion that shareholders are not unduly restricted in trading once the switch has taken effect would require support from evidence relating to venues located in more jurisdictions than the few, however relevant, considered in the studies illustrated above. Low liquidity, which is indeed a factor to be reckoned with, is generally considered as an established core market failure with SME listings.[87] Moreover, MTFs can be quite diverse in terms of liquidity, which is also a consequence of the large number of infrastructures that characterise the European share trading landscape.[88] For example, low liquidity on Euronext Growth Milan is regularly reported as a critical issue.[89] Conversely, liquidity on Euronext Growth Paris appears to be comparable to that on Euronext Paris.[90] Growth markets (and other MTFs) across the EU are also very different in size, with the largest growth markets, domiciled in Sweden and France, 'making up 70% of the total SME volumes on GMs'.[91] In addition, MTF share trading volumes are highly concentrated in a few countries: the Netherlands (63 per cent of MTF turnover volumes in 2022), France (24 per cent in 2022) and Germany (9 per cent in 2022).[92] While market fragmentation

[87] Technical Expert Stakeholder Group on SMEs (n 11) 12 f, 43; M Fenwick and EPM Vermeulen, 'The Effectiveness of Trading Venues in Facilitating Small and Medium-sized Enterprise Growth: An Examination of Liquidity and Regulatory Oversight' (May 2024) *ECGI Law Working Paper* No 768/2024. Available at: www.ssrn.com/abstract=4809704.

[88] See ESMA TRV Risk Analysis, *Evolution of EEA Share Market Structure since MiFID II* (n 50) 7 (at the end of 2022, the number of active infrastructures in the EEA stood at 158 trading venues: 59 regulated markets, 99 MTFs and 47 systematic internalisers. Share trading fragmentation is thus significantly more fragmented in EEA markets that in US markets, where only 24 national stock exchanges were active at the end of 2022 – out of which 20 belong to only four groups).

[89] See V Houlder, 'Private Trading Will Not Close London's IPO Gap' (London, Financial Times, 11 April 2024) *C* (reporting that Aim's daily trading volumes 'have recently averaged just 0.07 per cent of shares outstanding'); N Scoditti, 'The Euronext Growth Milan Market (EGM) at September 2023: A Detailed Analysis' (20 October 2023) *Hybris Corporate Finance*. Available at: www.hybriscf.it/articolo/34/il-mercato-euronext-growth-milan-egm-a-settembre-2023-unanalisi-dettagliata; and F Sabatini, E Chetrì and M Calusa, 'EGM Analysis 2023' (2024) *Banca Profilo Research*. Available at: www.bancaprofilo.it/wp-content/uploads/2024/01/Presentazione-EGM-4Q23-1601.pdf, 13 (both reporting that, in 2023, 50% of companies traded less than 0.1% of their market capitalisation on daily average).

[90] Annunziata and Lambiase (n 40) 31.

[91] ESMA, *EU Securities Markets 2023, ESMA50-524821-3149* (2024). Available at: www.esma.europa.eu/sites/default/files/2024-05/ESMA50-524821-3149_EU_Securities_Markets_2023.pdf, 13.

[92] ibid 15.

can be 'liquidity maximising for large capitalisation stocks', it can be 'detrimental for small and medium-sized enterprises (SMEs) and other less-actively traded stocks'.[93]

It is certainly true that MTFs are obliged to ensure the orderly execution of trading with exchange pricing in a manner as close as possible to that of regulated markets. In practice, however, different levels of market liquidity, depending on the specific trading venue, may affect the actual tradability of shares or the conditions for trading (mainly in terms of the price offered in relation to the intrinsic value of the shares) in one trading venue compared to another. Whether actual differences between MTFs operating in Europe should be a reason not to harmonise downlisting remains an open question, which would at least require a comprehensive comparative analysis of the venues concerned to be carried out.

Yet the EU legislator could consider the possibility of a rule that would exempt downlisting from the obligation to make a mandatory offer or cash compensation offer to minority shareholders, provided that the target unregulated market is sufficiently liquid.[94] Such a provision would leave room for the exchange to assess, on a case-by-case basis, when liquidity on the target venue is sufficient to prevent the application of major forms of investor protection; it would be a rule along the lines of those existing in some EU jurisdictions for migration of trading from one regulated market to another (domestic or European), which deactivate the compensatory remedy only if equivalent investor protection upon regular delisting is warranted in the target market (Article 133 CLF in Italy; section 39(2) phrase 2 lit b) BörsG in Germany).[95] In addition, EU law could provide for a reasonable waiting period between the date of announcement of the transfer and the date on which it takes effect to allow dissenting shareholders to sell their shares on the exchange.

It is instead far more questionable whether EU law should also give shareholders a say in the transfer and, if so, whether it should set out clear majority requirements. Requiring shareholder approval under EU law may affect the division of power between directors and shareholders, typically the province of non-harmonised and not to be easily harmonised company law. Any such requirement should therefore be left to national law.

However, a possible harmonisation of downlisting cannot be considered in isolation. The harmonised rule just hypothesised is based on the assumption that delisting from the regulated market requires some form of compensation to be offered to minority shareholders and that downlisting is treated as an exception. However, such an assumption would require some form of compensation obligation to be mandated upon voluntary delisting in all EU Member States. A harmonised regime for downlisting would therefore require that the rules applicable to voluntary delisting from regulated markets be harmonised. The very fact that only a minority of Member States provide for a national regime for delisting at the issuer's request illustrates the difficulty of introducing a harmonised delisting regime.

Further still, even voluntary delisting from exchange-regulated markets should be harmonised to allow for the possibility of regulating downlisting under a common

[93] ESMA TRV Risk Analysis (n 50) 5.
[94] See Thomale and Walter (n 62) 720.
[95] ibid.

EU-wide regime. On the issue of market exit, the rules for delisting from MTFs should indeed run in parallel with those for delisting from regulated markets.[96] If downlisting were to be exempt from a compensatory offer rule and no form of minority shareholder compensation were to apply to voluntary delisting from the MTF either, the resulting loophole would pave the way for 'staged' delisting from the regulated market, circumventing any compensation requirements otherwise triggered by voluntary delisting.[97] An issuer could take advantage of first moving trading to an MTF and then delisting from the MTF without having to offer compensation to shareholders at any stage of the process. Some form of compensatory remedy would therefore be needed not only in the case of pure delisting from regulated markets, but also in the case of delisting from exchange-regulated markets.

Moreover, as the same circumvention effect could also be achieved if, in the absence of common rules for delisting from MTFs, the issuer first moved trading from a regulated market to an exchange-regulated venue and then transferred trading to an MTF located in another Member State and subject to no or less stringent delisting rules,[98] a common anti-avoidance rule would additionally be needed.

Establishing a minimum common framework for investor protection in the case of delisting from MTFs would therefore seem to qualify as a (further) precondition for harmonisation of downlisting. If the EU were to move in this direction, it would arguably still have to leave room for national legislators, supervisors or market operators on many details of investor protection. For example, if EU law were to require a compensatory remedy for delisting from an MTF, pricing should not be more narrowly defined at EU level. Due to low liquidity, MTF prices may well not be meaningful or only marginally meaningful. The price would therefore need to be based on firm valuation, yet national rules for firm valuation – such as those for mergers – are not necessarily the same in all Member States.

In other words, EU intervention should, in principle, be more standards-based than rules-based, and should only set minimum standards. In this perspective, the recommendations made by the Technical Expert Group on SMEs back in 2021 in regard to delisting from Growth Markets could be considered by the European Commission: namely, that a harmonised set of good corporate governance principles related to minimum minority-protection requirements for delisting be introduced in EU legislation. Under one policy option proposed by the TESG, two layers of rules could be introduced, the first set of which, defined at EU level, would lay down general principles for SGM operators to build on when defining detailed provisions tailored to local conditions. Market operators would then be required to admit to trading only those issuers that comply with those detailed rules'. A second set of rules 'would then be developed by SGM operators and be applicable by issuers on a voluntary basis. Should these (voluntary) provisions not be complied with, SGM issuers would be required to issue a public document disclosing this arrangement'.[99]

[96] See Pilsl and Knoll (n 62) 186 for the German context.

[97] On staged delisting as a possible form of circumvention of the cash offer requirement under s 39 BörsG see Thomale and Walter (n 62) 719.

[98] ibid 720.

[99] Technical Expert Stakeholder Group on SMEs (n 11) 56.

If the challenge of harmonisation proved to be excessive, the Commission might still consider establishing an overarching principle that local markets operators implement appropriate transitional arrangements to facilitate the smooth shift to trading in both upward and downward directions.[100]

VII. Conclusion

Enhancing the attractiveness of European public equity markets is not solely reliant on the alleviation of regulatory costs and burdens associated with listing but also necessitates the consideration of the costs and burdens imposed on market exit. The implementation of viable downward market mobility could assist in reducing the listing gap within the EU. However, the disparate national regulatory frameworks currently set for downlisting can act as a hindrance. Empirical evidence appears to indicate that the need for investor protection is diminished in the context of downlisting in comparison to pure delisting. However, in order for the European Commission to reconsider the issue of the harmonisation of downlisting, it would be necessary to conduct further comprehensive empirical research on its effects, as well as of delisting from regulated markets and MTFs. Assessing liquidity across MTFs active within the Union would be beneficial too.

Nevertheless, the challenge of harmonisation requires a broader perspective to be adopted. Downlisting cannot be considered in isolation; rather, it requires that the rules governing voluntary delisting of securities from regulated markets and MTFs be consistent throughout the EU. Harmonisation in the field of market exit would need to be limited to securities law investor-protection remedies, without extending to any competing corporate law remedies. Regulatory intervention at the EU-level should be standards-based, rather than rules-based.

[100] As proposed by European Issuers, 'Comments on the EC Proposal on SME Listing Package' (2018). Available at: www.europeanissuers.eu/positions/files/view/5b5f049908fb6-en.

12

Delisting Rules and EU Capital Markets Integration

JONATHAN CHAN AND CARSTEN GERNER-BEUERLE*

I. Introduction

This chapter focuses on an under-appreciated feature of listing regimes – the 'regulatory costs' or difficulty of delisting, which can be understood as the regulatory barriers to exit.[1] This chapter argues that a delisting regime that is more difficult or costly for issuers – due to features such as the need in some jurisdictions to compensate dissenting minority shareholders, or prohibitively high shareholder approval requirements that make it near impossible to delist – has a negative effect on regulatory competition and may effectively impede the free movement of capital between EU Member States. More costly delisting regimes can be expected to lead to comparatively fewer voluntary delistings and could also theoretically result in fewer listings ex ante, if exit costs are high enough to deter entry for some firms. Thus, the first aim of this chapter is to understand how significantly the regulatory costs of delisting differ between jurisdictions. To do so, it constructs two indices that permit the measurement and comparison of delisting costs between jurisdictions. The first index, our Take Private Index, measures the regulatory barriers to take private transactions (voluntary delistings). The second index, our Market Migration Index, measures the regulatory barriers to market migrations

* Jonathan Chan, Assistant Professor at the Faculty of Law, McGill University, Canada, and Carsten Gerner-Beuerle, Professor of Commercial Law, Faculty of Laws, University College London. UK, and Global Distinguished Professor of Law, Notre Dame Law School, USA.We would like to thank Professors Rüdiger Veil and Vassilios Tountopoulos for organising the 'Delisting of Stock Corporations in Europe and Beyond' conference at the University of the Aegean in June 2023, at which this chapter was first presented. We are indebted to the conference participants for helpful comments and for sharing their delisting questionnaires, without which this research would not have been possible. All errors are our own. This chapter is adapted from J Chan and C Gerner-Beuerle, 'Delisting Costs and Corporate Mobility in Europe' (2024) 21 *European Company and Financial Law Review* 367.

[1] For example, in the current debate surrounding UK capital markets reform, a competitive listing regime is in the foreground, whereas delisting rules are largely absent from the discussion. See Financial Conduct Authority, *Primary Markets Effectiveness Review: Feedback to the discussion of the purpose of the listing regime and further discussion, Discussion Paper DP22/2* (May 2022). Available at: www.fca.org.uk/publication/discussion/dp22-2.pdf. Issues relating to competition and competitiveness are discussed on multiple occasions throughout the review, whereas cancellation of shares is only mentioned once (and not substantively).

where a firm moves from one market to another (eg, migrating a listing from Germany to the Netherlands).

If delisting rules can be described as a 'lobster trap' when entry is made easy, but exit is very difficult,[2] then this chapter compares, in relative terms, across a wide range of jurisdictions, just how trapped the lobsters are. We ultimately find that delisting costs differ significantly between listing regimes, which can be classified along a spectrum from 'prohibitive regimes' whereby voluntary delisting is extremely difficult due to high regulatory costs (eg, France, Netherlands, Finland) to 'permissive regimes' that facilitate exit by imposing few delisting requirements apart from a shareholder vote (eg, UK, Spain, Australia, Canada).

The second aim of this chapter is to set out the implications of these delisting costs for corporate mobility and capital allocation in the European Union (EU), with a particular focus on capital markets integration. Here we conceive of corporate mobility in a broader sense than the right of freedom of establishment as interpreted by the Court of Justice of the European Union (CJEU) in the *Centros* line of cases.[3] Corporate mobility should functionally include the possibility of migrating a listing between EU jurisdictions and the unfettered ability of a listed issuer in one Member State to exercise certain corporate powers (such as issuing securities to the public) in a different Member State through migration or cross-listing. The Treaty on the Functioning of the EU (TFEU) protects this type of corporate mobility by prohibiting restrictions on the free movement of capital within the EU (TFEU, Articles 63–66). We argue that delisting costs are so high in certain 'prohibitive regime' EU Member States that important components of corporate mobility are functionally impeded. We then evaluate a menu of policy options to ensure that delisting rules facilitate both efficient regulatory competition and corporate mobility, which is important given that delisting is the fate of most firms.[4] We also suggest that minority shareholder protection rights may be inefficiently strong in some EU jurisdictions, especially where they apply in cases of cross-border delistings.

The chapter is structured as follows. Part II contextualises our chapter within the broader law and finance literature on delistings. We review the reasons why public firms delist, as well as the characteristics of firms associated with a higher probability of going private. This chapter complements a strand of literature focusing on how higher regulatory compliance costs of maintaining a listing, such as following the passage of the Sarbanes–Oxley Act in the US, may contribute to delistings. Part III explains how we construct two indices to measure delisting costs. The first, our Take Private Index, allows for relative comparison of the difficulty of voluntary delisting in connection with an M&A (merger and acquisition) transaction. The second, our

[2] EB Rock, 'Securities Regulation as Lobster Trap: A Credible Commitment Theory of Mandatory Disclosure' (2002) 23 *Cardozo Law Review* 675.

[3] C Gerner-Beuerle and MA Schillig, *Comparative Company Law* (Oxford, Oxford University Press, 2019) 118–30.

[4] G Meeks and G Whittington, 'Death on the Stock Exchange: The Fate of the 1948 Population of Large UK Quoted Companies, 1948–2018' (2023) 65 *Business History* 679. Meeks and Whittington find that in a sample of 1,513 listed companies in 1948 (admitted to the Official List of the London Stock Exchange and some provincial exchanges), only 19 firms (1.26%) were still listed in 2018.

Market Migration Index, measures the difficulty of voluntary delisting in connection with the migration of a listing from one public trading venue to another. Part III also analyses UK regulation governing voluntary delistings. Part IV considers the implications of disparate delisting costs for the free movement of capital and the efficiency of capital allocation in the EU. Part V concludes and suggests that lower regulatory barriers to delisting would benefit EU capital markets integration by facilitating corporate mobility and increasing the efficiency of capital allocation within the EU.

Finally, a brief remark on terminology. By 'delisting', we mean the indefinite cancellation (as opposed to temporary suspension) of an issuer's listing and admission of securities to trading on a stock exchange. In jurisdictions such as the UK this results in the end of a public market for the issuer's securities, whereas in the US securities can be deregistered with the Securities and Exchange Commission (SEC) while still being publicly traded in over-the-counter markets.[5]

II. A Law and Finance Perspective on Delisting

A. Categorising Different Types of Delisting

Delisting can be voluntary or involuntary.[6] A delisting is voluntary if it is initiated at the will of the issuer. Most voluntary delistings occur in connection with a change in control transaction (eg, M&A), which we occasionally describe throughout this chapter using the term 'going private'.[7] Voluntary delistings also occur outside of M&A in the context of listing migrations or restructurings (eg, changing listing venue or moving from a dual to single listing), or in the case of a voluntary liquidation.[8] A delisting is involuntary if it results from firm failure (eg, non-strategic bankruptcy) or is initiated by the market operator against the will of the issuer (eg, exchange discipline). In some jurisdictions like the US, involuntary delistings are undertaken by the exchange rather

[5] In the US, a firm can deregister its securities with the Securities and Exchange Commission (SEC) to avoid reporting requirements ('going dark') while continuing to trade in over-the-counter markets (eg, Pink Sheets). This is not possible in the UK. See C Leuz, A Triantis and TY Wang, 'Why Do Firms Go Dark? Causes and Economic Consequences of Voluntary SEC Deregistrations' (2008) 45 *Journal of Accounting and Economics* 181; A Marosi and N Massoud, 'Why Do Firms Go Dark?' (2007) 42 *The Journal of Financial and Quantitative Analysis* 421; JM Fried, 'Firms Gone Dark' (2009) 76 *The University of Chicago Law Review* 135. On OTC trading, see R Davis et al, 'Modern OTC Market Structure and Liquidity: The Tale of Three Tiers' (2023) 64 *Journal of Financial Markets* 100815.

[6] JR Macey, M O'Hara and D Pompilio, 'Down and Out in the Stock Market: The Law and Economics of the Delisting Process' (2008) 51 *The Journal of Law & Economics* 683. NYSE Regulation also distinguishes between 'Exchange-Initiated Delisting' and 'Issuer-Initiated Delisting', see NYSE Regulation, 'Removal From Listings' (2023). Available at: www.nyse.com/regulation/delistings?market=NYSE.

[7] On the definition of going private transactions, see I Martinez and S Serve, 'Reasons for Delisting and Consequences: A Literature Review and Research Agenda' (2017) 31 *Journal of Economic Surveys* 733, 737.

[8] Macey and others note that 'voluntary delistings occur as the natural consequence of a merger, a decision to take the firm private, a voluntary liquidation, or a company's decision to list only in its home market'. See Macey, O'Hara and Pompilio, 'Down and Out in the Stock Market' (n 6) 689.

than the public securities regulator.[9] We therefore assign delistings into one of the four categories below (see Table 12.1).[10]

Table 12.1 Delisting Typology

A: Voluntary (in connection with M&A)	*B: Voluntary (no M&A)*
• Acquisition (eg, merger or scheme where surviving entity is a private company) • Take-private transaction (eg, MBO)	• Dual listing to single listing (eg, Ryanair) • Migration of single listing, either between market segments or across markets • Voluntary liquidation (eg, strategic bankruptcy)
C: Involuntary (financial distress)	*D: Involuntary (no financial distress)*
• Bankruptcy • Exchange discipline due to financial distress	• Exchange discipline for violation of listing rules (not related to financial health)

B. A Brief Review of the Literature on Delisting

The question 'Why do public firms delist?' has a seemingly straightforward answer: firms delist when the costs of listing exceed the benefits. A considerable body of work has been devoted to examining this cost–benefit calculus. Corporate finance theorists conceive listing costs as including all features that decrease firm value,[11] and listing benefits as including the private benefits of control.[12] A firm's decision to go private can be modelled as the flip side of the decision to go public via an initial public offering (IPO) – a controller might weigh delisting costs such as less liquidity against benefits such as having more control in decision-making.[13] This cost-benefit calculus can be framed as a wealth-maximisation problem, whereby a founder's decision to go public (or private) results from whichever trade-off of cash flow rights against control rights maximises their wealth.[14] Lower delisting costs should negatively affect firms' cost–benefit ratio of remaining publicly listed, and result in more public firms going private.

[9] ibid 710 f.

[10] Martinez and Serve also have a helpful delisting typology, which differs most notably from ours by categorising voluntary delistings into those with and without subsequent trading, rather than categorising based on a change in control transaction. See Martinez and Serve, 'Reasons for Delisting and Consequences' (n 7) 736–38. Onesti et al have also proposed a classification of voluntary and involuntary delistings. See T Onesti et al, 'On Delisting of Corporations: A Three-Dimensional Classification Framework for Voluntary Delistings' (2014) 4 *World Review of Business Research* 1.

[11] C Doidge, GA Karolyi, and RM Stulz, 'Why Do Foreign Firms Leave U.S. Equity Markets?' (2010) 65 *The Journal of Finance* 1507, 1509. Doidge, Karolyi and Stulz write that: 'Listing costs include all costs incurred as a result of the listing that reduce firm value.'

[12] ibid 1508.

[13] ST Bharath and AK Dittmar, 'Why Do Firms Use Private Equity to Opt Out of Public Markets?' (2010) 23 *The Review of Financial Studies* 1771 f.

[14] L Zingales, 'Insider Ownership and the Decision to Go Public' (1995) 62 *The Review of Economic Studies* 425.

In a review of the literature, Bharath and Dittmar identify five theoretical drivers behind a firm's listing/delisting decision: '(i) information considerations [eg, adverse selection problems that reduce firm valuations]; (ii) access to capital; (iii) control; (iv) liquidity; and (v) agency and other considerations [eg, reduced managerial agency costs after going private].'[15] These reasons have been empirically tested in a significant body of research on which firm-specific characteristics are most relevant in explaining why firms go private. In a thorough literature review of the research on delisting, Martinez and Serve summarise these findings, noting which studies find positive/negative/null relationships between delistings and variables such as firm size, financial performance, risk of financial distress, firm valuation (specifically under-valuation), growth prospects, debt levels/leverage, financial visibility (analyst coverage), and liquidity.[16] In canvassing the literature, Martinez and Serve suggest that these firm-specific characteristics are relevant because they 'influence their [firms'] ability to afford listing costs'.[17]

For example, one prominent study of US firms going private between 1980–2003 finds that firms are more likely to go private when, compared to their peers, they have less analyst coverage, fewer institutional investors, more concentrated ownership and less liquidity.[18] Another recent study of German delistings from 2003–15 suggests that 'cost–benefit considerations are an important explanatory factor' in delistings, and finds that 'decreasing growth opportunities, liquidity and profitability as well as increasing regulatory costs' are associated with a higher probability of firms either down-listing (migrating from a more to less regulated market) or going private.[19] The empirical research on whether high free cash flows are associated with an increased likelihood of going private is mixed.[20]

C. Background to how Regulatory Costs Influence Delisting

Our research is situated within the significant body of research exploring how regulatory costs are relevant to the listing and delisting cost–benefit calculus. Much of this research examines whether the passage of the Sarbanes–Oxley Act of 2002 ('SOX') in the US – which occurred in the wake of scandals such as Enron and WorldCom and instituted more rigorous financial reporting requirements, corporate governance disclosure, and structural corporate governance requirements, among other reforms – contributed to more firms exiting public markets as the regulatory compliance costs

[15] Bharath and Dittmar, 'Why Do Firms Use Private Equity' (n 13) 1776.

[16] Martinez and Serve (n 7) 740–43.

[17] ibid 742.

[18] Bharath and Dittmar (n 13) 1774.

[19] W Bessler et al, 'Why Do Firms Down-List or Exit from Securities Markets? Evidence from the German Stock Exchange' (2023) 17 *Review of Managerial Science* 1175, 1207.

[20] K Lehn and A Poulsen, 'Free Cash Flow and Stockholder Gains in Going Private Transactions' (1989) 44 *The Journal of Finance* 771. But see L Renneboog, T Simons and M Wright, 'Why Do Public Firms Go Private in the UK? The Impact of Private Equity Investors, Incentive Realignment and Undervaluation' (2007) 13 *Journal of Corporate Finance* 591. Renneboog, Simons and Wright find that firm undervaluation (connected with informational asymmetries) and reduced agency costs are the most important drivers of UK public to private transactions, with no evidence for the excess free cash-flow hypothesis.

of maintaining a listing increased and the private benefits of control correspondingly decreased (due to more stringent corporate governance requirements such as having audit committees entirely constituted of independent directors).[21]

Many of the studies find that the post-SOX increase in compliance costs for listed firms contributed to more delistings, sometimes called the 'SOX cost hypothesis'.[22] Hostak et al observe that more than three-quarters of the firms in their sample (foreign firms who voluntarily deregistered their American Depositary Receipts between 1997–2006) cited compliance costs in their deregistration announcement.[23] Leuz, Triantis and Wang attribute an increase in securities deregistration with the SEC ('going dark') to the passage of SOX and its internal control requirements (eg, section 404), suggesting that, in addition to higher compliance costs, 'some firms exit the SEC reporting system because their insiders face more scrutiny and higher penalties after SOX'.[24] Chaplinsky and Ramchand find that the probability of foreign firms delisting in the US after SOX is higher for firms who are domiciled in countries with stronger corporate governance, suggesting that bonding and other benefits of a cross-listing were outweighed by increased costs post-SOX for some firms.[25] Conversely, Gao, Ritter and Zhu contest the SOX cost hypothesis,[26] as do Doidge, Karolyi and Stulz, the latter attributing the decline in US listings to an increased rate of M&A activity rather than regulatory costs.[27]

D. Contribution to the Delisting Literature

As highlighted above, most of the delisting literature focuses on finance-related drivers of delisting that are either firm-specific (eg, valuations, analyst coverage, turnover, etc) or market-wide (eg, availability of private capital, the need for larger firms/economies of scope, etc). The delisting research that engages with regulatory costs tends to use panel data to explore how changes in compliance costs or corporate governance requirements affect delistings (eg, rates of listing/delisting following SOX).

However, the emphasis in the literature is on whether the regulatory costs of *being listed* contribute to delistings, rather than analysing the regulatory costs of *terminating a listing* and considering how the costliness of exit and the delisting process itself could influence listing and delisting activity. The importance of regulation governing the

[21] For a discussion of the SOX requirements, see Gerner-Beuerle and Schillig, *Comparative Company Law* (n 3), 274 f.

[22] Martinez and Serve (n 7) 743f.

[23] P Hostak et al, 'An Examination of the Impact of the Sarbanes–Oxley Act on the Attractiveness of U.S. Capital Markets for Foreign Firms' (2013) 18 *Review of Accounting Studies* 522, 524.

[24] Leuz, Triantis and Wang, 'Why Do Firms Go Dark?' (n 5).

[25] S Chaplinsky and L Ramchand, 'What Drives Delistings of Foreign Firms from U.S. Exchanges?' (2012) 22 *Journal of International Financial Markets, Institutions & Money* 1126f. Chaplinsky and Ramchand measure corporate governance quality using the index developed by De Nicolò, Laeven and Ueda. See G De Nicolò, G Laeven and K Ueda, 'Corporate Governance Quality: Trends and Real Effects' (2008) 17 *Journal of Financial Intermediation* 198.

[26] X Gao, JR Ritter and Z Zhu, 'Where Have All the IPOs Gone?' (2013) 48 *Journal of Financial and Quantitative Analysis* 1663.

[27] C Doidge, GA Karolyi and RM Stulz, 'The U.S. Listing Gap' (2017) 123 *Journal of Financial Economics* 464, 466f.

delisting process has not gone without appreciation, though in the context of voluntary delistings it has been under-theorised.[28] Vismara, Paleari and Ritter remark that 'the difference in the rate of delisting must also consider regulatory differences', noting that 'delisting is more difficult and "costly" in continental Europe' due to requirements to buy out minority shareholders.[29] We continue in the line of inquiry raised by Vismara, Paleari and Ritter, who, investigating the difference between primary markets (EU regulated markets) and second markets (typically multilateral trading facilities or 'MTFs'), demonstrate that 'IPOs that list on second markets are more likely to be subsequently delisted or targeted by an acquiring firm'.[30]

Within the legal literature that focuses on delisting regulation, Zetzsche analyses the similarity in regulatory costs for cold delistings (eg, a public-to-private freeze-out) versus regular delistings faced by controlling shareholders in German listed companies.[31] Maume compares UK and German delisting regulations with detail and clarity, proposing reform suggestions for the German regime.[32] Zmysłowska compares how minority shareholders are protected in delisting across different EU regimes.[33]

Our delisting indices allow future research to empirically test hypotheses on the association between the regulatory costs of delisting and the number of firms entering and exiting public markets in a range of jurisdictions, thereby complementing the studies mentioned above. Intuitively, the regulatory costs of delisting – ie, how onerous or permissive the regulatory requirements are in allowing an issuer to cancel its listing and shares admitted to trading – makes delisting more or less *sticky*. This can be expected to influence firms' delisting decisions and affect corporate mobility if, in addition to the usual costs and benefits of maintaining a listing, firms factor in the costliness of exit in the delisting decision calculus. In this vein, one may expect that the *stickier* the delisting regime (ie, higher costs imposed by regulation to exit), the fewer voluntary delistings there would be.

Figure 12.1 Delisting decision timeline

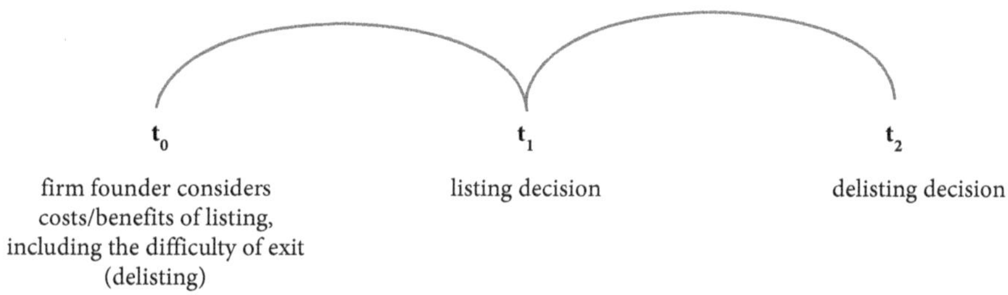

[28] For a seminal analysis of involuntary delistings, see Macey, O'Hara and Pompilio (n 6).

[29] S Vismara, S Paleari and JR Ritter, 'Europe's Second Markets for Small Companies' (2012) 18 *European Financial Management* 352, 371.

[30] ibid 383.

[31] DA Zetzsche, 'Going Dark Under German Law – Towards an Efficient Regime for Regular Delisting' (29 January 2014). Available at: papers.ssrn.com/sol3/papers.cfm?abstract_id=2387712.

[32] P Maume, 'The Parting of the Ways: Delisting Under German and UK Law' (2015) 16 *European Business Organization Law Review* 255.

[33] M Zmysłowska, 'Protection of Interests of Minority Shareholders in the Case of the Delisting of a Company in the Light of Regulations Binding in Europe' (2023) 18 *Capital Markets Law Journal* 391.

Relatedly, if private firm owners perceive the delisting regime to be *sticky* (ie, more costly to exit at t_2), they may be less likely to list in the first place (at t_1), because the future costs of delisting are higher in these regimes relative to the benefits of a listing (see Figure 12.1). This intuition builds on work by Chemmanur, Signori, and Vismara, who demonstrate that different post-IPO scenarios, such as the likelihood of being acquired, influence private firm founders' decision to go public.[34]

III. Constructing Indices to Measure the Regulatory Costs of Delisting

Many studies rely on corporate governance or investor protection indices to either control for or examine the role of corporate law and regulation on delisting. For example, delisting studies employ the World Bank governance ratings,[35] La Porta et al's investor protection index,[36] Djankov et al's anti-director rights index,[37] and De Nicolò's corporate governance index.[38] However, we have not yet come across an index capturing how difficult or costly it is to delist.

We create two bespoke delisting indices, distinguishing between take-private transactions (voluntary delistings) and market migrations where a firm moves from one market segment to another. We make this distinction because most EU jurisdictions (not the UK) regulate take-private transactions and market migration differently; the former often more stringently, such as imposing different shareholder approval requirements or waiving the requirement to make a tender offer to minority shareholders in the case of market migrations. Our Take-Private Index (TPI) and Market-Migration Index (MMI) examine delisting requirements in EU 'regulated markets' (larger exchanges such as Euronext or the Frankfurt Stock Exchange),[39] and therefore do not measure how costly it is to delist from MTFs (so-called 'second markets' such as AIM). The two indices allow for the comparison and ranking of delisting regimes from *most to least costly to exit*, with a high index value representing comparatively high regulatory costs.

[34] TJ Chemmanur, A Signori and S Vismara, 'The Exit Choices of European Private Firms: A Dynamic Empirical Analysis' (2023) 65 *Journal of Financial Markets* 100821.

[35] S Thomsen and F Vinten, 'Delistings and the Costs of Governance: A Study of European Stock Exchanges 1996–2004' (2014) 18 *Journal of Management & Governance* 793; Chemmanur, Signori and Vismara, 'The Exit Choices of European Private Firms (n 34).

[36] Thomsen and Vinten, 'Delistings and the Costs of Governance' (n 36). Thomsen and Vinten use the LLSV index as updated by Pagano and Volpin (2005).

[37] Doidge, Karolyi, and Stulz, 'Why Do Foreign Firms Leave U.S. Equity Markets?' (n 11).

[38] Chaplinsky and Ramchand, 'What Drives Delistings?' (n 25).

[39] For an explanation of 'regulated markets' under MiFID II, see D Busch, 'MiFID II and MiFIR: Stricter Rules for the EU Financial Markets' (2017) 11 *Law and Financial Markets Review* 126 f.

A. Index Codex Criteria

The Take-Private Index (TPI) is composed of the following 10 indicators:

Variable	**Coding criteria**
1. tp_codified	Takes the value zero if the requirements for a take-private transaction are set out in law or regulations, and one otherwise. [eg, a law that provides for the possibility of a delisting, but does not set out the requirements to be fulfilled to delist an issuer (eg, a law that does not specify which corporate organ is responsible for the delisting decision), will receive the value of one. Likewise, a law that does not provide for a delisting procedure but requires companies to pursue another corporate transaction that makes it impossible for the issuer to retain a listing (eg, a takeover followed by a squeeze-out), will receive the value one.]
2. tp_quorum	Quorum in the general meeting to delist; takes the value zero if no shareholder vote or no minimum quorum is required and expressed as the percentage of the share capital that must be represented at the meeting otherwise.
3. tp_majority	Majority in the general meeting to delist; takes the value zero if no shareholder vote is required, 0.5 for a simple majority, 0.67 for a two-thirds majority, and the percentage of votes required for a delisting resolution otherwise.
4. tp_veto	Takes the value zero if a delisting resolution is not conditional on approval by a majority of the minority and no comparable minority veto rights exist, and one otherwise.
5. tp_discretion	Takes the value zero if a market regulator/operator has no discretion in approving an application for delisting, provided a set of formal requirements are satisfied, and one otherwise. [eg, where a market regulator has the power to reject an application because it would be detrimental to the interests of the investors or the orderly functioning of the market, the variable will take the value one.]
6. tp_buyout	Takes the value zero if the issuer or majority shareholder is not required to buy out dissenting shareholders in the case of a delisting, and one otherwise.
7. tp_buyout_price	Takes the value zero if the issuer or majority shareholder is not required to buy out dissenting shareholders or there are no appraisal rights or other mechanisms to ensure that shareholders receive fair value (such as calculating the buyout price with reference to the average market price before the delisting decision), and one otherwise.

(continued)

(Continued)

Variable	Coding criteria
8. tp_substantive	Takes the value zero if shareholders cannot challenge a delisting decision of the company (taken by the board of directors and/or the general meeting, as appropriate) on substantive grounds, for example by claiming that the delisting decision encroaches on their rights as shareholders (eg, is prejudicial to their interests, etc), other than according to general directors' duties or duties imposed on shareholders; takes the value one if shareholders can challenge a delisting decision on such grounds.
9. tp_foreign_issuers	Takes the value of zero if foreign issuers are subject to no additional requirements, and one otherwise.
10. tp_time_delay	Takes the value of zero if no precondition for delisting imposes minimum time requirements of 180 days or more relating to any feature (eg, liquidity), and one otherwise.

The Market Migration Index (MMI) is composed of the following 11 indicators:

Variable	Coding criteria
1. mm_codified	[Same as tp_codified]
2. mm_quorum	[Same as tp_quorum]
3. mm_majority	[Same as tp_majority]
4. mm_veto	[Same as tp_veto]
5. mm_EU_listing	Takes the value zero if it is not a precondition for a delisting that the shares are listed on another regulated market in the EU (but they can be listed outside the EU), and one otherwise.
6. mm_discretion	[Same as tp_discretion]
7. mm_buyout	[Same as tp_buyout]
8. mm_buyout_price	[Same as tp_buyout_price]
9. mm_substantive	[Same as tp_substantive]
10. mm_foreign_issuers	[Same as tp_foreign_issuers]
11. mm_time_delay	[Same as tp_time_delay]

B. Index Values

Our TPI and MMI indices for the countries listed in Table 12.2 below are coded based on country questionnaires specifying aspects of delisting law, regulation and jurisprudence. The questionnaires were completed by experienced legal academics in each jurisdiction and circulated for comments and discussion. Index values are presented in the Appendix.

Table 12.2 Jurisdictions in the TPI and MMI

Jurisdiction	TPI Score (highest to lowest)	MMI Score
1. France (Euronext Paris)	8.8	7.5
2. Netherlands (Euronext Amsterdam)	6.9	3
3. Finland (Nasdaq Helsinki)	5.8	5.8
4. Sweden (Nasdaq Stockholm)	5	3.5
5. Greece (Athens Stock Exchange)	4.9	4.8
6. Italy (Borsa Italiana/Euronext Milan)	4.87	2.87
7. Austria (Wiener Boerse)	4.75	3.75
8. Belgium (Euronext Brussels)	3.95	4.25
9. Cyprus (Cyprus Stock Exchange)	3.9	3.9
10. Australia (Australian Securities Exchange)	3.5	1
11. Germany (Börse Frankfurt)	3	2
12. Spain (BME Exchange)	2.75	2.75
13. UK (LSE) (premium segment)	1.75	1.75
14. Canada (Toronto Stock Exchange)	1.5	1
15. UK (LSE) (standard segment)[40]	0	0

The TPI scores indicate that when it comes to voluntary delisting, France has the highest delisting costs (8.8 out of 10) and the UK has the lowest (when averaging the premium and standard segment TPI scores of the LSE Main Market).[41] The mean TPI score is 4.09 ($\sigma = 2.20$) and the mean MMI score is 3.19 ($\sigma = 1.96$). Eleven of the 13 jurisdictions sit within one standard deviation of the mean TPI score, and 10 of the 13 jurisdictions sit within one standard deviation of the mean MMI score. Fewer jurisdictions require a mandatory tender offer to dissenting shareholders in the case of market migrations when compared to conventional going private transactions: the mean mm_buyout value (.33) is considerably lower than the mean tp_buyout value (.73). Shareholder approval requirements are lower on average for market migrations than take private delistings: the mean mm_majority value (.47) is lower than the mean tp_majority value (.63), as is the mean mm_quorum value (.18) when compared to the mean tp_quorum value (.33). Most jurisdictions explicitly provide for a delisting procedure (separate from a squeeze-out procedure) in law or regulations (mean

[40] Our indices reflect UK delisting regulation at the time of writing, prior to the UK Financial Conduct Authority's enactment of a simplified listing regime in July 2024. Under the recently enacted UK Listing Rules (UKLR) in July 2024, the premium and standard segments of the LSE are replaced by a single segment: Commercial Companies (Equity Shares) or ESCC. Commercial companies previously listed on the premium segment will be 'mapped' to the ESCC category, and commercial companies previously listed on the standard segment of the LSE will be 'mapped' to a transition category or secondary listing category. See Financial Conduct Authority, *Primary Markets Effectiveness Review: Feedback to CP 23/31 and final UK Listing Rules, Policy Statement PS24/6* (July 2024). Available at: www.fca.org.uk/publication/policy/ps24-6.pdf.

[41] Standard-listed securities on the LSE Main Market can be cancelled without a shareholder vote, so long as 20 business days' notice is provided to shareholders. See Listing Rule 5.2.8.

tp_codified value is. 33), grant the regulator or market regulator discretion in refusing a voluntary delisting (mean tp_discretion and mm_discretion values are. 53), and do not provide shareholders with statutory or regulatory recourse to challenge a voluntary delisting that is otherwise compliant with the applicable requirements (mean tp_substantive and mm_substantive values are. 40).

We categorise jurisdictions as having a *prohibitive*, *permissive*, or *differential* regulatory approach to voluntary delistings. A regime is prohibitive if it sets out requirements that effectively preclude voluntary delistings, such as a very high (≥ 90 per cent) quorum or shareholder approval requirement, or if the cost of a voluntary delisting is prohibitively high because of the cumulative effect of multiple delistings requirements (as reflected by the aggregate value TPI and MMI indices). This is illustrated in the first column of Table 12.3 below, whereby all of the 'prohibitive delisting' jurisdictions, which represent the nine jurisdictions with the highest TPI scores pursuant to Table 12.2, have quorum or shareholder approval requirements higher than 90 per cent *and* require a mandatory buyout of minority shareholders in all cases.[42]

Permissive regimes impose less-stringent requirements for voluntary delisting than prohibitive regimes. A regime is permissive if its most onerous requirement is a moderately high shareholder vote (≤ 75 per cent), coupled with relatively few other requirements (such as a majority of the minority vote or providing the regulator with discretion to reject a voluntary delisting application), but it does not require a mandatory buyout of dissenting minority shareholders. Extremely permissive delisting regimes, like the LSE standard segment in the UK, do not impose issuers with any material regulatory obstacles to delisting: shareholder approval is not required, nor can dissenting minority shareholders effectively challenge a delisting decision. The decision is left in the hands of the directors whom the shareholders appointed. Moderately permissive regimes such as the LSE premium segment (UK) and Canada require a majority of independent shareholders to approve a voluntary delisting when the issuer has a controlling shareholder, and Australia provides shareholders with a statutory remedy to challenge voluntary delistings with the Takeovers Panel.[43]

The jurisdictions in column 3 of Table 12.3 have regulatory requirements that substantially differ for take-private transactions and market migrations, as indicated by their different TPI and MMI scores. All these jurisdictions have a considerably lower MMI score than TPI score, suggesting that the approach to regulating market migrations is more permissive than for voluntary delistings. For example, some jurisdictions lower or remove altogether otherwise very high shareholder approval requirements upon a market migration, such as in the Netherlands. In some jurisdictions, such as Austria and Italy (as well as Germany and Spain), more lenient requirements only apply if the issuer migrates to another EU/EEA regulated market specifically.

[42] Germany and Spain require a mandatory buyout of minority shareholders, but do not impose high shareholder approval requirements, and therefore are more borderline classifications.

[43] In addition to the oppression remedy, adjudicated by the courts (and a feature of UK and Canadian company law), Australian shareholders can and have relied upon the 'unacceptable circumstances' remedy to challenge a delisting with the Takeovers Panel. See Corporations Act 2001 Pt 2F.1 and Pt 6.10 div 2 subdiv B.

Table 12.3 Classifying delisting regimes

Prohibitive	Permissive	Differential (prohibitive for take privates, permissive for market migrations)
France	Australia	Netherlands
Finland	Canada	Sweden
Greece	UK (both MM segments)	Italy
Belgium	Germany (borderline)	Austria
Cyprus	Spain (borderline)	

C. Methodological Challenges to Index Construction

In this section, we discuss possible challenges to the methodology underlying the construction of our TPI and MMI scores. A first issue in the construction of an index or composite indicator – whether it be the World Economic Forum's Global Competitiveness Index, LLSV's anti-director rights index (ADRI), or our indices – is whether the variables contained in the index validly measure the systematised concept (in our case, delisting costs).[44] All the variables in the TPI and MMI measure how difficult or costly it is to delist in some regard. Variables concerning shareholder voting requirements or additional requirements for foreign issuers or minimum time requirements measure one component of delisting difficulty: satisfying more onerous ex ante conditions to delist. Other variables concerning legal challenges by shareholders measure a different component of difficulty: withstanding challenges after the initial conditions have been satisfied. Variables concerning whether a market regulator has discretion to approve a delisting or whether the delisting requirements are codified measure the legal certainty of a delisting application. More uncertainty increases delisting difficulty because the probability of an unsuccessful application increases, as do time and information-gathering costs. Variables concerning requirements to buy out dissenting shareholders measure the costliness of delisting, since making a tender offer to dissenting shareholders materially increases the financial costs of delisting, and more capital is needed to delist. Costliness and difficulty are related concepts and go hand in hand, since a costlier delisting (whether financially or in terms of opportunity costs) is more difficult, all else being equal.

A second issue in index construction is how to appropriately weight different variables. While acknowledging potential pitfalls, we weight all of the variables equally to minimise researcher subjectivity.[45] In doing so, we follow established

[44] On construct validity, see R Adcock and D Collier, 'Measurement Validity: A Shared Standard for Qualitative and Quantitative Research' (2001) 95 *American Political Science Review* 529.

[45] We employ a linear aggregation method whereby each indicator value is added to arrive at a composite score, rather than other methods, such as contingent indexing, which are employed to measure the interaction of different indicators (eg, legal rules) with each other. See D Ferreira et al, 'Management Insulation and Bank Failures' (2021) 47 *Journal of Financial Intermediation* 100909. Discussing index weights and aggregation, the Organisation for Economic Co-operation and Development (OECD) acknowledges that 'weights are essentially value judgements'. See OECD, European Commission and Joint Research Centre, *Handbook on Constructing Composite Indicators: Methodology and User Guide* (2008). Available at: www.oecd.org/

methods of index construction used by the World Bank, Organisation for Economic Co-operation and Development (OECD), and others.[46] However, by including two binary variables that account for whether regulation requires an issuer to make a cash offer to minority shareholders to delist (eg, Austrian law requires a buyout offer that must not be lower than the issuer's average trading price over the last six months) and that should always move together – the presence of a tender offer requirement (tp_buyout) as well as a separate variable that receives a one if regulation includes a codified offer appraisal mechanism (tp_buyout_price) – we double weight what we perceive to be the most costly delisting indicator in our index.[47]

A third issue with any index is ensuring that the coding and index values are accurate. For example, Spamann's recoding and correction of the 1998 ADRI 'diverges substantially' from the original LLSV index (the correlation coefficient is 'only 0.53'), undermining some of LLSV's original claims.[48] To reduce the probability of coding errors due to misunderstanding the questionnaires, we contacted the questionnaire authors to seek clarification when we felt it necessary.

D. UK Regime for Voluntary Delistings

In this section we consider salient elements of the UK delisting regime as it applies to premium-listed issuers on the Main Market of the London Stock Exchange (LSE) to provide an example of a jurisdiction with comparatively lenient or permissive delisting regulation.[49]

Delisting is governed by the listing rules contained in the Financial Conduct Authority (FCA) Handbook, and is referred to as 'cancellation' of listing.[50] The listing rules were formerly administered by the London Stock Exchange (LSE), but are now public regulation administered by the FCA since the passing of the Financial

content/dam/oecd/en/publications/reports/2008/08/handbook-on-constructing-composite-indicators-methodology-and-user-guide_g1gh9301/9789264043466-en.pdf, 31.

[46] The World Bank *Doing Business* report weights all topics equally in its composite indicator. See World Bank, *Doing Business 2020, Comparing Business Regulation in 190 Economies* (Washington, DC, World Bank, 2020) 81. See also OECD, European Commission and Joint Research Centre, *Handbook on Constructing Composite Indicators* (n 45) 31–33. Widely used indices such as Bebchuk, Cohen and Ferrell's entrenchment index ('E-index') also use equally weighted components. See eg LA Bebchuk, A Cohen and A Ferrell, 'What Matters in Corporate Governance?' (2009) *The Review of Financial Studies* 783.

[47] Collinearity among indicators is not a problem if double weighting is intentional, since 'weights should ideally reflect the contribution of each indicator to the composite'. OECD, European Commission and Joint Research Centre (n 45) 32.

[48] H Spamann, 'The "Antidirector Rights Index" Revisited' (2010) 23 *The Review of Financial Studies* 467, 483. See also M Graff, 'Law and Finance: Common Law and Civil Law Countries Compared – An Empirical Critique' (2008) 75 *Economica* 60.

[49] Our discussion of UK delisting regulation and calculation of index values for the LSE Main Market (premium and standard segments) were conducted prior to the UK Financial Conduct Authority's enactment of a simplified listing regime in July 2024. While changes to the UK listing regime are sweeping, the rules relating to delisting ('cancellations') were not significantly reformed: the core shareholder approval requirements, notice, and independent shareholder vote requirements for issuers with a controlling shareholder all remain the same. See FCA Handbook, UK Listing Rule 21.2.8 (July 2024).

[50] FCA Handbook, Listing Rule 5.2.

Services and Markets Act (FSMA) 2000.[51] The process of cancelling a listing is relatively straightforward: first, at least 20 business days in advance of the anticipated date of cancellation, the issuer (authorised by the board of directors) must issue a circular to shareholders calling for a general meeting.[52] The circular must contain an extensive list of information, including 'a clear and adequate explanation of its subject matter giving due prominence to its essential characteristics, benefits and risks'.[53] Then, at the general meeting, at least 75 per cent of shareholders must vote to approve the resolution for the delisting.[54] If, however, the issuer has a 'controlling shareholder', defined as a shareholder who controls more than 30 per cent of the votes to be cast at the general meeting, then at the general meeting a majority of independent shareholders voting on the resolution must also approve the delisting.[55] Notably, in comparison to other European jurisdictions, there is no minimum shareholder quorum requirement for the general meeting at which the delisting resolution is voted on. Once the cancellation of shares is effected, shareholders will be stuck with illiquid shares, making it imperative for shareholders to sell their shares during the notice period prior to the delisting vote. However, this is not problematic for shareholders in the majority of voluntary delistings on the LSE Main Market, which are M&A-related take-private transactions whereby shareholders receive either cash or shares in the buyer as consideration.[56]

The above features of the UK delisting regime for LSE premium-listed companies – a shareholder vote requiring 75 per cent approval (though without a quorum requirement) at the general meeting, and additional majority approval by independent shareholders for issuers with controlling shareholders – are relatively minimal regulatory barriers that facilitate delistings while maintaining a sufficient baseline of investor protection. These requirements also apply to downlisting from the premium segment to the standard segment or Alternative Investment Market (AIM), with the additional requirement that the issuer migrating its listing will also need a letter from its listing sponsor.[57]

The UK delisting regime is more permissive in comparison to many other EU regulated markets in that it does not:

- impose regulatory barriers involving discretion by the competent authority to refuse delistings;

[51] The UK Companies Act 2006 does not regulate delisting, though it contains a procedure for minority shareholder squeeze-outs following 90% shareholder acceptance of a takeover offer (see Pt 28 ch 3 of the Companies Act 2006).

[52] FCA Handbook, Listing Rule 5.2.5.

[53] ibid Listing Rule 13.3.

[54] ibid Listing Rule 5.2.5.

[55] ibid Listing Rule 5.2.5(2)(b).

[56] The FCA reviewed delistings on the LSE Main Market and Alternative Investment Market (AIM) from 2010–16, finding that on the Main Market the most commonly provided reason for a delisting was the issuer being acquired (141 issuers), followed by overseas companies cancelling their secondary listing (89 issuers), insolvency (53 issuers), market migrations/down-listings (44 issuers), and voluntarily going private (20 issuers). See Financial Conduct Authority, *Review of the Effectiveness of Primary Markets: The UK Primary Markets Landscape, Discussion Paper DP17/2* (February 2017). Available at: www.fca.org.uk/publication/discussion/dp17-02.pdf, 45.

[57] FCA Handbook, Listing Rule 8.4.14R.

- require a tender offer to buyout dissenting shareholders in the delisting; or
- contain capital maintenance requirements which prevent voluntary delistings such as a typical take-private transaction.

The FCA (as competent authority) is not formally empowered with discretion to delay or deny a voluntary delisting provided that the issuer has satisfied all the applicable requirements.[58] However, the FCA does have a degree of discretion over whether all the applicable requirements have been satisfied, so it is not practically possible to delist without the FCA's consent. Additionally, unlike many other EU regulated markets, UK delisting regulation does not require a mandatory buyout of dissenting shareholders upon a voluntary delisting. However, the UK Companies Act 2006 provides that when a public company has passed a resolution to re-register as a private limited company, minority shareholders may apply to the court to cancel the resolution. Upon this application, the court may make any order, including requiring 'the purchase by the company of the shares of any of its members [shareholders]'.[59] This provision would not be triggered automatically by a voluntary delisting so long as the public company does not re-register as a private company. Further, an issuer seeking to voluntarily delist from the LSE would not normally be restricted by provisions relating to the maintenance of share capital, save for if a delisting is combined with a restructuring that results in the cancellation of shares.[60]

IV. Delisting Regulation and EU Capital Allocation

As we have seen, some delisting rules impose significantly higher costs on issuers than others. This may affect the frequency with which companies move between capital markets in the EU and thus impact market integration. The question therefore arises how delisting rules should be evaluated in terms of the free movement provisions of the Treaty, and whether costly delisting regimes, or certain particularly demanding rules, for example 90–95 per cent shareholder approval requirements, are in conformity with the economic freedoms.

Our discussion will focus on the free movement of capital under Articles 63–66 of the TFEU.[61] Article 63 prohibits all restrictions on the movement of capital

[58] In contrast, the FCA is formally empowered with discretion to deny a voluntary *suspension* (rather than cancellation) of securities. See FCA Handbook, Listing Rule 5.1.4.

[59] Companies Act 2006, s 98.

[60] Companies Act 2006, s 641. See also *Re Unilever Plc* [2018] EWHC 2546 (Ch).

[61] Delistings that are part of a corporate reorganisation may also implicate the right of establishment, Arts 49–55 TFEU. The right of establishment extends to transfers of shares that result in a shareholder gaining 'definite influence' over a company, Case C-231/05 *Oy AA* ECLI:EU:C:2007:439, [2007] ECR I–6373, para 20; Case C-251/98 *Baars* ECLI:EU:C:2000:205, [2000] ECR I–2787, para 22. The Court of Justice considers the intended purpose of national legislation to differentiate between the free movement of capital and the right of establishment where the two freedoms overlap, Case C-543/08 *Commission v Portugal* (EDP) ECLI:EU:C:2010:669, [2010] ECR I-11241, para 40. It examines national legislation solely pursuant to Art 49 if the challenged law is intended to apply only to shareholdings that enable the holder to have a definite influence over a company's decisions. Laws concerning shareholdings that do not reach this threshold (ie, portfolio investments) are examined solely pursuant to Art 63, and where it is possible that the challenged law affects both shareholders exerting a definite influence and other shareholders, the Court applies Arts 49 and 63

between Member States, subject only to certain provisions of a Member State's tax law and general overriding requirements in the public interest.[62] The provision therefore captures both (directly and indirectly) discriminatory and non-discriminatory national measures. It is uncontroversial that discriminatory measures that concern capital movements, for example the differential tax treatment of residents and non-residents,[63] are in breach of Article 63 unless they can be justified under the Treaty.

Non-discriminatory measures are more difficult to assess. The Court of Justice established in its so-called Golden Shares jurisprudence that indistinctly applicable laws that restrict the free movement of capital fall in principle within the scope of the free movement of capital.[64] As a result of this broad interpretation, Article 63 potentially captures a wide array of national legal rules, which would then need to be justified by a Member State under the *Gebhard* conditions.[65] Since the proportionality test required pursuant to *Gebhard* and related case law is demanding and puts the onus on the Member States to show that no less restrictive measure would have been available to attain the objective pursued and the measure does not have a disproportionate effect on protected interests,[66] the free movement provisions would leave little room for diversity in policy preferences and national experimentation.[67]

This problem is not unique to the free movement of capital. All four economic freedoms have been interpreted equally broadly by the Court of Justice. The Court has made efforts to formulate workable tests to determine 'the outer limits of EU law'[68] and to differentiate between rules that are unlikely to substantially hinder free movement and rules that require further scrutiny (that is, justification under *Gebhard*). These efforts have not (yet) produced a coherent system, and they differ somewhat between the four freedoms, but certain common themes have emerged that are reflected in the free movement of capital case law. For example, the Court frequently asks whether a national legal rule hinders 'access to the market'. This formulation stems from the free movement of goods decision in *Keck*,[69] where the Court introduced a distinction between product requirements and rules prohibiting certain selling arrangements to define a sphere of national law that was 'beyond the scrutiny of the Court of Justice'.[70] Selling arrangements, the Court held, were outside the scope of the free movement of goods, provided they affected all traders in the same manner, in law and in fact, since

concurrently, ibid para 43. Since we are interested in the effects of delisting rules on corporate mobility generally, rather than solely on M&A transactions, we centre our discussion on the free movement of capital as the more general freedom in the present context.

[62] Art 65 TFEU and the jurisprudence of the CJEU following Case C-55/94 *Gebhard v Consiglio dell'Ordine degli Avvocati e Procuratori di Milano* ECLI:EU:C:1995:411, [1995] ECR I-4165.

[63] Case C-443/06 *Hollmann v Fazenda Pública* ECLI:EU:C:2007:600, [2007] ECR I–8491.

[64] On the Court's Golden Shares jurisprudence, see C Barnard, *The Substantive Law of the EU: The Four Freedoms* 7th edn (Oxford, Oxford University Press, 2022) 519 f; L Flynn, 'Free Movement of Capital' in C Barnard and S Peers (eds), *European Union Law*, 4th edn (Oxford, Oxford University Press, 2023) 482, 487.

[65] See n 62.

[66] Barnard, *The Substantive Law of the EU* (n 64) 177–92 (free movement of goods) 542–44 (free movement of capital).

[67] On this problem, see C Gerner-Beuerle, 'Shareholders Between the Market and the State. The VW Law and Other Interventions in the Market Economy' (2012) 49 *Common Market Law Review* 97, 107.

[68] Barnard (n 64) 114.

[69] Joined Cases C-267/91 and C-268/91 *Keck and Mithouard* ECLI:EU:C:1993:905, [1993] ECR I-6097.

[70] Barnard (n 64) 114.

their application to foreign products was 'not by nature such as to prevent their access to the market or to impede access any more than it impedes the access of domestic products'.[71]

Since delisting rules are typically indistinctly applicable, at least in relation to migration between regulated markets within the EU,[72] defining the protected sphere of national law where policy decisions do not have to withstand scrutiny under the Treaty is important for our analysis. The next section describes the approach the Court has traditionally taken to delimit the scope of the free movement of capital. In section A, we argue that existing legal tests, stemming primarily from the Court's Golden Shares case law, are difficult to apply to the present context. Section B proposes an alternative approach, inspired by the Court's right of establishment jurisprudence, which is, arguably, more closely aligned with the problem at hand, the migration of companies between capital markets. Section C goes beyond a doctrinal analysis and provides another rationale for scrutinising delisting rules under the free movement provisions. When the capital needs of a company change, regulatory impediments to migrating to another market may negatively affect the efficient allocation of capital in the EU. Suppose a company seeks to finance a growth strategy but finds it difficult to raise the necessary funds in its home market because of a small investor base, or its operational focus has changed, perhaps as the result of an M&A transaction, and the local investor base lacks familiarity with the industry and geographic market that is now the company's focus. In the first case, a lack of funding would impede the company's growth; in the second case, reliance on the local investor base is likely to increase the company's cost of capital. In both cases, capital allocation in the EU is inefficient.

Assuming that migrating to a more appropriate market is not feasible because of a restrictive delisting regime, two alternative solutions are conceivable. The issuer may seek a secondary listing on another market or rely on investors migrating to its home market. The first of these alternatives comes with disadvantages. A secondary listing increases compliance and other costs, may receive less analyst coverage than a primary listing, and may not reach stock index inclusion thresholds, with the result that the issuer does not benefit from the positive stock price effects that are typically associated with index inclusion.[73] Section C explores whether the second alternative – supply-side capital mobility – can be expected to mitigate the risk of inefficiency in capital allocation. In theory, perfect supply side capital mobility would remedy capital allocation problems resulting from restrictive delisting regimes, but in practice there are significant capital mobility frictions in the EU which limit the effectiveness of this solution.

[71] *Keck and Mithouard* (n 69) para 17.

[72] There are exceptions. For example, Art 17(5) of Greek Law 3371/2005 on Capital Markets Issues and Other Regulations, Official Gazette A 178/14.7.2005, provides for exemptions to the delisting requirements if an issuer migrates to another regulated market in Greece, but not in the case of migration to another regulated market abroad.

[73] WB Elliott et al, 'What Drives the S&P 500 Inclusion Effect? An Analytical Survey' (2006) 35 *Financial Management* 31.

A. Delisting and the Free Movement of Capital under Article 63 TFEU

Capital movements pursuant to Article 63 TFEU include both direct investments in companies, that is, investments with a view to participating in the management and control of a company, and portfolio investments.[74] As mentioned above, the Court of Justice held in its Golden Shares jurisprudence that measures that make it less attractive for potential investors to hold equity in a company, for example because the company has a dual class share structure or certain shareholders have special control rights, such as veto rights, fall within the scope of the free movement of capital even if they apply irrespective of the nationality of an investor. It may be argued that the issue here is different: measures of a regulatory body or the legislator make it more difficult and thus less attractive for an issuer to raise capital in another market (be this another public or a private capital market), than for an investor to provide capital. However, this is only a difference of perspective. A rule that renders delistings more costly and potentially prevents an issuer from migrating to another market or going private impedes the deployment of capital that would otherwise be available in these markets as much as a rule that discourages investors from investing.[75] In both cases, there is the risk that the resultant allocation of capital is inefficient.[76] Delisting rules are therefore relevant to capital movements within the meaning of Article 63 TFEU.

However, whether delisting rules that are indistinctly applicable fall within the scope of the free movement of capital is a more complex question than establishing that economic activity associated with a delisting qualifies as a capital movement.[77] The first case to address the issue at some length was Case C-98/01 *Commission v United Kingdom*,[78] which concerned special rights retained by the British government

[74] Case C-367/98 *Commission v Portugal* (Golden Shares I) ECLI:EU:C:2002:326, [2002] ECR I–4731, para 38; Joined Cases C-282/04 and 283/04 *Commission v Netherlands* (KPN/TPG) ECLI:EU:C:2005:712, [2006] ECR I–9141, para 19.

[75] In other contexts, the Court has confirmed that the issuer perspective is as relevant as the investor perspective, see Case C-315/02 *Lenz v Finanzlandesdirektion für Tirol* ECLI:EU:C:2004:446, [2004] ECR I–7063, para 21 (holding that the differential tax treatment of dividend payments of Austrian and foreign companies 'produces a restrictive effect in relation to companies established in other Member States, inasmuch as it constitutes an obstacle to their raising capital in Austria').

[76] The net social welfare effects of mechanisms that disincentivise investment, such as multiple voting rights and other corporate governance arrangements that lead to board entrenchment, are difficult to assess. Empirical evidence shows that control-enhancing mechanisms are negatively associated with firm value. For an overview of the evidence, see LA Bebchuk and K Kastiel, 'The Perils of Small-Minority Controllers' (2019) 107 *The Georgetown Law Journal* 1453, 1471–73. However, these studies may not account for all effects that are relevant to a comprehensive social welfare assessment, for example positive externalities of higher research and development expenditure. For a critical evaluation of the empirical evidence, see also Institutional Shareholders Services Inc. (ISS), European Corporate Governance Institute (ECGI), Shearman & Sterling LLP, *Report on the Proportionality Principle in the European Union, External Study Commissioned by the European Commission* (2007). Available at: www.ecgi.global/system/files?file=2024-02/_osov_final_report_en.pdf, 6.

[77] See the text to nn 64–72 above.

[78] Case C-98/01 *Commission v United Kingdom* ECLI:EU:C:2003:273, [2003] ECR I-4641 (*BAA*).

as a shareholder in the process of privatising the British Airports Authority. The UK Government argued that control-enhancing mechanisms contained in the articles of association of the privatised successor company to the British Airports Authority, BAA plc, were compatible with EU law, 'since they appl[ied] to all Member State nationals without discrimination on grounds of nationality and [did] not restrict access to the market'.[79]

This argument relies on the Court's approach to delimiting the scope of the free movement of goods and explicitly references the decision in *Keck*.[80] The Court of Justice seemed receptive to the UK Government's attempt to define 'the outer limits' of the free movement of capital by reference to *Keck* and the market access test, although it came to a different conclusion. Embracing the dichotomy between product requirements and selling arrangements, the Court held:

> The measures at issue are not comparable to the rules concerning selling arrangements which were found in [*Keck and Mithouard*] not to fall within the scope of [the free movement of goods]. ... In this instance, although the relevant restrictions on investment operations apply without distinction to both residents and non-residents, it must none the less be held that they affect the position of a person acquiring a shareholding as such and are thus liable to deter investors from other Member States from making such investments and, consequently, affect access to the market.[81]

In subsequent free movement of capital cases, also concerning special rights established in favour of the state as a shareholder in privatised enterprises, the Court continued to entertain the *Keck* analogy. It consistently held that control-enhancing mechanisms affected shareholdings 'as such' and were therefore not equivalent to selling arrangements.[82] The Court simultaneously complicated the taxonomy in response to Member State arguments that dual class stock and other special shareholder rights were 'wholly in accordance with the normal rules of company law in force' in the Member State and that general company law was outside the purview of the Court of Justice.[83] The Court argued that the challenged special rights in the Golden Shares cases were reviewable because they 'derogated' from ordinary company law, either because special rights were established in favour of certain classes of shareholders in law[84] or in the articles of association (or a shareholders' agreement) *and* the special right in the articles or shareholders' agreement could be traced back to the exercise of the state's public authority, rather than being the product of a private act.[85]

These two tests work in opposite directions in the present context. It may be argued that costly (or at least *prohibitively* costly) delisting rules affect the position

[79] ibid para 27.

[80] See n 69 and the accompanying text.

[81] Case C-98/01 *Commission v United Kingdom* ECLI:EU:C:2003:273, [2003] ECR I-4641, paras 45–47.

[82] For example, *EDP* (n 61) paras 65–68; Case C-212/09 *Commission v Portugal* (GALP) ECLI:EU:C:2011:717, [2011] ECR I-10889, paras 62–65.

[83] *BAA* (n 78), para 31. The same argument can be found in many other Golden Shares cases, for example Case C-112/05 *Commission v Germany* (Volkswagen) ECLI:EU:C:2007:623, [2007] ECR I-8995, paras 32–33; *EDP* (n 61) paras 29, 33; *GALP* (n 82) paras 35, 39.

[84] *Volkswagen* (n 83) paras 46, 60 f; Joined Cases C–463/04 and C-464/04 *Federconsumatori v Comune di Milano* ECLI:EU:C:2005:805, [2007] ECR I–10419, paras 17, 34.

[85] For example, *EDP* (n 61) para 62; *GALP* (n 82) para 53.

of issuers 'as such', since they prevent issuers from meeting their financing needs by raising capital in another market.[86] They may thus be compared to product requirements rather than rules that concern the manner in which capital is raised. On the other hand, in contrast to the provisions that are scrutinised under the *Keck* test, delisting rules are imposed by the home state of an issuer (in the sense of the issuer's current listing state), not by the market which the issuer seeks to access.[87] Maintaining the free movement of goods analogy, they are therefore comparable to requirements in force in the Member States where goods are produced. In accordance with the principle of equivalence or mutual recognition,[88] a delisting that is lawful in one Member State needs to be recognised in other EU states, but what constitutes a lawful delisting is subject to the regulatory discretion of the home state. Given these considerations, it is perhaps more natural to rely on the Court's 'derogation of company law' test to determine whether the free movement of capital encompasses delisting rules (and more generally capital markets regulation). Since the delisting rules we have analysed entail no favourable treatment for specific issuers it would follow that they do not engage Article 63 TFEU.

However, this, of course, does not resolve the problem that costly delisting regimes restrict access to capital markets in the EU. A delisting regime that stipulates a very high quorum or majority requirement of 90–95 per cent effectively eliminates the possibility of migrating to another capital market outside of an M&A transaction. A better analogy to the problem at hand may therefore be the case law of the Court of Justice on companies that seek to reincorporate in another Member State. Delistings and reincorporations are two facets of corporate mobility that pose a similar legal question, namely, how to define the sphere of regulatory activity of the *home* state that is beyond the scrutiny of the Court of Justice. We turn to this question next.

B. Delisting and the Right of Establishment under Articles 49 and 54 TFEU

Several landmark rulings of the Court of Justice have interpreted the rights of companies to exercise their freedom of establishment pursuant to Articles 49 and 54 TFEU, which are now relatively well defined. In contrast to the free movement of capital, the Court has developed bespoke principles that distinguish between inbound and outbound corporate movements.[89] We are interested in the latter case: the 'protected sphere' of national law where the home state can regulate without the need to justify (indistinctly applicable) restrictions on corporate mobility. In its first seminal decision concerning outbound mobility, *Daily Mail*, the Court famously stated

[86] This argument holds irrespective of whether a delisting occurs for purposes of market migration or to take a company private. In both cases a prohibitively costly delisting restricts access to another market.

[87] The *Keck* test concerns the question whether provisions of the *target* market fall within the scope of the free movement of goods, see the text to nn 69–71 above.

[88] Case C-120/78 *Rewe-Zentral AG v Bundesmonopolverwaltung für Branntwein* (Cassis de Dijon) ECLI:EU:C:1979:42, [1979] ECR 649.

[89] For an overview, see Barnard (n 64) 402–08.

that companies were 'creatures of the law and, in the present state of Community law, creatures of national law'.[90] Naturally, given that a company is an artificial legal person, a legal system (which, in the absence of harmonisation, is a national legal system) must be able to define the requirements that determine a company's incorporation, that is, the rules that need to be satisfied to establish a company. It would have been conceivable to apply the right of establishment from this point onwards, since a legal person has then come into existence that should, in principle, be able to benefit from the right of establishment. However, the Court of Justice in *Daily Mail* seemed to draw the ambit of reserved national law more widely, stating that national law 'determines [a company's] incorporation and functioning'.[91] While some questions remain unclear, the regulatory sphere within which a Member State can operate without the need for *Gebhard* justification consequently encompasses incorporation rules as well as provisions pertaining to the internal management of a company.[92]

The Court further held that the home state's regulatory authority includes the power 'not to permit a company *governed by its law* to retain that status if the company intends to reorganise itself in another Member State by moving its seat to the territory of the latter' (emphasis added).[93] However, importantly, this does not mean that the home state can prevent a company from 'converting itself into a company governed by the law of [another] Member State, to the extent that it is permitted under that law to do so', for example by requiring the winding up or liquidation of the company.[94] In other words, the regulatory authority of the home Member State ends when a company migrates to another Member State *and* the move entails a change in the applicable law.

It is not entirely clear from the case law of the Court of Justice what the cut-off point is that triggers the reviewability of home Member State law by the Court. In a strict application of the *Daily Mail* rationale, it may be thought that home Member State law governing the decision whether to move (ie, the relevant internal corporate governance requirements, for example, the requirement to obtain shareholder approval) falls outside the scope of Articles 49 and 54 TFEU, since these matters concern the 'functioning' of a company. However, in more recent decisions, the Court seemed to define the scope of the right of establishment more broadly. In *Cartesio*, it stated that 'legislation [of the home state] on the incorporation and winding-up of companies [did not enjoy] any form of immunity from the rules of the … Treaty on freedom of establishment' if such rules prevented a company from migrating to another Member State.[95] In *Polbud*, the Court used even more inclusive language. It held that '*all measures* which

[90] Case C-81/87 *The Queen v HM Treasury and Commissioners for Inland Revenue, ex parte Daily Mail and General Trust plc* ECLI:EU:C:1988:456, [1988] ECR 5483, para 19.

[91] ibid.

[92] For a detailed discussion of these issues, including more recent case law, see C Gerner-Beuerle et al, 'The Illusion of Motion: Corporate (Im)Mobility and the Failed Promise of *Centros*' (2019) 20 *European Business Organization Law Review* 425, 454–62.

[93] Case C-210/06 *Cartesio Oktató és Szolgáltató bt* ECLI:EU:C:2008:723, [2008] ECR I-9641, para 110.

[94] ibid para 112.

[95] ibid.

prohibit, impede or render less attractive the exercise of freedom of establishment must be considered to be restrictions on that freedom' (emphasis added).[96] These two cases dealt with requirements of the home Member State for winding up or liquidating a company before it could be converted into a company governed by the law of another Member State. However, the rulings suggest that such requirements are merely examples of the types of measures that can impede the freedom of establishment in the case of outbound movements.

This interpretation is supported by the Court's approach to delimiting the regulatory authority of a host Member State where a company seeks to reincorporate under the laws of that state. In *VALE*,[97] the Court qualified the *Daily Mail*'s 'creature of national law' argument. It recognised that, in the absence of harmonised rules, it was a matter for the domestic legal order of each Member State to determine the requirements for the incorporation or conversion of companies under their law.[98] However, this does not mean that 'such national provisions [can] escape all review in the light of [the] Treaty provisions'.[99] Rather, in the view of the Court, the Treaty requires that the relevant rules 'are not less favourable than those governing similar domestic situations (principle of equivalence) and that they do not render impossible in practice or excessively difficult the exercise of rights conferred by the European Union legal order (principle of effectiveness)'.[100]

Translating these considerations to the context of listings and delistings, three points may be made. First, Member States should have discretion to regulate capital markets located within their territory without full scrutiny under the Treaty where capital markets regulation is not harmonised (thus, for example, in relation to delisting rules). Similar to *Daily Mail*'s 'creature of national law' argument, markets cannot function properly without a regulatory framework that determines the 'rules of the game'. Since it is easy to conceive of ways to make an existing regulatory regime more accommodating to market participants, full regulatory scrutiny under the Treaty would necessitate *Gebhard*-justification for virtually all of a Member State's non-harmonised capital markets law.

Second, we know from both the *Keck*-inspired free movement of capital case law and *Cartesio*, *Polbud*, and *VALE* that the reserved area of Member State law is not unlimited, including in relation to legal requirements that are a precondition for the exercise of free movement rights, such as laws on the incorporation or conversion of a company. Scrutiny under the Treaty is warranted, particularly when laws prohibit or impede movement from one market to another. At least the set of rules that we capture with our market migration index should therefore be subject to a review by the Court. The legal rationale that motivated the Court in *Cartesio* and *Polbud* is equally applicable to the present context. Market migration is characterised by the decision to exit the jurisdiction of one Member State's regulatory authority to submitting to that of another. The

[96] Case C-106/16 *Polbud* ECLI:EU:C:2017:804, para 46.
[97] Case C-378/10 *VALE Építési kft* ECLI:EU:C:2012:440.
[98] ibid paras 48, 51 f.
[99] ibid para 45.
[100] ibid para 48.

Court held in *Cartesio* and *Polbud* that this must be possible and cannot be impeded unduly by the home Member State.

Third, it is not clear from the right of establishment case law on outbound movements whether a home state's laws are fully reviewable, or an intermediate standard of review applies, for example the principles of equivalence and effectiveness on which the Court relied in *VALE* to assess a host state's law on conversions. We suggest that the latter approach is more convincing. Full review under the Treaty would be tantamount to a comprehensive harmonisation of delisting rules, favouring the adoption of the least restrictive regime unless individual rules that make access to capital markets less attractive can be justified. The Treaty's free movement provisions are not the right vehicle to bring about such comprehensive harmonisation, and Member States may object to the strong deregulatory tendency that is inherent in the structure of the economic freedoms. Additionally, it is useful to leave space for regulatory experimentation where conflicting interests are involved and it is not immediately clear how these interests should be reconciled, as here with the interests of issuers, controlling shareholders and minority investors. Consequently, if the solution suggested here is adopted, delisting rules that render market migration 'impossible in practice or excessively difficult'[101] are subject to review under the Treaty. Arguably, the rules we classify as prohibitively costly fall into this category.

The prohibitively high cost of a delisting regime may result from the cumulative effect of multiple rules operating in combination (as reflected by the aggregate value of our two indices) or from specific rules that are individually difficult to satisfy, for example a very high quorum or shareholder approval requirement. In principle, it is irrelevant for purposes of the principle of effectiveness whether one rule individually or several rules in combination renders an exercise of the free movement of capital excessively difficult. However, the distinction will affect the potential policy responses of Member States. It is difficult to see how a rule that requires, say, the approval of 90 per cent of the outstanding share capital (or indeed 90 per cent of the voting share capital)[102] for market migration within the EU can be justified. On the other hand, where no individual rule is prohibitively costly, but the overall regime renders a delisting excessively difficult (as is, arguably, the case with the French market migration regime[103]), a policy maker has discretion to retain certain requirements, even if they are not widely shared in the EU, while modifying others.[104]

C. Prohibitive Delisting Rules under EU Capital Mobility

A costly delisting regime can be conceptualised as a restriction on the free movement of capital that operates on the demand side. The negative implications of such a

[101] *VALE* (n 97) para 48.

[102] For example, Cyprus, Finland, and Greece, see Part III above and the scores of the MMI in the Appendix.

[103] See Part III, Table 12.2 above.

[104] For example, as discussed in Part III above, only a minority of Member States require a mandatory buyout when an issuer migrates to another market within the EU. Yet, it is hard to contend that this requirement alone renders delistings prohibitively costly.

restriction for an efficient allocation of capital within the EU would be mitigated if the supply of capital was perfectly mobile. Consider the case of a company that intends to delist to migrate to another stock exchange. If that company was prevented from migrating because of a restrictive delisting regime, but the supply of capital was perfectly mobile, its cost of capital would not be higher than in the intended destination market for the sole reason that fewer domestic providers of capital were present in the market of the company's current listing. Restrictions on delistings would therefore not lead to a misallocation of capital (they may, of course, lead to other costs, for example higher transaction costs because of more costly communication with the issuer's shareholder base).[105]

However, it is well established that the mobility of capital continues to be low in the EU in comparison with other internal markets, such as the United States. This is despite sustained efforts to create a capital markets union – a truly integrated market for capital. The European Central Bank (ECB) assesses financial integration in the Euro Area regularly. In its biannual reports, it examines four market segments, the money, bond, equity and banking markets.[106] In all four segments, financial activity occurs predominantly in domestic markets, often outstripping transactions with other Eurozone countries by a significant margin. Notably, the share of debt and equity securities of non-domestic Eurozone issuers held by institutional and retail investors ranges between no more than 10 and 20 per cent, while domestic holdings amount to between 50 and 60 per cent.[107] In a potentially concerning sign for the project of Capital Markets Union, the home bias that can be observed in the debt and equity markets (and also in the banking market[108]) has remained at broadly the same level since the financial crisis.[109]

Limited mobility on the supply side makes a regulatory regime particularly important that facilitates demand-side mobility. While in theory a perfectly free supply of capital between EU Member States would remedy capital allocation inefficiencies stemming from prohibitively costly delisting rules, in practice there are significant frictions to capital mobility in the EU, therefore increasing the importance of delisting rules which are supportive of market migration.

[105] The calculus would also be different in the case of a take-private delisting. Here, misallocations may arise between public and private markets even if the supply of public equity capital is perfectly mobile.

[106] European Central Bank, *Financial Integration and Structure in the Euro Area* (April 2022). Available at: www.ecb.europa.eu/pub/pdf/fie/ecb.fie202204~4c4f5f572f.en.pdf and European Central Bank, *Financial Integration and Structure in the Euro Area, Statistical Annex* (April 2022). Available at: www.ecb.europa.eu/pub/pdf/fie/ecb.fie202204_annex~b0778eef8f.en.pdf?0b8abf9f4561f1a555000a9963f0c7b7. For the most recent data, see the Statistical Annex, in particular section 2.3.1 (money market), section 2.3.2 (debt and equity securities markets), and section 2.3.3 (banking market).

[107] European Central Bank, *Statistical Annex* (n 106) 18, 20 (charts 14, 16). Investment funds are an exception, since they typically hold broad, internationally diversified portfolios, see ibid 19 (chart 15).

[108] Financial integration in the retail banking sector is low, with more than 80% of loans to non-financial borrowers coming from domestic lenders and banking institutions tending to concentrate their assets in their home states, ibid 21, 23 (charts 17, 21).

[109] For example, the percentage of equities held by domestic investors was around 65% in 2008 and has been flat at around 55% since 2013, ibid 20 (chart 16).

V. Conclusion: The Benefits of Lower Delisting Barriers to EU Capital Markets Integration

This chapter has focused on an often-overlooked feature of listing regimes – the regulatory costs of delisting – which refer to the regulatory barriers to cancel an issuer's listing on a public trading venue. We have constructed two indices to understand and compare how significantly these regulatory costs differ between jurisdictions, which include 11 European jurisdictions (all 'EU regulated markets') and three non-EU jurisdictions. Our Take Private Index (TPI) measures the difficulty of voluntary delistings in a given jurisdiction, and our Market Migration Index (MMI) measures the difficulty of transferring from one listing venue to another. Our results indicate that, based on their TPI and MMI scores, regulatory variation between delisting regimes is significant. Given this variation, we classify delisting regimes as 'prohibitive' (ie, effectively precluding voluntary delistings), permissive' (ie, facilitating voluntary delistings with less onerous requirements), and 'differential' (ie, prohibitive for take private transactions but permissive for market migrations).[110]

Considering the lack of harmonised delisting rules in the EU and wide variation in the regulatory costs of delisting among EU Member States, we examine whether prohibitively costly delisting regimes are in conformity with Articles 63–66 TFEU on the free movement of capital. We apply doctrinal tests from the EU Court of Justice's Golden Shares and corporate mobility jurisprudence and suggest that while delisting rules do not engage Article 63 TFEU, they likely engage the rights of companies to exercise their freedom of establishment pursuant to Articles 49 and 54 TFEU by analogy. Ultimately, we suggest that an EU home state's rules contained in our market migration index should be subject to review by the Court of Justice, on an intermediate standard of review (as in *VALE*), since the legal rationale that motivated the Court in *Cartesio* and *Polbud* is equally applicable in the context of a company seeking to delist in one EU Member State and migrate its listing to another. Finally, we suggest that regardless of one's view on whether delisting regimes engage the freedom of establishment provisions in Articles 49 and 54 TFEU, regulatory impediments to delisting and migrating to another market negatively affect the efficient allocation of capital in the EU. Lowering the regulatory costs of delisting in prohibitive regimes where voluntary delisting is excessively difficult is therefore an appropriate policy response to facilitate corporate mobility and increase capital allocation efficiency in the EU.

[110] For a list of each jurisdiction's classification, see Part III Table 12.3: Classifying delisting regimes.

Appendix

Take-Private Index (TPI)

Country	country_ code	tp_ total	tp_ codified	tp_ quorum	tp_ majority	tp_ veto	tp_ discretion	tp_ buyout	tp_ buyout _ price	tp_ sub stantive	tp_ foreign_ issuers	tp_ time_ delay
Australia	AU	3.5	0	0.75	0.75	0	1	0	0	1	0	0
Austria	AT	4.75	0	0	0.75	0	0	1	1	1	0	1
Belgium	BE	3.95	0	0	0.95	0	0	1	1	1	0	0
Canada	CAN	1.5	0	0	0.5	1	0	0	0	0	0	0
Cyprus	CY	3.9	0	0	0.9	0	0	1	1	0	0	1
Finland	FI	5.8	1	0.9	0.9	0	1	1	1	0	0	0
France	FR	8.8	1	0.9	0.9	0	1	1	1	1	1	1
Germany	DE	3	0	0	0	0	1	1	1	0	0	0
Greece	GR	4.9	0	0.95	0.95	0	1	1	1	0	0	0
Italy	IT	4.87	1	0.2	0.67	0	1	1	1	0	0	0
Netherlands	NL	6.9	1	0.95	0.95	0	1	1	1	1	0	0
Spain	ES	2.75	0	0.25	0.5	0	0	1	1	0	0	0
Sweden	SE	5	1	0	0	0	1	1	1	1	0	0
UK premium	UK_p	1.75	0	0	0.75	1	0	0	0	0	0	0
UK other	UK_o	0	0	0	0	0	0	0	0	0	0	0

Market-Migration Index (MMI)

Country	country_code	mm-total	mm_codified	mm-quorum	mm-majority	mm_veto	mm-EU_listing	mm-discretion	mm-buy out	mm-buyout_price	mm-sub stantive	mm-foreign_issuers	mm-time_delay
Australia	AU	1	0	0	0	0	0	0	0	0	1	0	0
Austria	AT	3.75	0	0	0.75	0	1	0	0	0	1	0	1
Belgium	BE	4.25	0	0.5	0.75	0	0	0	1	1	1	0	0
Canada	CAN	1	0	0	0	1	0	0	0	0	0	0	0
Cyprus	CY	3.9	0	0	0.9	0	0	0	1	1	0	0	1
Finland	FI	5.8	1	0.9	0.9	0	0	1	1	1	0	0	0
France	FR	7.5	1	0	0.5	0	0	1	1	1	1	1	1
Germany	DE	2	0	0	0	0	1	1	0	0	0	0	0
Greece	GR	4.8	0	0.9	0.9	0	0	1	1	1	0	0	0
Italy	IT	2.87	0	0.2	0.67	0	1	1	0	0	0	0	0
Netherlands	NL	3	0	0	0	0	0	1	0	0	1	0	1
Spain	ES	2.75	0	0.25	0.5	0	1	1	0	0	0	0	0
Sweden	SE	3.5	1	0	0.5	0	0	1	0	0	1	0	0
UK_ premium	UK_p	1.75	0	0	0.75	1	0	0	0	0	0	0	0
UK_other	UK_o	0	0	0	0	0	0	0	0	0	0	0	0

13

Cold Delistings

ELIF HÄRKÖNEN AND JESSICA ÖSTBERG*

I. Introduction

A public limited liability company that meets certain requirements relating to the negotiability and liquidity of shares, the financial situation, and the organisation of the company, may apply to a stock exchange for admission to trading. In the European Union (EU), rules governing listing requirements are based on Article 51 of MiFID II.[1] In short, shares may be admitted to trading only if the conditions for fair, orderly and efficient trading exist. In several jurisdictions, the legislator delegates the development of more specific listing requirements to stock exchanges, which both implement and enforce these detailed rules.[2]

A listing of the shares may bring several advantages for the company. It may enable growth since it facilitates the raising of capital, and it normally increases the public awareness and goodwill of the company. From the perspective of shareholders, a listing facilitates the transfer of shares and increases transparency. Founding individuals can use an initial public offering (IPO) as an exit strategy. A listing is, however, also costly and resource-demanding, mainly due to the heavy, regulatory burden for listed companies. This may be a problem for companies in financial distress and for smaller growth companies that cannot allocate significant resources to regulatory compliance. Other disadvantages are that company founders need to relinquish control, at least to a certain extent, if the admission to trading is accompanied by an IPO. Furthermore, going public may limit the company from making long-term investments if investors are focused on short-term returns. In addition, publicly traded companies can become undervalued because of overall market conditions.[3]

* Elif Härkönen, Senior Associate Professor, Linköping University, and Jessica Östberg, Associate Professor, Linköping University. Unless otherwise indicated, this analysis reflects the legal framework in force across the jurisdictions discussed as of mid-2024.

[1] Directive 2014/65/EU on markets in financial instruments amending Directive 2002/92/ EC and Directive 2011/61/EU [2014] OJ L173/34 (Dir 2014/65/EU).

[2] See eg Securities Market Act (*lag 2007:528 om värdepappersmarknaden*) ch 15 s 1 (SWE).

[3] See J Macey, M O'Hara and D Pompilio, 'Down and Out in the Stock Market: The Law and Economics of the Delisting Process' (2008) 51 *The Journal of Law & Economics* 683; D Zetzsche, 'Going Dark Under German Law – Towards an Efficient Regime for Regular Delisting' (2013) 4 *Revue trimestrielle de droit financier* 1.

A delisting occurs when a company's shares are removed from trading on a stock market. Delistings can be divided into exchange-initiated delistings, so-called mandatory or involuntary delistings, and issuer-initiated delistings, commonly referred to as voluntary delistings. Mandatory delistings can be initiated by the stock exchange for different reasons, for example, if the issuer files for bankruptcy, if the liquidity of the shares is too low, or if the issuer doesn't follow the listing rules. Voluntary delistings can be motivated by the issuer's desire to change to a different trading venue, merge with another unlisted company, or take the company private to reduce public scrutiny as well as the regulatory burden and costs associated with the listing.

In this chapter, we will focus on so-called cold delisting transactions (as defined below). In the literature, the term has predominantly been used in a continental European context. Depending on the author, different transactions are included in the cold delisting category. Both Maume and Rampos refer to cold delistings when they discuss transactions consisting of mergers between listed stock companies and unlisted stock companies, resulting in a single unlisted company.[4] Maume does not include takeover squeeze-outs in his definition of a cold delisting, while Zetzsche includes going-private transactions which are the side effect of a transaction with a different key motive, such as a squeeze-out.[5] In addition, both Zetzsche and Nordhues use the term for going-private transactions where a listed company changes to another business association form with ownership interests that cannot be traded on a stock exchange. For example, a public company can change into a private company or, in German law, an *Aktiengesellschaft* can change into a *Gesellschaft mit beschränkter Haftung* (*GmbH*).[6] Tutino, Panetta, and Laghi include in their definition of cold delistings a wide variety of corporate restructurings where the company does not meet the listing criteria anymore. Their definition of cold listings includes involuntary delistings linked to corporate restructurings such as mergers and acquisitions, integration into the parent company as well as reverse stock splits and share purchases.[7]

As the short literature overview suggests, the term 'cold delisting' is not a settled concept. There is no legal definition of cold delistings, and the term has not been defined in judicial precedents, as far as we know. In this chapter, we will use the term cold delisting transaction (CDT) (the term CDT is used interchangeably with the term cold delisting, depending on the context) for all corporate restructuring transactions, where the securities of the corporation are no longer traded on a stock exchange or another similar trading facility after the transaction. The term 'going-private transaction' is broadly used to encompass all types of transactions that result in the company's delisting, including, for example, tender offers and squeeze-outs. Even though some aspects of going-private transactions are discussed, the focus is on CDTs. To introduce

[4] P Maume, 'The Parting of the Ways: Delisting Under German and UK Law' (2015) 16 *European Business Organization Law Review* 255, 271. See also D Rampos, 'Squeeze-Outs Arrive – Greece has Entered the Modern Era, with Effective Squeeze-Outs and Even Back-Door Delistings Now Possible' (2007) 26 *International Financial Law Review* 30, 31.

[5] Maume (n 4) 274; Zetzsche (n 3) 1.

[6] Zetzsche (n 3) 1; P Nordhues, 'Breaking into Germany' (2015) 34 *International Financial Law Review* 46, 47.

[7] M Tutino, IC Panetta and E Laghi, 'Key Factors in Delisting Process in Italy: Empirical Evidence' (2013) 2 *GSTF Journal on Business Review* 218.

some delimitations, we will focus on three categories of CDTs. Firstly, we will discuss transactions structured in the form of a merger, amalgamation or a scheme of arrangement, where a listed company merges into an unlisted entity, resulting in a delisting due to the surviving company being an unlisted business entity. Secondly, we will discuss spin-offs, in which a subsidiary's separation from a listed holding company leads to its delisting. Finally, we will include a discussion of delistings which are a side effect of a conversion from a listed entity to another business association form where the securities are not transferable and freely negotiable.

The topic of cold delistings received a lot of attention in continental Europe after the German *Macrotron*[8] and *Frosta*[9] cases. However, the topic is not only of interest in jurisdictions influenced by the German developments. In the United States (US), the Sarbanes-Oxley Act (SOX) was adopted in the same year as the *Macrotron* judgment was rendered in Germany.[10] Several of the new corporate governance requirements of the SOX were perceived as too arduous by smaller listed companies, leading to a wave of delistings and an interest in the benefits and drawbacks of different going-private transactions.[11]

The legal framework covering CDTs can be found in both company law and securities law, depending on the jurisdiction. There are considerable differences between jurisdictions when it comes to shareholder protection and the protection of other constituencies in such transactions. Our chapter will make a comparative evaluation of legal rules in different jurisdictions, with a focus on the legal framework in the US and the EU. In particular, the aim is to assess the legal protection awarded to shareholders in CDTs. The aim is also to contribute to the debate on whether a further harmonisation of the national regimes would contribute to the EU's project of a Capital Markets Union (CMU).

In the US, legislation covering going-private transactions can be found both at the federal level, when it comes to securities law, and at the state level, when it comes to company law. When discussing state-level legislation in the US, our focus will be on legislation in the state of Delaware. The main reason is that Delaware has succeeded in attracting more than half of all listed corporations registered in the US.[12] In addition, the legal rules in Delaware have an impact well beyond the borders of the state. The Delaware General Corporate Law (DGCL) has been described as a *lingua franca* for corporate lawyers in the US.[13] It is considered one of the most advanced and flexible

[8] Judgment of the German Federal Court of Justice of 25 November 2002 (BGH, Urt v 25.11.2002 – II ZR 133/01, BGHZ 153, 47, 53).

[9] Judgment of the German Federal Court of Justice of 8 October 2013 (BGH, Urt v 08.10.2013 – II ZB 26/12, NJW 2014, 146).

[10] Sarbanes-Oxley Act of 2002, Pub L 107–204, July 30, 2002, 116 Stat 745, codified at 15 USC, ss 7201–66 (2023).

[11] For example, 15 USC s 7241 (s 302 in Sarbanes-Oxley Act) and 15 USC s 7262 (s 404 in Sarbanes-Oxley Act) (2024). The exact impact of Sarbanes-Oxley Act is disputed (companies can delist for other reasons than Sarbanes-Oxley Act compliance) but, during the period 1996–2012, the total number of US listed companies halved from 8,025 in 1996 to 4,101 in 2012, see C Doidge, A Karolyi and RM Stulz, '*The U.S. listing Gap*' (2017) 123 *Journal of Financial Economics* 464, 467.

[12] Delaware Division of Corporations, 'About the Division of Corporations'. Available at: www.corp.delaware.gov/aboutagency.

[13] LS Black, Jr, *Why Corporations Choose Delaware?* (Dover, Delaware Department of State Division of Corporations, 2007) 1 f.

company laws in the world, influencing other US states as well as many EU Member States. Furthermore, the state has a court system that is considered effective and experienced, in addition to a well-developed body of case law.[14]

Concerning the EU, we will discuss EU-level legislation, supplemented by examples from company and securities law at the national level in different Member States. In particular, the Swedish regulatory system is often used as an example in discussions. The Swedish system has regulated CDTs in both company and securities law, making it an intriguing hybrid system of regulation. In addition, the regulation of the Swedish stock market is composed of a mixed law and self-regulatory system, allowing a multifaceted analysis of the benefits and drawbacks of different regulatory techniques. A special feature of the Swedish stock market regulation is that the rulings of the self-regulatory body, the Swedish Securities Council (SSC), concerning good practice in the Swedish stock market must be followed by listed companies according to the listing agreement. A breach of the SSC rulings can result in fines and sanctions under the relevant listing agreement.[15] The rulings of the SSC are, to a very large extent, followed by companies listed in Sweden. In addition, from September 1, 2025, the new Rules on Voluntary Delistings issued by the Stock Market Self-Regulation Committee will take effect on the Swedish stock market.

The chapter is structured as follows. In Part II, we describe different transactions structured as CDTs as well as their effects. Part III focuses on some theoretical aspects, including the different agency conflicts between the board of directors and the shareholders as well as the agency conflict between controlling and minority shareholders. In Part IV we make a comparative analysis of the prevalence of different minority shareholder protection techniques in connection with CDTs. Part V focuses in more detail on some of the prevailing problems in regulating CDTs. Part VI concludes the analysis.

II. CDTs and their Effects

A. The Transactions

CDTs may be structured through mechanisms such as mergers, amalgamations or schemes of arrangement between a listed company and an unlisted company. In such arrangements, the listed company transfers all its assets and liabilities to the unlisted company, indirectly leading to a delisting of the listed company. Alternatively, a similar outcome may be achieved through the division of a company into an unlisted entity.

The EU directive relating to certain aspects of company law (the Company Law Directive) requires Member States to make rules for mergers by acquisition and mergers by formation of a new company.[16] There are, however, no specific rules governing

[14] Delaware Division of Corporations (n 12).

[15] Nordic Main Market Rulebook for Issuers of Shares, Supplement D, Nasdaq Stockholm paras 34–36 (rules applicable from 1 January 2025).

[16] Directive (EU) 2017/1132 relating to certain aspects of company law [2017] OJ L169/46 (Dir 2017/1132) Art 88.

mergers resulting in a cold delisting. A merger by acquisition is defined as a transaction where one company transfers all its assets and liabilities in exchange for shares in the acquiring company and a cash payment, not exceeding 10 per cent of the nominal or accounting par value of the shares so issued. A merger by the formation of a new company is a transaction where several companies are wound up and transfer their assets and liabilities in exchange for shares in the new company. Such mergers are covered by similar limitations on cash payments which cannot exceed 10 per cent of the nominal or accounting par value of shares issued.[17] EU Member States may, in addition to mergers by acquisition and by formation of a new company, also permit mergers with cash payments exceeding 10 per cent. The same procedural rules and requirements on general meeting approval as for mergers covered by the directive apply if a Member State decides to allow cash-out mergers at the national level.[18] As will be further outlined in Part IV, some EU countries do not provide for specific rules when a merger results in a delisting, whereas other jurisdictions provide for special protections for shareholders in such CDTs.

In the US, similar rules apply to mergers, where two companies may either merge into a single surviving corporation or consolidate into a new resulting corporation formed by the consolidation. There are no restrictions in the US on cash-out mergers.[19] In some jurisdictions influenced by Anglo-Saxon law, such as India, Canada, South Africa, and New Zealand, the term amalgamation is used to describe a transaction, where two companies form a new company, continuing their existence as a single company.[20] Some jurisdictions also allow company restructurings through a scheme of arrangement. Usually, court-ordered schemes of arrangements are less flexible than mergers and amalgamations.[21] Despite this, schemes of arrangements have been the most popular way for listed companies in the United Kingdom (UK) to structure a going-private transaction. Compared with takeovers, the UK scheme of arrangement requires a more cumbersome process requiring both shareholder and court approval; however it allows the offeror to acquire 100 per cent of the company in a single transaction.[22]

In addition to transactions structured as mergers, amalgamations and schemes of arrangements, a CDT can be structured as a spin-off. It is not unusual for a listed company to conduct a part of its business via an unlisted subsidiary. In some cases, all business operations are conducted this way. Such issuers may delist the shares via a spin-off, in which the assets of the listed entity are transferred to the unlisted subsidiary and the shares of the latter are distributed as a dividend to the shareholders of the listed entity. The second step of the transaction can be structured as a part of a back-door listing with new shareholders in the listed entity, for example if the listed entity distributes shares as payment in a merger with a third party, or as a two-step process where the listed entity lacks a clear business strategy and is unable to demonstrate any business

[17] ibid Arts 89 f.

[18] ibid Art 116.

[19] Del Code Ann tit 8 s 251 (2024).

[20] Companies Act of 2013, ss 230–35 (IND); Canada Business Corporations Act ss 181–87; Companies Act of 2008, ss 113, 115–16 (RSA); Companies Act 1993 ss 219–25 (NZ).

[21] See eg Companies Act of 2006, ss 895–901L (UK); Companies Act of 2008, ss 114 f (RSA).

[22] J Yu and C Sutton, 'Structuring Public Takeovers in the UK' (2022). Available at: www.armstrongteasdale.com/content/uploads/2022/03/Structuring-Public-Takeovers-in-the-U.K.-Table-1.pdf.

operations following the transfer of assets to a non-listed subsidiary through a spin-off, leading to a mandatory delisting.[23]

A company could also effect a delisting by changing its business association form to an entity where the shares are not (easily) transferable and freely negotiable, as this would forfeit one of the principal requirements of listed companies.[24]

B. The Effects of a Cold Delisting

One obvious effect of a delisting, voluntary or mandatory, including a cold delisting, is that there will no longer be an effective trading market for the sale of the shares.[25] This has implications for the liquidity and, often, the pricing of the shares. Since shareholders normally invest in a listed company to maximise returns, the lack of liquidity and the price decline in connection with a CDT are normally detrimental to shareholders and may, in the long run, have an impact on investor confidence for the whole market. In addition, a CDT may, depending on the type of transaction, result in ownership in a different type or size of business, a factor that holds significant importance for many shareholders. Moreover, access to information about company operations and financial performance will normally be much more limited in an unlisted company. Additionally, many of the rules protecting shareholders apply only to public or listed companies, including, but not limited to, the takeover regulatory framework. Consequently, shareholder protection will be more limited. It should, however, be stressed that a core set of company law minority protection rules apply in both listed and private companies. The shareholders will accordingly still be protected, however to a somewhat lesser extent.

From the company's perspective, the regulatory burden will decrease with a delisting. The company will no longer be covered by stock market trading rules, disclosure and market abuse rules, takeover rules, corporate governance rules applicable to listed companies or other similar securities rules. This will lead to cost reductions and greater flexibility. The management[26] might be better off after a CDT as there will be less compliance work to do and they could consequently spend more time and resources on product development and marketing of the products. There will be no pressure from the stock market with respect to short term earnings. The rules governing remuneration and related party transactions are furthermore, at least in the EU, normally less strict in unlisted companies. The accountability and risk with respect to sanctions will decrease to some extent. However, there will still be a duty of loyalty for directors in

[23] For an example of a spin-off and backdoor listing on the Swedish stock market, see the Swedish Securities (SSC) Council decision in AMN 2019:03, discussed in more detail in section IVA.

[24] Dir 2014/65 Art 51. See also Zetzsche (n 3) 1. In certain jurisdictions, such as Sweden, shares in private companies must not be listed on a stock market or trading facility, see Companies Act of 2005, ch 1 s 8 (SWE).

[25] For a law and economics analysis of the effects of delisting, see Macey, O'Hara and Pompilio (n 3). See, for the reasons and effects, I Martinez, S Serve and C Djama, 'Reasons for Delisting and Consequences: A Literature Review and Research Agenda' (2015). Available at: ssrn.com/abstract=2591449.

[26] The term management used in this chapter includes the board of directors, the managing director and the oversight body, if any, and any other persons who have a decision-making power with respect to the management of the company, ie the directors and officers of the company.

most jurisdictions, which limits their discretion, including in relation to related party transactions.[27] Moreover, it is often more difficult to attract investors, and the company might lose some credibility and goodwill in connection with a delisting.

III. Theoretical Framework

A. CDTs and the Principal-Agency Problem

One problem that arises primarily, but not exclusively, in companies where ownership and control are separated, such as in listed companies, is the so-called principal-agency problem.[28] In particular, minority shareholders of such companies have very limited insight into and influence over the company's activities. Instead, the business operations are run by the management, who, at least in theory, possess the expertise required and contacts that may benefit the company. The board of directors often has a right to an extensive insight into the company's business and extensive authority to make business decisions and to represent the company in transactions with third parties. The essence of the principal-agency problem is that the agent, ie, the management, holds an information advantage in addition to controlling the company's business. These factors, combined with the assumption that human beings are utility maximisers, create the risk that the agent may prioritise their own interests at the expense of those of the principal (the shareholders).[29] When management acts in their self-interest to the detriment of the shareholders, the company's loss is referred to as agency costs.[30]

The principal–agent problem may be of relevance in connection with a CDT. There is a risk that, for example, a merger with an unlisted company is performed to enable the director to extract benefits for himself or a related party. It should, however, be noted that the principal–agent problem is not necessarily connected with the delisting, but rather with the transaction that leads to the delisting. The measures that may be taken to reduce agency costs can be divided into regulatory strategies and governance strategies.[31] The duty of loyalty and the rules regarding decision-making, the majority rules, and the principle of equality are examples of regulatory strategies aimed at reducing agency costs.[32] The duty of loyalty implies, inter alia, that the management should

[27] See, for a recent study of the duty of loyalty and care with comparative outlooks eg J Östberg, 'The Duty to Act in the Interest of the Company' in HS Birkmose, M Neville and KE Sørensen (eds), *Instruments of EU Corporate Governance, Effecting Changes in the Management of Companies in a Changing World* (Alphen aan den Rijn, Wolters Kluwer, 2023).

[28] See regarding the principal-agency problem eg AA Berle and GC Means, *The Modern Corporation and Private Property* (New York, The Macmillan Company, 1932) 71; MC Jensen and WH Meckling, 'The Theory of the Firm: Managerial Behavior, Agency Costs and Ownership' (1976) 3 *Journal of Financial Economics* 305 and J Armour, H Hansmann and R Kraakman, 'Agency Problems and Legal Strategies' in R Kraakman et al (eds), *The Anatomy of Corporate Law: A Comparative and Functional Approach*, 3rd edn (Oxford, Oxford University Press, 2017) 29.

[29] See Armour, Hansmann and Kraakman (n 28) 29.

[30] ibid.

[31] ibid 31.

[32] ibid 31f.

act in the interests of the company, and not in, for example, their own interests, the interests of a related party or the majority.[33]

The principal–agent problem may also arise between the majority and the minority, the so-called second agency problem.[34] In such an agency relationship, the minority is the principal and the majority the agent.[35] The majority holds the power to decide on several important matters for the company, creating an obvious risk of abuse to the detriment of the company and/or the minority shareholders. The majority may consequently promote its interests at the expense of the minority.[36] The principal–agent problem between the majority and the minority is particularly relevant in connection with a CDT, where there is a risk that the majority holds an economic interest in the CDT transaction and may extract benefits in connection therewith to the detriment of the minority shareholders.

The second agency problem is mainly dealt with through minority protection rules.[37] As further discussed in Part IV below, the minority protection rules differ depending on the type of transaction and the relevant jurisdiction. In some jurisdictions, abuse of power by the majority is also curtailed by a general rule or principle prohibiting abuse of rights or by imposing fiduciary duties upon the majority.[38]

B. The Principles of Free Transferability and Negotiability

In many jurisdictions, the free transfer of shares constitutes an important principle for incorporated companies.[39] The principle is consequently closely related to the status as a legal entity and the limited personal liability.[40] In some jurisdictions, the principle is codified.[41] According to the principle, shareholders may at any time sell off their

[33] See eg Östberg (n 27). Governance strategies, such as incentive programs for management, are not examined in this chapter.

[34] See Armour, Hansmann and Kraakman (n 28) 30; BR Cheffins, *Company Law: Theory, Structure and Operation* (Oxford, Oxford University Press, 1997) 64 f.

[35] See Armour, Hansmann and Kraakman (n 28) 30.

[36] See Z Goshen and A Hamdani, 'Majority Control and Minority Protection' in JN Gordon and WG Ringe (eds), *The Oxford Handbook of Corporate Law and Governance* (Oxford, Oxford University Press, 2018) 449, 452.

[37] See Goshen and Hamdani (n 36) 459 f; Armour, Hansmann and Kraakman (n 28) 30 and L Enriques et al, 'The Basic Governance Structure: Minority Shareholders and Non-Shareholders Constituencies' in R Kraakman et al (n 28) 79–89.

[38] See eg Enriques et al, ibid 84 f; KE Sørensen, 'Duty of Loyalty for Shareholders – A Possible Remedy for Conflicts in SMEs?' in M Neville and KE Sørensen (eds), *Company Law and SMEs* (Copenhagen, Thomson Reuters, 2010) 127–70; PH Conac, 'The Shareholders' Duty Not to Abuse Rights', in HS Birkmose (ed), *Shareholders' Duties* (Alphen aan den Rijn, Wolters Kluwer, 2017) 363–76.

[39] See eg J Armour et al, 'What Is Corporate Law?' in R Kraakman et al (n 28) 10.

[40] See eg Armour et al, ibid 10 f and PL Davies, S Worthington and C Hare, *Gower: Principles of Modern Company Law*, 11th edn (London, Sweet & Maxwell, 2021) 45.

[41] See eg Companies Act (*Aktiebolagslag 2005:551*) ch 4 s 7 (SWE) and Companies Act (*Osakeyhtiölaki 624/2006*) ch 1 s 4 (FIN). Under Norwegian law the principle is applicable in relation to public companies, so called *allmennaksjeselskaper*, see Companies Act (*Lov om allmennaksjeselskaper 1997*) ch 4 s 15 (NO). For private companies on the other hand there are restrictions with respect to transferability, unless the articles stipulate free transferability, see Companies Act (*Lov om aksjeselskaper 1997*) ch 4 s 15 (NO).

shares and the company's operations can be continued independently of changes in ownership.[42]

A shareholder meeting decision, taken by a qualified or special qualified majority, is normally required to restrict the free transferability of shares. Under Swedish law, such a restriction may only be adopted with a majority consisting of all of the shareholders present at the meeting, representing at least 90 per cent of the shares in the company.[43] The same qualified majority is also required for a decision to transform a company from a public to a private company.[44] Although Swedish law does not by default restrict the transfer of shares in private companies, a conversion of a public company to a private company will in practice influence the possibility to transfer the shares since there is often no market for the sale of the shares in such a company. In close companies, where the owners are engaged in the business and the success is normally dependent on the competence and cooperation among the shareholders, the transfer of shares is often further restricted by law or through provisions in the articles of association.[45]

The free transferability of shares should be distinguished from the concept of negotiable financial instruments. According to Article 51 of MiFID, the rules regarding the admission of financial instruments to trading on a regulated market must ensure that transferable securities are freely negotiable. In some jurisdictions, only certain categories of companies may be listed on a stock exchange or other marketplace, as is the case, for example, under Swedish law. Consequently, the shares of private companies are freely transferable according to Swedish law, but they are not considered transferable securities that are negotiable on the capital market.[46] The free negotiability of shares on the capital market enhances the liquidity of the shares. If a shareholder is dissatisfied with the management, it may simply exit by selling their shares. In addition, the negotiability enables a diversification of the portfolio, simplifies capital raising efforts for the company, and can significantly influence the share price through enhanced liquidity.[47]

IV. Shareholder Protection in CDTs

A. Voting Requirements

In the EU, qualified voting requirements are a popular mechanism for shareholder protection. For example, according to Article 93 of the EU Company Law Directive, Member State law shall provide that a merger approval decision is approved by 'a majority of not less than two-thirds of the votes attached either to the shares or to the subscribed capital represented'. Member States may, however, provide that a simple majority of votes

[42] See eg Armour et al (n 39) 10.
[43] Swedish Companies Act (*Aktiebolagslag 2005:551*) ch 7 s 43(2) (SWE).
[44] ibid ch 26 s 6.
[45] See eg Davies, Worthington and Hare (n 40) 45 f.
[46] ibid ch 1 s 8.
[47] See eg Armour et al (n 39) 10.

is sufficient if at least half of the subscribed capital is present at the general meeting. Each class of shares affected by the merger transaction votes separately.[48] In Germany, the approval of a merger resolution requires a majority of 75 per cent of the votes cast at the general meeting.[49] Under Finnish law, a merger resolution must be supported by at least two-thirds of the votes cast and the shares represented at the meeting.[50]

Similar qualified majority voting requirements have also been introduced in non-EU countries. For example, the Bermuda company law threshold for approval of an amalgamation or merger requires that 75 per cent of those voting approve the resolution, and the quorum necessary shall be two persons holding at least one-third of the issued shares.[51] Similarly, the UK Companies Act requires approval of schemes of arrangement by shareholders representing at least 75 per cent in value and headcount at the shareholder meeting approving the scheme.[52]

Some jurisdictions provide for higher qualified majority requirements for mergers and divisions resulting in a delisting. Under Greek law, for example, a merger of a listed company with a non-listed company must be approved by the general meeting with 95 per cent majority of the total voting share capital.[53] In addition, the Swedish Companies Act has special rules on mergers when a company with shares listed on a regulated market is absorbed by a company that is not listed on a regulated market. Although the transaction is not prohibited per se, the rules are so strict that it would practically be impossible to adopt such a merger decision. A decision is valid only if it has been supported by all the shareholders who are present at the general meeting and these together represent at least 90 per cent of all shares in the company.[54] Identical rules apply to divisions.[55] Companies listed on a multilateral trading facility that are merged with a private company are covered by rulings of the SSC stipulating the same special qualified majority requirement.[56] The special qualified majority requirement also applies with respect to cross-border mergers, but not with respect to cross-border divisions. With respect to cross-border divisions, the normal two-thirds majority rule applies to all kinds of divisions, even if the acquiring company is a non-listed company.[57] Moreover, there are rules providing for appraisal rights in connection with cross-border mergers and cross-border divisions under Swedish law.[58] Considering this, the special qualified majority rules for cross-border mergers resulting in a delisting seems to be unnecessarily strict.

[48] Dir 2017/1132 Art 93(2). In a merger by acquisition, the Member States can introduce rules according to which the general meeting of the acquiring company does not need to approve the merger, unless a minority requires it, see ibid Art 94.

[49] Transformation Act (*Umwandlungsgesetz*) s 50(1) (GER).

[50] Companies Act (*Osakeyhtiölaki 624/2006*) ch 5 s 27 (FIN).

[51] Companies Act s 106 (BER).

[52] Companies Act 2006 s 899 (UK).

[53] Law 4601/2019 on Corporate Transformations Art 18 (GRC); Law 3371/2005 on the admission of securities to official stock exchange listing and on information to be published on those securities, Art 17(5) (GRC). (The same qualified majority rules apply with respect to a voluntary delisting according to Art 17(5)). Art 17 was changed in 2013 to include mergers, splits or conversions which result in a delisting, see Law 4141/2013 (GRC).

[54] Companies Act (*Aktiebolagslag 2005:551*) ch 23 s 17 (SWE).

[55] ibid ch 24 s 19.

[56] See eg the statements in SSC decisions AMN 2019:03 and AMN 2021: 50.

[57] ibid ch 23 s 36, ch 24 s 31.

[58] ibid ch 23 s 50, ch 24 s 55.

Swedish company law does not regulate spin-offs, but the SSC has considered under what conditions spin-off transactions may be contrary to good practices on the stock market.[59] In *AMN 2019:03 Indentive*, a Swedish company listed on the Swedish MTF Nasdaq First North, planned a three-step restructuring, where they had first transferred the business of the company to a subsidiary. In the second step, shares in the subsidiary were supposed to be distributed to the *Indentive* shareholders, where after *Indentive* would buy the shares of *Artificial Solutions*, an unlisted company, and pay for the shares by issuing new shares in *Indentive* to the shareholders of *Artificial Solutions*. The motive was to conduct a back-door listing by *Artificial Solutions*. The former shareholders in *Indentive* would, after the transaction, be owners of the unlisted subsidiary, while the owners of *Artificial Solutions* would be the new owners of *Indentive*. The SSC stated that the same requirements as in the case of a complete delisting of the company's shares should be applied in spin-off cases involving a major part of the listed company's value. It emphasised that whoever acquires shares in a listed company does so under the assumption that there is a functioning market for the company's shares until the listing requirements are no longer met. The board of directors must act in the interests of the company and of all the shareholders and not just the majority when making such a decision. If the listing requirements are still met, the reasons for the delisting must be of such strength that it can be considered justified to expose the other shareholders to the disadvantages of a delisting.[60] Otherwise, the spin-off contravenes good practice on the stock market, unless it has been adopted by the general meeting of shareholders with a majority consisting of all shareholders present at the general meeting, provided they represent at least 90 per cent of the shares in the company.[61] A similar level of minority protection as that provided in the context of a voluntary delisting should consequently be applicable. In addition, the shareholders have to be clearly informed of the qualified majority requirement in the notice to the general meeting.[62]

A CDT structured as a conversion from a company with freely tradable shares and an unlimited number of shareholders to a business association form with restrictions regarding negotiability is often covered by qualified, or special qualified majority voting requirements. For example, under German law, a conversion of an Aktiengesellschaft into a GmbH leads to a cold delisting, since the shares of a GmbH cannot be publicly traded.[63] This principle also applies under Swedish law, if a public company is transformed into a private company, since the shares of a private company may not be

[59] See SSC decisions AMN 2019:03 and AMN 2021:50.

[60] SSC decision AMN 2014:33. Similar statements have also been made in SSC decision AMN 2004:29 (delisting did not consider the rights of minority shareholders); SSC decision AMN 2006:02 (change of market place was allowed, since the company risked a mandatory delisting); SSC decision AMN 2010:15 (change to a market place with lower liquidity was criticised, not in the interest of minority shareholders); SSC decision AMN 2012:17 (not published); SSC decision AMN 2016:21 (not published) and SSC decision AMN 2018:54 (delisting was allowed, due to an economic crisis of the company).

[61] See SSC decisions AMN 2016:21 and AMN 2019:03 See, however, p 242 regarding the Rules on Voluntary Delistings effective from September 1, 2025 with inter alia new majority rules, also applicable to spin-offs.

[62] The decision was confirmed and considered to apply equally in SSC decision AMN 2021:50 which also concerned a spin-off.

[63] Transformation Act (*Umwandlungsgesetz*) ss 226–34 (GER); J Semler, A Stengel and N Leonard (eds), *Umwandlungsgesetz*, 5th edn (Munich, CH Beck, 2021) s 226 margin no 11; Zetzsche (n 3) 4.

listed for trading.[64] Such a decision is, pursuant to chapter 26 section 6 of the Swedish Companies Act, valid only if it has been supported by all shareholders who are present at the general meeting if they together represent at least 90 per cent of all shares in the company.

In other countries, such as the UK and France, a special resolution approving the conversion decision must be passed by a majority of not less than 75 per cent.[65] In addition, some countries include additional restrictions concerning the number of shareholders in the private company. In France, an SA converting into an SARL first needs to fulfil the requirements of an SARL, including the requirement that an SARL cannot have more than 100 shareholders.[66] If a listed company were to reduce its shareholders to less than 100 shareholders, it would already be in breach of stock market rules on liquidity and spread, why the conversion decision in itself would not be the reason for the delisting of the stock, but the reduction in the number of shareholders.

In the US, the conversion of a corporation into another entity is not covered by any qualified majority voting requirements. If a majority of the outstanding shares vote for the adoption of the resolution, the conversion shall be authorised.[67] Similarly, merger rules only require that a majority of the outstanding stock of the corporation approve the merger.[68] In addition to traditional short-form mergers, DGCL includes rules on a simplified two-step intermediate merger process, which has become a popular second step for the acquisition of a listed Delaware company after a tender offer. If an acquirer in a tender offer receives the required majority of shares to complete a merger, usually a majority of the shares, it is allowed to complete a back-end merger with an unlisted entity without shareholder approval as the second step in a tender offer, simplifying the going private transaction after consummation of a tender.[69]

Minority shareholder protection in the US is primarily achieved by requiring the board of directors to consider their fiduciary duties when proposing a conversion, merger or in a takeover setting, in addition to extensive appraisal rights. When it comes to mergers and takeovers, different fiduciary duty standards apply depending on whether the transaction involves controlling shareholders or whether it is between two unrelated parties.[70] However, even if US company law does not require that a qualified

[64] Companies Act (*Aktiebolagslag 2005:551*), ch 1 ss 7 f (SWE).

[65] Commercial Code (*Code de Commerce*) ss L223–230, L225–245 (FR). Furthermore, an SA cannot change its legal form in the first two years of operation, see Commercial Code (*Code de Commerce*) s L225–243 (FR). A conversion of an SA to an SAS needs to be approved unanimously, see Commercial Code (*Code de Commerce*) s L227-3 (FR). Similarly, according to the UK Companies Act, a public company may be re-registered as a private limited company if the special resolution is passed by a majority of not less than 75%, see Companies Act 2006 ss 97, 283 (UK). A public company limited by shares can be re-registered as an unlimited private company if all members of the company have approved to the re-registration, see Companies Act 2006 s 109 (UK). Publicly listed companies in France also have to follow the AMF Regulations, including additional rules on corporate restructurings.

[66] Commercial Code (*Code de Commerce*) s L223–3 (FR).

[67] Del Code Ann tit 8 s 266(b) (2024).

[68] ibid tit 8 s 251(c) (2024).

[69] ibid tit 8 s 251(h) (2024). A traditional short-form merger requires 90% of the target's outstanding shares, see ibid tit 8 s 253 (2024).

[70] See eg *Aronson v Lewis* 473 A2d 805, 812 (Del 1984); *Smith v Van Gorkom* 488 A2d 858, 872–873 (Del 1985) for a development on the business judgment rule standard. See *Unocal Corp v Mesa Petroleum*

majority approve a transaction, qualified majority voting requirements are often invoked as procedural safeguards. The Delaware Supreme Court has held in several cases that if a decision is approved by a majority of disinterested informed shareholders, a majority of the minority and/or a majority of disinterested directors, board decisions are, in most cases, reviewed only according to the business judgment rule standard. Without a qualified majority vote, the board decision will be scrutinised according to a higher standard of review, an enhanced scrutiny or an entire fairness standard.[71]

B. Shareholder Protection Through Exit Rights

Several jurisdictions globally protect shareholders by providing exit rights, either in the form of appraisal rights or in the form of a requirement to make a public offer to buy the shares of shareholders who dissent from a CDT.[72]

Appraisal rights are applied, for example in the US and Canada.[73] In Delaware, all dissenting shareholders are provided appraisal rights in all mergers, consolidations and conversions, and consequently not only in such transactions resulting in a delisting.[74]

The EU has been much more restrictive in introducing appraisal rights as a remedy for majority oppression. For many years, the Company Law Directive and its predecessors mainly included procedural rules on information, expert reports, and voting during a general meeting, leaving it up to the Member States to introduce more comprehensive minority protection rules.[75] It was not until 2019 that the EU introduced limited appraisal rights in the context of cross-border transactions through the Directive on cross-border conversions, mergers and divisions.[76] In cross-border mergers, conversions, and divisions, Member States must ensure that at least the shareholders who voted against the transaction have the right to dispose of their shares for adequate compensation.[77] At the Member State level, some EU jurisdictions offer appraisal rights for all types of mergers

Co 493 A2d 946, 958 (Del 1985); *Revlon, Inc v MacAndrews Forbes Holdings* 506 A2d 173 (Del 1986) for fiduciary duty standards between two unrelated parties. See *Weinberger v UOP, Inc* 457 A2d 701, 710–711 (Del 1983); *Kahn v Lynch Communication Systems* 638 A2d 1110, 1117 (Del 1994) for fiduciary duty standards when there is a controlling shareholder involved.

[71] See eg *Corwin v KKR Financial Holdings LLC* 125 A3d 304, 312 (Del 2015); *In re Volcano Corp Stockholder litigation* 143 A3d 727, 738 (Del Ch 2016); *Larkin v Shah* 2016 WL 4485447, 8 (Del Ch 2016); *Kahn v Worldwide Corp* 88 A3d 635, 644 (Del 2014); *In re Pure Resources Shareholder litigation* 808 A2d 421, 445 f (Del Ch 2002); *In re CNX Gas Corp Shareholders Litigation* 4 A3d 397, 413 (Del Ch 2010).

[72] Appraisal rights are rights of shareholders who dissent from a transaction to receive the fair value of their shares, as determined by a court, see eg JE Fisch, 'A Lesson from Startups: Contracting Out of Shareholder Appraisal' (2022) 107 *Iowa Law Review* 941.

[73] Canada Business Corporations Act ss 190; Del Code Ann tit 8 ss 262, 266 (2024).

[74] Del Code Ann tit 8 ss 262, 266 (2024).

[75] European Commission, 'Proposal for a Directive of the European Parliament and of the Council amending Directive (EU) 2017/1132 as regards cross-border conversions, mergers and divisions' COM (2018) 241 final, 6.

[76] Directive (EU) 2019/2121 amending Directive (EU) 2017/1132 as regards cross-border conversions, mergers and divisions [2019] OJ L321/1 (Dir 2019/2121).

[77] Dir 2017/1132 Arts 86i, 126a, 160.

while others still include appraisal rights only in the limited circumstances required by the Directive on cross-border conversions, mergers and divisions.[78]

In addition to the limited company law appraisal rights at the EU level, the Takeover Directive includes appraisal rights in connection with tender offers, where the offeror holds shares representing not less than 90 per cent of the capital and voting rights in the target.[79] The lack of appraisal rights as a minority protection feature in EU company law might reflect the prevailing attitude in Member States that shareholders cannot in general be cashed out in a merger. Even if the Company Law Directive allows Member States to introduce rules on cash-out mergers, most Member States prohibit such transactions.[80]

A few jurisdictions have additional appraisal rights in, inter alia, CDTs. Under German law, section 29(1) *Umwandlungsgesetz* stipulates that when a legal entity merges, by way of absorption by a legal entity having a different form, or when a listed company merges onto an unlisted company, the acquiring company must offer shareholders who object to the merger the option to sell their shares in exchange for appropriate cash compensation. The appropriateness of the offered cash compensation must always be authorised by the merger auditors under section 30(2) *Umwandlungsgesetz*. In addition, if a shareholder asserts that a cash compensation which was to be offered to him is not appropriate, the court must, at his request, determine the appropriate cash compensation. The same applies if the cash compensation was not offered or was not offered properly.[81]

Other jurisdictions provide rules requiring a mandatory bid to be made in case of, inter alia, a CDT. For example, in France, a buyout obligation in a listed corporation is triggered by three different categories of corporate events in addition to the standard squeeze-out appraisal rights. Firstly, when the company changes its legal form from a listed company (*société anonyme*) to a limited partnership with shares (*société en commandite par actions*), the controlling shareholder or the active partners in the limited partnership with shares are required to make a buyout offer to the shareholders. Secondly, in companies with a controlling owner, the financial supervisory authority (*Autorité des marchés financiers or AMF*) is explicitly allowed to request a buyout remedy when the controlling party decides to propose significant amendments to the articles of association or bylaws. Thirdly, the AMF can request a buyout remedy if a controlling owner decides to conduct a merger with a parent company or another company under the parent company's control, to sell all or most of the company's assets,

[78] For example, Swedish company law requires that shareholders are given appraisal rights in connection with cross-border mergers, divisions and conversions, but not domestic mergers, see ch 23 s 50, ch 24 s 55 and ch 24a s 34 Companies Act (*Aktiebolagslag 2005:551*) (SWE). In addition, the Swedish Companies Act (ch 22) includes appraisal rights when a majority owner owns more than 90% of the shares. Under ch 16 s 13 of the Finnish Companies Act (*Osakeyhtiölaki 624/2006*) shareholders voting against a merger have a right to demand the redemption of their shares. The general principles of ch 1 s 8 of the Finnish Companies Act also apply which means, inter alia, that the board of directors of the merging company has a duty to ensure that the merger consideration is in the best interests of the company and its shareholders.

[79] Directive 2004/25/EC on takeover bids [2004] OJ L142/12 (Dir 2004/25) Arts 15(2) and 16.

[80] M Ventoruzzo, 'Freeze-Outs: Transcontinental Analysis and Reform Proposals' (2010) 50 *Virginia Journal of International Law* 842, 878.

[81] Transformation Act (*Umwandlungsgesetz*) ss 29, 34 (GER). See also Companies Act of 2013 s 232(3)(h)(B) (IND) (with similar rules).

to reorient the company's business or to suspend dividends for several years. Since the AMF Regulation covers all significant amendments to the articles of association and bylaws, CDTs with others than affiliated parties may also trigger the buyout remedy in companies with a controlling owner.[82]

Under Spanish law CDTs are to be treated as voluntary delistings, implying that a public tender offer shall be made under the terms of the regulation on takeover law, unless the shares are not listed within a period of three months from the registration in the company register.[83] Similar rules apply under Columbian law.[84] Also, Austria provides rules governing a mandatory bid to be made in CDTs.[85] It should be noted that the legitimacy of CDTs was highly disputed in Austria until the delisting regime came into force in 2018. In 2017, the Austrian Supreme Court ruled that a merger to achieve a delisting is not per se unlawful. However, a merger would according to the Court be considered an abuse of rights if its sole purpose was to achieve a delisting and if there was a massive imbalance between the assessed interests of the corporation and those of the shareholders.[86]

C. Other Rules and Principles Protecting Shareholders

In addition to qualified majority voting requirements and exit rights, CDTs are almost always governed by requirements on disclosures. There is no specific distinction between civil law and common law countries, but all countries seem to view disclosure rights as an important part of the regulatory framework for going private transactions, including CDTs. In both common and civil law countries, disclosures often form part of securities regulation, including the relevant listing agreement. In addition, company law rules on mergers and conversions provide for disclosure rules. The Company Law Directive for example includes extensive information rights in connection with mergers.[87] In the US, going private transactions are, in addition to the state level, regulated at the federal level in securities law. Rule 13e–3 transactions cover share purchases by the issuer or an affiliate, tender offers by the issuer, and solicitation of proxies on behalf of the issuer regarding a merger, reorganisation, recapitalisation, or similar transaction, causing a class of securities which is subject to federal securities rules to be eligible to terminate

[82] General Regulation of the AMF (*Règlement général de l'AMF en vigeur du 01/01/2024–28/03/2024*) Arts 236-1, 236-5, 236-6 (FR). See also R Papadima, M Gherghe and R Valeanu, 'Shareholder Exit Signs on American and European Highways: Under Construction' (2016) 18 *University of Pennsylvania Journal of Business Law* 1059.

[83] Law RD 1066/2007 (*Real Decreto 1066/2007, de 27 de julio, sobre el régimen de las ofertas públicas de adquisición de valores*) Art 10(1) (ES).

[84] Law 222/95 (*Ley 222 de 1995 Regimen de Sociedas*) Arts 12(3), 14, 15, 16 (CO).

[85] Under Austrian law, protection of minority shareholders is stipulated in special provisions, such as the Stock Corporation Act (*Aktiengesetz*) s 225(2a) (mergers), s 240(3) (conversions), s 148(2a) (other changes which result in a delisting); EU Reorganisation Act (*EU-Umgründungsgesetz*), s 21(5); Division Act (*Spaltungsgesetz*) s 12(3) (divisions).

[86] See OGH 23 June 2017, 6 Ob 221/16t; M Winner, 'Verschmelzung zum Zweck des Delisting rechtsmissbräuchlich' (2017) 12 *Zeitschrift für Finanzmarktrecht* 387, 389; R Wolfbauer, '§ 38. Zulassungsverfahren zum und Widerrufsverfahren vom Amtlichen Handel' in M Gruber (ed), *BörseG 2018/MAR, Band 1: BörseG 2018* (Vienna, MANZ, 2020) margin no 46.

[87] See eg Dir 2017/1132 Arts 86d–86g, 86k, 91–92, 95–97, 122–25, 126c, 137 f, 141–43, 160d–g, 160k.

such a registration. The rule thus covers most going private transactions, requiring additional disclosures to shareholders.[88]

A CDT is normally prepared, proposed, and/or executed by the board of directors. In most jurisdictions, the directors are, as set forth above, obliged to observe their duty of loyalty and care to the company when preparing the transaction. They may consequently not promote the interests of the majority, or another party if that interest contravenes the interest of the company. In addition, in connection with a delisting, including a CDT, it could also be discussed, at least with respect to jurisdictions that do not provide exit rights, such as for example Sweden and Greece, if the duty of loyalty should be interpreted as to include not only the interest of the company, but also the interest of the shareholders in holding shares in a listed company. At least the rulings of the Swedish SSC have emphasised the importance of such considerations in connection with a delisting.[89] The principle of free negotiability is, as outlined in Part III above, typically of paramount importance for shareholders in listed companies. The loss of liquidity resulting from a delisting of the shares fundamentally alters the nature of the investment, often leaving the shareholders unable to sell their shares, a fact that may adversely affect the share price. Interpreted in this manner, the directors should, when preparing the CDT, weigh the company's interest against the interest of the shareholders in holding shares in a listed company.

In addition to abusive behaviour by the directors, there is a risk that a controlling shareholder abuses his/her power in connection with a CDT. As mentioned above, most jurisdictions provide voting rules or exit rights protecting the minority in connection with a CDT. However, these rules do not always guarantee that the interests of minority shareholders are adequately safeguarded. In many jurisdictions, specific principles and rules exist to protect shareholders from abuse of power by the majority, which could be applied in cases concerning such misconduct.

V. Considerations Regarding the Regulation of CDT

A. The Possible Harmonisation of Company and Securities Law in the EU

As the comparative outlook shows, countries have chosen to regulate CDT in several ways. A basic distinction is made between rules formed as part of securities law and rules enacted as part of company law. There are distinct advantages and disadvantages to each approach. Minority protection rules adopted in a company law setting have the disadvantage of only covering domestic companies. A fundamental principle in company law is the conflict of laws principle, according to which only one state should regulate the internal affairs of the corporation. In the US, this is recognised as

[88] 17 CFR s 240.13e-3 (2024).
[89] See eg SSC decisions AMN 2014:33 and AMN 2004:29.

the internal affairs doctrine.[90] The case law of the ECJ has mainly been concerned with how the freedom of establishment in EU law should be interpreted when companies are involved in cross-border transactions, but it seems that the fundamental principle that Member State law governs the internal affairs and legal status of a company is as firmly established in the EU as in the US.[91]

The fact that foreign companies on national stock exchanges are not covered by domestic company laws makes the case for enacting specific CDT rules as part of company law less appealing. Companies listed on the same stock market would be covered by different CDT rules depending on the country of origin, leading to a fragmented regulatory system.[92] If additional shareholder protection features are introduced in company law, the territorial nature of the legislation, ie, the fact that the rules are only applicable to domestic listed companies, may leave a gap in minority protection. This gap in protection could be significant, depending on the exposure of the stock market to foreign listings. The problem is evident in countries which attract a large number of foreign firms to its capital markets. In an EU context, it presents a problem when certain parts of company law are not harmonised, and, at the same time the aim is to increase cross-border trading between Member States.

The benefits of regulating CDTs in company law would be that company laws provide a powerful sanctioning mechanism, when the registration of a transaction,[93] such as a merger, can be made dependent on the company following minority protection rules.

In addition, there is a strong home country bias when a company chooses where to list its securities. In 2018, domestic companies accounted for 86 per cent of listing on the EU stock markets. Similar home bias exists at a global level.[94] The drawback of introducing shareholder protection in connection with CDT in domestic company laws is thus marginal for most capital markets, if an analysis is made only of cross-border listings. However, the advancements in information and communication technology, coupled with the deregulation of capital flows have increased foreign investment in the stock market globally. For example, more than 40 per cent of the capital in listed companies in the Netherlands and the UK is owned by foreign investors.[95] Investors are often

[90] *CTS Corp v Dynamics Corp of America* 481 US 69, 89 (1987); see also *Edgar v MITE Corp.* 457 US 624 (1982).

[91] Case 81/87 *The Queen v HM Treasury and Commissioners of Inland Revenue, ex parte Daily Mail and General Trust plc* ECLI:EU:C:1988:456 [1988] ECR 5483 para 19; Case 210/06 *Cartersio Oktató és Szolgáltató bt*, ECLI:EU:C:2008:723 [2008] ECR I-09641 para 124. The court, however, also notes that national legislation on incorporation and winding-up of the company does not enjoy any form of immunity from EU law. See also Case 106/16 *Polbud – Wykonawstwo sp.* ECLI:EU:C:2017:804 where it was considered a restriction on the freedom of establishment when a company was not allowed to change its registered office to another Member State without the winding-up of the company.

[92] An example of the problems with cross-border company listings is the *Alliance Oil* case, SSC decision AMN 2013:35, which concerned a Bermuda-registered company, Alliance Oil, listed on the Swedish stock market NASDAQ Stockholm.

[93] See eg Companies Act (*Aktiebolagslag 2005:551*) ch 23 s 21 (SWE).

[94] Oxera Consulting LLP, *Primary and secondary equity markets in the EU* (2020). Available at: www.oxera.com/wp-content/uploads/2020/11/Oxera-study-Primary-and-Secondary-Markets-in-the-EU-Final-Report-EN-1.pdf, 90.

[95] A De La Cruz, A Medina and Y Tang, *Owners of the World's Listed Companies* (2019). Available at: www.oecd.org/content/dam/oecd/en/publications/reports/2019/10/owners-of-the-world-s-listed-companies_6f8bda93/ed7ca2f3-en.pdf, 14.

drawn to countries with a high level of minority protection, contributing to more liquid capital markets.[96] While investors in the US are the largest cross-border investors, those from continental Europe investors ranked second worldwide in cross-border equity investments.[97]

The case for using securities law as a regulatory mechanism for CDTs seems appealing if the purpose is to cover cross-border listings. The EU securities law framework routinely includes in its realm third-country firms providing services in the Union.[98] However, the problem from an EU perspective is that corporate governance and minority shareholders issues have been notoriously difficult to regulate in securities laws at the EU level. As an example, the European Commission proposed in its 1985 White Paper a detailed text in the field of takeover bids.[99] The Takeover Directive took 14 years to negotiate and was finally adopted when a compromise was reached on several key corporate governance measures.[100] Most of the securities laws at the EU level have focused on market structure, market abuse, or disclosure rules for companies instead of corporate governance rules. However, there are exceptions. Corporate governance rules for listed companies have to a certain extent undergone harmonisation in the EU through the Shareholder Rights Directive (SRD), which includes rules on shareholder protection in listed companies.[101] For example, according to the 2017 amendments to the SRD, related party transactions of a certain size need to be approved by the general meeting in listed companies.[102] Furthermore, fundamental transactions, such as mergers, divisions, cross-border mergers, and cross-border divisions are, as set forth above, already partly harmonised in the Company Law Directive.[103]

An alternative would be to regulate minority protection matters in connection with CDTs at the national level in securities laws. However, with the ambition of EU securities regulation to create a European CMU with harmonised rules at the EU level, there is little room for national securities regulation. Most countries have been reluctant to adopt securities laws when the regulatory area is dominated by the harmonised securities law structure at the EU level. In addition, from an EU perspective, national regulation of CDTs would further fragment the EU securities market and would be contrary to the aim of the EU to foster cross-border offers by harmonising securities laws.[104]

[96] R La Porta et al, 'Legal Determinants of External Finance' (1997) 52 *The Journal of Finance* 1131; WA Reese Jr and MS Weisbach, 'Protection of Minority Shareholder Interests, Cross-listings in the United States, and Subsequent Equity Offerings' (2002) 66 *Journal of Financial Economics* 65.

[97] De La Cruz, Medina and Tang (n 95) 15.

[98] See eg Dir 2014/65/EU Art 1.

[99] European Commission, 'Proposal for a Directive of the European Parliament and of the Council on takeover bids' COM 2002/0534 final.

[100] Dir 2004/25.

[101] Directive 2007/36/EC on the exercise of certain rights of shareholders in listed companies [2007] OJ L184/17 (Dir 2007/36).

[102] ibid Art 9c. See also Directive (EU) 2017/828 amending Dir 2007/36/EC as regards the encouragement of long-term shareholder engagement [2017] OJ L132/1 Art 1.

[103] Dir 2017/1132 Arts 86a–160u.

[104] See eg European Commission, 'Proposal for a regulation to make public capital markets in the Union more attractive for companies and to facilitate access to capital for small and medium-sized enterprises' COM (2022) 762 final, 7.

B. Striking the Right Balance of Shareholder Protection in CDTs

Our evaluation of the different measures taken in the context of CDTs takes as its starting point the four main minority protection measures: qualified majority voting rights, the right to exit the company, the duty of loyalty and care and disclosure requirements.

Many of the French-origin, German-origin, and Scandinavian civil law countries have introduced protection for shareholders in CDTs in the form of qualified majority voting rights. In some countries, such as Sweden, the qualified majority requirements when a listed company is absorbed by an unlisted entity are so strict that they would normally be impossible to achieve. It is doubtful if excessive qualified majority requirements provide for the best available solution to the conflict between majority and minority shareholders. CDTs can under certain circumstances generate efficiency gains and cost reductions, despite the conflicts that they entail.[105] A regulatory framework such as the Swedish one in practice effectively prohibits a CDT, even though it might in certain cases be beneficial for the shareholders, for example, if the liquidity is very low and the share price does not reflect a fair market value of the company.

Minority protection through decision rights during shareholders' meetings is less prominent in the US. As mentioned above, DGCL does not have any requirements on qualified majority voting for mergers between public and private companies.[106] The decision regarding transformation to another business association form similarly only requires that a majority of the outstanding stock vote for the adoption of the proposal.[107] In addition, Delaware law includes rules on intermediate merger transactions after a tender offer, where shareholders do not have any voting rights. Neither of the two biggest US stock markets impose any additional requirements on shareholder approval for voluntary delistings. An explanation could be that shareholder-protective measures focusing on protection from the abuse of the majority are more important in countries with large controlling owners, while the US system, with its more dispersed ownership, is more focused on the relationship between the directors and shareholders, and potential abuse from the management of the company.[108] Contrary to civil law countries, the US minority protection rules are focused on directors' and officers' fiduciary duties, a standard which is applicable both when there is a conflict of interest between directors and officers on the one hand and shareholders on the other hand, as well as when the transactions involves a controlling shareholder. The legal strategies in civil law and common law countries thus seem to be influenced at least partly by the agency conflict they try to address.[109]

Even though there are differences between civil law and common law countries when it comes to shareholder protection in CDTs it should be noted that both civil

[105] E Rock et al, 'Fundamental Changes' in R Kraakman et al (n 28) 174.
[106] Del Code Ann tit 8 s 251(c) (2024).
[107] ibid tit 8 s 266(d) (2024).
[108] PP Lele and MM Siems, 'Shareholder Protection: A Leximetric Approach' (2007) 7 *Journal of Corporate Law Studies* 17, 35 f.
[109] Rock et al (n 105) 172. See, however, Companies Act 2006 s 899 (UK).

law and common law jurisdictions usually combine minority protection features from different categories elaborated on in our chapter. For example, in many jurisdictions exit rights are combined with disclosure obligations and, in some jurisdictions, also with qualified majority voting requirements. However, it seems that the US has more extensively focused on ex-post remedies to abusive majority shareholder transactions resulting in a delisting, including judicial review of the transaction and appraisal rights. At the EU level, the focus has instead been more on ex-ante protections, such as decision rights and disclosures before the transaction.

VI. Conclusion

During the last decades, shareholder protection has been on the rise globally. Our chapter on CDTs shows that minority shareholders are protected through both ex-ante protection measures and ex-post remedies to abusive CDTs, depending on the jurisdiction. It should be acknowledged that more shareholder protection is not always equal to better legal systems or more growth and an increase in economic welfare. The results of our comparison on minority shareholder protection in CDTs do not show if a certain measure is 'better' for the country, i.e., results in more liquid stock markets and economic growth. Likely, the optimal mix is likely to vary across countries and depends on various factors, such as the composition of the shareholder base and the most prominent agency conflicts within domestic companies. However, a harmonisation of CDTs at the EU-level would contribute to the CMU, which would likely make the transaction costs lower for companies considering cross-border listings. In addition, cross-border investors would benefit from similar shareholder protective measures in all EU countries.

PART V

Global Perspectives

14

Delisting in the United States

MARTIN GELTER AND STEVE THEL*

I. Overview

The United States has the largest securities markets in the world with thousands of publicly traded firms (issuers) whose composition constantly changes. Both voluntary and involuntary delisting are a natural part of this process. Involuntary delisting is a sanction used by the stock exchange and the Securities and Exchange Commission (SEC) against an issuer. The threat of a potential delisting is part of the arsenal of instruments that help to induce compliance.

Voluntary delisting can occur for multiple reasons, such as a merger or bankruptcy. A firm – usually with a controlling shareholder – might decide to 'go private' to escape from the continuous disclosure and other requirements of the Securities Exchange Act of 1934 and to eliminate any minority ownership. A firm might also 'go dark' by reducing the number of shareholders of record below the minimum number required for the Exchange Act's disclosure requirements to apply. To understand the delisting process and its consequences, it is necessary to understand the legal context more broadly, including the corporate and securities law framework. While corporate law mainly seeks to protect outside shareholders in the going-private transactions, the Exchange Act provides for disclosure and other requirements.

Broadly speaking and, as explained below, the reporting requirements of the Securities Exchange Act of 1934 apply when an issuer has had an effective registration statement under the Securities Act, when its securities are traded on a national securities exchange, or when it exceeds certain quantitative thresholds regarding a firm's size and number of record security holders. To escape the disclosure requirements of the federal securities law, it therefore does not suffice to delist, but an issuer needs to take steps under the securities laws to deregister so that none of the three prerequisites continue to apply.

This chapter explores all of these legal questions. After briefly surveying the US securities market and securities law in section II, this chapter discusses voluntary delisting

* Martin Gelter, Professor of Law, Fordham University School of Law, and Steve Thel, Wormser Professor of Law, Fordham University School of Law. The authors thank Caroline Gentile and Sean Griffith as well as participants of the 2023 Delisting Conference for helpful comments. This chapter describes the law as of 31 December 2024. Recent developments, especially Delaware's SB 21, are not taken into account. Errors remain our own.

in section III. It discusses both the securities law framework as well as the going-private process under corporate law, which will typically involve a freezeout merger. Section IV explores involuntary delisting. Section V summarises and concludes.

II. The Securities Markets and the General Legal Framework

A. The US Securities Market

The United States has the largest securities market in the world. Today, there are slightly less than 4,000 publicly traded firms, down from a peak of about 7,000 in 1996.[1] Despite the declining number, market capitalisation has risen relative to the US GDP, corresponding to about 150 per cent or a dazzling figure of USD 38 trillion in 2022.[2] The reasons for the decline in the number of listed corporations are not entirely clear. Explanations include the consolidation of industries through M&A activity, reduced antitrust enforcement, 'killer acquisitions' and an increased regulatory burden. Not all explanations are equally plausible or able to provide more than a partial explanation.[3] Most likely, a combination of economic factors has led to this reduction, which does not appear to indicate that the securities market is in decline.

However, there have been a number of remarkable changes to patterns of investment and stock ownership during the past decades. Berle and Means' famous 1933 book 'The Modern Corporation and Private Property' described a market characterised by a separation of ownership and control, where publicly traded firms had a highly dispersed shareholder base, leading to very powerful management.[4] This characterisation was true throughout the second half of the twentieth century, maybe even more so than at the time of Berle and Means' study.[5] In the traditional picture, a large proportion of stockholders were retail investors. During the last few decades, retail investors have been replaced partly by institutional investors, such as mutual funds, ETFs and hedge funds.[6] Retail investors still hold much of the stock, although indirectly through mutual funds and index funds, the latter being characterised as 'passive' investors because they just commit to holding stock corresponding to an index rather than managing a portfolio. Large firms now still tend to have a dispersed ownership

[1] MJ Roe and CCY Wang, 'Half the Firms, Double the Profits: Public Firms' Transformation, 1996–2022' (2023) 8 *Journal of Law, Finance & Accounting* 211, 217–219.

[2] ibid 227.

[3] KM Kahle and RM Stulz, 'Is the US Public Corporation in Trouble?' (2017) 31 *Journal of Economic Perspectives* 67, 83–86; Roe and Wang, 'Half the Firms, Double the Profits' (n 1) 16–32.

[4] AA Berle Jr and GC Means, *The Modern Corporation and Private Property* (New York, The Macmillan Company, 1933); see RC Clark, 'The Four Stages of Capitalism: Reflections on Investment Management Treatise' (1981) 94 *Harvard Law Review* 561.

[5] See MJ Roe, *Strong Managers Weak Owners* (New Jersey, Princeton University Press, 1994).

[6] Kahle and Stulz, 'Is the US Public Corporation in Trouble?' (n 3) note 7 at 81.

structure. Still, they also often have 'common ownership', meaning that some of the largest shareholders are funds belonging to the same families of fund advisors.[7]

A narrower but not less important phenomenon of recent years is that of firms permanently characterised by a controlling shareholder.[8] In the tech industry in particular, dual-class structures often allow founders to hold shares giving them multiple voting rights (as long as they hold this stock).[9] Some of the largest firms are today thus controlled, which was not true 50 years ago.

Finally, a significant concern is that some companies are not publicly traded on large, registered exchanges such as the NYSE or NASDAQ, but instead are bought and sold by investors in the over-the-counter (OTC) market. Historically, the OTC market consisted of the 'pink sheets' named after the papers on which prices were quoted daily.[10] Today, the OTC market has moved to electronic platforms.[11] The securities of a company that is delisted but still has public stockholders will be traded 'over the counter'. Whether such securities will trigger disclosure requirements depends on whether the issuer has filed an effective registration statement under the Securities Act, or, alternatively, whether the issuer exceeds certain thresholds in terms of total assets and securities holders of record (see section III.A). If such an issuer falls below a certain threshold, it may deregister and escape disclosure even if it still has public shareholders (see section III.C.iv). Firms that 'go dark' often fail to disclose information to investors.[12]

B. Corporate Law and Securities Law

Publicly traded corporations in the United States are subject to two levels of legislation and case law: corporate law and securities law. Corporate law is state law, leaving it for the corporation to decide where to incorporate regardless of their place of business or location of headquarters. Two thirds of the *Fortune 500* and half of all publicly traded corporations are incorporated in Delaware.[13]

Securities law in this context is largely federal law. The federal securities laws were first enacted during the Great Depression as part of President Roosevelt's New Deal. The Securities Act of 1933 established registration and disclosure requirements applying when an issuer offers securities to the public. The Securities Exchange Act of 1934

[7] M Backus, C Conlon and M Sinkinson, 'Common Ownership in America: 1980–2017' (2021) 13 *American Economic Journal: Microeconomics* 273.

[8] BV Reddy, 'More than Meets the Eye: Reassessing the Empirical Evidence on U.S. Dual-Class Stock' (2021) 23 *University of Pennsylvania Journal Business Law* 955, 963–68 (summarising data on tech IPOs); A Gurrea-Martínez, 'Theory, Evidence, and Policy on Dual-Class Shares: A Country-Specific Response to a Global Debate' (2021) 22 *European Business Organization Law Review* 475, 479 f (observing the increasing of dual-class firms in the US over time).

[9] See Z Goshen and A Hamdani, 'Corporate Control and Idiosyncratic Vision' (2016) 125 *Yale Law Journal* 560, 588–91 (interpreting dual-class stock as a way for entrepreneurs to protect their business plans vision from shareholder pressure).

[10] Eg, DC Langevoort and RB Thompson, 'Publicness in Contemporary Securities Regulation after the JOBS Act' (2013) 101 *Georgetown Law Journal* 337, 348 (discussing the history of the OTC market).

[11] See ibid at 349 (describing electronic OTC market platforms).

[12] Eg JM Fried, 'Firms Gone Dark' (2009) 76 *University of Chicago Law Review* 135, 150.

[13] See eg WJ Moon, 'Delaware's Global Competitiveness' (2021) 106 *Iowa Law Review* 1683, 1693.

created the SEC (Securities and Exchange Commission) as a powerful regulator and added periodical disclosure requirements. The SEC has adopted numerous rules and regulations to implement and further specify the requirements of the two acts.[14] The federal nature of securities law also means that federal courts have subject matter jurisdiction over it, contrary to the state courts' competence to adjudicate on corporate law issues. There are also state securities laws, but these are of limited significance for the issues discussed here.

The first of the current federal securities statutes, the Securities Act of 1933, was largely devoted to requiring the registration of securities offered to the public. As discussed below, this 1933 Act registration can have consequences for Exchange Act reporting. The key to the Exchange Act as originally enacted in 1934 was the registration of securities exchanges with the SEC, which was created by the Act, and their regulation.[15] The registration of exchanges was limited to a relatively small number, but other provisions of the Act had more far-reaching consequences. It was, and is, unlawful for brokers, dealers and exchange members to trade a security on an exchange unless that security has been registered under the Exchange Act registration.[16] The Act did not require companies to register their securities, presumably because of concerns about the limits of federal power at the time, but companies had to 'voluntarily' register in order to preserve the liquidity that exchange trading provided. Once they registered securities under the Exchange Act, exchange-traded companies became subject to a sort of federal corporate law. They were required to prepare and file with the SEC such periodic reports as the SEC required.[17] The solicitation of proxies for Exchange Act registered securities was subjected to SEC regulation.[18] Finally, the officers, directors and principal shareholders of Exchange Act registered securities are required to report their trading of those securities and to disgorge their short-swing profits.

As originally enacted, the Exchange Act focused on exchange-traded securities and left the over-the-counter market to regulation by the SEC. In 1936, however, Congress added section 15(d) to the Act, requiring issuers with an effective registration statement under the *Securities Act* to file periodic reports as required by section 13, but did not subject them to the other provisions of the Exchange Act just discussed. The section 15(d) reporting requirement ceased any year after the first year in which the number of registered security holders fell below a certain number.

In 1964, section 12(g) was added to the Exchange Act to require companies with 500 or more shareholders of record and a certain amount of assets to register under section 12. The effect of this registration was to subject the issuers to the reporting, proxy and short-swing trading rules of the Exchange Act. Thus, larger issuers in the over-the-counter market were made subject to the Exchange Act's requirements

[14] See FA Gevurtz, 'United States: The Protection of Minority Investors and Compensation of their Losses' in P-H Conac and M Gelter (eds), *Global Securities Litigation and Enforcement* (Cambridge, Cambridge University Press, 2019) 109, 114 f.

[15] Exchange Act s 6. Brokers, dealers and exchanges cannot use jurisdictional means to use an Exchange unless the Exchange is registered with the SEC, ibid s 5.

[16] Exchange Act s 12(a), (b).

[17] Exchange Act s 13(a). Over time, s 13 has been amended to require reports of substantial investors.

[18] Exchange Act s 14(a). Over time, s 14 has been amended to require reports to shareholders and to provide for SEC regulation of tender offers for Exchange Act registered securities.

for exchange-listed companies. In 2012, section 12(g) was amended to substantially increase the record-holder threshold.

Corporate law governs powers of directors and shareholders, including requirements for votes[19] (eg, for merger transactions aimed at going private), but not explicit disclosure requirements relating to such votes, which are governed by securities law.[20] Directors' fiduciary duties, which are essential in determining what course of action they may take in going-private transactions, are governed by corporate law. In the following, this chapter will discuss federal securities laws and the corporate law of Delaware (where relevant).[21]

The stock exchanges have enacted rules on delisting; this chapter will refer exclusively to New York Stock Exchange (NYSE) rules, specifically section eight of the NYSE Listed Company Manual.

III. Voluntary Delisting

A. 'Delisting', 'Deregistration', 'Going Private' and 'Going Dark'

We need to clarify some terminology before discussing voluntary delisting, defined as a removal from the stock exchange initiated by the issuer. In the United States, it is important to clearly distinguish between going-private transactions, the process of 'delisting' and 'deregistration',[22] which is sometimes described as 'going dark'.[23]

'Delisting' is the removal of a corporation's stock from a securities exchange (such as NYSE); 'deregistration' refers to the removal of the securities from registration with the SEC, which is necessary to remove an issuer from the reach of securities law and to escape disclosure requirements. Registration under the Exchange Act is not automatically linked to being traded on the stock exchange. An issuer can become subject to the Securities Exchange Act's reporting requirements in several ways, namely (1) by listing a class of securities on a national stock exchange (Securities Exchange Act, section 12(b)), (2) by exceeding certain quantitative thresholds regarding shareownership and total assets (section 12(g))[24] and (3) by having filed an effective registration statement under the Securities Act (section 15(d)). Delisting only eliminates registration under section 12(b). The other two forms of registration, which are

[19] In some cases, stock exchange rules establish additional voting requirements.

[20] State corporate legislation does not typically establish disclosure requirements. However, when analysing the fiduciary duties of directors and controlling shareholders, courts are typically more deferential toward stockholder approval if the vote was, among other things, based on adequate disclosure of the relevant facts.

[21] The Securities Exchange Act is quoted by its original section numbers rather than by its location in the US Code.

[22] See eg D Bakst, T Kollar and C Naidu, 'Current Developments to the Process of Delisting and Deregistration of Securities from U.S. Exchanges' (2020) *PLI Current: The Journal of PLI Press* vol 4, No 3, art 14.

[23] See eg C Leuz, A Triantis and TY Wang, 'Why Do Firms Go Dark? Causes and Economic Consequences of Voluntary SEC Deregistrations' (2008) 181 *Journal of Accounting and Economics* 181, 182.

[24] In short, USD 10M and more than 2,000 shareholders (or more than 500 shareholders) of record who are not accredited investors). For more details, see below III.C.iv.

suspended while a company is exchange traded, reemerge, meaning that disclosure requirements persist.[25]

A voluntary delisting will typically be preceded by a going-private transaction that eliminates minority shareholders from the firm. Ideally, a going-private transaction (governed chiefly by corporate law), such as a freezeout merger, will bring the number of security holders under the thresholds established in the Securities Exchange Act[26] (see below section C.iv). If a firm does not eliminate all outside shareholders, its stock may continue to be traded in the over-the-counter market.[27] If it then 'goes dark' by falling under the thresholds of section 12(g) and section 15(d) and then deregisters, it may escape disclosure requirements even if there are significant numbers of beneficial securities holders (section C.iv). Typically, such companies will continue to trade in the OTC market, often with adverse effects for outside investors.[28]

Empirically, the number of voluntary delisting decisions is substantial. Min and Jin surveyed 8-K disclosures under Item 3.01 (which includes voluntary and involuntary delisting) in 2019, finding 112 delistings from the NYSE, 115 from NASDAQ, and 12 others. They note that these include outcomes of mergers as well as transfers to different exchanges.[29] Macey, O'Hara and Pompillo report that there were between 77 and 225 voluntary delistings from NYSE each year between 1998 and 2004 and between 235 and 433 voluntary delistings on NASDAQ.[30]

The following sections, therefore, begin with going-private transactions (section B), which logically precede delisting and deregistration (section B.v).

B. The Going-private Transaction

(i) The Decision to Delist

SEC rules explicitly require that 'the issuer must comply with all applicable laws in effect in the state in which it is incorporated … governing an issuer's voluntary withdrawal of a class of securities'.[31] Rule 806.02 of the NYSE Listed Company Manual stipulates that an issuer may delist 'after its board approves the action'.[32] The DGCL (Delaware General Corporation Law) or other state laws do not require shareholder authorisation for delisting. However, going-private transactions (such as freezeout mergers) that allow delisting and deregistration will typically require approval. Formally, shareholders are not involved in the decision to delist.[33]

[25] Bakst, Kollar and Naidu, 'Current Developments to the Process of Delisting' (n 22).

[26] Securities Exchange Act ss 12(g) and 15(d).

[27] Eg SEC, *No-action letter (Orbit International Corp.)* (13 November 2014) 2014 SEC No-Act. LEXIS 394, *5 (describing how Orbit's common stock traded on the OTC Pink after its delisting from NASDAQ).

[28] Leuz, Triantis and Wang, 'Why Do Firms Go Dark?' (n 23) 186.

[29] G Min and K-Y Jin, 'Relational Enforcement of Stock Exchange Rules' (2021) 47 *BYU Law Review* 149, 179.

[30] J Macey, M O'Hara and D Pompillo, 'Down and Out in the Stock Market: The Law and Economics of the Delisting Process' (2008) 51 *Journal of Law and Economics* 683, 691.

[31] R 12d2-2(c)(2)(i).

[32] See also NASDAQ Rule Series 5000 (listing rules).

[33] Eg, Fried, 'Firms Gone Dark' (n 12) 141.

In the absence of specific corporate law rules governing delisting, general principles for such decisions apply. The quorum for a board resolution will be provided for in the corporation's certificate of incorporation or (more likely) its bylaws.[34] By default, the quorum in a Delaware corporation is a majority of the total number of directors. The certificate or bylaws can set a higher number; the certificate may authorise the bylaws to set a smaller number, which must be at least one third of the total number of directors.[35] A decision is made with a majority of the directors present in the meeting unless the certificate or bylaws require a higher number.[36]

(ii) Structuring the Going-Private Transaction

(a) Freezeout Merger

The corporate going-private transaction is typically structured either as a one-step merger or a two-step transaction consisting of a tender offer followed by a merger.[37]

In the case of a one-step merger transaction, the target corporation (ie, the entity going private) is merged with a wholly owned subsidiary of the acquirer (ie, of the controlling shareholder). Typically, the operating company going private (rather than the special-purpose entity) will survive the merger (reverse triangular merger).[38] Minority shareholders normally receive cash or acquirer stock as compensation for their shares.[39] The transaction must be initiated by a resolution of each board of the two corporations constituent to the merger.[40] Stockholders must (normally) vote on it,[41] with the required majority for approval being the majority of all outstanding stock.[42]

[34] The certificate (or articles) of incorporation is the corporation's founding document and must be submitted to the secretary of state, where is a matter of public record. DGCL ss 101(a), 102, 103. The bylaws are typically and longer, more technical document and can be amended more easily. DGCL s 109. On the amendment of the certificate, see DGCL s 242(a), on the amendment of bylaws s 109(a). See W T Allen, R Kraakman and V S Khanna (eds), *Commentaries and Cases on the Law of Business Organization,* 6th edn (2021) 104 f.

[35] DGCL s 141(b).

[36] ibid.

[37] See eg G Subramanian, 'Freezeouts in Delaware and Around the World' (2023) 24 *University of Pennsylvania Journal of Business Law* 803, 804. Wisconsin and California have enacted statutes specifically addressing going- private transactions. Wis Admin Code DFI-Sec s 6.05; Cal Corp Code s 1203, see Securities Practice Portfolio Series, *Corporate Practice, Portfolio 235: Corporate Stock Repurchases & Going Private* (2023) II.D.7.b. This discussion here focuses on Delaware.

[38] In a forward triangular merger, the single-purpose subsidiary survives. See eg, Allen, Kraakman and Khanna, *Commentaries and Cases* (n 34) 514 (discussing the distinction between the two types of triangular mergers).

[39] Typically, the parent will have placed the merger consideration in the subsidiary: FA Gevurtz, *Corporation Law*, 3rd edn (St Paul, West Academic Publishing, 2021) 672 at n 59.

[40] DGCL s 251(b).

[41] DGCL s 251(f) provides for some exceptions when no vote is required by the stockholders of the surviving corporation. These will not apply here, however, because stockholders will have to trade in their shares for the merger consideration (cash or stock in the parent). Section 251(f)(2).

[42] DGCL s 251(c). If there are multiple classes of stock and the merger agreement involves an amendment of the issuer's certificate that affects the rights of a specific class of stockholders, this class will need to approve the merger separately. F A Gevurtz and C M Sautter, *Mergers and Acquisitions Law* (St Paul, West Academic Publishing, 2019) 86; *Dalton v American Investment Co* [1985] 490 A.2d 574, 586; aff'd [1985] 501 A.2d 1238; DGCL s 242(b)(2).

No vote would be required if a parent company merges with a subsidiary pursuant to DGCL section 253, which requires 90 per cent ownership.

In the case of a two-step tender offer, the acquirer would first offer to shareholders to purchase their stock and subsequently initiate a merger if the threshold is reached. Typically, the offer would be contingent on reaching the necessary percentage. DGCL section 251(h), which was introduced in 2013, permits a merger without a vote if the preceding tender offer fulfills specific requirements if the merger agreement provides for it. Pursuant to this section, the offer must be for all shares entitled to vote on a merger and may be contingent on reaching the necessary threshold for a merger vote. The offeror must promise to consummate the merger as soon as practicable after the tender offer, and the remaining minority shareholders must be paid out in the merger at the same price as those who accepted the tender offer. The effect of this provision is that the acceptance of the tender offer supplants the vote on the merger in cases where the acquirer does not have the voting power to approve the transaction unilaterally.[43]

(b) Other Methods

Another method is a reverse stock split, where many stockholders would receive only a fractional share.[44] A sale of all assets followed by dissolution is another method.[45] Both of these would require at least one shareholder majority vote in Delaware.[46] However, outside public shareholders are not needed for approval.[47]

A corporation with a small shareholder base might use a stock repurchase to get below the shareholder thresholds of sections 12(g) and 15(d) to 'go dark'.[48] This is the one method where the corporation's capital matters. Under DGCL section 160(a)(1), a repurchase is not permissible when it is impaired or when the repurchase would impair the capital.[49] Moreover, section 160(a)(1) allows a repurchase (regardless of impairment of capital) also when the corresponding shares are retired and the capital is reduced accordingly pursuant to sections 243, 244 (both of which require a board resolution, but not a shareholder vote).[50] A repurchase tender offer does not require a shareholder

[43] Gevurtz and Sautter, *Mergers and Acquisitions Law* (n 42) 85 f.

[44] Law Journal Press, *Going Private* (2023) s 3.02(3).

[45] ibid s 3.02(4).

[46] A reverse stock split would require a vote because requires an amendment of the certificate, which records the number and denomination of stock. DGCL s 102(4), s 242. Both a sale of substantially all assets and a dissolution require a vote. DGCL ss 271, 275.

[47] Fried (n 12) 142.

[48] Securities Practice Portfolio Series, *Corporate Practice* (n 38) II.D; see also r 12g5-1 (definition of held of record).

[49] Note, however, that the published balance sheet based on GAAP is not necessarily decisive for whether a company's capital is impaired. Eg, *Klang v Smith's Food & Drug Centers, Inc* [1997] 702 A.2d 150; see also B Manning and J J Hanks, *Legal Capital*, 4th edn (Minnesota, Foundation Press, 2013) 194 (discussing how the Model Business Corporation Act allows the use of accounting principles 'reasonable under the circumstances').

[50] DGCL s 244(b) prohibits a reduction of capital when the firm's assets after the reduction are not sufficient to pay the corporation's debt. In this situation, it is therefore not possible to retire shares (s 243(c)), which means that the firm also cannot repurchase them. On the discussion, see D A Drexler, L S Black Jr and A G Sparks III, *Delaware Corporation Law and Practice* (New York, Matthew Bender & Company, 2022) 1 at s 19.01.

vote.[51] Not accepting the offer might be risky if a firm aims to deregister: if the repurchase brings the number of record holders below the required thresholds, the remaining holdouts may be stuck with an illiquid investment in a company not subject to any disclosure requirements.[52]

When making a self-tender offer to repurchase stock, an issuer must follow rule 13e-4 and Schedule TO (which provides for the same disclosures as third-party offers). Rule 13e-4 stipulates some substantive conditions for the tender offer, including the offer must be open for 20 business days, that it must be non-discriminatory, and that each person tendering must be paid the highest price paid during the offer period.[53]

(iii) Fiduciary Duties and the Significance of Due Process

Historically, freezeout mergers (as the primary method of going private) were not always as easy as today. Courts sometimes adjudicated that a freezeout transaction must have a colorable business purpose (besides eliminating the minority).[54] The 'business purpose' requirement was abandoned in Delaware in *Weinberger v UOP*.[55]

Today, a going-private transaction in the form of a freezeout merger is typically negotiated between the acquirer and an independent committee negotiating on behalf of minority shareholders.[56] The reason is fiduciary duties, specifically the duty of loyalty. Given that the controlling shareholder has the power to push through the transactions with its voting power, such a deal is inherently conflicted. By default, the Delaware courts would apply the 'entire fairness' standard to such a transaction.[57] In this context, 'fairness' means a combination of fair dealing and fair price.[58] The defendants (ie, the directors and the controlling shareholder) have the burden of proof to show entire fairness.[59] Even with a controlling shareholder present, the courts have held that approval by an independent committee (which must fulfil certain requirements) or informed approval by a majority of disinterested minority shareholders can shift the burden of proof.[60] In recent years, the courts have gone even further: In *Kahn v MFW*, the Delaware Supreme Court found that approval of both an independent committee *and* the majority of minority shareholders can give the transaction the protection of the

[51] Fried (n 12) 142.
[52] ibid 143.
[53] R 13e-4(f)(1)(i), (3), (8).
[54] *Singer v Magnavox Co* [1977] 380 A.2d 969 (ruling that a long-form merger is improper if its sole purpose is to freeze out minority shareholders).
[55] *Weinberger v UOP, Inc* [1983] 457 A.2d 701, 715.
[56] Subramanian, 'Freezeouts in Delaware and Around the World' (n 37) 804.
[57] Eg, AR Brownstein, AJ Nussbaum et al, 'Going Private Guide (August 2022)' in Practicing Law Institute, *Doing Deals 2023: The Art of M&A Transactional Practice* (2023) 359, 379. Available at: www.plus.pli.edu/Browse/title?fq=title_id%3A(357747).
[58] *Weinberger v UOP, Inc* (n 55) 711; eg, *Cede & Co v Technicolor, Inc* [1983] 634 A.2d 345, 361, modified [1994] 636 A.2d 956; *Wiegand v Berry Petroleum Co* [1991] CA No 9316.
[59] Eg, *Citron v E. I. duPont de Nemours & Co.* [1990] 584 A.2d 490, 499–500; *Cinerama, Inc. v Technicolor, Inc.* [1995] 663 A.2d 1156; *Kumar v Racing Corp. of Am., Inc.* [1991] CA No 12039; *Sealy Mattress Co of N J v Sealy, Inc* [1987] 532 A.2d 1324. In re *MultiPlan Corp. S'holders Litig* [2022] 268 A.3d 784, 792; see R F Balotti and J A Finkelstein, *Delaware Law of Corporations and Business Organizations*, 4th edn (New York, Wolters Kluwer, 2021) s 9.56.
[60] *Kahn v Lynch Commc'n Sys, Inc* [1995] 669 A.2d 79.

business judgment rule. To qualify, a certain number of conditions must be met. The business judgment rule applies:

> if, but only if:
> (i) the controller conditions the procession of the transaction on the approval of both a Special Committee and a majority of the minority stockholders;
> (ii) the Special Committee is independent;
> (iii) the Special Committee is empowered to select its own advisors freely and to say no definitively;
> (iv) the Special Committee meets its duty of care in negotiating a fair price;
> (v) the vote of the minority is informed; and
> (vi) there is no coercion of the minority.[61]

This case is often understood as part of a broader trend in Delaware jurisprudence reducing substantive judicial scrutiny of transactions by permitting boards to structure the decision-making process pursuant to a process that facilitates arm's-length negotiation and deference to market actors.[62] If a well-informed committee negotiates the transaction and well-informed stockholders approve it, it will receive the benefit of the business judgment rule, meaning that 'the claims against the defendants must be dismissed unless no rational person could have believed that the merger was favorable to … minority stockholders'.[63]

(iv) Appraisal as an Alternative Mechanism to Review Price

In addition to a lawsuit based on fiduciary duties, minority shareholders in a freezeout may also have the option of appraisal. Appraisal means that shareholders in a company constituent to a merger can have the compensation valued by the court and receive a corresponding amount of cash. The conditions governing the availability of appraisal rights are complex and hard to explain from a policy perspective. In Delaware, appraisal rights are, as a general rule, not available for shares of a publicly traded corporation.[64] However, an exception applies when stockholders are to receive compensation in a form other than shares of a surviving entity or (broadly speaking) of a publicly traded corporation.[65] Thus, in a going-private merger, stockholders can request appraisal if they receive stock of a privately held parent corporation or cash. Stockholders cashed out in a short-form merger can request appraisal regardless of the form of compensation.[66] However, in Delaware, appraisal is not available for other

[61] *Kahn v M&F Worldwide Corp.* [2014] 88 A.3d 635, 645. But see In re *Dell Techs. Inc. Class* v *S'holders Litig.* [2020] CA No 2018-0816-JTL (finding that the special committee was not sufficiently empowered to negotiate because it was offered only two proposals while a third one was eliminated from consideration).

[62] Eg, Z Goshen and S Hannes, 'The Death of Corporate Law' (2019) 94 *NYU Law Review* 263, 285.

[63] *Kahn v M&F Worldwide Corp* (n 61).

[64] DGCL s 262(b)(1).

[65] ibid s 262(b)(2).

[66] ibid s 262(b)(3). A short-form merger under s 253 allows a 90% controlling stockholder to merge with the subsidiary without requiring a stockholder vote.

transactions that might be used for going private, such as a reverse stock split, sale of all assets, or liquidation.[67]

The procedure to receive appraisal is cumbersome.[68] Stockholders must submit a written demand for appraisal before the shareholder meeting and then vote against the merger.[69] Only stockholders who follow this process will receive appraisal, which makes the instrument relatively toothless because the other minority shareholders will receive the compensation provided in the merger agreement. Unlike a class action based on fiduciary duty violations, appraisal does not have what Europeans would call an *erga omnes* effect.[70] Another disadvantage is that the fair value established by the court can occasionally be lower than the price set in the merger agreement (whereas in a fiduciary duty action, shareholders can only gain).[71] In the early and mid-2010s, appraisal rights still became commonly used by strategic investors who bought the stock of companies where a merger was announced ('appraisal arbitrage').[72] Part of the reason was the high interest rate (relative to low interest rates at the time) available to petitioners for the period between the effective date of the merger and the payment of appraisal under Delaware law.[73]

In an appraisal procedure, the valuation is decided by the court. Under DGCL section 262(h),

> the Court shall determine the fair value of the shares exclusive of any element of value arising from the accomplishment or expectation of the merger, together with interest, if any, to be paid upon the amount determined to be the fair value. In determining such fair value, the Court shall take into account all relevant factors.

This means that going concern value is considered, but not normally synergies. The court is free to adopt valuations provided by the parties' expert witnesses. The Delaware courts famously abandoned the previous 'Delaware block method' in *Weinberger* (1983) and instead required the use of methods accepted in the 'financial community'.[74]

In recent years, appraisal has become less attractive in part because of cases relating to valuation. While the Delaware Supreme Court stopped short of establishing a presumption in favour of a negotiated deal price, the court has stated that

> economic principles suggest that the best evidence of fair value [is] the deal price, [if] it result[s] from an open process, informed by robust public information, and easy access to deeper, non-public information, in which many parties … had a chance to bid.[75]

[67] *Hariton v Arco Electronics, Inc* [1963] 188 A.2d 123 (declining to apply a 'de facto merger' doctrine to apply appraisal rights in a sale of all assets).

[68] CR Korsmo and M Myers, 'Appraisal Arbitrage and the Future of Public Company M&A' (2015) 92 *Washington University Law Review* 1551, 1560–66 (summarising critiques of appraisal).

[69] DGCL s 262(d)(1).

[70] Korsmo and Myers, 'Appraisal Arbitrage and the Future of Public Company M&A' (n 68) 1562 ('shareholders seeking judicial appraisal must "opt-in"').

[71] Balotti and Finkelstein, *Delaware Law of Corporations and Business Organizations* (n 59) s 9.62.

[72] Korsmo and Myers (n 68) 1566–72.

[73] JD Cox and TL Hazen, *Business Organizations Law*, 5th edn (St Paul, West Academic, 2020) 647; Korsmo and Myers (n 68) 1579–80.

[74] *Weinberger v UOP, Inc* (n 55) 712 f. The Delaware Block Method employed a weighted average of discounted earnings, market value and asset value.

[75] *DFC Global Corporation v Muirfield Value Partners, L.P.* [2017] 172 A.3d 346, 349; see also *Dell, Inc. v Magnetar Global Event Driven Master Fund Ltd.* [2017] 177 A.3d 1, 21.

Other factors likewise play a role, including 'the presence of competing bidders, the length of time accompanying the negotiations, the publicity surrounding the negotiations, [and] the restrictions of any deal protection provisions'.[76]

(v) The SEC's 'Going-Private' Rule

Disclosure requirements preceding a voluntary delisting are governed by the SEC's 'going-private' rule (rule 13e-3).[77] Rule 13e-3 applies to transactions or series of transactions involving (a) purchases of equity securities, (b) tender offers, and (c) proxy solicitation relating to certain types of transactions (such as mergers and reverse stock splits) by the issuer and its affiliates. These transactions must have a reasonable likelihood of an effect or purpose of causing the class of equity securities to be eligible for delisting or deregistration (among other things).[78]

The issuer must file a so-called Schedule 13E-3, which includes a comprehensive list of disclosures, including the identity and background of the issuer and affiliates initiating the transactions, terms of the transaction, contracts relating to the transaction, post-transactions plans, and the source of funds, and the purpose of the transaction, managers' belief about the fairness of the transaction.[79] While this is a mere disclosure provision that will not result in substantive scrutiny of the issuer's plans or the merits of the purpose of delisting, the provision is sanctioned with antifraud rules that could result in enforcement actions and civil and criminal liability. The timing of the disclosure depends on the type of the planned transaction; it may have to be made in conjunction with the planned tender offer or proxy solicitation but in no event later than 20 days in advance of, eg, an open market purchase.[80]

Rule 13e-3(b) and (c) explicitly prohibit fraudulent, deceptive, and manipulative acts or practices in connection with a going-private transaction subject to this rule by the issuer and its affiliates and to make untrue material statements or to omit a material fact to make the statement misleading.[81] These subsections parallel other antifraud rules under the Securities Exchange Act. The SEC has the authority to take enforcement actions against such violations and can impose a variety of sanctions. In a notable case involving Revlon, minority shareholders were offered preferred stock in place of their common stock, which would have allowed the company to reduce its debt to its controlling shareholder. The trustee of Revlon's 401(k) plan solicited an advisory opinion from a financial advisor that found that consideration was inadequate (which meant that beneficiaries of the plan could not tender their stock). The issuer took various measures to keep this information from its independent board members and minority

[76] Cox and Hazen, *Business Organizations Law* (n 73) 647.

[77] R 13e-3 is based on s 13(e) of the Securities Exchange Act, which makes it unlawful for issuers to purchase its own securities in contravention of rules and regulations issued by the SEC.

[78] R 13e-3(a)(3).

[79] See eg, TL Hazen, *Treatise on the Law of Securities Regulation* (St Paul, West Publishing Company, 2023) s 11:49. R 13e-3 also applies when a stock may subsequently be traded on a different exchange. *Shamrock Associates v Horizon Corp* [1986] 632 F Supp 566, 573.

[80] R 13e-3(f)(i).

[81] Sub-s (b) applies to issuer subject to s 12 of the Securities Exchange Act, which sub-s (c) refers to issuers governed by s 15(d).

shareholders. Revlon and the SEC settled these charges with a cease-and-desist order and a fine of USD 850,000.[82]

In addition, false and misleading disclosures can form the basis of a private lawsuit. The Court of Appeals for the 6th Circuit has recognised a private right of action under section 13(e) and rule 13e-3, meaning that minority shareholders could bring a lawsuit (potentially a class action) on this basis.[83] In addition, the issuer may have concurrently violated rule 10b-5 (false or misleading disclosures concerning the purchase and sale of a security) and rule 14a-9 (false or misleading statements in a proxy statement), which would also entail a liability risk. As in 14a-9 cases, plaintiffs in a 13e-3 case sometimes do *not* have a remedy under securities law if they still have one under state corporate law.[84] This is because a misleading disclosure will (depending on the applicable state law) mean that plaintiffs have a fiduciary duty claim (as discussed above in section iii). After all, the freezeout merger will still be assessed under the entire fairness test. Given that there is still a state law remedy, the violation of federal law lacks causation for an injury to plaintiffs.[85]

C. Delisting and Deregistration under Federal Securities Law

(i) Legal Basis

The securities law establishes procedures to remove securities from listing and for deregistration. Securities Exchange Act section 12(d), sentence 2, provides that

> [a] security registered with a national securities exchange may be withdrawn or stricken from listing and registration in accordance with the rules of the exchange and, upon such terms as the Commission may deem necessary to impose for the protection of investors, upon application by the issuer or the exchange to the Commission.

The SEC has adopted rule 12d2-2, which governs 'removal from listing and registration'.[86] It requires that 'the issuer must comply with all applicable laws in effect in the state in which it is incorporated and with the national securities exchange's rules governing an issuer's voluntary withdrawal of a class of securities'.[87] Rule 806.02 of the NYSE Listed Company Manual stipulates that an issuer may delist 'after its board approves the action'. The issuer must furnish the Exchange with the board resolution authorising the delisting and comply with the requirements of rule 12d2-2(c).

[82] *In the Matter* of *Revlon, Inc* [2013] 2013 SEC LEXIS 1693, 2013 WL 2641116; *see also* SEC, 'SEC Charges Revlon with Misleading Shareholders in Going Private Transaction' (2013) Press Release 2013-110. Available at: www.sec.gov/newsroom/press-releases/2013-2013-110htm; The New York Times, 'To Perelman's Failed Revlon Deal, Add Rebuke from S.E.C.' (13 June 2013). Available at: www.archive.nytimes.com/dealbook.nytimes.com/2013/06/13/s-e-c-charges-and-fines-revlon-for-misleading-shareholders/.

[83] *Howing Co v Nationwide Corp* [1987] 826 F2d 1470.

[84] *Howing Co v Nationwide Corp* [1992] 972 F2d 700 (finding that the plaintiffs had lost their appraisal remedy under Ohio law and therefore had a 13e-3 claim).

[85] See generally *Virginia Bankshares, Inc v Sandberg* [1991] 112 S Ct 39.

[86] 17 CFR s 240.12d2-2.

[87] R 12d2-2(c)(2)(i).

(ii) Disclosure and Notification Requirement

As a first step corresponding to what is known in Europe as an ad hoc disclosure, the registrant must file a Form 8-K when the board of directors (or a committee or officers) 'has taken definitive action to cause the listing of a class of its common equity to be withdrawn …'.[88] The firm has four business days to submit the filing.[89] In other words, the initial decision to trigger a going-private process must be made public.

The delisting process has two steps: first, written notice to the Exchange and information to the public, and second, filing Form 25 to the SEC as an application to delist a class of securities. Under rule 12d-2(c)(2)(ii), the issuer must 'provide written notice' to the exchange 'no fewer than 10 days' prior to filing the form. Contemporaneously, 'the issuer must publish notice of its intention to withdraw along with its reasons for such withdrawal, via a press release' and must post the notice on its website.[90] This written notice must 'set forth a description of the security involved, together with a statement of all material facts relating to the reasons for withdrawal from listing and/or registration.' The issuer must concurrently provide Form 25 to NYSE.[91]

(iii) Role of the SEC

The role of the SEC in the delisting process is relatively passive. During the 1970s, the SEC proposed a rule 13e-2 governing going-private transactions that would have enabled it to prohibit a transaction that would be unfair to shareholders. In light of controversy about whether the SEC had the statutory authority to enact such a rule, the proposal was never enacted.[92] Rule 13e-3, adopted in 1979 (see above section B.v) only requires disclosures.

Section 12(d) delegates the authority to determine the process and conditions for delisting to the SEC, both in general and in individual cases. However, by default, delisting is effective ten days after filing Form 25.[93] The SEC may postpone the effectiveness

> to determine whether the application on Form 25 to strike the security from registration under section 12(b) of the Act has been made in accordance with the rules of the exchange, or what terms should be imposed by the Commission for the protection of investors.[94]

While the most important reporting requirements end with delisting, the registration of securities under section 12(b) remains effective for 90 days after filing.[95]

This reflects a change compared to how delisting worked in the past. Before 2005, amendments to rule 12d2-2 came into force in 2006, the SEC needed to issue an order

[88] Form 8-K, Item 3.01(d). See generally r 13a-11 (establishing that issuers must file 8-K reports).
[89] Form 8-K, General Instructions, B.1.
[90] R 12d2-2(c)(2)(iii).
[91] R 806.02.
[92] On the historical development, see Hazen, *Treatise on the Law of Securities Regulation* (n 80) s 11:51; G Subramanian, 'Fixing Freezeouts' (2005) 115 *Yale Law Journal* 2, 9 f.
[93] R 12d2-2(d)(1).
[94] R 12d2-2(d)(3).
[95] R 12d2-2(d)(2).

granting a delisting application.[96] Today, Form 25 becomes effective if the Commission remains passive. In principle, the SEC can impose additional conditions for the protection of investors.[97] Reportedly, the SEC rarely intervenes at this stage.[98]

(iv) Deregistration and Suspension of Reporting Requirements

As previously discussed, a public listing suspends the disclosure requirements for issuers registered under section 12(g) or required to file reports under section 15(d). While disclosure requirements under this section are dormant during a listing on a national securities exchange, they reemerge with delisting: Reporting requirements remain in place if the issuer has a 12(g) registration or if the firm would be required to register under section 12(g).[99]

Consequently, an issuer cannot escape disclosure requirements if it is above the thresholds of that provision. Section 12(g) applies when the issuer has total assets of more than USD 10 million and more than 2,000 shareholders of record (or more than 500 shareholders of record who are not accredited investors). To deregister from section 12(g), an issuer can use Form 15 if it has fewer than 300 shareholders, or fewer than 500 shareholders and less than USD 10 million in assets.[100] According to the SEC, Form 15 can only be filed after Form 25 has become effective.[101] Form 15 is normally effective 90 days after filing;[102] however, disclosure requirements are suspended immediately. If deregistration is withdrawn or denied, the issuer has 60 days to file all reports that would have been required.[103]

If the issuer has registered securities under the Securities Act, it is subject to disclosure requirements under section 15(d) of the Exchange Act.[104] This requirement (which may apply in parallel to section 12(g)) can be avoided in two ways. First, it is automatically suspended if the registered class of securities has less than 300 shareholders of record (except in the year when the registration statement became effective).[105] To notify the SEC, the issuer must still file Form 15 within 30 days of the year when the suspension is effective.[106]

[96] Securities and Exchange Commission, *Removal from Listing and Registration of Securities Pursuant to Section 12(d) of the Securities Exchange Act of 1934* (2004) 70 FR 42456-57.

[97] See *Cavanagh Cmtys. Corp. v New York Stock Exch.* [1976] 422 F Supp 382, 384 ('once the security is approved for listing, neither the exchange nor the issuer may delist the security without SEC approval').

[98] Bakst, Kollar and Naidu (n 22).

[99] R 12d2-2(d)(6).

[100] R 12g-4(a)(1), (2). There are different thresholds for banks and savings and loans holding companies.

[101] SEC, *Exchange Act Forms* (30 September 2008). Available at: www.sec.gov/divisions/corpfin/guidance/exchangeactforms-interps.htm, Question 111.01.

[102] R 12g-4(a).

[103] R 12g-4(b).

[104] Disclosure requirements under s 15(d) are suspended as long as a security is registered under s 12 (including s 12(g)). In other words, s 15(d) captures only firms that are neither traded on a national securities exchange nor exceed the thresholds of s 12(g), but have had an effective Securities Act registration statement.

[105] Securities Exchange Act s 15(d)(1).

[106] R 15d-6.

Second, an issuer can suspend the reporting requirements of section 15(d) pursuant to rule 12h-3. There are slightly different requirements than under the statutory suspension. Most of all, under rule 12h-3(b)(1)(i), what matters is the number of holders of record at any time (rather than at the beginning of the year). Alternatively, reporting can be suspended if there are fewer than 500 holders of record and the issuer's assets have not exceeded USD 10 million on the last day of the preceding three fiscal years.[107] Because these thresholds are higher, companies typically rely on rule 12h-3.[108] Under both ways of escaping section 15(d) (the statutory method and rule 12h-3), the section 15(d) registration is only suspended: it automatically reemerges if the firm exceeds the threshold[109] (given that the registration statement remains effective).

One difficulty with the thresholds based on ownership of securities is the definition of 'held of record.'[110] In 1964, when section 12(g) was added, looking at holding records was a reasonable way of gauging whether a class of securities had broad public ownership, but this is no longer true today.[111] Most securities are held by the Depositary Trust Company (DTC), a clearinghouse for securities transactions, on behalf of broker-dealers. The 'street name' of the holder of record is thus not the beneficial owner (or investor) but the broker-dealer.[112] This is typically not an issue for growing startups that are at risk of exceeding the threshold and being required to register under section 12(g) because their investors and employee-stockholders will normally be 'holders of record.' However, for publicly traded firms seeking to delist, it results in an undercount of stockholders for the purpose of the numerical thresholds.[113] It is a significant concern that a firm may de facto have public ownership and be traded in the OTC market without being subject to disclosure requirements under the securities law any longer. Empirical research has found that going dark is associated with negative cumulative abnormal returns.[114] Given the growth of online platforms facilitating investment outside of traditional securities markets, we now have a situation comparable to the period before the introduction of section 12(g), where the disclosure of information is not always

[107] R 12h-3(b)(1)(ii). The thresholds are higher for banks, savings and loans holding companies, and bank holding companies.

[108] DM McMillan, *1 Securities Practice Guide § 9.05* (2023). Available at: www.advance.lexis.com/open/document/openwebdocview/-10-05-Going-Private-Transactions/?pdmfid=1000522&pddocfullpath=%2Fshared%2Fdocument%2Fanalytical-materials%2Furn%3acontentItem%3a523N-BN90-R03J-V2FT-00000-00&pdcomponentid=342619.

[109] SEC, *Exchange Act Forms* (n 101) Question 153.02.

[110] See r 12g5-1(a) ('securities shall be deemed to be 'held of record' by each person who is identified as the owner of such securities on records of security holders maintained by or on behalf of the issuer …'). While sub-s (b)(3) addresses circumvention intended to evade registration requirements under ss 12(g) and 15(d), this does not capture the conventional holding of securities in the form of a 'street name.'

[111] Langevoort and Thompson, 'Publicness in Contemporary Securities Regulation after the JOBS Act' (n 10) at 355–57.

[112] Securities and Exchange Commission, *Report on Authority to Enforce Exchange Act Rule 12g5-1 and Subsection (b)(3) 8-10* (2012) available at www.sec.gov/news/studies/2012/authority-to-enforce-rule-12g5-1.pdf.

[113] UR Rodrigues, 'The Once and Future Irrelevancy of Section 12(g)' (2015) *University of Illinois Law Review* 1542. See n 104.

[114] Leuz, Triantis and Wang (n 23) 198 f; see also Macey, O'Hara and Pompillo, 'Down and Out in the Stock Market' (n 30) 700 f (finding a reduced stock price associated with liquidity cost).

assured.[115] Revising the 'held of record' definition is currently on the SEC's rulemaking agenda.[116]

Rule 12h-6 facilitates deregistration for foreign private issuers.[117] Before the rule was enacted in 2007, it was difficult to escape registration under sections 12(g) and 15(d) because showing that they had fewer than 300 US shareholders of record was often difficult.[118] Under the new rule, a foreign private issuer qualifies for deregistration if the average daily trading volume in the US represents 5 percent or less of their worldwide trading volume over 12 months (irrespective of the number of US shareholders). However, such an issuer may still show that they have fewer than 300 US shareholders.

Under section 25(1) of the Securities Exchange Act, a

> person aggrieved by a final order of the [SEC] may obtain review of the order in the United States Court of Appeals for the circuit in which he resides or has his principal place of business ... within sixty days after the entry of the order, a written petition requesting that the order be modified or set aside in whole or in part.

The SEC may also order a hearing to decide about deregistration applications (sometimes upon the insistence of shareholders).[119]

IV. Involuntary Delisting

A. Reasons for Delisting

Delistings and suspensions of trading can be initiated by both the SEC and the stock exchange. Section 12(d) of the Securities Exchange Act, among other things, provides that a

> security registered with a national securities exchange may be ... stricken from listing and registration in accordance with the rules of the exchange and, upon such terms as the Commission may deem necessary to impose for the protection of investors, upon application by the issuer or the exchange to the Commission.

In addition, section 12(j) authorises the SEC 'to deny, to suspend the effective date of, to suspend for a period not exceeding twelve months, or to revoke the registration of a security' if the SEC has found that 'the issuer ... has failed to comply with any provision of [the Securities Exchange Act] or the rules and regulations thereunder'. The SEC must notify the issuer and give it the opportunity for a hearing and may then issue an order to

[115] Langevoort and Thompson (n 10) at 351.

[116] For an analysis of statutory constraints and recent reform attempts, see AI Platt, 'Legal Guardrails for a Unicorn Crackdown' (2022) 120 *Michigan Law Review* 89.

[117] See Langevoort and Thompson (n 10) at 360.

[118] A Belonick, '§ 4.01 Registration of Securities Under the Securities Exchange Act of 1934, (3)(b)(vi)' in *Federal Securities Exchange Act of 1934* (Matthew Bender Elite Products, 2024).

[119] See *In the Matter of Bacardi Corporation* [1989] Exchange Act Release No 34-27255 and [1990] Administrative Proceeding File No 3-7019 (hearing before an administrative law judge upon the insistence of a shareholder had set up 238 trusts to keep Bacardi above the share ownership threshold); *Order Granting an Application of BF Enterprises, Inc. under the Securities Exchange Act of 1934* [2012] Exchange Release No 34-66541 (granting an exemption from s 12(g) reporting because of the low number of beneficial owners).

suspend or revoke the registration (and hence the listing) of a security. As commentators have pointed out, delisting is a harsh sanction and typically unnecessary, given that the SEC has other enforcement tools available.[120] Typically, orders under this section have led to compliance rather than delisting.[121]

Rule 12d2-1(a) permits the Exchange to suspend a security from trading 'in accordance with its rules'. The Exchange must 'promptly notify the Commission of any such suspension, the effective date thereof, and the reasons therefor'.[122] NYSE rules provide that securities will be suspended or struck from the list if they fall below specific quantitative and qualitative criteria.[123] These include the number of total stockholders, trading volume, public float, market capitalisation and stock price.[124]

The Exchange also has the discretion to evaluate the issuer's continued listing, among other things, in cases of reduced operating assets and the scope of operations.[125] The issuer's intention to enter bankruptcy and liquidation gives NYSE the discretion to suspend and delist the issuer.[126] The same applies when the issuer violates the listing agreement with the NYSE.[127] Finally, the failure to file the financial reports under securities law (such as annual 10-K reports, quarterly 10-Q reports, both of which include financial statements) and severe problems with these reports as well as the auditor's report also set specific procedures in motion that can result in an issuers suspension or delisting.[128] This means that the Exchange, in cases of the violation of listing rules, does not necessarily have to delist the issuer. In many cases, the mere threat of delisting will coerce compliance.

B. Process

Under rule 12d2-2(b), the Exchange may file an application on Form 25 to delist a class of securities in accordance with its rules. These must provide for notice of the issuer of the Exchange's decision to delist the securities, an opportunity for appeal to the Exchange's board of directors or to a committee designated by the board, and public notice of the final determination to delist the securities by a press release and posting notice on the Exchange's website. This notice must be 'disseminated no fewer than ten days before the delisting becomes effective'. The delisting is effective ten days after the filing of Form 25.[129] The Exchange must promptly deliver a copy of Form 25

[120] L Loss and J Seligman, *Fundamentals of Securities Regulation*, 8th edn (New York, Wolters Kluwer, 2023) s 6.B.3.b.

[121] ibid.

[122] The SEC also the power to suspend trading for a period not exceeding ten business days under s12(k) because of market emergencies.

[123] NYSE Rule 801.00.

[124] NYSE Rules 802.01A, 802.01B, 802.01C.

[125] NYSE Rule 802.01D.

[126] ibid.

[127] ibid.

[128] NYSE Rule 802.01E.

[129] R 12d2-2(d)(1).

to the issuer.[130] The issuer must file an 8-K report to notify public of such a delisting action.[131]

As mentioned above in section III.C.iii, a delisting application submitted on Form 25 will be automatically effective since the 2006 amendments to rule 12d2-2. Before this change, the SEC had to issue an order of delisting. This is no longer true today. It may, however, decide to intervene. The SEC may postpone the effectiveness

> to determine whether the application on Form 25 to strike the security from registration under section 12(b) of the Act has been made in accordance with the rules of the exchange, or what terms should be imposed by the Commission for the protection of investors.[132]

C. Recourse

A person aggrieved by the Exchange's delisting decision (such as an issuer) can petition the SEC to review the Exchange's decision.[133] However, as Min and Jin explain,

> [u]pon such appeal, the SEC is to uphold the sanction if it finds that (1) the facts forming the basis for the sanction exist, (2) the sanction is in accordance with the rules of the exchange, and (3) such rules were applied in a manner consistent with the purposes of the Exchange Act.[134]

Similarly, the federal courts (in some older cases) have found that the Exchange followed its own rules in making the delisting decision and whether additional terms should be imposed for the protection of investors.[135] Consequently, the SEC will not perform a substantive review of the Exchange's exercise of discretion, making an appeal unlikely to succeed. However, the SEC may overturn an exchange decision based on a finding that the (factual) record on which the Exchange based its delisting decision. For example, in a case involving a company called *Cleantech*, the SEC found that the record did not support the fact that the issuer had withheld material information from NASDAQ's staff that was considering its application to list its shares.[136]

As discussed above in section III.C.iv, the SEC's determination can be further reviewed by the US Court of Appeals.[137] New York courts have, therefore, dismissed

[130] R 12d2-2(d)(2).
[131] Form 8-K, Item 3.01.
[132] R 12d2-2(d)(3).
[133] Securities Exchange Act s 19(d). See Securities and Exchange Commission, *Removal From Listing and Registration of Securities Pursuant to Section 12(d) of the Securities Exchange Act of 1934* (n 96).
[134] Min and Jin, 'Relational Enforcement of Stock Exchange Rules' (n 29) 163. See in detail Securities Exchange Act s 19(e)(2), (f).
[135] *Atlas Tack Corp v NY Stock Exch* [1957] 246 F2d 311; *Exch Buffet Corp v NY Stock Exch* [1957] 244 F.2d 507, 510 (also pointing out that the SEC could have challenged unreasonable rules when they were enacted); Belonick, '§ 4.01 Registration of Securities Under the Securities Exchange Act of 1934, (3)(b)(vi)' (n 119) s 4.01.
[136] *In Re Cleantech Innovations, Inc* [2013] SEC LEXIS 1998. The SEC subsequently approved NASDAQ's delisting of Cleantech successor firm. *6D Global Technologies, Inc* [2017] SEC LEXIS 2839.
[137] Securities Exchange Act s 25(1). See also *Cavanagh Cmtys Corp v NY Stock Exch* [1976] 422 F Supp 382.

a company's suit against the NYSE's decision to delist it.[138] An involuntarily delisted firm's securities may continue to trade in the OTC market.

In summary, involuntary delisting (as well as the threat of it) is an essential sanction in the arsenal of the SEC and stock exchanges to enforce their rules. In their survey of 2019 8-K disclosures, Min and Jin found 26 instances of delistings from NYSE and 91 from NASDAQ.[139] In 84 cases, the reason was a violation of the Exchange's quantitative criteria, in ten cases delinquency in filing periodic reports, in one case a persistent violation of corporate governance requirements,[140] and 22 times other violations such as failure to pay fees or bankruptcy.[141] Macey, O'Hara and Pompillo report between 18 and 65 involuntary delistings from NYSE each year between 1998 and 2004, and between 64 and 489 on NASDAQ.[142]

V. Conclusion

The overall picture of the law governing delisting in the United States is complex. Federal securities laws govern the delisting process but going-private transactions are largely controlled by state corporate law. In the going-private process, investors are reasonably well protected by lawsuits based on fiduciary duties. While the Delaware courts have moved away from substantive review as long as the decision-making process is sound, this has probably made planning easier while not undercutting the protection of minority shareholders too much. The fact that securities law still applies to delisted firms in many cases sets incentives to freeze out the minority against cash compensation.

Securities law adds an additional layer of complexity, with the distinction between delisting and deregistration as an extra step. It remains to be seen whether issue of firms with some public ownership 'going dark' and avoiding the securities law entirely will be addressed by the SEC in the coming years.

Involuntary delisting is, to a large extent, subject to the discretion of the Exchange, given that Form 25 becomes automatically effective and given that the SEC reviews the delisting decision mainly for consistency but does not review the Exchange's exercise of discretion. Still, firms and investors seem to be adequately protected, given the possibility of review by the SEC and federal courts.

[138] *Fifth Ave. Coach Lines, Inc. v NY Stock Exch* [1966] 26 AD2d 49, 270 NYS2d 852.

[139] Min and Jin (n 29) 179.

[140] This could include failure to constitute the board or required committees, failure to follow rules requiring shareholder approval.

[141] Min and Jin (n 29) 180 f.

[142] Macey, O'Hara and Pompillo (n 30) 691.

15

Delisting in Australia

PAMELA HANRAHAN*

I. Introduction

In Australia, delisting typically occurs at the intersection of three sets of rules. The first set – the listing rules of the relevant securities exchange – is largely contractual. The second and third – the corporate law and (where relevant) the laws regulating control transactions – are largely statutory. Which rules apply, and what they require of the proponents of a delisting and the exchange operator, vary depending on the circumstances. These include whether the proposed delisting is at the instigation of the entity or the exchange operator, whether it will follow a change-of-control event such as a merger or a take-private transaction, and whether the relevant entity is (or will be) listed on another exchange.

A person who acquires or holds quoted securities in an Australian listed entity is not entitled to expect that the entity will remain listed indefinitely. Delisting is seen as an ordinary and predictable part of the efficient functioning of equity capital markets (ECM); the Australian rules aim to facilitate voluntary or involuntary delisting in appropriate circumstances while protecting ECM integrity and the fair treatment of all security holders, including where the listed entity or some members oppose delisting. Of course, exchange operators and their owners have a commercial interest in maintaining or increasing the number of suitable entities that are listed and have the power to refuse an entity's request to delist; the recent increase in the rate of delisting from Australia's dominant exchange, the Australian Securities Exchange (ASX) makes that interest more acute. But exchange operators will not oppose or obstruct voluntary delisting if the request to delist is made for an acceptable reason and the applicable rules are followed; neither will Australia's national corporations and markets regulator the Australian Securities and Investments Commission (ASIC) or (where it has jurisdiction) the independent Takeovers Panel.

* Dr Pamela Hanrahan, Emerita Professor, University of New South Wales Business School, Senior Fellow at Melbourne Law School, and Consultant at Johnson Winter Slattery, Sydney, Australia.

This chapter focuses on the rules that govern delisting by an Australian public company whose securities are quoted on ASX.[1] It is organised as follows. This first Part introduces the broader legal and regulatory framework and provides some commercial context. Part II summarises relevant principles of the ASX Listing Rules, corporate law and laws regulating control transactions and explains when they apply to different categories of delisting. Part III deals in more detail with delisting that occurs at the instigation of the listed entity, with a particular emphasis on the rights of (and constraints on) dissenting members. Part IV looks at delisting at the instigation of ASX Limited, the operator of ASX. Part V concludes with some broader observations about how Australian law and market practice seeks to balance the competing interests of security holders who favour delisting and those who oppose it – what ASIC has described as 'the regulatory objective of avoiding both minority oppression and minority dictation'[2] – with the overarching goal of protecting ECM integrity.

A. The Broader Legal and Regulatory Framework

In Australia's federal system of government, legislative responsibility for corporate law and the regulation of securities markets belongs to the Commonwealth Parliament.[3] The principal Commonwealth statute, the *Corporations Act 2001* (Cth) (Corporations Act), relevantly includes chapters dealing with corporate personality and governance,[4] reporting,[5] reorganisations,[6] finance and fundraising,[7] takeovers,[8] collective investment schemes,[9] market misconduct,[10] the securities industry[11] and the operation of financial

[1] Noting that some ASX listed entities are not Australian public companies: for example, foreign companies and registered managed investment schemes: see n 48. Also, ASX is not the only listing exchange: see n 17. There are no major differences between the delisting rules of ASX and the other two main listing exchanges, each of which leave the delisting decision at the discretion of the exchange operator.

[2] ASIC, *Regulatory Guide 10: Compulsory Acquisitions and Buyouts* (March 2024) para 10.6. Available at: www.asic.gov.au/regulatory-resources/find-a-document/regulatory-guides/rg-10-compulsory-acquisitions-and-buyouts/.

[3] Full transfer of legislative responsibility for these matters from the States to the Commonwealth was completed in 2001; for an account of the history of federalisation and the current constitutional arrangements, see A Black and P Hanrahan, *Securities and Financial Services Law*, 10th edn (Sydney, LexisNexis Butterworths, 2021) paras 1.45–1.52. Many of the current legislative arrangements relevant to delisting are derived from predecessor State legislation, which was increasingly harmonised from the early 1960s onwards.

[4] Corporations Act chs 2A (registration of a company), 2B (basic features of a company), 2C (registers), 2D (officers and employees, including directors' and other officers' duties), 2E (related party transactions), 2F (members' rights and remedies) and 2G (meetings).

[5] ibid chs 2M (financial reports and audit), 2N and 2P (filings with ASIC), 6C (information about ownership of listed companies) and 6CA (continuous disclosure).

[6] ibid ch 5 (external administration, including members' schemes of arrangement).

[7] ibid chs 2H (shares), 2J (transactions affecting share capital), 2L (debentures), 6D (offers of securities) and pts 7.8A and 7.9 (offers of financial products other than securities).

[8] ibid chs 6 (takeovers), 6A (compulsory acquisition and buy outs) and 6B (rights and liabilities in relation to Chapter 6 and 6A matters).

[9] ibid chs 5C (managed investment schemes) and 8B (corporate collective investment vehicles).

[10] ibid pt 7.10 (including misleading conduct, market manipulation and insider trading). Conduct in relation to financial products and financial services is also regulated by pt 2, div 2 of the *Australian Securities and Investments Commission Act 2001* (Cth) (ASIC Act).

[11] ibid pts 7.6–7.8 (Australian financial services licensing).

markets.[12] The Corporations Act is lengthy and is both supplemented and modified by numerous subordinate legislative instruments, including instruments made by ASIC.[13] The Corporations Act is not a code; as in most other common law jurisdictions, law is also made by State and Federal courts which have concurrent jurisdiction in Corporations Act matters.[14]

Administratively, three bodies matter in any discussion about delisting from ASX.[15] They are ASX Limited, ASIC and the Takeovers Panel.

(i) Role of ASX Limited

The first is ASX Limited, the operator of ASX. ASX Limited is a widely-held public company (itself listed on ASX)[16] that is licensed by the Commonwealth Treasurer to operate a tier 1 financial market.[17] It was formed (and subsequently floated) by the merger last century of broker-owned local exchanges in State capital cities which had operated stock and futures exchanges and acted as self-regulatory organisations for member firms.[18] As the holder of an Australian markets licence issued under the Corporations Act, ASX Limited has been supervised by ASIC and the Reserve Bank of Australia since 2002.[19]

[12] ibid pts 7.2–7.5 (licensing and supervision of market operators and infrastructure providers).

[13] See Australian Law Reform Commission, *Confronting Complexity: Reforming Corporations and Financial Services Legislation, Report No 141* (November 2023). Available at: www.alrc.gov.au/wp-content/uploads/2024/01/ALRC-FSL-Final-Report-141.pdf.

[14] Corporations Act pt 9.6 (proceedings). The exception is takeover disputes that are adjudicated by the Takeovers Panel, discussed below.

[15] The other main exchange operators are National Stock Exchange of Australia Ltd (which operates NSX) and Sydney Stock Exchange Ltd (which operates SSX). The NSX Listing Rules provide for listing to be cancelled by the market operator under NSX Listing Rules 2.18–2.22. Delisting from SSX is covered by SSX Listing Rules 14.18–14.23.

[16] See ASX Listing Rules ch 20. Many of the same institutional and private investors that use ASX to trade securities are also the members (that is, shareholders) of ASX Limited. ASX Limited's business operations and governance are therefore subject to the same ultimate control by its owners as those of any other Australian public company.

[17] As at November 2024, there were 10 licensed tier 1 market operators in Australia: see www.asic.gov.au/regulatory-resources/markets/market-structure/licensed-and-exempt-markets/licensed-domestic-financial-markets-operating-in-australia/. Of these, only four operate markets on which securities (as distinct from other financial products) can be traded by retail as well as wholesale investors and traders. They are: ASX Limited (which operates ASX), Chi-X Australia Pty Ltd (which operates Cboe Australia), National Stock Exchange of Australia Ltd (which operates NSX) and Sydney Stock Exchange Ltd (which operates SSX). Cboe Australia is an alternative trading exchange through which ASX-listed securities can be traded. ASX, NSX and SSX serve different segments of the listing market. SSX states that its focus is on small, high-growth companies while NSX focuses on growth-stage companies; each is a fraction of the size of ASX.

[18] ASX Limited was demutualised and listed in 1998, making it the first exchange operator in the world to list on its own market. See T Cowan, R da Silva Rosa and T Walter, *The Demutualisation of the Australian Stock Exchange: Causes and Consequences* (Securities Industry Research Centre of Asia-Pacific, 2005). ASIC assumed responsibility for regulating market participants (including under the *ASIC Market Integrity Rules (Securities Markets) 2017*) in 2010, displacing ASX Limited as an SRO for market participants. See ASIC, *Regulatory Guide 265: Guidance on ASIC Market Integrity Rules for Participants of Securities Markets* (August 2022). Available at: www.asic.gov.au/regulatory-resources/find-a-document/regulatory-guides/rg-265-guidance-on-asic-market-integrity-rules-for-participants-of-securities-markets/. See also Black and Hanrahan (n 3) paras 9.19–9.24.

[19] The Australian markets licensing regime is established by Corporations Act pt 7.2. For a discussion of the oversight of ASX Limited, including in relation to its failed project to replace the Clearing House

ASX Limited makes the operating rules for its various markets; relevantly these include the ASX Listing Rules.[20] It also publishes detailed guidance on its expectations of listed entities and its approach to interpreting the ASX Listing Rules and to enforcing the contractual promise to comply with them made by entities on their admission to the official list. This guidance includes *Guidance Note 33: Removal of Entities from the ASX Official List* (ASX Guidance Note 33) discussed in detail in Parts III and IV below.

ASX Limited's capacity to enforce a listed entity's compliance with the ASX Listing Rules derives from the contract between it and the listed entity, ASX Limited's powers of suspension or delisting under the ASX Listing Rules, and the statutory recognition given to the ASX Listing Rules by legislation which allows for courts to make orders enforcing compliance.[21] The right to enforce the ASX Listing Rules against a listed entity, and to require ASX Limited to do so, also extends to anyone affected by a contravention or likely contravention, including a member of the entity.

If ASX Limited fails to exercise its functions as the market operator properly (for example by failing to delist a company when it ought to do so) and thereby contravenes its obligations as the holder of a Australian market licence,[22] it can be directed to do so by the responsible Minister.[23] Separately, ASIC can give directions to ASX Limited if it is considered necessary, or in the public interest, to protect people dealing in a financial product or class of financial products.[24]

(ii) Role of ASIC

The second body that matters is ASIC.[25] ASIC is an independent Commonwealth regulatory agency with an unusually broad mandate.[26] In addition to being the corporate, securities, and financial markets regulator, it is responsible for licensing and consumer protection in the provision of financial services and credit, for product disclosure and retail distribution of financial products (including banking, superannuation insurance, and credit products), for registration and regulation of collective investment schemes, and for licensing and supervision of market operators and market infrastructure providers (including ASX Limited and its licensed clearing and settlement subsidiaries).

ASIC has extensive powers under the Corporations Act and the *Australian Securities and Investments Commission Act 2001* (Cth) (ASIC Act) to enforce the corporate law

Electronic Subregister System (CHESS), see Commonwealth of Australia Parliamentary Joint Committee on Corporations and Financial Services, *Statutory Inquiry into ASIC, the Takeovers Panel, and the Corporations Legislation* (Report, April 2024).

[20] See Black and Hanrahan (n 3) paras 9.25–9.35.

[21] Specifically, Corporations Act ss 793C and 1101B.

[22] The duties of Australian market licensees are set out in Corporations Act s 792A. They include an obligation, to the extent that it is reasonably practicable to do so, to do all things necessary to ensure that the market it operates is fair, orderly and transparent. See Black and Hanrahan (n 3) paras 9.13–9.14.

[23] The responsible Minister is the Treasurer of the Commonwealth of Australia: Corporations Act s 794A. See Black and Hanrahan (n 3) para 9.16.

[24] Corporations Act s 794D. See Black and Hanrahan (n 3) para 9.17.

[25] In the Twin-Peaks architecture of financial regulation in Australia, ASIC as the conduct and disclosure regulator operates alongside the Australian Prudential Regulation Authority as the prudential regulator of the deposit-taking, superannuation (other than self-managed superannuation) and insurance sectors; both are independent of the central bank, the Reserve Bank of Australia.

[26] Black and Hanrahan (n 3) paras 2.12–2.26.

(including corporate disclosure laws) against companies (including listed companies) and their officers. It has wide information-gathering and investigative powers.[27] If it considers that a company or its officers has contravened the law, it can take appropriate enforcement action. Depending on the provision that has been contravened, this may include referring matters to the Commonwealth Director of Public Prosecutions for criminal prosecution,[28] bringing civil penalty proceedings,[29] bringing civil proceedings (including seeking declarations and injunctions),[30] accepting court enforceable undertakings[31] and issuing infringement notices.[32] As noted, ASIC can direct ASX Limited in the exercise of its functions in some circumstances.[33] ASIC also has power to enforce compliance with the listing rules against a person who is under an obligation to comply with them (like a listed company) or an obligation to enforce them (like ASX Limited). This is done by application to a court for an order requiring the person to comply and, where appropriate, requiring its directors to take reasonable steps to ensure it does so.[34]

Turning specifically to delisting, ASIC has no direct role in delisting decisions, which belong to ASX Limited. ASIC itself cannot delist companies for contraventions of the corporate law or the listing rules or require ASX Limited to do so. However, if an individual or company contravenes the corporate law in circumstances leading to, or in connection with, a delisting (for example, by contravening their duties as a director or by providing misleading disclosure), ASIC may use its extensive investigation and enforcement powers. ASIC regularly uses its powers to enforce aspects of corporate law (including disclosure law) and the securities laws in civil court, including in circumstances that in other jurisdictions are viewed almost exclusively as matters for private suit, such as ordinary negligence by company directors or innocent misrepresentations in connection with securities.[35]

[27] See ASIC, *Information Sheet 145, ASIC's Compulsory Information Gathering Powers* (March 2020). Available at: www.asic.gov.au/about-asic/asic-investigations-and-enforcement/asic-s-compulsory-information-gathering-powers/. See also Black and Hanrahan (n 3) paras 2.47–2.49 and 2.55–2.86.

[28] ASIC has power to prosecute some summary offences, but more serious offences (including those listed in Corporations Act sch 3) are prosecuted by the independent prosecutor established by the *Director of Public Prosecutions Act 1983* (Cth).

[29] The civil penalty regime is established by Corporations Act pt 9.4B and is available for contraventions of the provisions listed in Corporations Act s 1317E.

[30] Including under Corporations Act s 1324, which gives ASIC standing to apply for injunctive relief where a person (including a listed company or its officers) 'is engaging or is proposing to engage in conduct that constituted, constitutes or would constitute: (a) a contravention of this Act; or (b) attempting to contravene this Act; or (c) aiding, abetting, counselling or procuring a person to contravene this Act; or (d) inducing or attempting to induce, whether by threats, promises or otherwise, a person to contravene this Act; or (e) being in any way, directly or indirectly, knowingly concerned in, or party to, the contravention by a person of this Act; or (f) conspiring with others to contravene this Act'.

[31] ASIC Act 2001, s 93AA.

[32] Including under ASIC Act 2001, s 12GX and s 1317DAC. On enforcement generally, see Black and Hanrahan (n 3) paras 2.87–2.118.

[33] Under Corporations Act s 794D. See n 24.

[34] Corporations Act s 793C. An application may be made by ASIC, ASX Limited, or 'a person aggrieved by the failure'. There are no reported cases where ASIC is the applicant.

[35] Corporations Act s 180 requires corporate officers to act with reasonable care and diligence. Failure to do so contravenes a civil penalty provision and can attract a court-ordered pecuniary penalty of the greater of up to 5,000 penalty units (currently AUD $1.65 million) and, if the court can determine the benefit derived and detriment avoided because of the contravention, the amount of the benefit or detriment multiplied by three.

ASIC also has the power to grant exemptions from, or modify the operation of, specified provisions of the Corporations Act either on a case-by-case basis or by a legislative instrument that applies generally or to a specified class. Exemptions and modifications may be expressed to operate subject to conditions,[36] and may affect individual rights and entitlements, including property rights.[37] ASIC may be asked to exercise these powers on the application of a listed company in connection with a change-of-control transaction or proposal for voluntary delisting, where its particular circumstances make following the standard processes difficult.

(iii) Role of the Takeovers Panel

The third body that matters in the context of delisting involving a change-of-control transaction is the Takeovers Panel. The Takeovers Panel is established by legislation[38] to act as a peer review body in connection with parties' conduct in relation to control transactions.[39] Its primary function is to resolve disputes quickly and commercially in response to applications made to it by an affected party or by ASIC. An application diverts the dispute from the courts. The Takeovers Panel resolves applications by deciding whether 'unacceptable circumstances' have occurred in relation to the transaction, which it determines having regard to the statutory principles known as colloquially in Australia as the Eggleston Principles, the public interest, and other relevant considerations.[40]

There is no statutory definition of 'unacceptable circumstances'[41] and decisions of the Takeover Panel (while instructive of its approach) are not binding precedents in the

Misleading or deceptive conduct (even if unintentional) in relation to securities contravenes Corporations Act s 1014H and ASIC Act ss 12DA, 12DB and 12DF. This can be enforced by ASIC and form the basis for a claim for damages. Proceedings by private plaintiffs, including class actions funded by third-party litigation funders, are not excluded by ASIC's decision to commence regulatory action.

[36] Black and Hanrahan (n 3) paras 2.38–2.46.

[37] *Australian Securities and Investments Commission v DB Management Pty Ltd* (2000) 199 CLR 321; [2000] HCA 7.

[38] ASIC Act 2001, pt 10. The Takeovers Panel comprises approximately 50 members of the business and legal community that can be empaneled (generally in threes) to hear applications as they arise. The decisions of the Takeovers Panel are administrative in nature and are subject to judicial review under the *Administrative Decisions (Judicial Review) Act 1977* (Cth); s 5 of that Act stipulates the grounds of review which are, in essence, a reflection in summary form of the grounds on which administrative decisions are susceptible to challenge at common law. See eg *Eastern Field Development Ltd v Takeovers Panel* [2019] FCA 311.

[39] The Takeovers Panel's power to make a declaration of unacceptable circumstances extends beyond takeover bids to other control transactions: see Takeovers Panel, *Guidance Note 1: Unacceptable Circumstances* (July 2018). Available at: www.takeovers.gov.au/guidance-notes para 18. Schemes of arrangements are generally left to the relevant court, but see *Citect Corporation Ltd* [2006] ATP 6, [33].

[40] In deciding whether unacceptable circumstances exist, the Takeovers Panel must consider legal and policy issues as required by Corporations Act s 657A. The Eggleston Principles, developed in 1969, are set out in s 602 and include that the acquisition of control over voting shares takes place in an efficient, competitive and informed market; shareholders and directors know the identity of the acquirer, have a reasonable time to consider the proposal and have sufficient information to enable them to assess the merits of the proposal; as far as practicable, shareholders all have a reasonable and equal opportunity to participate in any benefits arising from the proposal; and an appropriate procedure is followed as a preliminary to compulsory acquisition. The Takeovers Panel decision-making responsibilities are explained in its Procedural Guideline 5.10. Available at: www.takeovers.gov.au/panel-process/procedural-rules-and-guidelines/guidelines#5-10.

[41] See Corporations Act s 657A. *The legislation gives the Takeovers Panel jurisdiction to declare circumstances unacceptable having regard to the purposes of Chapter 6 of the Act set out in* s 602: 'This is … designed to

traditional sense. The Panel's practical decision-making often turns on whether, in the context of a matter over which it has jurisdiction, circumstances exist or may exist that are 'unacceptable' in the sense they would (if allowed to arise or persist) interfere with the proper functioning of the market for control of a listed entity.[42]

B. The Commercial Context

These indicators provide some comparative commercial context for the discussion that follows.

On generally accepted measures, Australia is the world's sixth-largest country by landmass, and the 55th largest by population. It is the 14th largest economy by nominal gross domestic product (GDP) and the 19th largest by per-capita-adjusted GDP. Its stock market (at about 2.2 per cent of global markets) is in the top ten, dwarfed by the United States, then Japan, the United Kingdom (UK) and China, but within the band also occupied by France, Canada, Switzerland and Germany.[43] Its ratio of stock market capitalisation to GDP is closer to that of Japan and the UK. As a result of its decades-old compulsory superannuation system, Australia has the fifth-largest pool of domestic pension fund capital.[44]

Globally, ASX is the eighth largest securities exchange.[45] As at November 2024 there were 1,944 entities listed on ASX of which approximately 60 had a market capitalisation of more than AUD $10 billion and just over half had a market capitalisation of less than AUD $100 million.[46] Their quoted securities are held by foreign investors, domestic institutional investors, and households.[47] Most ASX listed entities are Australian public companies, but in 2024 ASX's official list also included approximately 150 foreign companies, 50 registered managed investment schemes operating in the real estate or infrastructure sectors, and more than 100 listed collective investment companies and trusts.[48]

ensure the Panel can address circumstances which impair those purposes, without having to also establish either a contravention of the Act or an effect on control or potential control of a company or on the acquisition or proposed acquisition of a substantial interest in a company.' See Explanatory Memorandum to the Corporations Amendment (Takeovers) Bill 2007, para 3.8.

[42] The history and role of the Takeovers Panel is usefully summarised in *Eastern Field Developments Limited v Takeovers Panel* [2019] FCA 311 at [83]–[99]. It must not make an order if it is satisfied that the order would unfairly prejudice any person.

[43] These countries sit between 2% and 3% of global market capitalisation: see www.statista.com/statistics/710680/global-stock-markets-by-country/.

[44] ASX Limited, *ASX Annual Report 2024* Available at: www.asx.com.au/content/dam/asx/annual-reports/asx-2024-annual-report.pdf.

[45] ibid 15.

[46] See www.asx.com.au/about/market-statistics/historical-market-statistics#number.

[47] Reserve Bank of Australia, *Background on the Australian Listed Equity Market: Submission to the House of Representatives Standing Committee on Economics Inquiry into Common Ownership and Capital Concentration in Australia* (13 September 2021). Available at: www.rba.gov.au/publications/submissions/financial-sector/background-on-the-australian-listed-equity-market-2021-09/index.html.

[48] Managed investment schemes are a form of collective investment registered with ASIC under the Corporations Act ch 5C, usually structured as a trust with investors holding units that represent a beneficial interest in the trust property. Australian real estate investment trusts are referred to as A-REITs; many are structured as stapled entities with units in the trust stapled to shares in its operating company. Listed

In ASX Limited's financial year 1 July 2023 to 30 June 2024 there were 56 new listings and 156 delistings on ASX.[49] In the financial year 1 July 2022 to 30 June 2023 there were 57 new listing and 119 delistings, reversing the trend from 2021–2022 when there were 217 new listings and 128 delistings[50] and 2020–2021 when there were 176 new listings and 136 delistings.[51]

II. Delisting: Key Principles

A member who acquires ordinary shares in a company that is, or will be,[52] listed usually does so in the expectation that they will be able to trade those shares on ASX, subject to any temporary trading halts and asuming the shares are not suspended from quotation.[53] They also expect that the specific legal and contractual entitlements conferred on them as members of a listed entity by the Corporations Act and the ASX Listing Rules will be available to them for as long as listing continues.[54] A decision (by the company or ASX Limited) to delist impacts on the commercial – but not legal – character of their shareholding.

Delisting is ultimately a matter for ASX Limited and occurs either under ASX Listing Rule 17.11 (following a request from the entity) or Rules 17.12–17.16 (where the delisting is not at the entity's request). The former allows ASX Limited to remove an entity from the official list on request, while also providing that ASX Limited 'is not required to act on the entity's request, or may require conditions to be satisfied before it will act on the request'.[55] The conditions may include a shareholder vote in some circumstances.

investment companies (LICs) and listed investment trusts (LITs) are distinguished from other (quoted but not listed) investment products such as ETFs that are traded on ASX Limited's separate AQUA market. See P Hanrahan and I Ramsay, 'Regulation of Mutual Funds in Australia' in W Birdthistle and J Morley (eds), *Research Handbook on the Regulation of Mutual Funds* (Cheltenham, Edward Elgar, 2018).

[49] ASX Limited, *ASX Group Monthly Activity Report – June 2024* (4 July 2024). Available at: www.asx.com.au/about/media-centre. For information about recently delisted entities, see www.asx.com.au/listings/how-to-list/guides-rules-and-resources/delisted-entities; for information about entities delisted from ASX since 2001, see www.delisted.com.au.

[50] ASX Limited, *ASX Group Monthly Activity Report – June 2023* (6 July 2023). Available at the database indicated in n 49.

[51] ASX Limited, *ASX Group Monthly Activity Report – June 2022* (6 July 2022) available at the database indicated in n 49.

[52] As part of an initial public offering (IPO), the prospectus will state a company's intention to list: Corporations Act s 711(5). If listing is not achieved, s 724 applies and may require that amounts subscribed be repaid. To qualify for listing, the entity must meet 20 conditions set out in ASX Listing Rule 1.1. These include, for example, that the entity's structure and operations must be appropriate for a listed entity, its main class of securities (usually ordinary shares) must be granted quotation, it must have a free float of at least 20% and at least 300 non-affiliated security holders on admission, and it must meet minimum profit or assets tests.

[53] Short trading halts are made at the entity's request under ASX Listing Rule 17.1, for example pending an announcement. ASX Limited may suspend quotation of an entity's securities for a longer period at the entity's request under ASX Listing Rule 17.2 or on its own initiative under ASX Listing Rules 17.3–17.6. See ASX Limited, *Guidance Note 16: Trading Halts and Voluntary Suspensions* (August 2018). Available at: www.asx.com.au/about/regulation/rules-guidance-notes-and-waivers/asx-listing-rules-guidance-notes-and-waivers.

[54] For example, the requirement to produce a remuneration report covering key management personnel and to put it forward for a member vote at the annual general meeting applies only while the company is listed: Corporations Act s 300A.

[55] ASX Limited, *ASX Guidance Note 33: Removal of Entities from the ASX Official List* (December 2019). Available at the database indicated in n 53, para 2.1.

The reasons for, and bases upon, which ASX Limited will agree to voluntary delisting are explained in ASX Guidance Note 33 and discussed in Part III below. Delisting not at the entity's request can occur under ASX Limited's general delisting discretion (ASX Listing Rule 17.12), or automatically following a compulsory acquisition (ASX Listing Rule 17.14), or for non-payment of listing fees (ASX Listing Rule 17.15). These bases are also explained in ASX Guidance Note 33 and are discussed in Part IV below.

In any circumstances leading to delisting, ordinary corporate law principles apply. Three aspects of the Australian law are particularly relevant. The first is the legal duties and responsibilities of the company's directors and other officers. Actions they take (or fail to take) that lead to delisting must comply with their statutory and general law duties, including the duty to act with care and diligence, to act for a proper purpose and in the best interests of the company, and to manage conflicts of interest and duty.[56] The second is the strict corporate disclosure laws, which include a continuous disclosure obligation and statutory prohibitions on misleading conduct in relation to securities that cover deliberate, negligent or innocent misrepresentation.[57] The third is the right of individual members to bring proceedings for a remedy (such as an injunction or an order regulating the future conduct of the company's affairs) if the affairs of the company are being conducted in a manner that is 'contrary to the interests of the members as a whole', or 'oppressive to, unfairly prejudicial to, or unfairly discriminatory against, a member or members whether in that capacity or in any other capacity'.[58]

Often, delisting occurs following a control transaction such as a take-private transaction (where one member or a small syndicate of members buys out the others) or a merger with or acquisition by another entity. There are two main pathways by which a change of control of an Australian listed company can be achieved. The first is under a takeover bid made in accordance with chapter 6 of the Corporations Act.[59] The second is through a reorganisation of the company by way of a members' scheme of arrangement, conducted under the supervision of ASIC and the courts pursuant to part 5.1 of the Corporations Act.[60] There are pertinent commercial reasons for adopting one pathway

[56] For an explanation of the legal duties of directors and other officers, see P Hanrahan, *Directors' Legal Responsibilities: A Handbook for Australian Boards* (Sydney, AICD, 2022).

[57] The continuous disclosure laws in ASX Listing Rule 3.1 and Corporations Act ch 6CA require a listed entity to disclose price-sensitive information (subject to very limited exceptions) immediately to the market by announcement through the ASX platform. Corporate disclosures including announcements and notices of meeting (but not takeover documents, which are subject to a different liability regime) are covered by the general statutory prohibitions on misleading conduct in Corporations Act s 1041H and ASIC Act 2001, s 12DA and specific provisions relating to financial products in ASIC Act ss 12DB and 12DF. Carelessness in relation to disclosure can lead to individual civil penalty liability for corporate officers, for example under Corporations Act ss 180, 674A and 1308.

[58] Corporations Act pt 2F.1.

[59] For a brief overview of the takeover laws, see the Takeovers Panel, *Summary of Takeover Provisions*. Available at: www.takeovers.gov.au/resources/key-concepts/summary-takeover-provisions. The law works by Corporations Act s 606 prohibiting, subject to numerous exemptions set out in s 611, the acquisition of a 'relevant interest' in voting shares if, as a result of the transaction, a person's voting power in the company increases from under 20% to over 20%, or increases from a starting point that is above 20% and below 90%. The exemptions include acquisitions resulting from a formal takeover bid made on-market or off-market in accordance with Corporations Act ch 6 and acquisitions that result from a scheme of arrangement.

[60] For a brief explanation of schemes of arrangement and the respective roles of ASIC and the court see ASIC, *Regulatory Guide 60: Schemes of Arrangement* (September 2020). Available at: www.asic.gov.au/regulatory-resources/find-a-document/regulatory-guides/rg-60-schemes-of-arrangement/. See also Federal

over the other or running both processes simultaneously; speaking very generally, a scheme of arrangement may offer greater predictability as to the timing and outcome than a takeover bid in circumstances where all the target's shares will be acquired and the acquirer and the target company's board have agreed the terms of the transaction.

Corporations Act chapter 6 and part 5.1 each offer statutory protections to members affected by the control transaction. These include extensive information rights[61] and the right to have a say in whether the transaction goes ahead.[62] Takeover bids and schemes of arrangement also provide a mechanism for 'mopping up' the shareholdings of any dissenting minority. If the acquirer in a takeover bid achieves 90 per cent acceptance, they may move to compulsory acquisition.[63] If a scheme of arrangement is approved by special resolution of the members in general meeting and accepted by the court, it is binding on all members, including those who vote against it.[64] As Part III explains, ASX Limited takes the existence of these protections into account in deciding what conditions (for example, as to information or member consent) to impose on a delisting that occurs in the context of a control transaction.

III. Delisting at the Instigation of the Company

This Part looks in more detail at the rules that apply when a company makes a request pursuant to ASX Listing Rule 17.11 for removal from the official list. This is the most common basis for delisting.[65] ASX Guidance Note 33 gives examples of 'common and generally acceptable reasons why an entity might ask to be removed from the official list'; they include where:

- the entity is re-domiciling to another jurisdiction and intends to move its listing from ASX to an overseas exchange
- the entity has its primary listing on another exchange and no longer requires a secondary listing on ASX
- following a takeover bid, scheme of arrangement, or other change-of-control transaction, the entity has only one or a small number of remaining members
- the directors consider that the securities are trading materially lower than net asset value and an alternative (such as a redemption or buy-back) is proposed to allow members to exit the stock, or

Court of Australia, *Schemes of Arrangement Practice Note (GPN-SOA)* (October 2023). Available at: www.fedcourt.gov.au/law-and-practice/practice-documents/practice-notes/gpn-soa. For registered managed investment schemes, see Takeovers Panel, *Guidance Note 15: Trust Scheme Mergers* (May 2011). Available at: the database indicated in n 39.

[61] For example, the prescribed bidder's statement and target's statement in a takeover bid and the scheme booklet in a scheme of arrangement.

[62] In a takeover bid, it is for each member to decide whether to accept the bid and sell into the offer. In acquisitions approved by ordinary resolution of disinterested members and in schemes of arrangement, members have their say by voting in a general meeting.

[63] Under Corporations Act pt 6A.1.

[64] ibid pt 5.1.

[65] For example, of the 81 entities removed from the official list in the six months between May 2024 and November 2024, 53 were removed following a request under ASX Listing Rule 17.11; see www.asx.com.au/listings/how-to-list/guides-rules-and-resources/delisted-entities.

- the directors have determined for some other proper reason that it is no longer in the interests of the entity or its members to remain listed.[66]

Examples of unacceptable reasons are to avoid the application of ASX Listing Rules chapter 10 (requiring member approval for specified transactions), to avoid the continuous disclosure obligations, or to deny minority members a market 'in order to coerce them into accepting a current or planned offer from a controlling security holder to buy their securities at an undervalue'.[67]

The process begins with confidential discussions between the entity and ASX Limited, during which the conditions that ASX Limited plans to impose are discussed. Once an in-principle agreement is reached, the entity will go into trading halt, make a formal application for removal, and make a detailed market announcement containing the prescribed information.[68] That prescribed information includes an explanation of the remedies available to members through a court under Corporations Act part 2F.1 (if the removal is oppressive or contrary to the interests of members as a whole) or through the Takeovers Panel under Corporations Act part 6.10 (if the removal involves unacceptable circumstances in a control transaction).

As to the usual conditions imposed by ASX Limited, these depend on the circumstances. ASX Limited distinguishes between delisting where the entity's securities are readily able to be traded on another exchange[69] and where its securities are not readily able to be traded on another exchange.[70] In the latter case, ASX Limited's approach depends on whether delisting is preceded by a successful control transaction, including where a takeover bid has resulted in 75 per cent acceptances but has not met the conditions for compulsory acquisition.[71] In these circumstances, the conditions relate mostly to disclosure to members and to allowing adequate time (one month for the former, three months for the latter) for members to dispose of their securities (if they wish to) before ASX delisting takes effect. But if the delisting is not preceded by a successful control transaction (leading either to automatic delisting following compulsory acquisition or a request for voluntary delisting), ASX Limited will usually require that the entity obtain the approval of its members by way of special resolution and, if the resolution is passed, that the entity remains listed for at least one month after the date of the resolution.[72]

When it requires a members' resolution as a condition of delisting, ASX Limited prescribes the information to be provided to members in the notice of meeting and may restrict the entitlement of some members to vote. The voting exclusions are often closely

[66] ASX Guidance Note 33 (n 55) para 2.1.

[67] ibid para 2.1.

[68] ibid para 2.4.

[69] ibid para 2.6. Early in 2025, a proposal by Irish company James Hardie Industries Public Company Limited (JHX) to move its primary listing from ASX to NYSE without giving seeking JHX member approval attracted significant criticism from professional and institutional investors in Australia. As a result, ASX Limited announced on 27 April 2025 that it would review the circumstances in which it required, and granted waivers from requirements for, member approval of significant transactions affecting ASX listed entities. Available at: www.asx.com.au/content/dam/asx/about/media-releases/2025/27-apr-asx-commences-listing-rules-review.pdf.

[70] ibid paras 2.7 and 2.8.

[71] ibid para 2.10. If a takeover bid leads to compulsory acquisition, then ASX Listing Rule 17.15 applies.

[72] A special resolution requires the approval of at least 75% of votes cast by members who are eligible to vote, and who do vote, in person or by proxy.

negotiated. Under Australian corporate law, the usual position is that all members[73] are permitted to vote at a general meeting; they are entitled to exercise their votes as they see fit because members are not in a fiduciary relationship with each other or the company.[74] However, in ASX Guidance Note 33, ASX Limited specifies five cases where specified members will be excluded from voting, including a general catch-all where ASX Limited 'considers it appropriate in any specific case to impose a voting exclusion'. They also include where ASX Limited is concerned that the motive or effect of the delisting is to confer a benefit on some members at the expense of others.[75] In these cases, the votes of members who stand to benefit and their associates may be excluded.[76]

Given the complex interplay between ASX Listing Rules chapter 17, corporate law and the law regulating control transactions, it is helpful to consider the different policy considerations relating to member approval raised by: an entity re-domiciling and migrating their listing to another exchange or giving up an ASX secondary listing; delisting as part of a control transaction; and voluntary delisting for other acceptable reasons.

A. If the Entity is Listed on Another Exchange

While ASX Limited will impose information conditions in the form of a detailed announcement, this type of delisting does not usually require the approval of the entity's members as market trading will remain possible through a different venue. This is so even if the listing or operating rules of the other venue do not offer the same protections to members as primary listing on ASX. ASX Guidance Note 33 says that, in exercising its discretion to approve delisting, ASX Limited will 'look favourably' on the entity putting in place transitional arrangements (for say three months) with a local Australian broker who can facilitate sales on the other exchange and remit the sale proceeds in Australian dollars.[77]

[73] In ASX Guidance Note 33 (n 55) para 2.7 ASX Limited says 'including, for the avoidance of doubt, those with a 75%+ security holding who can secure the passage of a special resolution with their own vote'.

[74] In practice, the oppression remedy in Corporations Act pt 2F.1 and the equitable doctrine of 'fraud on the minority' operate as a constraint on the exercise of voting power. For a discussion of the latter doctrine, see *Catto v Hampton Australia Ltd (in liq) (No 3)* (2004) 89 SASR 234; [2004] SASC 242.

[75] The cases mentioned by ASX Limited in ASX Guidance Note 33 (n 55) para 2.7 include where it is 'concerned that the removal may be intended, in part, to avoid the application of the Listing Rules to a transaction or situation that … would otherwise attract a voting exclusion under Listing Rule 14.11' or where the company has been the subject of a takeover bid in the preceding 12 months that has not resulted in compulsory acquisition or satisfied the requirements of ASX Listing Rule 2.10.

[76] ASX Limited's discretion to exclude some shareholders from voting is contained in ASX Listing Rule 14.11.1. ASX Guidance Note 33 (n 55) para 2.7 says that ASX Limited will impose voting exclusions in five situations: as an anti-avoidance mechanism; where the delisting is to avoid the continuous disclosure laws; where the security holder or their associates is likely to obtain some other material advantage or benefit not available to other security holders; where there has been a takeover bid in the last 12 months that has resulted in a change of control; or if ASX Limited otherwise considers it appropriate. These exclusions are routinely adopted by proponents of delisting on the advice of experienced counsel without being insisted upon by ASX Limited.

[77] ASX Guidance Note 33 (n 55) para 2.6.

B. Delisting as Part of a Control Transaction

Often, the consequence of a control transaction – whether by takeover bid or scheme of arrangement – is that maintaining the target entity's listing is no longer appropriate. Because delisting is the last step in a broader process, the protections afforded to members are largely to be found in the law regulating the control transaction itself.

In a takeover bid, members are afforded the protections contained in Corporations Act chapter 6, which give effect to the Eggleston Principles.[78] It is for each member to decide for themselves whether to accept the bidder's offer up to the point of compulsory acquisition. The members' statutory protections include their right to receive prescribed information, to have adequate time to decide whether to accept the bid, and to have a reasonable and equal opportunity to participate in any benefits arising from the bid.

A person (including a member) who considers that unacceptable circumstances have arisen in relation to the bid can apply to have the Takeovers Panel intervene; there are many examples of security holders having asked for a declaration of unacceptable circumstances in relation to a proposed delisting.[79] However, the fact that an entity will be delisted is not of itself an unacceptable circumstance; ordinarily the Panel will look for an impact on control that offends the Eggleston Principles in section 602 of the Corporations Act. In *Re Flinders Mines Ltd (No 2 & 3)*, the Takeovers Panel said:

> The decision of a company's board to seek to de-list involves the exercise of business or commercial judgement, and may be subject to (among other things) requirements of the applicable listing rules, the discretions and policy of the relevant listing authority, director's duties and minority shareholders remedies. It is not the Panel's role, in the ordinary course, to opine on such judgements or enforce requirements for which other regulators or the courts have primary responsibility. However, the overlap of such requirements does not prevent the Panel exercising its jurisdiction in relation to matters that do fall within its jurisdiction and role. In our view, where de-listing has or is likely to have an effect on control or the acquisition of a substantial interest in a listed company, and appears inconsistent with the purposes in section 602, it is appropriate for us to consider whether it gives rise to unacceptable circumstances.[80]

If a successful takeover bid results in compulsory acquisition, delisting follows automatically.[81] Compulsory acquisition (that is, the right to force remaining members to sell their shares to the successful bidder at the bid price) is available when the bidder and their associates have relevant interests in at least 90 per cent (by number) of the securities in the bid class and have acquired at least 75 per cent (by number) of the securities that the bidder offered to acquire under the bid (whether or not the acquisitions happened under the bid).[82]

[78] See n 40.

[79] See eg the recent decisions of the Takeovers Panel in *Re Strategic Minerals Corp NL* [2018] ATP 2; *Re Flinders Mines Limited (No 2 and 3)* [2019] ATP 2; *Re Energy Resources of Australia Ltd 02R* [2020] ATP 2.

[80] *Re Flinders Mines Limited* [2019] ATP 2, [20].

[81] ASX Listing Rule 17.14. Of the 81 entities removed from the official list in the six months between May 2024 and November 2024, nine were removed following compulsory acquisition; see www.asx.com.au/listings/how-to-list/guides-rules-and-resources/delisted-entities.

[82] Compulsory acquisition and compulsory buy-out following a takeover bid are dealt with in Corporations Act pt 6A.1. General compulsory acquisition or buy-out is dealt with in pt 6A.2.

The protections for dissenting members whose shares are to be compulsorily acquired are contained in chapter 6A of the Corporations Act.[83] The Eggleston Principles include that an appropriate procedure is followed under the post-bid compulsory acquisition provisions; if a bidder satisfies the post-bid compulsory acquisition thresholds in a way that is not appropriate, the Takeovers Panel may make a declaration of unacceptable circumstances.[84]

If the bidder in a takeover bid (in which delisting was foreshadowed) reaches 75 per cent but not the threshold for compulsory acquisition, and fewer than 150 members holding at least 300 shares remain, ASX Guidance Note 33 indicates that delisting can occur without the separate approval of the remaining members if conditions (including that the offer remained open for at least two weeks after the bidder attained its 75 per cent stake) are met. The policy reason is that members 'had a reasonable opportunity to sell their holdings by accepting the bid after the bidder secured control of the entity and the entity is now at or near the margin where ASX may consider removing the entity from the official list for failure to maintain a sufficient spread of security holdings'.[85]

However, if an entity is the subject of a takeover bid that results in the bidder and its associates having effective control without meeting these conditions, the practice of ASX Limited is to require the removal to be approved by members and to impose a voting exclusion on the bidder and its associates.[86]

Schemes of arrangement are conducted under a different legal regime, in which the control transaction and resulting delisting occur under the supervision of ASIC and the courts. A scheme usually begins with negotiations between the acquirer and the company's board that culminate in a scheme implementation agreement. The company, with the acquirer's input, prepares disclosure in the form of a detailed 'scheme booklet' which is provided to ASIC for review (as to the adequacy of the disclosure, not the commercial merits of the transaction). The company then seeks the approval of the court for the scheme booklet to be dispatched to members, accompanied by orders convening a meeting of members to vote on the scheme, at which the acquirer and its associates typically do not vote. After the meeting, if the scheme is approved by special resolution of the members and of members in each relevant class, a second court hearing is held to approve its implementation. If it is contemplated by the scheme, that implementation will usually result in delisting within a few days of completion.

C. Other Voluntary Delisting

In other circumstances, where the company's board reaches the decision that delisting would be in the best interests of the company as a whole, ASX Limited will require the decision be approved by a special resolution of the company's members.[87] In some situations, voting exclusions apply.[88] The disclosure provided to members, including

[83] For a summary of the process, see ASIC, *Regulatory Guide 10* (n 2).

[84] Corporations Act ss 602(d) and 657A(2)(b).

[85] ASX Guidance Note 33 (n 55) para 2.9.

[86] ibid para 2.7.

[87] ibid para 2.7. The notice of meeting must include the information required by ASX Guidance Note 33 (n 55) para 2.11.

[88] ibid para 2.12. See n 76.

the extensive disclosure required by ASX Guidance Note 33, must be accurate and complete, and the entity's directors have statutory and general law obligations that go to the adequacy of that disclosure.[89]

In practice, voluntary delisting (outside a re-domicile or control transaction) is often a consequence of the listed entity being no longer willing or able to meet the ongoing requirements for listing in ASX Listing Rules chapter 12 (such as maintaining a spread of security holdings sufficient to ensure an orderly and liquid market); it may occur when the entity's securities have already been suspended from quotation.[90] There is therefore some overlap with the discussion in Part IV below.

A decision by a board to seek, or by the members in general meeting to approve, delisting is a commercial decision. That decision is open to challenge by a member or a dissenting member of the board of directors under the provisions of the Corporations Act only if it is oppressive, unfairly discriminatory, unfairly prejudicial or contrary to the interests of the members as a whole.[91] There is a significant body of case law interpreting and applying the oppression provisions in corporate law more generally. However, the mere fact of delisting is not oppressive; it will depend on the circumstances.[92] Relevant factors include how practicable and desirable it is to maintain listing and any arrangements proposed for allowing minority shareholders to exit (for example, by delaying delisting to allow time of an on-market sale, or by a selective buy-back or reduction of capital).[93]

There are oppression cases arising out of decisions to delist, but they rarely succeed. In *De Tocqueville Private Equity Pty Ltd v Linden & Conway Ltd*, a minority shareholder unsuccessfully challenged a decision to delist a thinly-traded company that was not in a position, without changing its strategy and operations, to meet the ongoing requirements for listing. The minority shareholder failed to establish that the directors' decision to seek delisting was 'made other than by resort to a properly exercised commercial judgment'. The Court observed that, while the minority shareholder 'may feel locked in to [the company], in the sense of having difficulty selling on the market, this is … not due to the current actions of the directors, but more to the nature of the strategies and constitution of [the company] which have been in existence for some time'.[94] The Court went on to say that:

> Having regard to the nature of the listing rules, it seems to me to be up to [the company] itself to make a decision whether to comply or not. It seems that to comply would involve a change in direction for [the company] which the directors themselves consider to be commercially inappropriate.[95]

[89] See Hanrahan (n 56) ch 7.

[90] Suspension is provided for in ASX Listing Rule 17.1 (at the entity's request) and 17.2 to 17.6 (by ASX Limited).

[91] Corporations Act pt 2F.1. The jurisprudence on the oppression remedy in corporate law is extensive. See RP Austin and I Ramsay, *Ford Austin & Ramsay's Principles of Corporations Law*, 17th edn (Sydney, LexisNexis Butterworths, 2024) paras 10.430–10.480.

[92] See, for example, *MF Lady Pty Ltd (Trustee) v Henry Morgan Limited* [2022] FCA 978.

[93] The procedures for selective reductions of capital and share buy-backs are set out in Corporations Act pt 2J.1.

[94] *De Tocqueville Private Equity Pty Ltd v Linden & Conway Limited* (2006) 59 ACSR 587; [2006] FCA 1309, [34].

[95] ibid [35].

There is no requirement in Australian law that, if delisting occurs outside the conditions for compulsory buy-out following a successful takeover bid,[96] dissenting shareholders are bought out by either the company or a controlling shareholder. But the entity has the option of making a commercial decision to offer an exit by way of a reduction of capital or share buy-back.[97]

IV. Delisting at the Instigation of ASX Limited

Listing is granted and maintained at the discretion of ASX Limited. ASX Limited will automatically remove an entity from the official list following a compulsory acquisition (discussed in Part III above) or for non-payment of its annual listing fee.[98] It is also empowered to remove an entity if the entity is unable or unwilling to comply with, or breaks, a listing rule; if the entity has no quoted securities; or if removal is 'appropriate for some other reason'.[99]

In exercising its power to delist, ASX Limited (like all listing exchanges) must strike a balance between protecting ECM integrity and depriving the entity's members of their ability to trade on-market. This is recognised in the detailed guidance provided in ASX Guidance Note 33.

A. Delisting for Non-Payment of Listing Fees

An entity that fails to pay its annual listing fee will be suspended after five days and then removed from the official list on the twentieth business day after the due date.

For a solvent entity,[100] the decision to pay (or not pay) its annual listing fee rests with the entity itself. ASX Limited recognises the risk that an entity wanting to be removed might seek to circumvent the member approval required for a voluntary delisting by choosing not to pay. Therefore, ASX Limited cautions that:

> Such conduct will not only breach the obligation of the entity to act in accordance with the spirit, intention and purpose of the Listing Rules, it is likely to raise issues as to whether the directors of the entity are complying with their statutory and common law obligations to discharge their duties with a reasonable degree of care and diligence and to exercise their

[96] Corporations Act pt 6A.1 div 2.

[97] See n 93. It depends on maintaining the company's solvency, and on following the prescribed statutory procedures.

[98] ASX Listing Rule 17.15. Of the 81 entities delisted between May 2024 and November 2024, 14 were removed under ASX Listing Rule 17.15; see www.asx.com.au/listings/how-to-list/guides-rules-and-resources/delisted-entities.

[99] ASX Listing Rule 17.12. Of the 81 entities delisted between May and November 2024, 5 were removed under ASX Listing Rule 17.12; see www.asx.com.au/listings/how-to-list/guides-rules-and-resources/delisted-entities.

[100] An entity in external administration will remain on the official list, although suspended: see ASX Guidance Note 33 (n 55) para 3.4.

> powers in good faith and for a proper purpose. In some cases, it could also leave the entity open to an action for oppressive conduct or 'just and equitable' winding up.[101]

ASX Limited reserves the right to take legal action to recover outstanding listing fees and to reinstate the entity to the official list when payment occurs.

B. Other Involuntary Delisting

The ASX Listing Rules give the market operator a broad discretion to remove entities from the official list. In ASX Guidance Note 33, ASX Limited observes that the power:

> is not one that ASX exercises lightly, since it takes away from the entity's security holders the ability to trade their securities on a licensed securities exchange. However, it is a power that ASX will exercise to protect the reputation and integrity of the ASX market and to prevent future investors from buying into a listed entity that in ASX's opinion should not be listed on the ASX market.[102]

The circumstances in which ASX Limited has exercised this power include where a listed entity has breached the Listing Rules (including 'persistent or egregious breaches' of the continuous disclosure requirement), where it failed to meet the on-going requirements for listing specified in ASX Listing Rule chapter 12 (including a sufficient spread of security holding, a sufficient level of operations, an adequate financial condition or a structure and operations appropriate for a listed entity), and (subject to some allowance) where the entity was suspended for a period exceeding two years or failed to lodge documents required under ASX Listing Rule 17.5 for over a year.[103]

No right of appeal lies to the ASX Appeal Tribunal for suspension or delisting decisions made by ASX Limited under the ASX Listing Rules. A listed company or other affected person that objects to a delisting decision by ASX Limited might complain to ASIC or the Minister about ASX Limited's conduct;[104] otherwise they must ask a court for relief.[105]

Given the significant impact that delisting might have on a listed entity, the legal controls over the exercise of ASX Limited's powers that arise from the contract between it and the listed entity are important.[106] During the 1990s, some delisted entities brought cases challenging the exercise by the exchange operator of its (then) delisting power;[107] more recent cases dealing with the power of ASX Limited to suspend listing

[101] ibid para 3.2 (footnotes omitted).

[102] ibid para 3.3.

[103] ibid para 3.4.

[104] See nn 23 and 24 above.

[105] See n 21 above.

[106] A Black, 'Judicial Review of Discretionary Decisions of Australian Stock Exchange Limited' (1989) 5 *Australian Bar Review* 91; M Gillooly, 'Public Law Review of ASX Delisting Decisions' (1995) 13 *Australian Bar Review* 221; P Latimer, 'Legal Enforcement of Stock Exchange Rules: Part II' (1996) 8 *Bond Law Review* 6.

[107] See *Chapmans Ltd v Australian Stock Exchange Limited* (1996) 67 FCR 402; *CTC Resources NL v Australian Stock Exchange Ltd* (1997) 23 ACSR 418. In *Chapman*, the Full Federal Court decided that delisting decisions, while reviewable at common law, cannot be challenged as decisions under an enactment pursuant to the *Administrative Decisions (Judicial Review) Act 1977* (Cth).

include *Hampton Hill Mining NL v ASX Limited* in 2020.[108] These decisions confirm that, in exercising these powers, ASX Limited is required to act honestly and fairly, and to accord procedural fairness (which usually includes an obligation to provide the listed entity with a proper opportunity to be heard). It may be required to given reasons for a decision. A brief statement of the reason for delisting will appear in ASX Limited's published announcement.

V. Balancing Competing Interests

Delisting decisions (in any jurisdictions) gives rise to competing interests. At a market level, rule-makers must balance considerations of ECM integrity with the commercial interests of market operators in encouraging entities to seek and maintain listing and the desire of institutional and private investors access a broad menu of liquid equity investments.[109] ECM integrity requires that entities listed on an exchange are suitable in the sense that trading in their securities can take place in a fair, efficient and informed market; this depends on the entity reliably complying with the law and listing rules. If an entity cannot be relied upon to maintain the standards for listing adopted for that market, delisting may be necessary to maintain trust and confidence in the market despite its deleterious effect on the individual entity and its members.[110] As the holder of an Australian market licence issued under the Corporations Act, ASX Limited must prioritise ECM integrity. It is required 'to the extent that it is reasonably practicable to do so, do all things necessary to ensure that the market is a fair, orderly and transparent market'. It must 'have adequate arrangements … for operating the market' including arrangements for 'handling conflicts between the commercial interests of the licensee and the need for the licensee to ensure' that its market operates in this way, and for 'monitoring and enforcing compliance with the market's operating rules'.[111]

At the level of individual entities, members may disagree on delisting. If delisting is to occur at the end of a control transaction, dissenting members may have declined

[108] *Hampton Hill Mining NL v ASX Limited* [2020] WASC 86, [32]–[35].

[109] The delisting dilemma for exchange operators is acknowledged in the literature. See, for example, I Martinez and S Serve, 'Reasons for Delisting and Consequences: A Literature Review and Research Agenda' (2017) 31 *Journal of Economic Surveys* 733. Public markets are in decline globally. There is an active debate over whether that decline is cyclical or structural. See ASIC, *Australia's Evolving Capital Markets: A Discussion Paper on the Dynamics Between Public and Private Markets* (February 2025). Available at: https://asic.gov.au/regulatory-resources/find-a-document/reports/dp-australia-s-evolving-capital-markets-a-discussion-paper-on-the-dynamics-between-public-and-private-markets/.

[110] The *CTC Resources* case (n 107) is an unusual example of a delisting said to be for market integrity reasons. In 1990 a listed entity announced a rights issue that had 'an element of a lottery'. Members could subscribe for preference shares; each preference share so taken up was to take part in a lottery through which 12 holders would share 50% of the proceeds of the raising of AUD $7.5 million. The proposal was 'not at all to the liking of' the exchange, which delisted the entity. The entity sued the exchange, and the matter was eventually compromised: see *Commonwealth v Davis Samuel Pty Ltd (No 7)* (2013) 282 FLR 1, [36]. The case was notorious for another reason because money improperly transferred from the Commonwealth ended up in the entity, which the Commonwealth then spent almost two decades attempting to recover: see *Commonwealth of Australia v CTC Resources NL* [2016] FCA 112.

[111] Corporations Act s 792A. This is a civil penalty provision for the purposes of Corporations Act pt 9.4B.

to sell into the takeover bid or voted against the scheme of arrangement at the scheme meeting. If the delisting is decided on by the entity's board outside a control transaction, dissenting members may have the opportunity to vote against it at a meeting of members (but only if a meeting is required by corporate law or by the rules or practice the exchange). In Australia, a shareholder vote is usually required to approve the board's decision to delist outside a successful control transaction, if the entity will no longer be listed on any public exchange.

When members disagree, rule-makers must strike a balance between 'minority oppression and minority dictation'.[112] While the interests of a dissenting minority must be considered,[113] in Australia members do not have a legal right to insist that listing be maintained if the entity's board, acting properly, decides it is in the best interests of the company to relinquish it.[114]

In the end, the fate of a dissenting member depends on the context. The key protections for members of Australian companies that are delisting from ASX, discussed in Parts III and IV above and summarised in Table 1, show how those interests are balanced.

Table 15.1 Dissenting Members' Rights in a Delisting

Context	Position of dissenting members
The entity is listed on another exchange	Members are given notice and time (usually one month) to sell their shares on-market before delisting from ASX occurs.[115]
ASX Limited decides to delist the entity and the board does nothing to prevent it	An individual member cannot challenge the decision by ASX Limited but has standing to apply for court orders requiring ASX Limited to enforce the ASX Listing Rules against the entity.[116] If the delisting decision by ASX Limited is the consequence of conduct by the board or members of the entity that is oppressive or there are unacceptable circumstances, the dissenting member can seek remedies.[117]

(continued)

[112] See n 2.

[113] Including the significance of a shareholder's interest in their shares recognised by the High Court of Australia in *Gambotto v WCP Ltd* (1995) 182 CLR 432. The *Gambotto* case concerned a proposal to amend the constitution of a company to achieve the compulsory acquisition by a controlling shareholder of a minority shareholding; for a useful analysis see I Ramsay and B Saunders, 'What Do You Do with a High Court Decision You Don't Like? Legislative, Judicial and Academic Responses to Gambotto v WCP Ltd' (2010–2011) 25 *Australian Journal of Corporate Law* 112.

[114] If directors breach their duties, they can be the subject of a civil prosecution by ASIC or a civil claim by the company. This may include scrutiny of the reasons for the delisting decision to determine whether the 'business judgment' safe-harbour in Corporations Act s 180(2) applies. A member may be able to cause the company to sue the directors by way of a statutory derivative action under Corporations Act pt 2F.1A.

[115] ASX Listing Rule 12.11 and ASX Guidance Note 33 (n 55) para 2.6.

[116] Corporations Act s 793C. This may be useful if the entity's compliance would remove ASX Limited's reason for delisting it.

[117] Corporations Act s 232 (court-ordered remedies for oppression); Corporations Act s 657A (declaration of unacceptable circumstances by the Takeovers Panel).

Table 15.1 ***(Continued)***

Context	Position of dissenting members
A controlling shareholder has acquired more than 90 per cent and wants the entity to delist	If the controlling shareholder has completed a takeover bid, it can compulsorily acquire the dissenters' shares (and the dissenters can require a buy-out).[118] In other circumstances, the controlling shareholder can move to compulsory acquisition if most outstanding members agree or the court approves.[119] Delisting is automatic after compulsory acquisition.[120] If there is oppression or there are unacceptable circumstances, the dissenting member can seek remedies.[121]
A controlling shareholder has acquired more than 75 per cent in a takeover bid and wants the entity to delist	The delisting will probably go ahead without member approval if the dissenting members are fewer than 150. The entity will remain listed for three months after notice is given to allow members to sell their shares on-market.[122] If there is oppression or there are unacceptable circumstances, the dissenting member can seek remedies.[123]
The majority has voted to approve a scheme of arrangement that will result in delisting	Affected persons have a right to be heard at the first and second court hearings. The scheme is binding on all members once it is approved by the court at the second hearing.[124]
The majority has voted to approve the board's decision to delist	The usual corporate law and disclosure law principles apply to the meeting. A dissenting member may have remedies if the meeting is not properly convened or held,[125] if the notice of meeting is defective,[126] if there is oppression,[127] or if there are unacceptable circumstances.[128] Where the approval meeting is held to satisfy a requirement imposed by ASX Limited as a condition of delisting,[129] it will impose requirements relating to the notice of meeting[130] and may impose voting exclusions.[131] The entity will remain listed for one month after the meeting to allow members to sell their shares on-market.[132]

[118] Corporations Act s 661A (compulsory acquisition) and 662A (compulsory buy-out). An affected member can apply to the court to prevent a compulsory acquisition under Corporations Act s 661E if the consideration is not fair value for the shares.

[119] Corporations Act s 664A. Compulsory acquisition can occur if members holding less than 10% of the outstanding shares object, or it is approved by a court under Corporations Act s 664F.

[120] ASX Listing Rule 17.14 and ASX Guidance Note 33 (n 55) para 3.1.

[121] Corporations Act s 232; Corporations Act s 657A.

[122] ASX Listing Rule 17.11 and ASX Guidance Note 33 (n 55) para 2.10.

[123] Corporations Act s 232; Corporations Act s 657A.

[124] ibid s 411.

[125] Corporations Act pt 2G.2.

[126] Including under Corporations Act s 1041H.

[127] Corporations Act s 232.

[128] ibid s 657A.

[129] ASX Listing Rule 17.11 and ASX Guidance Note 33 (n 55) para 2.7.

[130] ASX Guidance Note 33 (n 55) para 2.11. This includes 'reasonably detailed' information about the reasons for seeking delisting.

[131] ibid para 2.12.

[132] ibid para 2.7.

As Table 15.1 shows, members of an Australian listed company are not entitled to insist that it remains listed indefinitely. And rule-makers and dispute resolution bodies – including the courts and the Takeovers Panel – recognise that the decision by the company to remain listed (or by ASX Limited to allow it to remain listed) can be affected by a range of commercial, pragmatic, and policy considerations that justify delisting. Instead, individual members are protected by their corporate law rights – including to a remedy for oppression – and where relevant their rights under the control laws to relief where the delisting decision is made in unacceptable circumstances.

Ultimately, the decision by ASX Limited to delist a company (either at its request or involuntarily) should be determined having regard to the overarching consideration of maintaining ECM integrity. In practice, this often involves sensitive and complex judgements. In making those judgements, ASX Limited is given considerable discretion, but is ultimately accountable the Minister and ASIC, and to the courts, for the exercise of that discretion.

16

Delistings in Hong Kong

CHEE KEONG (CK) LOW AND TAK YIP LOW*

I. Introduction

The delisting of a public listed company involves the withdrawal or cancellation of its listing status on the Stock Exchange of Hong Kong ('SEHK') which motivation can be either 'involuntary' or 'voluntary'. The latter – which is often referred to as privatisations or 'going/taking private' – is less prevalent given the shareholding structure of public listed companies in Hong Kong where it is not uncommon for the substantial shareholder and/or family to hold up to 75 per cent of its issued capital as the minimum public float required for a listing on the SEHK is usually 25 per cent.[1]

This chapter is divided into three parts: The first examines involuntary delistings under which regime the SEHK cancels the listing of securities to protect investors and/or to maintain an orderly market. As a new 'hard deadline' regime was implemented for the resumption of trading from August 2018, this part will provide an overview of the previous framework before turning to an elaboration of the present to provide for a comparison. Although the present regime is relatively new – with a track record of less than six years at the time of writing – it has nonetheless been the subject of several judicial reviews.

The second part examines the privatisations of companies that were listed on the SEHK, a key consideration for which is usually the perception that its market capitalisation does not accurately reflect the 'true or potential' value of the company. While such a transaction is most commonly undertaken by way of a scheme of arrangement, other options include a compulsory acquisition, a general offer or a capital reorganisation – the latter two with requisite shareholders' approval for delisting.

* Chee Keong (CK) Low *FCG HKFCG*, BEc; LLB; GradDip Comm Law (Monash); LLM (Hong Kong), and Tak Yip Low, LLB (Hons) UCL England.

[1] Chs 2, 2A and 2B of the Rules Governing the Listing of Securities on the Stock Exchange on Hong Kong ('the Main Board Listing Rules'). Available at: www.en-rules.hkex.com.hk/sites/default/files/net_file_store/consol_mb.pdf and chs 2, 3 and 4 of the Rules Governing the Listing of Securities on the Growth Enterprise Market of the Stock Exchange on Hong Kong ('the GEM Listing Rules'). Available at: www.en-rules.hkex.com.hk/sites/default/files/net_file_store/consol_gem.pdf. The Listing Committees of the Main Board and of GEM have operated as a combined committee since 2003 and membership of these committees was fully unified in May 2006.

To provide for a better appreciation of how the foregoing has been implemented in Hong Kong, selected case studies on both involuntary delistings as well as privatisations are discussed in the last part.

While the focus of this chapter will be on the delistings of companies that are listed on the Main Board of the SEHK, references will be made to appropriate provisions of the Growth Enterprise Market or 'GEM' which Rules mirror in large part to those of the Main Board.[2] The terms 'public listed company' and 'issuer' are used interchangeably throughout this chapter, the latter reflecting the terminology as stated in the Listing Rules.

II. Involuntary Delistings

A. Pre-August 2018

Companies may request for a suspension of trading[3] or this may be imposed on them by either the SEHK and/or the Securities and Futures Commission[4] ('SFC'), the latter pursuant to Rule 8(1) of the Securities and Futures (Stock Market Listing) Rules.[5] Such suspension of trading serves a legitimate purpose, namely, to ensure a fair and orderly market which allows for trading to be undertaken on a fully informed basis as well as to avoid uneven dissemination of information which may give rise to opportunities for insider dealing. Under normal circumstances, the regulators – the SFC and/or the SEHK – will only suspend the trading of a company's shares where unexplained movements in price and/or trading volume arise, or where there are breaches or suspected breaches of the Listing Rules and/or of applicable securities laws and regulations.

The Main Board Listing Rule 6.01 empowers the SEHK to suspend or cancel the listing of any securities to protect investors or maintain an orderly market under three specified circumstances namely, where an issuer[6] (a) fails to maintain a sufficient public float; (b) fails to maintain sufficient operations or assets; and (c) is no longer suitable for listing.

The procedure is set out under Main Board Listing Rule 6.10 under which the SEHK may (a) issue a delisting notice specifying a remedial period (specific remedial period).

[2] With its comparatively lower eligibility requirements the GEM caters towards the needs of smaller and mid-sized companies desirous of seeking a listing on the SEHK. Although the GEM is operated by the SEHK, it is entirely distinct from the Main Board. As such the GEM Listing Rules apply only to GEM and the Main Board Listing Rules apply only to the Main Board. For a succinct overview of the listing processes see HKEX, 'Listing on the Main Board'. Available at: www.hkex.com.hk/Join-Our-Market/IPO/Getting-Started/Listing-on-the-Main-Board?sc_lang=en and HKEX, 'Listing on GEM'. Available at: www.hkex.com.hk/Join-Our-Market/IPO/Getting-Started/Listing-on-GEM?sc_lang=en.

[3] A suspension of trading differs from a trading halt the latter of which is used to allow material information to be adequately disseminated during trading hours and to allow adequate time for the public to evaluate that information. A listed company may request a trading halt if the price-sensitive information announcement is ready for publication within a certain period of time. If a trading halt exceeds a prescribed period it will become a trading suspension.

[4] The Securities and Futures Commission is the statutory regulator of capital markets in Hong Kong pursuant to the Securities and Futures Ordinance (ch 571) hereafter 'the SFO'. See also SFC, 'Regulatory Functions' for an overview of its role and functions at www.sfc.hk/en/Regulatory-functions/Corporates.

[5] SFO, Ch 571V. Available at: www.elegislation.gov.hk/hk/cap571V.

[6] The corresponding provisions for GEM are set out in GEM Listing Rules 9.01, 9.04 and 9.14 (n 1).

If the issuer fails to remedy the issues and resume trading before the end of the remedial period, the SEHK may cancel its listing; or (b) delist the issuer immediately.

Delistings are usually preceded by an extended period of trading suspension of the shares of the issuer on the SEHK. To preserve the integrity of the market and to ensure its efficiency, as well as to protect the rights of investors, the SEHK implemented certain measures to keep trading suspensions to a minimum.

In particular, it published Guidance Letters GL83-15 in December 2015[7] and GL87-16 in April 2016[8] to remind issuers about their responsibilities on good practices on trading suspension pending disclosures of material information and on their responses to rumours or market commentaries with allegations of material irregularities respectively. In essence, these highlighted the need for issuers to be diligent in avoiding trading suspensions or – should this be necessary – to keep the period of such suspensions to a minimum.

The procedure for delistings from the Main Board of the SEHK through 31 July 2018 was set out in Practice Note 17 Sufficiency of Operations and Delisting Procedures – commonly referred to as 'PN17'[9] – which provided issuers with guidance for the implementation of the then provisions of Chapter 6 of the Main Board Listing Rules.[10]

In essence, PN17 envisaged a four-stage procedure:

At the first stage, the SEHK will monitor developments in the initial period of six months following the suspension during which period the issuer must make quarterly announcements on its progress in meeting the qualitative requirements of Main Board Listing Rule 13.24,[11] namely whether it has attained a sufficient level of operations and assets of sufficient value to support its operations to warrant the continued listing of the issuer's securities.[12]

At the second stage, the SEHK will write to the issuer, drawing attention to its continued failure to meet the aforesaid Main Board Listing Rule 13.24 and requiring it to submit a resumption proposal within the next six months. During this period the directors of the issuer are required to submit monthly progress reports. The SEHK will consider the issuer's proposals and determine whether it is appropriate to proceed to the next stage.

At the third stage, the SEHK will announce that the issuer does not have sufficient assets or operations for listing and will impose a deadline – generally six months – for submission of resumption proposals. Throughout this stage the directors of the issuers are required to provide monthly progress reports to the SEHK.

At the fourth stage, if no resumption proposals are received at the end of the third stage the listing of the company will be cancelled and this will be announced by both the issuer and the SEHK.

[7] Available at: en-rules.hkex.com.hk/sites/default/files/net_file_store/gl8315.pdf.

[8] Available at: en-rules.hkex.com.hk/sites/default/files/net_file_store/gl8716.pdf.

[9] Available at: en-rules.hkex.com.hk/sites/default/files/net_file_store/HKEX4476_3736_VER10.pdf.

[10] There is no equivalent PN17 procedure for GEM. The provisions of ch 6 of the Main Board Listing Rules are mirrored in large part in ch 9 of the GEM Listing Rules. See n 1, especially GEM Listing Rule 9.04.

[11] See n 1.

[12] A similar requirement is set out under GEM Listing Rule 17.26, see n 1.

A Guidance Letter was issued in September 2013 to provide some insights to the criteria for resumption for long suspended companies.[13] Significantly, the foregoing neither set any hard deadlines – which may in any event be extended by the Listing Committee of the SEHK – nor did it require anything more than the submission of a resumption proposal by the company. While this does allow for some degree of flexibility for companies to continually develop and/or refine their resumption proposals, it nonetheless prevents their shareholders from trading in its securities given the suspension.

For these reasons, it was not uncommon for the trading of shares in some companies to be suspended for an inordinately long period which does not bode well for their shareholders who are deprived of the choice of an orderly and timely exit. Tables 16.1 and 16.2 below set out the particulars of trading suspensions as well as cancellations or withdrawals of listing on the Main Board of the SEHK and on the GEM respectively as at the last trading day of the calendar year from 2015 to 2018.[14]

Table 16.1 Summary of Suspensions and Delistings on the Main Board of the SEHK from 2015 to 2018

	2015	**2016**	**2017**	**2018**
Cancellations/Withdrawals of listing	1	2	3	10
Companies suspended for Three Months or more	51	53	53	71
Companies in the First Stage of Delisting[15]	6	4	2	6
Companies in the Second Stage of Delisting	8	6	4	3
Companies in the Third Stage of Delisting	2	11	14	16
Resumption of Trading of Securities	25	15	14	10
Total Number of Listed Companies[16]	1,644	1,713	1,794	1,925

[13] HKEX, 'Guidance Letter for Long Suspended Companies, HKEX-GL66-13'. Available at: www.en-rules.hkex.com.hk/sites/default/files/net_file_store/gl6613.pdf.

[14] Extracted from HKEX, *Annual Reports* for 2015, 2016, 2017 and 2018. Available respectively at: www.hkexgroup.com/-/media/HKEX-Group-Site/ssd/Investor-Relations/Regulatory-Reports/documents/2016/160321ar_e.pdf, 41; www1.hkexnews.hk/listedco/listconews/sehk/2017/0320/ltn20170320225.pdf, 35; www.hkexnews.hk/listedco/listconews/sehk/2018/0319/ltn20180319293.pdf, 38 and www.hkexgroup.com/-/media/HKEX-Group-Site/ssd/Investor-Relations/Regulatory-Reports/documents/2019/190319ar_e.pdf, 55. The number for cancellation/withdrawal of listing may not be limited only to delistings as these may include privatisations which are undertaken voluntarily.

[15] Data for the number of companies at the various stages of delisting from the Main Board of the SEHK were extracted from HKEX, 'Report on Initial Public Offering Applications, Delisting and Suspensions' for the years ending 2015, available at: www.hkex.com.hk/News/Market-Communications/2015/151231news?sc_lang=en; 2016 (available at www.hkex.com.hk/News/Market-Communications/2016/161230news?sc_lang=en); and 2017 (available at www.hkex.com.hk/News/Market-Communications/2017/171229news?sc_lang=en). With the transition to the 'hard deadline regime' data on the First and Second Stages of Delisting was only available up to 31 July 2018 (available at www.hkex.com.hk/News/Market-Communications/2018/180731news?sc_lang=en).

[16] HKEX, 'Hong Kong and Mainland Market Highlights'. Available at: www.hkex.com.hk/Mutual-Market/Stock-Connect/Statistics/Hong-Kong-and-Mainland-Market-Highlights?sc_lang=en#select3=8&select2=11&select1=30.

Table 16.2 Summary of Suspensions and Delistings on GEM of the SEHK from 2015 to 2018[17]

	2015	**2016**	**2017**	**2018**
Cancellations/Withdrawals of listing	1	2	2	0
Companies Suspended for Three Months or more	7	3	3	11
Companies Notified of the SEHK's intention to cancel their listing	3	0	2	3
Resumption of Trading of Securities	3	5	1	2
Total Number of Listed Companies[18]	222	260	324	389

The procedure for GEM differs from that of the Main Board in that there is only a 'one-stage' delisting procedure. In essence, the issuer is notified by the SEHK that the latter intends to cancel its listing due to the former's failure to maintain sufficient operations or assets to warrant its continued listing. The issuer is thereafter provided with a period of time – usually within 12 months – within which it is to rectify these deficiencies to the satisfaction of the SEHK failing which it will be delisted from GEM.

With the introduction of the new 'hard deadline regime' as discussed in the next section, PN17 became transitional in nature applying as it did strictly to 23 issuers that were already placed under the first, second or third stage of delisting as at 31 July 2018.[19] It was repealed following the completion of these outstanding cases of which only one – Primeview Holdings Limited – fulfilled its resumption requirements and was allowed to resume trading on the SEHK on 5 July 2019, almost exactly two years following its initial suspension.[20]

B. Since August 2018

In its Consultation Paper titled 'Delisting and Other Rule Amendments' issued in September 2017 it was highlighted that:

> In 2015, the Listing Committee reviewed the delisting policy and considered it necessary to adopt a more robust delisting policy in the interest of maintaining the reputation of the Hong Kong market. The existence of long suspended issuers in persistent breach of the Rules in a material manner, or suspected of illegal or improper activities, undermines the quality of our market and its reputation. A robust delisting policy with an effective delisting procedure will facilitate an orderly exit of poor quality issuers, incentivize suspended issuers to act promptly towards resumption and provide a deterrent effect against issuers committing

[17] As there is no equivalent of PN17 for GEM, there are no 'stages of delisting', see ch 9 of the GEM Listing Rules (n 1).

[18] See n 16.

[19] SEHK, *Monthly Prolonged Suspension Status Report (Main Board) (as at 31 December 2018)*. Available at: www.hkex.com.hk/-/media/HKEX-Market/Listing/Rules-and-Guidance/Disciplinary-and-Enforcement/Enforcement-Newsletter/psuspenrep_mb_20181231.pdf.

[20] Primeview Holdings Limited, 'Fulfilment of Resumption Conditions and Resumption of Trading' (4 July 2019). Available at: www.hkexnews.hk/listedco/listconews/sehk/2019/0704/ltn20190704568.pdf. The company has since changed its name to Artini Holdings Limited.

> material breaches of the Rules. This will also provide more certainty to the market on how the Exchange handles suspended issuers and brings its practice more in line with other major markets.[21]

The Conclusions to the aforesaid Consultation Paper were published on 25 May 2018 wherein the SEHK proposed a number of amendments to both the Main Board Listing Rules and the GEM Listing Rules to address the concerns over prolonged trading suspensions, couched upon the policy objectives as are succinctly stated at paragraph 28 namely:

> The Exchange does not agree with a respondent's view that the primary purpose of a delisting framework is to promote resumption of trading. Instead, an effective delisting framework enables the Exchange to meet its statutory obligation to maintain a fair, orderly and informed market for the trading of securities, by delisting issuers that no longer meet the continuing listing criteria in a timely manner, incentivizing suspended issuers to act promptly towards resumption and deterring issuers from committing material Rule breaches.[22]

Thus, it is about the maintenance of a quality market where every issuer is Rule compliant rather than about the continued listing of companies that are short of the mark. Nonetheless, the exit for the latter group must be achieved in a fair, orderly and transparent fashion with definitive timelines and objectively ascertainable deliverables. To this end, the SEHK implemented its proposals on the new 'hard deadline' delisting regime for long-suspended companies as of 1 August 2018 ('the Effective Date') which measures included:

For the Main Board the addition of a separate delisting criterion to allow the SEHK to delist an issuer after a trading suspension of 18 continuous months; allowing the SEHK to (i) publish a delisting notice stating its right to delist an issuer if the issuer fails to resume trading within the period specified in the notice, or (ii) delist the issuer immediately in appropriate circumstances; and removing of PN17 which will no longer be needed after the new delisting process takes effect.

For the GEM to make changes to align the delisting process with that of the Main Board except for allowing the Exchange to delist a GEM issuer after a trading suspension of 12 continuous months.

To ensure procedural fairness, transitional measures were introduced for issuers whose securities were under a trading suspension before 1 August 2018, namely that the new Rules would not apply to issuers under PN 17 – or other companies having been given a notice period before delisting – as these remain subject to the then applicable Listing Rules; and Main Board issuers which have been suspended for 12 continuous months or more – but were not then subject to PN17 – may be delisted if they fail to resume trading within 12 months from the Effective Date.

[21] HKEX, *Consultation Paper – Delisting and Other Rule Amendments* (2017). Available at: www.hkex.com.hk/-/media/HKEX-Market/News/Market-Consultations/2016-Present/September-2017-Consultation-Paper-on-Delisting-and-Other-Rule-Amendments/Consultation-paper/cp2017091.pdf, 7.

[22] HKEX, *Consultation Conclusions – Delisting and Other Rule Amendments* (2018). Available at: www.hkex.com.hk/-/media/HKEX-Market/News/Market-Consultations/2016-Present/September-2017-Consultation-Paper-on-Delisting-and-Other-Rule-Amendments/Conclusions-(May-2018)/cp2017091cc.pdf and HKEX, 'Exchange Publishes Conclusions from its Consultation on Delisting and Other Rule Amendments'. Available at: www.hkex.com.hk/News/Regulatory-Announcements/2018/180525news?sc_lang=en.

Save for the foregoing all other Main Board and GEM issuers are subject to the new Rules effective 1 August 2018.[23]

Thus, in a nutshell, the power to approve the delisting or the cancellation of listing of securities rests with the Listing Committee. Companies on the SEHK may be delisted immediately or delisted if they fail to remedy issues and resume trading before the end of the remedial period specified in the delisting notice.[24]

To assist affected long-suspended issuers[25] as well as to ensure a smooth transition to the new 'hard deadline regime' the SEHK published its Guidance Letter HKEX-GL95-18 Guidance on Long Suspension and Delisting[26] in May 2018 which explained its policy objectives in the following manner:

> The objective of the amended delisting Rules is to keep the necessary trading suspension to the minimum, by facilitating timely delisting of issuers that no longer meet the continuing listing criteria. This, in turn, provides certainty to the market on the delisting process. The delisting Rules are also aimed at incentivizing suspended issuers to act promptly towards resumption and deterring issuers from committing material breaches of the Rules.[27]

Significantly, the SEHK expressly states that:

> Under the Rules, the Exchange will cancel the listing of a long-suspended issuer upon the expiry of the remedial period (prescribed or specific) if the issuer has not remedied the issues causing the suspension and re-complied with the Rules. This remedial period sets a deadline referenced to the resolution of the relevant issues and resumption of trading, as opposed to submission of a resumption proposal as in the previous regime.[28]

With time of the essence, the underlying message is crystal clear – *Act Fast and Engage*. Issuers have a finite time period[29] within which to remedy its regulatory and/or business issues to the satisfaction of the SEHK. During this period, it should regularly engage with, or seek guidance from, the SEHK and update the market with quarterly announcements on its resumption process and business developments.

The mere submission of a resumption proposal is no longer acceptable as the actions to be taken by the issuer must address the relevant issues to ensure full compliance with the relevant Listing Rules *before* the end of the remedial period to avoid delisting. To this end, the SEHK has set out some steps that the suspended issuer should take including[30] promptly identify the key compliance issues and devise a resumption plan with clear timelines to re-comply with the applicable Listing Rule with the objective of resuming trading before the end of the remedial period; to keep the market duly informed with

[23] The marked-up amendments to the relevant Main Board Listing Rules are available at www.en-rules.hkex.com.hk/sites/default/files/net_file_store/Update_121_Attachment_1.pdf, while those of the GEM Listing Rules are available at www.en-rules.hkex.com.hk/sites/default/files/net_file_store/Update_56_Attachment_1.pdf.

[24] Main Board Listing Rule 6.01A and GEM Listing Rules 9.14–9.18 (n 1).

[25] 'Long suspended issuers' refers to issuers whose securities have been suspended from trading for three or more months.

[26] Available at www.en-rules.hkex.com.hk/sites/default/files/net_file_store/GL95-18.pdf. This replaces HKEX-GL66-13 (n 13).

[27] ibid 8 with respect to the Main Board and n 22.

[28] See n 26 above, 12.

[29] This being 18 months for Main Board listed companies and 12 months for issuers that are listed on GEM.

[30] See n 26 above, 14.

applicable announcements (if any) on corporate actions on top of the regular quarterly updates and publication of periodic financial results; maintain adequate internal controls and procedures to ensure full compliance with its continuing obligations under the Rules and applicable securities laws; and actively engage the SEHK with the provision of pertinent and timely information – including a draft resumption announcement for pre-vetting – for the latter to properly assess whether the issues have been addressed and the relevant Listing Rules have been re-complied with.

It is imperative for the issuer to act promptly and definitively for trading of its securities can resume only after the SEHK has confirmed that it has remedied the issues and re-complied with the Rules to its satisfaction.[31] Thus, the onus is now strictly upon the issuers to *resolve and resume* namely, to ensure that all of the relevant regulatory and/or business issues are resolved to the satisfaction of the SEHK to allow for its resumption of trading by the deadline of the remedial period.

During this period – in the discharge of its regulatory actions – the SEHK will, inter alia,[32] issue resumption conditions/guidance to the issuer; review the issuer's quarterly announcements published under Rule 13.24A and other announcements to monitor its on-going compliance with the Rules and resumption progress; pre-vet the issuer's announcements under Rule 13.52(2); and publish monthly long suspension reports on the HKEXnews website.

In addition, the SEHK shall – within ten business days after the receipt of the issuer's written request – confirm whether it is satisfied that the issuer has remedied the issues and re-complied with the Rules to meet the resumption conditions/guidance.[33]

The power to delist rests with the Listing Committee which will – generally – consider and decide on the matter administratively without conducting an adversarial hearing.[34] Decisions of the Listing Committee – together with its reasons – are communicated in writing to the issuer.

While it is within the powers of the Listing Committee to grant an extension of time, this is not a matter of right for the issuer and is only done in exceptional circumstances when factors outside of the control of the issuer prevent it meeting the planned timeframe despite having largely implemented the necessary steps to ensure its resumption of trading on the SEHK. In any event, the Listing Committee is not expected to grant a second extension to the remedial period.[35]

It is noteworthy that companies that are subject to a Rule 8 of the Securities and Futures (Stock Market Listing) Rules ('Rule 8 Suspension') namely, a suspension mandated by the SFC, are not exempt from the delisting procedures under the Listing Rules. However, although the SEHK may delist the company if it fails to resume trading after a continuous trading suspension of 18 months this right will only be exercised after discussions with the SFC.[36]

To assist issuers with their resumption process, the SEHK has provided detailed guidance for specific cases of trading suspension as follows:

[31] ibid 15.
[32] ibid 16.
[33] ibid 17.
[34] Main Board Listing Rule 2A.08 and GEM Listing Rule 3.09 (n 1).
[35] See n 26 above, 22 and 47.
[36] ibid 60–62. This is further discussed in the section titled 'Rule 8 Suspensions' under 'Case Studies' below.

(i) Failure to Maintain Sufficient Operations or Assets under Rule 13.24[37]

In essence, to resume trading an issuer must demonstrate to the satisfaction of the SEHK that it has a business that has substance and is viable and sustainable in the longer term. To this end, Guidance Letters have been issued to cater to a number of different scenarios including reverse takeovers, transformation into a substantially different business[38] and large issue of securities for cash.[39] In situations where a reverse takeover is envisaged, the SEHK will treat the resumption plan as a new application for an initial public offering in which case an A1 application would have to be filed by the issuer.[40]

During this period, the issuer is required to publish quarterly announcements on resumption progress as well as announcements on its financial results and reports to demonstrate its financial performance and position. To demonstrate its re-compliance with Main Board Listing Rule 13.24, the issuer must produce a circular with information supporting the viability and sustainability of its restructured business which meets with the requirements of the SEHK.

(ii) Failure to Publish Financial Results or Inside Information Due to Material Irregularities[41]

These irregularities include alleged material accounting or lapses in corporate governance practices or significant weaknesses in internal controls, pertaining to both periodic financial and/or inside information. Examples of material accounting irregularities that are detected by the auditors of the issuers include concerns about the authenticity of documents or the nature and commercial substance of material transactions, failure to keep proper books and records, lack of evidence to substantiate the existence and/or the ownership of material assets and discrepancies in accounting records. Apart from the above, it can also extend to actual or suspected corporate irregularities including potentially fraudulent activities.

To achieve re-compliance with the Listing Rules and resumption of trading the issuer would be expected take a number of affirmative steps including – where applicable – the setting up of an independent committee to review matters which involves involvement of director(s); engaging forensic accountants and/or independent control system experts should the issues revolve around internal control systems; actively engaging the company's auditors to resolve outstanding or unresolved issues or replacing them promptly where auditors have resigned; and continue to publish periodic results and reports.

[37] ibid 27–36.

[38] HKEX, 'Guidance on sufficiency of operations, HKEX Guidance Letter HKEX GL-106-19' (October 2019). Available at: www.en-rules.hkex.com.hk/sites/default/files/net_file_store/GL106-19.pdf. This issue has also been the subject of a number of Listing Decisions including LD115-2017 to LD117-2017. Available at: www.hkex.com.hk/-/media/HKEX-Market/Listing/Rules-and-Guidance/Interpretation-and-Guidance/Consolidated-PDFs/Listing-Decisions/ld_2017.pdf.

[39] HKEX, 'Guidance on large scale issues of securities, HKEX Guidance Letter HKEX-GL-105-19'. Available at: www.en-rules.hkex.com.hk/sites/default/files/net_file_store/GL105-19.pdf.

[40] HKEX, 'Guidance on application of the reverse takeover rules, HKEX Guidance Letter HKEXGL-104-19' (October 2019). Available at: www.hkex.com.hk/-/media/HKEX-Market/Listing/Rules-and-Guidance/Interpretation-and-Guidance/Guidance-Letters/gl104_19_preversion.pdf?la=en. Form A1 Listing Application Form (For Equity Securities and Debt Securities). Available at: www.en-rules.hkex.com.hk/rulebook/listing-application-form-equity-securities-and-debt-securities.

[41] See n 26 above, 37–46.

Importantly, to restate the obvious, when the issuer seeks a resumption of trading on the SEHK the onus rests on it to show that it has satisfactorily addressed all the relevant issues supported by all relevant information to attest to the issuer's suitability for listing.[42]

(iii) Insufficient Public Float

Where the reason for the trading suspension is an insufficient public float, the SEHK would expect the issue to be resolved within a reasonably short period of time and may impose a specific remedial period of not more than six months.[43] This is so as the SEHK is of the opinion that prolonged suspensions due to insufficient public float are mostly caused by major shareholders' refusal to cooperate with the management of the issuer to resolve the issue.[44] In order for trading to be resumed the issuer must announce the completion of relevant transactions and arrangements causing the issuer to restore sufficient public float.[45]

Despite the uncertainties brought about by Covid-19, interest in listing on the Main Board of the SEHK has not dampened in recent years as evident by the 10 per cent increase in the number of listed companies to 2,283 over a five-year period ending 31 December 2023. However, as illustrated in Tables 16.3 and 4 below, there has also been an increase in the number of delistings as well as of companies which trading has been suspended for at least three months on both the Main Board as well as GEM of the SEHK over the same period.

Table 16.3 Summary of Suspensions and Delistings on the Main Board of the SEHK from 2019 to 2023[46]

Year	**2019**	**2020**	**2021**	**2022**	**2023**
Cancellations of listing	13	23	21	37	34
Companies suspended for three months or more	42	43	83	78	53
Companies given notice for delisting	0	8	4	11[47]	8
Total number of listed companies[48]	2,071	2,170	2,219	2,257	2283

[42] HKEX, 'Listing Decision LD114-2017'. Available at: www.en-rules.hkex.com.hk/sites/default/files/net_file_store/ld114-2017.pdf.

[43] See n 26 above, 58.

[44] ibid 57.

[45] ibid 59.

[46] HKEX, 'Report on Initial Public Offering Applications, Delisting and Suspensions' for the years ending 2019 (available at: www.hkex.com.hk/News/Market-Communications/2019/191231news?sc_lang=en); 2020 (available at: www.hkex.com.hk/News/Market-Communications/2020/201231news?sc_lang=en); 2021 (available at: www.hkex.com.hk/News/Market-Communications/2021/211231news?sc_lang=en); 2022 (available at: www.hkex.com.hk/News/Market-Communications/2022/221230news?sc_lang=en) and 2023 (available at: www.hkex.com.hk/News/Market-Communications/2023/231229news?sc_lang=en).

[47] With the repeal of PN17 the Listing Committee is empowered under Main Board Listing Rule 6.01A and GEM Listing Rule 9.14A to cancel the listing of companies whose securities have been suspended from trading on the SEHK for a continuous period of 18 months for the former and 12 months for the latter. This period may be shortened by the SEHK.

[48] See n 16 above.

Table 16.4 Summary of Suspensions and Delistings on GEM of the SEHK from 2019 to 2023[49]

Year	2019	2020	2021	2022	2023
Cancellations of listing	6	8	13	10	10
Companies suspended for three months or more	12	13	15	16	17
Companies given notice for delisting	1	1	0	1	0
Total number of listed companies[50]	378	368	353	340	326

The initial success of the 'hard deadline' regime in meeting its stated policy objectives namely, to keep the necessary trading suspension to the minimum by facilitating timely delisting of issuers that no longer meet the continuing listing criteria as well as to incentivise suspended issuers to act promptly towards resumption is evident from the following excerpt from the Listing Committee Report 2020 at the conclusion of the first full year of its implementation:

> For the year ended 31 December 2020, 15 suspended companies successfully resolved their regulatory issues and resumed trading (12 of them were subject to the New Delisting Regime) and 31 suspended companies were delisted (14 of them were subject to the New Delisting Regime). The New Delisting Regime also effectively shortens the suspension periods by incentivising issuers to re-comply with the Listing Rules and delisting issuers in persistent breach of the Listing Rules. Of the 12 resumed companies, nine were able to resolve their regulatory issues and resumed trading within one year after the trading suspension. The average suspension period of the 14 delisted companies was around 1.6 years.[51]

Recent uncertainties have surfaced in global financial markets which has seen, *inter alia*, the collapse of Silicon Valley Bank,[52] a Californian based bank that specialises in the provision of loans to tech start-ups, as well as the material weaknesses in reporting and control procedures at Credit Suisse leading to the takeover of the second largest bank in Switzerland by UBS.[53]

From the perspective of the SEHK, it is not unreasonable to expect the reverberations to adversely affect companies in terms of their operations and/or cash flow, at least in the short term, which could lead to an increasing number of trading suspensions. This may further compound the trend of long-suspended companies which is evident since the start of the Covid-19 pandemic in 2020 namely, those that have trading suspensions of at least three months as well as those that have been given notices for delisting.

This trend will be of particular significance given the efficacy of the 'hard deadline' regime that has been in place since 1 August 2018 as time will be of the essence to an

[49] See n 46 above.

[50] See n 16 above.

[51] Available at: www.hkex.com.hk/-/media/HKEX-Market/Listing/How-We-Regulate/Listing-Committee/Listing-Committee-Report/AnnualRpt_2020dec.pdf, 77.

[52] A Hetler, 'Silicon Valley Bank Collapse Explained: What You Need to Know' (*TechTarget*, 13 March 2024). Available at: www.techtarget.com/whatis/feature/Silicon-Valley-Bank-collapse-explained-What-you-need-to-know.

[53] UBS Group AG and UBS AG, 'UBS to acquire Credit Suisse'. Available at: www.ubs.com/global/en/media/display-page-ndp/en-20230319-tree.html?campID=SEM-UBSADVICE-HK-ENG-Google-UBSAdvice_Lead_Gen_SEM_HK_ENG_BrandCSMerger_Exact-Brand_CSMerger-ubs%20takeover%20credit%20suisse-Exact-c.

increasing number of issuers which have to ensure re-compliance with the applicable Listing Rules within a prescribed period or risk being delisted from the SEHK.

III. Reviews and Judicial Pronouncements

Prior to 6 July 2019, reviews of Listing Committee decisions were initially undertaken by the Listing (Review) Committee or the Listing (Disciplinary Review) Committee which comprised the same members as the Listing Committee albeit with a panel consisting of different, non-conflicted members to review the decision. To enhance the structural independence in decision-making, and to further improve efficiency by reducing the review of decisions of material significance to only one level, a new independent Listing Review Committee ('LRC') was established on 6 July 2019 in line with the Consultation Conclusions on Review Structure in relation to Listing Committee Decisions.[54]

Significantly – to ensure independence – membership of the revamped LRC expressly excludes current members of the Listing Committee as well as members or representatives of the SFC or HKEX.[55] Thus, upon its establishment, the LRC became the independent and final review body for decisions made by the Listing Committee. The single-level LRC replaced the two-level review structure that had previously been in place comprising initially the Listing (Review) Committee or the Listing (Disciplinary Review) Committee, and ultimately the Listing Appeals Committee.[56] However, as a transitional measure, any reviews that had started prior to the establishment of the LRC would continue until their resolutions under the then applicable Listing Rules.

Under the Listing Rules if the issuer is dissatisfied with the outcome it is entitled to apply for a review of the decision to the LRC.[57] When initiated, the LRC will conduct a *de novo* review on the merits by considering the issuer's case and deciding it afresh – after taking into account all the relevant evidence and arguments that may be advanced by the issuer in writing and/or orally – at an oral hearing.[58]

Table 16.5 below summarises the outcomes of appeals on Listing Committee decisions on delisting of issuers by the LRC since its establishment through to 31 December2023.[59]

[54] Available at: www.hkex.com.hk/-/media/HKEX-Market/News/Market-Consultations/2016-Present/August-2018-Review-Structure-to-LC-Decisions/Conclusions-(January-2019)/cp201808cc.pdf. For details of the LRC see HKEX, 'Listing Review Committee', see https://www.hkex.com.hk/Listing/How-We-Regulate/Listing-Review-Committee?sc_lang=en.

[55] The Hong Kong Exchanges and Clearing Limited ('HKEX') is the listed holding company of the SEHK, see HKEX, 'About HKEX'. Available at: www.hkexgroup.com/about-hkex/about-hkex?sc_lang=en.

[56] Main Board Listing Rule 2B.07. Available at: www.hkex.com.hk/-/media/HKEX-Market/Listing/Rules-and-Guidance/Listing-Rules-Contingency/Amendments-to-Main-Board-Listing-Rules/2018/Update-No-121/mb_delist_1805.pdf on the powers of the Listing Appeals Committee.

[57] Main Board Listing Rule 2A.27K and GEM Listing Rule 3.38K (n 1). The SFC may also request a review of any matter.

[58] Main Board Listing Rule 2A.27L and GEM Listing Rules 3.38L (n 1). In the interests of transparency and accountability the non-disciplinary decisions of the LRC are routinely published and available at www.en-rules.hkex.com.hk/rulebook/listing-review-committee-decisions.

[59] Extracted from the annual reports of the Listing Committee for 2019. Available at: www.hkex.com.hk/-/media/HKEX-Market/Listing/How-We-Regulate/Listing-Committee/Listing-Committee-Report/AnnualRpt_2019dec.pdf, 87; for 2020 (www.hkex.com.hk/-/media/HKEX-Market/Listing/How-We-Regulate/

Table 16.5 Summary of Decisions on Delistings by the Listing Review Committee

Year	2019	2020	2021	2022	2023
Number of cancellation of listings approved by the Listing Committee (LC)	8	19	14	11	19
Number upheld by LRC	8	16	14	10	13
Expressed as a percentage of cases brought to LRC	100	84.2	100	90.9	68.4
Number of decisions of LC overturned by LRC	0	3	0	0	6
Remitted back to LC	0	0	0	1	0

As evident from Table 16.6 below, the implementation of the 'hard deadline' regime has also incentivised issuers to work promptly on their re-compliance with the Listing Rules within the Remedial Period to address their regulatory issues to resume trading on the SEHK.

Table 16.6 Number of Resumption of Trading of Long-Suspended Companies on the SEHK[60]

Year Ending	2019	2020	2021	2022	2023
Number of Issuers	8	15	32	38	53

There has been an upsurge in the number of applications for judicial reviews – with no less than 24 cases by the end of 2023 – brought by issuers following the introduction of the Revised Delisting Regime with its 'hard deadline' in August 2018, the establishment of the LRC in July 2019, and the revised test for sufficient level of assets and operations under Main Board Rule 13.24 and GEM Rule 17.26 introduced in October 2019.

A. The *Bolina* Case

As at the time of writing there were a total of five such applications in 2020, six in 2021, four in 2022 and a further nine in 2023. Of these judgments, that of the Court of First Instance in *Bolina Holding Co Ltd (in Liquidation) v SEHK*[61] ('Bolina') is instructive on the legal status of the current delisting framework.

The facts in *Bolina* are relatively straightforward. The company was listed on the SEHK on 13 July 2012 and its shares was suspended from trading on 17 September 2018 when a winding-up order was made against the company on the grounds that it was unable to pay its debts. Liquidators were appointed by an order of the High Court

Listing-Committee/Listing-Committee-Report/AnnualRpt_2020dec.pdf, 114; for 2021 (www.hkex.com.hk/-/media/HKEX-Market/Listing/How-We-Regulate/Listing-Committee/Listing-Committee-Report/AnnualRpt_2021dec.pdf, 118; for 2022 (www.hkex.com.hk/-/media/HKEX-Market/Listing/How-We-Regulate/Listing-Committee/Listing-Committee-Report/AnnualRpt_2022dec.pdf, 101; and for 2023 (AnnualRpt_2023dec.pdf, 95.

[60] ibid 50, 77, 88, 43 and 56 respectively.

[61] *Bolina Holding Co Ltd (in Liquidation) v The Stock Exchange of Hong Kong Limited* [2021] HKCFI 460; HCAL2328/2020. Available at: https://legalref.judiciary.hk/lrs/common/search/search_result_detail_frame.jsp?DIS=133785&QS=%24%28Bolina%2Choldings%29&TP=JU.

on 3 October 2018. Subsequently on 26 October 2018 and 3 April 2019, the SEHK set a trading resumption deadline of 16 March 2020 subject to satisfactory re-compliance with the Listing Rules by addressing four key areas. First, publish all outstanding financial results and address any audit modifications; second, demonstrate that it has sufficient operations and assets under Rule 13.24; third, have the winding-up order against the company withdrawn or dismissed and the appointment of the liquidators discharged; and fourth, inform the market of all material information.

Despite this, the company's financial adviser only submitted a resumption proposal lacking in certain specifics to the SEHK on 16 March 2020 – the stated resumption deadline – which claimed, inter alia, that the planned audit schedule had been delayed by the outbreak of COVID-19. On the basis of the resumption proposal, the company applied for an extension of the Remedial Period to December 2020. The application was rejected by the Listing Committee and – on appeal by the company – affirmed by the LRC which 'noted that the Company had not met all the resumption guidance and had not resumed trading in its shares, either by the resumption deadline of 16 March 2020 or by the date of the hearing'.[62]

On 27 November 2020 the company applied – on the strength of five grounds – for leave for a judicial review of the LRC decision. These grounds included alleged errors on the part of the SEHK in procedural matters, in not finding the existence of exceptional circumstances to extend the Remedial Period and in finding that there were significant uncertainties with the resumption proposal as well as the decision of the LRC being unreasonable, unfair and inconsistent.[63]

The Hon Chow J was not convinced that the grounds for judicial review had a realistic prospect of success and dismissed the application with costs. The judgment of his Lordship is of particular significance in the following areas which reaffirms and endorses the legal foundations underpinning the present delisting framework:

> … it is clear from that the Guidance Letter that the Prescribed Remedial Period is intended to be strict, and the period would be extended only in exceptional circumstances. Second, whether the circumstances are "exceptional" for this purpose is primarily a matter for the Exchange, not the court, to decide.[64]
>
> The Resumption Guidance laid down four conditions to be satisfied by the Company for the resumption of trading of its shares. It is not in dispute that the Company failed to satisfy at least three of the four conditions[65] … it should have been clear to the Company that it was required to comply with all four conditions before the suspension of trading of its shares would be lifted.[66]
>
> The Resumption Guidance was issued by the Exchange in October 2018 (and supplemented in April 2019). The COVID-19 pandemic did not, however, begin to affect China or Hong Kong until late 2019/early 2000. There was, *prima facie*, time for the necessary audit work to be carried out prior to the outbreak of the COVID-19 pandemic[67] … In my view, the claim that the

[62] ibid 14.
[63] ibid 15.
[64] ibid 34.
[65] ibid 43.
[66] ibid 46.
[67] ibid 47.

> COVID-19 pandemic constituted an exceptional circumstance justifying an extension of time for the Company to comply with the Resumption Guidance has no substance whatsoever.[68]
>
> The Listing Review Committee was, I consider, entitled to take the view that there still existed 'a lot of uncertainties' and the Company had not demonstrated 'with sufficient certainty that it could fulfil all the outstanding resumption guidance within a short period of time or at all'. This view of the Listing Review Committee is in accordance with the relevant legal requirement and reasonable.[69]
>
> The question of whether an issuer should be granted an extension of time to comply with the relevant resumption conditions in any given case depends on the facts and circumstances of that case. The decision in any particular case represents an exercise of judgment by the Listing Review Committee, and should not be treated as setting any binding precedent for future cases.[70]
>
> The Listing Review Committee is far better placed than the court to determine the deleterious effect, in terms of the quality and reputation of, and investors' confidence in, the market, of allowing such companies to continue to be listed on the Exchange.[71]

B. The *Tenwow* Case

In rejecting leave to apply for judicial review in *Tenwow International Holdings Limited (in Provisional Liquidation) v SEHK*[72] ('Tenwow'), the Hon Coleman J provided some important insights on some of the factors that need to be considered on what might constitute 'exceptional circumstances' wherein his Lordship opined as follows:

Delays should not be self-inflicted and issues should be addressed on a timely basis by the company as

> … the slippage in timetable, and the Company's failure to have met its own various milestone dates, leading to what it regarded as substantial necessary further delay. The reasoning that such a further delay could not be considered 'short', and that the various issues remaining were not merely procedural in nature is express.[73]

Due consideration must be given to the totality of the process leading to the decision as

> … focusing on only one paragraph (§41) of the Decision to seek to make good the suggestion that these points were not taken into account is an unfair and inappropriate ignoring of the remainder of the Decision.[74]

[68] ibid 48. This remains a comparatively high bar as to avail itself of this the issuer must demonstrate its inability to meet the resumption conditions/guidance and re-comply with the Rules within the remedial period is caused by disruptions arising directly from the COVID-19 outbreak and not from other substantive issues.

[69] ibid 50.

[70] ibid 52.

[71] ibid 54.

[72] *Tenwow International Holdings Limited (in Provisional Liquidation) v The Stock Exchange of Hong Kong Limited* [2020] HKCFI 2982; HCAL2294/2020. Available at: https://legalref.judiciary.hk/lrs/common/search/search_result_detail_frame.jsp?DIS=132275&QS=%24%28HCAL%2C2294%2F2020%29&TP=JU. Similar to *Bolina*, the application for leave was premised on the decision of the LRC not to grant an extension of time to the company which resulted in the cancellation of its listing under Main Board Listing Rule 6.01A.

[73] ibid 50.

[74] ibid 55.

The exercise of discretion should not be unlawfully fettered by the adoption of rigid policies to the exclusion of individual circumstances as we should

> … accept that a decision-maker must not maintain a policy so rigidly to affect a fettering of its discretion in individual cases. Nor must the policy be blindly applied; the decision-maker must always be willing to listen to anyone with something new to say.[75]

Claims of arbitrariness, irrationality and/or challenges on grounds of *Wednesbury* unreasonableness require a high threshold of proof and

> it does not seem to me to be reasonably arguable to suggest that the LRC acted irrationally or *Wednesbury* unreasonably in reaching its conclusion that the Company's situation did not fall within the exceptional circumstances in § 19 of GL95-18 as might warrant the grant of an extension of the remedial period.[76]

C. The *Cai* Case

The policy objective underpinning the judicial approaches in *Bolina* and *Tenwow* has since been accepted by the Court of Appeal in *Cai Zhenrong v SEHK*[77] ('Cai'). In *Cai*, the appellant – a substantial shareholder who held 25.13 per cent of the shares in Blockchain Group Company Limited – had sought an interim injunction after Coleman J had refused leave for judicial review against the SEHK from proceeding with the cancellation of the company's listing.

As the applicant had indicated that he would appeal the decision to the Court of Appeal, the SEHK agreed to withhold the deadline of the delisting to 4 August 2021. However, a day prior to this deadline, the appellant requested that SEHK extend withholding the delisting to 13 August 2021, claiming that there was insufficient time to prepare his application to the Court of Appeal. The SEHK refused and announced on 5 August 2021 – pursuant to Main Board Listing Rule 6.01A – that the listing of the company's shares would be cancelled effective from 9.00 a.m. on 10 August 2021.

On learning of the refusal of the SEHK on 4 August 2021, the appellant lodged an application for the injunction late that afternoon requesting for the court to dispose of the application on paper. This request was rejected by the learned judge who could not discern any valid reason why his legal team, which had been with him throughout, was unable to make such an application on a timely basis. Kwan VP expressed that: '[T]he impression I gained from the papers is that the applicant is quite used to delay making his application to the court in an attempt to delay or prevent the delisting of the Company'[78] and gave leave to the SEHK to lodge submissions by 10 a.m. on 9 August 2021, the day before the delisting of the company was to take effect.

On that date, having read the papers, Kwan VP agreed with the findings of the learned trial judge below and refused to grant the injunction sought as there was no

[75] ibid 57.
[76] ibid 66.
[77] *Cai Zhenrong v The Stock Exchange of Hong Kong Limited* [2021] HKCA 1179; CACV359/2021. Available at: https://legalref.judiciary.hk/lrs/common/search/search_result_detail_frame.jsp?DIS=137733&QS=%2B%7C%28cacv359%2F2021%29&TP=JU.
[78] ibid 5.

evidence adduced of irreparable harm, to whom would such harm be brought, or of the impact of the delisting. Her Lordship opined that

> … delaying the delisting process is contrary to the policy of SEHK to create a fixed deadline for resumption of trading to ensure that listed companies whose shares have been suspended from trading for a lengthy period should have the listing cancelled. In the present situation, the delisting of the Company has been delayed by more than a year past the original deadline.[79]
>
> As to the contention that withholding the delisting of the Company pending this appeal would only go to enhance Hong Kong's reputation as an international financial centre, this has only to be stated to be rejected. To the contrary, the grant of an interim injunction in these circumstances would have adverse impact on the effectiveness of the current delisting regime, not to mention the reputation of the Hong Kong stock markets.[80]

Significantly, Kwan VP made an order *nisi* that Cai was to pay the costs of SEHK on an indemnity basis as the 'application is clearly devoid of merits'.[81] The law is now well settled and the legality of the current 'hard deadline' delisting framework should not be in dispute.

Thus, the message should be crystal clear: *Act Fast and Engage*. Rather than draw down the clock by challenging the decisions of the Listing Committee and/or the LRC in court – unless these are patently unreasonable when assessed objectively – it would be in the interests of the company and of its stakeholders for its board of directors to diligently and expeditiously address the issues to ensure re-compliance with the applicable Listing Rule to allow for the resumption of trading on the SEHK.

Significantly, the courts have affirmed that the LRC's decisions are not binding on subsequent Committees and that each Resumption Guidance is independent and carries equal weight. The fulfilment of one – or indeed of the majority – but not of all is insufficient and does not automatically justify an extension of time unless the circumstances are truly and objectively 'exceptional'.

It is trite that both the Listing Committee and the LRC draw their membership from a diverse group of market practitioners whose expertise and experience the courts are unlikely to second guess save in the most egregious of scenarios which, given the diversity and composition of these committees, are unlikely to arise. Its members are well placed to make independent assessments of whether there is sufficient certainty about the fulfilment of resumption conditions and courts have consistently deferred to their collective expertise in what are, by their very nature, often subjective judgment calls.

IV. Privatisations

With market uncertainties following the COVID-19 pandemic and the emergence of a potential debt crisis brought about by bank failures with interest rates continuing with its upward trajectory as central banks respond to stubborn inflationary pressures, it is not unreasonable to foresee an increase in the number of 'take private' transactions

[79] ibid 11.
[80] ibid 12.
[81] ibid 13.

leading to their delisting on the SEHK. The catalyst could be a number of factors including unpredictability around the speed and robustness of economic recovery; substantial depression in the share prices of listed companies leading to the perception amongst key shareholders that they are undervalued; the increasing burden and costs of compliance compounded by pressure from shareholder activists; and the availability of private equity funds seeking to deploy their capital for better returns.

This section examines the principal modes of privatisation or 'going private' that are available to companies listed on the SEHK namely, by a scheme of arrangement or by a general offer, which resulting delistings on the Main Board of the SEHK over a six-year period from 2018 is set out in Table 16.7 below.

Table 16.7 Voluntary Delistings and New Listings from 2018 to 2023[82]

Year	2018	2019	2020	2021	2022	2023
Withdrawal of listing by privatisations	2	10	21	18	13	0
Voluntary withdrawal of listing	5	0	3	9	2	13
Newly listed companies	149	161	165	129	89	73

A. Scheme of Arrangement

In a nutshell, a scheme of arrangement is a court-sanctioned arrangement pursuant to the provisions of the Companies Ordinance[83] for shareholders to cancel or to transfer all their shares in the company to the acquirer or the bidder. This is the most common form of privatisation in Hong Kong as it is implemented by the target company, invariably after an agreement between the acquirer and the substantial or controlling shareholders of the target company. Given that this is effectively a takeover of the target company, compliance with the provisions of the Code on Takeovers and Mergers and Share Buybacks ('the Takeovers Code')[84] will also be required.

A key consideration when contemplating a scheme of arrangement is that it is essentially an 'all or nothing' model, meaning that if the scheme is approved, it will be binding on all shareholders regardless of how they voted. Thus, the thresholds are set relatively high to ensure the protection of shareholders; failure to attain this will mean that the offer will fail in its entirety. Significantly, a scheme of arrangement is not suitable for bidders who wish to retain the listing status of the target company as it would not meet the requirements of the Listing Rules once the offer is successfully closed.

In a nutshell, a scheme of arrangement requires the passing of three principal approvals for companies that are incorporated in Hong Kong namely: under the *Companies*

[82] See n 46 above.

[83] Ch 622 of the Laws of Hong Kong. Available at: www.elegislation.gov.hk/hk/cap622.

[84] Available at: www.sfc.hk/-/media/EN/assets/components/codes/files-current/web/codes/the-codes-on-takeovers-and-mergers-and-share-buy-backs/the-codes-on-takeovers-and-mergers-and-share-buy-backs.pdf?rev=64b15447c2aa4132a0f301286cb6f2e1. The Takeovers Code applies where the target is a public company.

Ordinance – approval by shareholders of the company representing at least 75 per cent of the voting rights present and voting at the scheme meeting. In addition, the votes cast against the scheme should not exceed 10 per cent of the total voting rights attached to all 'disinterested shareholders', broadly defined as (a) shares not owned by the Offeror and parties in concert;[85] (b) under the Takeovers Code, by at least 75 per cent of the votes attaching to 'disinterested shares' present at a duly convened meeting with no more than 10 per cent of the votes attaching to all disinterested shares cast against the scheme; and (c) on the attainment of these approvals, the scheme must be sanctioned by the court as approval is not always automatic (as evident in the proposed privatisation of PCCW) (see 'Case Studies' below). In considering whether to sanction a scheme of arrangement, the Court would have regard to (a) whether the scheme is for a permissible purpose; (b) whether members who were called on to vote as a single class had sufficiently similar legal rights that they could consult together with a view to their common interest at a single meeting; (c) whether the meeting was duly convened in accordance with the court's directions; (d) whether members have been given sufficient information about the scheme to enable them to make an informed decision whether or not to support it; (e) whether the necessary statutory majority has been obtained; and (f) whether the court is satisfied in the exercise of its discretion that an intelligent and honest man acting in accordance with his interests as a member of the class within which he voted might reasonably approve the scheme.[86]

While the second limb seems identical under both the Companies Ordinance and the Takeovers Code, due care should be taken in view of the slight difference in the definition of the term 'disinterested shares'. Under the latter, the term is defined as:

> [S]hares in the company other than those which are owned by the Offeror or persons acting in concert with it. Where an offeree company has more than one class of share capital, the requirements in Rules 2.2, 2.10 and 2.11 will normally apply separately in respect of each class.[87]

In essence, the Companies Ordinance defines 'disinterested shares' as being shares held by 'non-interested parties' which groups would include (a) the company which makes the buy-back offer and the non-tendering member, plus their associates and nominees; and (b) the Offeror and his associates and nominees.[88] The term 'associate' of an Offeror or member is defined in section 667.

Although it is the responsibility of the company to decide whether to hold a single or separate class meetings, the court is nonetheless required to consider a number of factors at the 'Directions Stage' including

> … the test for classification of shareholders and whether it is necessary to convene separate class meeting. It is incumbent upon the company to consider whether the similarity or

[85] Companies that are incorporated outside Hong Kong would have to undertake the necessary procedures in their respective 'home jurisdiction'. The most common places of incorporation for companies listed on the SEHK include the Cayman Islands, Bermuda and the People's Republic of China.

[86] *Re Enice Holding Company Limited* [2018] HKCFI 1736; HCMP2705/2017. Available at: https://legalref.judiciary.hk/lrs/common/search/search_result_detail_frame.jsp?DIS=116784&QS=%2B%7C%28HCMP2705%2F2017%29&TP=JU para 37.

[87] See n 84 above, Notes to Rule 2.

[88] See n 83 above, s 674(3).

> dissimilarity of the rights of (a) the disinterested shareholders and (b) the concert parties against the company, and the way those rights are affected by the scheme are such that these two groups can sensibly consult together with a view to their common interest as to constitute the same class, or different classes.[89]

(i) Sanction by Court

As regards sanction by the court, the Court of First Instance has arrived at seemingly opposite conclusions on how to deal with the votes of concert parties. This is set out in Rule 2.10 of the Takeovers Code which, insofar as it is relevant, provides that (a) the scheme or the capital reorganisation is approved by at least 75 per cent of the votes attaching to the disinterested shares that are cast either in person or by proxy at a duly convened meeting of the holders of the disinterested shares; and (b) the number of votes cast against the resolution to approve the scheme or the capital reorganisation at such meeting is not more than 10 per cent of the votes attaching to all disinterested shares.

In *Re Cosmos Machinery Enterprises Limited*,[90] Harris J delivered his opinion on the scope of Rule 2.10 of the Takeovers Code namely, whether the Offeror concert parties should be excluded from voting at the Court Meeting – until then – an important, yet undecided, legal issue. Therein, his Lordship advanced two schools of thought on the meaning of Rule 2.10 of the Takeovers Code:

> First, Rule 2.10 prohibits the offeror concert parties from voting ('Prohibition View'). This seems to have been accepted by Mr Justice Segal in *Re Tonly Electronics Holdings Limited* ['Tonly'].[91] Under rule 2.10 of the Hong Kong Takeovers Code only …, the Disinterested Scheme Shareholders, that is shareholders of the Company other than the Offeror and Concert Parties, are permitted to vote on the Scheme. Second, Rule 2.10 does not prohibit the offeror concert parties from voting as such, but their vote cannot be counted for the purposes of complying with the Takeovers Code ('Non-Prohibition View').[92]

Although the 'Prohibition View' had been assumed to be the norm – and indeed although Harris J was himself the presiding judge in two other privatisations that had adopted this approach[93] – his Lordship nonetheless expressed his preference for the 'Non-Prohibition View' holding that:

> (1) It is more consistent with the natural and ordinary meaning of Rule 2.10. Rule 2.10 does not say in terms that the offeror concert parties cannot vote. Rule 2.10 is only concerned with ensuring that the offeror concert parties' votes are not counted towards the requisite

[89] *Re Chong Hing Bank Limited* [2021] HKCFI 3091; HCMP 968/2021. Available at: https://legalref.judiciary.hk/lrs/common/search/search_result_detail_frame.jsp?DIS=139465&QS=%2B%7C%28HCMP968%2F2021%29&TP=JU, para 43.

[90] *Re Cosmos Machinery Enterprises Limited* [2021] HKCFI 2088; HCMP 601/2021. Available at: https://legalref.judiciary.hk/lrs/common/search/search_result_detail_frame.jsp?DIS=137241&QS=%2B%7C%28hcmp601%2F2021%29&TP=JU.

[91] *Re Tonly Electronics Holdings Limited* [2021] Cayman Grand Court 9 March 2021, para 10. Details of this scheme of arrangement are available at: www1.hkexnews.hk/listedco/listconews/sehk/2020/1030/2020103002084.pdf and a brief write-up by Counsel is available at https://dvc.hk/news/cases-detail/guidance-on-concert-parties-vote-in-privatisation-schemes-re-cosmos-machinery-enterprises-ltd.

[92] See n 90 above, para 2.

[93] *Re Dah Chong Hong Holdings Ltd* [2020] HKCFI 274 and *Re Joyce Boutique Group Ltd* [2020] HKCFI 800.

> majorities. (2) The Non-Prohibition View is also more consistent with the natural and ordinary meaning of section 674(2) of the Companies Ordinance, Cap 622.[94]

His Lordship opined that '[I]n my view it should not be permissible for the notice of meeting to exclude these offeror concert parties because they are also parties to the scheme,'[95] further elaborating that:

> (1) If parties acting in concert with the offeror are part of the scheme, they must be allowed to vote as a matter of scheme law because there must be a meeting of those shareholders subject to the scheme: section 670(2)(b) of the (Companies) Ordinance. (2) *Tonly* is a case on point. There the Cayman incorporated, Hong Kong-listed entity promoted a privatisation scheme with all its shareholders (other than the offeror). Thus the scheme applied to two classes of shareholders, namely shareholders acting in concert with the offeror, and the remaining shareholders ('Disinterested Scheme Shareholders'). The company requested the Cayman court to order that the scheme be treated as a scheme between the company and all its shareholders (save for the offeror), but that only a meeting of the disinterested scheme shareholders be convened in order to comply with Rule 2.10.[96]

Taking the view that the opinion of Harris J in *Re Cosmos Machinery Enterprises Limited* was obiter dicta, Chan J – with the appointment of two Senior Counsel as amici curiae who considered the nature and purpose as well as the genesis of Rule 2.10 – expressed her preference for the 'Prohibition View' in *Re Chong Hing Bank Limited.*[97]

Her Ladyship premised her judgment on submissions of Counsel that had been grounded upon the interplay between section 674(2) of the Companies Ordinance and Rule 2.10, taken together with the natural and ordinary meaning as well as the policy objectives and drafting history of the latter.[98] In light of the foregoing Chan J opined that three types of meetings could be ordered by the Court under Rule 2.10 which involve parties acting in concert with the Offeror namely:

> (1) One Court meeting for all the shareholders to be bound by the scheme with the concert parties undertaking to the Court not to attend and vote at the meeting (*Tonly* §15; *China Netcom*[99] §11).
>
> (2) Two Court meetings for the disinterested shareholders and the concert parties respectively. The Court, however, may dispense with ordering the second meeting if the concert parties have agreed with the company or given an undertaking to the Court at the time when the company sought an order to convene meetings that they will be bound by the terms of the scheme (*Tonly* §§2, 5 & 16).
>
> (3) If the concert parties have agreed with the company or the Offeror to be bound by the terms of the scheme or the offer, then the scheme may simply be entered into between the company and the disinterested shareholders, in which case there is only one Court meeting for these shareholders (*Re Citic International Financial Holdings Ltd*, HCMP1686/2008, 6 November 2008, §1).[100]

[94] See n 90 above, para 3.
[95] ibid para 7.
[96] ibid para 6.
[97] See n 89 above.
[98] ibid paras 48–54, 57–61 and 63.
[99] *Re China Netcom Group Corporation (Hong Kong) Ltd* [2008] HCMP 1452/2008. Available at: https://legalref.judiciary.hk/lrs/common/search/search_result_detail_frame.jsp?DIS=62933&QS=%2B%7C%28HCMP1452%2F2008%29&TP=JU.
[100] See n 89 above, para 64.

Taking this into account and to be fully compliant – or at least as a prudent risk management strategy to minimise the risk of the proposed privatisation being judicially challenged – offerors must ensure that their concert parties irrevocably undertake to the offeror and the target company that they will neither attend nor vote at the Court Meeting; and expressly and irrevocably agree to be bound by the scheme.

Until the issue is definitively settled by a superior court, it is prudent for the judgment of Chan J in *Re Chong Hing Bank Limited* to be unequivocally and accurately reflected in properly constructed wording in all scheme-related documents and statements – especially in the Notice of Court Meeting – regarding the attendance, voting and irrevocable undertaking by such concert parties. This is even more important as Rule 31.1 of the Takeovers Code generally bars the making of another offer for the target company for at least 12 months from the withdrawal or lapse of the offer by offerors – and their concert parties – of failed privatisations.

Offerors should exercise prudence as the Takeovers Code defines 'acting in concert' – used interchangeably with the term 'concert parties' in this chapter – in broad terms as 'persons who, pursuant to an agreement or understanding (whether formal or informal), actively cooperate to obtain or consolidate "control" of a company through their acquisition of voting rights of the company.'[101]

Nine classes are set out, referring to classes of persons who are presumed to be acting in concert unless the contrary is established. However, this classification is not intended to be exhaustive and care should be taken to ensure compliance with the spirit of the Code in seeking to afford fair and equal treatment – so as to protect the rights – of shareholders.

B. General Offers[102]

In brief, a general offer is simply a contractual offer to acquire all the shares in the target company that are not already owned by the acquirer/bidder and its concert parties. These offers can be mandatory or voluntary, as well as being partial or full, and may not necessarily lead to a delisting of the target company from the SEHK.

Generally – given the tight shareholding structure of companies that are listed on the SEHK – takeovers in Hong Kong tend to be 'friendly' rather than hostile. Thus, to succeed the Offeror – or acquirer – needs to secure the support of the target company, or offeree, and of its major shareholders.

General offers are governed under the non-statutory Takeovers Code which sets out 10 Principles and 36 Rules that apply these general principles. Despite being

[101] See n 84 above. Many of the provisions of the Takeovers Code apply to those who are 'acting in concert' with the offeror. This is especially significant as the mandatory offer obligations under the Takeovers Code can be inadvertently triggered and binding on the parties, ibid Note 7A to Rule 26.

[102] SFC, 'Practice Note 20 (PN20) – Guidance note on announcements and documents under the Codes on Takeovers and Mergers and Share Buy-Backs (Codes)' for an informal and non-exhaustive guidance and checklist. Available at www.sfc.hk/-/media/EN/files/CF/pdf/Practice_Notes/PN20EN20250201OK_Clean.pdf?rev=ef6cc813e55c4fff8a8ed94740d1e18c&hash=A96814FBDD5D7830DE9C2AE81E403511).

a 'voluntary' Code without the force of law, it nonetheless represents a consensus of opinion among Hong Kong market participants and the SFC regarding standards of commercial conduct and behaviour considered acceptable for takeovers and mergers, privatisations and share buy-backs, breach of which may be subject to administrative actions including public statements involving criticism, disciplinary actions, suspensions and 'cold shoulder' treatments by the SFC. In certain circumstances, the SFC may also order the payment of compensation to shareholders who have suffered losses as a result of the breach.[103]

Administratively, the Takeovers Code falls under the purview of the Executive Director of the Corporate Finance Division of the SFC ('the Executive') and operates principally to ensure fair and equal treatment of all shareholders in relation to takeovers. Its scope is jurisdiction specific, applying as it does to three types of companies namely public companies in Hong Kong as assessed by the economic or commercial test; companies with a primary listing of their equity securities in Hong Kong; and Real Estate Investment Trusts ('REITs') with a primary listing of their units in Hong Kong.

Designed to provide an orderly framework within which takeover, merger, privatisation and share buy-back activities take place, it affords protection to shareholders by ensuring that there is equality of treatment of shareholders; timely and adequate information is disclosed to enable shareholders to make an informed decision as to the merits of an offer; and a fair and informed market is ensured in the shares of companies affected by takeovers, mergers, privatisations and share buy-backs.

C. Mandatory Offer

In essence – unless a 'whitewash waiver' which is discussed below has been granted by the Executive – a mandatory offer will be required under Rule 26 of the Takeovers Code when a person or persons 'acting in concert' acquires 30 per cent or more of the voting rights in the target company, or undertakes a 'creeping takeover'. The latter refers to situations where a person – or persons acting in concert – acquires more than 2 per cent of the target company within a 12-month period while at that material time having a shareholding of between 30 and 50 per cent.

Save with the consent of the Executive, a mandatory offer under Rule 26 can only be made conditional when the Offeror and its concert parties have received acceptances of more than 50 per cent of the voting rights, commonly referred to as the acceptance condition.[104] However, 'creeping takeovers' under this Rule must normally be unconditional. In any event, general offers must be extended to holders of any class of[105] equity

[103] See n 84 above, para 13.13 of the introduction to the Takeovers Code which specifically applies to rr 13, 14, 16, 23, 24, 25, 26, 28, 30 and 31.3.

[104] ibid r 26.2.

[105] Offers for different classes of equity share capital must be comparable and the Executive should be consulted in advance for such cases: ibid r 14.

share capital of the Offeree whether or not the class carries voting rights and voting non-equity share capital in which the Offeror or concert parties hold shares.

General offers that are made under Rule 26 must either be in cash or have a cash alternative at a price not less than the highest price paid by the Offeror or its concert parties within the six-month period of its commencement.[106] An independent valuation is required whenever the offer price is being satisfied for a consideration other than cash. In addition, should the Offeror or its concert parties purchase shares of the target during the Offer Period, the 'highest price window' will extend into this period.

An Offeror may make an application to the Executive to waive the requirements of Rule 26 under certain specified circumstances. A 'Whitewash Waiver' may be obtained from the Executive if this is separately approved by the shareholders with the underlying transaction.[107] This arises when the issue of new securities as consideration for an acquisition or a cash subscription or the taking of a scrip dividend would otherwise trigger a mandatory general offer under Rule 26.

To get the Whitewash Waiver, the shareholders must pass separate resolutions for (a) the waiver by a vote of at least 75 per cent of independent shareholders at the General Meeting, and (b) the underlying transaction by more than 50 per cent of the independent votes. An independent vote refers to the vote cast by shareholders who are neither involved nor interested in the transaction. Where shareholders approve only of the underlying transaction but not of the Whitewash Waiver, the former may still proceed, coupled with a general offer, provided that the condition for the latter is waivable.

The Executive will normally grant a waiver where the company is in such a serious financial position that a Rule 26 waiver is necessary to allow for the issue of securities without the approval of a vote of independent shareholders. Similarly, a waiver can be granted where a person makes an inadvertent mistake and undertakes to dispose of sufficient voting rights within a limited period to unconnected parties. It is also normally granted where a shareholder who, together with concert parties, holds 50 per cent or less of the voting rights of the company enters into a Placing and Topping-up Transaction with an independent person.

That said, the Executive will normally not grant a waiver if the person to whom the new securities are to be issued, or any person acting in concert with them, has acquired voting rights in the company (save for subscriptions for new shares which have been fully disclosed in the Whitewash circular) in the six months prior to the announcement of the proposals but subsequent to negotiations, discussion,s understandings or agreements with the directors of the company (which would include informal discussions) in relation to the proposed issue of new securities. A waiver will not be granted or, if it is granted, will be invalidated if, without the prior consent of the Executive, any acquisitions or disposals of voting rights are made by such persons between the announcement of the proposals and the completion of the subscription.

[106] ibid r 26.3(a). The consent of the executive is required to vary or dispense with the 'highest price' requirement.

[107] ibid sch VI ('Whitewash Guidance Note').

D. Voluntary General Offer ('VGO')

Any person can make a VGO provided that this would not trigger the thresholds for a mandatory offer as discussed above. A VGO is different from a mandatory offer in that the Offeror can incorporate any conditions except for those which depend on the judgments of the Offeror or the Offeree or the fulfilment of which is in their respective control or discretion.[108] Otherwise the offer would just be a complete sham as the Offeror could withhold fulfilling the conditions to ensure that the offer lapses.

To protect the interests of shareholders, the consideration payable on the acquisition of shares pursuant to a voluntary offer is subject to a number of rules, namely:

> It should not be for a discount of more than 50 per cent to the target company's market price determined as being the lesser of the closing price on the day before the announcement of a firm intention to make an offer under Rule 3.5 and the 5-day average closing price prior to such day.[109]
>
> Where the Offeror or concert parties have purchased shares in the target company within 3 months of the start of the offer period or during the period between the start of the offer period and the Rule 3.5 announcement, the offer must be on no less favourable terms.[110]
>
> If the Offeror or concert parties buys shares in the target company at above the offer price after the announcement of a firm intention to make an offer and during the offer period, the Offeror must make a revised offer which must be announced immediately and this entitlement will be backdated to allow persons who have accepted the original offer to benefit from the revised terms.[111]
>
> Consideration may be in cash or securities unless the Offeror or concert parties have bought for cash shares in the target company carrying more than 10 per cent of the voting rights during the offer period and within six months before the start of the offer period. If this is triggered, the general offer must be in cash or accompanied by a cash alternative at not less than the highest price paid for such shares.[112]
>
> If shares in the target company have been acquired by the Offeror with exchange of securities, this option must be similarly extended to all shareholders with a cash alternative.[113]

A VGO may be made conditional upon an acceptance level of shares carrying a higher percentage of voting rights, failing which the Offeror is entitled to withdraw.[114] For example, the Offeror may set the acceptance level at 70 per cent which operates a condition precedent.

A VGO may not necessarily lead to the delisting of the target company since the public float may still meet the minimum required by the SEHK following the conclusion

[108] ibid r 30.1.
[109] ibid definition of 'Offer'.
[110] ibid r 24.1(a).
[111] ibid rr 16.1 and 24.3.
[112] ibid r 23.1.
[113] ibid rr 23.1 and 23.2.
[114] ibid r 30.2.

of the Offer Period. A resolution by 75 per cent of the disinterested shareholders – with no more than 10 per cent of this group voting against – is required to approve the delisting following a general offer. To protect the rights of minority shareholders against the possibility of holding illiquid shares in an unlisted company, Rule 2.2 of the Takeovers Code on compulsory acquisition by the Offeror applies.

E. Compulsory Acquisition

If the objective is to take the company private with a disinterested shareholders' resolution, the VGO should be set at 90 per cent acceptance; this would allow the Offeror to invoke the statutory compulsory acquisition – or squeeze-out – rights under the applicable law of the place of incorporation to buy out the non-accepting shares.

When the Offeror has acquired at least 90 per cent of the voting rights of the target company, it can rely on section 693 of the Companies Ordinance to compulsorily acquire the remaining shares. This intention must be communicated to the shareholders within four months of posting the initial offer document; the Offeror must provide this notice before the earlier of (a) three months after the end of the offer period of the takeover offer; or (b) six months from the date of the takeover offer.[115] A shareholder may apply to court within two months of receiving such a notice for an order that the Offeror is not entitled to acquire the shares or for an order to vary the terms of the acquisition. Where no such application is made, the Offeror must acquire the remaining shares on the terms of the takeover offer.

A similar right is extended to the minority shareholder to be bought out. Under section 700 of the Companies Ordinance, the shareholder may write to the Offeror to require it to acquire his or her shares. When such a section 700 right arises, the Offeror must notify all the relevant shareholders of their rights. These must be exercised within three months after the later of (a) the end of the offer period; and (b) the date of the Offeror's notice. The Offeror is bound to acquire the shares on the terms of the offer or on such terms as it may agree.

Certain jurisdictions – including Mainland China – do not grant compulsory acquisition rights to the Offeror. Here, the Executive requires that the Offeror (a) allow any minority shareholders to exit their investment and (b) require that when the offer becomes or is declared unconditional it must remain open for a longer period than normally required under Rule 15.3; shareholders who have yet to accept the offer must be notified in writing of the intended closing date and the implications if they choose not to accept the offer; and the resolution to approve the delisting must be subject to the Offeror receiving valid acceptances from 90 per cent of the disinterested shareholders.

Table 16.8 sets out some salient similarities and differences between a scheme of arrangement and a general offer.

[115] See n 83 above, s 694(1).

Table 16.8 Comparison Between a Scheme of Arrangement for Hong Kong Incorporated Companies and a General Offer

Factors	Scheme of Arrangement	General Offer
Delisting	Yes	Yes with Mandatory Offers Not necessarily with Voluntary General Offers
Threshold for Delisting	75 per cent of votes by disinterested shareholders with no more than 10 per cent of all disinterested shares voting against If attained the resolution is binding on all shareholders including those who have voted against the scheme	Acceptance in respect of 90 per cent of the shares to which the offer relates so as to initiate the compulsory acquisition provisions or A resolution by 75 per cent of the disinterested shareholders – with no more than 10 per cent of this group voting against – is required to approve the delisting following a general offer.
Court Sanction	Yes	No
Permissible Irrevocable Undertakings	To vote in favour of scheme	To accept the offer
Restrictions on voting	Offeror and concert parties cannot vote	Offeror and concert parties cannot vote
Shareholders Ability to Block Delisting	Vote by 10 per cent of Disinterested Shares	Vote by 10 per cent of Disinterested Shares unless compulsory acquisition is triggered

V. Case Studies

This section highlights some of the delistings – or attempts thereat – under both the 'old' and the 'new' regimes in Hong Kong.

A. PCCW Limited[116]

This involved the proposed privatisation of PCCW by way of a scheme of arrangement ('Scheme') in 2009 and confirmation of the reduction in the company's share capital which required sanction by the court under the provisions of the *Companies Ordinance*. The proxy advisers – Glass Lewis – analysed the proposal and advised independent shareholders not to approve the Scheme which at that time required a two-tier approval process namely, 75 per cent in value and 50 per cent in number of votes by independent shareholders.

[116] *Re PCCW Limited* [2009] CACV85/2009. Available at: https://legalref.judiciary.hk/lrs/common/search/search_result_detail_frame.jsp?DIS=65708&QS=%2B%7C%28CACV%2C85%2F2009%29&TP=JU.

Prior to the meeting, anonymous allegations – which were reported separately to the SFC and the Independent Commission Against Corruption – arose that Fortis Insurance agents had been given shares in PCCW to induce them to vote in favour of the Scheme. Subsequently, following a random review of the PCCW shareholder list by a reporter, it was reported in the media that there was a large number of new shareholders whose names corresponded to agents of Fortis Insurance, giving rise to allegations of a share splitting scheme involving up to 500,000 shares to assist in the privatisation of PCCW. The article continued that Fortis Insurance Asia had formerly been known as Pacific Century Insurance and had been a listed company in Hong Kong with links to PCCW.

At final count, 1,404 shareholders voted in favour of the Scheme while 859 voted against. On review of the facts and of the evidence – in a case in which the SFC intervened – the Court of Appeal refused to sanction the Scheme holding that:

> If the court knows that there has been some form manipulation of the vote and it cannot be satisfied that the result of the vote has not been achieved by manipulation, it is impossible for the court to give its sanction;[117] in view of the evidence of vote manipulation, that the court could not be satisfied that the vote had been reflective of the proper majority, it would not be right for the court to exercise its discretion on other bases independently of that because the factual basis would not be clear;[118] and if the court is not satisfied that the statutory majority had not come to a decision representative of the class in question, it simply means that the petitioner has failed to discharge his burden with the consequence that the court cannot find it appropriate to approve the scheme. Such a decision on the part of the court cannot be equated with a finding made by the court in a piece of ordinary adversarial civil litigation by a claimant against a particular defendant that such defendant had manipulated the votes.[119]

Although the 'head count test' is no longer required for approvals of schemes of arrangements, the decision of the Court of Appeal in *PCCW* is nonetheless instructive as it confirms – citing with approval Buckley on the Companies Acts (14th edition) – that it is for the petitioner to satisfy the court that

> [there is] compliance with the statute; the class is fairly represented and the statutory majority are acting bona fide and not coercing the minority in order to promote interests adverse to those of the class; and the scheme may reasonably be approved by an intelligent and honest man of that class acting in respect of his interest.[120]

Significantly, the court retains a discretion – and while it should not substitute its view on the commercial merits of a corporate proposal – it is 'not obliged to adopt the view of the statutory majority. This is particularly so when the court is not satisfied that the statutory majority was achieved without vote manipulation practices.'

B. SCMP Group Limited

Following the exercise of an option on 7 February 2013, the two substantial shareholders of SCMP Group ended up with combined shareholding of some 89.4 per cent leaving

[117] ibid 70.
[118] ibid 97.
[119] ibid 122.
[120] ibid 113.

the company with a public float of just 10.6 per cent, well short of the minimum of 25 per cent as prescribed under the SEHK Main Board Listing Rules.[121] As a result, trading in the shares of the company was suspended on 26 February 2013 with a closing price of HKD 1.95 per share on the last trading date prior to its suspension.[122]

To address the issue of the public float, management approached the two substantial shareholders to initiate discussions to ascertain their views on, and their willingness to support, proposals to rectify the same so that trading in the shares of the company on the SEHK could be resumed. Neither party could come to an agreement so the stalemate dragged on.

After more than a year into its trading suspension, the Board initiated a possible delisting proposal on 9 May 2014 with an exit cash offer to be made by the Company which may be made by share buy-backs by general offer. As the company could not reach an agreement with its substantial shareholders on the price at which they would both be prepared to support the proposal, it was terminated 10 months later on 9 January 2015. As a result of the termination, Rule 31 of the Takeovers Code applied to prevent the company from announcing any further offer for the shares for a period of six months.[123]

Whilst the trading suspension of the company's shares continued into its third year, it – now renamed as Armada Holdings Limited having sold its media assets to Alibaba Investment Limited[124] – announced on 5 July 2016 that one of its substantial shareholders, namely KML, which held approximately 74.19 per cent of the total shares of the company had signed a Memorandum of Understanding with an independent third party for a possible sale of the stake.[125]

With the posting of the Composite Offer and Response Document on 4 November 2016, Great Wall Pan Asia (BVI) Holding Limited made an unconditional offer for the company[126] expressing stating therein that as it intended to maintain the listing of the company on the SEHK, it did not intend to compulsorily acquire any shares at the close of the offer acknowledging that:

> Upon the close of the Offer, trading in the Shares will continue to be suspended until a sufficient level of public float is restored, and the sole director of the Offeror and the new Directors

[121] SCMP Group Limited, 'Announcement'. Available at: www.hkexnews.hk/listedco/listconews/sehk/2013/0121/ltn20130121330.pdf.

[122] SCMP Group Limited, 'Status of Public Float and Suspension of Trading'. Available at: www.hkexnews.hk/listedco/listconews/sehk/2013/0226/ltn20130226051.pdf.

[123] SCMP Group Limited, 'Termination of the Possible Share Buyback Offer'. Available at: www.hkexnews.hk/listedco/listconews/sehk/2015/0109/ltn20150109396.pdf.

[124] SCMP Group Limited, 'Very Substantial Disposal in Relation to the Media Business and Special Cash Dividend and Termination off Discloseable Transaction'. Available at: www.hkexnews.hk/listedco/listconews/sehk/2015/1214/ltn20151214049.pdf. See also C Chow, 'Alibaba buys the South China Morning Post: Full Q&A with executive vice chairman Joseph Tsai. Available at: www.scmp.com/news/hong-kong/article/1890057/alibaba-buys-south-china-morning-post-full-qa-executive-vice-chairman.

[125] Armada Holdings Limited, 'Possible Acquisition of Shares of the Company'. Available at: www.hkexnews.hk/listedco/listconews/sehk/2016/0705/ltn201607051158.pdf.

[126] Amada Holdings Limited, 'Composite offer and Response Document Relating to the Mandatory Unconditional Cash Offer by Boci Asia Limited on Behalf of Great Wall Pan Asia (BVI) Holding Limited to Acquire All of the Issued Shares in Armada Holdings Limited'. Available at: www.hkexnews.hk/listedco/listconews/sehk/2016/1104/ltn20161104015.pdf. The offeror is ultimately owned by GWAMC, which is one of the four asset management companies (AMCs) in Mainland China responsible for the acquisition and disposal of distressed assets of the five largest state-owned banks to facilitate the reform and commercialisation of such banks. The sole shareholder of GWAMC is the Ministry of Finance of the People's Republic of China.

> of the Company have undertaken to the Stock Exchange jointly and severally to take appropriate steps to ensure that sufficient public float exists in the Shares after closing of the Offer, which may include the Offeror selling some of its Shares.[127]

The company subsequently announced the restoration of the minimum float requirement under Main Board Listing Rule 8.08(1)(a) with the successful placing of 393,727,502 shares representing about 25.11 per cent of its issued share capital to independent shareholders and a resumption of trading from 15 December 2016 – ending a period of almost four years as a 'long suspended company' on the SEHK.[128]

It is evident that, had the stalemate between the two substantial shareholders taken place after 1 August 2018, the outcome would have been completely different; companies that are suspended due to a failure to maintain their minimum public float would generally be given six months to remedy the situation so that trading in their shares can resume.

In the case of SCMP – instead of being delisted, its remedial process took almost four years to implement given the stalemate between the two substantial shareholders. In the interim, while trading in its shares remained suspended, the company disposed of its media business and assets, leaving its shareholders with a very different company from than that in which they had invested prior to 26 February 2013.

C. China First Chemical Holdings Limited

Trading in the shares of the company was suspended on 31 August 2018 – within the first month of the introduction of the 'hard deadline' regime – which meant that it would be delisted under Main Board Listing Rule 6.01A if trading were not resumed by 29 February 2020 namely 18 months after the date of its initial suspension.

The principal ground for the suspension of trading was the delay in the publication of its 2018 interim results as its auditors had raised concerns regarding some USD 33.4 million in receivables from a co-operative partner of a subsidiary of the company and more time was required to complete the necessary review procedures. This was compounded by the resignation of the chairman of its Audit Committee on 15 August 2018 which meant that the company did not have the minimum number of independent non-executive directors on its board.[129] The delay in publishing the interim results constituted a non-compliance with Main Board Listing Rule 13.49(6) for which a suspension of trading of shares was necessitated.[130]

[127] ibid 17. The company subsequently announced that it received acceptances for 97.57% of the issued shares as at the close of the offer: see the joint announcement at.portalvhds1fxb0jchzgjph.blob.core.windows.net/press-releases-attachments/1224815/ltn20161125425.pdf.

[128] Armada Holdings Limited, 'Completion of Disposal of Shares by the Controlling Shareholder and Resumption of Trading'. Available at: portalvhds1fxb0jchzgjph.blob.core.windows.net/press-releases-attachments/1224810/ltn20161214532.pdf.

[129] China First Chemical Holdings Limited, 'Progress on Appointment of Independent Non-Executive Director'. Available at: www.hkexnews.hk/listedco/listconews/sehk/2018/1030/ltn201810309983.pdf.

[130] China First Chemical Holdings Limited, 'Delay in the Publication of the Interim Results of the Group for the Six Months Ended 30 June 2018' Available at: www.hkexnews.hk/listedco/listconews/sehk/2018/0831/ltn201808319991.pdf.

On 6 November 2018 the SEHK notified the company of the Resumption Guidance which required rectification of the following to ensure re-compliance with the applicable Listing Rules namely (i) to conduct an appropriate investigation into the issues identified by the auditor of the Company, announce the findings, address the auditor's concerns and take appropriate remedial actions; (ii) to publish all outstanding financial results and address any audit modifications; and (iii) to inform the market of all material information for shareholders and investors to appraise the Company's position.[131]

Following some changes to the membership of its board of directors as well as its company secretary in the interim period the company announced on 20 January 2020 that a winding-up petition had been presented by a creditor to the Grand Court of the Cayman Islands which sought to appoint a joint official liquidator as well as to wind-up the company.[132]

As the company had not satisfied all of the requirements of the Resumption Guidance by the mandated date it was notified by the SEHK on 2 March 2020 that the Listing Committee would – on the recommendation of the Listing Division – be making a decision to cancel the listing status of the company under Main Board Listing Rule 6.01A.[133] This highlights that the SEHK will neither tolerate any inaction nor consider submissions of 'partial compliance' as the fulfilment of the requirements as set out in the Resumption Guidance is in essence 'all or nothing' which operates within a strictly defined time period of 18 months.

Subsequently on 6 March 2020 the SEHK informed the company that the Listing Committee had decided to cancel the listing of the company's shares with effect from 9.00 a.m. on 23 March 2020 – which meant that the last day of its listing would be on Friday 20 March 2020 – following 18 months and 20 days of continued suspension of trading of its shares since 31 August 2018.

The expediency of the delisting of China First Chemical clearly illustrates how the current delisting procedure is supposed to work in line with the policy objectives of removing long-suspended non-Listing Rules-compliant companies from the SEHK. In 'plain vanilla' cases – which do not have any special or specific externalities that may warrant an extension of time – companies must satisfactorily address all of the deficiencies as outlined in the Resumption Guidance issued by the SEHK to ensure full re-compliance with the Listing Rules within a strict period of 18 months from the date of their initial trading suspension, failing which it would entirely be within the powers of the Listing Committee to cancel their listing under Main Board Listing Rule 6.01A.

[131] China First Chemical Holdings Limited, 'Resumption Guidance'. Available at: www.hkexnews.hk/listedco/listconews/sehk/2018/1109/ltn201811099989.pdf.

[132] China First Chemical Holdings Limited, 'Announcement in Relation to Presentation of the Petition for the Winding-Up Against the Company'. Available at: www.hkexnews.hk/listedco/listconews/sehk/2020/0120/2020012001029.pdf.

[133] China First Chemical Holdings Limited, 'Update on Delay in Publication of 2018 Interim Results, 2018 Annual Results, 2019 Interim Results and 2019 Annual Results and Despatch of 2018 Interim Report, 2018 Annual Report, 2019 Interim Report and 2019 Annual Report'. Available at: www.hkexnews.hk/listedco/listconews/sehk/2020/0304/2020030401566.pdf.

D. CW Group Holdings Limited (In Provisional Liquidation)

The facts of CW Group Holdings Limited are largely similar as regards the duration of its trading suspension to those of China First Chemical Holdings Limited except that the company applied for a review of the Listing Committee's decision to the Listing Review Committee which ultimately delayed its delisting by some eight months.

Trading in the company's shares was initially suspended as a trading halt at 3.22 p.m. on 11 July 2018[134] – a few weeks earlier than that of China First Chemical Holdings Limited – pending the release of inside information with respect to the appointment of provisional liquidators for one of its subsidiaries, CW Advanced Technologies Limited ('CWATL').[135] However, the trading suspension continued and the company subsequently announced that it was placed in provisional liquidation by a creditor on 4 August 2018.[136]

As the company sought to challenge these actions it received a Resumption Guidance from the SEHK on 4 September 2018 to attend to the following issues to ensure re-compliance with the applicable rules by 31 January 2020, failing which its listing status could be cancelled pursuant to Main Board Listing Rule 6.01A: (a) to demonstrate its compliance with Main Board Listing Rule 13.24 which is a qualitative test to show a business has a level of operations and assets of sufficient value to support its operations to warrant its continued listing on the SEHK; (b) have the winding up petitions (or orders, if made) against the Company withdrawn or dismissed and the appointment of any liquidators (provisional or not) discharged; (c) to publish all outstanding financial results and address all audit modifications; and (d) to inform the market of all material information for the Company's shareholders and other investors to appraise its positions.[137]

Subsequently, some five months later, on 3 January 2019, even as the company continued to operate under the administration of the joint provisional liquidators and after some changes to its board of directors and senior management, the liquidation of CWATL by the Court of First Instance in Hong Kong on 5 December 2018[138] was announced by the company not the court.

On 17 February 2020 – after the 're-compliance date' of 31 January 2020 had passed with the company not having met all of the requirements set out in the Resumption Guidance mandated by the SEHK – it announced that it had (a) been actively – through its joint provisional liquidators – negotiating and formulating a restructuring plan with potential investors and creditors; (b) successfully applied for a moratorium

[134] CW Group Holdings Limited, 'Trading Halt'. Available at: www1.hkexnews.hk/listedco/listconews/sehk/2018/0711/ltn201807119985.pdf.

[135] CW Group Holdings Limited 'Inside Information in Respect of Updates on the Appointment of Provisional Liquidators Regarding CW Advanced Technologies Limited'. Available at: www.hkexnews.hk/listedco/listconews/sehk/2018/0711/ltn20180711978.pdf.

[136] CW Group Holdings Limited (In Provisional Liquidation), 'Inside Information in Respect of Updates on the Applications for the Appointment of Provisional Liquidators to CW Group Holdings Limited'. Available at: www.hkexnews.hk/listedco/listconews/sehk/2018/0807/ltn20180807326.pdf.

[137] CW Group Holdings Limited (In Provisional Liquidation), 'Resumption Guidance'. Available at: www.hkexnews.hk/listedco/listconews/sehk/2018/0917/ltn201809179985.pdf.

[138] CW Group Holdings Limited (In Provisional Liquidation), 'Winding-up of CW Advanced Technologies Limited (In Provisional Liquidation)'. Available at: www.hkexnews.hk/listedco/listconews/sehk/2019/0103/ltn201901031139.pdf.

to 31 May 2020 against enforcement actions by creditors against the company and two of its subsidiaries in Singapore pursuant to section 211B(1) of the Singapore Companies Act (Cap 50); (c) applied to the SEHK for an extension of time to submit its resumption proposal on 31 January 2020; (d) received a reply from the SEHK on 7 February 2020 that this application had been rejected and that the Listing Committee had decided to cancel the listing of the company under Main Board Listing Rule 6.01A; and (e) applied to the Listing Review Committee for a review of the aforesaid decision.[139]

In essence section 211B of the Companies Act (Cap 50) in Singapore is an enhanced moratorium in relation to a court-sanctioned scheme of arrangement between a financially distressed or insolvent company and its creditors where the former is unable to pay its debts. Introduced in May 2017 it was intended to make it easier for financially distressed companies to be rescued in line with the government's policy objectives of making Singapore the corporate restructuring hub for Asia.

Significantly, creditors outside of Singapore are not bound by the automatic stay which is effective upon the filing of the application under section 211B(1) of the Companies Act. Such creditors may continue to pursue other remedies in other jurisdictions outside of Singapore without breaching the automatic stay order which duration can be extended by the court in Singapore. Thus, even if the debtor company were to obtain a worldwide *in personam* stay – by way of an ex parte application filed at the same time as the application for a stay – this will not prevent creditors who are not subject to or within the jurisdiction of the Singapore court from seeking remedies in other jurisdictions.

As was to be expected under the circumstances and taking into account the policy objectives of the 'hard deadline' delisting regime, the company's application to the Listing Review Committee was unsuccessful and its share listing was cancelled with effect from 9 a.m. on 12 October 2020. This meant that the last day of its listing was on Friday 9 October 2020 – almost exactly 27 months since the initial suspension of its shares on 11 July 2018.

It is abundantly clear from CW Group Holdings Limited that – unlike the previous Practice Note 17 regime – the mere submission of a resumption proposal is insufficient and will not affect the time frame that has been set. In short, companies that have been placed under a period of long suspension must fulfil to the satisfaction of the SEHK all requirements set out in the Resumption Guidance and must be fully compliant with the Main Board Listing Rules within 18 months of the date of its initial suspension.[140]

Equally important is the fact that the clock starts to run from the date of the initial suspension of the company's shares – which might be a trading halt in anticipation of the release of material price-sensitive information – and not from the date of the receipt of the Resumption Guidance from the SEHK. Time is of the essence and, barring exceptional circumstances, no extension will be granted. Even so, this is likely to be strictly 'one off' to allow the company some time to address issues that are largely outside of its control in circumstances where it can demonstrate to the satisfaction of the SEHK that it is largely compliant with the Main Board Listing Rules.

[139] CW Group Holdings Limited (In Provisional Liquidation), 'Updates on the Development in Suspension of Trading'. Available at: www.hkexnews.hk/listedco/listconews/sehk/2020/0217/2020021700862.pdf.
[140] *Cai Zhenrong v SEHK* (n 77).

VI. Rule 8 Suspensions

By coincidence, the two longest trading suspended companies on the SEHK as of 31 December 2023 were both subject to Rule 8 of the Securities and Futures (Stock Market Listing) Rules namely, suspensions mandated by the SFC.[141]

Rule 8 provides that where it appears to the Commission that:

(a) any materially false, incomplete or misleading information has been included in any

  (i) document (including but not limited to any prospectus, circular, introduction document and document containing proposals for an arrangement or reconstruction of a corporation) issued in connection with a listing of securities on a recognised stock market; or

  (ii) announcement, statement, circular or other document made or issued by or on behalf of an issuer in connection with its affairs;

(b) it is necessary or expedient in the interest of maintaining an orderly and fair market in securities traded through the facilities of a recognised exchange company on the recognised stock market it operates;

(c) it is in the interest of the investing public or in the public interest, or it is appropriate for the protection of investors generally or for the protection of investors in any securities listed on a recognised stock market; or

(d) there has been a failure to comply with any condition imposed by the Commission under section 9(3)(c), the Commission may, by notice to the recognised exchange company, direct the company to suspend all dealings in any securities specified in the notice.

The issuance of such a Rule 8 notice by the SFC mandates compliance by the SEHK without delay.

The trading of shares in both of these companies – China High Precision Automation Group Limited and China Longevity Group Company Limited (formerly known as Sijia Group Company Limited) – has now been suspended for more than a decade.

A. China High Precision Automation Group Limited[142]

An initial trading suspension on 2 August 2012 was at the request of the company 'pending the release of an announcement in respect of certain price sensitive information' – which appears to have been linked to alleged inconsistencies identified

[141] HKEX, 'Monthly Prolonged Suspension Status Report (Main Board) (updated monthly)'. Available at: www.hkexnews.hk/-/media/HKEXnews/Homepage/Exchange-Reports/Prolonged-Suspension-Status-Report/psuspenrep_mb.pdf.

[142] Listed Company Information can be found via the search function on the HKEX website, which is available at www.hkexnews.hk/search/titlesearch.xhtml?lang=en. The SEHK Stock Code of China High Precision is 0591.

by its then auditor leading to a disclaimer of opinion of scope limitation[143] – with trading resuming the following day. The Rule 8 suspension was not imposed by the SFC until some three weeks later on 22 August 2012.

Per the SEHK, the resumption condition was simply stated as 'Approval of resumption by Securities and Futures Commission (SFC)'.[144] Significantly, a desk review of the four announcements by the company since then has not disclosed the reasons for its extended suspension under Rule 8; its most recent announcement stated that:

'The Company had made a resumption application under section 9 of the Securities and Futures (Stock Market Listing) Rules in order to address the regulator with the aim of resuming trading in the shares of the Company. Up to the date of this announcement, save as disclosed, there is no material update in relation to the Suspension. The Company will continue to comply with the relevant Listing Rules, and will make further announcements as and when appropriate. It is expected that the Company will publish an updated quarterly announcement by the end of April 2023.'[145]

Therein the company also stated that

> as disclosed in the announcement dated 19 June 2019, the Company received a letter from the Stock Exchange (the 'Letter') on 13 June 2019, in which the Stock Exchange stated, among other things, that subsequent to its consultation with the SFC, the Stock Exchange will, until further notice, withhold exercising its right to delist the Company under Rule 6.01A(2)(b)(ii) of the Listing Rules should trading in the Company's securities remain suspended on 31 July 2019.

Thus, even though the company has been long-suspended since 22 August 2012 and that the 'normal delisting date' under the then PN17 procedures would have resulted in its delisting on 31 July 2019, this action has been deferred until a decision on the same is made by the SFC despite more than four years having elapsed since the notice by the SEHK.

In fact, during its decade-long Rule 8 suspension, the company has only made a total of four announcements to update the market on its status, namely on 15 September 2017, 1 August 2018, 19 June 2019 and 31 January 2023. Companies are normally expected to publish quarterly updates under the current 'hard deadline' regime which commenced on 1 August 2018.

This is a grossly unacceptable standard of governance in general and of disclosure because its shareholders are effectively 'locked in' due to their inability to trade their shares on the SEHK. At a minimum it should be incumbent for such long-suspended companies to keep their shareholders apprised of the developments on a timely basis – consistent with the applicable rules as enforced by the SEHK – failing which, the SFC should act to mandate the same.

[143] China High Precision Automation Group Limited, 'Further Clarification Announcement in Respect of Annual Results for rhe Year Ended 30 June 2011 and Announcement for Resumption of Trading' available at www.hkexnews.hk/listedco/listconews/sehk/2012/0802/ltn201208021102.pdf.

[144] See n 143 above.

[145] China High Precision Automation Group Limited, 'Quarterly Update on Recent Development of Suspension' available at www.hkexnews.hk/listedco/listconews/sehk/2023/0131/2023013100197.pdf.

B. China Longevity Group Company Limited[146]

The company initially requested a suspension of trading of its shares on 14 February 2013 ostensibly to clarify 'the announcement of the Company dated 8 February 2013'[147] pertaining to disagreements over some audit opinions and a proposal to remove the auditor. This status remained until it announced via a short Exchange Notice – without any elaboration – that:

> Under Rule 8(1) of the Securities and Futures (Stock Market Listing) Rules, the Securities and Futures Commission, has directed the Stock Exchange of Hong Kong Limited to suspend all dealings in the shares of Sijia Group Company Limited (stock code: 1863) from 9 a.m. today (4/12/2014).[148]

Unlike China High Precision, as discussed briefly above, there appears to be some further clarity with the resumption conditions set by the SEHK for China Longevity namely that the company was required to receive approval of resumption by the SFC, inform market of material information and publish outstanding financial results and address any auditors' concerns.

Despite its decade-long trading suspension, the company does not appear to be taking much action to comply with these conditions, stating in its latest announcement dated 31 January 2023 that:

> As previously provided in the Company's Announcement on 18 June 2019, the Stock Exchange had confirmed that it would, until further notice, withhold exercising its right to delist the Company under Rule 6.01A(2)(b)(ii) should the trading in the Company's securities remain suspended on 31 July 2019. As of the date of this announcement, the Company has not received any notice from the Stock Exchange stating that it is proceeding to delist the Company.

According to a letter from the Commission Secretary to its Enforcement Divisions ('ENF') and the Company dated 5 March 2021, the company's Board had 'considered the Resumption Application at its adjourned meeting on 22 February 2021. The said meeting was again adjourned pending further information from the Company. The Company understands that up to the date hereof the Board has not made a decision on the Resumption Application and may seek further information from the Company'.[149]

Based on this, it does not appear that the company is taking any concrete steps towards resuming the trading of its shares on the SEHK despite the SFC suggesting in 2019 that the company should submit 'a written representation to the Board of the Commission pursuant to Section 9 of the Securities and Futures (Stock Market Listing)

[146] See n 143 above. The SEHK Stock Code of China Longevity is 1863.

[147] Sijia Group Company Limited (as it was known then), 'Suspension of Trading'. Available at: www.hkexnews.hk/listedco/listconews/sehk/2013/0214/ltn20130214124.pdf.

[148] HKEX, 'Listed Company Information'. Available at: www.hkexnews.hk/listedco/listconews/sehk/2014/1204/ltn20141204051.htm.

[149] China Longevity Group Company Limited, 'Update on Suspension of Trading'. Available at: www.hkexnews.hk/listedco/listconews/sehk/2023/0131/2023013100732.pdf. It has made a total of 22 announcements on the subject between 13 June 2014 and 28 October 2022, with the last six from 28 July 2020 being on a quarterly basis.

Rules to address the concerns raised by the Commission in its 'Show Cause Letter' dated 24 November 2014.[150]

More than four years have passed – double the 18-month 'Remedial Period' provided under the 'hard deadline' involuntary delisting regime – since the suggestion by the SFC, yet the company has seen fit to remain unresponsive. Absent publicly available information that is proffered by the company, it would be unjust to draw any inferences save to highlight the difference with China High Precision which announced that it had submitted its resumption application to the SFC with a further update forthcoming 'in April 2023'.

A desk review of the Annual Reports of the SFC[151] over the past decade from 2012/13 reveals an interesting statistic: in the nine years to 31 March 2021, it had only directed the SEHK to impose a trading suspension on issuers under Rule 8 on 26 occasions. Yet, this power was exercised no less than 220 times in 2021–2022 representing an almost 8.5-fold increase over the combined total for the preceding nine financial years. As none were reported under the monthly statistics compiled for 'long suspended companies' by the SEHK, it can be assumed these Rule 8 suspensions were for a period of less than three months.

A number of interesting facts arise from the desk review of Rule 8 suspensions as published by the SEHK and the SFC. The SFC's approach to 'Rule 8 Suspension' issuers appears similar to the previous PN17 delisting regime. Given that these companies are invited to submit written representations to the Board of the SFC akin a resumption proposal, the requisite degree of disclosure appears to differ between actions taken by the SEHK and those imposed by the SFC. The former adopts a more transparent approach in setting out the resumption conditions or guidance, while the SEHK has deferred to the SFC in not delisting these companies despite their having exceeded the remedial period which would normally have resulted in their delisting from the SEHK under 'non-Rule 8' circumstances. There has been no delisting of a 'Rule 8 suspended company' during the six years to 31 December 2023.

VII. Conclusion

The process of 'involuntary' delisting of companies from the SEHK has come a long way. Before 1 August 2018 – when the 'hard deadline' regime was introduced – the process could take years, as all the issuer had to do was to submit a 'resumption proposal' for the consideration of the SEHK. The policy objective seemed to revolve around the facilitation of resumption of trading of the suspended shares, perhaps a result of the more relaxed rules on 'backdoor listing' which gave rise to the significant economic value of 'shell companies'.[152]

[150] ibid.

[151] Consistent with the tax year in Hong Kong the SFC has a financial year ending on 31 March.

[152] SFC, 'Statement on the SFC's approach to backdoor listing and shell activities'. Available at: www.sfc.hk/en/News-and-announcements/Policy-statements-and-announcements/Statement-on-the-SFCs-approach-to-backdoor-listings-and-shell-activities. See also HKEX, 'Exchange Publishes Conclusions on Proposed Rule Changes Associated with Backdoor Listing and Shell Activities to Strengthen Long-term Health, Quality

Time is now of the essence under the new regime. Companies whose shares are suspended from trading must ensure that they meet all of the Resumption Guidance set by the SEHK to ensure re-compliance with the applicable Listing Rules for its shares to resume trading within 18 months of the date of its initial suspension – or an even shorter period of six months if the breach is an insufficient public float – whether this is at the request of the company or imposed by the SEHK or the SFC. It is no longer sufficient for the issuer just to submit a resumption proposal sometime during the third stage of delisting as was the common practice when PN17 was in effect.

Two distinct trends seem to be emerging as regards long-suspended companies on the SEHK since the introduction of the 'hard deadline delisting regime' on 1 August 2018. These may attest to the realisation of SEHK's policy objectives, namely that the process of delisting 'non-Listing-Rules-compliant' issuers is being done on a more timely and transparent manner; and the incidence of companies meeting the resumption guidance to be 'Main Board Listing Rule complaint' within the mandated 18-month remedial period is gradually increasing.

The courts have consistently ruled in favour of the SEHK in judicial reviews brought by issuers, upholding both the policy objectives as well as the framework; this has a rigorous process grounded in the expertise of the experienced market practitioners who make up the Listing Committee and the Listing Review Committee. Absent egregious abuses of process, it is highly unlikely that the courts would seek to substitute their views over those arrived at by senior practitioners in the capital markets. So, the regulatory message on involuntary delistings from the SEHK comes through loud and crystal clear: *Act Fast and Engage*.

Companies can also be voluntary delisted from the SEHK or 'privatised' by way of court-sanctioned schemes of arrangement or through takeovers by way of a mandatory offer or a voluntary general offer (although it should be noted that the last does not guarantee delisting). While seemingly identical, care must be taken to ensure complete compliance with provisions of both the Companies Ordinance as well as the Takeovers Code to minimise risks of judicial challenges, especially when it comes to documentation and voting.

Given current market volatility, it is likely that the incidence of privatisations will increase and it is imperative that Offerors are aware that they – and their concert parties – will be prevented from making another bid for the target company for at least 12 months should their attempt at 'going private' fail.

While there is a need to balance the interests of the issuers and the regulators, better clarity of policy objectives and transparency of disclosure would benefit the 'Rule 8 regime' administered by the SFC. It may, perhaps, be an appropriate time to review the consistency of policy objectives such as applying a common 'remedial period' as well as mandating written submissions by the company in manner that is similar to the 'Resumption Guidance' practiced by the SEHK since 1 August 2018.

Thus, the SFC can and should exercise broad powers under Rule 8 by specifying the breaches that it alleges of the issuer as does the SEHK in its Resumption Guidance.

and Sustainability of the Market'. Available at: www.hkex.com.hk/News/Regulatory-Announcements/2019/190726news?sc_lang=en.

Thereafter, the clock starts to run with the SEHK administering the process leading to either a resumption of trading of the company's shares or its delisting – as may be premised on the established processes – within an 18-month period.

This could address the apparent anomaly and present a clear regulatory regime whereby the SFC undertakes the exercise of its regulatory functions while leaving the SEHK to attend to the 'business end' of the delisting process within a common rigorous framework set up by experienced practitioners.

17

Delisting in India

HARPREET KAUR*

I. Introduction

Globalisation has made it mandatory for countries to have an advanced market-based financial system with highly functioning equity markets and stock exchanges as catalyst for economic growth.[1] Markets, being self-functioning entities, are expected to regulate the actions of the market players, by instilling market discipline through ex ante regulations.[2] However, on the basis of previous experiences of financial market scams, an amalgam of market discipline and regulatory discipline is being followed worldwide.[3] Regulatory intervention in the market involves stringent compliance-based regulations and corporate governance frameworks, which are aimed at ensuring safe and fair transactions.[4] Compliance with these regulations is intricately linked with stock exchanges as continuous compliance with regulations is a necessary precondition for companies to be listed on an exchange, and non-compliance is punished by exchanges. Sometimes the cost of complying with these regulations often outweighs the benefits accrued from raising finance through stock exchanges.[5] This, amongst many other reasons, propels companies to delist their securities from stock exchanges.

The listing of a company's securities means that the securities are listed on a stock exchange by virtue of a listing agreement between the stock exchange and the company. Once the securities are listed, they are made available to all traders on the exchange for trading via the exchange.[6] Conversely, the delisting of a company involves the removal of the securities of a listed company from the stock exchange. Delisting in India is regulated by the SEBI (Delisting Regulations) 2021 (Delisting Regulations). The Delisting

* Vice-Chancellor, National Law University, Jodhpur, India. Divyanshu Sharma provided the research assistance.

[1] C Hartwell, 'Do (Successful) Stock Exchanges Support or Hinder Institutions in Transition Economies?' (2013) 2 *Cogent Economics and Finance*. Available at: www.tandfonline.com/doi/full/10.1080/23322039.2014.946620.

[2] T Lane, 'Market Discipline' (1993) 40 *Staff Papers (International Monetary Fund)* 53.

[3] ibid.

[4] L Turner, 'Lessons Learned from the Failure of Market Discipline and Regulatory Lapses: How to Prevent Future Busts' (2008) 4 *Current Developments on Monetary and Financial Laws, International Monetary Fund.*

[5] S Thomsen and F Vinten, 'Delisting and the Costs of Governance: A Study of European Stock Exchanges 1996–2004' (2013) 18 *Journal of Management and Governance* 793, 795.

[6] K Mohanty, *Delisting of Equity Shares: Law and Practice*, 1st edn (New Delhi, ICSI, 2016) 1.

Regulations define delisting as the 'permanent' removal of the 'equity' shares of a company from a 'recognised' stock exchange.[7] The definition itself provides for different methods of delisting ie, voluntary and compulsory delisting.[8] Voluntary delisting, as the name suggests, is the volitional delisting of the company's shares from the stock exchange, pursuant to a volition of a company's acquirer or promoter.[9] Compulsory delisting, on the other hand, is a penal action undertaken by a stock exchange for non-compliance with the applicable regulations, pursuant to which the securities of a company are indefinitely removed from the stock exchange.[10] Post the delisting, be it voluntary or compulsory, the shares of the company are no longer traded on the stock exchange's platform; consequently, the company is no longer bound to adhere to SEBI regulations.

Delisting is often wrongly conflated with two other concepts – buy-back of shares and suspension of a company's membership on a stock exchange. Buy-back of shares is a process through which a company purchases its own securities from its security-holders, and then extinguishes securities.[11] Hence, post the completion of a buy-back, the securities purchased by the company cease to exist. The securities extinguished by the company cease to be a part of the company's capital. However, while delisting involves the process of buying-back shares from the shareholders, they are bought by the promoter/acquirer who initiates the delisting and not by the company. The delisted shares continue to exist and remain a part of the company's capital though not traded on the stock exchange. According to the Delisting Regulations, no delisting can be undertaken pursuant to a buy back.[12] Coming to suspension of a company's membership on a stock exchange, it is a punitive measure wherein a stock exchange can suspend a company's membership for a specified duration, for non-compliance with the byelaws of the exchange.[13] Byelaws refer to the rules made a stock exchange for regulating the conduct of the companies listed on its platform. These rules are specific to a stock-exchange and can vary from exchange to exchange.[14] Compulsory delisting, on the other hand, can be undertaken for certain specified reasons (which are not related to the byelaws of the exchange), and the company is delisted for at least 10 years, only after which the company can against apply for listing of its securities.[15] A company can be compulsorily delisted for violating the provisions of certain specified statutes and the rules made thereunder,[16] but not for the violation of byelaws of stock exchanges. These statutory provisions and rules are applicable on all listed companies in India, irrespective of the stock exchange on which they are listed. In the case of *Discovery Wealth Management*

[7] Securities And Exchange Board of India (Delisting of Equity Shares) Regulations [2021] (Delisting Regulations) reg 2(1)(j).

[8] ibid reg 2(1)(j).

[9] ibid reg 2(1)(bb).

[10] ibid reg 2(1)(g).

[11] There is a provision for extinguishment of the securities bought back under Companies Act [2013] s 68.

[12] Delisting Regulations (n 7) reg 4(1)(c).

[13] Securities Contracts (Regulation) Act [1956] s 9(3)(b)(iii).

[14] ibid s 9.

[15] Delisting Regulations (n 7) reg 34(1).

[16] See Securities Contract (Regulation) Rules [1957] Rule 21(d) which provides that a company can be compulsorily delisted for violating the provisions of Securities Contract (Regulation) Act (n 13); Securities and Exchange Board of India Act [1992]; and the Depositories Act [1996]; and the rules, regulations, and agreements made thereunder.

Services v Padmini Engineering Pvt Ltd, the Hon'ble Supreme Court of India clarified that a company can be compulsorily delisted if it does not comply with a condition provided in the listing agreement between the company and the stock exchange, even if the condition is not provided in the applicable statutory provisions.[17]

In light of these nuances of delisting of shares in India, the chapter aims to provide a theoretical and statistical study of delisting trends in India. To that end, Section II discuss the nuances, reasons, and consequences of delisting, as a managerial decision and a corporate action. Section III delves into the Delisting Regulations, delineating the trajectory of delisting regulation in India and the process presently applicable. Finally, in Section IV, the chapter examines the author's statistical research on delistings undertaken on the National Stock Exchange (NSE) from 2009–2022, to shed some light on delisting trends in India.

II. The Delisting Desiderata

A. Types of Delisting

As stated above, delisting in India can be either voluntary or compulsory under the Delisting Regulations. Voluntary delisting refers to the process of removing a company from a stock exchange on the volition of the company's promoter or acquirer.[18] While in the United Kingdom and the United States of America,[19] it is the issuer company which has the option to voluntarily delist itself, in India this option is not exercised by the company, but by those acquiring the company. A promoter is a person or an entity responsible for the establishment and operations of a company. In India, promoters wield considerable influence over a company.[20] Legally, a promoter is an entity/individual who is recognised as a promoter in the offer documents and the annual reports of the company; who has a direct or indirect control over the company; or in accordance with whose advice or direction the board of directors of a company is accustomed to work.[21] Under the Delisting Regulation, an acquirer refers to any person who is desirous of making an offer for delisting of the company's securities and who is an acquirer according to the SEBI Takeover Code or is a promoter of the company.[22]

[17] *Discovery Wealth Management Services Pvt Ltd & Ors v Padmini Engineering Private Limited & Ors* [2014] 16 SCC 158.

[18] Delisting Regulations (n 7) reg 2(1)(bb).

[19] See Code of Federal Regulation, s 240.12d2-2 (USA); Financial Conduct Authority, Listing Rules, r 5.2.4 (UK).

[20] H Kaur, 'Promoters and Corporate Governance under the Companies Act, 2013 and Allied Acts in India' (2015) 3 *Journal of National Law University Delhi* 53.

[21] Securities and Exchange Board of India (Issue of Capital and Disclosure Requirements) Regulations [2018] reg 2(1)(oo).

[22] Delisting Regulations (n 7) reg 2(1)(b). See Securities and Exchange Board of India (Substantial Acquisition of Shares and Takeovers) Regulations [2011] reg 2(1)(a) which defines an acquirer as 'a person who, directly or indirectly, acquirers or agrees to acquire whether by himself, or through, or with persons acting in concert with him, shares or voting rights in, or control over a target company'.

In India, there has been a perceptible rise in the number of delistings over the years.[23] It is usually believed that the listed status of a company is highly advantageous due to easy access to large amounts of capital, investor wealth maximisation, and higher managerial remuneration per the success of the company.[24] Broadly speaking, the decision to delist is the outcome of the company's failure to extract the benefits of being listed at an optimal cost.[25] However, there are multiple nuances to the decision to delist, which shall be discussed in the latter part of this section.

This cost–benefit analysis of the decision to delist might not always be uniform across all the stock exchanges where the company is listed. This means that sometimes a company might benefit from continuing its membership on certain stock exchanges as compared to the others. As a result of this, the Delisting Regulations provide for situations when a company might delist its shares from all platforms on which it was listed or might decide to remain listed on at least one recognised stock exchange with nationwide trading terminals.[26] The difference between the two, in terms of the procedure, is that the former requires the acquirer to mandatorily provide an exit opportunity to the shareholders of the company[27] while, in the latter case, no such exit opportunity is mandatory.[28]

The second kind of delisting recognised under the Delisting Regulation is compulsory delisting. In such a delisting, a company's securities are removed from the stock exchange by the exchange itself due to the failure of the company to meet its listing requirements.[29] In this kind of delisting, the company or its promoter/acquirer has no role in the decision to delist. The only role of the company is limited to infractions which push the stock exchange to take such a radical step.[30] According to the Delisting Regulations, a stock exchange can order the compulsory delisting of a company's shares if any of the grounds prescribed in the Securities Contract (Regulations) Act, 1956 are met.[31] However, this order cannot be issued without recognising the due process rights of the company namely, the right to make a representation before the order is passed, the right to be heard, and the mandate on the exchange to issue a reasoned order.[32] Once an order for compulsory delisting is issued, the company, its whole-time directors, promoters, the persons responsible for ensuring compliance with the securities laws, and other companies promoted by such persons are barred from accessing the securities

[23] A Coutinho, 'Number of Delisted Companies on the Rise; Bourses May See More Exits' (31 March 2018) *Business Standard*. Available at: www.business-standard.com.

[24] R Giovannini et al, 'Voluntary Delisting? A Valid Option for Firms Restructuring' (2011) *Midwest Finance Association 2012 Annual Meeting Papers*. Available at: www.papers.ssrn.com/sol3/papers.cfm?abstract_id=1928851.

[25] EK Pour and M Lasfer, 'Why do Companies Delist Voluntarily from the Stock Market?' (2013) *University of Birmingham Discussion Paper 2013-05*.

[26] Delisting Regulations (n 7) ch III.

[27] ibid reg 7.

[28] ibid reg 5.

[29] I Martinez and S Serve, 'Reasons for Delisting and Consequences: A Literature Review and Research Agenda' (2017) 31 *Journal of Economic Surveys* 733.

[30] J Macey, M O'Hara and D Pompilio, 'Down and Out in the Stock Market: The Law and Economics of the Delisting Process' (2008) 51 *Journal of Law and Economics* 683.

[31] Delisting Regulations (n 7) reg 32(1).

[32] ibid reg 32.

market or having their securities listed, either directly or indirectly, for a period of 10 years from the date of delisting.[33]

Another kind of delisting which is not directly recognised under the Delisting Regulations is cold delisting, a form of delisting where a listed company is delisted as a consequence of its merger with an unlisted entity.[34] The resulting unlisted company is required to make an adequate offer to the minority shareholders of the previously listed company before completing the merger.[35] This method of delisting is usually adopted to circumvent the cumbersome requirements of the delisting procedure under the applicable law.[36] Cold delisting differs from regular delisting as the aim of the latter is exclusively to delist the company's securities, but the former can have other aims along with the objective of delisting the company.[37]

As stated above, the Delisting Regulations do not use the term 'cold delisting' in India. However, the concept is indirectly recognised under the Indian legal framework. Under section 232(3)(h) of the Companies Act 2013, if a listed company amalgamates with an unlisted company, the resultant entity is an unlisted company.[38] According to the SEBI Takeover Regulations, in such an acquisition/merger, the listed company would be required to make an open offer to the public shareholders of the company before the merger is completed.[39]

B. Why do Companies Delist?

The decision to voluntarily delist is based on a cost–benefit analysis of the stock exchange membership for a company. There are numerous factors which can push a company to voluntarily delist itself, the broad category being that the company is no longer able to extract the benefits of the stock exchange membership at a reasonable cost.[40] Specifically, there are factors relating to the compliance burden of being listed, difficulty in raising finance from the public, and the leverage status of the company. Even in the Indian context, while there is not much academic work relating to delisting reasons for companies, in 1997 the *Dr K R Chandratre Committee* of SEBI, enlisted some reasons for delisting by Indian companies. According to the committee, the main reasons for Indian companies to delist are – the disproportionate economic and compliance cost of being listed; a high compliance burden; the low number of public

[33] ibid reg 34(1).
[34] P Maume, 'The Parting of the Ways: Delisting Under German and UK Law' (2015) 16 *European Business Organization Law Review* 255.
[35] ibid.
[36] I Martinez and S Serve, 'The Delisting Decision: The Case of Buyout Offer with Squeeze-out (BOSO)' (2011) 31 *International Review of Law and Economics* 228.
[37] D Zetzsche, 'Going Dark Under German Law – Towards an Efficient Regime for Regular Delisting' (2013) 0053 *Working Paper CBC-RPS* 1.
[38] Companies Act (n 11) s 232(3)(h)(A).
[39] Substantial Acquisition of Shares and Takeover Regulations (n 22) reg 5A.
[40] Pour and Lasfer, 'Why do Companies Delist Voluntarily from the Stock Market?' (n 25).

shareholders of the company; very low trading volume in the company's shares; and mergers and takeovers.[41]

Coming to the specific reasons, one of the fundamental reasons for companies to delist is the high cost of compliance associated with the listed status of a company.[42] Listed companies, all over the world, have to comply with a large number of regulations, make regular disclosures, constantly comply with corporate governance requirements, and ensure profitable operations at the same time.[43] In the Indian context, listed companies are required to comply with governance norms under SEBI (Listing Obligations and Disclosure Requirements) Regulations,[44] and ensure constant vigilance and compliance with the Insider Trading Regulations.[45] The overall cost of compliance with these requirements becomes greater for companies with lower profits and less liquidity.[46] In such a situation, delisting becomes a reasonable and profitable option for companies.

Apart from compliance costs, there is also an economic cost of being listed. Companies are required to pay fees to a stock exchange for their continued membership. In India, the quantum of fees payable depends on the market capitalisation of the company and its paid-up capital.[47] While the fees might not seem to be high for firms who can attract a greater number of investors on the stock exchange, firms with less 'financial visibility' see the listing fees as an unreasonable expenditure.[48] Thus, if a listed entity is no longer able to arrange the desired amount of liquid funds from the exchange, which is the main purpose of listing,[49] then the continued economic cost of remaining listed seems futile.[50] Similarly, listed firms have to bear the economic cost of undertaking regular audits. According to *Marosi and Massoud*, even a miniscule increase in audit-related costs can push companies towards delisting.[51]

There are some specific factors related to the internal composition and future plans of firms which affect their decision to delist. If the controlling shareholder feels that the level of risk is not extremely high, which the shareholder wants to share with the public, and intends to consolidate his control within the firm, he might propose delisting the firm.[52] Similarly, if the company has future growth plans and is able to fund its current

[41] Ministry of Corporate Affairs, *Chandratre Committee of the Working Group on the Companies Act* (1997) available at www.mca.gov.in/mca/html/mcav2_en/home/dataandreports/reports/library/library.html.

[42] A Marosi and N Massoud, 'Why Do Firms Go Dark?' (2007) 42 *The Journal of Financial and Quantitative Analysis* 421.

[43] ibid.

[44] See, generally, Securities and Exchange Board of India (Listing Obligations and Disclosure Requirements) Regulations [2015].

[45] See, generally, Securities and Exchange Board of India (Prohibition of Insider Trading) Regulations [2015].

[46] Martinez and Serve, 'Reasons for Delisting' (n 29) 733.

[47] See Bombay Stock Exchange, *Listing Fees*. Available at: www.bseindia.com/Static/about/listing_fees.aspx; National Stock Exchange, *Listing Fees – Main Board*. Available at: www.nseindia.com/companies-listing/raising-capital-public-issues-listing-fees.

[48] Martinez and Serve, 'Reasons for Delisting' (n 29) 733.

[49] L Zingales, 'Insider Ownership and the Decision to Go Public' (1995) 62 *The Review of Economic Studies* 425; A S Mello and J E Parsons, 'Going Public and the Ownership Structure of the Firm' (1998) 49 *Journal of Financial Economics* 79.

[50] ST Bharath and AK Dittmar, 'Why do Firms Use Private Equity to Opt Out of Public Markets' (2010) 23 *The Review of Financial Studies* 1771.

[51] Marosi and Massoud, 'Why Do Firms Go Dark?' (n 42) 421.

[52] Martinez and Serve, 'The Delisting Decision' (n 36) 228.

projects internally, at a lesser cost, then delisting might seem to be a prudent choice.[53] Lastly, if a firm is highly leveraged, it would be able to finance its operations at a lower cost from avenues other than the stock exchange. Thus, the firm might decide to delist.[54]

Coming to reasons for compulsory delisting, they are quite straightforward – non-compliance with the listing requirements by a company and the unprofitable membership of the company on the stock exchange.[55] Even in the Indian context, the main causes for compulsory delisting are the non-payment of the listing fees, non-compliance with the listing requirements, negligible trading volume, and improper market practices of the company.[56] Unlike in the US, where stock exchanges themselves decide the delisting criteria for companies,[57] in India the grounds for mandatory delisting are statutorily provided: if the company has incurred losses for three consecutive years and has a negative net worth; trading of the company's securities has been suspended for more than six months; the securities have been infrequently traded for the last three years; the company, its promoters, or its directors have been penalised for a regulatory/statutory/contractual infraction with fine of not less than one crore rupees or imprisonment of not less than three years;[58] the minimum public shareholding is below the specified threshold and has not been rectified within the provided time; and if the address of the company, its promoters, or directors is not known.[59]

According to *Martinez and Serve*, involuntary delisting arises where the firm is no longer able to manage the costs of its stock exchange members and is therefore 'obliged by the market to delist'.[60] This failure to manage its cost is hinted by the poor performance of the company's securities on the stock exchange. This poor performance of the company's shares is linked to the fall in the productive activity of the firm.[61] As per *Charitou et al*, the ownership structure of the firm also plays a crucial role in pushing the firm towards involuntary delisting. If the management does not involve sufficient number of outside directors, there is a high probability that the company will fail to meet the listing compliance requirements, and eventually be delisted.[62] From the stock exchange's perspective, the exercise of involuntary delisting power is to instil market discipline, by penalising firms for their non-compliance with the market regulations (which does not include the exchange's byelaws).[63]

[53] Bharath and Dittmar, 'Why do Firms Use Private Equity to Opt Out of Public Markets' (n 50) 1771.

[54] Pour and Lasfer, 'Why Do Companies Delist Voluntarily from the Stock Market?' (n 25).

[55] Martinez and Serve, 'Reasons for Delisting' (n 29) 733.

[56] Ministry of Corporate Affairs, *Chandratre Committee of the Working Group on the Companies Act* (n 41).

[57] Macey, O'Hara and Pompilio, 'Down and Out in the Stock Market' (n 30) 683.

[58] See Securities Contract (Regulation) Rules (n 16) r 21(d) which provides that a company can be compulsorily delisted for failure to company with Securities Contract (Regulation) Act (n 13); SEBI Act (n 16); and the Depositories Act (n 16); and the rules, regulations, and agreements made thereunder. The term agreement essentially includes the listing agreement as well.

[59] Securities Contract (Regulation) Rules (n 16) r 21.

[60] Martinez and Serve, 'Reasons for Delisting and Consequences' (n 29) 733.

[61] ibid.

[62] A Charitou, C Louca and N Vafeas, 'Boards, Ownership Structure, and Involuntary Delisting from the New York Stock Exchange' (2007) 26 *Journal of Accounting and Public Policy* 249.

[63] Macey, O'Hara and Pompilio (n 30) 683.

C. The Consequence of Delisting

The most immediate and direct consequence of delisting, be it voluntary or compulsory, is that the securities of the company are no longer traded on the stock exchange. The decision to delist a company has to be carefully thought-out by the stock exchange, as compulsory delisting negatively impacts not only the company but also the interests of the investors and the shareholders.[64] While voluntary delisting often leads to enhanced value creation for the public shareholders of the company, involuntary delisting is considered to be 'bad news' for public shareholders as there is a massive erosion of shareholder wealth post the involuntary delisting.[65]

Moreover, after the completion of the delisting process, the relisting of securities is not an immediately available option for companies. There is a cooling-off period provided under the Delisting Regulations only after which can a company apply for delisting. In case of compulsory delisting, 'the company, its whole-time directors, person(s) responsible for ensuring compliance with the securities laws, its promoters and the companies which are promoted by any of them to directly or indirectly access the securities market or seek listing of any equity shares or act as an intermediary in the securities market for a period of 10 years from the date of such delisting'.[66] Similarly, the securities voluntarily delisted, pursuant to the Delisting Regulations, are ineligible for relisting for a period of three years from the date of delisting.[67] Further, the delisting also has an impact in terms of value loss to existing shareholders with reduced liquidity due to absence of disclosure requirements and an inability to trade on the stock exchange.[68]

Apart from this, the decision to delist has an effect on the interests of the minority shareholders of the company during and after the delisting process. These shareholders are unable to sell their shares on delisting due to reduced protection with limited transparency.[69] The decision to delist may be skewed in favour of controlling shareholders' interests who may focus on consolidating their own shareholding at any cost.[70] Further, the managerial conflict of interest in delisting transactions may lead to unfair treatment of minority shareholders as the management has greater bargaining power and the incentive to minimise the fair value offered to the minority public shareholders.[71] As stringent SEBI regulations, which afford higher protection to minority shareholders, are no longer applicable post-delisting, minority shareholders are often placed in a vulnerable position.

[64] ibid.

[65] Martinez and Serve, 'Reasons for Delisting and Consequences' (n 29) 733.

[66] Delisting Regulations (n 7) reg 34(1).

[67] ibid reg 40(1)(a).

[68] Marosi and Massoud, 'Why Do Firms Go Dark?' (n 42) 439.

[69] M Florig and O Gossner, 'Unintended Consequences of German Stock Delisting Legislation' (2023) 1 *Centre for Research in Economics and Statistics Working Paper* 16. Available at: www.crest.science/RePEc/wpstorage/2023-01.pdf.

[70] C Lez, A Triantis and T Wang, 'Why Do Firms Go Dark? Causes and Economic Consequences of Voluntary SEC Deregistration's' (2008) RHS-06-045 *University of Maryland Working Paper* 37. Available at: www.papers.ssrn.com/sol3/papers.cfm?abstract_id=592421.

[71] H DeAngelo, L DeAngelo and E Rice, 'Going Private: Minority Freezeouts and Stockholder Wealth' (1984) 27 *The Journal of Law and Economics* 367, 368.

From the company's perspective, delisting might not lead to the absence of minority shareholders. Under the Indian legal system, minority squeeze-out may be difficult after the delisting, as a company can delist by buying out 90 per cent of the holding, leaving certain minority shareholders, post-delisting, with increasing compliance challenges.[72] Section 236 of the Companies Act provides that if an acquirer has obtained 90 per cent or more of the shareholding of the company, he can offer to purchase the remaining shares of the minority shareholders.[73] However, the provision does not mandate the minority to sell their shares pursuant to the acquirer's offer. Thus, even if a company is aiming to reduce its compliance cost through delisting, the same might not always happen, especially if the minority shareholders of the company have not provided their shares to the promoter/acquirer who initiated the delisting. Hence, the decision to delist should be well planned, especially considering the cumbersome procedure for delisting, which is discussed in the following section.

III. Delisting Trajectory in India: Regulations and the Process

Before the beginning of the twenty-first century, delisting in India was not subject to any regulation. This posed a problem as companies manipulated the process to the advantage of the majority shareholders/promoters of the company, leaving minority shareholders holding unliquidated shares at unfair prices.[74] This lack of oversight also allowed for market manipulation and limited transparency casting a shadow over the delisting process. In 2002, a committee constituted by SEBI took note of these manipulative practices, and the consequent threat posed to the interests of minority shareholders. Hence, it proposed the introduction of detailed regulations governing the delisting procedure in India.[75]

Consequently, SEBI introduced the Delisting Guidelines in India in 2003.[76] This framework established elements like minimum shareholding requirements, a reverse book-building mechanism for price discovery, and a mandatory open offer for minority shareholders to exit. SEBI further strengthened the delisting framework in 2009 with the introduction of the Delisting Regulations.[77] These regulations introduced a few major changes in the delisting procedure, making the procedure more stringent for the promoter/acquirer initiating the delisting, and introducing greater safeguards for minority shareholders of the company. These regulations were amended multiple times between 2015–2018. Finally, SEBI introduced the 2021 Delisting Regulations, which are presently applicable in India.

[72] S Sanghai, 'Minority Squeeze-out Rules in Delisting Process: What's the Way Forward?' (21 July 2023) *The Economic Times*. Available at: www.economictimes.indiatimes.com/markets/stocks/news/minority-squeeze-out-rules-in-delisting-process-whats-the-way-forward/articleshow/102006331.cms?from=mdr.

[73] The Companies Act (n 11) s 236.

[74] K Khatiwada, 'A Study on Trends in Delisting of Shares and Its Reasons' (2015) *Bombay Stock Exchange*. Available at: www.bseindia.com/downloads1/astudy_on_trends_in_delisting.pdf.

[75] Securities and Exchange Board of India, *Report of the Committee on Delisting of Shares – Part I* (13 August 2002). Available at: www.sebi.gov.in/reports/reports/aug-2002/report-on-delisting-of-shares-pdf-file-_13159.html.

[76] Securities and Exchange Board of India (Delisting of Securities) Guidelines [2003].

[77] Securities and Exchange Board of India (Delisting of Equity Shares) Regulations [2009].

In this section, the changes introduced by SEBI in the delisting procedure from 2003 to 2021 through successive regulations will be delineated, followed by the existing procedure of delisting as provided under the 2021 Delisting Regulations. At the end of the section, the changes which SEBI is presently contemplating regarding the delisting procedure will be discussed.

A. Navigating the Trajectory of Delisting Regulations in India

Regulation of the delisting procedure was the outcome of the realisation of the harm caused to investors in the Indian market. This first came to light with the constitution of the *KR Chandratre Committee* in 1997, which exposed the harm caused to the company's minority shareholders by the delisting decision of the majority shareholders. The Committee proposed the inclusion of stock exchanges as neutral arbiters who granted final approval for any delisting proposals.[78]

This was followed by the *Pratip Kar Committee*, established by SEBI in 2002. This committee was constituted at a time when there was high anxiety amongst Indian shareholders due to the inadequate exit prices offered by companies at the time of delisting; this essentially deprived minority shareholders of the company of their rightful value. The committee proposed the introduction of stringent regulations to curb the freedom of companies to decide the exit price offered to the public shareholders.[79] This committee's report led to the introduction of SEBI's Delisting Guidelines in 2003.

(i) SEBI (Delisting of Securities) Guidelines, 2003

The 2003 Guidelines provided mechanisms for voluntary and compulsory delisting. It permitted voluntary delisting of a company, provided it had been listed for at least three years.[80] In light of the report of the *Pratip Kar Committee* it provided a stringent mechanism for protecting the interests of minority public shareholders. For this, the Guidelines mandated companies to give an exit opportunity at a price determined according to the book-building mechanism provided in Schedule II.[81] Furthermore, the Guidelines instilled transparency in the delisting procedure via two mechanisms – mandatory public announcement and a detailed stringent mechanism for calculating the exit price. Under the guidelines, any promoter/acquirer who proposed the delisting of a company was mandated to issue a public announcement.[82] The exit price of the shares had to be calculated according to the book-building procedure.[83] The Guidelines mandated stock exchanges to create specialised infrastructure facilities to disseminate an exit price and delisting details to all the shareholders trading on that platform.[84]

[78] Ministry of Corporate Affairs, *Chandratre Committee of the Working Group on the Companies Act* (n 41).
[79] SEBI, *Report of the Committee on Delisting of Shares – Part I* (n 75).
[80] SEBI (Delisting of Securities) Guidelines (n 76) Proviso I to Guideline 5.1.
[81] ibid Proviso II to Guideline 5.1.
[82] ibid Guideline 7.
[83] ibid Guideline 8 r/w sch II.
[84] ibid Guideline 8.4.

Originally, the rules governing the delisting of securities were merely intended to serve as a framework for guidance allowing for an exit option at a predetermined price with the Stock Exchange monitoring compliance. The Guidelines were ultimately replaced by Regulations in 2009.

(ii) SEBI (Delisting of Equity Shares) Regulations, 2009

The 2003 delisting guidelines of SEBI broadly covered all aspects of delisting procedure. The first set of adjustments that suggested greater systemic clarity were made available for public feedback in April 2004. Opinions were received on important provisions and comments were received from a variety of sources. Based on this, SEBI released a concept paper to receive public feedback on the proposed delisting regulations.[85] This led to the introduction of the Delisting Regulations in 2009 which radically changed the procedure of delisting.

While the 2003 Guidelines permitted delisting of securities in general, the 2009 Regulations were applicable only to equity shares. Public shareholders were defined as equity shareholders of the company, other than promoters and holders of depository receipts.[86] Certain changes were introduced, which made the delisting procedure more stringent, thereby reducing the scope of manipulation by a company's majority shareholders/promoters. For instance, an enhanced threshold for shareholder approval from just a special resolution (ie, 75 per cent of shareholders approving the delisting procedure) to a special resolution coupled with twice the number of approval than the rejections,[87] the introduction of a mandatory requirement to seek in-principle approval from the stock exchanges before the exit price of the shares were announced,[88] and an increase in the minimum number of days for bidding from three to five.[89] The Regulations introduced a special framework for the delisting of small companies, which was less stringent.[90]

Stringency was further enhanced by amending certain previously existing provisions. The 2009 Regulations prohibited delisting through preferential allotment along with a buy-back of shares by the company.[91] Earlier, the prohibition was limited to delisting through the buy-back of shares.[92] The exit offer procedure was brought in line with the SEBI Takeover regulations, where the regulations now required a mandatory letter of offer,[93] a prohibition on the use of company funds for delisting,[94] and introduced the concept of a specified date for identifying the public shareholders of the company

[85] Securities and Exchange Board of India, *Concept Paper and Draft Regulations on Delisting of Securities for Public Comments* (23 November 2006). Available at: www.sebi.gov.in/reports/reports/nov-2006/concept-paper-and-draft-regulations-on-delisting-of-securities-for-public-comments_10830.html.
[86] SEBI (Delisting of Equity Shares) Regulations (n 77) reg 2(v).
[87] ibid reg 8(1)(b).
[88] ibid reg 8(1)(c).
[89] ibid reg 13(2).
[90] ibid reg 27.
[91] ibid reg 4(1).
[92] SEBI (Delisting of Securities) Guidelines (n 76) Guideline 4.2.
[93] SEBI (Delisting of Equity Shares) Regulations (n 77) reg 12.
[94] ibid reg 4(4).

eligible to receive the offer letter.[95] The Regulations enhanced the consequences of a delisting decision by increasing the relisting ban period for companies who delisted voluntarily to five years from two, and for companies who compulsorily delisted to 10 years from two.[96]

(iii) SEBI (Delisting of Equity Shares) Regulations, 2021

While the 2009 Regulations were holistic and were strengthened through several amendments during 2015–2018, the 2021 Regulations introduced several new concepts and made the delisting process even more stringent. New safeguards were introduced to protect the interests of public shareholders. For instance, the 2021 regulations introduced the concept of a committee of independent directors, which must provide its recommendations to the delisting proposal. The working of this committee must be transparent; the votes casted by the committee's members and the reasons for its recommendation must be published in a newspaper and shared with the stock exchange.[97] Companies are now required to obtain a certificate of a Peer Review Company Secretary, which must certify that the buying and selling activity of the promoter/acquirer, before the delisting proposal, are in accordance with the Regulations' requirements.[98] The public shareholders can inspect all the documents mentioned in the offer letter[99] to create lien over the depositories account opened by the Manager to the offer.[100] Even the Manager to the offer must now protect the public shareholders of the company by making disclosures regarding the remaining public shareholders and sending follow-up communications.[101] The Manager is also entrusted with the funds in the escrow account and must ensure that the remaining funds are not released to the acquirer/promoter before the completion of a until year from the successful completion of delisting, or until payment is made to the remaining public shareholders, whichever is earlier.[102]

The new terms like indicative price and counteroffer were introduced. The indicative price is required to be higher than the floor price calculated under the Takeover regulations[103] and it depicts the amount of premium that the acquirer/promoter is willing to offer, over and above the floor price. The amount to be deposited in the escrow account must be calculated in accordance with the indicative price offered by the acquirer.[104] Similarly, an acquirer has been empowered to offer a counteroffer to the discovered price,[105] if this is higher than the floor price or the indicative price. Lastly, the 2021 Regulations provided a different procedure for delisting of a listed subsidiary

[95] ibid reg 10(3).
[96] ibid reg 30(1); SEBI (Delisting of Securities) Guidelines (n 76) Guideline 18.
[97] Delisting Regulations (n 7) reg 28.
[98] ibid reg 10(2).
[99] ibid reg 16(5).
[100] ibid sch II.
[101] ibid reg 27(1).
[102] ibid reg 26(4).
[103] ibid reg 20(4).
[104] ibid reg 14(1).
[105] ibid reg 22(4).

of a listed holding company, where both the companies are in the 'same line of business' and the shares of the listed subsidiary are frequently traded.[106]

The Regulations introduced stringency in the process by specifying timelines for certain steps in the process which were missing in the 2009 regulations – like the timeline for obtaining board approval,[107] the passing of the special resolution,[108] opening of the escrow account,[109] the receipt of in-principle approval from the stock exchange,[110] and the return of shares in case of failure of delisting.[111] The Regulations expressly provide that all expenses pertaining to the delisting shall be borne by the acquirer/promoter, not the company.[112] To ensure that the price-sensitive information regarding the delisting of the company is made accessible to all the shareholders of the company, the 2021 Regulations have mandated an initial public announcement to be made at all the stock exchanges where the company is listed, by the acquirer/promoter, on the date when the acquirer/promoter decides to delist the company.[113] Previously, the promoter/acquirer used to inform the board of the company, which would then forward the same to the stock exchanges.[114] Furthermore, an acquirer is now barred from initiating another round of delisting until six months from the date of the failure of the previous delisting proposal.[115]

While the 2021 Regulations have introduced changes to strengthen the position of minority and public shareholders of the company it has relaxed certain requirements for the acquirer/promoter. For instance, the cooling-off period in a voluntary delisting has been reduced from five years to three years.[116] Similarly, now greater time is available to an acquirer/promoter to arrange the funds to be deposited in the escrow account. Now only 25 per cent of the total consideration needs to be deposited within seven working days from the date of shareholders' approval[117] while the remainder is required to be deposited before making the detailed public announcement,[118] as against the previous requirement of a 100 per cent deposit.[119]

B. The Procedure of Delisting in India

As has been previously mentioned, the 2021 Delisting Regulations are a holistic set of procedural guidelines, which provide a detailed mechanism for delisting a company's

[106] ibid reg 37.
[107] ibid reg 10(1), wherein board approval to be received in 21 days from the date of initial announcement.
[108] ibid reg 11(1), wherein shareholder approval to be received within 45 days of the board's approval.
[109] ibid reg 14(1), wherein escrow account should be opened within seven days of receipt of shareholders' approval.
[110] ibid reg 12(1), wherein application for in-principle approval to be made within 15 working days from the date of the shareholders' approval or regulatory approvals, whichever is later in time.
[111] ibid reg 23(2).
[112] ibid reg 23(2)(b).
[113] ibid reg 8(1).
[114] SEBI (Delisting of Equity Shares) Regulations (n 77) reg 8(1A).
[115] Delisting Regulations (n 7) reg 23(2)(c).
[116] ibid reg 40(1).
[117] ibid reg 14(1).
[118] ibid reg 14(3).
[119] ibid reg 11(1).

equity shares, while protecting the interests of public shareholders, who might be threatened by an unregulated delisting procedure, as happened before 2003. The previous sub-section has already highlighted the procedural safeguards and nuances of the 2021 Regulations. This sub-section intends to briefly delineate the procedure required for delisting equity shares of a company in India.

The Regulations provide for certain qualifications which must be fulfilled to pursue a delisting. It is required to have a mandatory listing history of three years, no delisting through buy-back and preferential allotment, and no sale in the six months prior to the initial public announcement to be undertaken by the acquirer proposing the delisting to be undertaken.[120] As has been previously mentioned, an acquirer includes both a promoter of the company and an acquirer per the SEBI Takeover Regulations.[121] The Regulations outrightly prohibit any proposal of delisting to be used as a fraudulent or deceptive scheme.[122] The purpose of such prohibition is to ensure that promoters and acquirers do not misuse the delisting procedure to defraud investors and earn undue profits at the cost of these investors. For instance, in the case of *in re Riddhi Siddhi Gluco Biols Ltd*,[123] SEBI imposed a penalty upon a company and its promoters for inflating the trading volume of the company's shares to offer a lower exit price to the shareholders. This was held to be a fraudulent scheme delisting for which penalties were imposed upon the company and its promoters. Similarly, *in re ECE Industries Ltd*,[124] the company initiated a buy-back of securities followed by a delisting proposal by the company's acquirers. These acquirers participated in the buyback and, through fraudulent intra-trading, created false trade volumes. These affected the exit price offered to the public shareholders, who were denied their rightful price. SEBI found the whole scheme of buy-back followed by delisting to be a fraudulent scheme.

The Regulations provide the procedure for voluntary and compulsory delisting. It provides different procedures for those voluntary delistings where the shares of a company are sought to be delisted from all the stock exchanges on which the shares are listed, and those voluntary delistings wherein the shares are sought to be delisted not from all stock exchanges having nation-wide terminals.[125] In the former case, the acquirer proposing to delist the shares has to provide an exit opportunity, which is not required in the latter case.[126]

In a delisting where it is mandatory to provide an exit opportunity, the procedure begins with the appointment of the Manager to the offer,[127] who is responsible for ensuring compliance with every provision of the 2021 Regulations. Once the Manager has been appointed, the acquirer is required to make an initial announcement of delisting to all the stock exchanges where the company's shares are listed.[128] This needs to be made on the same day that the acquirer decides to delist the shares of the company.[129]

[120] ibid reg 4.
[121] ibid reg 2(1)(b).
[122] ibid reg 4(5).
[123] *In Re Riddhi Siddhi Glico Biols Ltd & Ors* [2021] SCC Online SEBI 190.
[124] *In Re ECE Industries Ltd & Ors* [2021] SCC Online SEBI 112.
[125] ibid ch III.
[126] ibid.
[127] ibid reg 9(1).
[128] ibid reg 8.
[129] ibid reg 8(1).

The initial announcement is followed by the receipt of approval from the company's board, which includes the provision of a certificate of compliance from a Peer Review Company Secretary and a declaration from the board specifying compliance with the Regulations and that the proposed delisting is in the best interest of the company's shareholders.[130] Once the approval is received from the board, the acquirer is required to seek the shareholders' approval, in which the proposal must be approved by 75 per cent of the shareholders with at least twice the number of shareholders approving the proposal than those rejecting it.[131] Lastly, the acquirer is required to file for in-principle approval of the stock exchange; the stock exchange cannot 'unfairly withhold' the application for approval but can mandate some requirements to be fulfilled before approval is granted.[132]

Apart from the approvals needed and the process for each approval, the 2021 Regulations provide a detailed mechanism for the grant of an exit opportunity to the company's shareholders.[133] The acquirer is must open an interest-bearing escrow account with a Scheduled Commercial Bank, in which the total consideration needs to be deposited before the release of the detailed public statement.[134] This detailed public statement can be in the form of cash or a bank guarantee.[135] Post the opening of this account and the receipt of the in-principle approval from the stock exchange, the acquirer is required to release a detailed public statement, which shall specify the details mentioned in Schedule I of the Regulations along with the 'specified date', which is the cut-off date for ascertaining the shareholders who shall be sent the letter of offer.[136] Once the letter of offer is sent to all the shareholders of the company, the bidding process begins.[137]

The exit price is determined through the reverse book-building process which is mentioned in Schedule II of the Regulations. All public shareholders holding equity shares of the company have a right to participate in this process.[138] The exit price determined through this process is called the discovered price. If the discovered price is equal to the floor price or the indicative price, then the acquirer is bound to accept the equity shares tendered by the public shareholders.[139] Similarly, if the discovered price is higher than the floor price and less than the indicative price, the acquirer is bound to accept the shares at the indicative price.[140] But if the discovered price is more than the indicative price, then the acquirer can either reject the shares or make a counter offer.[141] The Regulations provide that if the acquirer rejects the discovered price or does not meet the requirement of a 90 per cent shareholding post the exit offer (as per Regulation 21), then the delisting proposal shall deemed to have failed.[142] The Regulations also specify

[130] ibid reg 10.
[131] ibid reg 11(1).
[132] ibid reg 12(4).
[133] ibid ch IV.
[134] ibid reg 14.
[135] ibid reg 14(5).
[136] ibid reg 15.
[137] ibid reg 17.
[138] ibid reg 19(1).
[139] ibid reg 22(1).
[140] ibid reg 22(2).
[141] ibid reg 22(3).
[142] ibid reg 23.

the mechanism for making payments, if the delisting is successful,[143] and for return of shares tendered if the delisting fails.[144] Once the payment is made, a final application is required to be made to the stock exchange for approval of delisting.[145]

Coming to compulsory delisting, the grounds are provided in Rule 21 of Securities Contract (Regulations) Rules 1957, as discussed in Section II.B.II. The 2021 Regulations provide for due process in this regard which includes public notice of proposed compulsory delisting, invitation of objections to the same, and the mandate of a reasoned order for delisting.[146] If an order for compulsory delisting is passed, then an exit opportunity needs to be provided by the promoters of the company on a value ascertained by an independent valuer within three months of the order of compulsory delisting except in a situation where the public shareholders intend to retain their shares.[147] The purpose of putting such an obligation on the company's promoters is to ensure that compulsory delisting of the company does not penalise the company's investors, who have no role in the company's infractions contrary to the company's promoters and directors. The obligation to provide the exit opportunity penalises the promoters for the company's infractions, as they are considered to be in control of the company's operations.[148]

An essential element of the procedure for compulsory delisting is that of natural justice. Regulation 32 of the Delisting Regulations provides that an opportunity of being heard needs to be mandatorily given to every interested entity in the proposed delisting.[149] Moreover, the stock exchange is mandated to 'consider' the representations made by the company and other interested entities before making the delisting order.[150] Failure to comply with the requirement of providing an opportunity of being heard before passing the delisting order can lead to dismissal of the compulsory delisting order.[151] Considering that natural justice is an essential element of the right of equality under the Constitution of India, an entity aggrieved by the non-observance of it by a stock exchange can avail of constitutional remedies if the statutorily provided options fail to provide the adequate remedy.[152]

C. Recent Development: A Possible Shift to Fixed-Price Method

In August 2023, SEBI released a consultation paper which proposed a shift from the reverse book-building mechanism to the fixed-price method of exit-price discovery.[153]

[143] ibid reg 24.
[144] ibid reg 23(2).
[145] ibid reg 25.
[146] ibid reg 32.
[147] ibid reg 33.
[148] Securities and Exchange Board of India, *Report of the Committee on Delisting – Part I* (29 April 1998) para 4.33. Available at: www.sebi.gov.in/sebi_data/attachdocs/1293169446788.pdf.
[149] Delisting Regulations (n 7) reg 32(3).
[150] ibid reg 32(4).
[151] See *Divine Multi Media (India) Ltd v BSE Ltd* [2019] OnLine SAT 193; *Chokhani International Limited v BSE Ltd* [2019] OnLine SAT 373; *Padmini Technologies Ltd v BSE Ltd* [2017] SCC OnLine SAT 72.
[152] *Ashoka Marketing Limited & Anr v The Calcutta Stock Exchange Limited & Ors* [2017] SCC OnLine Cal 15508.
[153] Securities and Exchange Board of India, *Report of the Sub-group on the Securities and Exchange Board of India (Delisting of Equity Shares) Regulations, 2021* (8 August 2023). Available at: www.sebi.gov.

According to the *Keki Mistry Committee*, which has proposed this shift, the existing reverse book-building mechanism delays determination of the exit price, which increases speculative trading of the company's shares. The Committee believes that a shift to fixed-price method would bring certainty in the process, enabling shareholders to decide at the outset of the delisting announcement on whether to tender their shares or not, and better enabling the acquirer to arrange funds in light of a pre-determined exit price.[154] The Committee has proposed for a shift towards to the fixed price method, wherein the fixed price offered by the acquirer shall not be less than the floor price of the shares, and if the delisting fails, then the acquirer shall have the option to re-initiate delisting after six months using either the fixed-price method or the reverse book-building method.[155]

The intention of SEBI behind this proposal is clearly to curb market malpractices in relation to manipulation of the floor price of shares. SEBI aims to curb the malpractice of certain traders which misuse the reverse book-building process. These traders purchase a bulk of shares of a company which is proposing to delist itself and then increase the floor price by bidding exorbitantly in the reverse book-building process. Thus, in effect, these handful of traders control the entire process of exit-price determination leading to high losses for the acquirer.[156]

However, it seems that the proposal has lost sight of the main reason that reverse book building was incorporated in the delisting regulations in the first place. Back in 2002, SEBI preferred reverse book building over fixed-price method of exit-price determination to ensure transparency in the price-determination process and enable greater shareholder participation in the process.[157] The author has argued that the existing reverse book-building process is the only safeguard available to minority shareholders of the company to fight for their interests in the proposed delisting by sometimes bidding an egregiously high price to thwart a delist which they deem to be against the interest of the company.[158] This can be exemplified through the proposed delisting of Vedanta Resources Ltd of 2020, where the shareholders by bidding a very high price were able to ensure that the acquirer was not able to achieve the threshold of 90 per cent.[159] Due to the concentrated shareholding pattern in the Indian corporate landscape and vulnerable position of minority shareholders along with the absence of any veto power given to the minority shareholders,[160] the author believes that the

in/reports-and-statistics/reports/aug-2023/consultation-paper-on-review-of-voluntary-delisting-norms-under-sebi-delisting-of-equity-shares-regulations-2021_75335.html.

[154] ibid at 7.

[155] ibid at 8.

[156] Mint, 'Regulator proposes to ease delisting norms' (15 August 2023) *Live Mint*. Available at: www.livemint.com/market/regulator-proposes-to-ease-delisting-norms-11692038697098.html.

[157] SEBI, *Report of the Committee on Delisting of Shares – Part I* (n 75).

[158] H Kaur, 'Delisting Regulations in India and the Position of Minority Shareholders' (27 September 2023) *Oxford Business Law Blog*. Available at: www.blogs.law.ox.ac.uk/oblb/blog-post/2023/09/delisting-regulations-india-and-position-minority-shareholders.

[159] A Ramarathinam and N Sultana, 'Vedanta's shares slump 21% after failed delisting' (12 October 2020) *Live Mint*. Available at: www.livemint.com/market/stock-market-news/vedanta-shares-slump-21-after-failed-delisting-11602510326627.html.

[160] T Nashier and A Gupta, 'Ownership Concentration and Firm Performance in India' (2023) 24 *Global Business Review* 353.

proposed shift to fixed-price method of price determination might go against the interest of minority shareholders.

Hence, while SEBI might be aiming to curb market malpractices and enhance ease of business in India through its proposal, it needs to analyse the proposal from the lens of minority shareholders' interests before adopting the same.

IV. Statistical Analysis of the Companies Delisted from the National Stock Exchange

A. Methodology

Stock exchanges are mandated to maintain an updated list of all the companies which are delisted from their platform. To understand trends and facts related to delisting within the Indian landscape, the author has engaged in a data collection of all the companies which have been delisted from the main board of the National Stock Exchange (hereinafter 'NSE'), during 2009–22. As on 31 December 2022, there were around 2,000 companies listed on the NSE. The online data maintained by the NSE provides only limited details about the delisted companies which include the company name, trading name, place of delisting, date, and type of delisting.

To provide a holistic analysis of delisting trends in India, the author collected further information regarding the exit price offered by the companies, the last known public issue by the company before delisting, the entity on whose initiative the delisting was undertaken (namely the promoter, acquirer, stock exchange, or liquidator), whether the delisting was undertaken at that time only from NSE or from other stock exchanges as well, and whether the delisted company ever relisted itself. All this data was collected from the information available on the NSE website, annual reports of respective companies, public announcements of delisting issued by the companies and NSE, and financial newspapers. Despite the best efforts of the author, there were numerous companies for which either no information was available online or only partial information was available on a few of the listed parameters.

B. Results

(i) Types of Delisting – Compulsory, Voluntary, and Liquidation

In the data collected, there were a total of 346 companies delisted from the NSE mainboard during 2009–22. Of these 346 companies, 137 or 39.59 per cent companies were compulsorily delisted by NSE, 116 or 33.52 per cent companies were delisted due to liquidation of the company. Lastly, 93 of the 346 or 26.89 per cent companies were delisted voluntarily, either by the company's promoters or acquirers. The percentage values have been rounded off to the second decimal for convenience.

Figure 17.1 Types of Delistings in Past Years

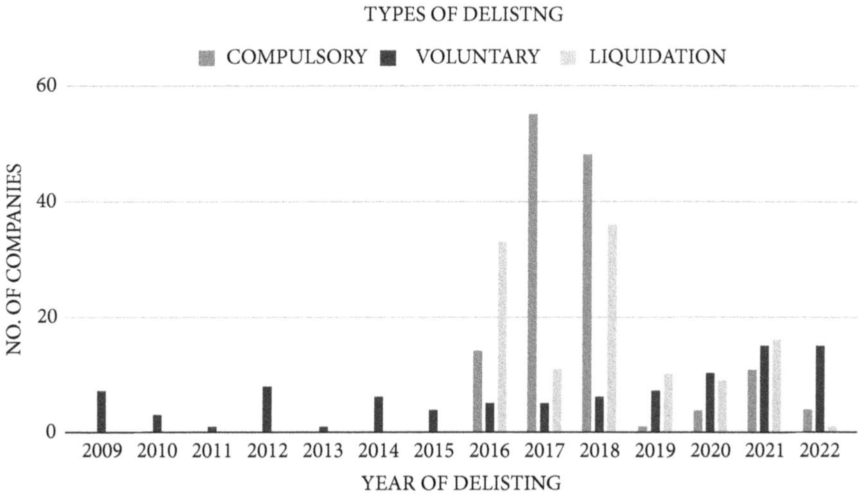

In the above graph (Figure 17.1), the black bars represent voluntary delisting; the dark grey bars represent compulsory delisting; and the light grey bars represent delisting due to liquidation. As is visible from the graph, compulsory and liquidation induced delisting are absent during the period of 2009–15. During the next three years, the voluntary delisting threshold was the same as the previous years. However, during the last four years, ie, 2019–22, there has been a constant increase in the number of voluntary delisting.

The compulsory and liquidation induced delisting were extremely high during the period of 2016–18. However, a sharp fall in the number of liquidation-induced delisting from 36 to 10, and compulsory delisting from 48 to 1 is observed between 2018 to 2019. From 2019–21, there has been an increase in the liquidation induced delisting, but from 2021 to 2022, liquidation induced delisting sharply reduced from 16 to 1. Similarly, during 2019–21, there was an increase in the number of compulsory delisting, which reduced from 11 to 4 between 2021–22.

(ii) Delisting Initiated by Whom?

Delisting in India can be initiated by promoters of the company, acquirer of the company along with persons acting in consort, liquidator of the company, successful resolution application under the Insolvency and Bankruptcy Code, 2016 (hereinafter 'IBC'), and the stock exchange itself. Under the 2021 Delisting Regulation, voluntary delisting can be acquirer-initiated or promoter-initiated whereas a stock exchange can initiate delisting as a penal measure. Under the IBC, a resolution applicant who has successfully taken over a company, and if in its resolution plan has proposed the delisting of the company, such resolution applicant is also empowered to initiate delisting. While the

Delisting Regulations 2021 do not apply to such kinds of delisting,[161] stock exchanges do maintain their records as well. Lastly, a liquidator under the IBC is also empowered to delist a company at the time of liquidating the company's assets.[162]

Out of the 346 companies delisted in India during 2009–22, data regarding the entity which initiated the delisting procedure is available for 330 companies. Of these, a total of 137 were delisted by the stock exchange, under the provision of compulsory delisting, constituting 41.51 per cent of the 330 companies: 116 of the 330 companies were delisted due to their liquidation, ie, at the behest of the companies' liquidators. Resolution applicants instituted only a limited number of delistings during the period of study, which was a mere 6.1 per cent or 20 of the 330 companies. Details of this division can be better understood from the pie chart given below (Figure 17.2):

Figure 17.2 Companies Delisted

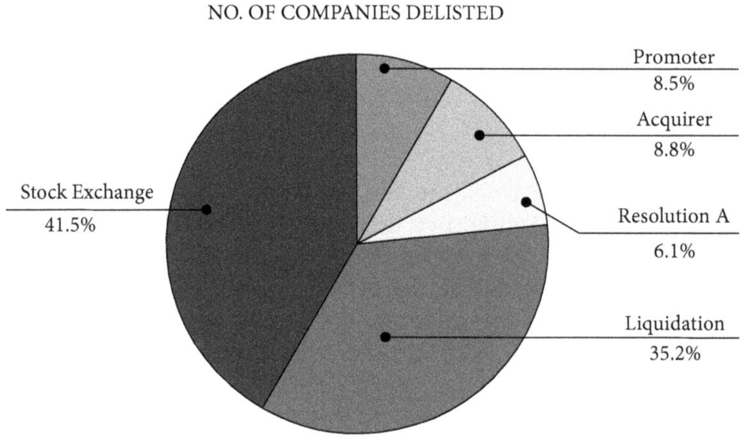

Interestingly, until the introduction of the Insolvency and Bankruptcy Code, 2016, all delistings were initiated either by the promoters of the companies or their acquirers. This agrees with our previous finding that, during 2009–15, companies only engaged in voluntary delisting. During 2009–15, a total of 30 companies were delisted; data regarding the entity initiating the delisting is not available for three. Out of the remaining 27 companies, while eight (29.62 per cent of the 27 companies) were delisted at the behest of the companies' promoters, 19 (70.38 per cent of the 27 companies) were delisted by the acquirers of the companies.

(iii) Companies Offering an Exit Price to Shareholders

As has been discussed in the previous section, all applicable regulations or guidelines on delisting in India (from 2003 to 2021) provided for an exit price to be paid by the promoter/acquirer to the company's public shareholders. Its purpose was to ensure that public shareholders of the company should be provided with fair value for their shares if they intended to exit the company due to the proposed delisting. However, the

[161] Delisting Regulations (n 7) reg 3(2)(b).
[162] Insolvency and Bankruptcy Code of India [2016] s 35(1)(m).

regulations never mandated the promoter or acquirer to initiate the delisting to offer an exit price to the shareholders. The final decision was left to the commercial wisdom of the parties.

In the data set, the details of the exit price offered by the promoter/acquirer were available for 266 out of the 346 delisted companies.[163] Of these 266 companies, merely 88 companies (ie, their promoters/acquirers) offered an exit price to their shareholders constituting 33.06 per cent of 266 companies. Rest of the promoters/acquirers of 178 companies decided not to offer any exit price to its shareholders. This means that if these shareholders wanted to exit the company due to the proposed delisting, they would not be offered any value for their shares.

Figure 17.3 Companies Offering an Exit Price

If we look at the above graph (Figure 17.3), it can be discerned that for the years 2009–13, every promoter/acquirer who proposed and went ahead with a delisting offered an exit price to the company's shareholders. During 2014–15, the number of companies whose promoters/acquirers did not offer any exit price was less than the ones offering an exit price. However, majority of the companies' promoters/acquirers decided not to offer any exit price from 2016–22. These companies constituted 72.42 per cent of the 243 companies, which were delisted during that period and whose details of exit price are available.

(iv) Year of Delisting vis-à-vis Last Public Issue

The author has tried to trace a link between the year in which a company decides to delist itself and the year in which the company made its last public issue. Such a link would help to explain the reasons which led to the decision to delist. Logically, a

[163] The graph (Figure 17.3) includes some companies which opted for partial delisting. However, the exact number of those is not available due to lack of information in the public domain.

company which has recently made a public issue of its shares would be seeing a high trading volume of its shares if the issue has been successful. As a result, it makes less sense for such a company to delist itself within a few years from the date of its last issue. However, there can be situations when a company might be constrained to delist itself soon after its last known issue, like change in profitability and market conditions, which can increase the cost of business for the company.

Figure 17.4 Delistings and Last Public Issue

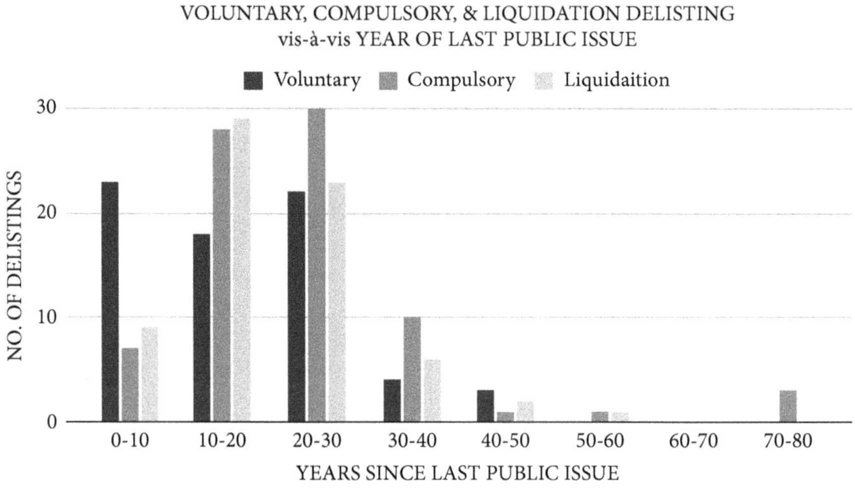

For this analysis, data of last public issue was available only for 220 out of the 346 companies which delisted during 2009–22 (Figure 17.4). A study of the above graph reveals that the highest number of voluntary delistings took place within the first 10 years of the last public issue of shares. At the maximum, a company could voluntarily delist itself within 50 years of its last public issue. For compulsory delisting, the same quantum is lower in the first 10 years, but there are very high number of compulsory delistings within 10–30 years of its last issue. Similarly, liquidation-induced delistings were highest within 10–20 years of the last known issue. However, no such delisting took place 60 years after the last issue.

C. Analysis

The Delisting Guidelines, 2003,[164] Delisting Regulations, 2009,[165] and Delisting Regulations, 2021[166] had empowered stock exchanges to delist companies as a penal provision. However, as discussed previously, this power was not used by the National Stock Exchange until 2015. The sudden surge in the number of compulsory delisting

[164] Securities and Exchange Board of India (Delisting Guidelines) [2003] Guideline 15.
[165] Securities and Exchange Board of India (Delisting Regulations) [2009] reg 22.
[166] Delisting Regulations (n 7) reg 32.

can be justified based on two inter-linked factors – increased compliance obligations for listed companies from 2015 onwards and the heightened vigilance of SEBI and stock exchanges to ensure compliance by companies. Coming to the first factor, 2015 saw the introduction of two major compliance-based regulations like the Insider Trading Regulations[167] and SEBI (Listing Obligation and Disclosure Requirements) Regulations.[168] With the coming in effect of these regulations in 2016, SEBI introduced a clean-up operation across stock exchanges, where it ramped up the management of stock exchanges to use this power of compulsory delisting to remove companies which have been suspended from trading for seven years or more due to penal reasons.[169] Consequently, large number of delisting orders were passed by the National Stock Exchange and the Bombay Stock Exchange (hereinafter 'BSE') in 2016.[170]

The SEBI introduced another major compliance-based regulation, SEBI (Issue of Capital and Disclosure Requirements) Regulations in 2018.[171] At that time, another clean-up operation was initiated, in which both BSE and NSE were engaged in large-scale delisting of shell companies to curb the flow of illicit funds in the securities market.[172] This clean-up was initiated after SEBI empowered stock exchanges in 2018 to impose monetary penalties, freeze shares of promoters, and even compulsorily delist companies which were not complying with the SEBI (Listing Obligation and Disclosure Requirements) Regulations. SEBI explicitly asked stock exchanges to initiate compulsory delisting procedure if a defaulting company fails to pay the fine imposed or remedy their non-compliant actions.[173] As a result, there were a large number of compulsory delisting in 2018 as well.

These stringent compliance requirements introduced by SEBI coupled with greater vigilance by stock exchanges led to voluntary delisting post-2015, as the increased cost of compliance made it expensive for companies to continue to remain listed. Coming to the case of liquidation induced delisting, while the same was absent till 2016, it was only with the introduction of the IBC that liquidation induced delisting came in the picture. Until June 2020, according to official data, almost 955 companies were referred for liquidation as they could not be salvaged under the Code.[174] In 2020 itself, a total of 189 companies were referred for liquidation under the Code and around 59 companies

[167] SEBI (Prohibition of Insider Trading) Regulations (n 45).

[168] SEBI (Listing Obligations and Disclosure Requirements) Regulations (n 44).

[169] N Kiran, 'Operation Clean-up' (17 July 2016) *Business Today*. Available at: www.businesstoday.in/magazine/features/story/sebi-move-to-delist-over-4000-companies-148181-2016-07-01; PTI, 'SEBI to encourage delisting of suspended companies' (12 March 2016) *The Economic Times*. Available at: www.economictimes.indiatimes.com/markets/stocks/news/sebi-to-encourage-delisting-of-suspended-companies/articleshow/51372655.cms.

[170] ibid.

[171] SEBI (Issue of Capital and Disclosure Requirements) Regulations (n 21).

[172] PTI, 'Bombay Stock Exchange to delist 222 companies from tomorrow' (3 July 2018) *The Economic Times*. Available at: www.cfo.economictimes.indiatimes.com/news/bombay-stock-exchange-to-delist-222-companies-from-tomorrow/64838574; PTI, 'NSE to delist Kingfisher, Plethico Pharma, 16 others from May 30' (21 May 2019) *Times of India*. Available at: www.timesofindia.indiatimes.com/articleshow/64261551.cms?utm_source=contentofinterest&utm_medium=text&utm_campaign=cppst.

[173] Securities and Exchange Board of India, *Non-compliance with provisions of SEBI (Listing Obligations and Disclosure Requirements) Regulations, 2015 and Standard Operating Procedure for suspension and revocation of trading of specified securities* (3 May 2018) SEBI/HO/CFD/CMD/CIR/P/2018/77.

[174] MS Sahoo, 'Insolvency Reforms: A Road Under Construction' (2022). Available at: www.ibbi.gov.in/uploads/resources/ab85b78f0ae05938cae4a7c6bae0c225.pdf.

underwent voluntary liquidation as an outcome of the COVID-19 Pandemic.[175] Such large number of liquidations under the IBC explain the perceptible rise of liquidation induced delisting in India since 2016.

These push factors from SEBI for removal of non-compliant companies from stock exchanges and the high rates of liquidation in the Indian corporate setup are also the reasons due to which the largest number of delistings in India were initiated by the stock exchange itself (as compulsory delisting) and then by liquidators during the period of study. This surge in compulsory and liquidation-induced delisting is the reason for the small share of promoter/acquirer/resolution applicant-induced delistings since 2016. During 2009–22, only 26.89 per cent of delistings were voluntary, rest being either compulsory or liquidation induced. Of these total 93 voluntary delistings, 32.25 per cent took place before 2016. During 2016–22, there were only 63 voluntary delistings vis-à-vis 253 compulsory and liquidation induced delistings. Thus, with the emergence of compulsory and liquidation induced delistings, there was a huge fall in the share of voluntary delistings in India, which were initiated by promoters, acquirers, and resolution applicants.

Coming to the pattern of exit-price offerings, during the period of 2009–15, it can be seen that majority of the companies were offering exit price to their public shareholders. This can be justified by the fact that the majority of these voluntary delistings were done pursuant to the acquisition of the delisted company. During this period, 30 companies were delisted, out of which data is available for 27. Of these 27 companies, 19 companies were delisted pursuant to an acquisition offer, which constitutes around 70.37 per cent. According to the works of *Viral Pandya,*[176] *Natika Poddar,*[177] *and Pradip Banerjee et al,*[178] acquisition pricing in India, prior to 2015, was done at a very high threshold because for the acquirer, the proposed merger or acquisition was crucial for enhancing their market share and operational synergy. Thus, Indian acquirers preferred to offer very high premiums to get the desired shareholder approval. This justifies the fact that all the acquirer-initiated delisting, during 2009–15, gave high exit offers to their public shareholders. However, no such explanation can be provided for the exit offers given by promoters, who initiated the delisting during that period.

Post 2015, while there is surely an increase in the number of companies offering an exit price to their shareholders, there is a relatively greater increase in the number of companies not offering an exit price. This can be ascribed to the fact that, post 2015, as previously explained, there was a surge in liquidation-induced delisting, where it can be reasonably assumed that nothing was left for the company's shareholders post the liquidation of the company's assets. This assumption is based on the fact that, before referring a company to liquidation under the IBC, the aim is to salvage the company through the resolution process, and if the resolution process fails then only a company

[175] Ministry of Corporate Affairs, *Bankrupt Companies after lockdown was imposed due to COVID-19 pandemic* (22 March 2021). Available at: www.pib.gov.in/PressReleasePage.aspx?PRID=1706640.

[176] VU Pandya, 'Mergers and Acquisitions Trends – The Indian Experience' (2018) 9 *International Journal of Business Administration* 44.

[177] N Poddar, 'A Study on Mergers and Acquisition in India and Its Impact on Operating Efficiency of Indian Acquiring Company' (2019) 9 *Theoretical Economic Letters* 1040.

[178] P Banerjee et al, 'Acquisition pricing in India during 1995–2011: Have Indian acquirers really beaten the odds?' (2014) 38 *Journal of Banking and Finance* 14.

is referred for liquidation.[179] Coming to compulsory delisting post-2015, as per the Delisting Regulations, 2021, an independent valuer determines the fair value of the shares, which is to be offered by the company's promoters.[180] However, according to the data, in 51 out of 105 companies compulsorily delisted (for which data of exit price offered is available out of the total 137 compulsory delistings), no exit price was offered to the shareholders. This shows that numerous companies which were compulsorily delisted did not have a positive value for their shares, which could be offered to the companies' shareholders.

Coming to the data for the year of delisting vis-à-vis the year of last public issue, the reason for the majority of voluntary delistings during the first 30 years since the last public issue can be a decline in the profitability of the company since its last issue, making it expensive for the company to remain listed. Similarly, within this period, when voluntary delistings are the highest, the issued shares might lose their attraction to investors, thereby reducing their trading volume making delisting a reasonable decision. The pattern of liquidation-induced delisting indicates that usually within 20 years of a company's last public issue, the business becomes unprofitable, pushing the company towards liquidation, thereby leading to its delisting. This can be because of factors such as increased cost of production, sectoral and regulatory changes and reduced competitiveness. Lastly, the pattern of compulsory delisting can be justified based on the assumption that in the initial 10 years from the last public issue, companies prefer to comply with SEBI regulations and byelaws of stock exchanges to avail themselves of its benefits and improve the company's financial position; however, over time, they become lax and end up being compulsorily delisted.

However, a better analysis of this parameter can be made with an in-depth study of the specific reasons which led to the delisting of the companies in the sample. Such a study would help to understand the numerous factors at play during the interregnum period of the last public issue and the year of delisting. However, information regarding the specific reasons for a company's delisting is not available publicly. The author of the present study restricted the scope of the work to publicly available information.

V. Conclusion

The chapter aimed to discuss the legal and practical landscape of delisting in India. Since the dawn of the twenty-first century, SEBI has been actively working towards refining the delisting process through successive regulations and amendments. The primary objective of SEBI has been to introduce greater transparency in the delisting process and strengthen the position of public shareholders in the process. At the same time, being cognisant of the rationale behind delisting, as a business decision, SEBI has tried to balance the ease of businesses in availing the option to delist. This has culminated in a set of holistic delisting regulations.

[179] VK Rajshekhar, 'Resolution Plan Approval and Effect of Interlocutory Application on Disposal of Cases' in *IBC-Ideas, Impressions, and Implementation* (New Delhi, IBBI, 2022) 87.

[180] Delisting Regulations (n 7) reg 33.

Through the data collected from the NSE regarding the companies delisted from 2009–22, the author has tried to substantiate the previously discussed theoretical underpinnings of delisting and delisting regulation in India. The author has established that the number of companies delisting depends on the stringency compliance requirements in a market. It was because of the introduction of the IBC and the SEBI regulations pertaining to compliance requirements of listed companies that NSE witnessed a dramatic surge in the number of companies being delisted. Moreover, SEBI has strengthened stock exchanges over time to ensure discipline in the market through rigorous use of compulsory delisting provisions.

While the existing regulations seem to be exhaustive and stable, they will be subject to revision in light of changing market dynamics. However, the ultimate aim of SEBI should be to achieve an optimal balance in the ease of business and shareholder protection. This is necessary in light of the fact that, while the option to delist should be available for a company, it should not be exercised at the cost of the company's public and minority shareholders. The Indian corporate landscape, unlike that in the UK and the US, still has concentrated ownership patterns, which requires SEBI to considerate of the interests of minority shareholders.

18

Delisting in Colombia, with Reference to Argentinean and Chilean Regulations

JUAN PABLO GONZÁLEZ*

I. Introduction

Delisting in Colombia, as well as in Chile and Argentina, is mainly a matter of law, specifically securities and corporate law.[1] Although exchanges retain the discretion to stipulate criteria for listing and delisting, such prerogative is seldom exercised, particularly in Colombia, rendering the criteria for delisting essentially nonexistent at the exchange level. Consequently, delisting requisites are associated with the cancellation of registration in the national registries (Colombia and Chile) or the rescission of authorisation for public offerings (Argentina).

Delisting in Colombia and Argentina intertwines with both corporate and securities law, raising some interesting questions. In contrast, Chilean delisting is confined to corporate law.

Historically, delisting has not precipitated significant litigation within these jurisdictions, as the regulations are characteristically clear-cut, refrain from imposing burdensome requirements on issuers, and generally afford investors an exit strategy, most commonly via a public acquisition offer from the issuer or endorsing shareholders.

Listing in these countries is predominantly a voluntary act, hence voluntary delisting is permissible. In the rare instances where registration in the national registry is compulsory, issuers may only proceed with voluntary deregistration if the statutory reasons to register have been extinguished. Mandatory delisting as a punitive measure by securities authorities is unusual.

Despite concerted efforts to augment the allure of securities markets for issuers and investors, there has been an uptick in delisting, with Colombia witnessing a

* JD Universidad Javeriana, LLM Cornell University, Professor of Securities Law at Pontificia Universidad Javeriana, Colombia and Partner at Esguerra JHR. Special thanks to HD Legal and Tanoira Cassagne, who provided information on the Chilean and Argentinean regulatory frameworks, respectively.

[1] Unless specifically stated, all mentions to listing and delisting requirements will refer to shares and other variable income instruments.

marked decline in issuers, primarily due to voluntary delisting. The consolidation of major exchanges in Chile, Peru, and Colombia seeks to reinvigorate regional markets by providing incentives for issuers to either list or maintain their listings, accessing a broader investor base.

Delisting of securities other than equities has some relevancy, particularly in Colombia, where fixed-income instruments are actively traded in regulated markets. Accordingly, a brief mention will be made in that respect.

This chapter unfolds in three segments: The initial part sets the stage and delineates the overarching regulatory landscape. The subsequent segment expounds the specific delisting regulations in Colombia and undertakes a comparative analysis with Chilean and Argentinean frameworks. The concluding segment contemplates the efficacy of these regulations in equilibrating the divergent interests inherent in delisting procedures, principally between controlling parties and minority shareholders.

A. Current Situation and Trends

In Latin America's economic spectrum, Brazil claims the apex of market capitalisation, boasting a respectable USD 931 billion, followed by Mexico at 576 billion, Chile at 180 billion, Colombia at 79 billion, and Argentina at 48 billion.[2] Equities trading in 2022 mirrored this hierarchy, with Brazil dominating at 1.2 trillion US dollars, trailed by Mexico at 102 billion, Chile at 38 billion, Colombia at seven billion, and Argentina at three billion.

Annual turnover tends to be low in all Latin American markets, except Brazil. According to the World Bank's statistics, Argentina's turnover ratio is 7.6, Colombia is somewhat higher at 9.4, while Mexico and Chile are very similar at 20.7 and 21.5, respectively. Brazil is more in line with developed markets standards, with a very acceptable turnover ratio of 87.5.[3]

As of December 2023, Brazil's Bovespa comprised 361 issuers,[4] Santiago's Bolsa registered 297, Mexico tallied 136, while Argentina and Colombia counted 88 and 64 respectively. Two decades ago, the number of issuers in these exchanges was 372, 241, 237, 110 and 108, respectively.[5] Among these exchanges, the Chilean case is unique. Although the number of domestic listed companies decreased over the last 20 years to a total of 192, 106 foreign companies were listed during that period.[6] Most of them are ETFs that track US stocks.

Colombia's issuer count has dwindled more than in any other sizable market in the region, both in absolute and relative terms. While it is challenging to single out the cause for this decline, several commonalities pervade the delisting processes. Primarily, share ownership often resides with a limited group of holders, often tied by family bonds,

[2] FIAB, *Monthly Statistics Tables* (December 2023). Available at: www.fiabnet.org/images/upload/post-1418.pdf.

[3] The World Bank, *Stocks traded, turnover ratio of domestic shares (%)*. Available at: www.data.worldbank.org/indicator/CM.MKT.TRNR.

[4] FIAB, *Monthly Statistics Tables* (n 2).

[5] FIAB, *Annual Statistical Summary* (2004). Available at: www.fiabnet.org/anuarios/Anuar-04.pdf.

[6] FIAB (n 2).

leaving a scant percentage for public trading. Furthermore, for the majority of firms, the equity market is not the principal conduit for obtaining funding. Lastly, the scarcity of minority shareholders simplifies and economises the delisting procedure.

These same elements have also stymied the influx of new market entrants. In response, the Colombian exchange has expended considerable efforts to expand its investor base and enhance its attractiveness to potential issuers. Its most recent endeavour, an amalgamation with exchanges in Santiago and Lima, known as Nuam Exchange, promises to bolster investor and issuer appeal. The venture's triumph will hinge on a myriad of factors, not least the readiness of regulatory bodies to synchronise present market legislations.

B. General Regulatory Framework

The legislative bedrock of Colombia, Chile, and Argentina is firmly rooted in civil law traditions, where codification is paramount. The venerated Chilean Civil Code, crafted by the distinguished jurist Andrés Bello in the nineteenth century, has had a profound influence on the Colombian and Argentinean codices. Nevertheless, corporate and securities law are relatively recent developments in these jurisdictions.

In Colombia, corporate law is encapsulated within the 1971 Code of Commerce and further refined by Laws 222 of 1995 and 1235 of 2008. The scarcity of governmental decrees is a testament to the comprehensive nature of these legal instruments, which sufficiently address the intricacies of corporate governance. Chile's corporate legal landscape is governed by Law 18.046, the Corporations Act, promulgated in 1981 and subject to subsequent modifications to address specific concerns. Argentina's corporate framework, under the aegis of Law 19.550, has also been subject to several amendments, providing a regulatory scheme for all corporate forms, inclusive of corporations.

Securities legislation in Colombia constitutes an elaborate structure, anchored by Law 964 of 2005, which serves as the framework statute, supplemented by an array of ordinary laws and governmental decrees. The latter has been compiled into a single decree, 2555 of 2010, that addresses, among many other aspects of financial regulation, all facets of securities listing and delisting. Absent an independent regulatory entity, the helm of financial regulation is held by government, ie the President and the Minister of Finance and Public Credit. Oversight functions are consolidated within the Financial Superintendence, which succeeded the Banking and Securities Superintendences in 2005, with a focus on supervision and a limited scope for regulatory intervention. The Superintendent, appointed by the President, operates with constrained independence.

Chile's framework for securities is contained in Law 18,045, known as the Securities Market Act, enacted in 1981. The Financial Market Commission, inaugurated in 2017, subsumed the supervisory and regulatory duties formerly held by the Superintendence of Banks and Financial Institutions. In stark contrast to Colombia's Financial Superintendence, the Commission is an autonomous entity, composed of a quintet of commissioners, four of whom are selected by the Senate, and a chair appointed by the President of the Republic. Their terms are fixed, safeguarding their roles from arbitrary dismissal, save for specific legal causes.

In Argentina, the structural provisions governing securities markets are articulated in Law 17.811, the Public Offering Act, subsequently amended by Law 26.831, the Securities Act. The National Securities and Exchange Commission, abbreviated as CNV, is endowed with expansive supervisory and regulatory powers. Though its members are presidential appointees, they are vested with fixed terms and are insulated from removal except for narrowly defined legal reasons. The decisions and regulations of the CNV are compiled into a unified codex, termed the CNV's Norms.[7]

In terms of securities law, delisting is closely related to the regulation of each country's national securities registry.[8] Thus, delisting is not merely conceptualised as the cessation of negotiation on a particular exchange but as the revocation of a security's registration with the competent national authority, which, in turn, precludes its trading on the public secondary market.

In Colombia and Argentina, the procedure for delisting securities is entwined with both corporate and securities law frameworks. From the perspective of corporate law, delisting precipitates a significant juncture that enables dissenting shareholders to exercise their right to withdraw from the company. Concurrently, securities law levies specific obligations on shareholders who initiate the delisting procedure. This bifurcated approach, which will be scrutinised in greater detail subsequently, is designed to afford minority shareholders substantial means to protect their interests, though it may also impede the delisting initiative in certain scenarios.

The Bolsa de Valores de Colombia ('BVC') and the Bolsa de Santiago are the most prominent exchanges in Colombia and Chile, respectively.[9] Notably, neither imposes any explicit restrictions on voluntary delisting. The BVC retains the authority to suspend the listing of a security, particularly where the issuer fails to fulfil its disclosure obligations. Yet, the BVC's regulations do not endorse permanent punitive measures or obligatory delisting. Similarly, its provisions remain silent on any specific criteria for voluntary delisting, deferring instead to statutory law and directives from the Financial Superintendence.[10]

Similarly, the Bolsa de Santiago's Issuer's Rights and Obligations Handbook authorises the suspension of listing and trading of non-compliant issuers' securities, albeit temporarily, extending up to five days or longer with the Financial Market Commission's

[7] Available at: www.cnv.gov.ar/sitioWeb/MarcoRegulatorio?panel=3.

[8] In Colombia, registration in the Securities and Issuers National Registry is mandatory for securities to be offered publicly or to be traded in a negotiation system (Decree 2555/2010, Art 5.2.1.1.1). In Chile, securities that are going to be offered publicly also have to be previously registered in the Securities Registry, as well as shares of every company that has 2,000 or more shareholders during 12 consecutive months (Law 18.045, Art 5). In Argentina, securities have to be admitted to the Public Offering Regime before launching a public offer. These registries are administered by the supervisory authorities of each country, very much in line with IOSCO's guidelines (among them, *The Role of Securities Commissions*. Available at: www.iosco.org/library/pubdocs/pdf/IOSCOPD9.pdf (September 1990)).

[9] After consolidation of the Bogotá, Medellín and Occidente Stock Exchanges in 2001, the BVC is the only securities exchange operating in Colombia. In Chile, the Bolsa Electrónica de Chile trades a fraction of the Bolsa de Santiago.

[10] BVC, *General Rulebook*, arts 1.3.1.6–1.3.1.10. Available at: https://media.graphassets.com/aP6CeV1RIeDw78SvJK5Z.

endorsement. The Handbook does not articulate any exceptional prerequisites for voluntary delisting.[11]

In stark contrast, Bolsas y Mercados Argentinos ('BYMA'), the preeminent Argentinean exchange established in 2018, enforces a more rigorous regime. BYMA possesses discretionary power to suspend or nullify the listing of securities independently, without prior consent from the CNV. Moreover, the pathway to voluntary delisting is contingent upon fulfilling a series of stringent stipulations.

Finally, it must be acknowledged that delisting requirements also exist for publicly traded fixed-income instruments. In the contexts of Colombia and Chile, it is a prevailing principle that such instruments cannot be delisted while they remain in active circulation.[12] In Argentina, however, the general assembly holds the capacity to delist publicly traded fixed-income instruments. Here, dissenting or discontented creditors are vested with the right to secure reimbursement, mirroring the shareholders' prerogative to withdraw from the company.[13]

II. Delisting Rules in Colombia: A Comparative Analysis with Chile and Argentina

A. Voluntary Delisting

(i) The Decision to Delist

The prerogative to cancel the registration of a company's shares in the national registry, and thus to delist from the local exchanges, resides with the shareholders' assembly, embodying a fundamental safeguard for minority shareholders' interests.[14] This mandate is mirrored in the regulatory frameworks of Chile and Argentina, albeit with subtle differences in execution.

The general assembly must be summoned and 15 days' prior notice given indicating that the decision to delist will be put forward to the shareholders. Additionally, shareholders shall be made aware of their right to withdraw from the company as well as the ensuing buyout offer.[15]

Argentina takes a similar approach, with two additional requirements: the board of directors must provide shareholders with an opinion on the advisability of delisting and

[11] Bolsa Santiago, *Manual de Derechos y Obligaciones de Emisores* [Issuer's Rights and Obligations Handbook]. Available at: https://servicioscms.bolsadesantiago.com/Normativas%20Bolsa%20de%20Comercio/Manual%20de%20Derechos%20y%20Obligaciones%20de%20Emisores.pdf.

[12] Decree 2555/2010, Art 5.2.6.1.1 (Colombia); CMF's General Rule No 30, Art 5.2 (Chile).

[13] Law 23.576, Art 15 (Argentina).

[14] The fact that the shareholders assembly is the only corporate body that can adopt the decision to delist also serves as a safeguard for board directors, who would be subject to litigation if they were to adopt such decision while obliged to act in the best interest of all shareholders. Under Colombian law, no such obligation, or other fiduciary duties, reside upon the shareholders assembly as a whole or the shareholders individually.

[15] Decree 2555/2010, Art 5.2.6.1.3 (Colombia).

the convening notice shall include the price of the buyout offer. These provisos enhance the transparency and informed nature of the shareholders' deliberative process, particularly as knowledge of the proposed acquisition value equips shareholders with critical data to inform their decision-making.

In Colombia, the resolution to delist may be enacted by a simple majority vote within the Assembly, indicative of a more streamlined corporate decision-making framework. Chile and Argentina, however, adopt a more stringent stance, as they both require a supermajority – precisely, two-thirds[16] and 75 per cent of extant voting rights,[17] respectively – for the motion to delist to pass. Moreover, in Argentina, dissenting shareholders must represent no more than 10 per cent of the voting rights, ensuring a substantial consensus is achieved before such a significant corporate action is approved.[18]

As explained above, the BVC and the Bolsa de Santiago do not impose any explicit restrictions on voluntary delisting, other than cancellation from the national registry. Conversely, BYMA builds upon the statutory requirements for cancellation from the public offer regime, adding certain obligations for the delisting issuer. Among them, the assembly's quorum to validly decide to delist is raised to 75 per cent of the existing shares, adding that the dissenting shareholders shall not exceed 10 per cent of those shares. Moreover, the board of directors must provide the shareholders with an opinion on the reasonableness of the tender offer's price and its recommendation to accept or reject this offer, accompanied by the opinion of the audit committee and the auditor, as well as two valuations of the company from independent appraisers. Finally, the shareholders that voted in favour of the delisting proposition must immobilise their shares until the buyout offer is completed.[19]

(ii) Minority Shareholders Protection

(a) Public Acquisition Offer

Subsequent to the general assembly's resolution to delist a Colombian company, the affirmative voting bloc is tasked with initiating a public acquisition offer targeting dissenting or non-participating shareholders.[20] This offer must be launched within three months following the delisting decision. Absent such an offer within this prescribed period, the decision will cease to produce any effects.

The price of the acquisition offer must be determined by an independent appraiser, whose credentials are subject to preliminary assessment by the Financial Superintendence, upon application by any endorsing shareholder of the delisting motion.[21] The issuer bears financial responsibility for the valuation service.

[16] Corporations Act, Law 18.046, Art 2 (Chile).

[17] BYMA, *Listing Rulebook*, Art 48 (Argentina). Available at: www.byma.com.ar/wp-content/uploads/dlm_uploads/2019/08/BYMA-Reglamento-de-Listado-2020-02-04.pdf.

[18] ibid.

[19] ibid Art 49.

[20] Only the shareholders that voted against the decision to delist or were absent from the assembly's meeting have the right to participate in the buyout offer. This right is non-transferable, even if the dissenting or non-participating shareholders transfer their shares (Decree 2555/2010, Art 5.2.6.1.2).

[21] According to Decree 2555/2010, Art 5.2.6.1.4 the shareholder that submits the appraiser's name to the SFC shall be responsible for launching the buyout offer. If no shareholder acts accordingly within the 30 days

The Argentinean framework delineates several distinct provisions in comparison to its Colombian counterpart. Primarily, the onus to extend the acquisition offer rests with the issuer, which in turn must prove the CNV it has enough liquid earnings to undertake the buyout process, in accordance with the principle of capital maintenance. Nonetheless, the predominant shareholder, should one exist, may volunteer to underwrite this obligation. Moreover, the independent valuator is mandated to incorporate specific statutory criteria,[22] to determine the buyout price, which shall be a 'fair price'.[23] Thirdly, the CNV reserves the right to object to the proposed valuation under certain conditions established by law.[24] Finally, the shareholders have the right to contest judicially the offered price.[25]

Upon comparison of the Colombian and Argentinean regimes, it is apparent that the latter erects additional fortifications in favour of minority shareholders. The efficacy of such measures is open to debate. Nonetheless, detractors could contend that the Colombian appraisal mechanism lacks robust safeguards for minority interests, given the inherent subjectivity of valuation methodologies and the fact that the appraiser's remuneration emanates from the issuer, predominantly under the control of the majority shareholder. Moreover, there is scant justification to prevent the company from launching the acquisition offer, consonant with share repurchase provisions under the Code of Commerce.[26]

(b) Right of Withdrawal

Numerous legislations confer shareholders the right to withdraw from a company, yet the conditions that precede this right vary widely. This analysis is focused on the decision to delist, as a trigger for the right of withdrawal. The commercial and securities statutes of the three countries studied in this chapter afford shareholders the possibility to exercise this right upon the assembly's decision to cancel the registration of the company's shares from the public registry (or, in the case of Argentina, the authorisation for public offering). In Chile, this is the only statutory recourse available to minority shareholders once the delisting resolution is passed. Meanwhile, in Colombia and

following the assembly's decision to delist, all shareholders who voted in favour shall be responsible for launching the buyout offer, in proportion to their voting rights, and for submitting the appraiser's name to the SFC within 10 days after the initial 30-day period has expired.

[22] These criteria include (i) prior negotiations by the offeror, (ii) the market price during the preceding semester, (iii) the equity value, (iv) discounted cashflow, and (v) liquidation value. In no instance shall the valuation be inferior to criteria (i) and (ii), unless the offeror demonstrates the company is in financial hardship. (Law 26.831, Art 88).

[23] ibid.

[24] ibid, the CNV may object the price in light of extraordinary circumstances affecting market price, apparent price manipulation or if the market price does not reflect the full compensation obtained by sellers.

[25] Dissenting and absent shareholders in Colombia do not have a specific judicial action to contest the buyout price and must resort to the ordinary processes and general principles of law to raise their claims. In the case of *Ruberto, Guillermo M. v Atanor S.A.* [2007], the Argentinean Commercial Chamber examined the criteria to establish a fair price contained in Decree 677/2001. This Decree provided the appraiser some discretion to determine the applicable criteria to establish the buyout price. Under Law 26.831, the appraiser lacks such discretion and must choose the highest price resulting from the applicable criteria.

[26] Code of Commerce, Art 396 (Colombia). However, under this provision the buyback must be approved by a supermajority of 70 per cent of the existing shares.

Argentina, stockholders have the alternative to accept the mandatory buyout offer, as described in the preceding paragraphs.

The beneficiaries of the right of withdrawal are the shareholders that opposed the decision to delist and those absent from the assembly's meeting.[27] The shareholders that voted in favour of the decision, and those that were present in the assembly and abstained from voting forfeit the prerogative to withdraw. The right to withdraw must be exercised within the eight days following the assembly's decision to delist and has immediate effects upon notification to the company.[28] However, if the assembly revokes its decision within 60 days or the buyout offer is not initiated within three months, the seceding shareholders will reacquire their rights, with retroactive effects.[29] Given the brief period of time provided to Colombian companies' shareholders to exercise their withdrawal right, they often have to choose whether to retire from the company or accept the ensuing buyout offer without full knowledge of the latter's conditions. Argentinean shareholders, on the other hand, are spared this quandary, as the price of the tender offer must be disclosed alongside the assembly call.

Once the company receives the notice to withdraw, the stocks shall be offered to the other shareholders. If they express no interest in acquiring them, the company will repurchase the stocks, provided it has liquid earnings from previous exercises or special reserves for that purpose. Otherwise, the company shall reimburse the withdrawing shareholder's equity.[30] In any case, the price shall be agreed upon by the parties. If there is no consensus, it will be determined by an appraiser designated by the Societies Superintendence. Payment shall be made within two months after the parties' agreement or the appraisal's result.[31]

In Chile, the company is not required to make an offer to remaining shareholders and, where the shares are actively traded, the price shall be equal to the average market price over 60 trading days between the thirtieth and ninetieth trading day prior to the shareholders meeting approving delisting. If the company's shares are not actively traded, their book value will be the repurchase price.[32] Remarkably, under Argentinean law, the shareholders opting for withdrawal receive only their shares' book value.[33] In most scenarios, these shareholders can secure more favourable terms if they accept the buyout offer, considering its price is defined according to criteria more advantageous to their interests.

The obligation to reimburse shareholders equity poses potential risks for a company and its creditors. Therefore, Colombian legislation incorporates some safeguards in order to prevent depletion of the company's assets. If the issuer demonstrates that its financial stability is endangered, it may request the Superintendence to extend the term

[27] Law 222/1995, Art 12 (Colombia); Corporations Act, Art 2 (Chile); Law 19.550, Art 245 (Argentina).

[28] Law 222/1995, Art 14 (Colombia). In Argentina the limit is five days for the dissenting shareholders and 15 for the absentees (Law 19.550, Art 245). In Chile, its 30 days (Law 18.046, Art 70). In Chile, the shareholder may defer the effects of his withdrawal until the company pays the full price of the shares (Decree 702/2012, Art 129).

[29] Law 222/1995, Art 14 (Colombia); Law 19.550, Art 245 (Argentina).

[30] In this case, the company's equity will be reduced.

[31] Law 222/1995, Arts 15 and 16 (Colombia).

[32] Decree 702/2012, Art 130 (Chile).

[33] Law 19.550, Art 245 (Argentina).

to pay the seceding shareholder for up to a year. Moreover, the Superintendence may determine that the withdrawal shall not proceed, if the issuers' ability to pay its creditors is substantially impaired.[34] In such instances, minority shareholders can resort to the buyout offer as an exit strategy. Chile provides a distinct safeguard for creditors: the right to withdraw shall be suspended if the company undergoes insolvency procedures, until creditors are paid in full.[35] Likewise, Argentinean insolvency law obliges seceding shareholders to reimburse the price received for their shares if the company defaults on payments.[36]

(iii) Foreign Issuers

Foreign companies are allowed to register their shares in Colombia, Chile and Argentina and to offer them to the public.[37] These foreign issuers are not bound by the local companies' law, thereby their shareholders are not entitled to the right of withdrawal under such laws. In Argentina, their registration's cancellation is governed by special rules that exempt the issuers and their controllers from the obligation to undertake a buyout offer.[38] This exemption also applies in Colombia, provided the company's shares remain listed on a foreign exchange and the issuer offers local investors with a mechanism that enables them to trade their shares on that exchange for at least for six months.[39]

B. Involuntary Cancellation

(i) Statutory Causes

As explained above, the Colombian, Chilean and Argentinean securities legislations are structured around the issuers obligation to register publicly offered securities with the competent authority. There are few statutory causes for cancellation of securities registration in Colombia. Beyond the absence of a public offering, the only causes for cancellation provided by the law are the issuers liquidation or a material breach of its obligations as an issuer.[40] In contrast, Chile's Securities Market Acts enumerates a comprehensive array of compulsory delisting causes,[41] including:

(a) when the issuer lacks 2,000 or more shareholders for a period of six months;

[34] Law 222/1995, Art 16 (Colombia).

[35] Corporations Act, Art 69 (Chile).

[36] Law 24.522, Art 149 (Argentina).

[37] Securities issued by foreign entities may also be negotiated in secondary markets in the form of deposit certificates, ETFs or similar vehicles. Additionally, local exchanges have been allowed to create secondary markets for non-registered foreign securities (eg Colombia's foreign securities quotation systems). Delisting of these securities in the local markets is tied to noncompliance of the listing requirements or their delisting in their countries of origin (Decree 2555/2010, Art 2.15.6.15).

[38] Comisión Nacional de Valores, *Resolución General 930/22*, Art 1.K (Argentina).

[39] Decree 2555/2010, Art 5.2.6.1.2 para 5.

[40] Decree 2555/2010, Art 5.2.6.2.1 and Law 964/2005, Art 51 (f) (Colombia).

[41] Securities Act, Law 18.045 Art 15 (Chile).

(b) a decision of the Financial Markets Commission, undertaken to safeguard public interest or the investors' welfare; and
(c) the Financial Markets Commission's decision, grounded in instances where (i) the registration relied on false information or facts, (ii) the issuer disseminated false information to the market, the Securities Registry, the stock exchanges or the securities intermediaries, or (iii) the issuer fails to meet the requirements that made the securities' registration necessary.

Argentina's CNV similarly delineates several causes for cancellation from the public offering regime,[42] encompassing:

(a) the issuer's dissolution for various reasons, including a merger;
(b) the issuer's bankruptcy;
(c) substantial alteration of the conditions prompting permission for a public offering.

There is significant asymmetry among these statutory causes for delisting. However, they tend to converge. In all countries, the issuer's breach of its obligations, be it during the registration process or afterwards, permits the supervisor to cancel its registration. In Argentina, the company's dissolution derived from its merger[43] is explicitly enumerated as one of the causes for cancellation from the public offering regime. No such cause for deregistration exists in Colombia or Chile. However, in all countries the outcome is similar. If a listed company is an absorbing participant in the merger, its registration as securities issuer is not affected. On the contrary, if the listed company is the absorbed party, it's up to the merging companies to decide whether to continue as a registered issuer. Where the decision is to cancel the registration, the dissenting and absent shareholders have the right to exercise their right to withdraw from the company.[44]

The only significant difference among these regimes resides in Chile's compulsory listing under certain circumstances and the consequences of their cessation. An illustrative example is the criterion tied to the number of shareholders, compelling all companies with 2,000 or more shareholders to register their shares with the CMF, and the cancellation derived from the decrease thereof.[45]

(ii) Delisting on the Exchange's Decision

The Rulebook of the Colombian Exchange does not stipulate any delisting measures that the Exchange may enforce upon issuers. Mandatory delisting occurs solely when

[42] CNV, *Norms* (n 7), Title III, ch I (Argentina).

[43] The dissolution of the company precedes its liquidation. In the case of a merger, the company is dissolved without liquidation.

[44] In Chile and Argentina, the company's merger always gives rise to the right of withdrawal. In Colombia, the shareholders will have this prerogative whenever the shareholders economic rights are deteriorated because of the merger (Law 222/1995, Art 12).

[45] Initially, the Securities Act (Law 18.045) required all companies with 500 or more shareholders to register as issuers. Law 21.521 (the Fintech Act) raised this threshold to 2,000 shareholders and required the companies to register their shares, not as issuer themselves, facilitating the process.

an issuer's registration is cancelled in the National Registry.[46] The Bolsa de Santiago's Issuer's Rights and Obligations Handbook assigns the board of directors the authority to establish causes for delisting and to impose punitive measures upon issuers. BYMA exercises broad discretion to delist any security whenever it concludes that the issuer lacks an administrative organisation capable of fulfilling the requirements of its Rulebook and that such a measure is in the investors' interest, the issuer has materially breached its obligations under the market's Rulebook, or another exchange has delisted the securities.[47]

(iii) The Balance of Interests

The legal frameworks of Colombia, Chile and Argentina exhibit a high degree of similarity in their approach to delisting. The obligations imposed upon the issuers seeking to delist, alongside the correlative rights of minority shareholders, show little variation across these countries at the statutory level. All jurisdictions authorise voluntary delisting upon the shareholders assembly decision and grant dissenting and absent shareholders the right to withdraw from the company. Colombia and Argentina also mandate a buyout offer, albeit the responsibility to launch the offer rests on different subjects. Mandatory delisting regulation is similarly consistent, with nearly identical causes enabling the supervising authority to enact such measures.

However, these similarities end at the exchange level, particularly with BYMA, which imposes several requirements upon delisting issuers, in excess of those provided by the law. The supermajority required for the shareholders' assembly to approve the delisting motion and the numerous internal and independent opinions required to support the decision might deter a controlling party from seeking to delist. Moreover, the Argentinean exchange is endowed with ample powers to suspend and cancel the negotiation of listed securities, in contrast to its Colombian and Chilean peers, which possess very limited powers in this regard. Still, BYMA has not been immune from the delisting trend that has impacted most Latin American equity markets, experiencing a decrease in issuers by approximately 20 per cent over the last two decades. Yet, it is speculative to consider whether that decline would have been more pronounced absent such rules, given the severe grievances that have plagued the Argentinean economy during that period.

It's open to debate whether any of these countries has struck the right chord in this balancing act among the competing interests of majority and minority shareholders. The absence of significant litigation might support the notion that they have succeeded. However, this may well be the result of clear regulations and the fact that, in most cases, delisting is the result of substantial concentration of voting rights among controlling parties. Perhaps a more accurate indicator of the success of the current delisting rules is that in none of these countries is there an apparent call for their amendment. That may well change in the foreseeable future. Except for Brazil, Latin American countries

[46] BVC, *General Rulebook* (n 10) Art 1.3.1.6.
[47] BYMA, *Listing Rulebook*, Art 46.

have struggled to create deep, liquid equity markets. Despite numerous efforts to boost investor confidence and attract new issuers, the anticipated response has not materialised. Exchanges have proved to be resilient players, consolidating at a regional level and venturing into new segments of the market. In their pursuit of new business, they are reaching out to non-traditional issuers that are not able or willing to meet the existing listing requirements. Should these standards be amended, a comprehensive review of delisting procedures will undoubtedly be necessary.

PART VI

Conclusions

19

Common Grounds on Delisting

ULRICH TORGGLER AND DANIEL MERT YILMAZ*

I. Introduction

In this chapter, we aim to provide a synthesis of the previous chapters and, thereby, lay the groundwork for the following chapter on future legislation. The Questionnaires and Country Reports provided by the participating jurisdictions served as the basis for this analysis.

In addition, insights gained at our conference in 2023 proved very valuable and account was also taken of these in the following.

First, the issues regarding delisting not only concern retail investors holding a couple of shares in a company but rather also concern bondholders and – more importantly – institutional investors, which never want (or are allowed) to hold shares of a private company.[1]

Second, delisting is not a repetitive und cooperative 'game'. On the contrary, it is very much an end-time game. It is a veritable 'swimming with sharks', because some market participants will exploit every available loophole pursuing their own interests, which obviously differ from those of legislators/regulators.

As to the questions we examined in greater detail, we will first follow up with the different possibilities of a Voluntary Delisting (II). Then, a brief summary on the Legal Grounds (III), the Competent Decision Body of the Issuer (IV) and the Competent Public Institution (V) will follow. Subsequently, we will consider Mandatory Bids and (other) Exit Options (VI) before turning to Mandatory Delistings (VII). Finally, in our Conclusion, we will identify the Common Grounds on Delistings in the various jurisdictions (VIII).

* Dr Ulrich Torggler, LLM, Professor at the Department of Commercial and Business Law at the University of Vienna, Austria, and Daniel Mert Yilmaz, Research Assistant and Doctoral Candidate at the University of Vienna, Austria.

[1] Even though Art 2(e) of Directive (EU) 2017/828 amending Directive 2007/36/EC as regards the encouragement of long-term shareholder engagement [2017] OJ L132/1 (SRD 2) provides a definition of institutional investors, this definition is too narrow, cf MB Madsen, 'Articles 1 and 2: Scope and Definitions' in HS Birkmose and K Sergakis (eds), *The Shareholder Rights Directive II: A Commentary* (Cheltenham, Edward Elgar, 2021) 2.35. For instance, according to Art 50 of Directive 2009/65/EC on the coordination of laws, regulations and administrative provisions relating to undertakings for collective investment in transferable securities (UCITS) (recast) [2009] OJ L302/32 (UCITS-Directive), UCITS in general may only invest in transferable securities.

II. Voluntary Delisting

A. Voluntary Delisting

First of all, it is worth noting that voluntary delisting is legally recognised in almost all of the jurisdictions under survey. The only exception is Italy, where the law explicitly only enables market migration.[2] However, the Italian doctrine nonetheless argues that delisting is permissible, as it is not explicitly forbidden.[3] In practice, a voluntary delisting is conducted through a 'cold delisting' (see II.B. below).[4]

Figure 19.1 Is Voluntary Delisting Explicitly Allowed by National Laws or Jurisprudence?

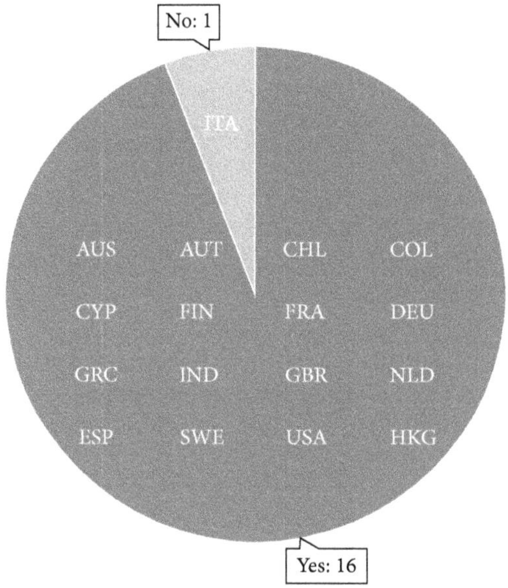

B. Cold Delisting

This leads us to the so-called 'cold delisting'. Pursuant to the Questionnaires, there is no legal definition for a 'cold delisting' in any of the jurisdictions under survey. The expression is used in most of the countries,[5] although with some variations as to its precise meaning.[6] The general (European) understanding of the term seems to be in line with Questions 18 and 19 of the Questionnaire regarding the merger of a listed company with an absorbing company without listing.[7] Throughout the jurisdictions, such a merger

[2] See G Balp, Questionnaire Italy Q 1.

[3] See ibid.

[4] See ibid Q 1 and Q 18.

[5] However, see also as to Finland, H Marjosola, Questionnaire Finland Q 18: 'alien'.

[6] See – among others – Balp, Questionnaire Italy (n 2) Q 18, where differences between Italian and German law are explained.

[7] See eg for the Austrian definition of a 'cold delisting' (which does not differ from the general understanding) U Torggler, Questionnaire Austria Q 18; see also P Nutz, *Delisting und Anlegerschutz: Der freiwillige Rückzug von der Börse und seine Folgen* (Vienna, Bank Verlag, 2022) 26, 27.

appears to be the simplest way to achieve a cold delisting, especially by merging the listed company with its subsidiary. However, the term 'cold delisting' also covers other corporate measures (eg demergers), which do not directly aim at, but nonetheless lead to, delisting. In most of the jurisdictions, a merger with an absorbing company that is not listed will result in a cessation of the listing of the shares of the other transferring company. One exception is Cyprus.[8]

Figure 19.2 Does the Merger of a Listed Company with a Non-listed Company Lead to Delisting?

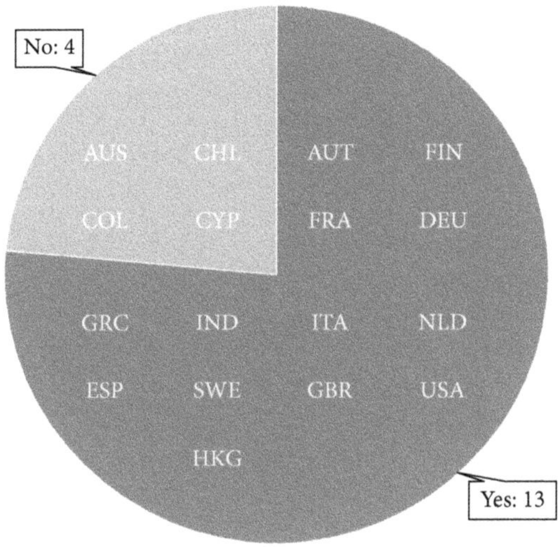

In many cases, a merger leading to a cold delisting is subject to the same prerequisites and restrictions regarding minority protection as a voluntary delisting, ie a withdrawal right of dissenting shareholders on a preceding mandatory bid.[9] However, if the cold delisting is to be achieved through other corporate measures, other exit options – such as an appropriate cash settlement – can be available.[10]

It must be borne in mind that any and every difference in standards will be exploited – it is, after all, a case of swimming with the sharks. A recent example is the German regulation StaRUG,[11] which implemented Directive EU 2019/1023 on Restructuring and Insolvency.[12] It became public knowledge that an increasing number of public companies use capital measures, ie reduce the capital to zero and then increase it with a simultaneous exemption of subscription rights, for restructuring purposes. At least in

[8] See T Papadopoulos, Questionnaire Cyprus Q 18, Q 19; cf also C Van der Elst, Questionnaire Netherlands Q 18, Q 19: delisting request initiated.

[9] See JP González, Chapter 18, II.B.i. Torggler, Questionnaire Austria (n 7) Q 18, Q 19.

[10] For instance, see Torggler (n 7) Q 13, Q 18.

[11] Unternehmensstabilisierungs- und -restrukturierungsgesetz of 22 December 2020 (BGBl. I S. 3256), which was recently amended by Art 7 of the Law of 15 July 2024 (BGBl. 2024 I Nr. 236).

[12] Directive (EU) 2019/1023 on preventive restructuring frameworks, on discharge of debt and disqualifications, and on measures to increase the efficiency of procedures concerning restructuring, insolvency and discharge of debt, and amending Directive (EU) 2017/1132 (Directive on restructuring and insolvency) [2019] OJ L172/18.

some cases, the real motivation behind such measures is to achieve a takeover and to delist without a tender offer or without having to compensate shareholders.[13]

In Finland, there is no special legislation on mergers leading to delisting; whether they are permitted is decided on a case-by-case basis by the NASDAQ Helsinki Listing Committee.[14] Similarly, in France, the consequences of certain corporate measures/transactions will be assessed by the Autorité des marchés financiers (AMF) and can trigger a mandatory buyout offer.[15]

Nevertheless, as was pointed out in the course of the discussions at the conference, this is a question of corporate law as opposed to financial markets law.[16] Such a harmonisation would *per se* not apply to non-EEA corporations.[17]

C. Downlisting and Market Migration

(i) Downlisting

Figure 19.3 Are there any Specific Provisions or Rulings on Downlisting?

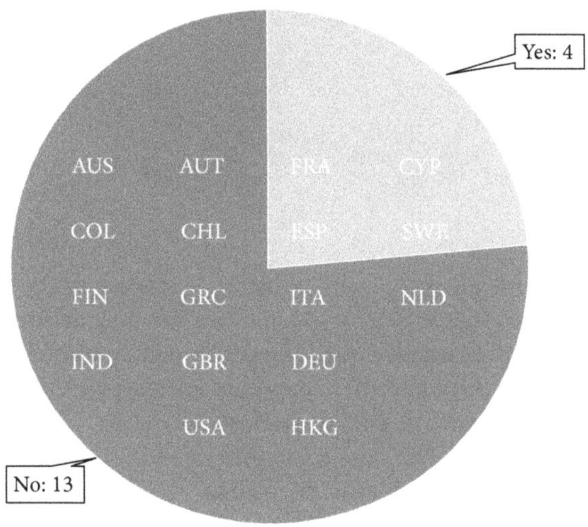

Based on the Questionnaires it became clear that the majority of the participating jurisdictions share a common understanding of the term 'downlisting':[18] A downlisting occurs when a security listed on the regulated market is no longer traded

[13] For a detailed legal analysis, see S Mock, '(Einseitige) Bezugsrechtsgewährung in Restrukturierungsplänen – Restrukturierungsübernahmerecht ante portas?' (2024) 27 *Neue Zeitschrift für Gesellschaftsrecht* 769.

[14] See Marjosola, Questionnaire Finland (n 5) Q 19.

[15] See K Deckert, Questionnaire France Q 18.

[16] For an economic analysis, see E Härkönen and J Östberg, Chapter 13, II.

[17] See III below.

[18] Exceptions seem to be USA and HKG.

on that market, but on secondary markets – such as MTFs in the EU.[19] Contrary to cold delistings, some jurisdictions provide regulations for downlistings.

For instance, in Spain, there is a regulation which stipulates that downlistings are to be treated in the same manner as regular delistings.[20] Despite the lack of legal provisions, this also applies to Austria and Germany.[21] In Sweden, there are no specific statutory rules, but there are rulings from the Swedish Securities Council regarding downlistings.[22] A different situation presents itself in Cyprus, as downlistings appear to be treated like market migrations.[23]

Downlisting is dealt with in more detail in Chapter 11 and Chapter 4.[24]

(ii) Market Migration

Figure 19.4 Are there Any Specific Provisions or Rulings on Market Migration?

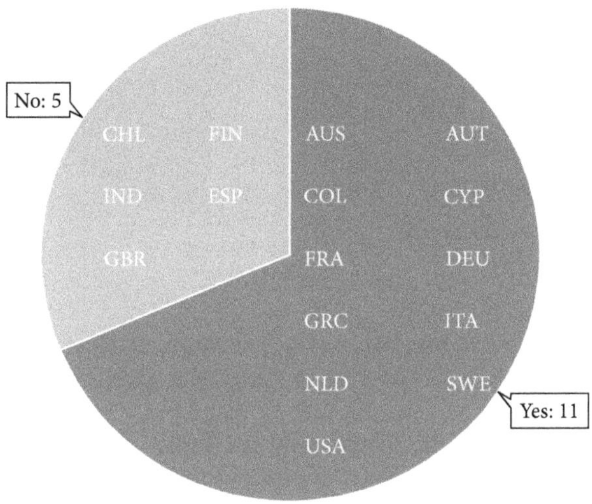

According to the common understanding of the Questionnaires, market migration occurs if a traded security is delisted from a regulated market and listed on another regulated market. Most jurisdictions under survey contain provisions on market migration.[25] As with regard to downlisting, there are no Swedish provisions regarding market migration, although the Swedish Securities Council has ruled on this issue.[26]

[19] This definition also aligns with the definition by G Balp, Chapter 11, I.
[20] See A Recalde and M Ataun, Questionnaire Spain Q 14.
[21] See Torggler (n 7) Q 14; K Çavuşoğlu, Questionnaire Germany Q 14.
[22] See J Östberg, Questionnaire Sweden Q 14.
[23] See Papadopoulos, Questionnaire Cyprus (n 8) Q 14.
[24] See Balp (n 19); cf also A Recalde and M Ataun, Chapter 4, III.D.ii., on downlistings from MTFs.
[25] An exception may be HKG.
[26] See Östberg, Questionnaire Sweden (n 22) Q 15.

III. Legal Grounds

Figure 19.5 What are the Legal Grounds for a Voluntary Delisting?

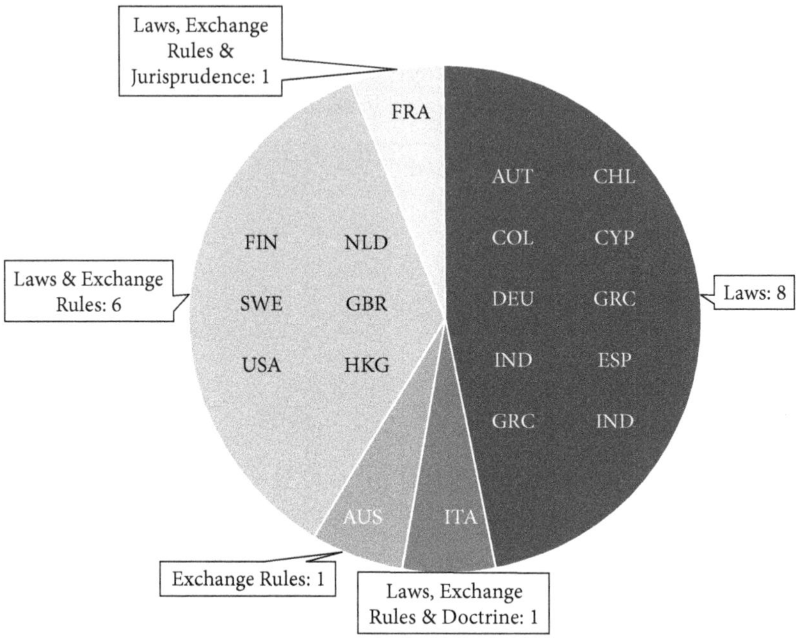

Substantial differences exist between the jurisdictions as to the legal grounds of a voluntary delisting, which is covered by statutory law, exchange rules of a private or regulatory character, case law, and soft law, to name but a few. As highlighted in the chart, the legal grounds are not limited to only one basis,[27] but there can be an interplay between different rules: eg Italian legal doctrine deduces the legitimacy from existing statutory laws and exchange rules.[28]

A fundamental question in this context is, in our view, whether the delisting regime can be left to the market for issuers and investors, ie to self-regulation by the market operators.[29]

At first glance, market operators do not seem to have an interest in letting their customers go. However, to attract listings, they should make it clear to prospective issuers that listings are not a one-way street. Nevertheless, when corporations decide whether and where to go public, delisting is a rather minor issue[30] and behavioural studies suggest that distant and improbable events tend to be over-discounted.[31]

[27] For a fundamental rights analysis in light of the ECHR, see Y Ktistakis, Chapter 2.

[28] See Balp (n 2) Q 1.

[29] This issue is also reflected in the Questionnaires, for instance, see Deckert, Questionnaire France (n 15) Q 7, Q 24; see H Marjosola, Chapter 8, III.

[30] See H DeAngelo, L DeAngelo and EM Rice, 'Going Private: Minority Freezeouts and Stockholder Wealth' (1984) 27 *Journal of Law and Economics* 367, 374: 'there is no reason to expect that a firm currently operating with a given (public or private) ownership structure will always find the current structure to be most efficient'.

[31] See generally, D Kahneman and A Tversky, 'Intuitive Prediction: Biases and Corrective Procedures' (1979) 12 *TIMS Studies in Management Science* 313; R Buehler, D Griffin and M Ross, 'Inside the Planning Fallacy:

Therefore, the effect of competition for issuers is likely to be flawed and will not produce efficient results. For similar reasons, rational-apathetic investors will probably not exert considerable market pressure on market operators to introduce efficient rules on delisting.[32] However, the opposite may be true for institutional investors.[33] In any case, we must bear in mind the risk of opportunistic behaviour by market operators with respect to corporations that are already listed, especially when granting discretion about whether an issuer is allowed to delist.[34] Ultimately, it is the disinterested shareholders who will suffer.

This leads to the second basic question: do we want financial market regulations or corporate law ensure minority protection? In other words: should the place of listing or the place of incorporation determine the applicability of shareholder-oriented rules?

The answer is: probably both. However, in our view, the case for European regulation is much stronger as regards investor protection under financial market laws, which also cover bondholders' interests. Shareholder protection, on the other hand, can arguably be left to the Member States to regulate. To preserve some competition between stock exchanges, EU financial regulation should consist of minimum standards, allowing market operators to be stricter depending on the market segments offered.

IV. Competent Decision Body of the Issuer

Figure 19.6 What is the Competent Decision Body of the Issuer?

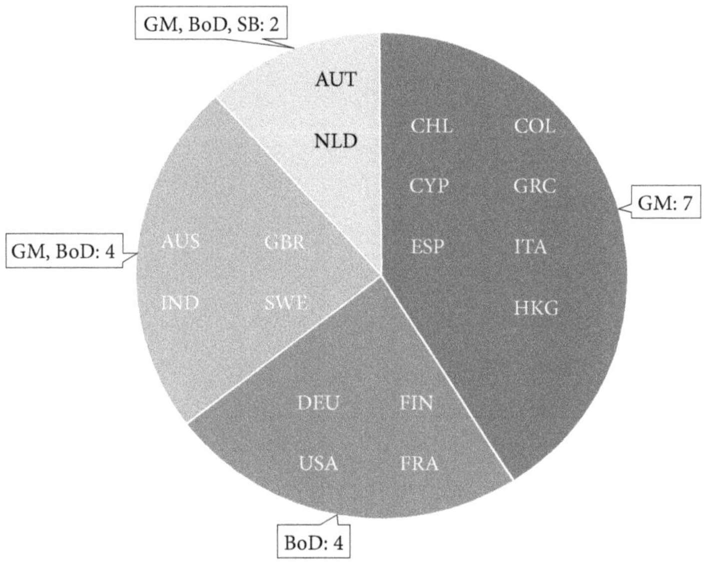

The Causes and Consequences of Optimistic Time Predictions' in T Gilovich, D Griffin and D Kahneman (eds), *Heuristics and Biases: The Psychology of Intuitive Judgment* (Cambridge, Cambridge University Press, 2002) 250 ff.

[32] On rational apathy in general, see RC Clark, 'Vote Buying and Corporate Law' (1979) 29 *Case Western Reserve Law Review* 776, 779.

[33] See I. above.

[34] See V. below.

The decision regarding delisting can be a management decision or one made by the shareholders.[35] However, there are also jurisdictions where both bodies must consent or additional corporate bodies, such as a supervisory board, must participate in the decision-making process. Most of jurisdictions require, at the very least, the approval of the general meeting (GM).

Finland, France and Germany are the only European jurisdictions in which the delisting decision is one taken by management alone.[36] However, a resolution by the GM is required in France in the case of a downlisting.[37] In the Netherlands, the decision to request a delisting lies within the competences of the board of directors (BoD), which is monitored by the supervisory board (SB). However, shareholders holding 95 per cent of the voting rights can also request a delisting if the issuer agrees to the delisting.[38]

In Sweden, the concrete circumstances are decisive: in general, the BoD will decide on a delisting.[39] However, according to the Swedish Securities Council, special circumstances may require a resolution by the GM.[40]

In our view, although concerning corporate finance due to its impact on shareholders, the delisting of shares should not be a mere management decision. The opposite is true with regard to bonds.

Figure 19.7 GM Majorities (if applicable)

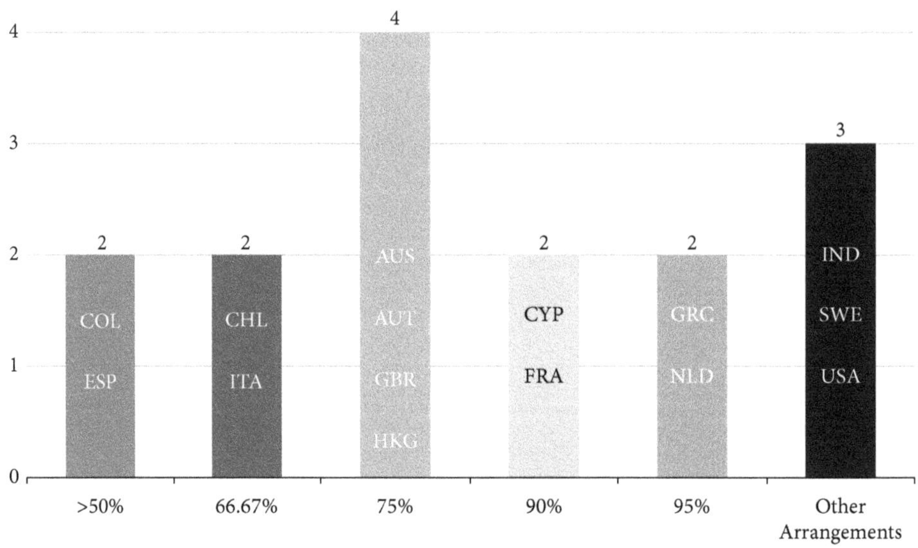

[35] For an in-depth analysis, see C Van der Elst, Chapter 3; Härkönen and Östberg (n 16) III.A. provide a detailed analysis of the agency conflicts in this matter.

[36] See Marjosola (n 5) Q 2; cf Çavuşoğlu, Questionnaire Germany (n 21) Q 2; Deckert (n 15) Q 2.

[37] Deckert (n 15) Q 2, Q 4.

[38] Van der Elst, Questionnaire Netherlands (n 8) Q 2.

[39] For further details, see Östberg (n 22) Q 2.

[40] See ibid Q 4.

In jurisdictions where a voluntary delisting requires the approval of the GM or its request, the necessary voting majorities range from 50 per cent to 95 per cent.

In Sweden, although as a general rule the GM decides by simple majority, the Securities Council requires a 90 per cent majority as good practice in the stock market.[41] In Spain, a simple majority suffices in most cases.[42] Indian law requires a 75 per cent majority, with at least twice as many shareholders approving rather than rejecting the proposal.[43]

The topic is dealt with by Van der Elst in more detail in Chapter 3 of this book. Therefore, we only make two observations: first, the risk of arbitrage versus squeeze-out is to be borne in mind. Second, it does make an important difference whether the majority of decisions are based on the *total capital* or on the *votes cast* in the GM.

V. Competent Public Institution

Figure 19.8 Which is the Competent Public Institution?

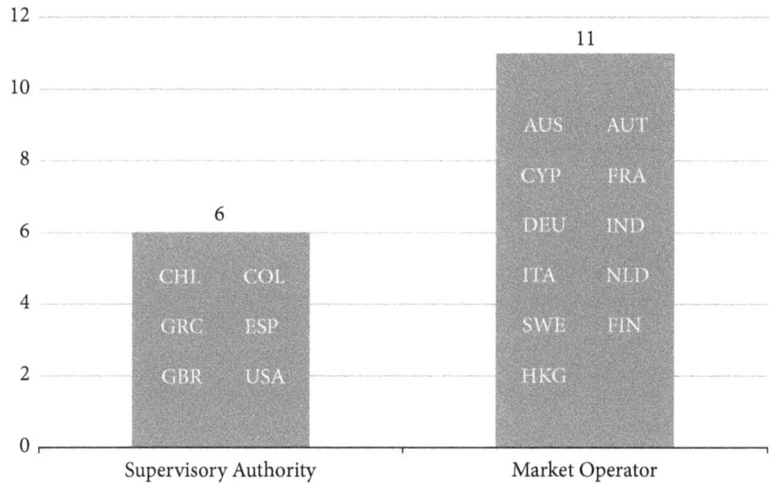

In about two-thirds of the jurisdictions under survey, the market operator acts as the competent public institution with regard to delisting procedures. This can also include the competence to grant a delisting application. However, it has to be pointed out that not every market operator exercises its decision with public authority *(imperium)*.[44] This is important, inter alia, with regard to the appeal mechanisms.[45]

[41] See Östberg (n 22) Q 4.
[42] See Recalde and Ataun, Questionnaire Spain (n 20) Q 4.
[43] See H Kaur, Chapter 17, III.B.
[44] For instance, the Austrian market operator acts by *acta iure imperii*, see Torggler (n 7) Q 8.
[45] For instance, see Deckert (n 15) Q 23, where the decisions of the *Autorité des Marchés Financiers* (AMF) and the decisions of the Chairman of the AMF have to be appealed at different (civil and administrative) courts. However, as pointed out, this is rather a theoretical problem. However, see eg Papadopoulos (n 8) Q 26 for an administrative appeal.

Figure 19.9 Is it Required that the Competent Public Institution Approves the Voluntary Delisting?

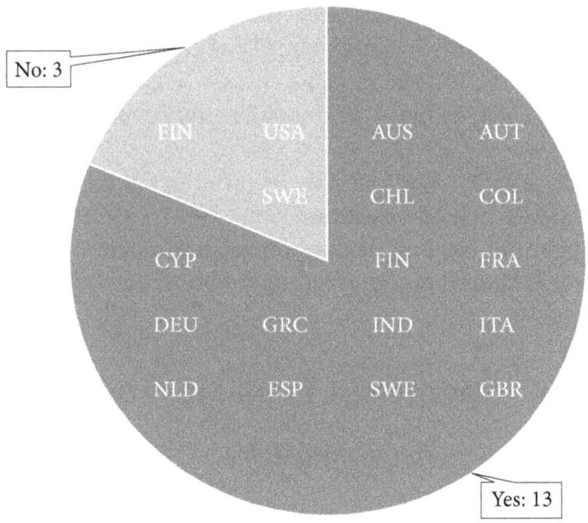

Figure 19.10 Does the Competent Public Institution have any Competence to Verify the Reasons for Delisting (if applicable)?

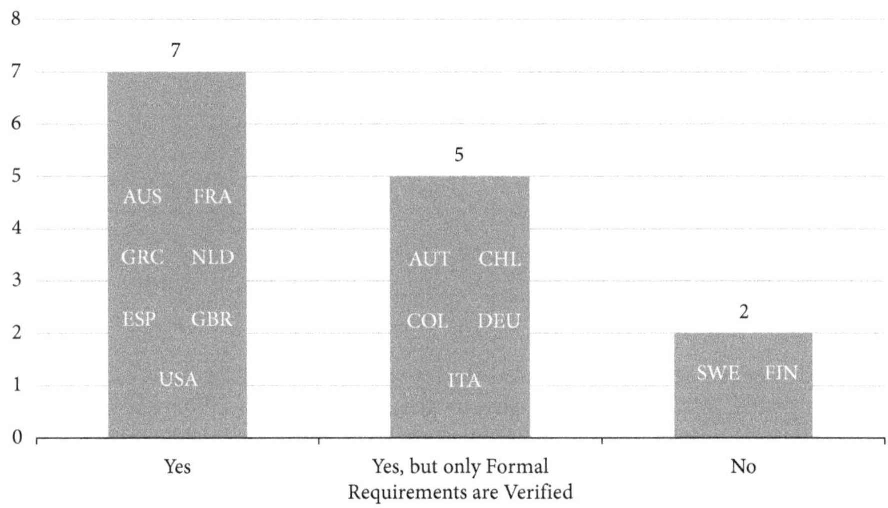

In most jurisdictions under survey, approval by the competent public institution is required. However, as highlighted in Figure 19.10, in about 50 per cent of these jurisdictions, the competence of the verification of the delisting application is limited to formal requirements, whereas in the other 50 per cent, the competent public institutions have discretion in their decisions on the merits of the particular case. In our view, material discretion in this sense also exists if a competent public institution decides if the interests of investors are adequately protected in a concrete delisting plan.[46] *De lege ferenda* it has to be borne in mind that market operators may be inclined to deny delisting of their customers.[47] This point is particularly critical in jurisdictions where the market operator acts as a private institution and, in addition, has discretionary power.[48]

Uncommon rules exist in the USA and in Finland. In the USA, a delisting becomes effective 10 days after the required 'Form 25' has been filed. However, the United States Securities and Exchange Commission (SEC) may postpone the effectiveness under special circumstances.[49] In Finland, the market operator may request the Finnish Financial Supervisory Authority (FIN-FSA) to verify its decision.[50]

VI. Mandatory Bid and Exit Options

A. Exit Options

Figure 19.11 Is there an Exit Opportunity Available to Shareholders?

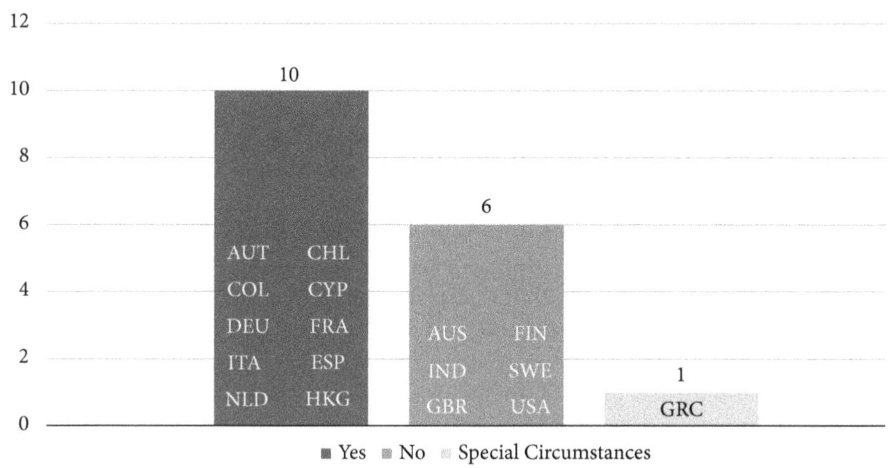

[46] For instance, this is the case in Australia. See P Hanrahan, Chapter 15, I.A.iii.; also see eg J Chan and C Gerner-Beurle, Questionnaire UK Q 8.

[47] See III. above; especially Marjosola (n 29) III.; also cf J Mohamed, 'Delisting nach dem Entwurf eines Zweiten Zukunftsfinanzierungsgesetzes (ZuFinG II)' (2025) 25 *Zeitschrift für Bank- und Kapitalmarktrecht* 1, 4, according to which the German legislator wants to remove the discretionary power of the market operator.

[48] This seems to be the case in France and Italy. See Deckert (n 15) Q 8, Q 24; Balp (n 2) Q 8, Q 21, Q 22.

[49] M Gelter, Chapter 14, III.C.iii.

[50] Marjosola (n 5) Q 8.

Apart from institutional oversight, the most effective means of shareholders' protection in the case of a delisting is likely an exit option, which enables them to leave the company which is going private and receive full compensation. About two-thirds of the jurisdictions under survey provide such an option, with most of them stipulating a mandatory bid.[51]

Figure 19.12 Is a Mandatory Bid Required in the case of a Voluntary Delisting?

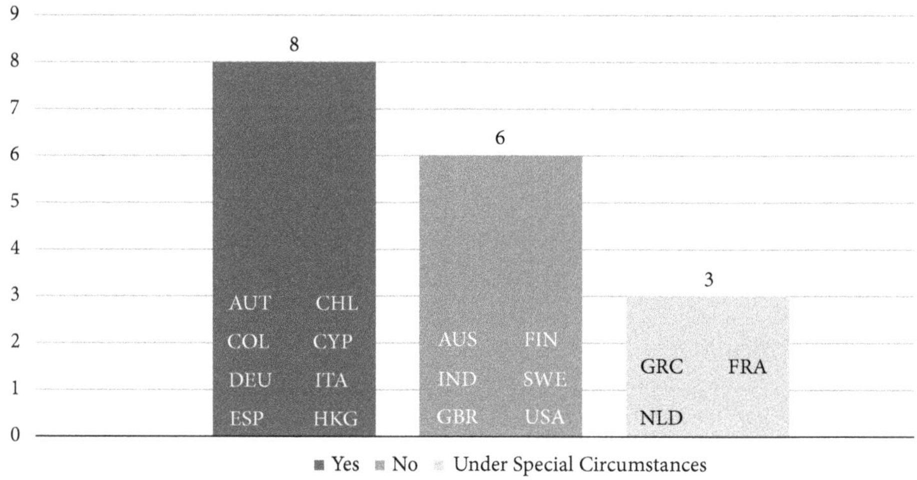

However, the devil is in the detail.[52] For instance, the circumstances under which a mandatory bid is required are complex in France and in the Netherlands.[53] In Greece, the law does not stipulate a mandatory bid, but nonetheless the competent public institution does request one.[54]

In our view, the basic question here is whether the law should provide for a put-option at a fair price after the decision to delist has been made. This could even make sense in addition to a mandatory bid if shareholders can show that the offered price was not fair. In this context, it must also be borne in mind that institutional investors will, in most cases, be required to sell their shares if the corporation is about to delist.[55]

If such a put-option is granted, the law must deal with the price, ie the valuation of the shares. In our opinion, it is imperative to regard two arising questions: (i) Who sets the price? (ii) How is the price calculated? We understand these are the most difficult questions of all, as most information on the prospectus of the company's business is in the hands of the company itself and, therefore, controlled, de facto, by its dominating shareholder, who, of course, has an incentive to keep the price it must pay low. In addition, the controlling shareholder can dictate the timing of the delisting.[56]

[51] Cf Recalde and Ataun (n 24) II.E. for further details. For the role of banks in delistings, see I Linaritis, Chapter 10.

[52] See also Recalde and Ataun (n 24) II.E. for further details on this matter.

[53] See Deckert (n 15) Q 9, Q 11; Van der Elst (n 8) Q 9, Q 11.

[54] See A Kouloridas, Questionnaire Greece Q 9.

[55] Cf I. above.

[56] For issues deriving from this matter, see P Giudici, Chapter 5, III., and Recalde and Ataun (n 24) I.B., III., III.E. Also see Linaritis (n 51) IV.B. for the role of banks in that respect.

Figure 19.13 How is the Price Calculated?

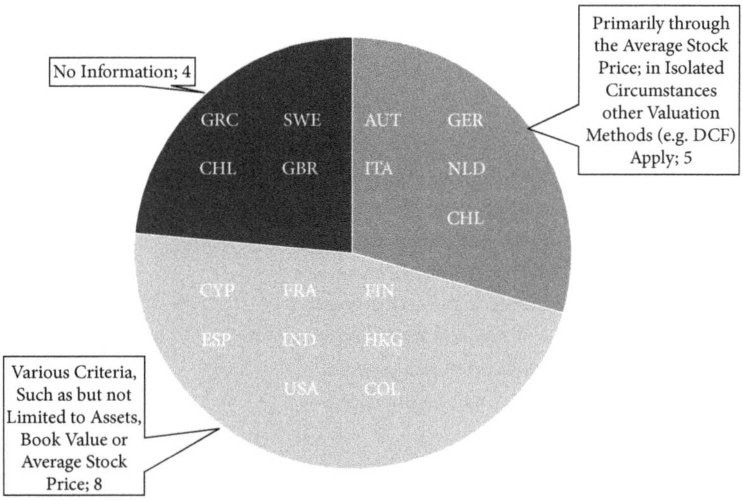

Figure 19.14 Who Sets the Price?

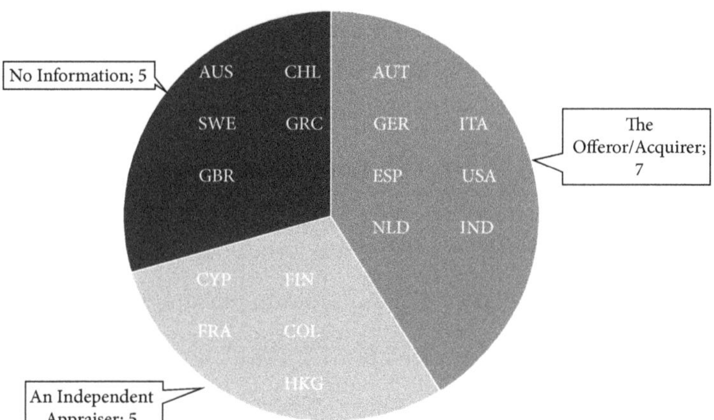

At least as a starting point for valuation, about one half of the countries rely on the average price of the stock involved, while the other half takes into account additional criteria. At first glance, the stock exchange price seems more adequate considering the object of valuation than fundamental values. Also, the stock exchange price is an easy and cheap way to set the price, which in most jurisdictions is left to the offeror. However, it can be problematic in some cases, especially in illiquid markets.[57] Also, as mentioned above, institutional investors may be obliged to dispose of their shares if the company goes private, which may distort the mechanism of price building.[58] Therefore, even market-oriented countries provide for additional valuation methods in special circumstances, possibly in combination with granting shareholders the right to challenge the valuation.

[57] For instance, see J Mohamed, 'Delisting reloaded (?) – Eine Bestandsaufnahme der rechtspolitischen Diskussion' (2023) 44 *Zeitschrift für Wirtschaftsrecht* 1975, 1980.

[58] See also Giudici (n 56) III. and Recalde and Ataun (n 24) III.

B. Shareholder Protection Mechanisms

Figure 19.15 How Are Dissenting Shareholders Protected in Voluntary Delistings? (Multiple Selections; not Exhaustive)

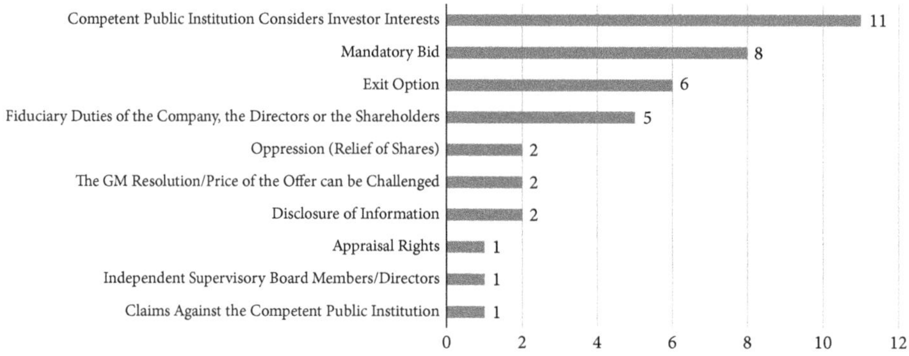

In addition to exit options, there are quite a few other measures to ensure investor protection.[59] Clearly, there are no common grounds here. Although the mandatory bid and the oppression (relief of shares) are both exit options, they have different underlying mechanisms.[60] Therefore, they have been listed separately. The same is true as to appraisal rights versus the possibility to challenge a GM resolution approving the delisting.[61]

VII. Mandatory Delisting

A. Reasons for Mandatory Delisting

Figure 19.16 Common Reasons for a Mandatory Delisting (Multiple Selections; not exhaustive)

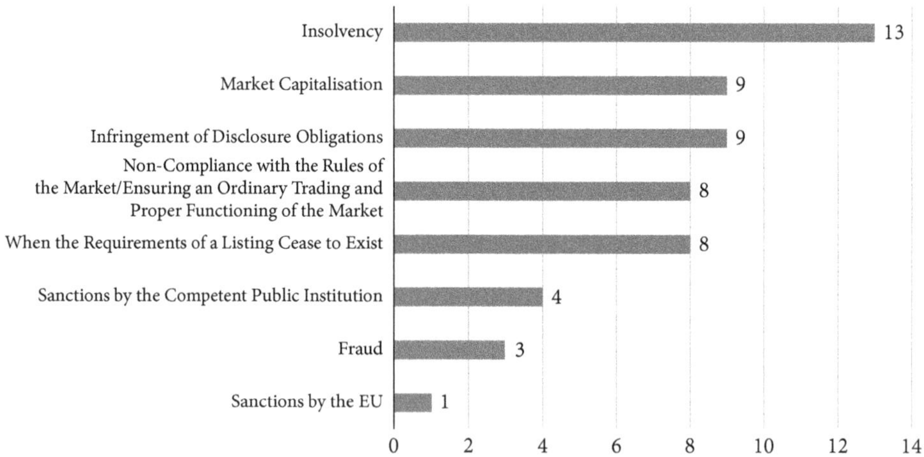

[59] See Van der Elst (n 35) IV. and Recalde and Ataun (n 24) III. for a detailed analysis of this issue.
[60] For instance, see the oppression mechanism in Cyprus in Papadopoulos (n 8) Q 9, Q 13.
[61] See M Gelter (n 49) III.B.iv.

In most states, major violations of listing requirements – including free float and transparency rules – will lead to delisting. Also, in almost all jurisdictions under survey, the insolvency[62] of the issuer can be a reason for a mandatory delisting. At first glance, this might seem self-explanatory, as insolvency can contravene the ordinary trading and proper functioning of the market. This can almost be seen as common ground due to the harmonisation provided by Article 52 of MiFID II.[63] However, even a small chance of a successful restructuring will, under some circumstances, make trading meaningful.[64]

B. Shareholder Protection Mechanism

Figure 19.17 How are Shareholders Protected in a Mandatory Delisting? (Multiple Selections; not Exhaustive)

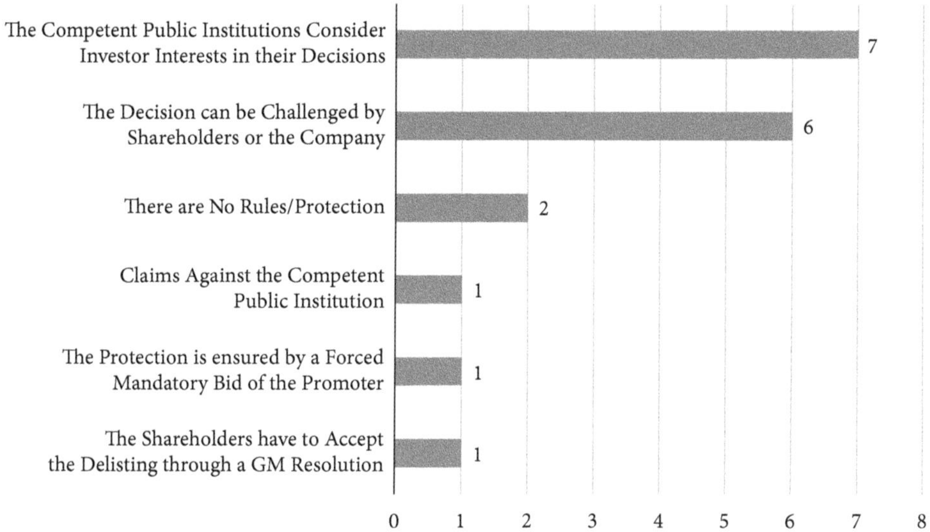

As to the means of shareholder protection, there is great diversity among the jurisdictions under survey. For example, in Chile, the mandatory delisting has to be approved by the GM.[65] This reduces the risk of arbitrage. This might be good news for existing shareholders, but bad news for future investors. The most widespread solution is what basically is already provided for in Article 52 of MiFID II: the competent public institution has to take into account the interest of investors and can, in particular, grant a grace period. Besides that, the risk of mandatory delisting is 'part of the game' of investing in publicly traded firms.

[62] For a definition, see JH Binder, Chapter 9.
[63] For an analysis pursuant to Art 52 MiFID II, see Marjosola (n 29) IV. and V.
[64] For a detailed examination, see Binder (n 62).
[65] See González (n 9) at II.A.iii.

VIII. Conclusion

Let us return to the main question of the introduction: What are the common grounds for delisting? In our view, there are not so many, except for the widely shared conviction that delisting in general and the protection of investors in particular must be addressed by the law.

Therefore, in a common capital market, the lack of common grounds of delisting does not weaken but arguably provides an even stronger case for EU regulation. However, the devil is in the detail, and the lack of common ground makes future legislation at least difficult. Therefore, in our view, the right time for EU regulation will likely be at some point in the future.

20

Delisting of Stock Corporations: Legal Fragmentation, Competition and Harmonisation Strategies

RÜDIGER VEIL*

I. Introduction

In European Member States, delisting is subject to divergent regulations. Although a number of similarities can be identified, these are limited to fundamental issues. It is generally accepted that shareholders should be adequately protected in the event of a delisting. This view is also reflected in the legal situation outside Europe. However, no further common ground can be identified. There are already differences in the legal bases. While some Member States subject delisting to company law requirements, others refer to takeover law. It is therefore hardly surprising that the protective instruments diverge: the requirement of a resolution by the general meeting of a stock corporation and exit rights under corporate law on the one hand, and a public takeover offer under capital markets law on the other.

The different approaches provide grounds for a comparative analysis.[1] Thus, this book examines the legal situation in selected European jurisdictions (10 EU Member States[2] and the United Kingdom), in Australia, Hong Kong, India, several South American countries and the United States.[3] In addition, this book provides insights

* Professor for Corporate Law and Capital Markets Law at Ludwig Maximilian University Munich, Germany.

[1] There is also a lack of insights in international literature on other European and non-European jurisdictions. However, see for a comparative law perspective (Germany and the United Kingdom), P Maume, 'The Parting of the Ways: Delisting under German and UK Law' (2015) 16 *European Business Organization Review* 255 f. In addition, the German monographic literature offers some insights to other jurisdictions. For an overview on the regulation in England and Wales, see C von Berg, *Der Marktrückzug des Emittenten* (Tübingen, Mohr Siebeck 2018) 60f and 67f and, on market withdrawal in the USA, 67f.

[2] Austria, Cyprus, Finland, France, Germany, Greece, Italy, Netherlands, Spain and Sweden.

[3] The country reports on the EU Member States are published separately from the book V Tountopoulos and R Veil (eds), *Delisting in Europe and Beyond* (Oxford, Hart Publishing 2025). They can be accessed on the companion website.

into the different perspectives of companies, their shareholders and management and discusses possible solutions.

This chapter draws on these findings and looks at the fundamental question of whether competition between national legal systems in Europe should continue or whether the EU should harmonise national delisting regimes. European legal scholarship has not yet discussed the pros and cons of harmonisation versus competition in regard to the rules for delisting stock corporations.[4] However, this issue is also essential for the attractiveness of the access to capital markets. If prohibitive requirements for delisting cause companies to refrain from going public and if insufficient shareholder protection rules cause investors to refrain from (cross-border) investments, harmonisation of the Member States' regulations might even be necessary to advance the project of the Capital Markets Union.

II. European Law

A. The Harmonisation of Capital Markets Law in the EU (1966–2019)

The Segré Report, published in 1966, set the course for the integration of capital markets in the then European Economic Community (EEC).[5] It identified obstacles to capital market integration and made specific proposals to improve the efficiency of European capital markets. The long-term goal was for the EEC to create a unified European capital market structure to facilitate the mobility of capital and investment in Europe. The report did not address delisting issues; its focus was on the distribution of securities (through public offering and intermediaries) and their admission to trading on European markets.

Eddy Wymeersch pointed out as early as 1977 that the conditions for delisting in the EEC countries were described in general terms.[6] However, the European legislator did not address the issue. The EEC, then the EC and finally the EU limited itself to harmonising prospectus requirements and transparency obligations for secondary market trading and to creating a largely uniform supervisory regime for market infrastructures.

The Takeover Directive required for the first time the introduction of a mandatory bid in national takeover laws, albeit limited to an offeror obtaining control,[7] as well as a sell-out right for shareholders after a successful takeover bid[8] and the possibility of squeezing out shareholders following a bid made to all the holders of the

[4] See, however, recommending a European regulation, S Kalss, 'Geregelte Märkte dürfen keine Einbahnstraße sein!' (2016) 27 *Europäische Zeitschrift für Wirtschaftsrecht* 321.

[5] Commission of the European Communities, *Building a European Capital Market. Report of a group of experts set up by the Commission of the European Communities* (Segré Report) (1966).

[6] For a comparative law perspective, see E Wymeersch, *Control of Securities Markets in the European Economic Community* (Brussels, Commission of the European Communities, 1977) 102.

[7] Art 5(1) Directive 2004/25/EC on takeover bids [2004] OJ L142/12.

[8] ibid Art 16.

offeree company's securities for all of their securities following a public takeover of a company.[9] But the Takeover Directive does not address the delisting of shares.

The only provisions relating to delisting by the market operator are set out in MiFID II,[10] which allows a trading venue to suspend or exclude trading in a financial instrument if the instrument no longer meets the necessary requirements or if trading in that instrument no longer takes place to a sufficient extent. Market operators must notify investors and the relevant supervisory authorities of this at an early stage.[11]

Finally, the EU company law directives do not address the delisting of shares. The European legislature has gradually harmonised the requirements for the conversion of corporations and provided for compensation rights to protect minority shareholders,[12] and has also harmonised shareholder rights in two steps through the Shareholder Rights Directive I and II.[13] But these legal acts do not cover delisting. We can therefore conclude that delisting has not yet been high on the European legislative agenda.

B. Political Discussion under the CMU Action Plan 2015/2020

The discussion on a Capital Markets Union, initiated in 2015 under the presidency of Jean-Claude Juncker and continued in 2020 under the presidency of Ursula von der Leyen, was the first to address voluntary delisting as a potential subject for harmonisation through European law. The European Commission found that a majority of stakeholders in its public consultation on a proportionate regulatory framework for SME listing saw added value in providing for minimum requirements for delisting at EU level. This assessment was based on the idea that harmonisation would promote regulatory competition and create legal certainty for multilateral trading venues, thereby encouraging cross-border investment in SME instruments in particular.[14] According to stakeholders, barriers to equal access to capital markets in Europe would be removed. Yet the calls of the stakeholders fell on deaf ears.

The Action Plan 2020 for a Capital Markets Union again emphasised the need for further market integration. The Commission announced that it would promote and diversify capital market access for small and innovative companies by proposing an improved regulatory framework.[15] The Technical Expert Stakeholder Group (TESG)

[9] ibid Art 15.

[10] Art 52(2) on delisting by order of the market operator and Art 69(2) of MiFID II on the power of the competent authorities to demand the exclusion of trading, Directive 2014/65/EU on markets in financial instruments [2014] OJ L173/349.

[11] H Marjosola, Chapter 8, VI. on the divergent implementation in the Member States.

[12] Directive (EU) 2017/1132 relating to certain aspects of company law [2017] OJ L169/46. Title II provides rules on conversions, mergers and divisions of limited liability companies.

[13] Directive 2007/36/EC on the exercise of certain rights of shareholders in listed companies (SRD I) [2007] OJ L184/17 and Directive (EU) 2017/828 amending Directive 2007/36/EC as regards the encouragement of long-term shareholder engagement (SRD II) [2017] OJ L132/1.

[14] European Commission, *Public consultation on building a proportionate regulatory environment to support SME listing* (May 2018).

[15] European Commission, *A Capital Markets Union for people and businesses – new action plan* [2020] COM (2020) 590 final, actions 2 and 16.

commissioned by the European Commission took up the ball and discussed measures to facilitate capital market access for SMEs.[16] It is noteworthy that the TESG also recommended a minimum harmonisation of delisting rules in order to provide adequate protection to minority shareholders. The TESG proposed a reform of the Transparency Directive 2004/109/EC to include requirements for voluntary delisting from both multilateral trading venues and regulated markets.[17] However, the EU Listing Act[18] did not take up this proposal when it was adopted in 2024. Delisting did not play a role in this reform discussion.

C. Delisting Regimes in the Member States

In 2021, the TESG criticised the fact that some Member States do not provide sufficient rules for shareholder protection in the event of a delisting. The experts based their criticism on the legal situation in Italy and the United Kingdom, which they used as examples of divergent regulatory approaches. The TESG was not able to draw on a comprehensive comparative law study. However, it correctly recognised that protection can be ensured, on the one hand, by requirements for a resolution of the general meeting and, on the other hand, by means of compensation rights.[19] Although it is internationally recognised that shareholders should be protected in the event of a delisting, there is no agreement as to whether it is more efficient to implement protection in company or capital markets law.

Delisting is a multifaceted phenomenon.[20] This makes it challenging to provide for a consistent regime for all types of a delisting. A delisting can be voluntary, either through an application by the issuer for revocation of admission[21] (which plays the greatest role in practice) or as a result of a merger or other conversion measure (so-called cold delisting);[22] in both cases, a delisting can take place either through a transfer of shares to another market segment (from the regulated market to a multilateral trading facility, so-called downgrading or downlisting)[23] or in such a way that shareholders are no longer able to trade the shares on any organised trading venue.[24] Furthermore, a delisting can occur involuntarily – against the will of the company or its major shareholder – because the revocation is either carried out at the initiative of

[16] Technical Expert Stakeholder Group (TESG) on SMEs, *Empowering EU capital markets for SMEs, Making listing cool again* (May 2021). Available at: https://finance.ec.europa.eu/document/download/ebb1a257-9ef2-4416-87b5-a1235157c351_en?filename=210525-report-tesg-cmu-smes_en.pdf.

[17] ibid 102.

[18] Regulation (EU) 2024/2809 amending Regulations (EU) 2017/1129, (EU) No 596/2014 and (EU) No 600/2014 to make public capital markets in the Union more attractive for companies and to facilitate access to capital for small and medium-sized enterprises [2024] OJ L series.

[19] Technical Expert Stakeholder Group (TESG) on SMEs, *Empowering EU capital markets for SMEs* (n 16) 101.

[20] Tountopoulos, Chapter 1, III.

[21] ibid III. Tountopoulos emphasises that a voluntary delisting is distinguished by the fact that the delisting is based on a decision by the listed company.

[22] Harkönen and Östberg, Chapter 13.

[23] Balp, Chapter 11.

[24] Tountopoulos (n 20) III: Prevailing Form of a Delisting.

the market operator (based on the rules of the market place) or ordered by a regulatory authority to enforce public interests.[25]

It would be impossible to consider all different kinds of delisting in this chapter. We will focus on the main case of withdrawal from the regulated market, which results in a cessation of organised multilateral trading.[26] We deem the delisting to be 'voluntary' if 'the company takes the decision or agrees with the initiative to delist its securities with voting rights from the trading activities of the stock exchange'.[27] The technicalities of such a delisting are irrelevant for the discussion on regulatory competition between EU Member States versus harmonisation by the European legislator. However, we can conclude that the EU jurisdictions examined in this research project share a common understanding that the issuer's management applies to the market operator for revocation of admission.[28]

(i) Similarities

What similarities exist in the legal systems examined for a delisting of shares? The authors of the final chapter of this book (summarising the findings of the research project) conclude that there are not so many, except for the widespread belief that investors should be protected adequately.[29]

It is noteworthy *that* shareholder protection is considered essential everywhere, although in most countries no empirical (statistically significant) findings exist regarding the relevance of a delisting for the value of shares. Germany is an exception in this respect. Delisting was one of the few reform topics on which empirical research was carried out in the wake of the decision by the Federal Court of Justice in the *Frosta* case.[30] The Federal Court of Justice ruled that shareholders have no rights to compensation in the event of a delisting or are otherwise protected. As a result, many companies delisted. Empirical research examined these cases. Although the studies produced different results, they prove that the view of the Federal Court of Justice shareholders should have no reason to fear price losses in the event of a delisting[31] is incorrect.[32] The German legislator therefore introduced provisions into the Stock Exchange Act to provide investors with effective protection.[33]

[25] Marjosola (n 11).

[26] In Germany, however, it is possible that shares can be traded on the open market at the request of a trading participant. At least at the Hamburg Stock Exchange, this does not require the issuer's consent to inclusion in the open market. See K Çavuşoğlu, Questionnaire Germany.

[27] See Van der Elst, Chapter 3, I.

[28] The research project also examined how the management's decision is made, in particular, what majorities apply and whether other bodies (supervisory board) are involved in the decision.

[29] Torggler and Yilmaz, Chapter 19.

[30] BGH, Ruling of 8 October 2013 – II ZB 26/12 – Frosta.

[31] ibid.

[32] B Karami and R Schuster, 'Eine empirische Analyse der Kurs- und Liquiditätseffekte auf die Ankändigung eines Börsenrückzugs am deutschen Kapitalmarkt im Lichte der "Frosta"-Entscheidung des BGH' (2016) *Corporate Finance* 106, 119.

[33] The German Ministry of Finance had initially put a research contract out to tender but withdrew the request after it became clear that politicians wanted to regulate delisting, irrespective of the results of economic research. Nevertheless, economists carried out a series of empirical studies. See M Doumet, P Limbach and E Theißen, 'Ich bin dann mal weg: Werteffekte von Delistings deutscher Aktiengesellschaften

If many countries lack empirical evidence on the consequences of delistings, why then do they regulate them? The view that shareholders need protection in the event of a delisting is probably based on cases perceived as scandalous from the perspective of minority shareholders.[34] Even if there are no cases in a jurisdiction that have triggered a political debate on delisting, it makes good sense to subject delisting to similar rules as other measures that may be disadvantageous for minority shareholders, such as a squeeze-out.[35]

With regard to the regulatory approach, we observe two solutions that prevail in a large majority of jurisdictions. Firstly, two-thirds of the jurisdictions examined (11 countries in Europe, as well as Australia, Hong Kong, India, various states in South America and the United States) provide for the right of shareholders to exit as a result of a delisting.[36] However, there are significant differences re the legal basis of the claim (whether it is a statutory claim or a settlement offered by the market operator as a prerequisite for revoking admission) and the criteria used to determine the fairness of the price offered. The exit (in non-technical terms) is also subject to different mechanisms, whether as a mandatory offer under capital markets law by the controlling shareholder, or as a sell-out right vis-à-vis the company or the controlling shareholder under corporate law.

Secondly, in almost all jurisdictions, the requirement of a shareholders' resolution is an essential element in the system of shareholder protection. These countries assume that the impact of a delisting on the tradability of shares significantly affects the shareholders.[37] Thus, delisting should not be at the sole discretion of the management. This is remarkable from a German perspective. In the academic discussion, scholars argued a delisting would not affect shareholders' membership rights but only the tradability of the shares, which is not protected under the German constitution.[38] This interpretation was later adopted by the Federal Constitutional Court[39] and, ultimately, by the Federal Court of Justice in the *Frosta* case.[40]

With regard to the majorities required for the resolution of the general meeting, there is no clear picture; a simple majority is sufficient in a few countries, while others require 66.6 per cent, 75 per cent, 90 per cent or even 95 per cent of the votes cast.[41]

nach dem Frosta-Urteil' (2015) *CFR Working Paper* No 15–14. Available at: www.econstor.eu/bitstream/10419/121254/1/836336690.pdf; Karami and Schuster, 'Eine empirische Analyse' (n 32) 106 f; L Pilsl and L Knoll, 'Delisting und Börsenkurs' (2016) 69 *Der Betrieb* 181.

[34] In Germany, the discussion has not ceased after the regulation of delisting in sec 39 BörsG but has flared up again due to spectacular cases. See on the consequences of Rocket Internet's withdrawal from the stock exchange F Fromholzer, 'Aktuelle Fragen und Beoachtungen zum Delisting' in R Veil, HC Grigoleit and M Habersack (eds), *Öffentliche Unternehmensübernahmen* (Tübingen, Mohr Siebeck 2022) 221 f.

[35] Kouloridas, refers to the impact on the value of the shares, Chapter 6, I (a) (iv).

[36] Recalde and Ataun, Chapter 4, D.

[37] ibid B. Recalde and Ataun argue that 'this kind of concern is well known in general company law, that usually provides for mechanisms applicable to the amendment of the articles of association restricting the free transferability of shares.'

[38] P Mülbert, 'Rechtsprobleme des Delisting' (2001) 165 *Zeitschrift für das gesamte Handelsrecht und Wirtschaftsrecht* 104, 113 f; G Spindler and L Klöhn, 'Delisting einer börsennotierten Aktiengesellschaft' (2003) 8 *Zeitschrift für Japanisches Recht* 75, 87 f; de Vries, K, *Delisting: Gesellschaftsrecht, Kapitalmarktrecht, Umwandlungsrecht* (Cologne, Otto Schmidt, 2002) 115.

[39] BVerfG, Judgment of 11 July 2012–1 BvR 3142/07.

[40] BGH *Frosta* (n 30).

[41] See Torggler and Yilmaz (n 29) IV; on supermajority rules, see Recalde and Ataun (n 36) E.

The different majority requirements are likely due to differences in corporate governance. It is not surprising that the legal remedies against the resolution of shareholders vary, as this depends largely on whether collective redress mechanisms exist under corporate or capital markets law.

(ii) Different Approaches in Shareholder Protection

What is the legal situation regarding shareholders in the 10 EU Member States and the United Kingdom examined in this research project?[42] If one approaches the question from the perspective of shareholder protection through exit or tender rights, the countries can be categorised into three groups. The first group includes countries which subject delisting to takeover law. The countries make a delisting contingent on a takeover bid (among other things). The second group includes those countries in which shareholders do not have a right to sell their shares by law, but in which a market operator may request it, or a supervisory authority or court can order it. Finally, one country does not provide for specific shareholder protection by way of a compensation payment but relies on the general rules under company law that require the management to act in the best interest of shareholders.

Austria, Germany and Italy belong to the first group. These countries provide for special statutory rules that determine the appropriateness of the compensation on the basis of the weighted average stock exchange price in the last six months,[43] as does Spain, which, however, has established a five-step test with regard to the appropriateness of the price, in which the stock exchange price is only one of five criteria.[44] France can also be included in this group. However, the legal situation in France is complex as delisting can occur in four ways: (i) as a result of a squeeze-out, (ii) through a squeeze-out following a buyout offer, (iii) a squeeze-out following a public takeover offer and (iv) upon application by the management to revoke the admission to trading.[45] The latter option is provided for in the stock exchange rules. It requires a takeover bid by the major shareholder and is only considered if the major shareholder owns at least 90 per cent of the shares and the proportion of shares in free float is low. In this case, as in the other four countries, shareholder protection is ensured by the offer to purchase the shares of the remaining shareholders.[46]

The second group includes jurisdictions that do not provide a statutory basis for compensation but instead ensure that shareholders are protected in the event of a delisting by granting powers to the market operator, the national supervisory authority

[42] The findings on the legal situation in the EU Member States and the United Kingdom are based on the country reports written by the authors in the research project. The country reports are available (open access) on the Hart Publishing companion website.

[43] See Çavuşoğlu, (n 26) Q 9: average domestic stock exchange price during the last six months (however, three exceptions apply); Balp, Questionnaire Italy Q 9 and 13: average market price of the shares in the last six months; Torggler, Questionnaire Austria Q 9: average stock exchange price in the last six months.

[44] See Recalde and Ataun, Questionnaire Spain Q 9: weighted average price of the shares in the last six months is one criterion out of five.

[45] See Deckert, Questionnaire France Q 9.

[46] ibid Q 9 referring to Euronext Rulebook.

or courts to ensure protection of minorities. In Finland, Greece and the Netherlands, shareholder protection is in the hands of the market operator.[47] The management of the exchange will only grant an application for revocation of admission if shareholders are protected. In doing so, the market operator takes into account whether the shareholders are offered compensation. Consequently, Finland and Greece do not provide for statutory provisions that regulate how to assess the compensation. The legal situation in the Netherlands is similar. Delisting is subject to the Euronext Rulebook. Shareholder protection depends, inter alia, on whether the company itself or a supermajority shareholder requests the delisting.[48] However, the company can only delist when the free float has become very small – a 'strategy less common [in other countries] than one could expect'.[49] In the United Kingdom, minority shareholders can apply to the court (after challenging the resolution) that the company is to purchase the shares.[50] Thus, the UK does not provide for a statutory right to compensation either. The legal situation in Cyprus is similar, where minority shareholders can mount a defence against delisting on the grounds of unfair disadvantage. If the delisting is deemed to be an oppression of minority shareholders, a court is entitled to order the company to acquire the shares of the (dissenting) shareholders.[51]

Finally, Sweden does not provide for statutory provisions governing the right to a compensation payment in the event of delisting. Delisting is subject to self-regulation, which is characterised by the notion that the management weighs the various interests against each other based on its fiduciary duties under general corporate law. The Swedish Securities Council, a self-regulatory body, 'has developed a very restrictive practice regarding applications for delisting if the admission requirements are still met'. The board of directors is expected to act in the interests of the company and of all shareholders when taking the decision for a delisting. If the admission requirements are still met, 'the reasons for the application must be of such strength that it can be considered justified to expose the other shareholders to the disadvantages of a delisting'.[52]

(iii) Conclusion

The EU Member States examined in the research project and the United Kingdom take different approaches to shareholder protection. The countries with a mechanism based in takeover law (group 1) have established a legal basis for a compensation (takeover bid).[53] In addition, they refer to the stock market price in order to determine the appropriateness of the compensation. The appropriateness of the price

[47] See Marjosola, Questionnaire Finland Q 9; Kouloridas, Questionnaire Greece Q 9 (national supervisory authority 'customarily asks for [a takeover bid], in order to approve the delisting').

[48] See Van der Elst, Questionnaire Netherlands Q 9.

[49] See Giudici, Chapter 5, B.

[50] See Chan and Gerner-Beuerle, Questionnaire UK Q 9.

[51] See Papadopoulos, Questionnaire Cyprus Q 9.

[52] See Östberg, Questionnaire Sweden Q 1.

[53] The revocation of admission requires that the bidder has made a takeover offer in accordance with the provisions of national takeover law.

is determined largely on the basis of the average weighted stock exchange price of the last six months.

The countries that leave the protection of shareholders to the market operator or the courts (group 2) do not provide a legal basis for fair compensation. The market operators, when deciding to revoke admission to trading, do not have to consider specific requirements regarding the appropriateness of a compensation offer. This is similar to the former legal situation in Germany following the Macrotron ruling by the Federal Court of Justice (BGH). The II. Senate had made delisting dependent on a mandatory offer, among other things, but left open the question of by whom this offer should be made (according to the ruling, the offer should be made either by the company or by the major shareholder) and what requirements apply to its appropriateness.[54] In legal literature, this shareholder protection was viewed as 'a mechanism unknown to German stock corporation and transformation law'.[55] It is therefore hardly surprising that the fundamental question of how to determine the appropriateness of the compensation – relevance of the stock market price and/or compensation of the intrinsic value to be determined on the basis of economic valuation methods – remained controversial after the court ruling.

III. Europeanisation of Delisting Regimes

The considerable regulatory differences in shareholder protection raise the question of whether the requirements for revoking the admission of shares to trading on a regulated market (initiated by the company or the major shareholder) should be harmonised.[56] Several forms of EU action could be considered. Firstly, the European Commission could issue recommendations to the Member States as to which aspects they should take into account in their national legal systems to ensure shareholder protection.[57] This can be done through soft law (recommendations and opinions)[58] or other mechanisms of exchange of best practices (open method of coordination).[59]

Secondly, the EU legislature could harmonise national delisting regimes, either by adopting a directive that requires minimum or maximum harmonisation of national delisting regimes or by enacting a regulation, thus implementing a unified legal situation

[54] The BGH merely stated that sufficient protection of minority shareholders can only be ensured if the minority shareholders are reimbursed for the value of their shares and if they are given the opportunity to have the correctness of the valuation reviewed in court proceedings.

[55] Spindler and Klöhn, 'Delisting einer börsennotierten Aktiengesellschaft' (n 38) 82.

[56] Balp (n 23) VI. discusses harmonisation of downlisting. A major consideration here is whether the target market (MTF) is liquid or not.

[57] H Fleischer, 'Corporate Governance in Europa als Mehrebenensystem' (2012) 41 *Zeitschrift für Unternehmens- und Gesellschaftsrecht* 160 f on the methods of 'soft' coordination; T Kahnert, *Rechtsetzung im Europäischen Gesellschaftsrecht* (Tübingen, Mohr Siebeck, 2012) 285 f.

[58] See Art 288 TFEU.

[59] Examples: (i) Takeover Bid Networks, comprising the national competent authorities under the TOD; (ii) Corporate Governance Forum, established by Commission Decision 2004/706/EC of 15 October 2002, the Forum should enhance the convergence of national codes of corporate governance and provide strategic advice to the Commission (mandate ended 2011).

across the EU. Finally, a possible outcome of a reform discussion might be that everything should remain the same, ie the European legislature maintains that regulatory competition takes place in Europe in the future.

With the debate on coordination, competition and harmonisation of national laws about delisting, we are breaking new ground. So far, there has been no in-depth discussion in academia that places delisting in a harmonisation context. In particular, the European Company Model Act developed by European scholars[60] does not provide principles or rules a European legal act could be based on or adopt. Thus, the comparative research project presented in this book opens up new insights into the legal situation in European and non-European countries and may serve as a reference not only for reform options, but also for thorough analysis of a harmonisation strategy.

A. The Need for a Europeanisation of Delisting Regimes

The need for a Europeanisation of national delisting regimes must be discussed with regard to the legislative powers of the EU. Which provisions of the TFEU provide for an EU competence to address the issue in a harmonising manner? Two norms come into consideration. Firstly, it may be necessary to coordinate the Member States' protective provisions that are prescribed in the interests of shareholders in order to make these provisions equivalent,[61] or, secondly, it may be necessary to harmonise the laws, regulations and administrative provisions of the Member States relating to the establishment and functioning of the internal market.[62] The first competence is limited to minimum harmonisation through directives, while the second also allows for unification through regulations.

What are the arguments in favour of harmonisation? If we look at the issue from the perspective of shareholder protection (addressed by both competency norms), the general reasons for developing a level playing field come into play: a divergent legal situation results in market fragmentation, makes cross-border investments more difficult and increases the home bias (especially of private investors).[63] The European legislature has therefore been focusing on investors' investment decisions since the beginning of European harmonisation. Finally, from 2014 to 2017, it transferred important directives governing access to capital markets and trading of securities on secondary markets into regulations (Prospectus Regulation; Market Abuse Regulation), resulting in a largely uniform legal situation in the EU. The level playing field is in the interests of issuers, whose capital costs decrease in a single internal market, and in the interests of investors, who can trade innovative financial products in a single internal market without cross-border friction and at low transaction costs.

Would the harmonisation of delisting open a completely new chapter in the development of European law? The answer is a clear no! Investment and divestment are

[60] European Model Company Act (EMCA) 2017.

[61] Art 50(2) lit (g) TFEU.

[62] Art 114(1) TFEU.

[63] See A Brüggemeier, *Harmonisierungskonzepte im europäischen Kapitalmarktrecht* (Tübingen, Mohr Siebeck, 2018).

two sides of the same coin. The idea that protecting divestment also safeguards investment has already been established in EU legislation. We can demonstrate this using the example of the mandatory bid rule under the Takeover Directive. If a bidder has gained control, shareholders have the right to exit the company at an appropriate price. Protection is provided through information (offer document) and a mandatory offer by the bidder to acquire the shares of shareholders of the target company. The rationale of the mandatory bid rule is to protect the investor's decision to invest in an independent company.[64] Thus, investment and divestment are closely linked under European takeover law: protective rules for divestment (sell-out right) also ensure protection of the investment decision. Therefore, scholarship and courts interpret the mandatory bid rule as a protective instrument under capital markets law.[65]

Harmonisation of delisting would follow the same narrative. When an investor acquires securities that are admitted to trading, they do so on the assumption that they can sell the securities on a secondary market. If the bidder (or the company itself) deprives the shareholders of the organised market for trading, protection should be provided through information and an offer by the company or a controlling shareholder. The rationale would be to also protect the investors' decision to invest in a company that issued *tradable* securities. An EU-wide harmonisation of shareholder protection in the event of a delisting would thus fit into the existing already harmonised European capital markets law.

If we look at Article 114 of TFEU as a competence norm for the European legislator, it becomes clear that harmonisation of national delisting regimes would also serve the interests of issuers in selling securities and thus contribute to the single market. A divergent legal situation makes it more burdensome for issuers to make an EU-wide public offer and consequently request admission for trading on trading venues outside the domestic legal system. Some Member States impose prohibitive requirements on delisting,[66] which has a deterrent effect not only on the decision of companies in the respective Member State to go public, but also on the decision of companies from other Member States to reach out to investors in the respective Member State. Listing must not be a one-way street for companies. If companies with a multiple listing nevertheless seek to withdraw from stock exchanges in other Member States, they will look

[64] H Krause and T Pötzsch, '§ 35' in HD Assmann, T Pötzsch and UH Schneider (eds), *WpÜG Commentary*, 4th edn (Cologne, Otto Schmidt, 2024) para 32; F Gegler, *Übernahmerechtliche Kontrolle* (Tübingen, Mohr Siebeck, 2019) 15 f.

[65] However, a uniform understanding of the rule throughout the European Union has not yet been developed. Using Germany as an example, we can illustrate that literature understands the mandatory bid rule in many ways. In particular, some authors interpret it as an instrument under corporate law. See KJ Hopt, *Europäisches Übernahmerecht* (Tübingen, Mohr Siebeck, 2013) 36 f, but also acknowledging, that the mandatory bid rule ensures proper functioning of capital markets. The Federal Court of Justice classifies the rule as part of capital markets law. See BGH, Ruling of 11 June 2013 – II ZR 80/12.

[66] Greece requires a majority of 95% of the total voting share capital for the delisting decisions, see Tountopoulos, (n 47) Q 3; same approach in the Netherlands, see Van der Elst, (n 48) Q 1; similarly, Cyprus requires approval of delisting decision by 90% of the shareholders, see Papadopoulos (n 51) Q 1. Finland also takes a restrictive stance, requiring that certain conditions be met, namely (i) that the share or the issuer no longer fulfils the requirements of the Nasdaq Main Market Rulebook or (ii) delisting is otherwise necessary based on the issuer's actions being in contradiction with the legislation or regulations on the operation of the exchange, see Marjosola (n 47) Q 1.

for ways to delist through mergers or other restructuring measures.[67] This results in unnecessary transaction costs for the company and its major shareholder as well as for the minority shareholders.

It is therefore reasonable for us to conclude that harmonisation of national regimes dealing with the voluntary withdrawal from regulated markets could be based on Article 114(1) of the TFEU.[68] One might counter that Member States already provide for rules protecting shareholders. However, there are significant differences in national laws in the EU regarding the protection of financial interests of shareholders. In particular, the varying regulation of compensation in the countries covered by the second group of European countries[69] proves to be disadvantageous. Experience has shown that shareholders do not receive an offer for a cash settlement if the market operator decides on delisting at its own discretion.[70] While the protection of shareholders' property rights is theoretically possible (on request by the market operator or ordered by a court), it does not occur in practice. In addition, a comparison of national laws in the EU reveals that there are significant differences regarding the requirement and the prerequisites of a resolution by the general meeting. The significant differences make it necessary to harmonise the rules to adequately protect shareholders on the one hand, and to make multiple listings in the EU easier for issuers on the other.[71]

Would competition between Member States be a preferable strategy? The willingness to implement rules from other legal systems in one's own legal system presupposes that the Member States are facing competitive pressure. In company law, competition between legal systems has proven to be an effective harmonisation mechanism. In the mid-2000s, Member States were willing to implement regulatory models (innovate legal transplants) from other jurisdictions in their own legal systems because they were exposed to competitive pressure. Companies often chose the legal form of a limited liability company under English law because they considered it more attractive than the legal forms in their own country.[72]

So far, there has been no comparable competition between regulatory systems in the EU with regard to delisting. Interestingly, four of the ten Member States examined

[67] The example of Italy shows that issuers and major shareholders are creative. Italy does not provide for any explicit regulation of voluntary delisting. Therefore, companies help themselves by 'creating' the conditions for the market operator to carry out a delisting on its own initiative. See Balp (n 43) Q 1: 'Given the uncertainty still surrounding the legitimacy of pure delisting under national law, voluntary delisting initiated by a shareholder or the company … is actually achieved in the practice, indirectly, through a transaction for the purchase of a number of shares such as to eliminate the requirements for maintaining the listing (reduction of free float below the minimum threshold …) or a transaction following which the issuer itself is extinguished (merger into a non-listed company.'

[68] See S Kastl, *Der Rückzug kapitalmarktfähiger Unternehmen* (Baden-Baden, Nomos, 2016) 302.

[69] Finland, Greece and the Netherlands.

[70] We can show this again using the example of Germany. After the Federal Court of Justice's Frosta decision, shareholder protection was limited to the market operator being able to make a delisting dependent on a cash settlement offer to shareholders. However, this has not happened in any of the numerous cases. see K Krug, *Der Rückzug von der Börse* (Baden-Baden, Nomos, 2019) 54.

[71] Tountopoulos (n 20) VII: 'It makes no sense to regulate listing [in Union law] while leaving delisting unregulated.'

[72] This competition, which has been fostered by the case law of the ECJ, has been widely researched. See C Gerner-Beuerle and M Schillig, *Comparative Company Law* (Oxford, Oxford University Press, 2019) 112 f.

in this book invoke takeover law in order to ensure adequate investor protection.[73] However, it is not possible to assess whether these countries have experienced mutual competition in this respect or at least learned from each other how best to deal with shareholder protection issues. This presupposes that a pioneer is identifiable and that other countries adopted the regulatory model of the pioneer to prevent companies from seeking a listing in the country where the takeover law model was first implemented. We cannot find any evidence in the legislative materials of reform acts in the Member States. On the basis of publicly available information, we are unable to conclude that competition has taken place between the Member States.

However, it is obvious that Austria, Germany, Italy and Spain provide protection that is essentially the same, as it is linked to a takeover bid (by the major shareholder or the company) and rules under takeover law governing the adequate price in case of a mandatory bid. It is conceivable that they have learned from each other in this respect. But the effectiveness of this coordination is likely to be low. There is not even anecdotal evidence that the four countries were under any competitive pressure. It is therefore unlikely that regulatory competition between EU Member States will lead to further coordination of the Member States' legal systems in the short or medium term.

B. Obstacles to the Europeanisation of Delisting Regimes

The Europeanisation of delisting regimes, whether through an EU directive or coordinating soft law instruments, is taking place against the backdrop of divergent approaches in the Member States, in company law on the one hand and in takeover and capital markets law on the other.[74] It is obvious that this makes harmonisation more difficult.[75] The problem is exacerbated by the fact that the approaches are largely path-dependent, as they reflect different philosophies about regulation in general and traditional experiences with company law in particular.

For example, it is common practice in the Nordic countries to rely on self-regulation by market participants to achieve certain regulatory objectives instead of imposing mandatory requirements, as market participants value a flexible and pragmatic regime.[76] Interestingly, this approach can also be observed in Australia and the USA.[77] In Sweden, it is considered sufficient that the general protective provisions of company law apply. This may explain why Sweden has not provided for a specific regime on delisting but refers instead to general fiduciary duties of the board of directors under company law.[78]

[73] Austria, Germany, Italy and Spain. France can also be added to this list, although other procedures are available there.

[74] See Van der Elst (n 27) C.: 'wide variety of regulations for securities delisting'.

[75] M Brellochs, 'Der Rückzug von der Bäre nach "Frosta"' (2014) *Die Aktiengesellschaft* 633, 646 argues it would be obvious that the European law should not only regulate market entry but also market exit, at least in principle. However, it would be another question whether this would be possible given the national differences and the experience with the Takeover Directive.

[76] See on the role of self-regulation in Sweden R Veil and F Walla, *Schwedisches Kapitalmarktrecht* (Hürth, Carl Heymanns Verlag, 2010) 12 f; in the delisting context Östberg (n 52) Q 1 and 17.

[77] See Recalde and Ataun (n 36) B: 'Self-regulatory Model'.

[78] Östberg (n 52) Q 1.

In Germany, there is a greater willingness to introduce a separate regime for the purpose of shareholder protection. However, the reform did not take place in company law. The legislator has taken into account that it is still common in Germany that some shareholders (also described as predatory shareholders) challenge resolutions of the general meeting with the aim of obtaining payments (without a legal basis) from the company.[79] The practice of abusive shareholder lawsuits makes it seem far-fetched to ensure shareholder protection by making a delisting subject to a resolution by the general meeting. Therefore, the legislator decided to safeguard the financial interests of shareholders by means of a mandatory takeover bid.

In contrast, France places delisting in the context of squeeze-out regimes, with the result that shareholder protection is primarily enshrined under company law.[80] It is also possible that a major shareholder achieves delisting by submitting a takeover bid.[81] However, this further delisting regime merely reflects deficits in the French corporate law regimes. Delisting through a takeover bid is not the typical avenue.

C. Strategy

Do these obstacles prevent the appreciation of delisting at European level and the development of a harmonised legal framework?[82] The EU has experienced different outcomes with the harmonisation of company law, takeover law and capital markets law. Capital markets law has already been unified (through regulations instead of directives) to a large extent. This was possible because the Member States did not provide for rules that are shaped by traditional regulatory approaches – the EU legislator did not experience any path dependencies with regard to insider trading and market manipulation prohibitions, disclosure obligations and conduct of business rules for investment firms! Instead, the European legislature has introduced new laws for most Member States.[83]

However, the EU has so far harmonised only core areas of company and takeover law, leaving the Member States with a great deal of discretion for implementation. Firstly, this is because the EU's legislative powers are limited. Article 50(2) lit (g) TFEU limits the competence of the EU to *coordinate* (and not unify!) the safeguards which, for

[79] In 2005, the German legislator enacted the 'Law on Corporate Integrity and Modernisation of the Right to Bring an Action for Annulment'. In 2009, the German legislator introduced a further reform to counter abusive lawsuits with the Act on the Implementation of the Shareholders' Rights Directive. However, a comprehensive reform has not yet been successful. Thus, shareholder lawsuits continue to be filed against resolutions of the general meeting for abusive reasons. This also explains why the legislator is hesitant to implement more shareholder democracy in the stock corporation by involving them in fundamental decisions of the board of directors.

[80] See Deckert (n 45) Q 9.

[81] ibid 'Euronext market rules provide for the possibility of pure and simple delisting from the Euronext Paris and Euronext Growth markets, i.e. without a squeeze-out, unless such a measure is likely to significantly harm the interests of investors or compromise the orderly functioning of the market.'

[82] Van der Elst (n 27) II. argues that 'balancing all interests of all involved parties in a voluntary delisting decision cannot be captured in one harmonised approach'.

[83] Even basic rules such as insider trading prohibitions and the prohibition of market manipulation did not yet exist in many Member States when the European legislator first adopted harmonising legislation (in 1989 on insider trading prohibitions and in 2003 on the prohibition of market manipulation).

the protection of the interests of members and others, are required by Member States. Secondly, this is because regulatory approaches in company law and takeover law are very different in the Member States, due to divergent corporate governance systems (including shareholder rights) and different understandings of the fundamental principles of company law, such as the principle of 'one share one vote', etc. Nevertheless, despite divergent legal situations, the EU has been able to harmonise core areas of company law and (politically sensitive) takeover law. The minimum requirements of the directives provide equivalent safeguards. This has been possible because EU legal acts are limited to establishing equivalent safeguards through principles. This leaves Member States with some discretion as to how they should be implemented into national laws, and what should be done to provide for their options.

With this in mind, the delisting should also be brought to the European stage. Harmonisation of core areas would be an important first step to facilitate access to capital markets for both issuers and investors and thus contribute to the goal of an internal market.[84] Regardless of whether a directive is based on Article 50(2) lit (g) TFEU or Article 114(1) TFEU, the European legislator should limit itself to harmonising the principles for delisting.

D. Core Areas of Harmonisation

The most pressing task is to protect shareholder confidence in the prospect of being able to sell shares on a trading venue at any time. Involuntary loss of share tradability due to a delisting makes it necessary to provide shareholders with adequate protections, given that Article 6(1) of the ECHR ensures that shareholders have the right to effectively challenge relevant decisions on the matter before a national court.[85] National legislators should be required to explicitly regulate that shareholders have the right to sell their shares at a fair price. Placing this protection in the hands of market operators who decide about delisting at their own discretion is insufficient to strengthen investor confidence in cross-border investments.[86] Although the approach requiring a takeover bid conditioned to a voluntary delisting is considered as an effective mechanism to protect minority investors[87] and is probably 'omnipresent in most jurisdictions of continental Europe, whether explicitly or implicitly',[88] Member States should be free to implement a sell-out right in company law as well.

The adequate price is the most important, but also the most difficult question of all delisting issues.[89] European company and takeover law do not yet provide any specific requirements for the appropriateness of a compensation payment. However, a Union-wide regulation of delisting should determine minimum requirements for the exit price. The national legislators should be obliged to introduce a minimum level

[84] See Kalss, 'Geregelte Märkte' (n 4) 321.
[85] Ktistakis, Chapter 2, II.
[86] Tountopoulos (n 20) VI. criticises the fact that the power of market operators to remove financial instruments from trading if they do not comply with the listing rules is not used the same way by all.
[87] Recalde and Ataun (n 36) V.
[88] Kouloridas (n 35) I. C. ii).
[89] Torggler and Yilmaz (n 29) VI A.; Tountopoulos (n 20) VI; Van der Elst (n 27) II.

of protection in the form of a compensation at the average weighted share price of the recent past, namely (three to six) months. Consequently, the selling price would generally be based on the stock market price. Whether and under what conditions the appropriate selling price is to be ascertained differently (for example by determining the value of the company using economic valuation models) should be left to the discretion of the Member States. In order for shareholders to be able to make a meaningful decision regarding the right to sell, the bidder should be obliged to provide more detailed information on the reason for delisting and the fairness of the price. However, there is no need to harmonise the financing of the offer by banks and other financial intermediaries[90] across the EU.

We have learned that the requirement of a general meeting resolution is another essential element of shareholder protection in a number of EU Member States.[91] Looking further afield, the legal situation in Asia,[92] Australia,[93] South America[94] and the US[95] confirms that the requirement of a resolution is considered essential for delisting worldwide. Should this aspect also be covered by an EU directive? The question is more complex than the question of whether to protect financial interests by means of a sell-out right.

European legislation has so far been reluctant to require Member States to make certain measures of the board of directors subject to a decision by the general meeting. This requirement is provided for in the case of mergers, divisions and changes of the legal form (conversion).[96] However, these are structural measures, which cannot be entrusted to any other organ than the general meeting. Thus, harmonising the competence of the general meeting for these decisions does not represent a major intervention in national laws.

The situation is different for business transactions. In Member States which provide for a two-tier system, the general meeting does not have authority to decide on such measures. Instead, the supervisory board (representing the shareholders) is involved in the decision.[97] European legislation has already taken the different corporate governance systems into account: The Shareholder Rights Directive II[98] allows

[90] See, in more detail, on the role of banks, practices and conflicts of interests, Linaritis, Chapter 10.

[91] In the following EU countries, the shareholder meeting decides on a voluntary delisting: Cyprus, Greece, Italy (regarding market migration), Spain. In other EU countries examined in this research project, the board of directors decides on a voluntary delisting: Finland, France, Germany, the Netherlands. However, in Finland delisting is possible only under very limited prerequisites. See Marjosola (n 47) Q 1. In France, the articles of association of the company may require a decision of the general meeting approving a delisting, see Deckert (n 45) Q 2. In Sweden, the predominant view is that a decision to delist may be taken by the board of directors. However, there is no case law confirming this interpretation. Östberg (n 52) Q 1.

[92] Low and Low, Chapter 16.

[93] Hanrahan, Chapter 15: 'Shareholder Vote in Some Circumstances'; Kaur, Chapter 17, B.

[94] González, Chapter 18, II A i.

[95] Gelter and Thel, Chapter 14, explain, regarding the US, that formally, shareholders are not involved in the decision to delist. However, going-private transactions (such as freeze-out mergers) that allow delisting and deregistration will typically require approval by shareholders.

[96] Directive (EU) 2017/1132 (n 12). Art 86h requires approval of a cross-border conversion. In case of a merger, Arts 93 and 126 require approval by the general meeting of each of the merging companies. In case of divisions, Arts 139 and 160h require approval by the general meeting of each company involved in a division.

[97] German Stock Corporation Act, s 111(4).

[98] Directive (EU) 2017/828 (n 13).

Member States to stipulate that related party transactions require the approval of the supervisory board rather than the general meeting.[99]

In view of the fundamental differences in the governance of companies in national laws of the EU, it is not advisable to make a Union-wide delisting dependent on a resolution of the general meeting.[100] We recommend that it should be left to the Member States to decide whether the general meeting or the supervisory board should be involved in the decision to delist. Consequently, Member States should not be bound by EU law regarding further requirements for a resolution of the general meeting (simple majority; qualified majority; majority of the minority) or the supervisory board (simple majority; qualified majority).

IV. Conclusion

Delisting touches the foundations of the investment decision. Both the objective of adequate shareholder protection and that of promoting cross-border investments argue in favour of harmonising the national regimes. We should not expect harmonisation to result from competition between the Member States.

We recommend a harmonisation of core areas of voluntary delisting. It is not necessary to harmonise in detail the procedure and the requirements for delisting by means of an EU legal act. However, a directive based on Article 50(2) lit g) and Article 114(1) of the TFEU should require the Member States to implement a minimum level of shareholder protection in the national legal systems. The EU directive should recognise fundamental principles and require Member States to implement these into their national laws.

Firstly, the EU directive should be based on the principle that going private is a right of both the company (issuer) and a majority shareholder. Usually, the majority shareholder will initiate a delisting of shares. It should be noted as a matter of principle (at least in the recitals of the EU legal act) that both the company and the majority shareholder are pursuing legitimate interests when seeking to delist.[101]

Secondly, the EU directive should be based on the principle that shareholders must be protected adequately in the event of a delisting. Shareholders should have the right to sell their shares at a fair price, either to the company or the major shareholder. Member States should be free to decide whether they enshrine protection in company, takeover or capital markets law.

Thirdly, the EU directive should recognise that the decision to delist is subject to a resolution of the shareholder meeting in many jurisdictions. However, Member States should not be obliged to provide for such a requirement. Member States with a two tier-system should be free to involve the supervisory board in the decision instead of subjecting delisting to a shareholder vote. Furthermore, the requirement of

[99] ibid Art 9c (4). Germany and Austria have made use of this power. German Stock Corporation Act, s 111b and Austrian Stock Corporation Act, s 95.

[100] Similarly, Balp (n 23) VI. re harmonisation of downlisting.

[101] See, in more detail on the grounds for going private, Recalde and Ataun (n 36) A; more specifically, on the interests of the company going private, Kouloridas (n 35) I (a)(ii).

a resolution of the general meeting should not lead to a situation in which delisting is practically impossible. Member States should not be allowed to impose disproportionate requirements on the majority of the resolution.

Fourthly, a harmonisation of core issues of voluntary downlisting from regulated markets would form the basis for a harmonisation of downlisting.[102] In this respect, too, the aim would be to ensure investor protection on the one hand, while enabling the company and its major shareholder to discontinue organised trading for cost reasons on the other.

[102] Balp (n 23) VI: 'On the issue of market exit, the rules for delisting from MTFs should indeed run in parallel with those for delisting from regulated markets.'

INDEX

www.ingramcontent.com/pod-product-compliance
Ingram Content Group UK Ltd.
Pitfield, Milton Keynes, MK11 3LW, UK
UKHW020229290926
15470UKWH00001B/427

9 781509 974788